1994 GOLF ALMANAC

The All-In-One Golf Resource

EDITED BY:
Don Cronin and Jerry Potter

With contributions from Steve Hershey, USA TODAY Golf Reporter, and the USA TODAY Sports staff

Managing Editor / Sports, USA TODAY, Gene Policinski

Managing Editor, Duncan Bock
A Balliett & Fitzgerald Book

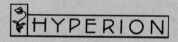

New York

Text Copyright © 1994 USA TODAY
Illustrations Copyright © 1994 USA TODAY

All rights reserved. No part of this book may be used or reproduced in any manner whatsoever without written permission of the Publisher. Printed in the United States of America. For information address Hyperion, 114 Fifth Avenue, New York, New York 10011.

USA TODAY is a registered trademark of Gannett Co., Inc.

ISBN # 0-7868-8007-4

FIRST EDITION
10 9 8 7 6 5 4 3 2 1

Acknowledgments
We are grateful, first of all, for the vision, support, skill and good humor of Susan Bokern, Silvia Molina, Michelle Mattox and Mark Jenkins at Gannett New Business, without whom this book would not have been possible; also many thanks to the sports staff at USA TODAY, especially
Don Cronin, Jerry Potter and Steve Hershey.
We send kudos to everyone at Hyperion, especially publisher Bob Miller.
We could never have completed this book without our own hard-working and talented production staff. We truly appreciate the efforts of designer and systems consultant Steven Johnson; production assistant Philip Chin; and B&F managing editor Lilly Golden.
—Balliett & Fitzgerald

Senior Tour and PGA Tour statistics provided by PGA Tour.
LPGA tour statistics provided by LPGA tour.
Record book and historical statistics by PGA, LPGA, Senior PGA tours.
Photographs of tour players are used with the permission of
PGA Tour, LPGA tour, and Senior PGA Tour.

Contents

Teeing off
Introduction, a look at 1993 5
Around the tour
Issues, news, opinions 9
Majors
1993 major event wrap-ups 25
Team events
Walker, Ryder and Dunhill Cup reviews 65
Tour report 73
   PGA Tour 74
   LPGA 117
   Senior PGA Tour 149
USGA report 189
PGA of America report 197
Players on tour 201
   PGA Tour (career highlights of more than 100 top players) 202
   LPGA (career highlights of more than 50 top players) 232
   Senior PGA Tour (career highlights of more than 50 top players) . . . 249
Final player statistics 269
For the record 283
   All-time records 284
   Tournament histories 299
   1993 leaders 335
Minors
   Nike and T.C. Jordan Tours 343
College
   NCAA tournaments, and more 355
Hall of Fame 359
Courses 363
Equipment 367
Instruction 371
Tour preview 377

GOLF ALMANAC 1994

TEEING OFF

A LOOK BACK AT 1993 ...6
JOHNNIE WALKER CHAMPIONSHIP...7
1995'S RYDER CUP CAPTAIN...8

USA SNAPSHOTS®
A look at statistics that shape the sports world

At the top of the Open

Golfers who won or were runner-up most often at the U.S. Women's Open:

Golfer	1st	2nd	Total
Louise Suggs	2	5	7
JoAnne Carner	2	5	7
Betsy Rawls	4	2	6
Mickey Wright	4	1	5

Source: USA TODAY research

By Web Bryant, USA TODAY

GOLF ALMANAC 1994

A YEAR OF ALMOSTS IN GOLF

Sitting back at the end of the year, we could say 1993 was a great year for golf and for many golfers, particularly those who play for pay.

We could—but we won't.

We'll just say it was *almost* a very good year.

Greg Norman almost put together a year for the ages. That blistering 6-under-par 64 he threw on the board in the final round of the British Open left Royal St. Georges Golf Club gasping.

With that round, Norman appeared to be doing what we've all awaited—moving atop the world of golf. But, alas, it wasn't to be.

Norman's putter failed at the PGA Championship where he lost a playoff to Paul Azinger—earning him the rare distinction of losing playoffs in all four majors.

And speaking of Azinger, no one deserves more good fortune in 1994 than the pleasant, easy going, hotly competitive man. Diagnosed with cancer in his right shoulder blade in December, he faces chemotherapy and radiation treatments over the first six to seven months of '94.

Hurry back, Paul. The world of sports, not just the PGA Tour, needs more like you.

Betsy King joined Norman in the almost category in 1993. She didn't win until the final tournament of the year, leaving her one victory short of qualifying for the LPGA Hall of Fame.

She took leads into the final round seemingly twice a month, but either couldn't hold on or was victimized by a career-making round by someone else.

Perhaps that closing '93 victory portends an excellent '94 for King. She certainly is capable of obliterating the field any week she plays.

John Daly may be the biggest story of them all, however. Daly, who had his usual No. 1 finish in driving distance, finished in the money 15 times in 24 starts but was in the top 10 just once—third at The Masters!

Then he walked off the course in mid-round twice, at the Buick Southern Open in late September and the Lincoln-Mercury Kapalua Invitational Nov. 5. The second early out cost him an indefinite suspension, which could stretch into April '94.

If Daly ever decides to get serious about golf, he could do great things. He has tremendous talent, but isn't using it. And the fans love him, so tournament sponsors and charities—and the ever-needed television audiences and ratings—stand to benefit if he ever reaches maturity.

Dave Stockton vaulted full-speed onto the Senior PGA Tour and showed the over-50 crowd he's more than just one of the boys. Stockton led the Seniors in victories (five) and money earned ($1,115,944).

With one stroke fewer at the season-ending Senior Tour Championship, he could have surpassed Lee Trevino's Senior PGA Tour earnings record ($1,190,518 in 1990).

But two victories stood out.

One was the USA's victory in the Ryder Cup matches. The victory not only was accomplished by a talented group of players of varying ages—but with the class befitting the sport.

Credit U.S. captain Tom Watson for bringing a competitive fire and a gentleman's demeanor to the matches.

The second victory occurred Dec. 12 in Sydney, Australia: Curtis Strange won a golf tournament for the first time since the 1989 U.S. Open.

Strange won the Greg Norman Holden Classic. It wasn't a major, but the field included Norman, Vijay Singh, Steve Elkington, Ray Floyd, Peter Senior, Sandy Lyle, Robert Allenby and Brett Ogle—all successful in '93.

Strange seems to have overcome physical ailments and is regaining the mental toughness we saw in the late '80s. He's becoming upset with himself when he hits poor shots—a sign the Curtis Strange we remember is about to climb back to the top of golf's pecking order.

For '94? Who can say?

But as we all know, it's pretty tough to have a truly bad day at the golf course.

—*by Don Cronin, golf editor,*
USA TODAY

1993 Johnnie Walker Championship

- **Course:** Tryall Country Club
- **Location:** Montego Bay, Jamaica
- **When:** Dec. 16-19, 1993
- **Weather:** Windy and warm the first three days. Calm, warm perfect conditions for the final round.
- **Purse:** $2.7 million
- **Par:** 71
- **Yards:** 6,760
- **Defending champion:** Nick Faldo defeated Greg Norman on the first playoff hole.
- **Tournament record:** 18-under-par 266, Larry Mize, 1993

Larry Mize had to do a bit of last-minute holiday shopping.

"I guess I ought to get Greg Norman a present," Mize said after earning $550,000 for his 10-shot, runaway victory in the Johnnie Walker Championship.

If it weren't for Norman, Mize wouldn't have made the elite 28-man field at this ambitious event that is self-billed as the World Championship. He got in as an alternate three weeks beforehand when Norman, the British Open champion, withdrew to spend the holidays in his native Australia.

Mize, 35, who has won four times in 12 seasons on the PGA Tour—including the 1987 Masters with a famous chip-in birdie to beat Norman in a playoff—made the most of his unexpected opportunity.

"That's as good as I've ever played. The other guys will kill me if I don't say that. I won't soon forget this round today," Mize said after shooting 65 in the final round.

After he established a three-shot lead in three rounds, Mize ran away from the field in his bogey-free, 6-under-par finish. He did not have a 5 on his card.

It was a race for second all the way.

"I never even thought about catching Larry," said Fred Couples, who eventually was runner-up.

"I'm second and I'm 10 shots back. That's hilarious," Couples said after a 65 that included nine birdies and a double-bogey 7. His 276 total took second when

Larry Mize left behind the world's best golfers after entering as a replacement for Greg Norman.

Masters champion Bernhard Langer of Germany dropped out of a tie with a three-putt bogey on the final hole. Langer closed 69-277.

The missed, 5-foot second putt cost Langer $50,000. A tie for second would have been worth $250,000. But Couples won $300,000, Langer $200,000.

Scotland's Colin Montgomerie was three shots behind at the start of the final round and the only man who ever had a chance to overtake Mize. But that chance evaporated when Montgomerie bogeyed the third and fourth holes while Mize birdied, putting the margin at seven.

"Colin had a tough day, got off to a bad start," Mize said. "That gave me some room and I just kept the pedal down."

Montgomerie played the front side in

40—hitting two spectators with a single shot on the eighth hole—while Mize was out in 32.

"I hit more spectators than fairways," Montgomerie said. "It's the worst nine holes I've played all year."

He finished with a 74, alone in fourth at 278. Curtis Strange, continuing a year-end comeback, came on with a 66 for fifth at 279, 13 strokes back. No one else was within 15.

The victory margin was exceeded in 1993 only by Nick Price's 12-stroke triumph in the Sun City Million Dollar challenge in South Africa.

Mize also won the Northern Telcom Open in Tucson, and the Buick Open in Grand Blanc, Mich., breaking a six-year non-winning streak. He earned $724,660 on the PGA Tour and $1.3 million world-wide.

Scores and earnings

Player	Scores
Larry Mize, $550,000	67-66-68-65–266
Fred Couples, $300,000	71-69-72-64–276
Bernhard Langer, $200,000	71-68-69-69–277
Colin Montgomerie, $130,000	67-69-68-74–278
Curtis Strange, $100,000	73-68-72-66–279
Nick Faldo, $87,500	70-72-69-70–281
Brad Faxon, $87,500	69-69-71-72–281
Vijay Singh, $75,000	72-70-71-69–282
Steve Elkington, $75,000	68-65-87-72–282
Ernie Els, $75,000	66-73-70-73–282
Fulton Allem, $65,000	69-69-72-73–283
Sam Torrance, $64,000	73-74-67-70–284
Gordon Brand Jr., $62,500	70-76-72-67–285
Corey Pavin, $62,500	72-75-70-68–285
Tom Kite, $59,000	73-74-72-68–287
Lee Janzen, $59,000	73-76-70-68–287
Steven Richardson, $59,000	73-71-73-70–287
Jeff Maggert, $59,000	76-67-70-74–287
Costantino Rocca, $59,000	71-66-74-76–287
David Frost, $56,000	69-74-76-70–289
Jesper Parnevik, $54,500	74-74-71-72–291
Ben Crenshaw, $54,500	75-71-72-73–291
Ian Woosnam, $52,500	73-73-74-72–292
Davis Love III, $52,500	73-70-76-73–292
Jim Gallagher, $51,000	73-76-70-74–293
Seiki Okuda, $50,000	79-72-72-74–297
Bradley Hughes, $50,000	76-74-76-77–303
Peter Baker, $50,000	74-78-79-76–307

Lanny Wadkins named Ryder Cup captain

Lanny Wadkins returned to the scene of one of his best shots to attain one of his biggest goals.

In the 1983 Ryder Cup matches at PGA National Golf Club, the USA and Europe were tied after 10 singles matches on the final day.

Wadkins, 1 down to Jose Maria Canizares going to the 18th hole, knocked a pitching wedge within a foot of the hole. He made birdie to halve his match and set up a one-point U.S. victory when Tom Watson won his match.

"That shot had to be the highlight of my Ryder Cup career," he said. "I know it was the most nervous I've ever been over one shot in my life. It had to be the most important shot I ever hit."

Wadkins was announced as the 1995 Ryder Cup captain Dec. 1, 1993, at PGA of America headquarters in Palm Beach Gardens, Fla.

"I started thinking about being a Ryder Cup captain in the mid-80s," he said. "As a former PGA Champion, I thought I would get a shot somewhere along the line, but I didn't know when. I think it's a wonderful way for the PGA to honor its champions."

Wadkins made his Ryder Cup debut in 1977 after winning the PGA Championship with a sensational back nine at Pebble Beach, Calif. Trailing Gene Littler by five shots, Wadkins, then 28, pulled even with a birdie at 18, then won with a 6-foot par putt on the third playoff hole.

Since then, he missed only one, in '81, going 20-11-3 in matches, including 2-1-1 in 1993 at Sutton Coldfield, England, to close within two of Arnold Palmer's record for wins by a U.S. player. His eight appearances tie Billy Casper's record.

Though still playing on the PGA Tour full-time, it seems unlikely Wadkins will qualify as a player for the '95 matches at Oak Hill Country Club in Rochester, N.Y. He was a wild-card selection in '89 and '91.

Wadkins may have clinched the job in September at the '93 Ryder Cup. He volunteered to sit out the final-day singles matches after Scotland's Sam Torrance had to withdraw because of an injured toe.

"The toughest thing is to just stand by and watch," Wadkins said. "It's one thing to play and then go watch, but to sit out and not be able to help the team is something I wouldn't wish on anybody.

"If the captaincy is anything like that, I'll have enough stomach acid to wear the chrome off a set of irons."

—by Steve Hershey

GOLF ALMANAC 1994

Around the Tour

Minority golf ...11
Heather Farr...15
Tour wrap-ups...17
The year in review...21

USA SNAPSHOTS®
A look at statistics that shape the sports world

Most money won by a rookie on the PGA Tour

Player	Year	Amount
John Daly	1991	$574,783
Robert Gamez	1990	$461,407
Grant Waite	1993	$411,405
Brett Ogle	1993	$337,374
Keith Clearwater	1987	$320,007

Source: PGA Tour   By Suzy Parker, USA TODAY

PGA Tour should unleash foreign stars

Bernhard Langer, fresh from the traditional champions dinner at Augusta National Golf Club, was sipping a beer with a few late-nighters in the media lounge.

Still aglow from his smashing four-shot victory and second Masters title, he was kidding that his 1985 green jacket was a little tight and wondering if he could talk himself into a new style.

He also was talking about his home in Boca Raton, Fla. and how much he, his wife, Vikki, a former Eastern Airlines flight attendant, and their children enjoy Florida in the winter.

Yes, the Langers of Anhausen, Germany, spend part of their winters in Florida. But because of a controversial rule passed by the PGA Tour a few years ago, Bernhard can practice all he wants, yet his tournament appearances are restricted.

Foreign players who are not members of the PGA Tour are limited to six tournaments outside the three major championships on U.S. soil: The Masters, U.S. Open and PGA Championship.

Before this ruling in 1989, Langer used to play at least 15 tournaments a year on the PGA Tour. In 1985, when he won The Masters and Sea Pines Heritage Classic, he was 13th on the money list. The following year he was 10th, then 23rd. Langer was a popular attraction who drew crowds wherever he went.

That's all over. U.S. fans saw the Masters champion only twice after the MCI Heritage in 1993. He still finished 23rd, with the best money-per-shot average in golf.

"Sure, I'd like to play more over here, especially at the beginning of the year," Langer said. "There aren't too many tournaments in Europe that appeal to me before May."

Sandy Lyle is another who enjoys playing in the USA. He was a full-time player before the ruling, winning five times during a three-year span (1986-88), including the '88 Masters.

When the rule was passed by the Tour Policy Board, Lyle, another crowd pleaser, had to make a decision: play in the USA or Europe. Nobody can do both full time.

"I've always enjoyed playing here, particularly in Arizona and California," Lyle said. "I won at Greensboro (N.C.) twice, but now it doesn't make sense to come over just for that week. Once The Masters is over, that's it for me, except for the majors."

"The European Tour is growing and needs our support," two-time Masters champion Nick Faldo said. "Our children are getting older and it's tougher to get away for just a week at a time. If there was no limit, it would certainly help us plan our schedule."

We have suggested this before and now, with the fifth foreign winner in six years at The Masters, it's appropriate to bring it up again: Winners of major championships should be given carte blanche.

These champions should be allowed to play any PGA Tour event they want. If you think that's a double standard, fine. This handful of guys deserves it, and they certainly would enrich any field they join.

The argument from PGA Tour Commissioner Deane Beman is that these players shouldn't be allowed to "cherry pick" the best tournaments and not support the others.

First of all, that's what the PGA Tour's big money-winners do. You don't see many of them at Phoenix, Milwaukee or the Texas Open.

Second, there's concern the foreign players will bump card-carrying PGA Tour players at certain tournaments. We're only talking about a foursome at most and certainly sponsors would jump at the chance to promote a Langer, Woosnam or Faldo.

Third, remember, PGA Tour players are welcomed with open checkbooks at any and all European tournaments.

So let's return the favor, establish a free trade agreement. Let's modify the PGA Tour rule, loosen a few stiff shirts and give golf fans the opportunity they deserve to see the best players in the world.

—by Steve Hershey

Despite progress, golf remains exclusive

The first black U.S. Golf Association executive has no master key that will unlock the multibillion-dollar golf industry to minorities, but he's hoping his ideas will lead to reform.

"Things like country-club memberships and professionals on tour are issues," says John Merchant. "But the basic problem is young people and economic opportunities."

Merchant drew that conclusion after hosting a symposium on minorities in golf at Callaway Gardens in Pine Mountain, Ga.

"A plan of action did not come out of the symposium," Merchant says. "But that was not one of my goals. My first priority was discussion and communication; the second was generating ideas."

Merchant, a lawyer from Bridgeport, Conn., joined the USGA Executive Committee in the wake of the 1990 Shoal Creek controversy.

The haunting comment by Shoal Creek founder Hall Thompson—who said, shortly before the club hosted the PGA Championship, that accepting blacks into private clubs "was just not done in Birmingham, Ala."—pricked the nation's conscience.

Golf's governing bodies have since developed plans for making the sport more accessible to the estimated 400,000 U.S. minority golfers.

Not only do the PGA of America, PGA Tour, LPGA and USGA refuse to stage tournaments at clubs with restrictive membership, but each organization also supports junior golf programs nationwide.

"The awareness level is higher and more clubs are changing their policies," says Merchant. "I don't think it's moving fast enough."

The LPGA helps fund a $180,000-a-year program in Los Angeles that teaches city youngsters to play golf. It has about 300 golfers, ages 7-17, who get free lessons, equipment and greens fees at public courses in Orange County.

But such programs for inner-city youth don't help the growing group of middle-class blacks, who also need assistance. Golf expenses remain prohibitive: A set of clubs can cost up to $1,000, and country club memberships in metropolitan areas can cost $30,000 or more just for the initial fee.

The National Golf Foundation says the average cost for yearly membership in a private club is almost $10,000, while public course greens fees average about $25 on weekends.

"If we're going to solve the problem," says former UCLA star LaRee Sugg who attended the conference, "we're going to have to target black junior golfers who have the talent and give them the financial and moral support they need to succeed."

Sugg failed in her bid for a full-time LPGA card for 1994 but does have some exemptions. She was trying to become the first black on tour since Rene Powell in 1980.

Both Sugg and three-time Junior Amateur champion Tiger Woods come from middle-class backgrounds and both learned to play on military courses: Woods in California, Sugg in Virginia.

Sugg says the USGA needs to soften its rules on amateur status, allowing young people to receive corporate support for travel and equipment.

"It would help the image of the sport if we had some black golfers on the pro tours," Sugg says. "People are looking for someone to point to and say, 'This person went through the system and made it.'"

Among touring professionals, there are more black players on the Senior PGA Tour because they learned to play while working as caddies. That avenue ended when electric carts made caddying a dying profession.

Now, Merchant says blacks and other minorities must get the same opportunities as others, beginning with jobs in the $1.5 billion-a-year golf equipment industry and support from corporate America.

"I'm not asking for a handout," he says. "I want a partnership in resolving these difficulties."

—*by Jerry Potter;*
contributions from Carolyn White

Do pro golfers gamble on the side? You bet

"Gambling is part of the game. It always has been and it always will be."
—Paul Azinger

Friendly wagering and golf have gone hand in hand since gutta percha balls and long-nosed wooden clubs.

It's not difficult to imagine two pipe-smoking Scots, waving a gentle mist away from their faces and haggling about giving strokes before ever mounding the earth into a tee.

Betting has become such an accepted part of golf that every course has a handicap system, which is simply a method for making matches even—so golfers can set up wagers.

Unlike the other major country club sport, tennis, where if players are of unequal ability it's no fun for either, a competitive golf match can be struck among strangers—if they are honest about their handicaps.

Sam Snead may be golf's most famous hustler. Although he owns the most coveted PGA Tour record—most victories, 81—he always was able to lure "pigeons" to his roost at The Greenbrier in White Sulphur Springs, W. Va., with a variety of betting games.

"Heck, sometimes you got to give them pigeons a shot a hole," he says. "But I can usually figure out how to give 'em just one less than they need."

The most popular game is a simple Nassau, where a player, or two-man team, matches scores on each hole against the opponent(s). This is where the handicap system is so convenient.

To make betting easier and fairer, each hole is rated on its difficulty to par. For example, a 460-yard, uphill par-4 with water to carry might be the No. 1 handicap hole, while a 120-yard, downhill par-3 might be the 18th.

Therefore, if you are giving your opponent a stroke, it would come where he needs it most, at the most difficult hole.

Matches between a player who averages 75 (a 3-handicapper) and one who averages 85 (a 13) can be hotly contested if the high handicapper is getting a shot on each of the 10 most difficult holes.

The match can be exciting, and the 19th hole even more interesting, as golfers—but almost never tennis players, settle bets. A popular rule: Winners buy, so losers can go home happy.

Tom Watson, captain of the winning U.S. Ryder Cup team, shocked purists when he suggested his players engage in money games while preparing for tournaments because, he believed, it would sharpen their competitive skills.

As usual, Ryder Cupper Lanny Wadkins was more blunt: "Tom should make guys play $50, one-down presses in practice rounds. If a guy says it's against his religion, tell him to get another religion."

A few players may object to gambling, but the U.S. Golf Association has no problem—if players bet only on themselves.

According to *The Rules of Golf*, "The USGA does not object to participation in wagering among individual golfers or teams of golfers (when the group of) participants in the wagering is limited to the players. The players may only wager on themselves or their teams and the sole source of all money won by the players is advanced by the players. And the primary purpose is the playing of the game for enjoyment."

Wadkins is notorious at his home course of Preston Trail Country Club in Dallas, where the members try to hobble him with a plus-5 handicap.

"It's tougher to win there than on Tour," Wadkins says. "Generally, we play 1-down, automatic presses with a bunch of garbage on the side."

"Garbage" is a common term for side bets by weekend players. Generally, a player or a team is rewarded with a scorecard "dot" for: (1) a greenie—being closest to the hole on a par-3 or a par-5; (2) a sandy—making par after escaping a sand bunker; (3) a chippie—chipping in for par or better.

One of the favorites of PGA Tour bettors is "the hammer." It's an opportunity to double a bet on any hole, as Mark O'Meara explains it.

"Let's say Bruce Lietzke is playing Payne Stewart," O'Meara says. "If Lietzke hits a shot from the fairway on the green, he can give Payne the hammer so the hole goes from $10 to $20. If Payne doesn't want it, say Lietzke's shot is close, he forfeits the hole. If he takes it, then hits his ball closer and hammers Lietzke right back, now it's $40. It keeps your interest."

For PGA Tour players earning six or seven figures a year, $40 is like 40 cents to the weekend pull-cart brigade. But golfers everywhere will say, "it's not the money, it's winning or losing."

"I prefer practicing alone to playing for nothing," says Ray Floyd, who earned a reputation as a high-rolling gambler before he won his first PGA Tour tournament at St. Petersburg, Fla., in 1963.

"It's not the money. I'm not gambling on the golf course, I'm practicing winning. When you're one-on-one, there's no second or third or fourth. You have to win."

And that is Watson's reasoning for wanting the Ryder Cup players to risk some cash in a friendly Nassau while practicing. The popular biennial event is all match play—better-ball and alternate-shot two-man matches for two days, then a day of singles matches.

Paul Azinger, Fred Couples, Davis Love III, Floyd, Wadkins and Stewart don't have to be pushed into money matches. Neither do Greg Norman, Nick Price, Ben Crenshaw, Steve Elkington, Mark Calcavecchia, Ken Green, Billy Ray Brown and Blaine McCallister—some of the most avid bettors.

"I like to play with a guy like Lanny," Azinger says. "He'll play for anything. But it doesn't matter how much you're playing for, you just have to have something on the match."

Azinger always is looking for a game, sometimes to the resentment of his caddy, who muttered after a Tuesday

Payne Stewart is one of many players who do not have to be pushed into money matches.

match before the British Open, "I think Paul gets more pumped up for these matches than the tournament."

Before the U.S. Open, Azinger and Calcavecchia trounced Lee Janzen and Rocco Mediate. Janzen, of course, went on to win the Open. Eager for a rematch, Janzen and Mediate dusted their rivals at Royal St. George before the British Open.

At 64, Arnold Palmer still probably plays as much social golf as any PGA Tour player. When he's at his Bay Hill Club near Orlando, Palmer says he plays three or four times a week with members and guests.

"We have what we call a shootout at the club, 11:30 (a.m.) every day," Palmer says. "We choose up four-man teams and count three balls every hole. Three matches, $10 each. It's a lot of fun, I love it."

So even Palmer, perhaps the richest athlete in the world, still gets excited every day about playing for $30. He's insatiable. At the PGA Championship in August, he couldn't get a game with Tour pros on Monday, so he hustled up three club pros and got the action he craves.

That's what it's all about. Whether you're an 18-handicapper or Arnold Palmer, it's not the money, it's the action.

—by Steve Hershey

Around the Tour 1993: News

S&L Fallout: Posh Golf Resorts Auctioned

As part of the savings and loans crisis' continuing legacy, six of the country's most famous luxury golf resorts were put on the auctioning block and sold for more than $400 million.

At an auction by Resolution Trust Corp., four bidders (two paying cash to take advantage of a special discount) bought the former Oak Tree Savings properties for $395.4 billion. The auction in Dallas drew 400 people, including Marilyn Quayle.

Sold were PGA West ($140 million) and La Quinta Golf & Tennis Resort ($136.4 million), both in La Quinta, Calif.; Mission Hills ($35.6 million) in Rancho Mirage, Calif.; Palm Beach Polo and CC ($27.1 million) in West Palm Beach, Fla.; the Carmel Valley Ranch ($20 million) near Carmel, Calif.; and the Kiawah Island Resort ($45.1 million) near Charleston, S.C., minus its famed Ocean Course.

The Ocean Course—where the USA regained the Ryder Cup from Europe in 1991—was later sold in a three-way deal. Its buyer, the Audubon Society of New York—often confused with, but not the same as, the National Audubon Society—paid about $27 million.

Although the real estate's book value was $738 million, RTC assessed their investment value as nearer to $366 million.

Spalding to Guard Patent Aggressively

With unusual haste for golf, the U.S. Patent and Trademark Office is granting Spalding Professional Golf a patent for its oversize ball.

The Magna, 1.72 inches in diameter compared to 1.68 for the "standard" ball, was introduced January 1993 as an aid to weekend golfers.

Through size and construction, the Magna curves less in flight, allowing high-handicap players to keep it on line more easily. Better players, however, sometimes have difficulty adjusting to the ball because they often want shots to curve, under control.

"The Magna has been a tremendous commercial success; this (patent) is just great," Brendan Davis, Spalding Golf managing director, said. "The ruling, which we anticipate in January, precludes anyone else putting a modern dimple pattern on a large ball. Someone could create a larger ball, but not with the normal dimple pattern, which controls the flight aerodynamically."

Spalding has begun an ad campaign to advise consumers and potential competitors it will "aggressively protect our patent against infringement," Davis said.

The ad copy says the Chicopee, Mass., company will, if necessary, "drag our lawyers off the course and into court. And that puts them in a very nasty mood."

Golf's Brave New World

Arnold Palmer and Joseph Gibbs, a Birmingham, Ala., cable television operator, hope to launch an all-golf channel in 1995.

Gibbs, who says Golf Channel still needs to raise $100 million, says International Management Group is an investor and will be involved in production.

Thursday through Sunday, the channel will show tournaments. There will be plenty of instruction—along with news and talk shows that parallel regular TV.

Palmer, says Gibbs, will put his mouth where his money is: "I'm envisioning Arnie doing fireside chats."

—by Michael Hiestand

HEATHER FARR TOUCHED ALL WHO KNEW HER

On a hot day in Nashville, Bill Cecil and Ken Stilts, a couple of good ol' boys from Tennessee, stood at the foot of a bed in Stilts' home, where Heather Farr was resting a day before a benefit golf tournament was being staged for her.

"Now, Heather," said Cecil, "when you get over this cancer you're gonna meet somebody and get married. We want you to do us a favor."

"What's that," said Farr, who was weak, tired and nauseous from chemotherapy.

"We want you to name your first son after us," said Cecil.

Without delay, Heather replied, "Well, I hope I marry a Texan, because I don't know anybody else who'd want a kid named Billy Ken."

Farr's humor in the face of death is one of the many memories held by those who knew her and watched her struggle to overcome cancer and return to golf, the game she loved.

Farr died Nov. 20 at Scottsdale (Ariz.) Memorial Hospital-North after a 4½-year battle with cancer. She was 28.

Through the ordeal she tried to maintain a normal life. March, 20, 1993, she married Goran Lingmerth, not a Texan, but a Swede who came to the USA in 1981 and played college football before settling in Phoenix.

At the wedding reception, a projector clicked off slides that showed both Heather and Goran at various stages of their lives: Heather as a young golfer; Goran as a young football player.

Those who watched long enough couldn't help but notice how cancer had taken its toll on Heather. A little bit of her life seemed to be drained from each frame.

"The odds were against her," said Cecil, the President of the Sara Lee Classic and Farr's guardian angel since 1989. "But she never gave up hope that she'd get well enough to play golf again."

Farr, born March 10, 1965, in Phoenix, was a national junior champion and an All-American at Arizona State. She was only 20 when she qualified for the LPGA in 1986.

She played the pro tour for 3½ seasons before being diagnosed with breast cancer on July 3, 1989.

Farr underwent chemotherapy and had a mastectomy. She moved back into her parents home in Phoenix so her mother, Sharon, her father, Gerald, and her sister, Missy, could share in her care. It was a 24-hour-a-day job.

"All things considered we find a lot of things to laugh about," said Sharon Farr.

Heather recovered, even getting strong enough to go back to practicing with an eye toward joining the tour in early 1991. But in December, 1990, she noticed some soreness in her shoulder.

The first diagnosis was muscle strain, but another test revealed that her body was not free of cancer, that the cells had metastasized on her skull and spine.

There would be more surgery, more chemotherapy, more radiation treatment and a bone marrow transplant.

At one point in the chemotherapy, when Heather was having to count the minutes of the treatment, she told Sharon Farr: "Mom, I don't think I'm gonna make it."

"Yes, you are," said Sharon. "Just hang on a little while longer."

Heather recovered enough to go home. By mid-summer she was swinging a golf club again and hoping to rejoin the LPGA in one more year.

Her battle became a rallying point for the LPGA. The players drew strength from her stuggle and she drew strength from their victories.

When Meg Mallon won the LPGA Championship in 1991, the first call to her was from Farr.

"I love your car," said the 5-1 Farr, speaking of a Mazda Miata that went with the victory.

"You would," said Mallon. "You're small enough to fit into it."

They laughed, just as Bill Cecil and Ken Stilts laughed on that hot day in Nashville.

They laughed, as Cecil said, because "Heather touched your heart and my heart and the heart of everyone else who ever knew her."

—by Jerry Potter

FURTHER ADVENTURES OF JOHN DALY

John Daly has what most PGA Tour players wish they had: personality. For that—and his grip-it and rip-it game—fans mob him gratefully. Daly's many trials on and off the course seem to make him even more appealing. But in a roller coaster year, the tour's driving-distance king teed off PGA Tour officials one time too many and was suspended indefinitely. In December, Daly said he expected to play the Freeport McMoRan Classic.

DALY ON QUITTING BOOZE:
"I had been drinking since I was 14, but I quit whiskey when I was 23, and thought I was OK. But all I did was double the amount of beer I drank. . . .

"I've played drunk; I'm not the only one out here. But, God, I don't ever want to be that way again."

A DALY CHRONOLOGY:
▶**Dec. 20, 1992:** John Daly, 26, drank himself to the point of no return at a party in his former Colorado home.

He was accused of tossing his wife against a wall, pulling her hair and smashing various objects in his path.

Daly denies he hit his wife.

"The deal was off the wall," said Daly. "It was nothing but a bad lie. I hit a few pictures, hit the wall. But to say I hit my wife is ungodly. . . .

"The good thing is, I don't drink anymore. Their lying actually helped me. I realized I had to get myself straightened out."

▶**Jan. 28, 1993:** With Charles Barkley among his supporters, Daly returned from his brief stint in alcoholism rehabilitation to shoot 2-under-par 69 and sit three off the pace in the first round of the Phoenix Open.

Daly was mobbed by autograph-seeking fans, welcoming him back to the PGA Tour, including the Phoenix Suns' Barkley.

"Take care of yourself and keep playing well," said Barkley, before getting his cap autographed, too.

▶**March 3:** Daly pleaded not guilty to an assault charge stemming from the altercation with his wife. The trial was scheduled for May 25 in Castle Rock, Colo.

▶**May 19:** While preparing for the Kemper Open, Daly told USA TODAY that 20 Diet Cokes a day and tons of M&M's have kept him sober on the PGA Tour.

"It hasn't been easy. Not a day goes by that I don't crave a beer," Daly said. "The chocolate is a substitute for alcohol, I guess."

▶**May 20:** Daly shot an opening-round 6-over-par 77 in the Kemper Open, then tossed his scorecard in the scoring tent and walked away without signing it. Later, he called an official and said, "I forgot to sign my card." Official Glenn Tait replied, "You're disqualified."

▶**May 24:** Daly pleaded guilty to a lesser charge of misdemeanor harassment, the PGA Tour said in a release. According to the release, the misdemeanor plea would be withdrawn when Daly completed a counseling program for alcohol abuse. The original charge of third-degree assault was dismissed.

▶**Oct. 19:** Steve Elkington watched with interest as Daly threw his putter after missing a 5-foot putt on the first hole of the World Match Play Championship at Virginia Water, England, then beat the U.S. golfer, 5 and 4.

▶**Nov. 5:** Daly was disqualified for refusing to finish the the second round of the Kapalua International. Daly missed a birdie putt on the 11th green and picked up his ball; he had earlier shot three double-bogeys.

▶**Nov. 7:** PGA Tour comissioner Deane Beman suspended Daly from the tour indefinitely. Said Beman: "I care about him, I like him, but some of the things he does are unacceptable. John now knows emphatically he can't quit. You can't go out there and walk off the golf course."

Daly finished 76th on the money list with $225,591; his best finish was third at The Masters.

—contributions from Rachel Shuster and Steve Hershey

PGA Tour: Norman and Price, almost great

Oh, to have been on that fishing trip with Nick Price and Greg Norman in late October before the season-ending Tour Championship.

Many lines were dipped, many lagers were swilled, and many yarns were spun—some even about golf—as these two longtime friends were finally able to put their feet up and watch the waves.

As the sun sank into the horizon, lines were reeled in and cans were popped with increasing regularity. It was time for memories of a year when one player finally reached the heights many had expected years ago and the other culminated a great comeback—but still had to be dismayed at what could have been.

Price, a non-winner for seven-and-a-half years, broke through with two victories in 1991, including the Canadian Open. The following year, he won his first major, out-dueling John Cook to win the PGA Championship by three shots at Bellerive in St. Louis.

It was in 1993, however, that Price was compared with Nick Faldo, the reigning top player in the world. Before the British Open, there was much banter in the pubs and courses across the United Kingdom about which Nick was No. 1.

Faldo, himself, made the final pronouncement when he pulled out of the World Cup competition in Orlando in mid-November, saying: "Over the last year, I probably haven't been the best player in the world. This year Nick Price was probably the best. He won four tournaments in the U.S. and that's pretty impressive. It's very difficult to win that often."

Yes, Price became the first to win four times since Wayne Levi in 1990. Only two others have done it since 1982 and nobody has topped that mark since Tom Watson won six in 1980.

Not only did Price lead the PGA Tour in victories, he also topped the money list with a record $1,478,557 and won the Vardon Trophy for lowest scoring average at 69.11.

The Vardon Trophy and money title, were probably topics of conversation during that fishing expedition. You see, they were downright gifts from the boat's owner, Captain Shark. Norman not only served the refreshments, he also gave away those two honors in a year that could have been his greatest ever.

First, the Vardon Trophy.

Norman's problem was that he assumed if he entered the bare minimum of 15 tournament required to keep his PGA Tour card, he would qualify.

What he didn't count on was (a), missing the cut at the U.S. Open, thus losing two rounds, and (b), straining a muscle in his shoulder working out at home and having to withdraw from the Canadian Open. Therefore, when he showed up at the Tour Championship, he only had played 54 rounds and no matter how hard he tried, he could only squeeze in four that week.

"I'm extremely disappointed," Norman said. "I thought all I had to do was play 15 tournaments. If I had known, I probably would have scheduled another tournament at the end of the year."

Instead, he went fishing and, in the process, blew the award, which, he says, means the most to him.

"I don't really care about the money title," he said. "I've won that twice already (1986 and 1990). If I did, I would have played more tournaments. But the Vardon Trophy means a lot. Your scoring average is the true gauge of how you've played all year."

So, entering the final round of the year that magnificent autumn afternoon at the storied Olympic Club, the Vardon was out of reach. But the money title was a distinct possibility because the two ahead of Norman—Price and Paul Azinger—were struggling.

Pressure affects different players in different ways, but it seems to hit Norman above the neck.

At 16, he had 94 yards downwind to the flag and tried to hit a 60-degree wedge. He buried it in the bunker and had to make a five-footer for bogey.

"When you're 94 yards away, you think you can make birdie," he said afterward. "I tried to cut it too close."

Any schoolboy knows if you have a one-shot lead, you don't get cute around a bunker, you just knock it on the green, take two putts and move on.

So now Norman was tied and that changed his approach to 17. After a good drive, he went for the green and wound up in the sand with another difficult lie. The best he could do was blast 20 feet past the pin and two-putt for par.

Still, after 17 holes, the money title was in Norman's grasp. All he needed was a par on the 347-yard final hole to gain a playoff with Jim Gallagher. Instead, from 136 yards away in the middle of the fairway, he pushed an 8-iron over the green, made bogey and had to share second money with Scott Simpson, John Huston and David Frost.

Even a loss in a playoff would have left Norman alone in second place; and with a payoff of $324,000, it would have been enough to pass Price.

Any wonder who will be buying on the next fishing excursion?

—by Steve Hershey

PRICE JOINED THE FLY BOYS OF GOLF

Of all the theories explaining why Price won three PGA Tour starts in a row during the summer of '93, four total and leaped to the front ranks of world golf, perhaps that old philosopher Fuzzy Zoeller had the best idea.

"Nobody can beat Nick since he got that plane," said Zoeller—who has a little prop job of his own—after going head-to-head with Price at the Federal Express St. Jude's Classic and losing by four shots.

Yes, Price has joined the flyboys of golf: Arnold Palmer, Jack Nicklaus, Ray Floyd, Greg Norman, Chi Chi Rodriguez, Bill Glasson and David Edwards. They all own planes. It's the latest rage.

"I've always had an interest in flying," Price said. "I started looking for a plane after the PGA last year and, as the year went on, I started looking up in the price list."

After finishing fourth on the 1992 PGA Tour money list with $1,135,773, Price could afford a new mode of transportation. He settled on a 1978 Westwind in May.

"Arnie and Jack had the right idea years ago," he said. "I'm convinced it added years to their careers by having the luxury and convenience of traveling on their own plane.

"I don't know why more players haven't done it. A lot of guys are financially able to do it, and the wear and tear it saves is unbelievable. It's such a relief for me to know that I have a plane waiting for me in Orlando (where he lives).

"The thing that wears you down the most is airports. It's like a three- or four-shot advantage not having worry about flights to the tournament and what time your plane leaves on Sunday, making connections and, of course, losing luggage.

"I'm so much more relaxed. I truly believe that's one of the reasons I'm playing better."

—by Steve Hershey

PGA OF AMERICA PLAYER OF THE YEAR:

The PGA of America honors the PGA Tour Player of the Year through a point system based on victories, earnings and scoring average from Jan. 1 through the Tour Championship. The final standings:

	Wins	Money	Scoring	Total
Nick Price	50	20	20	90
Paul Azinger	50	18	14	82
Greg Norman	40	16	0*	56
David Frost	20	12	18	50
Lee Janzen	40	8	0**	48
Tom Kite	20	6	16	42
Fulton Allem	30	4	0**	34
J. Gallagher Jr.	20	14	0**	34
B. Langer	30	0**	0**	30
Payne Stewart	0**	10	12	22
Fred Couples	10	2	10	22

* played fewer than the required 60 rounds.
** not among top 10 to earn points.
Source: PGA of America

LPGA Tour: Many winners, stiff competition

In May, right after Europeans Helen Alfredsson and Trish Johnson combined to win three consecutive events, the talk around the LPGA tour was of the European Invasion.

By November, right after Betsy King won three awards with one birdie putt, the talk was not of invasion, but of the competition that emerged in 1993 when 24 different golfers won tournaments.

"We have the best women golfers in the world playing our tour every week," said King. "You'll see players win two or three events a year, but it'll be a long time before somebody wins five or six again."

King won six events in 1989 to be the Rolex Player of the Year, but in 1993 she picked up the title with one official win in the Toray Queens Cup in Japan. She also won the money title with $595,992 and the Vare Trophy with an 18-hole scoring average of 70.85 strokes.

But none of these titles were settled until King made a birdie putt on the 54th hole at Lions Country Club in Yokawa, Japan.

"Any year has to be good when you have the major awards literally come down to the last putt of the last hole of the last event of the year," said LPGA commissioner Charlie Mechem. "The level of competitiveness on our tour is obviously very high."

Several young players emerged in '93 to mix with such veterans as King and Patty Sheehan and give the LPGA a diversity of stars.

Brandie Burton, who joined the tour in 1991 and will be only 22 when the 1994 season begins, won three events, including a major championship at the du Maurier Classic.

Burton, who was Rookie of the Year in 1991, added another win in September and was challenging King for Player of the Year in November. She finished in the top 10 in 16 of the 26 events she played.

"I think she'd going to be the next great player on our tour," says King. "She's one of the few players of this era who could win 30 times and qualify for the Hall of Fame under the current system."

Patty Sheehan's entry into the Hall of Fame was another highlight. She wasn't inducted until November, but she qualified in March by winning the Standard Register Ping in Phoenix. In May, just for good measure, she won the Mazda LPGA Championship, making three of her 30 career victories in that event.

"I'm not ready to retire," says Sheehan, 37. "I've got a lot of golf left. I've never been the leading money winner and I'd like to be that. And I'd like to be Player of the Year again."

Joining Burton and Sheehan with major victories in 1993 were Alfredsson, who won the Nabisco Dinah Shore in March, and Lauri Merten, who won the U.S. Women's Open in July.

Alfredsson had a chance to win the Women's Open. She led going into the final round, but she shot 74 at Crooked Stick Golf Club in Carmel, Ind., and lost to Merten.

Alfredsson, from Sweden, was one of nine first-time winners in '93. The others were Johnson, Kristi Albers, Kelly Robbins, Hiromi Kobayashi, Missie Berteotti, Cindy Schreyer, Helen Dobson and Donna Andrews.

Suzanne Strudwick, from Stafford, England, was the Gatorade Rookie of the Year, following Alfredsson in '92 to give Europeans the award for two consecutive years.

"The quality of our foreign players and their importance to our tour continues to be apparent," says Mechem. "The Women's Open was one of the highest rated telecasts we've had and Alfredsson and Merten were part of the reason it was so popular."

"In many ways we're doing quite well," says King. "The thing that scares me is the economy. Corporations are cutting back big time. It's hard for them to say one day that they're spending $1 million on a golf tournament and then announce the next day that they're laying off 5,000 workers."

—*by Jerry Potter*

Down in sales, Mazda bowed out

An era ended on Aug. 18, 1993, when the LPGA announced its championship would no longer be sponsored by Mazda Motors of America, ending a relationship that began in 1980.

"We're experiencing a lot of grief," said Jan Thompson, vice president of sales operations for Mazda. "The LPGA Championship was not just a marketing tool for us. It was family. It was people."

In 1994, the tournament will be sponsored by McDonald's and played as the McDonald's LPGA Championship, May 12-15 at the DuPont Country Club in Wilmington, Del. The new agreement is for five years, with a purse of $1.1 million in 1994.

"The real villain is the economy," said LPGA Commissioner Charlie Mechem. "This is a major event with a very large price tag."

Over the years, the downturn in auto sales and the fall of the dollar against the yen forced Mazda to eliminate its title sponsorships in golf, tennis and motor sports.

Mazda's car and truck sales for the first seven months of 1993 were down 6.3% from the same period in 1992, while overall sales in the USA were up 7.9%.

"You can't pass that on to the consumers," said Thomson, "because to keep up we'd have to raise car prices 25%."

So Mazda has to absorb about $3,000 for each vehicle sold. To soften the loss, Mazda had to make cuts in its marketing program.

"We can't justify big-ticket professional events," said Thompson. "We had to take our resources to support our dealers."

Thompson built the LPGA program, taking the tournament from Cincinnati to the Washington, D.C., area in 1990 and giving it a $1 million purse.

Mazda spent about $3 million a year on the event and Thompson added other programs to support it. Her Team Mazda included the best players in women's golf—Beth Daniel, Pat Bradley, Patty Sheehan and Meg Mallon.

"Everyone in our organization believes we had the best sports marketing program," said Thompson. "We were well-recognized. We sold a lot of cars because of our involvement with women's golf."

McDonald's said yes in two seconds

The board of directors of the McDonald's Championship had some surprise business in August.

"It took about two seconds to say yes," said Betsy Rawls, the group's executive director. "Then the celebration began."

In replacing the departed Mazda with McDonald's, the LPGA got a sponsor and an organization that has staged an LPGA event for the last 13 years, the last seven in Wilmington, Del.

But there's a big difference in the framework of the two tournament organizations. "Mazda was involved to sell cars," said Rawls. "We're involved to raise money for charity."

The Ronald McDonald Children's Charities has been the beneficiary of the McDonald's Championship and will remain the beneficiary for the LPGA Championship.

"McDonald's doesn't own this tournament," explained Rawls. "The McDonald's charities own it. We're a non-profit corporation."

—*by Jerry Potter*

Hall of Famer Patty Sheehan had been a member of Team Mazda.

ON THE FAIRWAYS: THE YEAR IN GOLF

JANUARY

▶**Jan. 7:** *Quote of the day*—After torrential rains had drenched the course at La Costa Country Club, ducks gathered in a huge pond that used to be the 18th fairway.

Dave Stockton, instead of calling to see if the first round of the Infiniti Tournament of Champions had been delayed, simply asked PGA Tour official Duke Butler, "Can we duck hunt off the 18th green?"

▶**Jan. 7:** Fred Couples was named PGA Tour Player of the Year for the second year in a row. Lee Trevino was voted Senior PGA Tour Player of the Year. John Flannery was the Hogan Tour's top player. Mark Carnevale and Dave Stockton were top rookies in the PGA Tour and Senior PGA Tour, respectively.

▶**Jan. 11:** Ray Floyd failed to make a run in his bid to win both the senior and regular tour fields of the Infiniti Tournament of Champions.

"I think everybody I've talked to lately has mentioned the double-dipping at the Tournament of Champions," Floyd had said on the eve of the event. "I think it has been good for golf."

▶**Jan. 25:** Karsten Manufacturing Corp., makers of Ping golf equipment, filed suit in U.S. District Court in Los Angeles against Make and Supply Sports International Inc., and its president, Ping Kugi Niu. The suit charged the defendants with copying Karsten's "Ping Zing" iron by infringing on its patent rights.

▶**Jan. 28:** Legendary player Sam Snead, 80, settled a suit stemming from an auto accident that left Roy Jeffers, 30, of Waynesboro, Ga., paralyzed. The accident occurred April 7, 1992. Snead was on his way to The Masters, where he was to be an honorary starter. The Augusta (Ga.) Chronicle reported the settlement to be worth at least $2 million.

▶**Jan. 28:** Spalding Sports Worldwide, the largest manufacturer of golf balls, planned to sue companies that market remanufactured balls under the Spalding logo. Earlier in the week, U.S. marshals seized 125,000 balls from Daniel Hutson, whose company, Challenge Golf of Waxhaw, N.C., had sold repainted balls with the Spalding logo for the previous two years.

FEBRUARY

▶**Feb. 1:** Simon & Schuster announced that Harvey Pennick's *Little Red Book* had become the best-selling hardcover sports book of all time.

▶**Feb. 21:** A Florida Circuit Court judge ruled that Fred Couples had to pay ex-wife Deborah temporary support of $52,000 a month until their divorce settlement became final.

Deborah Couples, an accomplished polo player had asked for $168,000 a month until the polo season ended, then $55,000 a month. Fred Couples offered $17,500.

Couples said his wife's obsession with polo ended the marriage. The divorce became final in October.

MARCH

▶**March 7:** Brothers Jurgen Krueger, 56, of Fairfield, Calif., and Dieter Krueger, 58, of Germany each had a hole-in-one during the same round at Rancho Solano Golf Course in Fairfield, Calif.

▶**March 14:** J.C. Snead's victory at the Vantage at The Dominion was his first in two Senior PGA Tour seasons. It also came two days after a tree fell on his house on the storm-swept East Coast.

"My wife (Sue) said, 'Play hard. We need the money to fix the house,' " Snead said. "I hope that's enough."

▶**March 18:** Richard T. Miller, general chairman of the 1993 U.S. Open at Baltusrol Golf Club in Springfield, N.J., said there would be no female tournament marshals during the event in June because of safety concerns resulting from an incident in the 1980 U.S. Open at Baltusrol. Fans overran the 18th hole after Jack Nicklaus sank the tournament-winning putt.

▶**March 28:** George Bush had spectators ducking his first shot off the tee in the Doug Sanders Kingwood Celebrity Classic as it sailed over their heads and into the trees. His second shot whacked a fan in the leg.

The Bush foursome—which included former vice president Dan Quayle and golf pros Doug Sanders and Mike Hill—shot a 63 and tied for eighth place.

April

▶**April 2:** Ian Woosnam, 1991 Masters champion, had missed the cut in all three of his PGA Tour starts in 1993. After failing to reach the third round of the Freeport-McMoran Classic in New Orleans, a frustrated Woosnam handed over his clubs to a youngster in the gallery.

▶**April 14:** Karsten Manufacturing Corp. and the PGA Tour settled their legal differences about square-groove Ping Eye-2 irons: The PGA Tour would not prohibit use of square-groove clubs; it would establish an equipment advisory committee; and its insurers would pay $4.5 million toward its legal expenses and an undisclosed sum to Karsten Manufacturing.

▶**April 20:** Former LPGA player Cathy Gerring, severely burned almost a year before at a tournament near Nashville, sued six defendants for $25 million in damages. The suit charged that a cooking device used—a wok and burner with an open flame—violated the county fire code, and that two food-service workers caused an explosion and fire by trying to refill the burner with liquid fuel.

▶**April 25:** Wearing a brace on his sore left thumb, Lee Trevino tied for fourth at the Muratec Reunion Pro-Am. "I should be back full speed in a few weeks," Trevino said. He had surgery on the thumb in December 1992.

▶**April 28:** Hampered by two herniated disks he had injured lifting his children at an amusement park in March, Tom Kite withdrew from the Shell Houston Open, the second tournament he missed since failing to make the cut at The Masters.

"The doctor said it would be a three-, four-, or five-week period of treatment," said Kite, who received cortisone shots for the injury. "I'll just have to go week to week."

May

▶**May 19:** Former vice president Dan Quayle apparently had plenty of time after leaving office to hone his golf game. In a pro-am before the Kemper Open in Potomac, Md., Quayle beat his pro partner, Joey Sindelar, by four shots.

Sindelar, 16th on the PGA Tour money list at the time, shot 5-over-par 76, while Quayle, a 5-handicap at nearby Congressional Country Club, had four birdies and a 72.

"Yeah, he beat me," Sindelar said. "From the white (members) tee (the pros played the blue, or back, tees). He has a real good swing."

June

▶**June 6:** Randy Hawkins, 34, of Jackson, Mich., got his first hole-in-one at 10 a.m. on the par-3, 105-yard third hole at Lakeland Hills Golf Course in Michigan Center. Six hours later, his father, Larry, 57, aced the same hole.

▶**June 20:** By finishing second at the the Rochester International and winning $46,546, Patty Sheehan became only the third LPGA player to surpass the $4 million earnings mark. Pat Bradley and Betsy King are the others.

▶**June 20:** The Rhode Island Woman's Golf Association continued to bar Nathalie Price from its championship because she did not belong to a private club. Price was a three-time State Publinx champion. RIWGA bylaws state that membership shall consist of private 18-hole golf clubs within Rhode Island.

July

▶**July 4:** Former major league pitcher Rick Rhoden shot a 2-under-par 214 to win the $195,000 Chrysler Celebrity Classic in Brampton, Ontario. He beat former NFL running back Donny Anderson by three strokes.

▶**July 6:** The LPGA, which has had trouble filling the early part of its schedule, announced a new 72-hole tournament for spring '94 in Florida.

The tournament, for a select field of about 20, will take place March 2-5 at Grand Cypress Resort in Orlando.

The participants will be winners of events in the past year, plus active Hall of Famers. Money is $700,000.

▶**July 5:** Ian Woosnam, the 1991 Masters champion, was fined $3,320 and banned from driving for a year after a court in London ruled his blood-alcohol level was more than double the legal limit when he crashed his Mercedes June 24. Woosnam, 35, drove through a row of hedges in the English county of Shropshire.

▶**July 8:** *Quote of the day*—ABC on-course golf reporter, Mark Rolfing, on college roommate, and golf teammate, Dan Quayle: "In college we played on about the same level. But he never was a good golfer. That kind of frustrated him and maybe pointed him in the direction of politics."

▶**July 11:** Rick Rhoden won for the second time in a week, shooting 9-under par for 54 holes in the Isuzu Celebrity Golf Championship at Edgewood Tahoe Golf Course in Stateline, Nev. Rhoden beat baseball Hall of Famer Johnny Bench by four strokes and collected $75,000.

"The big key for me the whole tournament was that I putted well," said Rhoden. "I consider myself an OK putter. I just try not to give anybody anything."

▶**July 17:** A six-year-old who plays golf better than some adults was forced off the links because of an age rule. Brian Adam played only one hole with his parents, Leslie and Paul, at Crawford's Par Three Golf Course in Wildwood, Pa. Course owner Bill Crawford called local police, who asked the family to leave.

August

▶**Aug. 15:** Jane Geddes shot the lowest round ever at the Women's British Open—a final-round 64—but placed fourth behind Australia's Karen Lunn, whose 17-under 275 was also a record low.

▶**Aug 18:** The LPGA Los Coyotes Classic, scheduled for Sept. 30-Oct. 3 in Buena Park, Calif., was canceled because of economic conditions, LPGA commissioner Charlie Mechem said. The British Women's Open was added to the LPGA Tour schedule for 1994, though it would not count as a major event.

▶**Aug. 22:** Golfer Calvin Peete accused the Senior PGA Tour of racial prejudice in the GTE Northwest Classic at Bothell, Wash., saying a warning for slow play was "unjustified." Peete wasn't penalized but withdrew. Said rules official Bryan Naugle: "Our officials treat everyone the same."

September

▶**Sept. 1:** Juli Inkster, struggling through one of the worst years of her career, revealed at the LPGA du Maurier Classic that she was pregnant with her second child.

▶**Sept. 27:** Augusta, Ga. native Jim Dent, a star on the Senior PGA Tour, became the first black player selected for induction into the Georgia Golf Hall of Fame.

▶**Sept. 29:** Ray Floyd withdrew from the Senior PGA Tour Vantage Championship upon hearing of the death of his father-in-law and ended his PGA Tour career.

Moments before an interview in Clemmons, N.C., Floyd learned Tony Fraietta, 80, had died after an illness.

"I'm sorry I won't be able to play this week. I always enjoy coming back to North Carolina," said Floyd, 51, born and raised in the state.

He was the only player to win on the PGA Tour ('92 Doral Ryder Open) and Senior Tour (three events) in one year.

"I'm going to stop trying to play both," he said. "I'm going to cut out the regular tour except for some majors. I'll continue to play The Masters as long as I don't embarrass myself, but I'll basically be a Senior Tour golfer from now on."

October

▶**Oct. 5:** In taping the Wendy's Three-Tour Challenge for a Christmas broadcast, Ray Floyd fired a course-record, 10-under-par 62 at Colleton River Plantation. Floyd led the Senior PGA Tour team to victory.

Said Paul Azinger, who was on the PGA Tour team, five strokes back: "Ray almost shot his age."

▶**Oct. 24:** Corey Pavin didn't win his first major, but he became a world champion, beating Nick Faldo at the final hole to win the World Match Play Championship.

"Besides the major championships, this tournament is next in line," Pavin said. "I love match play. In a way, I wish we could play every tournament match play, but I think by the end of the year all my hair would fall out. It's so much stress."

NOVEMBER

▶**Nov. 4:** The United States Golf Association stripped Sharon (Ohio) Golf Club of a 1994 U.S. Open sectional qualifier because of its all-male membership. Instead the 36-hole qualifier will be at Sunnehanna Country Club in Johnstown, Pa., June 6, 1994.

▶**Nov. 7:** Colin Montgomerie took advantage of Nick Faldo's ailing wrists to relieve the world's No. 1 player of the European money title.

Montgomerie, a beefy 30-year-old Scot, won the PGA European Tour Volvo Masters at Spain's Valderrama Golf Club and leapt from fifth to first on the money list. He played 24 events to Faldo's 14.

"I'm beginning to think I'm actually quite good at this game," Montgomerie said. "I have doubted it before."

▶**Nov. 7:** Fred Couples made three birdies in four holes on the back nine to pull away from the field for a four-stroke victory at the Kapalua International. Though not an official PGA Tour event, it was Couples' second win of the year.

▶**Nov. 9:** Arnold Palmer was picked to replace suspended John Daly in the Skins Game at Bighorn Golf Club in Palm Desert, Calif.

"I'm excited," said Palmer. "I believe I can be very competitive in this format."

Palmer's last official victory was in the 1988 Crestar Classic, a Senior PGA Tour event, but he had won the Senior Skins Game three of the previous four years.

"One of the things I've had trouble with lately is keeping my concentration long enough to play three rounds," Palmer said. "But in The Skins Game, you just have to keep yourself in one hole. That's why I've had some success."

▶**Nov. 10:** Tiger Woods, 17, among the youngest players to compete in a PGA Tour event, signed a letter of intent to attend Stanford University.

▶**Nov. 10:** The PGA of America acquired an option to buy the Valhalla Golf Club in Louisville, as part of what PGA CEO Jim Awtrey called "a strategic directive to acquire a few world-class sites" for the PGA Championship. Valhalla has been selected to host the 1996 PGA Championship.

▶**Nov. 21:** Ray Floyd sank a 6-foot birdie putt on the 18th hole at the Sherwood Country Club in Thousand Oaks, Calif., to win the $1.1 million Franklin Funds Shark Shootout with partner Steve Elkington.

▶**Nov. 21:** Jenny Lidback topped a year which included three top 10 finishes with a record-shattering victory at the Mitsubishi Motors Invitational Pro-Am. Her final-round 6-under-par 66 at Troon North in Scottsdale, Ariz., was a course and tournament low.

DECEMBER

▶**Dec. 5:** *Quote of the day*—Upon ending a four-year victory drought with a win in the Greg Norman Holden Classic in Australia, Curtis Strange said, "I'm back for this week."

▶**Dec. 19:** After entering the Johnnie Walker Championship as a replacement for the vacationing Greg Norman, Larry Mize dusted the field at Tryall Country Club in Montego Bay, Jamaica, finishing 10 strokes ahead of runner-up Fred Couples.

*—contributions from
Deborah Barrington, Debbie Becker, Jerry Bonkowski, Erik Brady, Peter Brewington, Ben Brown, Jack Carey, Steve Hershey, Michael Hiestand, Pat Guy, Jerry Potter, Beth Tuschak, Jon Saraceno, Larry Weisman, Carolyn White and Cynthia Wilson*

GOLF ALMANAC 1994

MAJORS

PGA TOUR ...26

LPGA...46

SENIOR PGA TOUR...58

USA SNAPSHOTS®
A look at statistics that shape the sports world

Winning by a wide margin
Largest margins of victory for the four major tournaments:

Stroke	Player	Year	Margin
British Open	Tom Morris Sr.	1862	13
U.S. Open	Willie Smith	1899	11
The Masters	Jack Nicklaus	1965	9
PGA Championship	Jack Nicklaus	1980	7

Source: USA TODAY research By Regi Ransdell, USA TODAY

GOLF ALMANAC 1994

THE MASTERS

AT A GLANCE

- **Course:** Augusta National Golf Club
- **Location:** Augusta, Ga.
- **When:** April 8-11, 1993
- **Weather:** Sunny and warm mostly. Rain interrupted play Friday and Saturday.
- **Purse:** $1,675,301
- **Par:** 72
- **Yards:** 6,905
- **Defending champion:** Fred Couples
- **Tournament record:** 17-under-par 271, Jack Nicklaus, 1965; Ray Floyd, 1976
- **Format:** 72 holes stroke play; cut to low 44 and ties, plus all players within 10 strokes of the lead (62 players made the cut).
- **Field:** Invited pros and amateurs.

Bernhard Langer won his second green jacket handily, while the American competition struggled to keep pace. Breezing to victory at the Masters, Langer displayed the methodical style that has made him a world-class golf champion.

Langer started the final round with a four-shot lead after a third-round 69 and finished the same way with a near flawless 70, for an 11-under-par 277.

"After winning the first one (in 1985), I thought the second would be easier," Langer said. "I was starting to wonder if I would ever win another major championship."

He pulled it off with precision driving in windy conditions. The only fairway he missed in two days was the very last one, when he ignored his caddy's suggestion to hit a safe 3-wood and drove into the fairway bunker.

"Bernhard wasn't in trouble all day until it didn't matter," said Chip Beck, who shot 70 and finished second, two strokes in front of John Daly (69), Steve Elkington (71), Tom Lehman (68) and Lanny Wadkins (71).

"Langer is a tactician beyond description," said Dan Forsman. "He's intelligent, highly methodical, highly calculating. You know he's not going to beat himself."

After an opening bogey when he chipped too strongly, the German champion pieced together 11 consecutive pars before a 20-foot eagle putt at the par-5 13th gave him breathing room.

"Until then, I wasn't making any putts," he said. "But I felt good about my swing and was firing at the flags all day. I even surprised myself sometimes."

Langer never made a double bogey, never hit a ball into the water, and had one three-putt.

—*by Steve Hershey*

Bernhard Langer rolled to his second Masters win.

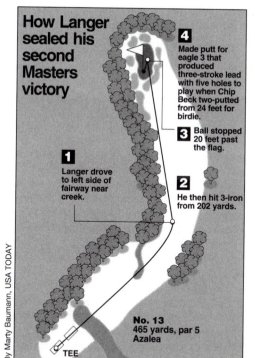

How Langer sealed his second Masters victory

1 Langer drove to left side of fairway near creek.

2 He then hit 3-iron from 202 yards.

3 Ball stopped 20 feet past the flag.

4 Made putt for eagle 3 that produced three-stroke lead with five holes to play when Chip Beck two-putted from 24 feet for birdie.

No. 13
465 yards, par 5
Azalea

TEE

By Marty Baumann, USA TODAY

'Three perfect shots' revised Langer's image

Bernhard Langer, 35, had been a world-class player for a decade, winning 37 times around the globe. Twice, he led the PGA European Tour money list, and in 1992 he was second.

In each of the previous 14 years, he had won at least once—and was topped only by Seve Ballesteros' 18 victories.

Still, until his four-shot triumph, he was best remembered in the USA not for winning the 1985 Masters, but for missing a 6-foot putt that cost the Europeans the '91 Ryder Cup.

Langer's victory put the missed Ryder Cup putt behind him. Two-time Masters champions deserve that privilege.

"I live in the future, not in the past," Langer said. "I know people won't let me forget it, but I'm satisfied that I gave my best effort. That's all I can do."

Langer's best was more than enough at Augusta. He sealed the victory with a 20-foot eagle putt on the par-5 13th hole, where he made what he called "three perfect shots."

First, he drew his drive down the left side, around the corner of the 465-yard hole, giving himself an opportunity to go for the green.

"I had 202 yards to the flag," he said. "There was no question I was going for it. I wasn't going to back off. I felt if I was going to win, I had to make some birdies."

At that stage, Langer had a two-shot lead on playing partner Chip Beck and had made only one birdie, at the downwind 555-yard second that yielded 28 birdies and only one bogey.

Beck missed his attempt to the left, then Langer drained his and raised his lead to three shots.

"Bernhard made a great putt," Beck said. "It was on line all the way."

Langer said he didn't feel victory was assured until he went four ahead with a birdie at 15. After his drive at the 500-yard hole, he had 243 yards to the flag against the wind. He laid up with a 5-iron, then hit a sand wedge to 7 feet.

"After that, I felt I would win if I didn't do something stupid," he said. "For the first time all day, I stopped aiming at the flags."

—by Steve Hershey

Strong showing makes Daly a comer for 1994

An early favorite for the 1994 Masters might be John Daly.

The 1991 PGA Championship winner left Augusta National buoyed by his performance, though he tied for third, six strokes back.

"I believe this golf course is set up for my game," he said. "I was proud of myself. I missed a couple of putts, but I hit the ball really well."

Daly has played two Masters. His highest score in eight rounds is 73, in the third round in 1992 and 1993.

He closed with a 69–283, matching his 1992 total.

"I was in contention on the back nine," said Daly, 6 under through 15 holes.

"That helps my confidence."

COMMENTARY: A FOREIGN AFFAIR?

Once again, a foreign player has won the Masters. Once again, most of the top players on the PGA Tour were non factors. This has become a spring ritual like azaleas blooming in Georgia.

With German Bernhard Langer's overwhelming four-shot win, foreign players have won five of the last six and six of the nine Masters since his 1985 victory.

Only Jack Nicklaus's brilliant back nine in '86 and Larry Mize's miraculous 140-foot chip-in in '87 kept Greg Norman or Seve Ballesteros from increasing foreign domination.

What is it about Augusta National that totally intimidates so many U.S. players? Why can't Lanny Wadkins, Tom Kite, Payne Stewart, Davis Love III, Paul Azinger, John Cook and others ever win?

The players have many theories, most of them cop-outs having to do with grass. I have another and it goes back to heritage, tradition, growing up in the good ol' USA.

Ever since Love, Azinger, Cook et al., had their first cut-down club in their hands as toddlers, they heard about the Masters, the breath-taking beauty and immaculate splendor of Augusta National.

The tournament quickly took on an almost mystic quality. As these young players grew, their putting green games were always "for The Masters." The vision of donning a green jacket becomes the dream of every youngster.

As their games improve and they become professionals, the dream intensifies. When a young player wins a PGA Tour event, one of the first things he says is "now I can go to Augusta." That means more than the money or trophy.

Love had talked of The Masters since January, how much winning it would mean.

"I'd trade all six of my victories for a win at Augusta," he said. "That's how people judge you—not by how many tournaments you win, but how you play in major championships."

Love, one of the world's longest hitters and most talented players, hasn't had a top-10 at The Masters. This time, he tied for 52nd, 10 over.

Azinger, a winner in each of the last seven years, never has contended at Augusta. His best finish was a tie for 14th in 1989. He missed the cut completely in 1993.

Cook never has finished higher than 21st (and that was in '81) and he has missed the cut in four of nine starts. This time, he started with a 76, then came back with a 67 before closing with a pair of 75s.

"I've got to start believing I can play around here," Cook said after his 67. "The first round, I got intimidated. I never got aggressive.

"This course makes you be very precise, but that's not me. I've got to fire at the flag and get what I get. But if you're not playing well, this place can intimidate you."

That seems to be the difference. U.S. players tiptoe into Augusta, thinking of all the negative things that can happen, remembering all the lore of disasters past at Amen Corner.

Foreign players breeze in, treating it as just another big tournament. They always refer to it as "the U.S. Masters" to differentiate it from, say, the German Masters, Volvo Masters or Dunhill Masters. Just another Masters. For uptight U.S. players, there is only one Masters.

—by Steve Hershey

BECK LAID UP ON NO. 15, FINISHED SECOND BEST

Chip Beck had a chance to gamble during the final round, but he chose to play it safe and finished second in The Masters.

The choice was whether to go for the green on the par-5, 500-yard 15th hole with his second shot or lay up. He chose to lay up, considering the risk too great.

"I'm happy with my decision," Beck said.

Beck trailed Langer by three strokes when they came to the 15th hole, an eagle possibility and probably his last chance to put pressure on Langer.

His tee shot left him 236 yards to the front of the green and 250 yards to the pin. A PGA Tour player can easily hit a 3-wood 236 yards, but Beck held off and made par.

His decision caught Langer by surprise.

"I was talking with my caddy," Langer said. "I told him, 'In this situation, he has to go for it.' If I had been in his shoes, I would have gone for it."

Langer made birdie, and that pretty much put the tournament out of Beck's reach.

—by Jerry Potter

COMMENTARY: BECK WILL REGRET IT

Finishing second in The Masters is not chopped liver. Nor is a 70 with the heat on for the final day. Lots of legends in other Masters would have died for a 70 on Sunday.

But Beck was not exactly George Patton coming down No. 15, was he? Behind three shots to Langer, it was time to start firing up three-pointers. Time to swing for the fences.

Americans prefer their history with a dash of daring. Damn the water, hand me a 3-wood.

But Beck is a precise young man, and having spent several minutes processing the data in his onboard computer, he decided he'd rather not. Too much wind. Too risky. So he laid up short. And settled for a par.

It would have been highly problematical for Beck to have gotten his eagle. It is unlikely he would have caught the resolute Langer had he gone at No. 15 with an Exocet missile.

But John Wayne did not get rich making movies about laying up.

In his interrogation Sunday, Beck was asked to explain how it could be he was seen actually smiling while walking with Langer during the round. Grit teeth and fire in the eyes seemed more telegenic.

"We're not in Herzegovina fighting a war," Beck answered. "If we can't enjoy it, when are we going to enjoy life? It's Easter Sunday, we're at Augusta, and we're playing well."

Perfectly sound answer from a man who probably was going to finish second no matter what he did. But I still wish he'd have gone for it. And so, I suspect, when all is said and done, will he.

—by Mike Lopresti

FORSMAN'S HOPES ENDED WITH DOUBLE DIP IN CREEK

Dan Forsman left himself a place in the lore of The Masters.

Unfortunately, he did it with a quadruple-bogey 7 on the par-3 No. 12, shortly after he had drawn within a stroke of leader Bernhard Langer.

The spectators gave Forsman a huge ovation at the 12th tee after he had saved par on No. 11.

Beck and Langer were on the 11th green. Playing partner Lanny Wadkins was safely on the green at 12.

"Lanny made it look so easy," Forsman said. "But I was having trouble with the yardage. I must have asked my caddy about the distance 15 times. My mind was racing and I wasn't able to slow down."

He had 162 yards to the pin. He chose a 7-iron and lofted the ball high.

"I knew it had no chance," he recalled.

It landed in the middle of Rae's Creek. He took his drop 100 yards short of the green and hit a sand wedge.

The ball hit the creek bank and spun back into the water.

He hit again, right and behind the pin, and two-putted for a 7.

Though he regrouped to birdie 13 and 14, his chance to win was gone.

—by Jerry Potter

MASTERS SHORT PUTTS

Handicapping The Masters

Who did you pick? Here's how USA TODAY sports analyst Danny Sheridan sized up the odds against winning The Masters:

Nick Faldo	7:1
Greg Norman	7:1
Fred Couples	8:1
Nick Price	8:1
Tom Kite	8:1
Davis Love III	10:1
Payne Stewart	12:1
Paul Azinger	12:1
Ian Woosnam	15:1
J. Maria Olazabal	18:1
Seve Ballesteros	20:1
Berhand Langer	25:1
Ian Baker-Finch	30:1
Mark McCumber	30:1
Brett Ogle	30:1
Steve Elkington	35:1
David Frost	35:1
Corey Pavin	35:1
Ray Floyd	40:1
John Cook	40:1
Ben Crenshaw	45:1
Chip Beck	45:1
Larry Mize	45:1
Phil Mickelson	50:1
Lanny Wadkins	50:1
Jeff Sluman	50:1
Mark O'Meara	50:1
Curtis Strange	60:1
Hale Irwin	60:1
Steve Pate	70:1
Rocco Mediate	75:1
Jeff Maggert	90:1
Craig Parry	100:1
Jack Nicklaus	250:1
John Daly	500:1
Arnold Palmer	1 million:1
Field	50:1
Any amateur	100,000:1

JACK 'N' ARNIE: A couple of old timers stirred visions of their glory days, upstaging the next generation during the opening round at Augusta.

Arnold Palmer shot birdie-birdie-birdie to begin the day, sending the crowd into a frenzy. "It was so loud, the ground was almost shaking up here (first tee)," said Ray Floyd, who was waiting to start.

Reality set in quickly for Palmer with a bogey at the 205-yard No. 4. Another at the par-3 sixth touched off a string of four in a row. Then he settled down and played the back side even, with birdies at 12 and 18 for 74. Still, he commanded a large media gathering outside the scoring tent.

"I was so pumped, I couldn't control my swing," he said of his once-in-a lifetime start. "The clubs started feeling like toothpicks on the fourth tee."

But the real show-stealer was Jack Nicklaus. He turned back the clock and performed from start to finish as he did in his prime, tying for the first-round lead.

Nicklaus' 5-under 67 equaled his best opening rounds at Augusta. In 1965, he shot 67 and went on to win. In '76, Nicklaus also had 67, but finished third to a fellow named Floyd, who also woke up the echoes during the first round. Floyd's only bogey came when he three-putted No. 10, and he finished at 68.

"In the old days, Jack was never off the leader board," Floyd said. "Guys like him and Arnold draw from positives on days like this, draw from the good things that have happened to them."

Nicklaus said he was inspired when he saw Palmer had birdied the first three holes, that it rekindled the old competitive fires.

" 'Hey,' I told myself, 'You can't let him be low senior,' " he said. "It got me in a positive frame of mind. I guess we still compete. We played practice rounds together the last two days and had a lot of fun."

CHAMPIONS' LOCKER ROOM: Just inside the front door of the Augusta National clubhouse, up the winding staircase to the right, past old photos of former presidents of this stately club is an unmarked room: the champions' locker room.

Before this year's tournament Fred Couples never knew where it was. When he went to the regular locker room, he was told summarily his locker would forevermore be in the main clubhouse, upstairs.

"It's kinda neat up there," he said. "There were a lot of old guys in there I don't normally hang around with. But it's quiet, out of the way, a good place to hang out."

GLAD IT WAS OVER: Couples, who finished 72–288 and 11 strokes back, was pleased to be defending champion but equally pleased when the tournament was over.

"I played well, but it wasn't good enough, and it wasn't near as good as I played a year ago," he said.

Couples said being the Masters defending champion is an especially tiring role, more than being the defending champion of the U.S. Open or PGA Championship.

"Those tournaments go different places each year," he said. "This one comes back to the same place, so there are more questions."

A year later, his recollections of his victory?

"It was a big, big win for me," he said of the '92 Masters. "All the media attention is fun, but I wouldn't want to do it every single week."

WATCHING: U.S. Amateur champion Justin Leonard hung around Augusta National for the weekend even though he didn't make the cut.

"I have a nonrefundable (airline) ticket," said the University of Texas junior the final day. "I'd rather be back home."

Leonard shot 76-73—149 and missed the cut by two strokes. For only the third Masters, no amateur made the cut.

BACKED OUT: Hampered by an injured back, Tom Kite, a pre-tournament favorite, failed to make the cut after shooting an opening-round 73. He walked gingerly on the course, bending only his knees to tee his ball or take it from cups.

Kite suffered from "a couple of herniated disks," he later said. He had injured his back two weeks earlier while at Disneyworld with his children and then aggravated it on the Augusta practice range two days before The Masters.

HOT ROOKIE: Tom Lehman, in his first Masters, couldn't get center stage on or off the course. Tied for the lead after the first round, he had to wait for Jack Nicklaus to finish his interview before starting his.

"I enjoyed listening to Jack," Lehman said. "I learned a lot from him. This game is like Jack says: You take it one shot at a time."

BENT GRASS: Augusta National

played longer in 1993 because the fairways had been mowed from green to tee, making players hit drives against the grain of the grass.

"You're getting at least 20 yards less roll on the drive," two-time winner Nick Faldo said before the tournament. "That will make a considerable difference."

CHIP-IN: Chip Beck shot 6-under-par 21 Wednesday to win the par-3 tournament. No par-3 winner has won The Masters the same year.

—*by Steve Hershey and Jerry Potter*

Scores and earnings

Bernhard Langer, $306,000	68-70-69-70–277
Chip Beck, $183,600	72-67-72-70–281
Steve Elkington, $81,600	71-70-71-71–283
Lanny Wadkins, $81,600	69-72-71-71–283
Tom Lehman, $81,600	67-75-73-68–283
John Daly, $81,600	70-71-73-69–283
Jose Maria Olazabal, $54,850	70-72-74-68–284
Dan Forsman, $54,850	69-69-73-73–284
Brad Faxon, $47,600	71-70-72-72–285
Payne Stewart, $47,600	74-70-72-69–285
Anders Forsbrand, $34,850	71-74-75-66–286
Seve Ballesteros, $34,850	74-70-71-71–286
Ray Floyd, $34,850	68-71-74-73–286
Corey Pavin, $34,850	67-75-73-71–286
Scott Simpson, $34,850	72-71-71-72–286
Fuzzy Zoeller, $34,850	75-67-71-73–286
Jeff Sluman, $24,650	71-72-71-73–287
Howard Twitty, $24,650	70-71-73-73–287
Ian Woosnam, $24,650	71-74-73-69–287
Mark Calcavecchia, $24,650	71-70-74-72–287
Mark O'Meara, $17,000	75-69-73-71–288
Fred Couples, $17,000	72-70-74-72–288
Larry Mize, $17,000	67-74-74-73–288
Sandy Lyle, $17,000	73-71-71-73–288
Jeff Maggert, $17,000	70-67-75-76–288
Russ Cochran, $17,000	70-69-73-76–288
Jack Nicklaus, $12,350	67-75-76-71–289
Hale Irwin, $12,350	74-69-74-72–289
Joey Sindelar, $12,350	72-69-76-72–289
Nolan Henke, $12,350	76-69-71-73–289
Greg Norman, $10,533	74-68-71-77–290
Bruce Lietzke, $10,533	74-71-71-74–290
Andrew Magee, $10,533	75-69-70-76–290
Gene Sauers, $8,975	74-71-75-71–291
Bob Gilder, $8,975	69-76-75-71–291
Phil Mickelson, $8,975	72-71-75-73–291
Craig Stadler, $8,975	73-74-69-75–291
Jay Haas, $8,000	70-73-75-74–292
Nick Faldo, $6,817	71-76-79-67–293
Duffy Waldorf, $6,817	72-75-73-73–293
John Cook, $6,817	76-67-75-75–293
Ted Schulz, $6,817	69-76-76-72–293
Keith Clearwater, $6,817	74-70-75-74–293
Lee Janzen, $6,817	67-73-76-77–293
Jumbo Ozaki, $4,940	75-71-77-71–294
Joe Ozaki, $4,940	74-70-78-72–294
Tom Watson, $4,940	71-75-73-75–294
Jay Don Blake, $4,940	71-74-73-76–294
Craig Parry, $4,940	69-72-75-78–294
Gil Morgan, $4,250	72-74-72-77–295
Brett Ogle, $4,250	70-74-71-80–295
David Peoples, $4,050	71-73-78-74–296
Colin Montgomerie, $4,050	71-72-78-75–296
Davis Love III, $3,900	73-72-76-77–298
David Edwards, $3,900	73-73-76-76–298
Ian Baker-Finch, $3,900	73-72-73-80–298
Gary Hallberg, $3,800	72-74-78-75–299
Charles Coody, $3,800	74-72-75-78–299
John Huston, $3,800	68-74-84-75–301
Gary Player, $3,700	71-76-75-80–302
Billy Andrade, $3,700	73-74-80-76–303

United States Open

AT A GLANCE

- **Course:** Baltusrol Golf Club (Lower Course)
- **Location:** Springfield, N.J.
- **When:** June 17-20, 1993
- **Weather:** Overcast and muggy Thursday. Very hot and humid Friday; even hotter (high of 102 degrees) and more humid Saturday. Temperatures in the 80s and a slight breeze Sunday.
- **Purse:** $1.6 million
- **Par:** 70
- **Yards:** 7,152
- **Defending champion:** Tom Kite, 3-under-par 285, at Pebble Beach (Calif.) Golf Links
- **Tournament record** : 8-under-par 272, Jack Nicklaus (63-71-70-68), 1980; Lee Janzen (67-67-69-69), 1993 (both at Baltusrol Golf Club, Lower Course, Springfield, N.J.).

Lee Janzen surprised many with his first majors win.

Taking advantage of three big breaks down the stretch, an unheralded Lee Janzen outdueled Payne Stewart at the 93rd U.S. Open.

"Some of the things that happened out there, I felt like maybe I was destined to win, because I got some of the greatest breaks you could ever get," said Janzen, who tied both Jack Nicklaus' U.S. Open record of 8-under-par 272 and Lee Trevino's mark of shooting four rounds in the 60s.

"I woke up with with a knot in my stomach, and it hasn't gone away yet."

At No. 10, Janzen tried to hit a 5-iron out of the rough over some trees but didn't hit it high enough. It miraculously went through the tree limbs and onto the green, where he two-putted for par.

In what was perhaps the turning point of his showdown with Stewart, Janzen hit a 5-iron shot in the rough on the par-3 16th and got lucky when it bounced into a good lie. Janzen then chipped in for a two-shot lead, showing uncommon nerve and determination.

"When I saw what a good lie I had," he said, "I felt like I had a good chance to chip it in."

The young challenger offered to let Stewart putt before he chipped. Ever-courteous, Stewart, about 45 feet away, told Janzen to come on, if he wanted.

"That's just golf etiquette," Stewart shrugged. "Even if you're away, if the other guy is off the green, you usually ask him if he wants to come on."

Janzen knew the possible consequences. If he chipped in, it would shrink the hole for Stewart and probably produce a commanding two-stroke lead.

"I wanted Payne to feel comfortable with his decision," Janzen said. "I asked him twice, and he gave me the option to go. I felt I had given him every opportunity to putt first, and if I chipped in, it was going to be a huge momentum swing."

(All manners aside, Janzen, 28, also betrayed true grit, saying, "I felt like any advantage I could get, I should take.")

He bore down and made a shot that will go down in Open history, along with Tom

Watson's chip-in to win in '82 and Tom Kite's pitch-in at the 1992 Open.

Stewart was stunned, of course.

With two par-5s left in the Open, he still was in contention. But after Janzen's chip-in, he was a long shot, at best.

"It wasn't what I was anticipating," Stewart said, smiling. "But that's what makes champions. You get the breaks, you win the golf tournament."

Janzen also benefited from a lucky stroke at 17. "I pushed my drive into the woods and it bounced out."

Another errant drive at 18 forced him to lay up with a sand wedge, then hit a 192-yard 4-iron to the green.

"I pushed it," Janzen said. "I was trying to hit a 4-iron to the middle of the green and I pushed it, but the wind held it up and I got a great bounce (to 8 feet, where he made birdie)."

Stewart, a runner-up for the third time this year after shooting 70, said with a shrug, "Those are things that win golf tournaments."

—by Steve Hershey

FRUSTRATION CONTINUED FOR PAYNE STEWART

In a year when he could have left marks that might not be equaled in today's era, Payne Stewart suffered, perhaps, his most bitter defeat.

On the verge of winning his second U.S. Open championship, he watched a relative unknown chip in on the 16th hole and go on to win a title he felt was his.

"All the credit in the world has to go to Lee Janzen," said a gracious Stewart, who finished two shots short of the title. "He just stood up there and he did it."

Stewart had said almost the same thing two weeks earlier when good friend Paul Azinger holed a miraculous bunker shot on the last hole to snatch away a win at the Memorial.

This was Stewart's third runner-up finish of 1993. He had also been third three times while trying desperately to collect his first win since his triumph in the 1991 U.S. Open.

"Ifs and buts don't win golf tournaments," he said. "I've got no regrets. I played well. I never shot over par all week. I'll keep knocking on that door and, by golly, one of these days that door will be open and I'll just bust right through it."

After his 3-iron shot ("I caught it a little heavy,") landed in a bunker in front of the 18th green, he still thought he had a chance to win.

"I had visions of Azinger in that bunker," he said. "I thought, 'You never know. If I hole this, he has to make that putt.' But it didn't go in and I'm not the champion this year."

It seemed many times he would be. After driving wildly on the front nine, he collected himself. He birdied the par-3 ninth with a 20-footer to close to a shot, then tied when Janzen bogeyed No. 12.

"I thought I'd made my (birdie) putt at 13," Stewart said. "Then he came back and made a great birdie at 14 and that super shot at 16. After he made that shot at 16, I told my caddy, 'We've been in this situation before.'"

Snake-bitten? Perhaps. Nobody had played more good tournaments at that point in 1993. He had won a lot of money, but that didn't interest him. Neither did runner-up finishes.

"Winning is what it's all about," he said. "That's why I'm out here, to win golf tournaments. And that's why I'll keep playing and keep practicing. Sooner or later, my day will come."

—by Steve Hershey

WATSON HAD TWO SOLID ROUNDS, TIED FOR FIFTH

Tom Watson, playing in the U.S. Open only on a special exemption, didn't match Hale Irwin's winning performance under the same circumstances in 1990 at Medinah, Ill. But he finished with a flourish nonetheless.

After he sank a 45-foot par putt, he threw both hands to the sky as the huge gallery around the 18th green roared.

Payne Stewart finished second at the U.S. Open.

"It was a great finish; it was fun," Watson said.

After making birdie at 17 and coming out of the woods for par at 18, he tied for fifth with Scott Hoch, at 2-under-par 278.

"Obviously, I'm happy," he said. "I'm thrilled to be back in the tournament next year without having to qualify or receive a special exemption. It's always been my favorite tournament."

The top 16 finishers received invitations to the 1994 championship at Oakmont Country Club near Pittsburgh.

Hale Irwin, who had won the 1974 and '79 U.S. Opens, received his only exemption in 1990 and won in a playoff with Mike Donald.

After a second-round 66, Watson was tied with Payne Stewart for second, two shots behind eventual winner Lee Janzen. Then, his old putting problems resurfaced as he missed three times from 5 feet or closer for a third-round 73.

"I got off to a terrible start (Sunday)," Watson said of his bogey–double bogey beginning. "I putted pretty well, but my driver didn't really react very well. It put me out of play on some key holes where you need to have birdies chances.

"But overall, I have to be pleased. One of these days, Watson will be back."

—by Steve Hershey

STRANGE BEAT FALDO WITH LESS AT STAKE THAN 1988

Five years before, they were at the pinnacle, two of the world's best golfers met in one of the ultimate showdowns—an 18-hole playoff for the 1988 U.S. Open at The Country Club in Brookline, Mass.

Curtis Strange and Nick Faldo met again at Baltusrol last year, paired in the final round of the Open. But there were no huge crowds, no media charting every shot.

They were dew sweepers, the seventh group off. They finished 90 minutes before Payne Stewart and Lee Janzen teed off.

Strange won that historic '88 duel, 71-75, the first of back-to-back U.S. Open victories. He won the final round solidly in 1993, too, 67-72.

In the locker room afterward, Fulton Allem, winner of the '93 Southwestern Bell Colonial, passed Strange and said, "Now we know how to get you playing well again: pair you with Nick."

Strange laughed, then said he really never thought about their classic confrontation. Knowing Strange, that seems difficult to believe. He even wore a red shirt, the color associated with many of his Sunday successes.

"This week is indicative of my whole year, so up and down," said Strange, 125th on the PGA Tour money list before the Open.

Strange's roller coaster Open: 73-68-75-67. Because he hasn't been able to put four rounds together (his best was a tie for 13th at Tucson), the struggling Virginian said he would not play in the upcoming British Open.

—by Steve Hershey

JANZEN SHOWED VETERAN'S POISE, POTENTIAL

Before Lee Janzen's thrilling victory, the last 28-year-old to win the U.S. Open was Andy North in 1978. Aside from his '85 Open win, he hasn't won since.

It seems unlikely the same fate could befall Janzen, who showed the poise and determination of a battle-hardened veteran as he outdueled Payne Stewart to win golf's most prestigious title.

"Lee's going to be around for a long time. He has a lovely golf swing, a great temperament and a beautiful putting stroke. He's a true champion," said Stewart.

"I have friends who have told me this kid is awesome for years, even before he came on tour," said Paul Azinger, who matched Janzen's closing 69 and tied Australian Craig Parry for third. "It may be a little early in his career for him to win a tournament this big, but I'm not surprised."

Major championships usually are won by wily veterans who can withstand the intense pressure. But once in a while a youngster breaks through.

Jack Nicklaus burst on the scene at age 22, winning the 1962 U.S. Open.

Billy Casper won the '59 Open at 27, Gary Player won the '65 Open at 29, Lee Trevino the '68 Open at 28, and Johnny Miller the '73 Open at 26.

All went on to sensational careers. It's premature to put Janzen in that category. But he certainly has a head start on a lot of his more heralded peers, who still are hoping for their first major championship.

Curtis Strange, a two-time Open champ, said, "Lee has the game to be a consistent winner. He hasn't been out here that long, but he's shown he has the guts to win."

Rick Smith, a highly respected teaching pro, who works with Janzen, Nicklaus and Rocco Mediate, was standing beside the No. 1 tee at Baltusrol the final morning of the Open, watching his protege prepare for the most important round of golf in his life.

"The thing I like best about Lee is that he has the mental ability to stay completely focused on the shot at hand," Smith said. "So many players have a tendency to look ahead, but Lee puts all his concentration on the shot he's hitting.

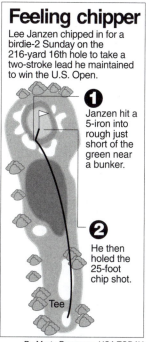

Feeling chipper
Lee Janzen chipped in for a birdie-2 Sunday on the 216-yard 16th hole to take a two-stroke lead he maintained to win the U.S. Open.

❶ Janzen hit a 5-iron into rough just short of the green near a bunker.

❷ He then holed the 25-foot chip shot.

By Marty Baumann, USA TODAY

"When we talked (Sunday) morning, I asked him what he was thinking about and he said, 'Hitting my drive on the first hole in the fairway,' and that's the way he is. That came first, then he would think only about the next shot."

An excellent example of how Janzen handles adversity came on the seventh hole when he drove into a fairway bunker, hit a 7-iron short, then a sand wedge short and pitched weakly. He faced a 10-footer for bogey and made it.

"That was a huge putt," he said. "Two shots would have been very tough to overcome, but I knew no matter what I did, I was going to play the rest of the round as hard as I could and as best I could and put everything behind me. I was able to put the poor play on the entire hole behind me and make the putt."

That might be easy to say, but how many 10-year veterans are able to do it? This was only Janzen's fourth year on the PGA Tour, but he played like he had been there all his life.

—by Steve Hershey

United States Open short putts

Janzen joined under 70-ers

In winning the U.S. Open, Lee Janzen joined an elite group: players who have broken 70 in all four rounds of a major championship.

▶ Arnold Palmer (1), 68-68-69-69–274; 1964 PGA Championship, Columbus (Ohio) CC.
▶ Lee Trevino, 69-68-69-69–275; 1968 U.S. Open Oak Hill CC, Rochester, N.Y.; and 69-68-67-69–273; 1984 PGA Championship, Shoal Creek CC, Birmingham, Ala.
▶ Ben Crenshaw (2), 69-67-69-67–272; 1979 PGA Championship, Oakland Hills CC, Birmingham, Mich.
▶ Betsy King, 68-66-67-66–267; 1992 Mazda LPGA Championship, Bethesda (Md.) CC.
▶ Lee Janzen, 67-67-69-69-272; 1993 U.S. Open, Baltusrol GC, Springfield, N.J.
▶ Greg Norman, 66-68-69-64–267; 1993 British Open, Royal St. George's GC, Sandwich, England; and (4) 68-68-67-69–272; 1993 PGA Championship, Inverness Club, Toledo, Ohio.
▶ Ernie Els (3), 68-69-69-68–274; 1993 British Open, Royal St. George's GC.
▶ Paul Azinger, 69-66-69-68–272; 1993 PGA Championship.
▶ Nick Faldo (5), 68-68-69-68–273, 1993 PGA Championship.

1- Tied for second behind winner Bobby Nichols.
2- Lost playoff to David Graham.
3- Tied for sixth.
4- Lost playoff to Paul Azinger.
5- Finished third.

"MISTAKES" UNDERMINED AZINGER: Once again, Paul Azinger challenged in a major championship and, once again, came up short.

Azinger, who has led both British Open and PGA Championships in the final round, birdied the second and third holes to get to 3 under par in the final round of the U.S. Open, then lost his momentum.

"I made a few mistakes out there (Sunday)," he said. "I made a few mistakes every day. Each day, it was holes 9 and 10. I had a good tournament, but it was never to be.

"I probably missed nine 5- to 7-foot putts the first two days, and you can't do that at a U.S. Open. I putted much better the last two days, but I had too much to make up."

Azinger's tie for third was his best finish in ten U.S. Opens and the first time he shot three rounds in the 60s.

YOUNG AM: U.S. Amateur champion Justin Leonard was a bit disappointed with his final-round 75 but pleased overall at his 8-over-par 288 finish.

"I feel very good about the way I played the first two days (69-71)," he said. "Even Saturday, I didn't hit the ball that well, but I got around in 73. (Sunday) I got off to a bad start (3 over after four holes) and never recovered.

"If I putt the way I did the first three days, I think I'll be in good shape. I'd like to get a little more distance, but I can play this golf course."

LO-O-O-NG: John Daly tamed the 630-yard No. 17th in two shots during the second round, the first time it has been reached in two shots in an Open.

He didn't do it Sunday but made birdie nonetheless.

PAIR OF ACES: Mike Hulbert made a first-round hole-in-one on the 198-yard 12th hole with a 5-iron. It was the 25th known U.S. Open ace.

"I three-putted the hole before and the one after," said Hulbert, who shot 71. "So all I was was even par for those three holes."

Three days later, Sandy Lyle aced the same hole, also with a 5-iron.

"It lightened the whole day a little bit," said Lyle, who shot 6-over 286. "I couldn't see it, but I heard the crowd noise as it got closer and closer.

"It's a lovely feeling."

FAVORABLE CONDITIONS: For the first time in years, players were rubbing their hands with glee over a U.S. Open course.

As practice rounds got underway, historic Baltusrol Golf Club looked benign: light rough and relatively flat greens.

"It's going to be the fairest Open I've ever played in," Greg Norman said. "They haven't tried to trick it up."

"This is probably the least amount of rough I've ever seen at an Open," 22-year PGA Tour veteran Tom Kite said. "It's a bit of a surprise."

OH! WHAT A FEELING: Ted Oh, a 16-year-old high school sophomore, Torrance, Calif., became the second youngest player in U.S. Open history.

"It's like, 'Oh my God, I get to see these guys, I get to talk to these guys,' " said Oh, who had qualified with a 36-hole 144 total at Valencia (Calif.) Country Club. "It's exciting. Everybody has heard of the U.S. Open. Even teachers were waving to me in the hallway saying, 'Way to go, Ted.' I guess I surprised a lot of people."

Suprised or not, Oh's teachers forced him to take his finals a week early before he could escape to Baltusrol.

The U.S. Golf Association believes Oh, who came with his parents from Korea eight years before, was the youngest to play in an Open since Tyrell Garth at age 14 in 1941.

Oh joined defending champion Tom Kite, one of eight in the field who played Opens before Oh was born, for a practice round Wednesday.

"He said, 'Just don't call me Mister.' He said I could call him Tom, but I still called him Mr. Kite."

As a freshman, Oh had defeated Eldrick "Tiger" Woods of Cypress, Calif., for the Southern California High School and Los Angeles City Open titles. (Woods became the first three-time U.S. Junior boys champion in 1993.)

In February 1993, Oh qualified for the Los Angeles Open with a 4-under-par 68. Woods received a sponsor's exemption. Neither made the cut, but Oh outplayed Woods by four strokes with 73-75–148.

Though he failed to make the cut at the Open, Oh overcame early nervousness and a triple-bogey at No. 10 for an opening 76. He birdied the 205-yard ninth and 630-yard 17th. In round two, he hit 79.

—by Don Cronin, Jeff Duncan and Steve Hershey

Scores and earnings

Player	Score
Lee Janzen, $290,000	67-67-69-69–272
Payne Stewart, $145,000	70-66-68-70–274
Craig Parry, $78,556	66-74-69-68–277
Paul Azinger, $78,556	71-68-69-69–277
Tom Watson, $48,730	70-66-73-69–278
Scott Hoch, $48,730	66-72-72-68–278
Ernie Els, $35,481	71-73-68-67–279
Raymond Floyd, $35,481	68-73-70-68–279
Nolan Henke, $35,481	72-71-67-69–279
Fred Funk, $35,481	70-72-67-70–279
David Edwards, $26,249	70-72-66-72–280
Nick Price, $26,249	71-66-70-73–280
John Adams, $26,249	70-70-69-71–280
Loren Roberts, $26,249	70-70-71-69–280
Jeff Sluman, $26,249	71-71-69-69–280
Barry Lane, $21,577	74-68-70-69–281
Fred Couples, $21,577	68-71-71-71–281
Mike Standly, $21,577	70-69-70-72–281
Ian Baker-Finch, $18,072	70-70-70-72–282
Steve Pate, $18,072	70-71-71-70–282
Blaine McCallister, $18,072	68-73-73-68–282
Dan Forsman, $18,072	73-71-70-68–282
Corey Pavin, $18,072	68-69-75-70–282
Tom Lehman, $18,072	71-70-71-70–282
Rocco Mediate, $14,531	68-72-73-70–283
Joe Ozaki, $14,531	70-70-74-69–283
Curtis Strange, $14,531	73-68-75-67–283
Chip Beck, $14,531	72-68-72-71–283
Kenny Perry, $14,531	74-70-68-71–283
Mark Calcavecchia, $14,531	70-70-71-72–283
John Cook, $14,531	75-66-70-72–283
Wayne Levi, $14,531	71-69-69-74–283
Steve Elkington, $11,052	71-70-69-74–284
Mike Donald, $11,052	71-72-67-74–284
Robert Allenby, $11,052	74-69-69-72–284
Davis Love III, $11,052	70-74-68-72–284
Lee Rinker, $11,052	70-72-71-71–284
John Daly, $11,052	72-68-72-72–284
Craig Stadler, $11,052	67-74-71-72–284
Colin Montgomerie, $11,052	71-72-73-68–284
Steve Lowery, $11,052	72-71-75-66–284
Bob Gilder, $11,052	70-69-75-70–284
Jumbo Ozaki, $11,052	71-71-72-70–284
Greg Twiggs, $11,052	72-72-70-70–284
Billy Andrade, $11,052	72-67-74-71–284
Brian Claar, $8,179	71-70-72-72–285
Mark Brooks, $8,179	72-68-74-71–285
Mark McCumber, $8,179	70-71-73-71–285
Scott Simpson, $8,179	70-73-72-70–285
Rick Fehr, $8,179	71-72-70-72–285
Larry Nelson, $8,179	70-71-71-73–285
Bob Estes, $6,526	71-73-69-73–286
Jeff Maggert, $6,526	69-70-73-74–286
Ian Woosnam, $6,526	70-74-72-70–286
Fulton Allem, $6,526	71-70-74-71–286
Vance Heafner, $6,526	70-72-73-71–286
Ed Kirby, $6,526	72-71-72-71–286
Kirk Triplett, $6,526	70-72-75-69–286
Michael Christie, $6,526	70-74-71-71–286
Keith Clearwater, $6,526	71-72-71-72–286
Sandy Lyle, $6,526	70-74-70-72–286
Joel Edwards, $5,940	71-73-70-73–287
Jay Don Blake, $5,940	72-70-71-74–287
Hale Irwin, $5,940	73-71-71-72–287
Mike Smith, $5,940	68-72-74-73–287
Arden Knoll, $5,940	71-70-73-73–287
Mike Hulbert, $5,940	71-73-72-71–287
Brad Faxon, $5,657	72-71-70-75–288
Fuzzy Zoeller, $5,657	73-67-78-70–288
Steve Gotsche, $5,657	70-73-71-74–288
#Justin Leonard	69-71-73-75–288
Duffy Waldorf, $5,405	71-72-71-75–289
Pete Jordan, $5,405	71-70-73-75–289
Jack Nicklaus, $5,405	70-72-76-71–289
Nick Faldo, $5,405	70-74-73-72–289
Grant Waite, $5,405	69-73-74-73–289
Jay Haas, $5,121	71-69-75-75–290
Barney Thompson, $5,121	71-73-71-75–290
Mark Wiebe, $5,121	71-72-77-70–290
Tony Johnstone, $5,121	71-72-74-73–290
Ted Schulz, $4,932	71-73-69-78–291
Wayne Grady, $4,932	69-75-70-77–291
Steve Stricker, $4,838	72-72-76-72–292
Stephen Flesch, $4,775	71-70-78-75–294
Doug Weaver, $4,680	70-73-77-75–295
John Flannery, $4,680	73-69-75-78–295
Robert Wrenn, $4,586	68-73-80-76–297
Robert Gamez, $4,523	72-70-78-78–298

- amateur

British Open

AT A GLANCE

- **Course:** Royal St. George's Golf Club
- **Location:** Sandwich, England
- **When:** July 15-18, 1993
- **Weather:** Sunny and some wind all weekend, except for brief showers early Thursday and early Sunday.
- **Purse:** $1 million
- **Par:** 70
- **Yards:** 6,860
- **Defending champion:** Nick Faldo
- **Tournament record:** 13-under-par 267, Greg Norman, 1993 (at Royal St. George's Golf Club, Sandwich, England)

After so many defeats and disappointments, Greg Norman knew he would eventually redeem himself. He finally did—at the 122nd British Open.

"I knew I could do it. And I did it. I did it my way," Norman said after posting the lowest score ever in the British Open—a 13-under-par 267—to beat defending champion Nick Faldo by two shots.

"This isn't going to be the last one," he said.

Norman may never play better than he played in the final round on the sandhills of Royal St. George's. It was the best round of a globe-trotting career that has produced 63 victories.

"It was perfect," Norman said.

He hit all the greens. He hit all the fairways. Furthermore, he hit the fairways where he wanted to, for the most advantageous shot to the flag.

"I was playing a chess game," he said. "I hit every shot on the middle of the clubface. I never hit a wrong shot."

There were only two glitches, both with the putter, one that failed to get up a steep ridge on the No. 7, and the miss from 14 inches on the 17th.

In the end, neither mattered. The driving and the ball-striking did the job, as Norman bettered the old British Open record of 268 (set by Tom Watson in 1977 at Turnberry, in Scotland).

Faldo played well, but with Norman playing flawlessly, the three-time champion had little or no chance. The Englishman's closing 67 gave him an 11-under-par total, which would have won in all but one of the 121 previous British Opens.

Also finishing with 67s were Masters champion Bernhard Langer of Germany and Australia's Peter Senior.

Langer fell victim to a double bogey-7 after pushing his tee shot out of bounds on the 14th and wound up alone in third at 270.

Senior, a first-round leader with Norman, Fuzzy Zoeller and Mark Calcavecchia, ran off a string of three consecutive birdies with his chin-high putter.

He and Corey Pavin tied for third at 272. Pavin shared the third-round lead but could do no better than 70.

Paul Lawrie of Scotland holed a 3-iron second shot on the 17th for an eagle. His closing 65 put him in a tie at 274 with 23-year-old Ernie Els of South Africa and Nick Price, who had won two straight tournaments coming into the Open.

Essentially, however, it was a three-man race—Norman, Faldo and Langer—until the Australian pulled away on the back nine.

"To be able to say I beat those two guys, it's one of the proudest days of my life," Norman said.

FIVE BIRDIES MADE UP FOR NORMAN'S SHAKY START

It would have been easy for Greg Norman to give up. The Australian's bid for a second British Open title got off to a dubious start.

Norman, who won the 1986 British Open and lost the '89 title to Mark Calcavecchia in a playoff, hit a poor tee shot and made double bogey on the first hole in round one.

At 1-over par after 12 holes, he then ral-

By Porter Binks, USA TODAY

Greg Norman was near perfect in his second British Open victory.

lied, ripping off five consecutive birdies to close at 4-under 66, in a four-way tie for the lead.

"After my double bogey, I said to myself, 'There are 71 holes to go, so be patient,'" said Norman. "How can you explain five birdies in a row? I hit it close, chipped one in and that was that. I did not know why it happened."

His birdies came from 18 inches on No. 13, 45 feet on a chip-in at 14 and 25 feet at 15. Then he put approach shots within 6 feet at 16 and 17.

Royal St. George's, rock-hard during practice rounds from lack of rain, was softened by rains opening day.

A total of 47 of the 156 players bettered par 70 on the same course where Sandy Lyle won the 1985 British Open at 2-over 282. Just 10 were under par in that first round.

Zoeller, who was in contention to win the last British Open at Royal St. George's until he double bogeyed the 13th hole the last day, said the field hasn't seen the course at its toughest: "The golf course can be a bear when the wind blows 40 to 50 miles an hour."

—*by Rick Remsnyder*

PLAYER

Things were pretty dull leading to the British Open—until **John Daly** walked into the press room Wednesday.

Earlier, pre-tournament favorites Nick Faldo and Nick Price dutifully paid homage to Royal St. George's and recited cliches.

But Daly talked about boozing, kicking M&Ms and putting from 50 yards off the green.

A recovering alcoholic, he said he's also trying to stay away from sweets: "I've now gone 11 days without eating chocolate. I went from one addiction to another."

Daly, 27, talked candidly about his bouts with alcohol.

"I'm very fortunate to be alive and playing golf and doing what I want to do," he said. "I have been drinking too much and you know how it is, you wake up feeling like crap."

Don't expect to see Daly in group counseling, however.

"Once you've been to rehab and heard some of the crap these guys have been through, you don't want to drink again," he said. "I'm not the sort of guy who can sit around talking about depressing things."

In his second British Open, he said he doubted his "grip it and rip it" style would fit the winds and funny bounces common on rock-hard British courses.

"The British Open is on a links course and is not made for the John Daly game," he said. "If the wind blows hard, there is no telling what I might do. I would certainly not be the favorite to win."

He didn't touch a club the week before the tournament, preferring to lounge at his new home in Orlando.

"Jack Nicklaus told me not to change my game," he said. "Jack said, 'Just hit the ball like you always do.' I came here to face the challenge and get the experience."

—*by Rick Remsnyder*

SPOTLIGHT

British Open short putts

BIG STICK: Peter Senior, trying to become the first to win a major championship using an elongated putter, rolled in birdie putts of 10, 15, 15, 25 and 30 feet during the opening round. Then he said he's tired of apologizing for his success with the 46½-inch putter.

"Some days I hole a lot of putts with the long one, and everybody seems to think you're cheating," he said. "They don't say that when you are putting badly."

LONG BALL: John Daly created a stir during Tuesday's practice round by driving the green on the 421-yard fifth hole.

"Daly flies it 40 yards past where I finish," said Ian Woosnam, who played a practice round the next day with Daly and Fuzzy Zoeller.

"I'm one of the biggest hitters, but he's way ahead of everyone else."

In that round, Daly putted from as many as 50 yards off the green.

"I tried chipping around the greens last year at Muirfield, but now I'm putting around them," he said. "You can't hit the ball close when you are chipping around here."

ROUGH TERRAIN: Until rains softened the course early Thursday, players were dreading the rock-hard fairways of Royal St. George's notoriously unforgiving layout.

Low scores have never been common at the 11-time Open host. Before Norman's victory, only one sub-par 72-hole score was posted at an Open, Bill Rogers' winning 4-under 276 in '81.

A true links course, Royal St. George's is disliked by some pros because it requires blind shots and offers unpredictable bounces off severely sloped fairways.

"It is one of the toughest courses I've played, an extremely difficult par 70," Bernhard Langer said. "It's possibly the hardest Open course if conditions are bad. In rain and strong wind, the ball just doesn't go anywhere."

—by Rick Remsnyder

Scores and earnings
Greg Norman, $154,000 — 66-68-69-64—267
Nick Faldo, $123,200 — 69-63-70-67—269
Bernhard Langer, $103,180 — 67-66-70-67—270
Peter Senior, $77,770 — 66-69-70-67—272
Corey Pavin, $77,770 — 68-66-68-70—272
Nick Price, $51,077 — 68-70-67-69—274
Paul Lawrie, $51,077 — 72-68-69-65—274
Ernie Els, $51,077 — 68-69-69-68—274
Fred Couples, $39,270 — 68-66-72-69—275
Wayne Grady, $39,270 — 74-68-64-69—275
Scott Simpson, $39,270 — 68-70-71-66—275
Payne Stewart, $33,110 — 71-72-70-63—276
Barry Lane, $31,570 — 70-68-71-68—277
Mark Calcavecchia, $23,430 — 66-73-71-68—278
Tom Kite, $23,430 — 72-70-68-68—278
Mark McNulty, $23,430 — 67-71-71-69—278
Gil Morgan, $23,430 — 70-68-70-70—278
Jose Rivero, $23,430 — 68-73-67-70—278
Fuzzy Zoeller, $23,430 — 66-70-71-71—278
John Daly, $23,430 — 71-66-70-71—278
Peter Baker, $15,400 — 70-67-74-68—279
Jesper Parnevik, $15,400 — 68-74-68-69—279
Howard Clark, $15,400 — 67-72-70-70—279
Rodger Davis, $12,936 — 68-71-71-70—280
David Frost, $12,936 — 69-73-70-68—280
Mark Roe, $12,936 — 70-71-73-66—280
Malcolm Mackenzie, $11,081 — 72-71-71-67—281
Yoshinori Mizumaki, $11,081 — 69-69-73-70—281
Des Smyth, $11,081 — 67-74-70-70—281
Larry Mize, $11,081 — 67-69-74-71—281
Mark James, $11,081 — 70-70-70-71—281
#Iain Pyman — 68-72-70-71—281
Seve Ballesteros, $11,081 — 68-73-69-71—281
Raymond Floyd, $9,517 — 70-72-67-73—282
Howard Twitty, $9,517 — 71-71-67-73—282
Wayne Westner, $9,517 — 67-73-72-70—282
Jean Van De Velde, $9,517 — 75-67-73-67—282
Paul Broadhurst, $9,517 — 71-69-74-68—282
Rocco Mediate, $8,205 — 71-71-72-69—283
Carl Mason, $8,205 — 69-73-72-69—283
Andrew Magee, $8,205 — 71-72-71-69—283
Greg Turner, $8,205 — 67-76-70-70—283
Duffy Waldorf, $8,205 — 68-71-73-71—283
Paul Moloney, $8,205 — 70-71-71-71—283
Anders Sorensen, $8,205 — 69-70-72-72—283
Darren Clarke, $8,205 — 69-71-69-74—283
Christy O'Connor, Jr., $8,205 — 72-68-69-74—283
Steve Elkington, $7,469 — 72-71-71-70—284
Lee Janzen, $7,469 — 69-71-73-71—284
John Huston, $7,469 — 68-73-76-67—284
Ian Garbutt, $6,709 — 68-75-73-69—285
Stephen Ames, $6,709 — 67-75-73-70—285
Miguel Jimenez, $6,709 — 69-74-72-70—285
Ian Woosnam, $6,709 — 72-71-72-70—285
Sam Torrance, $6,709 — 72-70-72-71—285
Frank Nobilo, $6,709 — 69-70-74-72—285
Manuel Pinero, $6,709 — 70-72-71-72—285
Jonathan Sewell, $6,709 — 70-72-69-74—285
Craig Parry, $6,198 — 72-69-71-74—286
Tom Lehman, $6,198 — 69-71-73-73—286
Vijay Singh, $6,198 — 69-72-72-73—286
Paul Azinger, $6,198 — 69-73-74-70—286
Ross Drummond, $5,929 — 73-67-76-71—287
Olle Karlsson, $5,929 — 70-71-73-73—287
James Spence, $5,929 — 69-72-72-74—287
Tom Pernice, $5,659 — 73-70-70-75—288
James Cook, $5,659 — 71-71-74-72—288
Magnus Sunesson, $5,659 — 70-73-73-72—288
William Guy, $5,659 — 70-73-73-72—288
Mike Miller, $5,416 — 73-68-76-72—289
Tom Purtzer, $5,416 — 70-70-74-75—289
Ian Baker-Finch, $5,416 — 73-69-67-80—289
Dan Forsman, $5,390 — 71-70-76-73—290
Peter Fowler, $5,390 — 74-69-74-73—290
Peter Mitchell, $5,390 — 73-70-72-75—290
Mike Harwood, $5,390 — 72-70-72-76—290
Mikael Krantz, $5,390 — 77-66-72-77—292
Ricky Willison, $5,390 — 73-70-74-76—293
- amateur

PGA Championship

AT A GLANCE

- **Course:** Inverness Club
- **Location:** Toledo, Ohio
- **When:** Aug. 12-15, 1993
- **Weather:** Hot and humid Thursday; fog delay Friday; hot and humid Saturday and Sunday.
- **Purse:** $1.6 million
- **Par:** 71
- **Yards:** 7,024
- **Playoff:** Paul Azinger defeated Greg Norman on the second playoff hole.
- **Defending champion:** Nick Price
- **Tournament record:** 9-under-par 271, 1964 (at Columbus Ohio CC)

Paul Azinger took his place among golf's elite when he rallied to win the 75th PGA Championship at Inverness Club, beating Greg Norman on the second playoff hole.

Norman suffered his second gut-wrenching loss in a PGA Championship at Inverness, missing a 5-foot par putt in the playoff after Azinger had two-putted for par.

In 1986, Norman was beaten at Inverness when Bob Tway holed an unforgettable bunker shot on the last hole. His loss to Azinger was also the Australian's fourth playoff defeat in major championships.

"In regulation, I had a putt exactly like Greg's on that hole, and I knew it had a lot of break," Azinger said. "I was ready to go to the next hole, but he missed."

For Azinger, his greatest triumph elevated him to the group of major championship winners and erased the only stigma in an 11-year career that now includes 11 victories.

"It brought tears to my eyes," Azinger said. "It's such a huge feeling of satisfaction. I felt like I had something to prove. I've always felt I was good enough to win a major championship, but I had to prove it."

Norman, playing in the last group, had two chances to win. At the 18th hole, he slid an 18-foot birdie try by on the left. On the first playoff hole (the 18th), he had almost an identical putt. It hit the hole but spun out.

"Two beautiful putts, they just didn't go in," the British Open winner said.

Of the second putt, Azinger said, "With two feet to go, I thought it was in. That was one of the nastiest lip outs I've seen."

On the second playoff hole, Norman said, he misread his 20-footer, leaving it about four feet short. On the second and losing putt, he said, "I just didn't give it enough speed."

—by Steve Hershey

Azinger overcame a major barrier

The weight Paul Azinger had been carrying around for years was hoisted off his shoulders. No longer could anyone call him the best player who hadn't won a major championship.

Since finishing bogey–bogey to lose the 1987 British Open by a shot to Nick Faldo, Azinger has lived with self-doubts about his ability to handle pressure.

In 1988, he led the PGA Championship after the second and third rounds before losing to Jeff Sluman. He has had a couple of chances to win the U.S. Open but his putter failed him when he needed it most.

All that is behind Azinger now, after his high-pressure performance at Inverness.

"I feel a huge burden off my shoulders," he said, showing obvious relief. "As a golfer, I felt I had something to prove. Recently, in pressure situations, I've been asking myself, 'Are you capable of dealing with this?'"

No one ever will question Azinger's intestinal fortitude again. Not after he made three consecutive birdies, starting at the 12th hole to catch Faldo and Norman. Not after he sank a 5-footer for birdie at 17 for what he thought was the lead. Not after he took on Norman in a playoff and outlasted the British Open champion.

"I was plenty nervous out there," said Azinger, one of the most popular players on the PGA Tour because of his frankness, sincerity and sense of humor.

"Walking off the seventh green after leaving a putt short for the third time, I asked myself if I could handle the pressure. Then, coming off the 16th tee, I questioned whether I would allow myself to perform or was I going to throw up. I was really sucking air, I'm not afraid to admit it.

"But I'm lucky, when I'm nervous, I don't have nervous arms, my hands don't shake. I can still putt, I usually just don't make too many.

"The funny thing was I wasn't a bit nervous in the playoff and I don't think Greg was either. It seems once you get to that point, you relax. When the guy was holding out the numbers we picked to see who teed off first, Greg laughed and said his hand was shaking more than ours."

Beating Norman made Azinger's first major championship even sweeter. They went head-to-head at the Doral-Ryder Open last March and Norman won by four shots. This time, the tables turned.

"We went at it for two days at Doral and he waxed me pretty good," Azinger said. "Afterwards, I told him I had never seen anyone play better (Norman was 23 under par) and that it was good to have him back."

When Nick Price won in 1992, he was generally described as one of the nicest guys in golf.

Well, if he has a rival in that area, it is the guy who succeeded him as the PGA Champion.

—*by Steve Hershey*

Paul Azinger won his first major championship.

Norman doomed to repeat history

Nobody has had a wider variety of playoff setbacks in major championships than Greg Norman.

After his loss to Azinger, Norman had suffered playoff defeats in all four major championships.

It started with the 67-75 thumping by Fuzzy Zoeller at the 1984 U.S. Open. Then, in 1987, there was the Larry Mize chip-in at The Masters that haunted him for years.

In 1989, Norman was beaten by Mark Calcavecchia in a four-hole British Open playoff after making birdies on the first two holes.

After letting his second PGA Championship at Inverness slip away (he lost to Bob Tway's bunker shot on the last hole in 1986), Norman didn't like it any more, but he was handling it better.

"At least I've been there, I suppose," Norman said softly when asked of his many near victories. "I'm going to go away from here with a positive attitude.

"Of course, I feel down now, but I know I played well all week. I shot a good score in the final round. I gave myself a chance to win and just got beat by a great player."

Norman started the final-round with a one-shot lead on five players. After a disastrous double bogey on the 210-yard, par-3 No. 6 when he left a bunker shot in the sand, he battled back with four birdies in the last 11 holes.

"I had a bit of a hiccup there on the front nine," said Norman, who followed his double bogey with a bogey. "But I thought I came back strong.

"I was three shots back of Nick Faldo after that, but I had 11 holes to go and never gave up. I thought 12-under would be good enough to win and it almost was."

Instead, he was headed for what would be still another in a remarkable string of playoff defeats.

"I've learned to handle adversity pretty well," he said, softly. "I'll be all right once I leave here and have a couple of beers."

—*by Steve Hershey*

Commentary: PGA is entry-level major

Hurry, hurry, hurry. Step right up. You want a major championship? Come on in, come one, come all to the PGA Championship.

The past six PGA winners didn't have a previous major in their resume: Jeff Sluman, Payne Stewart, Wayne Grady, John Daly, Nick Price and now Paul Azinger.

One-week wonders or budding superstars, take your pick. Sluman and Grady haven't won since. For Stewart, Daly and Price, however, it was a launching pad, the confidence booster that has propelled them to great heights. With 10 wins already under his belt, Azinger's win confirmed that he is entering his prime.

What is it about the PGA Championship? Why does it produce so many first-time winners as opposed to, say, The Masters?

Starting in 1988, Sluman's year, Masters champions have been Sandy Lyle, Nick Faldo (twice), Ian Woosnam, Fred Couples and Bernhard Langer. Lyle, Faldo and Langer had won previous majors. Woosnam and Couples were No. 1 in the worldwide Sony rankings.

Fluke winners are a rarity at The Masters because of the intimacy of Augusta (Ga.) National Golf Club. The best players know every break of the treacherous greens, because they putt them every spring. Familiarity breeds confidence, one of the most important assets of any champion.

"There are no surprises at Augusta," Norman said. "It's the best golf tournament in the world, because it's pure golf. That's why they get so many great champions."

In contrast, players arriving at recent PGA Championships rarely knew what to expect in recent years. Oak Tree? Kemper Lakes? Shoal Creek? Crooked Stick? Most players had never been to those courses before and haven't been back, so everybody starts from scratch.

Oak Tree Golf Club in Edmond, Okla., was rated one of the most difficult courses in the USA, but what made it so tough, usually, were the howling winds roaring across the plains.

So what happened? The wind didn't blow that week and scores were the second-lowest in PGA Championship history. Short-hitting Sluman holed a 100-yard wedge shot for an eagle on the last day and went on to shoot 6-under-par 65.

Kemper Lakes Golf Club near Chicago was the longest course in PGA Championship history (7,217 yards) at the time. So what happened? Short-hitting Mike Reid led for three rounds and had it won until he bogeyed the 16th hole, double bogeyed 17 and missed an 8-foot birdie putt at 18 to hand the title to Stewart.

Shoal Creek in 1990 was another aberration. The snarly, ankle-high Bermuda grass rough, plus brick-hard greens made pars precious. The first day, 123 players were over par, and there were 121 the second.

As the players staggered in Sunday, three—winner Wayne Grady, runner-up Fred Couples and Gil Morgan—were under par. Grady shot a miraculous, second-round 5-under 67 and won at 6-under. It's not a week the PGA of America recalls with pride.

As a last-minute replacement, Daly went to long and wide-open Crooked Stick and dominated. Now, Azinger perservered on a course designed in 1919 that favors precision putters and chippers, like himself.

Predictable? What were the odds of any of those five winning when the tournaments started? Keep that in mind in 1994. Whatever makes sense probably won't happen if it's the PGA Championship.

—*by Steve Hershey*

PGA Championship short putts

Handicapping the PGA

USA TODAY sports analyst Danny Sheridan sized up the competition at Inverness.

Nick Faldo	7:1
Greg Norman	7:1
Nick Price	8:1
Bernhard Langer	9:1
Fred Couples	10:1
Paul Azinger	12:1
Payne Stewart	15:1
Corey Pavin	20:1
Jose Maria Olazabal	25:1
Ian Woosnam	25:1
Steve Elkington	30:1
Tom Kite	30:1
Lee Janzen	30:1
Larry Mize	30:1
Chip Beck	30:1
Anders Forsbrand	30:1
Davis Love III	35:1
David Frost	35:1
Craig Parry	35:1
Fuzzy Zoeller	35:1
Jeff Maggert	40:1
Dan Forsman	40:1
Sandy Lyle	50:1
Ian Baker-Finch	50:1
Tom Watson	75:1
John Cook	100:1
Brad Faxon	100:1
Ray Floyd	125:1
Mark Calcavecchia	150:1
John Daly	175:1
Keith Clearwater	200:1
Field	7:1
Any club pro (40)	500:1

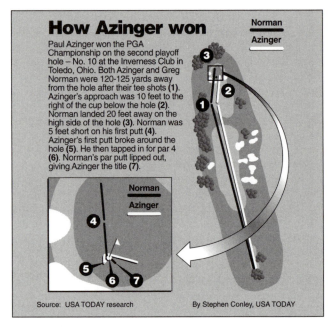

How Azinger won

Paul Azinger won the PGA Championship on the second playoff hole – No. 10 at the Inverness Club in Toledo, Ohio. Both Azinger and Greg Norman were 120-125 yards away from the hole after their tee shots **(1)**. Azinger's approach was 10 feet to the right of the cup below the hole **(2)**. Norman landed 20 feet away on the high side of the hole **(3)**. Norman was 5 feet short on his first putt **(4)**. Azinger's first putt broke around the hole **(5)**. He then tapped in for par 4 **(6)**. Norman's par putt lipped out, giving Azinger the title **(7)**.

Source: USA TODAY research — By Stephen Conley, USA TODAY

OFF TARGET: Those old putting woes that he thought he had beaten came back to haunt Tom Watson once again.

After playing three solid, under-par rounds, Watson finished with a final-round 1-over-par 72 to wind up fifth at 8-under-par 276. He had also tied for fifth at the U.S. Open.

"I'm playing better now than I was at Baltusrol," Watson said. "And I'm definitely putting better.

"I had my chances today on 11, 12 and 13. I was hitting it within 8-10 feet, but I couldn't make anything. I started off struggling. I three-putted the first hole and it's hard to get going after that."

WADKINS STRUGGLED: Lanny Wadkins, trying to win his way onto the Ryder Cup team, started off with 13 consecutive pars and then fell out of contention with a double bogey on the 14th hole. He shot 74 to fall from a tie for second to a 6-way tie for 14th.

"I was shut out," he said. "No birdies, I can't believe that. I have been making birdies all week and today nothing.

"At 14, I made a bad tee shot and it got me where I couldn't even play the hole. I had to lay up my third shot and I just never recovered."

MADE 'EM ALL: Thirteen players made the cut in all four major championships in 1993: Ian Baker-Finch, Mark Calcavecchia, Fred Couples, John Daly, Steve Elkington, Nick Faldo, Dan Forsman, Lee Janzen,

Craig Parry, Scott Simpson, Payne Stewart, Ian Woosnam and Fuzzy Zoeller.

Surprisingly absent from the list were Masters champion Bernhard Langer, who missed at the U.S. Open when he had neck problems, and British Open winner Greg Norman, who was cut at the U.S. Open.

HO HUM: Bob Tway made the most dramatic shot in PGA Championship history when he sank a bunker shot on the last hole to win the 1986 title.

Richard Zokol landed in the same sand trap and blasted into the hole for birdie and his final-round 70.

"I was in the bunker and told myself, 'Tway made it here and the feeling came over me,'" Zokol said. "I hit a great bunker shot and it went into the hole. It's not a difficult shot. Everything feeds down to the hole."

CHANGING THE GUARD: The PGA Championship may have seen the last of Seve Ballesteros. The Spaniard, 36, withdrew for the second year in a row, citing personal reasons. It seems likely he will end his brilliant career without winning this major championship.

In 1992, he said back problems kept him from coming, but he had missed three cuts in his last five starts. Winner of two Masters and three British Opens, Ballesteros has played in 10 PGA Championships with one top-five finish, fifth in 1984.

BIG SHOT: In the first round, Darrell Kestner, pro at Deep Dale Golf Club in Manhasset, N.Y., made the first double eagle in a PGA Championship. He holed his 222-yard, 5-wood second shot on the 515-yard 13th hole. He shot 1-under-par 70.

"It was so far away, I couldn't see," said 40-year-old Kestner. "When the crowd started screaming, I figured it must have hit the stick. When they didn't stop, I figured it went in. Needless to say, it was the first one I've ever made."

—*by Steve Hershey*

Scores and earnings

Player	Rounds
#Paul Azinger, $300,000	69-66-69-68—272
Greg Norman, $155,000	68-68-67-69—272
Nick Faldo, $105,000	68-68-69-68—273
Vijay Singh, $90,000	68-63-73-70—274
Tom Watson, $75,000	69-65-70-72—276
Bob Estes, $47,812	69-66-69-73—277
Hale Irwin, $47,812	68-69-67-73—277
Scott Simpson, $47,812	64-70-71-72—277
John Cook, $47,812	72-66-68-71—277
Dudley Hart, $47,812	66-68-71-72—277
Scott Hoch, $47,812	74-68-68-67—277
Nolan Henke, $47,812	72-70-67-68—277
Phil Mickelson, $47,812	67-71-69-70—277
Richard Zokol, $25,000	66-71-71-70—278
Steve Elkington, $25,000	67-66-74-71—278
Bruce Fleisher, $25,000	69-74-67-68—278
Gary Hallberg, $25,000	70-69-68-71—278
Lanny Wadkins, $25,000	65-68-71-74—278
Brad Faxon, $25,000	70-70-65-73—278
Eduardo Romero, $18,500	67-67-74-71—279
Jay Haas, $18,500	69-68-70-72—279
Lee Janzen, $14,500	70-68-71-72—281
Ian Woosnam, $14,500	70-71-68-72—281
Greg Twiggs, $14,500	70-69-70-72—281
Jim McGovern, $14,500	71-67-69-74—281
Frank Nobilo, $14,500	69-66-74-72—281
Gene Sauers, $14,500	68-74-70-69—281
Peter Jacobsen, $10,167	71-67-74-70—282
Billy Mayfair, $10,167	68-73-70-71—282
Loren Roberts, $10,167	67-67-76-72—282
Hal Sutton, $7,058	69-72-70-72—283
Craig Parry, $7,058	70-73-68-72—283
Fred Couples, $7,058	70-68-71-74—283
Nick Price, $7,058	74-66-72-71—283
Tom Wargo, $7,058	71-70-71-71—283
Fulton Allem, $7,058	70-71-70-72—283
Mike Hulbert, $7,058	67-72-72-72—283
Mark Calcavecchia, $7,058	68-70-77-68—283
Mark McCumber, $7,058	67-72-75-69—283
Davis Love III, $7,058	70-72-72-69—283
Stu Ingraham, $7,058	74-69-71-69—283
Fuzzy Zoeller, $7,058	72-70-71-70—283
Wayne Levi, $7,058	69-73-66-75—283
Fred Funk, $4,607	72-66-76-70—284
D.A. Weibring, $4,607	68-74-72-70—284
Russ Cochran, $4,607	69-74-70-71—284
John Huston, $4,607	68-69-75-72—284
Dan Forsman, $4,607	67-75-70-72—284
Payne Stewart, $4,607	71-70-70-73—284
Joe Ozaki, $4,607	73-68-66-77—284
Peter Senior, $3,600	69-70-70-76—285
Hubert Green, $3,600	70-71-69-75—285
John Daly, $3,600	71-68-73-73—285
Jeff Maggert, $3,600	72-69-71-73—285
Andrew Magee, $3,600	71-72-74-68—285
Jose Maria Olazabal, $3,110	73-69-73-71—286
Larry Nelson, $3,110	73-67-74-72—286
Tom Kite, $3,110	73-69-71-73—286
Rick Fehr, $3,110	70-71-72-73—286
Sandy Lyle, $3,110	69-73-70-74—286
Jeff Sluman, $2,800	74-69-72-72—287
Ben Crenshaw, $2,800	70-70-73-74—287
Michael Allen, $2,800	73-70-75-69—287
Donnie Hammond, $2,800	73-70-68-76—287
Mike Standly, $2,800	72-71-68-76—287
Ian Baker-Finch, $2,650	73-69-70-76—288
Mark Wiebe, $2,625	74-69-73-73—289
Bob Ford, $2,587	70-71-78-71—290
Rocco Mediate, $2,587	70-73-74-73—290
Steve Pate, $2,550	73-70-72-77—292
Kevin Burton, $2,512	69-73-76-76—294
Barry Lane, $2,512	67-74-77-76—294
Bob Borowicz, $2,475	72-71-80-72—295
John Adams, $2,450	72-70-76-78—296

- won on second playoff hole

Nabisco Dinah Shore

AT A GLANCE

- **Course:** Mission Hills Country Club, Old Course
- **Location:** Rancho Mirage, Calif.
- **When:** March 25-29, 1993
- **Weather:** Sunny but windy Thursday. Friday and Saturday, sunny and warm; a light breeze Sunday.
- **Purse:** $700,000
- **Par:** 72
- **Yards:** 6,437
- **Defending champion:** Dottie Mochrie defeated Juli Inkster on first playoff hole.
- **Tournament record:** 15-under-par 273, Amy Alcott, 1991

Helen Alfredsson broke a three-way tie to win.

A year before, Helen Alfredsson was on the outside looking in with the rest of the spectators at the Nabisco Dinah Shore.

After beating Betsy King in the first women's major championship of 1993, she became the ultimate insider.

Alfredsson, from Goteborg, Sweden, was the first foreign-born woman to win a golf major championship since South Africa's Sally Little in the 1988 duMaurier Ltd. Classic. The victory was also her first on the LPGA Tour.

"I was around last year," Alfredsson said. "I was out here watching. It's better to be inside the ropes than walking around outside."

Alfredsson broke a three-way tie to win. She shot par 72 in the final round to finish at 4-under 284, two strokes better than King, Amy Benz and Tina Barrett.

"Helen is a good player," said King, who was seeking her third Dinah Shore victory. "But it's a real misnomer to call her a rookie. She's 27 years old. She has played a lot of golf all over the world."

Alfredsson was 1992 LPGA rookie of the year, when she earned $262,115. She didn't win, coming closest at the Mazda Japan Classic in November, where she lost to King in a four-hole playoff.

Before joining the LPGA, she was a star in the Women's Professional Golf European Tour—Rookie of Year in 1989 and Women's British Open champion in '90. She helped Europe defeat the USA in the Solheim Cup in 1992 in Scotland.

Before turning pro, she played at U.S. International University in San Diego.

She was quite familiar with the Dinah Shore and Mission Hills before the tournament, having played it once while a member of the European tour.

Alfredsson received a sponsor's invitation to play in the 1991 Dinah Shore on the basis of her European success. But in 1992 she wasn't invited, and she wasn't high enough on the money list to qualify. So she watched from the gallery as Dottie Mochrie defeated Juli Inkster in a playoff.

"I didn't learn anything by watching last year," Alfredsson said. "But just being outside the ropes and not being a part of the tournament motivates you to want to be on the other side."

Alfredsson did not break par in the final 36 holes and was 1 under par for the final 54 holes. But none of the leaders made a last-day move.

King shot 74-286 and Dawn Coe-Jones shot 75-287.

"I decided to be patient today and just try to make pars," Alfredsson said. "It paid off."

—*by Jerry Potter*

PLAYER SPOTLIGHT

Betsy King didn't know for sure if it was fate or luck, but the golf ball wasn't heeding her commands in the first months of 1993.

Twice she had been in contention with 18 holes to play, and both times she had come away with second place.

"Last year, I didn't have too many chances to win, but every time I had a chance I won," said King, who won three times in 1992.

Because King had 28 wins, two shy of qualifying for the LPGA Hall of Fame, each missed opportunity was highlighted.

She shared the lead with Helen Alfredsson and Dawn Coe-Jones entering the final round of the Nabisco Dinah Shore. But she shot 74 and tied for second.

Earlier in March, she had a one-stroke lead entering the final round of the Ping/Welch's Championship in Tucson, Ariz., but lost by a stroke to Meg Mallon.

"As you get older, every year you think a little more about the Hall of Fame," said King, 37.

Patty Sheehan, who qualified for the Hall of Fame March 21, said winning No. 29 was a lot easier than winning No. 30.

"I don't think the Hall of Fame enters Betsy's mind when she's playing," Sheehan said. "She just wants to win."

"Betsy's age doesn't have any effect on her," Sheehan said. "You don't lose skills until you get well into your 40s."

Sheehan said, "What Betsy has experienced this year is typical of any good golfer. Success comes in spurts. It's not steady.

"Betsy is playing well. She's strong-willed. If she misses an opportunity to win I don't think it will be a problem."

—by Jerry Potter

MAJORS / NABISCO DINAH SHORE

Scores and earnings

Player	Earnings	Scores
Helen Alfredsson	$105,000	69-71-72-72–284
Amy Benz	$49,901	72-73-71-70–286
Tina Barrett	$49,901	70-73-72-71–286
Betsy King	$49,901	71-74-67-74–286
Hollis Stacy	$25,126	72-74-71-70–287
Missie Berteotti	$25,126	68-74-73-72–287
Dawn Coe-Jones	$25,126	72-68-72-75–287
Nancy Lopez	$15,762	68-78-72-70–288
Brandie Burton	$15,762	73-73-68-74–288
Trish Johnson	$15,762	74-68-72-74–288
Jane Crafter	$15,762	71-72-70-75–288
Patty Sheehan	$10,625	73-70-76-70–289
Debbie Massey	$10,625	70-74-74-71–289
Tammie Green	$10,625	72-73-72-72–289
Laura Davies	$10,625	72-72-73-72–289
Pamela Wright	$10,625	74-68-75-72–289
Pat Bradley	$10,625	71-69-75-74–289
Kris Monaghan	$8,806	76-71-74-69–290
Donna Andrews	$8,101	73-74-72-72–291
Karen Noble	$8,101	74-72-70-75–291
Nancy Scranton	$8,101	73-72-71-75–291
Michelle McGann	$7,237	78-70-75-69–292
Sharon Barrett	$7,237	69-77-72-74–292
Lori Garbacz	$6,304	75-75-72-71–293
Caroline Keggi	$6,304	74-74-73-72–293
D. Ammaccapane	$6,304	69-75-74-75–293
Cindy Schreyer	$6,304	75-70-72-76–293
Anne-Marie Palli	$6,304	70-71-76-76–293
Marta Figueras-Dotti	$6,304	68-72-75-78–293
D. Lofland-Dormann	$4,740	76-75-75-68–294
Dottie Mochrie	$4,740	77-73-74-70–294
Heather Drew	$4,740	79-70-74-71–294
Val Skinner	$4,740	73-75-74-72–294
Allison Finney	$4,740	70-73-79-72–294
Cindy Rarick	$4,740	76-75-70-73–294
Sherri Turner	$4,740	73-72-76-73–294
Terry-Jo Myers	$4,740	74-73-73-74–294
Joan Pitcock	$4,740	70-72-76-76–294
Sherri Steinhauer	$4,740	72-74-71-77–294
Liselotte Neumann	$3,173	72-76-72-75–295
JoAnne Carner	$3,173	78-73-71-73–295
Patti Rizzo	$3,173	74-77-71-73–295
Juli Inkster	$3,173	75-73-73-74–295
Maggie Will	$3,173	72-73-76-74–295
Shelley Hamlin	$3,173	73-74-73-75–295
Kathy Postlewait	$3,173	72-73-75-75–295
Barbara Mucha	$3,173	73-73-73-76–295
Jan Stephenson	$3,173	73-72-74-76–295
Florence Descampe	$2,117	76-74-74-72–296
Judy Dickinson	$2,117	74-76-74-72–296
Jane Geddes	$2,117	75-73-75-73–296
Colleen Walker	$2,117	71-74-77-74–296
Meg Mallon	$2,117	72-74-75-75–296
Sally Little	$2,117	72-70-79-75–296
Lisa Walters	$2,117	74-73-73-76–296
Alice Ritzman	$1,531	77-74-74-72–297
Amy Alcott	$1,531	72-74-76-75–297
Cindy Figg-Currier	$1,531	74-72-75-76–297
Alice Miller	$1,531	73-71-75-78–297
Kris Tschetter	$1,267	73-74-76-75–298
Deb Richard	$1,267	74-71-78-75–298
Rosie Jones	$1,103	75-75-76-73–299
Michelle Estill	$1,103	72-73-78-76–299
Vicki Fergon	$1,103	70-77-75-77–299
Susie Redman	$968	74-72-80-74–300
Stephanie Farwig	$968	75-76-74-75–300
Lynn Connelly	$968	73-75-77-75–300
Lynn Adams	$968	75-74-73-78–300
Elaine Crosby	$862	75-76-81-69–301
Beth Daniel	$862	76-72-76-77–301
Nina Foust	$769	72-79-77-74–302
Muffin Spencer-Devlin	$769	73-78-76-75–302
Patty Jordan	$769	72-78-75-77–302
Lauri Merten	$769	75-74-75-78–302
Marlene Hagge	$722	74-77-80-73–304
Chris Johnson	$692	72-76-78-79–305
Sandra Palmer	$692	73-74-78-80–305
Becky Pearson	$692	76-75-73-81–305
Ayako Okamoto	$664	73-78-77-79–307
Shirley Furlong	$650	76-75-81-76–308
#Vicki Goetze	$0	73-76-81-78–308

- amateur

Mazda LPGA Championship

AT A GLANCE

- **Course:** Bethesda Country Club
- **Location:** Bethesda, Md.
- **When:** June 10-13, 1993
- **Weather:** Temperature and humidity in the 90s Thursday. Hot and overcast with some wind Friday; 72 and sunny Saturday and Sunday.
- **Purse:** $1 million
- **Par:** 71
- **Yards:** 6,261
- **Defending champion:** Betsy King, 17-under-par 267
- **Tournament record:** 17-under-par 267, Betsy King, 1992

Patty Sheehan held on to win her fourth major.

Continuing to dominate the field in a year that had already seen her enter the LPGA Hall of Fame, Patty Sheehan survived a flawed finish to win the Mazda LPGA Championship. It was her 31st career victory and third in 1993 alone.

"I'm not going to roll over and play dead just because I'm in the Hall of Fame," said Sheehan.

After starting the final round tied for second, two strokes behind Jenny Lidback, Sheehan posted a final-round 69–276 and edged Lauri Merten by a stroke.

"I knew I had to get off to a good start and put some pressure on Jenny," Sheehan said. "She got in trouble right away, and I put some more pressure on her when I made birdie on the third hole."

Lidback, a non-winner, struggled to a 78–282 and tied for 17th. Sheehan struggled some, too, especially on the last three holes, but managed to earn the fourth major title of her career.

The first two came in 1983 and '84 at the LPGA Championship, played in Kings Island, Ohio.

"I'm 10 years older, my hair's gray and I wear knickers now," Sheehan said. "Otherwise, I haven't changed much."

Champagne flowed after the tournament, just like it flowed after all of the other big victories in Patty Sheehan's career.

But the sparkle was perhaps not quite the same.

"The U.S. Open last year was the most important victory of my career," said Sheehan, 36. "That's for two reasons: It got me five wins closer to making the Hall of Fame and psychologically, it eliminated the demons of the 1990 Open."

(She lost the 1990 Women's Open after leading by 12 strokes in the third round and 11 in the fourth.)

Some of the demons tried to resurface as Sheehan struggled home with a bogey and two pars in the final three holes.

"I was worried," she said. "I never felt comfortable. My hands were shaking on that last putt. The only problem with that is you never know which shake is going to hit the putt."

As third-round leader Lidback lost track of her game on the front nine, Sheehan played a steady round, making birdies on the third, ninth and 12th holes to get to 10-under-par.

She appeared to be in control. But a bogey on 16, and a charge by Merten, put some doubt into the finish.

"I knew I had to find a rhythm," Sheehan said. "I found it, but I lost it at the end. I just tried to shake off that bogey on 16 and finish up the tournament."

Sheehan sank the 4-foot par putt on 18 to finish 9-under and clinch the victory.

By winning her fourth major, Sheehan showed she had not lost her desire to compete, even though she had reached just about all the goals in her career.

"I haven't played extremely well since I got into the Hall of Fame," she said. "You don't want to get complacent and you don't want to quit trying, but making the Hall of Fame promotes that."

—by Jerry Potter

MERTEN WAS CLOSE WITHOUT KNOWING IT

Lauri Merten was in a dream world. After nine winless seasons, she was battling famed Patty Sheehan down the stretch at a major championship.

She was afraid her nerves couldn't handle it, so she denied herself the pleasure of seeing her name at the top of the leaderboard after her birdie at the eighth hole.

"I had no clue," she said. "I knew I was playing well, but I didn't know how anybody else was doing."

Third-round leader Jenny Lidback, playing with Sheehan, led a retreat by several contenders with a 78. Cathy Johnston-Forbes, tied with Sheehan at the start of the day, shot 74.

So, it was left to Merten to provide the drama and prevent a Sheehan runaway. She rose to previously unattained heights.

She had won, but that was back in 1984 when she was just starting her career. This was the LPGA Championship.

She flashed a signal that this might be her week with the best third round, a bogey-free 5-under-par 66. That still left her five shots behind Lidback and not on the final round leader board—at least, not to begin with.

"When I started out (Sunday), I really never thought about winning," she said. "But I knew I was putting well, and on the front nine, my putts just kept going in."

Merten birdied the second, fourth, sixth and eighth holes to move to 8 under par. Sheehan, playing three groups behind, also was at 8 under.

"I didn't want to look at the leaderboard," Merten said. "I think you know when to look."

Finally, heading to the 17th tee, Merten said she noticed a lot of the fans were dropping out of her gallery, so she figured she wasn't leading.

"I stole a look then and saw that Patty was 10 under, so I figured I needed to birdie the last two holes," she said.

Instead, she landed in two greenside bunkers, but blasted out for pars. After Sheehan bogeyed the par-3 16th and drove into the rough at 17, Merten headed for the practice range.

It was in that solitude she learned she wouldn't be in a playoff, but she had won the biggest check of her career: $93,093. That alone was more than she had won in any year since '84.

"I'm not disappointed," she said. "I'm really happy. I made a good (6-foot) putt for par on the last hole. I've never played this well in a major."

Before her lone bogey, when she three-putted the 13th, she had played 30 holes 10-under-par while shooting 66-67.

"This is definitely a stepping-stone for me," she said. "My driving has improved and my chipping and putting has improved. Now I have more confidence.

"I think I handled the pressure pretty well. I just tried to go out and have fun, and I did—for a while."

—by Steve Hershey

Mazda LPGA Championship short putts

EAGLE EYE: Michelle McGann didn't win the Mazda LPGA Championship in the last round, but she gave fans a thrill.

McGann sank back-to-back eagles, for 3s on the par-5 12th and 13th holes.

"After you make the first one, you want to make the second," said McGann, whose drives average 253.6 yards.

On the 445-yard 12th hole, she hit driver and a 4-iron, leaving her an 8-foot putt. On the 501-yard 13th, she hit driver and a 225-yard 5-wood to 10 feet.

The 3s put her 7-under, but bogeys on 15 and 17 left her tied for fourth at 70–279.

COLLAPSE: Jenny Lidback, the third-round leader after rounds of 69-67-68, skied to a 78 on the last day, dropping to an eight-way tie for 17th.

Lidback, 30, was non-exempt after finishing 124th on the '92 money list. She played only four other events this year, and inexperience under pressure was evident.

"Jenny was real nervous," said Sheehan, who played with Lidback in round four. "She got in trouble right away at No. 1 and that seemed to unsettle her."

Lidback made an 8-foot putt for bogey at No. 1, then bogeyed the third, sixth and ninth holes to fall back.

SUPER FAST: Players got a final-round surprise at the No. 1 tee. A memo notified them the greens had been triple-cut and rolled to make them faster and smoother.

Some players had complained earlier that greens were slower than in past years.

Tammie Green, who closed 70–279, said it was hard to read the greens after reading the memo.

"After you've seen they've been triple-cut, you don't know how hard to hit a putt," she said. "If I'd made about a yard more of putts, I'd have been right (in contention)."

—by Steve Hershey and Jerry Potter

Scores and earnings

Player	Earnings	Scores
Patty Sheehan	$150,000	68-68-70-69–275
Lauri Merten	$93,093	73-70-66-67–276
Barb Bunkowsky	$67,933	68-70-69-70–277
Betsy King	$40,130	72-66-72-69–279
Michelle McGann	$40,130	73-68-68-70–279
Tammie Green	$40,130	71-69-69-70–279
Patti Rizzo	$40,130	72-69-67-71–279
Nancy Scranton	$23,651	74-68-72-66–280
Trish Johnson	$23,651	68-73-69-70–280
Cathy Johnston-Forbes	$23,651	68-68-70-74–280
Terry-Jo Myers	$16,277	71-69-73-68–281
Kris Tschetter	$16,277	73-72-67-69–281
Joan Pitcock	$16,277	68-74-70-69–281
Jan Stephenson	$16,277	69-69-73-70–281
Donna Andrews	$16,277	70-72-68-71–281
Cindy Rarick	$16,277	68-67-73-73–281
Jane Crafter	$11,444	72-73-70-67–282
Nancy Ramsbottom	$11,444	71-71-72-68–282
Jane Geddes	$11,444	76-68-68-70–282
Elaine Crosby	$11,444	71-71-70-70–282
Pamela Wright	$11,444	68-72-72-70–282
Beth Daniel	$11,444	74-67-70-71–282
Rosie Jones	$11,444	70-71-69-72–282
Jenny Lidback	$11,444	69-67-68-78–282
Kim Williams	$8,947	72-70-72-69–283
Mary Beth Zimmerman	$8,947	73-68-72-70–283
Nancy Lopez	$8,947	68-73-72-70–283
Liselotte Neumann	$8,947	72-68-73-70–283
Judy Dickinson	$8,947	71-70-69-73–283
Angie Ridgeway	$7,243	72-72-72-68–284
Chris Johnson	$7,243	74-69-73-68–284
Dottie Mochrie	$7,243	71-70-74-69–284
Alison Nicholas	$7,243	70-72-70-72–284
Barb Thomas	$7,243	72-69-71-72–284
Dale Eggeling	$7,243	72-71-68-73–284
Cindy Figg-Currier	$7,243	74-67-67-76–284
JoAnne Carner	$5,609	69-73-73-70–285
Brandie Burton	$5,609	74-70-70-71–285
Ayako Okamoto	$5,609	73-71-70-71–285
Shelley Hamlin	$5,609	73-66-75-71–285
Colleen Walker	$5,609	73-70-70-72–285
Tracy Kerdyk	$5,609	69-69-72-75–285
Jill Briles-Hinton	$4,720	72-70-72-72–286
Lori Garbacz	$4,720	72-71-69-74–286
Missie Berteotti	$4,015	74-71-72-70–287
Suzanne Strudwick	$4,015	73-71-73-70–287
Meg Mallon	$4,015	71-70-73-73–287
Laura Davies	$4,015	72-69-71-75–287
Kristi Albers	$4,015	71-69-70-77–287
Danielle Ammaccapane	$3,260	69-74-74-71–288
Kelly Robbins	$3,260	72-69-76-71–288
Maggie Will	$3,260	70-68-71-79–288
Sally Little	$2,731	74-70-72-73–289
Dana Lofland-Dormann	$2,731	73-68-74-74–289
Tina Tombs	$2,731	70-70-74-75–289
Stephanie Farwig	$2,731	72-68-72-77–289
Karen Noble	$2,203	74-70-73-73–290
Caroline Pierce	$2,203	72-71-71-76–290
Pearl Sinn	$2,203	70-72-71-77–290
Lisa Walters	$1,901	73-70-78-70–291
Caroline Keggi	$1,901	70-69-74-78–291
Hiromi Kobayashi	$1,667	68-74-75-75–292
Stefania Croce	$1,667	73-70-73-76–292
Nina Foust	$1,667	69-76-70-77–292
Robin Walton	$1,499	72-73-75-73–293
Evelyn Orley	$1,499	68-75-75-75–293
Juli Inkster	$1,499	70-73-74-76–293
Diane Daugherty	$1,398	73-72-75-77–297
Patty Jordan	$1,348	72-73-78-76–299
Dina Ammaccapane	$1,298	76-68-78-80–302

United States Women's Open

AT A GLANCE

▸**Course:** Crooked Stick Golf Club
▸**Location:** Carmel, Ind.
▸**When:** July 22-25, 1993
▸**Weather:** Due to slow play, darkness caused play to be suspended at 8 p.m. Thursday with 15 players still on the course. Hot and humid; thunderstorms Saturday night felled several trees, and course cleanup delayed the start of Sunday's round by one hour.
▸**Purse:** $800,000
▸**Par:** 72
▸**Yards:** 6,311
▸**Defending champion:** Patty Sheehan defeated Juli Inkster 72-74 in an 18-hole playoff after they tied at 4-under-par 280.
▸**Tournament record:** 11-under-par 277, Liselotte Neumann, Baltimore Country Club (Five Farms East Course), 1988

Lauri Merten came from behind to win the Open.

Lauri Merten, who jokes that her life has been an uphill struggle, topped the grade and turned downhill by winning the U.S. Women's Open.

"My left leg is 3 centimeters shorter than my right leg," Merten said. "I wish it would have been the other way around because I'd have been on an uphill lie all my life."

Merten's shots might be downhill, but she used only 68 in her come-from-behind victory.

Starting the final round 4 under par and five strokes behind leader Helen Alfredsson, Merten made six birdies and two bogeys to finish at 8-under 280.

Down the stretch, Merten, runner-up in the Mazda LPGA Championship in June, birdied 16 and 18, two of the toughest holes on a course drenched by an overnight storm.

"I thought Crooked Stick was a long-hitter's golf course," she said, "but it became a shot-maker's course."

The change played to Merten's strengths. She averaged just 225 yards on her drives, but an excellent short game produced 18 birdies in 72 holes.

In the last round, she birdied No. 8 with a 60-foot putt and the 16th with a chip-in. Then she watched as Andrews and Alfredsson missed birdie putts on 18 that would have tied her.

The loss was especially disappointing for the Swedish star Alfredsson, who was vying for her second major championship of the year.

"I couldn't get comfortable and I couldn't make any putts," said Alfredsson, who was 8-under par before a bogey on 16. "You're not going to scare anyone in the Open unless you make birdies. I don't know if I've ever been this disappointed. All I had to do was shoot par today and I would have won."

—*by Jerry Potter*

Merten was helped by golf gurus

Lauri Merten has a golf game that's the handiwork of teaching pros Mike McGetrick and Ed Oldfield.

Their suggestions at Crooked Stick helped Merten snag the championship.

"I felt like I could play well in the Open," said Merten, 33, of Greenville, Del. "I like to gut it out. I never give up on anything."

In winning the Open, her third LPGA victory, Merten came from nowhere and accomplished a lot. After a divorce and golf swing problems, she wasn't sure she could compete on the LPGA tour.

That's when she went to McGetrick, who works with about a dozen LPGA players, including many of the best.

"Mike has a little test he gives you," she said. "It asks a lot of questions about your strengths as a player. At the end he asked me if I thought I could win again. I almost started crying."

That was on a Friday. McGetrick called off practice and told her to come back on Monday.

"I told Mike, 'I don't know if I can win anymore,'" she said. "He told me, 'I think you can win again.'"

McGetrick was at Crooked Stick before the Open to work with all his students. He told Merten to believe in herself and her swing. Saturday afternoon, Merten was on the practice green going through endless drills when Oldfield came by after a session with Betsy King.

"Ed gave me a few tips on putting," she said. "I tried to remember what he told me when I putted (Sunday)."

Merten made six birdies in the fourth round, including a 60-foot putt and a chip-in at No. 16.

"Mike always tells me not to think about the negatives," she said. "He says when I have a 6-iron shot that I should think I'm going to hit the best 6-iron of my life."

—*by Jerry Potter*

FOR 15 HOLES, ALCOTT RECALLED GLORY DAYS

Most golfers would want to forget Amy Alcott's opening round in the U.S. Women's Open.

Not Alcott. She wanted to remember every shot, every birdie, every bogey—and that she'd have been leading the Women's Open if not for Crooked Stick Golf Club's final three holes.

"I played incredibly well," said Alcott, who settled for 2-under 70, two strokes off the lead. "I made six birdies. A round like this has been coming for me a long time."

Alcott, who would finish the Open at 3-over 291, has been within a victory of the 30 she needs to qualify for the LPGA Hall of Fame since winning the Nabisco Dinah Shore on March 31, 1991.

In 1993 she missed the cut in seven of 14 starts before the Open. Her best finish: 19th at the Itoki Hawaiian Ladies Open, Feb. 20, 1993.

For 15 holes at Crooked Stick, Alcott was the class of the field. She chipped in for birdies on the eighth and 12th holes and was 5-under-par before she missed the green and made bogey at No. 16, then three-putted 17 and 18 for bogeys.

Alcott's sprint to the top of the leaderboard didn't surprise Jane Geddes, who finished at 70 while Alcott was playing the back nine.

"When Amy is on her game she's the best iron player there is," said Geddes, who won the 1986 Open. "You get on a golf course like this and you'd better stick your irons shots in the right places on the greens.

"Amy plays a shot every time she hits the ball. She says, 'I'm gonna bump this one in,' or 'I'm gonna turn this one over.'"

Alcott's problem in recent years has been mental more than physical—she admitted being tired of golf, but showed renewed interest at the Open.

"My game has slipped a little," she said. "The key to my career has been consistency. I got a little tired. If you get tired, you don't have motivation."

Alcott, 37, turned pro at 19. She has earned nearly $3 million in almost 19 years on the LPGA tour.

"This game has made me happy and rich with a lot of memories," she said. "I haven't had enough motivation to keep driving myself."

—*by Jerry Potter*

Crooked Stick Golf Club

Long-hitting John Daly won the 1991 PGA Championship playing Crooked Stick Golf Club in Carmel, Ind., at 7,289 yards. For the U.S. Women's Open in 1993, Crooked Stick was set up at 6,311 yards. Comparisons for each hole:

White line shows tee movement

Hole	Par	Yardage PGA	Yardage Open	Hole	Par	Yardage PGA	Yardage Open
1	4	343	345	10	4	453	375
2	4	432	376	11	5	533	502
3	3	196	152	12	4	395	368
4	4	457	385	13	3	180	127
5	5	600	525	14	4	468	390
6	3	195	168	15	5	507	462
7	4	441	370	16	4	469	407
8	4	438	349	17	3	212	175
9	5	525	435	18	4	445	400
Front	36	3,627	3,627	Back	36	3,662	3,206
				Total	72	7,289	6,311

By Web Bryant, USA TODAY

CROOKED STICK RAN FROM NICE TO NASTY

Even before the deluge that left Crooked Stick in tatters for the Open's final round, Pete Dye's hazard-frought design had many LPGA players scratching their heads.

After a practice round, Bob Kendall, caddy for Dottie Mochrie, remarked that "Pete must have been on valium when he built the front nine and then took a shot of acid when he went to the back nine."

The nines are distinct. The front side flows nice and easy, but the back nine is, said Betsy King, "a little funky" in some places.

Said King: "I'd hate to come to the 18th hole needing to make a birdie."

Added Tammie Green: "The 16th, 17th and 18th holes may be the toughest we ever play."

Crooked Stick, where John Daly won the 1991 PGA Championship, is known as a long-hitter's course. Daly played it at 7,289 yards. But shortened to 6,311 yards for the Women's Open, the premium switched to iron play—which helped Lauri Merten.

Crooked Stick was set up for the best women golfers, much like Oakmont (Pa.) Country Club in 1992, Judy Bell, secretary of the U.S. Golf Association, said.

"We wanted them to have to use all (14) golf clubs," she said before the Open began. "If, at the end of the tournament, that has happened, then the examination has been a success."

No doubt, it was a tough test.

"Very demanding," defending champion Patty Sheehan agreed. "You've got to drive the ball in the fairway; the rough is real deep. But I think the greens are what make this golf course difficult."

—*by Jerry Potter*

Loss left Lopez short one goal

By No. 15, most of the gallery had deserted her, bound for other holes, other golfers. Nancy Lopez, in the midst of another futile U.S. Women's Open, was left to battle Crooked Stick alone.

Sticking with her was the old man in the maroon hat, walking slowly through a steamy Indiana afternoon.

Domingo Lopez had smiled as his daughter sped through the first seven holes with seven pars, bowed when she hit into the water for a triple bogey on No. 8, and now stood by No. 15, resigned to her annual U.S. Open fate.

"It happens to her so many times," said the man who taught his daughter how to play and then unleashed her upon an unsuspecting world of golf. "She comes close. She doesn't win it. So many times."

She is 36 and has won nearly everything—47 tournaments, in the Hall of Fame by age 30.

Everything in golf has been hers—except the U.S. Open.

We have seen this frustrating malady before, holes in otherwise immaculate resumes. Palmer and Watson have the PGA. Snead the U.S. Open. Trevino the Masters.

The ailment crosses boundary lines to other sports. Ernie Banks never had his World Series, Bo Schembechler never a national championship.

Each had to handle the Missing Link in his way, lest disappointment become obsession.

Completing a final-round 74 that left her five strokes behind, Lopez's decision was to kiss her father on the cheek. And then smile at the world. She would smile at a mugger.

Her children in Cincinnati awaited her call. She had told them to keep their fingers crossed, but crossed fingers apparently weren't enough.

"I really used to let it bother me," she said of this U.S. Open business. "But it doesn't bother me anymore.

"It's just not that important to me. I would love to win the Open. But I'm not going to let it destroy my career or what I've accomplished. I think it's unfair to do that to any player."

Still, it had been a particularly frustrating week. She liked Crooked Stick as well as any Open course she could remember. She was hitting the ball well. She felt comfortable, and ready to break down the wall.

No. 8, a nasty par-4 that coils around a pond, was the booby trap. A double bogey Saturday. A triple bogey Sunday, when she hit a fat 9-iron. Give her a par both days and she probably finishes tied for the lead. She's in a Monday playoff. The quest may be over.

"That hole don't like Nancy," Domingo Lopez sighed.

"When do I last see her get a triple bogey? Let me think . . . let me think . . . I never see Nancy get a triple bogey before. Honestly."

Her chances foundered at No. 8. Not until No. 15 did she get her day's first birdie—"Look at her laugh," her father said softly—and a 20-foot birdie putt at 18 left fans cheering.

So she finished her 17th U.S. Open unfulfilled. The champion was Lauri Merten, playing in her fourth.

If there is any justice, Lopez's time will come. Given what she has meant to women's golf, for Lopez not to win the championship of her country would be counter to logic, or good taste.

"Maybe she never wins it," Domingo said. "But if she wins it once, she's probably going to win it three times."

Three times? A father's high hopes. One will do. One would plug the hole nicely.

"I feel I'm getting closer and closer," she said. "How much patience do I need? I have to keep waiting."

—*by Mike Lopresti*

United States Women's Open short putts

SNOWED IN: Betsy King, who shot 2-over-par 74 in the opening round, led at 3-under through seven holes, when up jumped the "snowman" on No. 8.

King's quadruple-bogey 8 (golfers call it a snowman) on No. 8 sent her from 3 under to 1 over in a 400-yard stretch.

"I made a bad tee shot and a bad decision," King said. "It all added up to 8." The details:

Tee shot: Far right into the high rough.

2nd shot: Moved ball about 3 feet with sand wedge.

3rd shot: Penalty shot taking an unplayable lie, dropped ball 188 yards from the hole.

4th shot: 5-wood into water on the left.

5th shot: Another penalty shot, dropping the ball 100 yards from the green.

6th shot: Pitching wedge to green, 15 feet from the hole.

7th shot: Putt to within 1 foot of the hole.

8th shot: Tapped in for quadruple bogey.

"It's a scary course," said the two-time Open winner who went on to finish the first round double bogey–birdie–bogey. "There's a lot of places you can hit the ball where you'll be penalized."

If not for the snowman, King would have been in contention on the final day.

MUDDY MESS: A violent thunderstorm swept the area on the eve of the final round, downing trees and flooding some greens and bunkers.

Six bunkers were marked as "ground under repair," allowing free relief, said David Eger, U.S. Golf Association Senior Director for Rules and Competition.

Alice Miller had never seen conditions like those she found on the 16th hole.

When she hit her approach shot into the flooded left bunker, the drop area was a mess.

Said Miller, "In essence you were dropping in mud."

—*by Jerry Potter*

Scores and earnings

Player	Rounds
Lauri Merten, $144,000	71-71-70-68–280
Donna Andrews, $62,431	71-70-69-71–281
Helen Alfredsson, $62,431	68-70-69-74–281
Pat Bradley, $29,249	72-70-68-73–283
Hiromi Kobayashi, $29,249	71-67-71-74–283
Patty Sheehan, $22,379	73-71-69-71–284
Betsy King, $17,525	74-70-72-69–285
Michelle McGann, $17,525	70-66-78-71–285
Nancy Lopez, $17,525	70-71-70-74–285
Ayako Okamoto, $17,525	68-72-71-74–285
Laura Davies, $13,993	73-71-69-73–286
JoAnne Carner, $13,993	71-69-73-73–286
Tina Barrett, $11,999	73-73-70-71–287
Chris Johnson, $11,999	71-75-69-72–287
Sherri Steinhauer, $11,999	73-67-75-72–287
Nina Foust, $11,999	71-71-71-74–287
Dottie Mochrie, $9,978	72-71-74-71–288
Gail Graham, $9,978	72-73-70-73–288
Barb Mucha, $9,978	75-69-71-73–288
Kris Tschetter, $9,978	73-71-69-75–288
Meg Mallon, $9,061	73-72-69-75–289
Danielle Ammaccapane, $8,334	73-74-73-70–290
Allison Finney, $8,334	74-72-73-71–290
Michele Redman, $8,334	75-71-72-72–290
Dawn Coe-Jones, $8,334	69-72-76-73–290
Lori West, $6,894	73-73-73-72–291
Alice Miller, $6,894	73-68-78-72–291
Laurie Brower, $6,894	73-73-72-73–291
Julie Larsen, $6,894	76-71-70-74–291
Amy Alcott, $6,894	70-74-73-74–291
Cindy Mah-Lyford, $6,894	73-73-70-75–291
Shelley Hamlin, $6,894	74-68-73-76–291
Kelly Robbins, $6,894	71-70-74-76–291
Dina Ammaccapane, $6,894	71-70-70-80–291
#Debbi Miho Koyama	70-74-72-75–291
Judy Dickinson, $5,907	74-73-72-73–292
Michelle Estill, $5,907	74-70-75-73–292
Missie Berteotti, $5,907	72-75-70-75–292
Melissa McNamara, $5,233	74-73-73-73–293
Cindy Rarick, $5,233	76-70-74-73–293
Elaine Crosby, $5,233	75-70-75-73–293
Deb Richard, $5,233	73-71-76-73–293
Juli Inkster, $5,233	71-72-76-74–293
Brandie Burton, $5,233	74-72-72-75–293
Missie McGeorge, $4,412	73-72-77-72–294
Pamela Wright, $4,412	73-73-74-74–294
Florence Descampe, $4,412	71-75-73-75–294
Nancy Ramsbottom, $4,412	71-76-71-76–294
Lenore Rittenhouse, $4,412	73-74-70-77–294
Lisa Walters, $3,814	75-72-76-72–295
Jane Geddes, $3,814	70-70-79-76–295
Vicki Goetze, $3,814	72-72-74-77–295
Amy Read, $3,442	70-72-79-75–296
Beth Daniel, $3,442	74-69-74-79–296
Barb Bunkowsky, $3,314	72-75-77-73–297
Kim Cathrein, $3,242	75-69-78-76–298
Jody Anschutz, $3,242	73-69-76-80–298
Kathy Guadagnino, $3,162	73-73-78-75–299
Amy Benz, $3,162	72-71-79-77–299
#Sarah Ingram	76-70-76-77–299
Alison Munt, $3,105	76-71-78-76–301
Liselotte Neumann, $3,074	77-70-79-77–303
Jennifer Myers, $3,105	74-73-76-82–305
# - amateur	

du Maurier Ltd. Classic

AT A GLANCE

- **Course:** London Hunt and Country Club
- **Location:** London, Ontario
- **When:** Aug. 26-29, 1993
- **Weather:** Mostly warm and comfortable. Rain suspended play briefly during round four.
- **Purse:** $800,000
- **Par:** 72
- **Yards:** 6,331
- **Playoff:** Brandie Burton defeated Betsy King on the first playoff hole.
- **Defending champion:** Sherri Stinehauer, 11-under-par 277
- **Tournament record:** 16-under-par 262, Jody Rosenthal, 1987

Like most young golfers, Brandie Burton always dreamed of winning a championship with a birdie putt.

"Not a tap-in," said Burton. "But a putt of something over 15 feet."

Burton's dream came true last August as she beat Betsy King on the first hole of a playoff in the du Maurier Classic, the final major championship of the season in women's golf.

Burton and King ended regulation at 11-under-par 277 at the London Hunt and Country Club.

Burton shot a final-round 2-under 70 and King shot 1-under 71 in constant rain that forced one brief suspension of play.

"Coming down the stretch," said Burton, "it was very hard to judge the speed of the putts."

Ironically, Burton wasn't certain of the length of that winning roll. She thought it was something over 20 feet and less than 25.

For sure it was uphill and downhill and breaking left to right through the water. The ball seemed to hang on the lip of the cup for a moment before falling in from the side.

"I didn't think the ball was going to get there," said Burton, 21, of Rialto, Calif.

"I can assure you that it wasn't going by the hole."

In regulation play, Burton three-putted the 18th hole for a double-bogey 6 to let King back into the tournament.

King, who entered the final round with a one-stroke lead, led Burton by three strokes through 10 holes, but she four-putted the 15th green and lost the lead.

"I went the whole week without a three-putt," said King, trying to make the best of the situation.

"If I had the 15th hole to play over again, I would have marked my ball after I missed the second putt."

King's first putt was from 35 feet, the second was from 8, the third from 4 and the fourth from 1 foot.

Still, she had a chance to win the tournament in regulaton on the 18th hole when she missed a birdie putt from 15 feet.

"I thought I'd made it," said King. "It just turned away at the end."

Continuing an agonizing streak, King lost for the seventh time after heading into the final round as a leader in 1993 and stayed two victories short of induction into the LPGA Hall of Fame.

In the playoff, King drove into a fairway bunker and then came up short of the green on her second shot.

Burton was on the green in two strokes, putting an 8-iron shot 20 feet from the cup on her approach.

Burton, who joined the LPGA in 1991 at age 19, credited her caddie, Chuck Parisi, with helping her regroup for the playoff hole.

"He's a positive person," said Burton. "After the 18th in regulation, he said, 'It's over. Let's go beat the ball again and see if we can do better.'"

Burton responded with the third victory of her career, her second this year and first win in a major championship.

"I think I lost to the next great player on the LPGA tour," said King. "She's going to win more tournaments than anybody in the next 10 years."

—by Jerry Potter

Brandie Burton may be the next LPGA great.

DU MAURIER IS SPECIAL TO COE-JONES AND KING

Both Dawn Coe-Jones, the first-round leader, and runner-up Betsy King have a special interest in the du Maurier, which is the Canadian national championship and the final major of the year in women's golf.

Only one Canadian, Jocelyn Bourassa, has won the championship since it began in 1973.

"You want to win every tournament," said Coe-Jones, a native of Campbell River, British Columbia. "But this is the only time I get to showcase my game in Canada, so a win here would be the ultimate."

King has 28 career victories, but the du Maurier is the only major championship that has eluded her.

"If you said at the beginning of the year that there's one tournament you want to win, this would be it for me because I've never won it," King said. "But no one is so good that she can pick one tournament, say 'I'm going to win it' and then go out and win it."

—by Jerry Potter

Scores and earnings

Player	Earnings	Scores
#Brandie Burton	$120,000	71-70-66-70—277
Betsy King	$74,474	65-70-71-71—277
Dawn Coe-Jones	$54,346	64-74-72-68—278
Dottie Mochrie	$42,269	68-69-71-71—279
Kris Monaghan	$31,198	72-71-71-66—280
Vicki Fergon	$31,198	67-73-68-72—280
Dana Lofland-Dormann	$23,751	68-68-73-72—281
Helen Alfredsson	$19,926	70-70-72-70—282
Kathy Guadagnino	$19,926	69-69-70-74—282
Danielle Ammaccapane	$14,894	72-72-73-66—283
Sherri Steinhauer	$14,894	73-69-71-70—283
Judy Dickinson	$14,894	70-71-71-71—283
Chris Johnson	$14,894	71-69-72-71—283
Gail Graham	$11,674	71-72-72-69—284
Tammie Green	$11,674	69-73-72-70—284
Lori West	$11,674	72-72-69-71—284
Tina Barrett	$9,862	74-72-70-69—285
Deb Richard	$9,982	72-74-70-69—285
Sally Little	$9,862	72-69-69-75—285
Beth Daniel	$9,862	69-70-68-78—285
Cindy Rarick	$8,302	73-73-70-70—286
Nancy Harvey	$8,302	75-70-71-70—286
Amy Benz	$8,302	73-70-71-72—286
Jenny Lidback	$8,302	70-73-68-75—286
Rosie Jones	$7,084	69-71-77-70—287
Dale Eggeling	$7,084	70-73-73-71—287
Kristi Albers	$7,084	70-72-72-73—287
Michelle McGann	$7,084	67-74-72-74—287
Amy Alcott	$7,084	70-70-73-74—287
Kelly Robbins	$5,317	76-71-72-69—288
Lynn Connelly	$5,317	76-71-71-70—288
Jody Anschutz	$5,317	73-74-71-70—288
Alicia Dibos	$5,317	73-71-73-71—288
Donna Andrews	$5,317	73-71-72-72—288
Stephanie Farwig	$5,317	71-73-72-72—288
Missie McGeorge	$5,317	72-73-70-73—288
Hiromi Kobayashi	$5,317	73-72-69-74—288
Lauri Merten	$5,317	75-69-70-74—288
Kim Williams	$5,317	70-73-71-74—288
Robin Hood	$5,317	71-70-73-74—288
Jane Crafter	$4,106	74-71-73-71—289
Nina Foust	$3,224	75-72-72-71—290
Caroline Pierce	$3,224	74-73-72-71—290
Lisa Walters	$3,224	72-73-74-71—290
Martha Nause	$3,224	71-73-75-71—290
Colleen Walker	$3,224	70-75-73-72—290
Muffin Spencer-Devlin	$3,224	71-72-75-72—290
Allison Finney	$3,224	73-71-73-73—290
Dina Ammaccapane	$3,224	71-73-72-74—290
Mary Beth Zimmerman	$3,224	69-74-72-75—290
Marianne Morris	$3,224	74-70-69-77—290
Ellie Gibson	$2,052	71-69-80-71—291
Karen Lunn	$2,052	74-73-72-72—291
Julie Larsen	$2,052	71-71-77-72—291
Hollis Stacy	$2,052	71-74-73-73—291
Stefania Croce	$2,052	75-68-75-73—291
Denise Baldwin	$2,052	71-72-74-74—291
Juli Inkster	$2,052	71-74-70-76—291
Jan Stephenson	$1,408	70-75-75-72—292
Tania Abitbol	$1,408	71-74-74-73—292
Cindy Schreyer	$1,408	73-71-75-73—292
Maggie Will	$1,408	74-73-70-75—292
Melissa McNamara	$1,408	71-69-75-77—292
Elaine Crosby	$1,127	71-75-72-75—293
Meg Mallon	$1,127	70-75-73-75—293
Katie Peterson-Parker	$1,127	70-73-75-75—293
Barb Bunkowsky	$1,127	73-73-71-76—293
Cindy Figg-Currier	$1,127	73-72-71-77—293
Lori Garbacz	$986	75-72-72-75—294
Nancy Ramsbottom	$986	73-72-74-75—294
Martha Faulconer	$891	74-73-71-77—295
JoAnne Carner	$891	72-74-71-78—295
Terry-Jo Myers	$891	71-73-73-78—295
Joan Pitcock	$826	73-74-76-73—296
Tracy Kerdyk	$826	69-77-75-75—296
Jean Zedlitz	$826	70-73-78-75—296
Judy Sams	$783	74-72-75-77—298
Michelle Mackall	$783	74-72-72-80—298
Liz Earley	$759	75-71-74-79—299
Sharon Barrett	$743	71-76-75-78—300

\# - won on first playoff hole

The Tradition

AT A GLANCE

- **Course:** Desert Mountain Golf Club, Cochise Course
- **Location:** Scottsdale, Ariz.
- **When:** April 1-4, 1993
- **Weather:** Sunny, cool and windy.
- **Purse:** $850,000
- **Par:** 72
- **Yards:** 6,869
- **Defending champion:** Lee Trevino
- **Tournament record:** 14-under-par 274, Lee Trevino, 1992

Tom Shaw sank a birdie putt on 18 to edge Mike Hill.

Tom Shaw found a course that fits his game, or a game that fits the Cochise Course at Desert Mountain.

"This is one course that fits me because I hit the ball so high," said Shaw, who shot a tournament-record 19-under-par 269.

"I felt everything was coming together for me. It was nice to prove it."

Shaw finished with consecutive rounds at 5-under-par 67 and sunk a crucial putt to edge Mike Hill by one stroke.

"I've played a lot of good rounds here," Shaw said. "But I've never put four good ones together."

"Tom can be proud of himself," said Hill, who finished 67–270—including an eagle on the final hole that forced Shaw to make a 12-foot birdie putt. "I put a lot of pressure on him today, but he hit some great shots."

"It's gotta be a lot like having to make a free throw to win the Final Four," Shaw said. "I didn't want to have any doubts about making it."

Shaw made the putt, earning his second win in four Senior PGA Tour seasons and his first since the 1989 Showdown Classic.

The major championship is the first of Shaw's career, which began on the PGA Tour in 1963. The $127,500 payoff is the largest of his career and almost doubles his '93 earnings.

"One of my favorite mottos is anything good is worth waiting for," Shaw said.

"I played pretty good the first two years I was on the Senior Tour, but last year I played awful. I've worked real hard to improve, and it's nice to see the work pay off."

Shaw and Gibby Gilbert were tied starting Sunday, but it became a Shaw-Hill race.

Shaw opened with four birdies to go 17 under and was 19-under through 12 holes. A bogey on the par-4 14th set the stage for the final hole, a 531-yard par-5.

Hill outdrove Shaw and had a 5-iron to the green. Shaw was 205 yards away and needed a 2-iron to get home.

"That was as good a 5-iron as I've hit in a long time," Hill said. "I needed to make that putt to put a little pressure on Tom."

Shaw's 2-iron shot hit the green but skipped to the back fringe, forcing a chip to set up the winning putt.

"That shot he hit with a 2-iron was as good as any you'll see," Hill said. "It took a lot of courage to hit a 2-iron because if he puts the ball in the back bunker he's gonna be, 'Adios, amigo.'"

Birdies, Rattlers: All in a Day's Work

On their way to a tie for the first-round lead, Lee Trevino and Dave Stockton took a nature walk on the Cochise Course at Desert Mountain.

They bagged birdies and saw some coyotes and one rattlesnake.

"What a day," said Trevino after shooting 6-under-par 66. "It was so relaxing."

Relaxing?

That's exactly what Trevino saw the rattler doing behind the 13th tee. Stockton saw it too and tried to kill it before taking a spectator's advice to leave it alone.

"I took a 2-iron and went back there to kill it," Stockton said.

"A lady told me not to kill it. She said, 'It won't bother you.' I said, 'It sure won't bother me dead.'"

Trevino, a group ahead of Stockton, had left the snake alone.

"They won't bother you," said Trevino, who learned a lot about rattlers as a young pro in El Paso. "They're the only snakes that warn you if you get too close to them."

Trevino said the snake was stretched out in the sun, watching golf. Neither he nor Stockton put on much of a show for it on No. 13, a 136-yard par-3.

Stockton two-putted from 20 feet for par. Trevino, 3-under through 12, didn't make another birdie until 15 but added birdies on 16 and 18 to take the lead. Stockton made four birdies on the back nine, including one on 18 to tie Trevino.

"I cannot remember being so relaxed while playing golf," said Trevino, who was recovering from left thumb surgery in December 1992. "I think it has something to do with not putting so much pressure on myself to win."

—by Jerry Potter

Scores and earnings

Tom Shaw, $127,500 — 70-65-67-67–269
Mike Hill, $74,800 — 69-68-66-67–270
Ray Floyd, $51,000 — 69-71-69-65–274
Dale Douglass, $51,000 — 69-66-69-70–274
Gibby Gilbert, $51,000 — 67-66-69-72–274
Isao Aoki, $34,000 — 69-65-71-70–275
Al Geiberger, $30,600 — 74-69-64-69–276
Tom Weiskopf, $27,200 — 68-67-69-73–277
Jack Nicklaus, $22,950 — 72-69-70-67–278
Charles Coody, $22,950 — 67-72-69-70–278
Miller Barber, $19,550 — 73-70-69-67–279
Bob Charles, $19,550 — 68-69-73-69–279
Lee Trevino, $17,000 — 66-70-72-72–280
Dave Stockton, $15,300 — 66-73-73-69–281
Dick Hendrickson, $15,300 — 74-67-70-70–281
Jim Colbert, $15,300 — 68-73-69-71–281
Tommy Aaron, $11,659 — 73-73-69-67–282
Terry Dill, $11,659 — 71-67-74-70–282
Gary Player, $11,659 — 67-73-71-71–282
Jim Albus, $11,659 — 67-70-72-73–282
Tom Wargo, $11,659 — 71-71-66-74–282
Jack Kiefer, $11,659 — 67-72-69-74–282
J.C.Snead, $9,138 — 73-69-72-69–283
Larry Laoretti, $9,138 — 69-73-70-71–283
Bob Wynn, $7,752 — 71-74-70-69–284
George Archer, $7,752 — 68-74-73-69–284
Don Bies, $7,752 — 70-69-74-71–284
Kermit Zarley, $7,752 — 70-73-71-70–284
Don January, $7,752 — 72-70-71-71–284
Chi Chi Rodriguez, $6,545 — 71-70-74-70–285
Mike Joyce, $6,545 — 70-72-72-71–285
Dewitt Weaver, $5,865 — 70-72-73-71–286
Dick Lotz, $5,865 — 74-68-72-72–286
Bruce Lehnhard, $5,865 — 70-70-73-73–286
Jim Dent, $5,228 — 72-72-75-68–287
Joe Jimenez, $5,228 — 72-73-72-70–287
Don Massengale, $4,675 — 72-70-76-70–288
Bruce Crampton, $4,675 — 75-68-73-72–288
Ken Still, $4,675 — 73-70-69-76–288
Dick Rhyan, $4,080 — 77-72-73-67–289
Larry Gilbert, $4,080 — 72-71-76-70–289
Rocky Thompson, $4,080 — 76-70-71-72–289
Bob Reith, $4,080 — 72-71-73-73–289
Babe Hiskey, $3,315 — 75-69-74-72–290
Orville Moody, $3,315 — 74-75-69-72–290
Bruce Devlin, $3,315 — 73-74-70-73–290
Bob Brue, $3,315 — 74-75-68-73–290
Rives McBee, $3,315 — 71-76-70-73–290
Jim Ferree, $2,635 — 74-74-74-69–291
Larry Mowry, $2,635 — 76-73-71-71–291
Bob Verwey, $2,635 — 72-76-70-73–291
Butch Baird, $2,210 — 75-74-73-70–292
Ben Smith, $2,210 — 68-77-74-73–292
Billy Casper, $1,998 — 73-73-76-71–293
Lee Elder, $1,998 — 71-76-71-75–293
Bobby Nichols, $1,870 — 68-78-73-75–294
Dave Hill, $1,700 — 77-77-71-70–295
Harry Toscano, $1,700 — 77-75-72-71–295
Arnold Palmer, $1,700 — 76-74-71-74–295
Roger Kennedy, $1,530 — 77-76-72-71–296
Doug Dalziel, $1,360 — 73-81-73-70–297
Bert Yancey, $1,360 — 76-74-74-73–297
Gay Brewer, $1,360 — 72-74-77-74–297
Larry Ziegler, $1,190 — 73-69-75-81–298
Simon Hobday, $1,020 — 70-75-78-76–299
Jimmy Powell, $1,020 — 72-74-76-77–299
Walter Zembriski, $1,020 — 72-73-75-79–299
Homero Blancas, $799 — 75-75-75-75–300
Bob Goalby, $799 — 74-80-70-76–300
William Viele, $799 — 71-75-76-78–300
Lou Graham, $646 — 74-78-78-71–301
Charlie Sifford, $646 — 76-76-77-72–301
Tom Joyce, $646 — 76-73-77-75–301
Frank Beard, $561 — 74-75-77-78–304
Phil Rodgers, $510 — 75-78-77-78–308
Dow Finsterwald, $510 — 78-73-78-79–308
Doug Sanders, $459 — 82-74-74-81–311
Jerry Barber, $425 — 73-79-81-80–313
Doug Ford, $425 — 82-82-75-76–315
Gene Littler — 77-71-78–WD

PGA Seniors' Championship

AT A GLANCE

- **Course:** PGA National Resort & Spa, Champion Course
- **Location:** Palm Beach Gardens, Fla.
- **When:** April 15-19, 1993
- **Weather:** Sunny, warm and windy, except for scattered showers Friday.
- **Purse:** $800,000
- **Par:** 72
- **Yards:** 6,704
- **Playoff:** Tom Wargo defeated Bruce Crampton on the second playoff hole
- **Defending champion:** Lee Trevino
- **Tournament record:** 17-under-par 271, Jack Nicklaus, 1991
- **Format:** 72 holes stroke play
- **Field:** 144 PGA of America club pros, age 50 and older, and Senior PGA Tour players

In recent years club pro Tom Wargo had watched his old playing partners Jim Albus and Larry Laoretti catch what he called "the golden nugget."

He mined a little gold himself when he won the PGA Seniors' Championship in a two-hole playoff with Bruce Crampton.

"This is all one big moment," said Wargo, pro at Greenview Golf Club in Centralia, Ill., after the victory. "How do you capture it? The significance hasn't sunk in yet, but it probably will tomorrow."

The former ironworker endured a psychological joust with Tom Weiskopf after round three and beat Crampton with a par-3 at the 152-yard 17th hole. Crampton hit his tee shot into the water and made 5.

They had tied at 13-under 275 after regulation 72 holes. Crampton shot a final-round 66, Wargo a 71.

Wargo joined Albus and Laoretti as former club pros to win major senior events. Albus won the 1991 Senior Players Championship, Laoretti the '92 U.S. Senior Open.

Laoretti hung around to congratulate Wargo the best way he knew—by buying him a beer and giving him a cigar.

"How many colds did you have last night?" Laoretti asked.

"Three," answered Wargo, puffing on a cigar.

Laoretti knew better than most what Wargo had accomplished. But Wargo may have surpassed Laoretti or Albus with his victory.

Wargo spent the last 25 years trying to learn to play golf. He had become one of the best-playing club pros, but a club pro is no touring pro.

Tom Weiskopf hinted as much Saturday when he said, "Until you win, you don't know what it's like to win."

Wargo, who read Weiskopf's comments the next morning, said, "You can take that either way. The only thing I can tell you is right now I've got one win and he's got zero on the Senior (PGA) Tour."

Weiskopf, like Wargo, was in his first Senior Tour season in 1993. Weiskopf won the Chrysler Cup in February, but it's an unofficial event.

Wargo's victory was very official, and it gave him a one-year exemption on the Senior PGA Tour. He planned to play in the Senior PGA Tour Murata Reunion Pro-Am in Frisco, Texas, the next week.

"I was going to play there anyway," he said, "because I had to go back to Dallas to get my car. I left it at the airport."

After Dallas, he said, he would take two weeks off and return to Centralia because, "I gotta get back home and cut some grass."

—*by Jerry Potter*

HOME CLUB ENTHRALLED BY BOSS'S VICTORY

Tom Wargo might have found the net receipts a bit short for April 19 when he returned to Greenview Golf Club in Centralia, Ill.

A crowd of 150 excited fans had enjoyed a beer "on the house" as Wargo, their boss, won the PGA Seniors' Championship.

Illinois club pro Tom Wargo won in two playoff holes.

"We're extremely excited and it's a little emotional in here right now," floor supervisor Patty Hollingsead said moments after the crowd watched the win on TV. "One of our local bankers just walked by with tears streaming down his face. Am I crying too? Oh yes. You better believe I am."

When Wargo parred the second playoff hole to defeat Bruce Crampton, "The windows were shaking, everybody was screaming and yelling," Hollingsead said.

There was some other screaming and yelling when NBC switched to the Spurs-Trailblazers NBA game during the playoff.

"Everybody started booing, hissing," Hollingsead said. "We were trying to figure out who to call. When they switched back, everybody hollered, 'Quiet! Quiet! Tom's back on.' And then it got real quiet."

The clubhouse planned to be open Monday after the event, as the boss would want. "Knowing Tom, we'd better not change our routine at all. It had better be business as usual," Hollingsead laughed.

The celebration would have to wait a week, when Wargo and his wife, Irene—who runs the clubhouse—got back from the next tournament.

—*Carolyn White*

Scores and earnings

#Tom Wargo, $110,000	69-69-67-70–275
Bruce Crampton, $80,000	73-67-69-66–275
Isao Aoki, $60,000	72-67-69-71–279
Bob Charles, $40,000	74-67-72-68–281
Tom Weiskopf, $40,000	73-64-72-72–281
Mike Hill, $30,000	72-71-72-67–282
Orville Moody, $22,500	72-70-71-70–283
Jim Albus, $22,500	70-68-73-72–283
Jack Nicklaus, $16,000	69-71-73-71–284
J.C. Snead, $16,000	68-69-75-72–284
Larry Mowry, $16,000	76-68-69-71–284
Harold Henning, $16,000	69-70-73-72–284
Tommy Aycock, $14,000	70-70-75-70–285
Ray Floyd, $14,000	77-67-72-69–285
Al Kelley, $14,000	75-66-72-72–285
Gary Player, $12,000	73-73-72-68–286
Rocky Thompson, $12,000	72-70-73-71–286
Jimmy Powell, $12,000	70-71-74-71–286
George Archer, $12,000	73-72-70-71–286
Dale Douglass, $12,000	74-69-70-73–286
Walter Zembriski, $10,250	73-69-76-69–287
Kermit Zarley, $10,250	73-71-72-71–287
Dave Stockton, $9,000	79-72-69-68–288
Dewitt Weaver, $9,000	72-76-73-67–288
Lee Trevino, $9,000	72-68-73-75–288
Larry Gilbert, $8,000	76-74-71-68–289
Gibby Gilbert, $6,500	73-73-74-70–290
Simon Hobday, $6,500	72-73-74-71–290
Dick Hendrickson, $6,500	70-75-75-70–290
Harry Toscano, $6,500	77-71-72-70–290
Arnold Palmer, $6,500	76-73-67-74–290
Ken Still, $4,050	74-71-74-72–291
Jim Dent, $4,050	73-70-76-72–291
Tommy Horton, $4,050	74-73-70-74–291
Chi Chi Rodriguez, $4,050	76-74-73-68–291
Rives Mcbee, $4,050	69-75-72-75–291
Miller Barber, $2,950	70-75-75-72–292
Tom Shaw, $2,950	72-67-77-76–292
Don Massengale, $2,650	74-71-76-72–293
Larry Ziegler, $2,650	66-76-75-76–293
Mike O'Sullivan, $2,650	71-74-72-76–293
Bob Murphy, $2,650	74-75-74-70–293
John Frillman, $2,400	77-70-74-73–294
Stan Thirsk, $2,300	72-73-71-79–295
Terry Dill, $2,063	74-70-73-79–296
Jack Kiefer, $2,063	74-74-75-73–296
Jim Colbert, $2,063	72-77-74-73–296
Seiichi Kanai, $2,063	77-71-76-72–296
Joe Jimenez, $1,775	78-68-74-77–297
Gay Brewer, $1,775	71-72-75-79–297
Jim King, $1,775	76-75-72-74–297
Don January, $1,775	75-70-79-73–297
David Philo, $1,775	77-73-74-73–297
Mike Joyce, $1,775	77-72-77-71–297
Masaru Amano, $1,600	78-73-74-73–298
Brian Huggett, $1,525	74-75-78-72–299
Charles Coody, $1,525	73-76-78-72–299
Ed Dalton, $1,463	68-76-81-75–300
Larry Laoretti, $1,463	75-76-78-71–300
Lee Elder, $1,400	75-69-74-83–301
Bob Brue, $1,400	78-73-72-78–301
Lloyd Monroe, $1,400	79-72-77-73–301
Dave Ragan, $1,338	74-74-79-75–302
Bobby Nichols, $1,338	74-76-78-74–302
Odell Trueblood, $1,300	74-73-79-77–303
Hisashi Suzumura, $1,270	79-71-76-78–304
Chuck Workman, $1,270	72-78-77-77–304
John Paul Cain, $1,270	77-73-77-78–305
Ryosuke Ohta, $1,230	73-73-84-75–305
Al Krueger, $1,200	75-75-78-79–307
Doug Dalziel, $1,170	75-76-80-77–308
Hiroshi Ishii, $1,170	76-73-83-76–308
Tommy Aaron, $1,140	79-71-75-84–309
Doug Sanders, $1,120	76-75-82-79–312

- won on second playoff hole

Ford Senior Players Championship

AT A GLANCE

- **Course:** TPC of Michigan
- **Location:** Dearborn, Mich.
- **When:** June 24-27, 1993
- **Weather:** Windy, cool and rainy with play interrupted Saturday.
- **Purse:** $1.2 million
- **Par:** 72
- **Yards:** 6,876
- **Defending champion:** Dave Stockton, 11-under-par 277
- **Tournament record:** 27-under-par 261, Jack Nicklaus, Dearborn (Mich.) CC, 1990

Jim Colbert played almost flawless golf as he built a three-shot lead with three holes to play in the Senior Players Championship and had enough left to survive a late stumble.

Colbert made bogey on the 72nd hole, but Raymond Floyd's birdie on that hole was too little, too late. Colbert held his one-stroke lead for his seventh Senior PGA Tour victory and second in 1993. It was his first in a major championship.

"When I was walking off the 17th, I heard a roar from the crowd up on the 18th green," Colbert said. "It didn't quite sound like a 'he holed it' roar. But I said, 'Boy, I hope Raymond putts.'"

Floyd's birdie putt, from 1 foot, put him in the clubhouse with a 68—279, cutting Colbert's lead to two strokes.

"You don't play any round without some adversity," Colbert said. "I figured the 18th was my adversity."

Colbert, who had pulled his drive into wetlands and made a double-bogey on 18 the day before, hit a perfect drive in the final-day pressure-cooker. But, instead of a safe 3-iron onto the green, he hit a 5-wood into a bunker. He blasted out, but needed two putts to finish at 69—278.

That still left him a stroke—and $74,400—ahead of Floyd.

Colbert's career golf earnings reached $3.7 million, with $2.2 million courtesy of the senior circuit.

Scores and earnings

Player	Rounds—Total
Jim Colbert, $180,000	67-72-70-69—278
Ray Floyd, $105,600	68-72-71-68—279
Al Geiberger, $86,400	72-73-69-66—280
Rocky Thompson, $72,000	68-71-70-72—281
Jim Ferree, $49,600	72-69-70-72—283
Isao Aoki, $49,600	71-69-71-72—283
Bob Charles, $49,600	66-74-70-73—283
Jim Dent, $36,000	73-75-67-69—284
Larry Gilbert, $36,000	70-76-68-70—284
Tom Weiskopf, $31,200	70-71-74-70—285
Dave Stockton, $27,600	68-77-71-70—286
Babe Hiskey, $27,600	73-71-71-71—286
Mike Hill, $23,400	76-72-70-69—287
Tom Wargo, $23,400	74-72-70-71—287
Jim Albus, $21,000	66-73-77-72—288
Bob Murphy, $21,000	68-73-75-72—288
Dick Rhyan, $18,040	71-78-71-69—289
Bob Betley, $18,040	73-74-70-72—289
George Archer, $18,040	71-75-71-72—289
J.C. Snead, $15,360	74-75-70-71—290
Chi Chi Rodriguez, $15,360	72-71-73-74—290
Charles Coody, $12,069	73-76-77-65—291
Jack Nicklaus, $12,069	67-75-78-71—291
Dave Hill, $12,069	72-71-76-72—291
Dick Hendrickson, $12,069	71-75-71-74—291
Kermit Zarley, $12,069	72-70-74-75—291
Larry Mowry, $12,069	69-71-74-77—291
Jack Kiefer, $12,069	70-70-73-78—291
Orville Moody, $9,480	75-67-80-70—292
Don January, $9,480	71-75-75-71—292
Walter Zembriski, $9,480	72-71-76-73—292
Tom Shaw, $8,640	73-73-75-72—293
Gary Player, $7,740	73-74-75-72—294
Gibby Gilbert, $7,740	71-75-77-71—294
Don Bies, $7,740	76-72-72-74—294
Tommy Aaron, $7,740	69-77-74-74—294
Billy Casper, $6,840	74-71-75-75—295
Larry Ziegler, $6,480	70-73-82-71—296
Harold Henning, $6,480	73-75-75-73—296
Lee Trevino, $5,760	74-76-78-69—297
Terry Dill, $5,760	71-76-79-71—297
Gay Brewer, $5,760	72-74-75-76—297
Homero Blancas, $5,760	74-72-74-77—297
Dick Lotz, $4,800	72-75-79-72—298
Bob Reith, $4,800	73-76-75-74—298
Dick Goetz, $4,800	74-77-70-77—298
Arnold Palmer, $4,800	72-76-78-72—298
Simon Hobday, $3,960	75-75-76-73—299
Ben Smith, $3,960	71-79-75-74—299
Bob Brue, $3,960	73-72-75-79—299
Al Kelley, $3,072	74-78-77-71—300
J.C. Goosie, $3,072	72-79-75-74—300
Joe Jimenez, $3,072	72-77-77-74—300
Walter Morgan, $3,072	71-78-76-75—300
Dale Douglass, $3,072	77-73-74-76—300
Rives McBee, $2,520	74-77-77-73—301
Miller Barber, $2,520	75-75-74-77—301
Dewitt Weaver, $2,520	74-72-74-81—301
Mike Joyce, $2,160	76-74-79-73—302
Bill Kennedy, $2,160	74-74-76-78—302
Ken Still, $2,160	74-80-70-78—302
Tommy Aycock, $1,860	78-78-76-71—303
Butch Baird, $1,860	79-80-73-71—303
Bobby Nichols, $1,560	76-77-75-76—304
Larry Laoretti, $1,560	73-77-77-77—304
Bert Yancey, $1,560	75-74-76-79—304
Jim O'Hern, $1,320	78-80-74-73—305
Jimmy Powell, $1,128	79-76-76-76—307
John Paul Cain, $1,128	84-74-70-79—307
Harry Toscano, $1,128	72-77-76-82—307
Don Massengale, $948	72-78-80-79—309
Frank Beard, $948	73-80-75-81—309
Bruce Devlin, $840	78-71-82-79—310
Bob Wynn, $792	72-77-78-87—314
Doug Dalziel, $720	81-81-74-79—315
Lee Elder, $720	73-81-80-81—315
John Brodie, $648	79-79-77-82—317
Mike Fetchick, $600	76-82-78-85—321

United States Senior Open

AT A GLANCE

- **Course:** Cherry Hills Country Club
- **Location:** Englewood, Colo.
- **When:** July 8-11, 1993
- **Weather:** Partly cloudy Thursday with play suspended for nearly two hours in early afternoon because of lightning in the area; suspended again because of darkness with 21 players on the course. Hot and humid Friday and Saturday; light drizzle Sunday.
- **Purse:** $750,000
- **Par:** 71
- **Yards:** 6,915
- **Defending champion:** Larry Laoretti, 9-under-par 275, four strokes ahead of Jim Colbert.
- **Tournament record:** 14-under-par 270, Gary Player, Brooklawn CC, Fairfield, Conn., 1987

Jack Nicklaus showed he could still putt under pressure in winning his fourth senior tour major.

Needing to two-putt from 35 feet on the treacherous 18th green to win, Jack Nicklaus and many in the gallery might have thought the outcome of the U.S. Senior Open was still very much in doubt.

Not Tom Weiskopf.

Nicklaus had sank a 12-foot birdie putt at the 16th hole to inch ahead of Weiskopf, and he maintained his one-stroke advantage to the 18th. When Nicklaus hit the green, Weiskopf knew his courageous bid was over.

"Who can tell me when Jack Nicklaus has ever three-putted to lose a major championship or missed a putt under pressure?" Weiskopf said. "The guy is the greatest putter under pressure of all time, bar none."

Nicklaus got his par, making a 2½-footer to capture his first title since winning this event in 1991.

Asked if he ever remembered three-putting to lose a tournament, Nicklaus paused and said, "I don't recall one. I've blown a few tournaments, but I don't think I've blown too many of them that way. Actually, I didn't three-putt a green all week. I three-putted once or twice from the fringe, but not from on the green."

Nicklaus, 53, finished with a 1-under-par 70 for a 72-hole total of 6-under 278. Weiskopf, who closed with a 67, wound up at 279. Kermit Zarley was third, another stroke back, and Dale Douglass tied Chi Chi Rodriguez at 281.

Nicklaus, who entered the final round leading Douglass by one shot and Weiskopf by four, saw his advantage dissipate in the face of a furious flurry by Weiskopf, who birdied five of his first eight holes.

Taming the putting paralysis that had gripped him for three rounds, Weiskopf vaulted to 6-under-par for the tournament and climbed ahead of Nicklaus and Douglass.

Weiskopf's 5-under 30 on the front nine tied a Senior Open record.

Nicklaus, however, drew back into a tie for the lead with a 2-foot birdie putt at the seventh hole.

While Douglass slipped back with bogeys at the 10th and 12th holes, Nicklaus and Weiskopf, both former Ohio State golfers, stayed within a stroke of each other.

Weiskopf, a two-time runner-up to Nicklaus in the Masters who continually has played in Nicklaus' shadow, reclaimed the lead with his sixth birdie of the day at No. 13. But he fell back into a tie when his tee shot at the par-3 15th stopped on the edge of the green and he three-putted for bogey.

Weiskopf failed to take advantage of a birdie opportunity at the par-5 17th hole when his tee shot sailed into the right rough and his second shot to the island green was partially blocked by trees. He had to lay up and settle for par.

Nicklaus then went ahead, hitting an 8-iron 12 feet behind the hole at No. 16 and making the putt.

"When I got to my ball in the 16th fairway, there was mud on the right side of the ball," Nicklaus said. "I remember Johnny Miller saying if there's mud on the right side, the ball will go left. I don't know if it's true or not. I just decided I wasn't going to play to the middle of the green. If it's going off line, it's going off line, but it's going at the hole to start with. It went right over the pin."

On the putt, Nicklaus said he reminded himself not to move his head, which he had done on several previous missed putts during the round.

"As soon as it left the putter, I thought, 'I've made it if I read it right.' I didn't look up until it was six feet from the hole."

He played the 17th conservatively, laying up for a safe par. With thunder rumbling overhead, he two-putted the difficult 18th for his sixth Senior Tour title, all in majors.

Under cool, cloudy conditions on a course softened by early-morning rain, Weiskopf had threatened to run off and hide.

"I gave it the best run I possibly could," he said. "I played the best four rounds of golf I have ever played under these types of conditions. I know in my mind no one played better than I did from tee to green. I just didn't putt as well as some of the other guys. Jack was just one stroke better than I was. Sure, I'm disappointed, but this has happened to me before."

Scores and earnings

Player	Scores
Jack Nicklaus, $135,330	68-73-67-70—278
Tom Weiskopf, $72,830	73-69-70-67—279
Kermit Zarley, $42,346	70-71-69-70—280
Chi Chi Rodriguez, $27,723	67-70-75-69—281
Dale Douglass, $27,723	70-71-68-72—281
Miller Barber, $21,289	70-70-73-69—282
Tommy Aycock, $18,210	72-71-73-67—283
Ray Floyd, $18,210	70-73-70-70—283
Lee Trevino, $15,864	69-73-73-69—284
Simon Hobday, $14,268	71-70-74-70—285
Larry Ziegler, $14,268	69-73-70-73—285
Jim Colbert, $13,023	69-74-72-71—286
Bob Charles, $12,111	72-72-75-68—287
Tommy Aaron, $12,111	70-72-74-71—287
Bob Murphy, $11,025	69-75-76-68—288
Dewitt Weaver, $11,025	75-71-73-69—288
Gibby Gilbert, $9,867	76-73-73-67—289
Tom Wargo, $9,867	73-76-72-68—289
Gary Player, $9,867	70-74-74-71—289
Don Bies, $8,817	73-75-71-71—290
Al Geiberger, $8,817	74-72-70-74—290
Isao Aoki, $8,817	70-68-76-76—290
Terry Dill, $8,121	76-71-74-70—291
Rocky Thompson, $8,121	71-70-77-73—291
Ben Smith, $7,553	74-77-70-72—293
Harold Henning, $7,553	74-70-75-74—293
Larry Gilbert, $7,553	76-70-73-74—293
Bob Menne, $7,027	74-72-75-73—294
Bob Betley, $7,027	77-71-72-74—294
Larry Mowry, $6,640	73-77-74-71—295
Dave Stockton, $6,640	76-68-71-80—295
Frank Beard, $6,285	79-72-76-70—297
Brian Waites, $6,285	79-72-75-71—297
Tom Shaw, $6,285	74-72-77-74—297
Orville Moody, $5,792	73-77-78-70—298
Billy Casper, $5,792	74-76-74-74—298
#Marvin Giles III	71-75-77-75—298
Jim Albus, $5,792	72-75-74-77—298
Charles Coody, $5,792	77-72-72-77—298
J.C.Snead, $5,232	74-72-78-75—299
Gary Cowan, $5,232	74-76-73-76—299
Jim Stefanich, $5,232	71-79-73-76—299
Bruce Crampton, $5,232	74-75-73-77—299
Joe Mcdermott, $4,882	75-76-76-73—300
#Robert Housen	78-73-73-76—300
#Jackie Cummings	76-71-78-76—301
Larry Laoretti, $4,673	75-75-74-77—301
#Joel Hirsch	74-76-74-77—301
Walter Zembriski, $4,673	75-76-72-78—301
Chuck Thorpe, $4,393	77-73-75-77—302
Bob Reith, $4,393	75-74-72-81—302
Arnold Palmer, $4,113	75-75-78-75—303
Robert Cornett, $4,113	76-72-79-76—303
#Ken Cromwell	76-75-74-78—303
Bob Thatcher, $3,764	73-78-81-72—304
Clayton Cole, $3,764	74-77-77-76—304
Lloyd Moody, $3,764	75-74-75-80—304
Paul Moran, $3,484	71-79-80-76—306
Art Proctor, $3,434	75-74-83-80—312

- amateur

TEAM EVENTS

RYDER CUP ...66

WALKER AND DUNHILL CUPS...70

HEINEKEN WORLD CUP...71

PREVIEWS...72

USA SNAPSHOTS®
A look at statistics that shape the sports world

Where a round of golf costs most

- Japan: $150.26
- China: $132.24
- Cayman Islands: $100.06
- Spain: $96.76
- United States: $29.83

(Weekend rate for 18 holes with motorized cart rental on public course)

Source: Runzheimer International By Elys A. McLean, USA TODAY

Ryder Cup

AT A GLANCE

- **Course:** The Belfry (Brabazon Course)
- **Location:** Sutton Coldfield, England
- **When:** Sept. 24-26, 1993
- **Weather:** Partly sunny and cool.
- **Par:** 72
- **Yards:** 7,176
- **Defending champion:** USA

Payne-demonium broke out on the lush 18th green at The Belfry as the USA completed a rousing comeback to win the Ryder Cup on British soil for the first time since 1981.

Payne Stewart shook a double magnum of champagne, then sprayed it over well-wishers and teammates celebrating a 15-13 victory that will go down as one of the best matches in the 66-year history of the biennial golf competition.

After falling behind by three points, the U.S. strung together five victories and a closing tie to retain the cup it won in equally dramatic fashion two years before at Kiawah Island, S.C.

Europe's top five players—Nick Faldo, Bernhard Langer, Seve Ballesteros, Jose Maria Olazabal and Ian Woosnam—were winless on the final day. Faldo and Woosnam earned halves, the others were beaten in a closing U.S. rush.

"We had one of the great Ryder Cups of all time," captain Tom Watson said. "My team performed with guts that typifies teams from America."

Raymond Floyd, at 51, the oldest player to compete in a Ryder Cup, provided the surge for the USA, which trailed 7 1/2 to 4 1/2 after the opening morning matches. The 1989 captain won two matches on Saturday, then outbattled Spain's brilliant young star Olazabal 2 up Sunday in the clinching match.

Floyd sank the putt that assured the cup stays in U.S. hands until the 1995 matches at Oak Hill Country Club in Rochester, N.Y.

"It was so exciting for me to be here at 51 and be a part of this spectacle," Floyd said.

"Kiawah (Island, S.C., in '91) was the biggest sporting event in America for a decade and this must rank alongside it."

Continuing the trend of recent years—the last four matches were decided by two or fewer points—eight of the 12 matches went to the treacherous, 474-yard, dogleg, water-guarded final hole.

In redemption for '89, when five U.S. players lost on the final hole, this time Chip Beck, Davis Love III, and Floyd won, and Paul Azinger earned a satisfying halve against Faldo.

The stage was set for the comeback when Europe won three of four two-man alternate-shot matches Saturday morning to take a three-point lead.

"We have to win three matches this afternoon to get back in contention," Lanny Wadkins said then.

That the U.S. did, led by John Cook and Beck, who came off the bench to ignite the rally. The first team off, Cook dropped birdie putts on top of Faldo's at the first and fourth holes, then sank another for a 1-up lead they didn't lose.

"It showed Nick right from the start, it wasn't going to be a walkover," Cook said.

Over nine consecutive, pressure-packed holes, Beck and Cook held off Faldo, golf's No. 1-ranked player, and his hand-picked partner, Colin Montgomerie. Often, Faldo birdie putts brushed the hole. None fell.

Rejuvenated, the USA came alive. Corey Pavin and Jim Gallagher crushed Mark James and Costantino Rocca 5 and 4 in the second match and Floyd and Stewart turned back Olazabal and Sweden's Joakim Haeggman 2 and 1.

The U.S. was back. Down a point, the match would be decided in Sunday's 12 singles, a U.S. strong point.

There was concern about the opening match, however. By his own admission, Fred Couples played poorly for two days, losing three of four matches and halving one on Paul Azinger's strong play. He was the underdog against Woosnam, who was 4-0.

Couples sank a 12-foot birdie putt on the 13th to cut Woosnam's lead to 1 up.

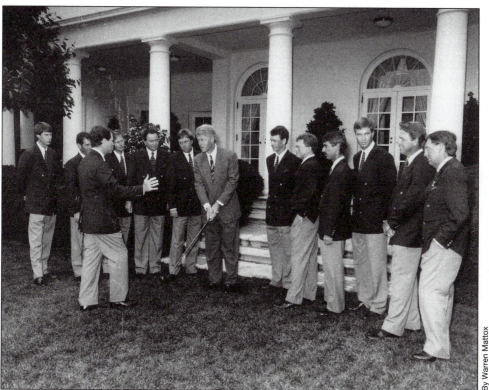

Ryder Cup team members advised President Bill Clinton on the fine points of golf before leaving for the U.K.

A 2-iron to 18 feet on the 548-yard 15th set up a two-putt birdie and a tie.

At 18, Couples hit an 8-iron to 10 feet, but missed the birdie try. Woosnam's 8-iron rolled to 7 feet, but he, too, missed and the USA escaped with a half—and a jump start.

"I played a great match against a great player and it was close all the way," Couples said. "I wouldn't have cared if I did not get any points, as long as the team won."

Again, Beck added a spark with the day's best comeback. He was 3 down after Barry Lane's 8-foot birdie at 13. But he won No. 14 when Lane three-putted; he won the par-5 15th with a 30-foot eagle putt and parred 16 to win again.

Another showdown at 18, and you have to hand it to Beck—which Lane did by hitting a 3-iron second shot into the lake.

Stewart, who sank two long birdie putts in a 3 and 2 victory Saturday, still was hot Sunday. He birdied four of the first eight holes to go 4 up and cruised past Mark James starting the string of five U.S. victories.

As shadows lengthened, Stewart's win was expected, as was Gallagher's 3 and 2 victory against the struggling Ballesteros, who couldn't hit a fairway and opened with four consecutive bogeys in perhaps his last Ryder Cup appearance as a player. Tom Kite also delivered, routing an injury-hindered Langer 5 and 3.

"I played well, but Langer is not 100 percent," Kite said. "When I didn't make the team last time, it was a big disappointment. I made up my mind to make it this time and come over here and play well."

It was left to Love, Floyd and Azinger. They all came through on the critical 18th: Love and Floyd winning, Azinger with a birdie to halve Faldo amid the celebration.

"Zinger got his wish," Wadkins said during the final-green festivities. "Before we started, he said, 'Please make my match not count.'"

—by Steve Hershey

Floyd went out with style

In 1969, Orville Moody won the U.S. Open, Frank Beard was the leading money winner on the PGA Tour and a youngster named Ray Floyd played in his first Ryder Cup.

Now, unfortunately, he says he's played in his last. If so, he went out like Ted Williams, who homered in his last at-bat.

At 51—the oldest Ryder Cup player ever—Floyd, quite appropriately, sank the clinching putt.

Even battling Spain's young sensation, Jose Maria Olazabal, Floyd reeled off three consecutive birdies after No. 11 to take control of the match. When he tapped in a 2-footer for par at the 16th hole, he closed out Olazabal and gave the USA the 14th point it needed to retain the Cup.

The night before, Floyd set a standard each player on the victorious U.S. team should forever etch in their minds.

After playing 36 holes Saturday, Floyd went out in the damp darkness and worked on his game. He made a slight adjustment in his swing and came back to play brilliantly in a 2-up victory against the Spaniard.

"I played well with Payne Stewart in the morning (winning 3 and 2), but I went out in the afternoon and lost it," Floyd said.

"After the match, I went to the practice tee and worked on my address position. I could only stay about 15 minutes because it got too dark. But when I went out this morning, I felt great."

The oldest player played the best Sunday. A wild-card captain's pick for the last two events, Floyd was the only player not to make a bogey.

"I played as good a golf as you can play and made three birdies when they were needed," said Floyd, who almost made a hole-in-one on the 189-yard 14th, lipping out a 5-iron.

"That's what I thought about when I picked Ray," U.S. captain Tom Watson said. "He's the kind of guy you want on your team."

There will be no more Ryder Cup thrills for Floyd, who bowed out with perhaps his finest performance, earning three of a possible four points in a record-tying eighth appearance.

"I'm done," he said shortly after defeating Olazabal. "This was it for me. I'm getting too old for this. I just won't be that good a player in two years. I'm finished."

Asked when he made the decision, Floyd flashed his familiar smile and said, "Right now.

"I'll probably still play a few regular tour events, but this is it for the Ryder Cup. I don't know how I could go out any better."

—by Steve Hershey

Ryder Cup short putts

LOVE'S MATCH: Davis Love III grew nervous when he saw several teammates and their wives at the 16th hole of his final-day match with Costantino Rocca.

"I'm a rookie; I couldn't figure out that scoreboard," Love said with a laugh. "But when I saw all those people, I knew my match would be critical."

The Italian made back-to-back birdies and was 1 up going to the 567-yard, par-5 17th, where long-hitting Love had the edge.

"I thought that was my chance," Love said. "But I missed my (30-foot) birdie putt." Rocca handed Love the hole nonetheless, missing from 3 feet.

"I wasn't surprised," Love said. "I knew he was thinking about it. He had so much pressure. I had given him a couple from about a foot or two, and he had made some long ones. His luck was due to run out."

At 18, Rocca drove into the right rough, was short with his approach, pitched 20 feet past the pin and missed his putt. Davis two-putted up a ridge from about 40 feet after leaving his first putt 6 feet short.

PAYOFFS: All weekend, the tricky

Ray Floyd played in a record-tying eight Ryder Cups.

267-yard, water-guarded, par-4 10th hole proved a tough decision: try to drive the green, or lay up with a 7- or 8-iron and try to wedge it close.

In better-ball play, the first player often would go for it. If he made it, the second tried.

Tom Kite, however, never hesitated in four matches. The first day, he hit a 3-wood to 5 feet (Love made the eagle).

"The guy who hits first drives the wagon," he said. "It totally determines what your opponent does."

Sunday, Kite put a 3-wood on the green, forcing Langer to hit a wood. He splashed it, and Kite coasted to a 5 and 3 win.

DEBUT: John Cook came to The Belfry not playing very well and was held out of the first three matches. But, when he got a chance, he contributed.

On his first hole, Cook answered Nick Faldo's 16-foot birdie putt with one from 14 feet. He topped Faldo's birdie again at the par-5 4th and made another at No. 6. He and Chip Beck edged previously unbeaten Faldo and Colin Montgomerie 2 up in a match Captain Tom Watson said turned the competition around.

Said Cook: "Tom said we needed the point, so we went out and got it."

VOLUNTEER: Lanny Wadkins volunteered to sit out Sunday's singles because of an injury to Europe's Sam Torrance.

By Ryder Cup rules, if a player is hurt, the other team puts a player's name in an envelope and withdraws him, creating a halve, or tie.

"I offered to Tom to put my name in the envelope," said Wadkins, 2-1 in pairs. "It would not have been fair to the guys who qualified (on points. Wadkins and Ray Floyd were wild cards). A lot of the guys came up to me and said I was crazy to do it. But those guys earned points to get on the team."

—*by Steve Hershey*

Results of the 30th Ryder Cup matches:

USA 15, EUROPE 13

FRIDAY—Foursomes: Lanny Wadkins-Corey Pavin (USA) d. Mark James and Sam Torrance 4 and 3; Ian Woosnam-Bernhard Langer (Europe) d. Paul Azinger-Payne Stewart 7 and 5; Tom Kite-Davis Love III (USA) beat Seve Ballesteros and Jose Maria Olazabal 2 and 1; Nick Faldo-Colin Montgomerie (Europe) d. Ray Floyd and Fred Couples 4 and 3. Fourball: Ian Woosnam-Peter Baker (Europe) d. Jim Gallagher-Lee Janzen 1-up; Lanny Wadkins-Corey Pavin (USA) d. Bernhard Langer-Barry Lane 4 and 2; Seve Ballesteros-Jose Maria Olazabal (Europe) d. Tom Kite-Davis Love III 4 and 3. Paul Azinger-Fred Couples (USA) and Faldo and Montgomerie halved.
SATURDAY—Foursomes: Nick Faldo-Colin Montgomerie (Europe) d. Lanny Wadkins-Corey Pavin 3 and 2; Ray Floyd-Payne Stewart (USA) d. Peter Baker-Barry Lane 3 and 2; Bernhard Langer-Ian Woosnam (Europe) d. Fred Couples-Paul Azinger 2 and 1; Seve Ballesteros-Jose Maria Olazabal (Europe) d. Tom Kite-Davis Love III 2 and 1. Fourballs: Corey Pavin-Jim Gallagher (USA) d. Mark James-Costantino Rocca 5 and 4; Ian Woosnam-Peter Baker (Europe) d. Fred Couples-Paul Azinger 6 and 5; John Cook-Chip Beck (USA) d. Nick Faldo-Colin Montgomerie 2-up; Ray Floyd and Payne Stewart (USA) d. Jose Maria Olazabal-Joakim Haeggman 2 and 1.
SUNDAY—Singles: Lanny Wadkins (USA) and Sam Torrance halved (Torrance withdrew injured, Wadkins designated to sit out); Fred Couples (USA) and Ian Woosnam halved; Chip Beck (USA) d. Barry Lane 1-up; Colin Montgomerie (Europe) d. Lee Janzen 1-up; Peter Baker (Europe) d. Corey Pavin 2-up; Payne Stewart (USA) d. Mark James 3 and 2; Joakim Haeggman (Europe) d. John Cook 1-up; Jim Gallagher (USA) d. Seve Ballesteros 3 and 2; Tom Kite (USA) d. Bernhard Langer 5 and 3; Davis Love III (USA) d. Costantino Rocca 1-up; Ray Floyd (USA) d. Jose Maria Olazabal 2-up; Paul Azinger (USA) and Nick Faldo halved.

Walker Cup

- **Course:** Interlachen Country Club
- **Location:** Edina, Minn.
- **When:** Aug. 18-19, 1993
- **Weather:** Hot and humid.
- **Par:** 72
- **Yards:** 6,721
- **Defending champion:** United States
- **Largest winning margin, team:** 14 (USA defeated Britain-Ireland 19-5 at Interlachen Country Club, Edina, Minn., 1993)
- **Format:** Match play.

Fred Couples returned to form, leading the USA to victories in the Dunhill and Heineken cups.

Five golfers finished unbeaten in leading the USA to a 19-5 victory against the British-Irish team in the Walker Cup Match. The 14-point margin was the greatest in the biennial competition that matches top amateur players since 1961, covering 15 tournaments.

John Harris, 41, an insurance executive from nearby Edina, Minn., defeated reigning British Amateur champion Iain Pyman 3 and 2 for the point that clinched the Cup for the USA. Many of Harris' neighborhood friends and golfing buddies walked the course during his matches.

"We expected good golf and we got it," Captain Vinny Giles said. "But we got a lot more. These guys really came together as a team, and as a family."

In the opening round, 1992 U.S. Amateur champion Justin Leonard helped the USA to a 6½-3½ lead.

Leonard, 21, of Dallas, one of seven U.S. players competing for the first time in the series, won seven of the first nine holes against Raymond Burns of Northern Ireland on the way to a 4 and 3 victory.

Jay Sigel of Collegeville, Pa., competing in a record ninth Walker Cup, suffered a rare loss. In eight previous Walker Cup tournaments, Sigel, 49, had a 10-3-3 singles record, but he lost in the opening round 3 and 2 to Dean Robertson of Scotland.

"I knew, unless (Britain-Ireland) played very, very well, they couldn't beat us," Giles said. "I felt we were 10 deep, and to the man, each one played extremely well."

Dunhill Cup

- **Course:** St. Andrews, Scotland
- **When:** Oct. 14-17, 1993
- **Weather:** Cold, windy and rainy.
- **Par:** 72
- **Yards:** 6,933
- **Defending champion:** England defeated Scotland 2-0-1.
- **Format:** Stroke-play matches among three-man teams.

Fred Couples defeated Nick Faldo 68-69 and John Daly defeated Peter Baker 70-73, leading the USA to victory over Britain at the Dunhill Cup. Mark James defeated U.S. Captain Payne Stewart 70-74.

In the second round, the USA fought off upset-minded Paraguay 2-1 on victories by Payne Stewart and Fred Couples.

In other second day results in the round-robin matches, Scotland downed Wales 3-0, Mexico edged South Africa 2-1, and England beat Taiwan 2-1.

Paraguay posted one of the biggest upsets in golf in the first round when it defeated host Scotland 2-1.

The USA opened its bid by beating Wales 3-0.

Heineken World Cup of Golf

AT A GLANCE

- **Course:** Lake Nona Golf Club
- **Location:** Orlando
- **When:** Nov. 11-14, 1993
- **Weather:** Sunny and warm.
- **Purse:** $1.1 million
- **Par:** 72
- **Yards:** 7,011
- **Defending champion:** USA
- **Tournament record, team:** 548, Jack Nicklaus and Arnold Palmer, USA, 1966 (Yomiuri CC, Tokyo); and Fred Couples and Davis Love III, USA, 1992 (La Moraleja II, Madrid, Spain).
- **Tournament record, individual:** 269, Roberto de Vicenzo, Argentina, 1971 (Jockey Club, Buenas Aires, Argentina)
- **Format:** Two-man teams, total strokes.

With Fred Couples leading the charge, the USA finished a sweep of 1993 international golf team events with a runaway win in the Heineken World Cup.

Couples shot 4-under-par 68, teaming with Davis Love III for a 20-under 556, five strokes ahead of Zimbabwe at Lake Nona Golf Club.

"It's great for American golf," Couples said. "It means a lot to win for your country. It's fun when you can share a win with a teammate."

"It doesn't surprise me that the U.S. won all those [international events]; it has so many good players to chose from," said Nick Price, who shot 68 for Zimbabwe.

Bernhard Langer made only two bogeys all week, shooting 69-68-66-69–272 to win the $75,000 individual prize, three strokes ahead of Couples. However, Germany finished eighth because Langer's partner, Sven Struver, was 11-over.

"I putted very well, but I couldn't help my partner," Langer said. "I felt bad when he dropped shots. If he had played as well as he can, we could have won."

Couples and Love teamed well, as they did winning in 1992 in Madrid, Spain. Both were under par each day.

"Davis played as well as Freddy; he just didn't make many putts," said Price, who was paired with the winners Saturday and Sunday. "All I said all weekend was 'nice shot' or 'well played.'"

For Couples, it was just a continuation of his outstanding play since the Ryder Cup.

"My life is skyrocketing forward," he said. "My game is getting back to where it was last year. When it's easy like this, I just feel I'm going to shoot a good score."

Couples had a sensational start Thursday when his 216-yard 2-iron from the rough rolled into the hole at the 532-yard ninth hole for his first double eagle. Sunday, he chipped in on the first hole for birdie and sank a 40-footer at No. 7 for another.

"I guess it was my week," he said. "I didn't hit many bad shots. I felt we'd be the team to beat if we played our game."

The '94 World Cup is scheduled for Dorado Beach, Puerto Rico.

—by Steve Hershey

Scores and earnings

Team—USA, $260,000 (team), 556; Zimbabwe, $150,000, 561; Scotland, $100,000, 565; Australia, $75,000, 566; Spain, $60,000, 567; South Africa and New Zealand, $37,500, 568; Germany, $25,000, 571; Ireland and Italy, $18,500, 573; England and Canada, $14,000, 574; Sweden and France, $10,500, 575; Paraguay, $9,000, 579; Wales, $8,000, 582; Brazil, $7,000, 583; Japan, $7,000, 588; Argentina, $7,000, 592; Hong Kong and Mexico, $7,000, 597; Netherlands, $7,000, 602; Greece, $7,000, 603; Taiwan, $7,000, 609; Bermuda, $7,000, 617; Puerto Rico, $7,000, 629; Jamaica, $7,000, 652; Fiji, $7,000, 646; Israel, $7,000, 682.

Individual (top 20)

Bernhard Langer, Germany, $75,000	69-68-66-69–272
Fred Couples, U.S. $50,000	66-71-70-68–275
Ernie Els, South Africa, $35,000	69-71-72-66–278
Nick Price, Zimbabwe, $35,000	70-69-71-68–278
Jean Van de Velde, France, $20,000	66-70-71-72–279
Robert Allenby, Australia, $15,000	72-68-70-70–280
Sam Torrance, Scotland	68-69-71-73–281
Davis Love III, U.S.	71-69-71-70–281
Anders Forsbrand, Sweden	71-69-74-68–282
Manuel Angel Jimenez, Spain	72-70-72-68–282
Costantino Rocca, Italy	71-75-67-70–283
Mark McNulty, Zimbabwe	71-68-72-72–283
Frank Nobilo, New Zealand	74-69-69-71–283
Ronan Rafferty, Ireland	71-69-73-71–284
Colin Montgomerie, Scotland	75-70-69-70–284
Dave Barr, Canada	74-70-70-71–285
Jose Rivero, Spain	73-72-66-74–285
Greg Turner, New Zealand	73-73-64-75–285
Mark Mouland, Wales	68-70-75-73–286

Preview: 1994 team cup matches

Solheim Cup

▶**Course:** The Greenbrier
▶**Location:** White Sulphur Springs, W.Va.
▶**When:** Oct. 21-23, 1994
▶**Par:** 72
▶**Yards:** 6,265
▶**Defending champion:** Europe
▶**Largest winning margin, team:** 7 (USA defeated Europe 11½-4½, 1990)

Charlie Mechem, the commissioner of the LPGA, will see if his prediction comes true this fall when the Solheim Cup comes back to the USA.

Shortly after the Europeans shocked the USA 11½ to 6½ in Edinburgh, Scotland, in 1992, Mechem said, "You know, this may be the best thing that ever happened to this event."

Mechem, ever the optimist, thought the European triumph would lend credibility to these fledging biennial matches between the best women professional golfers in the world.

Founded by Karsten Solheim, who invented Ping golf clubs, the matches are a way for Solheim to showcase women's professional golf.

In the first matches, held in 1990 at Lake Nona Golf Club in Orlando, Fla., the USA waltzed past the Europeans 11½ to 4½.

Another rout by the Americans in '92 could have relegated the matches to the monkey barrel of golf events. Now, the Solheim Cup has a chance to lift women's professional golf to a higher level.

The third meeting in the matches comes Oct. 21-23, 1994 at The Greenbrier in White Sulphur Springs, W.Va. In returning the matches to America, Solheim selected one of the world's most prestigious resorts.

It's the home of Sam Snead and site of the 1979 Ryder Cup, won by the USA 17-11.

To add another candle to the cake, the LPGA has selected JoAnne Carner, the LPGA Hall of Famer, to captain the team.

Carner, who will be 55 when the matches are contested, is a long-time student of Snead and is quite familiar with The Greenbrier.

Also, she's one of the best match-play competitors in the history of women's golf, having played on four Curtis Cup teams as an amateur.

Carner won't be competing, but she is respected for her knowledge by the USA's team. Although the final field won't be selected until later this year, Betsy King lead in points through 1993.

"A lot of things have been said in the last year about our founding players coming out and being a part of the tour," said King.

"That's nice, but the thing that impresses me most is how JoAnne plays week in and week out and is still competitive. She's just an amazing golfer."

—*by Jerry Potter*

Curtis Cup

▶**Course:** The Honors Course
▶**Location:** Chattanooga, Tenn.
▶**When:** July 30-31, 1994
▶**Defending champion:** Great Britain & Ireland
▶**Largest winning margin, team:** 11 (USA defeated Great Britain, 14½-3½, at Denver, Colo., 1982)

The Curtis Cup returns to the South for only the second time in its history in 1994. Designed by Pete Dye, Tennessee's Honors Course hosted the 1991 U.S. Amateur, in which Mitch Voges defeated then-University of Arizona student Manny Zerman 7 and 6 in the final match.

After winning only twice in the first 52 years of Curtis Cup competition, Great Britain & Ireland has triumphed in three of the last four matches.

GOLF ALMANAC 1994

Tour Report

PGA TOUR...74

LPGA TOUR...117

SENIOR PGA TOUR...149

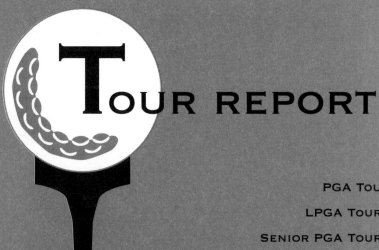

USA SNAPSHOTS®
A look at statistics that shape the sports world

What's a PGA Tour win worth?
How much does the winner of a $1 million-purse PGA Tour tournament receive?

A) $225,000
B) $180,000
C) $135,000
D) $100,000

Answer: B-$180,000; second gets $108,000; third is $68,000

Source: *1993 PGA Tour Book* By Sam Ward, USA TODAY

GOLF ALMANAC 1994

1993 PGA Player of the Year

Nick Price was first in victories with four and in money earned with $1,478,557. He won the Vardon Trophy with a scoring average of 68.90 and earned PGA of America's point-based award for player of the year.

PRICE WAS BEST—BY DEFAULT

As the sun was setting at picturesque Olympic Club on Oct. 31, 1993, Greg Norman was in position to win the $3 million Tour Championship while his two chief rivals for Player of the Year, Nick Price and Paul Azinger, were packing their bags.

The season's last official tournament was billed as the showdown between these three, 1-2-3 on the money list. It all came down to one tournament and whoever performed the best under pressure probably would win the coveted award.

Well, none of them distinguished themselves, although only Norman embarrassed himself.

Price went in as the leading money winner. He had only one sub-par round while tying for 18th at 2-over-par 286.

"It's hard not to be disappointed," he said. "I finished with a three-putt and that pretty well sums it up. I had six putts inside 7 feet and didn't make one. I was clueless."

Azinger, No. 2 on the money list—$17,701 behind Price—had a wonderful opportunity to take over the top spot. He needed only to finish in the top 12. But he never broke par and finished 21st at 4-over.

"I figured I needed to be 5-under. I didn't hit it well enough to shoot 5-under," he said. "I tried as hard as I could. I just didn't putt particularly well."

Norman had it balled in his fist walking to a 94-yard wedge shot at the par-5 16th hole. He needed only to par the last three holes to win the money title and, most likely, Player of the Year.

Instead, he went brain dead once again under pressure and finished 6-5-5 to tumble into a four-way tie for second.

"I knew there was a lot at stake," Norman said. "But I've won the money title before (1986, 1990) and I've won the Vardon Trophy before (1989, 1990). I played very well, I just screwed up the last three holes."

Norman, based on playing only 15 tournaments, had a fantastic year. His percentage of top-10s (12 in 15 starts) far surpassed anyone. He won the Doral-Ryder Open with a record-smashing 23 under par.

He saved his best performance in years for the British Open, coming from behind with a final-round 64 to win his second Claret Jug.

A month later, he came within a lip-out on the last hole of winning the PGA Championship. His accordion act at the Olympic Club still gave him four second-place finishes. His scoring average was 69.48.

"This might be the best year I've ever had," Norman said. "It was more satisfying than '86 when I won eight times around the world (two on PGA Tour, plus British Open) because then I was on the way up. This year, I came back after a dismal year in '91. It's tougher to come back and do it again."

Azinger also enjoyed the best year of his 11-year career, although he won four times in '87. He had three victories, including a playoff with Norman at the PGA Championship for his first major, and 11 top-10s in 24 events.

"I had my best year ever," he said. "But three guys had Player of the Year-type years. What if Norman had played a full schedule? What if Nick would have played more at the end of the year? What if I had putted better? Who knows?"

Price led in the most important category—victories—with four, including the Players Championship. He also won the money title with a record $1,478,557, the Vardon Trophy with a 69.11 18-hole average and the PGA of America's Player of the Year point race 90-84 over Azinger.

"Look at the three of us, we all played equally well," Price said. "I have more wins, but they each won a major. It's really such a close call."

Not really, Nick. The vote is easy. This time, Price is right.

—*by Steve Hershey*

Infiniti Tournament of Champions

AT A GLANCE

- **Course:** LaCosta Resort & Spa
- **Location:** Carlsbad, Calif.
- **When:** Jan. 7-10, 1993
- **Weather:** Rained out on Thursday, with two rounds played Friday. Because of light rain all day Sunday, the greens were squeegeed between groups.
- **Purse:** $800,000
- **Par:** 36-36—72
- **Yards:** 6,935
- **Defending champion:** Steve Elkington
- **Tournament record:** 21-under-par 267, Calvin Peete, 1986
- **Format:** Field includes only winners of 1992 PGA Tour events.

Scores and earnings

Player	Rounds—Total
Davis Love III, $144,000	67-67-69-69–272
Tom Kite, $86,400	69-71-69-64–273
Mark O'Meara, $46,400	70-70-68-67–275
Paul Azinger, $46,400	65-69-70-71–275
John Cook, $31,000	73-68-68-69–278
Brad Faxon, $31,000	71-69-67-71–278
Steve Pate, $27,225	73-66-71-69–279
Dan Forsman, $27,225	68-71-69-71–279
John Huston, $24,825	70-73-68-70–281
Fred Couples, $23,025	70-70-72-70–282
Mark Calcavecchia, $23,025	68-72-70-72–282
Chip Beck, $20,625	71-72-69-71–283
Greg Norman, $20,625	68-70-71-74–283
Bill Glasson, $19,225	67-75-70-72–284
Craig Stadler, $17,625	73-72-71-69–285
David Peoples, $17,625	70-71-72-72–285
Gary Hallberg, $17,625	70-71-69-75–285
Ben Crenshaw, $15,625	73-72-72-70–287
David Edwards, $15,625	71-70-74-72–287
Steve Elkington, $15,625	73-69-72-73–287
Fred Funk, $14,425	72-74-70-72–288
Ray Floyd, $13,825	71-72-73-73–289
Richard Zokol, $13,825	70-73-72-74–289
Bruce Lietzke, $13,225	74-70-73-73–290
Jay Haas, $12,625	72-75-73-71–291
Corey Pavin, $12,625	71-74-75-71–291
Lanny Wadkins, $12,625	71-76-70-74–291
Lee Janzen, $12,225	76-72-74-72–294
Mark Carnevale, $12,025	74-71-78-76–299
Billy Ray Brown, $11,825	78-79-75-72–304

Davis Love III triumphed in the tour opener.

After fruitlessly chasing Fred Couples all the previous year for the money title, Davis Love III reversed roles in the 1993 tour opener.

Despite extremely difficult conditions at La Costa Country Club after a week-long rain that washed out opening-day play and forced almost continual squeegeeing of the greens Sunday, Love made one bogey in his 67-67-69-69—272.

"I'm proud of not making many bogeys in these conditions," he said. "The greens weren't the best, but I never had a three-putt."

Tom Kite, three groups ahead, shot 32 on the front nine and birdied Nos 17 and 18 for 32 on the back, tying the course record and pressuring Love.

"I saw Kite finish at 15 (under par) when I was on the 16th tee," Love said. "I told myself to try to birdie the last three. You don't want to think about making three pars to win because of the alternative."

—*by Steve Hershey*

United Airlines Hawaiian Open

AT A GLANCE

- **Course:** Waialae Country Club
- **Location:** Honolulu
- **When:** Jan. 14-17, 1993
- **Par:** 36-36—72
- **Yards:** 6,975
- **Purse:** $1.2 million
- **Weather:** Perfect temperatures but breezy.
- **Defending champion:** John Cook
- **Tournament record:** 23-under-par 265, Hale Irwin, 1981, and John Cook, 1992

Scores and earnings (partial)
Howard Twitty, $216,000	63-68-70-68—269
Joey Sidelar, $129,600	71-68-66-68—273
Paul Azinger, $81,600	67-68-69-70—274
Brett Ogle, $49,600	67-70-70-70—277
Jeff Maggert, $49,600	68-71-68-70—277
Keith Clearwater, $49,600	72-66-68-71—277
Nolan Henke, $38,700	69-71-71-67—278
Davis Love III, $38,700	69-68-71-70—278
Mark O'Meara, $31,200	66-73-71-70—280
Duffy Waldorf, $31,200	69-69-71-71—280
Bill Glasson, $31,200	65-71-73-71—280
Wayne Levi, $31,200	72-65-69-74—280
Corey Pavin, $21,840	68-71-72-70—281
Russ Cochran, $21,840	72-71-68-70—281
David Edwards, $21,840	72-71-68-70—281
Brian Claar, $21,840	70-74-66-71—281
Fred Funk, $21,840	67-66-74-74—281
Steve Lowery, $16,200	67-76-69-70—282
Harry Taylor, $16,200	68-69-73-72—282
John Flannery, $16,200	71-69-70-72—282
Bob Eastwood, $16,200	69-73-67-73—282
Chip Beck, $12,000	71-71-72-69—283
Ben Crenshaw, $12,000	66-74-73-70—283
Dave Barr, $12,000	70-70-72-71—283
Richard Zokol, $12,000	72-71-68-72—283
Tony Sills, $9,060	70-71-73-70—284
Brad Bryant, $9,060	73-69-70-72—284
Donnie Hammond, $9,060	70-70-70-74—284
Loren Roberts, $9,060	73-69-68-74—284
Jay Haas, $6,410	74-70-71-70—285
Bob Gilder, $6,410	71-67-76-71—285
Mark Lye, $6,410	70-72-72-71—285
Mike Donald, $6,410	74-70-70-71—285
Tom Lehman, $6,410	66-73-74-72—285
Craig Stadler, $6,410	72-71-70-72—285
Mark Brooks, $6,410	71-71-71-72—285
Gene Sauers, $6,410	73-70-70-72—285
Hale Irwin, $6,410	70-71-71-73—285
Brian Henninger, $6,410	71-70-70-74—285
John Elliott, $6,410	72-68-71-74—285
Jim McGovern, $6,410	72-70-69-74—285
Robert Gamez, $4,440	70-74-72-70—286
Billy Andrade, $4,440	68-71-72-75—286
Eddie Pearce, $4,440	70-71-70-75—286
Jim Gallager, $3,514	70-71-75-71—287
Scott Simpson, $3,514	74-70-72-71—287
Barry Cheesman, $3,514	70-71-73-73—287
Neal Lancaster, $3,514	76-68-70-73—287
Craig Parry, $3,514	73-66-71-77—287

Northern Telecom Open

AT A GLANCE

- **Course:** Tucson National Golf Resort
- **Location:** Tucson, Ariz.
- **When:** Jan. 21-24, 1993
- **Par:** 36-36—72
- **Yards:** 7,148
- **Purse:** $1.1 million
- **Weather:** Sunny and warm.
- **Defending champion:** Lee Janzen
- **Tournament record:** 10-under-par 266, David Frost, 1988

Scores and earnings (partial)
Larry Mize, $198,000	68-66-70-67—271
Jeff Maggert, $118,800	70-66-70-67—273
Robin Freeman, $52,800	71-68-69-66—274
Jim Gallagher, $52,800	75-66-67-66—274
Michael Allen, $52,800	68-70-68-68—274
Dudley Hart, $52,800	66-66-69-73—274
Billy Andrade, $36,850	63-73-69-70—275
Craig Parry, $29,700	67-72-72-65—276
Robert Gamez, $29,700	69-67-72-68—276
Roger Maltbie, $29,700	70-68-70-68—276
Lennie Clements, $29,700	69-67-70-70—276
Phil Mickelson, $29,700	67-65-69-75—276
Payne Stewart, $20,020	71-70-68-68—277
Curtis Strange, $20,020	71-66-71-69—277
Nolan Henke, $20,020	66-72-70-69—277
Donnie Hammond, $20,020	70-71-67-69—277
John Flannery, $20,020	67-69-69-72—277
Brian Claar, $12,467	67-71-72-68—278
Dan Pohl, $12,467	73-67-70-68—278
Andy Bean, $12,467	69-68-72-69—278
Dave Rummells, $12,467	67-69-72-70—278
Mark Brooks, $12,467	68-68-71-71—278
Scott Gump, $12,467	67-68-72-71—278
Marco Dawson, $12,467	69-68-70-71—278
Harry Taylor, $12,467	70-67-69-72—278
Greg Twiggs, $12,467	68-67-70-73—278
Paul Goydos, $7,975	71-71-68-69—279
Ed Dougherty, $7,975	69-66-74-70—279
Lee Janzen, $7,975	70-68-70-71—279
Trevor Dodds, $7,975	69-71-66-73—279
Loren Roberts, $6,820	71-69-72-68—280
Gil Morgan, $6,820	68-68-72-72—280
Rick Fehr, $6,820	69-70-75-66—280
Duffy Waldorf, $5,437	70-71-70-70—281
Jeff Sluman, $5,437	71-71-70-69—281
Neal Lancaster, $5,437	72-68-72-69—281
Jim McGovern, $5,437	72-70-67-72—281
Willie Wood, $5,437	70-69-74-68—281
Bob Estes, $5,437	71-67-75-68—281
Mike Springer, $5,437	70-70-68-73—281
Steve Lowery, $3,850	69-71-71-71—282
Mark Lye, $3,850	72-68-71-71—282
Gene Sauers, $3,850	68-68-74-72—282
Billy Mayfair, $3,850	72-70-69-71—282
John Adams, $3,850	70-70-72-70—282
Dan Halldorson, $3,850	73-65-76-68—282
Bruce Fleisher, $3,850	69-71-75-67—282
Brad Fabel, $2,734	72-69-70-72—283

Phoenix Open

AT A GLANCE

- **Course:** Tournament Players Club of Scottsdale, Stadium Course
- **Location:** Scottsdale, Ariz.
- **When:** Jan. 28-31, 1993
- **Par:** 35-36—71
- **Yards:** 6,992
- **Purse:** $1 million
- **Weather:** Beautiful Thursday and Friday. Strong, gusty winds Saturday and Sunday.
- **Defending champion:** Mark Calcavecchia
- **Tournament record:** 21-under 273, Mark Calcavecchia, 1989

Lee Janzen, thriving in blustery weather that troubled others, birdied the final two holes to pull away for a two-stroke victory in the Phoenix Open.

His 3-under-par 68 final round was enough for the $180,000 first prize in light of how others fared under conditions reminiscent of a British Open, with wind gusts to 28 mph and 3-inch rough.

Robert Wrenn, the leader at 11-under after 54 holes, shot a 74 and finished in a four-way tie for third. He hasn't won since 1987.

David Frost had even worse luck. He started Sunday at 10-under, but double bogeyed three times and bogeyed once in a four-hole stretch, finishing at 3-under 281 for the tournament.

Andrew Magee, who shot 64 in similarly tough conditions Saturday and began the final round tied with Frost, was alone in second after sinking birdie putts on four of the six final holes.

Janzen's 72-hole, 11-under 273 was the highest ever for an Open-winner at the TPC of Scottsdale course, site of the tournament since 1987.

This victory affirmed soft-spoken Janzen's standing as one of the best-kept secrets on the tour. He had finished strong in 1992, placing at the Tour Championship and jumping from 115th to 72nd, then ninth on the money list in three years on the tour.

Scores and earnings

Player	Earnings	Scores
Lee Janzen	$180,000	67-65-73-68–273
Andrew Magee	$108,000	69-70-64-72–275
Mike Springer	$48,000	70-69-68-69–276
Michael Allen	$48,000	66-70-70-70–276
Kirk Triplett	$48,000	69-67-69-71–276
Robert Wrenn	$48,000	66-68-68-74–276
Keith Clearwater	$32,250	68-72-71-66–277
Mark Wiebe	$32,250	67-70-70-70–277
Gil Morgan	$28,000	71-65-74-68–278
Tom Lehman	$28,000	69-66-73-70–278
Jeff Maggert	$21,200	66-70-73-70–279
Jim Woodward	$21,200	67-69-72-71–279
Ed Dougherty	$21,200	67-69-71-72–279
Gary Hallberg	$21,200	70-69-67-73–279
Steve Lowery	$21,200	69-65-70-75–279
Chip Beck	$14,500	68-70-73-69–280
Peter Jacobsen	$14,500	70-70-71-69–280
Russ Cochran	$14,500	69-72-70-69–280
David Jackson	$14,500	69-70-71-70–280
Joel Edwards	$14,500	70-67-72-71–280
Mark O'Meara	$14,500	69-70-70-71–280
Scott Simpson	$9,600	66-70-74-71–281
Tommy Armour III	$9,600	69-67-74-71–281
Mark McCumber	$9,600	72-68-70-71–281
Phil Blackmar	$9,600	69-72-68-72–281
David Frost	$9,600	66-66-71-78–281
Billy Andrade	$7,100	72-68-71-71–282
Mike Donald	$7,100	66-71-73-72–282
Bruce Fleisher	$7,100	70-68-71-73–282
John Flannery	$7,100	70-70-69-73–282
Larry Mize	$7,100	67-71-71-73–282
Ronnie Black	$5,414	72-67-72-72–283
Gene Sauers	$5,414	72-68-71-72–283
John Adams	$5,414	71-70-69-73–283
Rick Fehr	$5,414	69-68-73-73–283
Larry Rinker	$5,414	68-72-73-70–283
Gary McCord	$5,414	66-69-73-75–283
R.W. Eaks	$5,414	72-64-70-77–283
Ed Humenik	$4,000	70-69-72-73–284
Brian Claar	$4,000	70-71-70-73–284
Paul Azinger	$4,000	69-70-73-72–284
Dillard Pruitt	$4,000	71-68-71-74–284
Steve Elkington	$4,000	69-72-72-71–284
Marco Dawson	$4,000	68-70-70-76–284
Robert Gamez	$2,753	69-68-73-75–285
Bob Lohr	$2,753	69-69-75-72–285
Scott Gump	$2,753	69-67-77-72–285
Tom Watson	$2,753	67-68-78-72–285
Dudley Hart	$2,753	68-72-68-77–285
Steve Pate	$2,753	70-67-71-77–285
Phil Mickelson	$2,753	67-70-78-70–285
Jim Carter	$2,753	70-71-75-69–285
Peter Persons	$2,315	71-67-74-74–286
Bill Glasson	$2,315	75-66-71-74–286
Howard Twitty	$2,315	67-74-72-73–286
Ted Schulz	$2,315	70-70-75-71–286
Lance Ten Broeck	$2,200	68-69-73-77–287
Tom Purtzer	$2,200	77-64-71-75–287
Fred Funk	$2,200	72-68-68-79–287
Jeff Sluman	$2,200	71-70-73-73–287
David Toms	$2,200	68-70-77-72–287
Hal Sutton	$2,200	68-73-74-72–287
Richard Zokol	$2,200	69-72-75-71–287
Bob Estes	$2,110	69-72-70-77–288
John Huston	$2,110	71-69-74-74–288
David Peoples	$2,080	70-69-74-76–289
Jay Delsing	$2,050	74-67-73-76–290
Duffy Waldorf	$2,050	74-67-76-73–290
Skip Kendall	$2,010	68-71-75-77–291
Bill Britton	$2,010	67-71-77-76–291
Bobby Wadkins	$1,950	69-69-77-77–292
Neale Smith	$1,950	72-68-77-75–292
Perry Moss	$1,950	74-67-76-75–292
Brian Henninger	$1,950	72-68-78-74–292
Ted Tryba	$1,890	69-70-75-79–293
Nolan Henke	$1,890	72-69-73-79–293

AT&T PEBBLE BEACH NATIONAL PRO-AM

AT A GLANCE

- **Courses:** Pebble Beach Golf Links, Spyglass Hill Golf Club, Poppy Hills
- **Location:** Pebble Beach, Calif.
- **When:** Feb. 4-7, 1993
- **Weather:** Sunny early Thursday but overcast and windy later. Sunny Friday; overcast and rainy all weekend.
- **Purse:** $1,250,000
- **Par:** all 72
- **Yards:** Pebble Beach GL 6,799 yards; Spyglass Hill 6,810 yards; Poppy Hills 6,865 yards.
- **Defending champion:** Mark O'Meara (1989, '90 and '92)
- **Tournament record:** Paul Azinger.
- **Format:** 72 holes, stroke play. Cut after three rounds to low 60 and ties for pros, low 20 and ties for pro-am teams.

Australian rookie Brett Ogle showed a veteran's poise while overcoming several setbacks to win the AT&T National Pro-Am by three strokes.

Ogle, 28, jammed his wrist, hit a ball onto the beach, bogeyed three of four holes in one stretch, trailed by a shot with seven holes to play and still pulled away from Billy Ray Brown with a 71 for a 12-under-par 276.

"After I hit it on the beach, I thought I was done," Ogle said. "But I pulled myself together and finished quite neat and tidy with three birdies in the last six holes."

Ogle, who won the 1990 Australian PGA Championship, plans to apply his $225,000 prize toward buying a house in the USA.

"This win means so much," he said. "This sets me up for three years on the PGA Tour. I'm going to Australia tomorrow and talk with my wife. We're thinking about Orlando."

—by Steve Hershey

Scores and earnings
(x-Spyglass Hill Golf Course; y-Poppy Hills Golf Course; z-Pebble Beach Golf Links)

Player	Score
Brett Ogle, $225,000	z68-y68-x69-z71–276
Billy Ray Brown, $135,000	y70-x68-z69-z72–279
Greg Twiggs, $65,000	y69-x72-z70-z69–280
Joey Sindelar, $65,000	y69-x70-z70-z69–280
Trevor Dodds, $65,000	z70-y68-x70-z72–280
Lee Janzen, $45,000	z71-y67-x72-z71–281
Grant Waite, $40,313	z71-y70-x72-z69–282
Chip Beck, $40,313	x72-z71-y69-z70–282
Brandel Chamblee, $27,969	y72-x73-z68-z70–283
Payne Stewart, $27,969	y72-x70-z71-z70–283
Bobby Clampett, $27,969	x73-z72-y68-z70–283
Steve Elkington, $27,969	z68-y71-x74-z70–283
Billy Andrade, $27,969	y70-x74-z68-z71–283
Dan Forsman, $27,969	z73-y71-x64-z75–283
John Flannery, $27,969	y70-x69-z70-z74–283
Gil Morgan, $27,969	y69-x70-z69-z75–283
Emlyn Aubrey, $18,125	z75-x70-y68-z71–284
Tom Watson, $18,125	y71-x75-z71-z67–284
Mark Carnevale, $18,125	x75-z70-y68-z71–284
David Frost, $18,125	z66-y72-x71-z75–284
John Inman, $12,089	y71-x74-z69-z71–285
Brad Bryant, $12,089	z70-y72-x71-z72–285
Fuzzy Zoeller, $12,089	y69-x72-z73-z71–285
Tom Purtzer, $12,089	y71-x73-z72-z69–285
Ken Green, $12,089	x70-z74-y69-z72–285
Fred Funk, $12,089	z69-y69-x72-z75–285
Mark Brooks, $12,089	z67-y70-x73-z75–285
Tom Lehman, $7,961	x73-z72-y68-z71–286
Tom Kite, $7,961	y72-x74-z69-z71–286
Kirk Triplett, $7,961	y71-x70-z73-z72–286
Rocco Mediate, $7,961	y71-x74-z69-z72–286
Dillard Pruitt, $7,961	z71-y72-x73-z70–286
Russell Beiersdorf, $7,961	z70-y73-x70-z73–286
Lennie Clements, $7,961	z70-y67-x75-z74–286
Davis Love III, $7,961	y68-x78-z71-z69–286
Bob Gilder, $5,508	x71-z77-y66-z73–287
Brian Kamm, $5,508	x72-z72-y70-z73–287
Jeff Wilson, $5,508	z71-y71-x73-z72–287
Mark O'Meara, $5,508	y71-x76-z69-z71–287
Larry Rinker, $5,508	y71-x71-z74-z71–287
Jay Haas, $5,508	x72-z72-y69-z74–287
Scott Simpson, $5,508	y75-x73-z68-z71–287
Stan Utley, $5,508	y68-x71-z72-z76–287
Bob Lohr, $3,613	y68-x72-z74-z74–288
Skip Kendall, $3,613	x70-z73-y73-z72–288
Peter Jacobsen, $3,613	y74-x72-z70-z72–288
Jay Delsing, $3,613	x70-z71-y72-z75–288
David Ogrin, $3,613	y70-x73-z74-z71–288
Donnie Hammond, $3,613	y72-x73-z72-z71–288
Howard Twitty, $3,613	z78-y71-x68-z71–288
Bill Kratzert, $3,613	x70-z73-y68-z77–288
Dave Peege, $2,900	x72-z72-y71-z74–289
Loren Roberts, $2,900	x71-z72-y74-z72–289
Robert Friend, $2,900	z69-y73-x71-z76–289
Keith Clearwater, $2,900	z69-y74-x69-z77–289
John Cook, $2,900	y70-x76-z71-z72–289
Bill Britton, $2,900	x74-z72-y71-z72–289
Larry Mize, $2,738	x70-z76-y69-z75–290
Brian Henninger, $2,738	y71-x75-z70-z74–290
Olin Browne, $2,738	x71-z74-y71-z74–290
Perry Moss, $2,738	y71-x72-z70-z77–290
Lon Hinkle, $2,738	z70-y72-x75-z73–290
Chris Perry, $2,738	z73-y72-x72-z73–290
Greg Cesario, $2,625	z69-y73-x73-z76–291
John Mahaffey, $2,625	z70-y75-x71-z75–291
John Adams, $2,625	y70-x78-z69-z74–291
George Burns, $2,550	x73-z71-y71-z78–293
Tim Loustalot, $2,550	z75-y73-x68-z77–293
David Toms, $2,550	z70-y73-x70-z80–293

AT&T PEBBLE BEACH NAT'L PRO-AM (CONT'D)

By Porter Binks, USA TODAY

Known as one of the tour's more stoic players, Scott Simpson benefited from Bill Murray's antics.

PLAYER SPOTLIGHT

Was it more than a coincidence that **Scott Simpson** went on to enjoy his best finish in 20 months after playing three rounds with Bill Murray at Pebble Beach?

To the amazement of many, Simpson, one of the more stoic players on the PGA Tour, volunteered to play with the zany comedian, whose nonstop banter with the crowd and unpredictable antics in the fairway could have been disconcerting.

"I thought it would be fun," Simpson said. "It may surprise a lot of people, but, hey, I like rock 'n' roll. I'm a Democrat."

When Murray was at his craziest, with the TV cameras rolling Saturday, Simpson maintained his concentration well enough to shoot 4-under-par 68. Playing in more serene conditions Sunday, he couldn't do better than 71.

At the next tour stop, the Bob Hope Chrysler Classic, Simpson tied the PGA West course record with 9-under-par 63 in the third round, then closed with 66 to finish third.

"I played real well, but Tom (Kite) never gave us a chance on Sunday," Simpson said. "Usually, a 66 on Sunday is pretty good, but not when the leader shoots 62."

Still, Simpson was very encouraged by his best finish since losing a playoff to Payne Stewart at the 1991 U.S. Open and eagerly looked forward to another shot at Torrey Pines. He was born and raised in the San Diego area before moving to Oahu, Hawaii.

"I'm hitting the ball real well right now," he said, smiling.

"It must be the lessons Murray gave me."

—*by Steve Hershey*

Pebble Beach Pro-Am team scores

Payne Stewart ($7,000) and Jim Morris, 63-65-63-66—257
Perry Moss ($4,750) and Ken Bowden, 62-65-67-68—258
Billy Andrade ($4,750) and Mark McGwire, 65-66-63-64—258
David Edwards ($4,750) and Mark Grace, 65-66-63-64—258
Willie Wood ($4,750) and John Zoller, 66-70-60-62—258
Olin Browne ($3,450) and Pandel Savic, 65-66-63-65—259
Brett Ogle ($3,450) and Peter Pocklington, 67-61-64-67—259
Larry Rinker ($2,833) and Richard Gelb, 64-64-66-66—260
John Inman ($2,833) and Stan Smith, 62-63-67-68—260
Andrew Magee ($2,833) and Jim Vickers, 63-66-60-71—260
Brandel Chamblee ($2,600) and James Rheim, 65-64-66-66—261
John Flannery ($2,250) and John McCoy, 67-67-62-66—262
Dillard Pruitt ($2,250) and Peter Fluor, 63-67-67-65—262
Patrick Burke ($2,250) and Tom Candiotti, 65-64-66-67—262
Andy Bean ($2,250) and John Purcell, 64-66-66-66—262
Barry Jaeckel ($2,250) and Stewart Francis, 67-66-64-65—262
Doug Tewell ($2,250) and Thomas Warde, 67-65-65-65—262
David Ogrin ($1,900) and Jason Bateman, 67-62-66-67—263
Joey Sindelar ($1,800) and James Griggs, 64-66-67-67—264
Jay Haas ($1,700) and John Harris, 66-66-65-68—265
Brad Bryant ($1,550) and Jay Swanson, 64-68-65-69—266
Ted Schulz ($1,550) and Howard Lester, 67-64-65-70—266
John Adamas ($1,350) and Bob Lurie, 67-67-61-72—267
Mark Brooks ($1,350) and Billy Timpson, 64-63-68-72—267
George Burns ($1,200) and Bruce Qvale, 65-66-63-74—268

Bob Hope Chrysler Classic

AT A GLANCE

- **Course:** Bermuda Dunes Country Club, Indian Wells Country Club, LaQuinta Country Club and PGA West (Palmer Course)
- **Location:** LaQuinta, Calif.
- **When:** Feb. 11-14, 1993
- **Weather:** Sunny and warm.
- **Purse:** $1.1 million
- **Par:** 72 (each course)
- **Yards:** Bermuda Dunes Country Club, 6,927; Indian Wells Country Club, 6,478; LaQuinta Country Club, 6,854; PGA West (Palmer Course), 6,931
- **Defending champion:** John Cook
- **Tournament record:** 29-under-par 331, Corey Pavin, 1991

At 43, an age when most golfers' careers are declining, Tom Kite may have reached his peak.

"I'm a better player now than I've ever been," Kite said after shooting a record-breaking 10-under-par 62 at PGA West to win the Bob Hope Chrysler Classic. He finished at 35-under-par 325, six strokes ahead of Rick Fehr.

"I'm not afraid to shoot a low number anymore," the defending U.S. Open champion said. "It's easy to get protective out here, get to 3-4 under par and sit on it. Now, when I get to 4 under, I want to go to 5, then 6. On the last hole (at PGA West), with a six-shot lead, I really wanted to make birdie."

Displaying his new relentless attitude during the final round, Kite increased his one-shot lead to four after only two holes when he opened with a pair of birdies and Rick Fehr bogeyed No. 1. Kite went on to birdie the final four holes, sinking a 20-footer on the par-3 15th, a 12-footer at 16, a 35-footer at the par-3 17th, and finishing with a 6-footer after driving into a fairway bunker on the par-5 final hole.

—*Steve Hershey*

Scores and earnings

Player	Earnings	Scores
Tom Kite	$198,000	67-67-64-65-62–325
Rick Fehr	$118,800	66-66-70-62-67–331
Scott Simpson	$74,800	71-69-66-63-66–335
Jim Gallagher	$43,313	69-68-67-69-63–336
Keith Clearwater	$43,313	68-66-68-70-64–336
Jay Haas	$43,313	66-66-71-65-68–336
Bob Lohr	$43,313	68-66-66-66-70–336
Bill Glasson	$34,100	70-64-66-67-70–337
Wayne Levi	$29,700	68-66-66-69-69–338
Steve Elkington	$29,700	69-63-66-68-72–338
Fred Couples	$29,700	68-64-68-66-72–338
Davis Love III	$20,271	70-70-67-65-67–339
Kelly Gibson	$20,271	67-67-66-69-70–339
Donnie Hammond	$20,271	65-73-64-67-70–339
Bob Estes	$20,271	67-66-72-63-71–339
John Cook	$20,271	66-67-70-65-71–339
Payne Stewart	$20,271	70-66-64-67-72–339
Gil Morgan	$20,271	69-66-67-65-72–339
Dennis Trixler	$13,332	67-69-69-68-67–340
Scott Hoch	$13,332	70-70-68-65-67–340
Jodie Mudd	$13,332	68-71-66-66-69–340
Tad Rhyan	$13,332	68-66-69-67-70–340
John Huston	$13,332	67-70-65-67-71–340
Neal Lancaster	$9,680	72-67-68-68-66–341
Lanny Wadkins	$9,680	69-66-66-69-71–341
Scott Gump	$9,680	68-65-67-67-74–341
Mike Standly	$7,645	67-70-68-68-69–342
Curtis Strange	$7,645	66-65-71-70-70–342
Fuzzy Zoeller	$7,645	76-69-63-67-67–342
Ed Humenik	$7,645	68-67-70-67-70–342
Corey Pavin	$7,645	70-70-67-67-67–342
John Flannery	$7,645	71-68-65-64-74–342
Ronnie Black	$5,451	67-67-69-70-70–343
Ted Tryba	$5,451	68-67-70-69-69–343
Grant Waite	$5,451	66-71-64-72-70–343
Mark O'Meara	$5,451	70-68-64-70-71–343
John Adams	$5,451	71-65-68-68-71–343
Mike Donald	$5,451	67-68-69-71-68–343
Dave Rummells	$5,451	63-69-69-69-73–343
Mike Springer	$5,451	69-70-71-66-67–343
Blaine McCallister	$5,451	71-67-71-68-66–343
Greg Twiggs	$4,180	70-68-68-68-70–344
Tommy Armour III	$4,180	71-66-70-69-68–344
Tim Simpson	$3,247	71-69-69-65-71–345
Bruce Fleisher	$3,247	71-67-68-69-70–345
Brian Henninger	$3,247	71-72-68-65-69–345
Harry Taylor	$3,247	70-68-71-67-69–345
Jay Delsing	$3,247	68-73-66-69-69–345
Jimmy Johnston	$3,247	70-68-68-70-69–345
Bill Britton	$3,247	70-65-72-70-68–345
Skip Kendall	$2,624	70-69-66-68-73–346
David Edwards	$2,624	69-66-69-69-73–346
Craig Stadler	$2,624	66-72-69-67-72–346
David Jackson	$2,624	68-70-70-66-72–346
Brian Claar	$2,486	66-69-70-67-75–347
Joel Edwards	$2,486	66-70-67-72-72–347
Peter Jacobsen	$2,486	69-68-68-66-76–347
Lennie Clements	$2,486	71-69-69-67-71–347
Steve Pate	$2,486	71-67-70-70-69–347
Fred Funk	$2,365	67-72-68-68-73–348
Robert Gamez	$2,365	71-70-69-65-73–348
Jeff Sluman	$2,365	68-67-71-65-77–348
Ed Dougherty	$2,365	73-67-66-69-73–348
Russell Beiersdorf	$2,365	71-70-64-71-72–348
Tom Lehman	$2,365	69-69-70-68-72–348
Jaime Gomez	$2,244	70-70-66-67-76–349
Billy Ray Brown	$2,244	68-68-67-70-76–349
Nolan Henke	$2,244	65-70-70-73-71–349
Hal Sutton	$2,244	71-68-71-68-71–349
Peter Persons	$2,244	66-71-70-71-71–349
Paul Goydos	$2,156	72-67-70-66-75–350
Robin Freeman	$2,156	67-73-69-67-74–350
John Inman	$2,156	69-73-68-68-72–350
Steve Lowery	$2,112	70-72-68-68-73–351
P.H. Horgan III	$2,090	72-70-72-64-74–352
Fulton Allem	$2,068	68-69-67-73-77–354

Buick Invitational of California

AT A GLANCE

- **Course:** Torrey Pines
- **Location:** San Diego
- **When:** Feb. 18-21, 1993
- **Weather:** Rain and fog Thursday to Saturday; clear Sunday.
- **Purse:** $1 million
- **Par:** 72
- **Yards:** North Course, 6,659; South Course:,7,021
- **Defending champion:** Steve Pate
- **Tournament record:** 22-under-par 266, George Burns, 1987

Phil Mickelson erased any doubts about his ability to play under pressure with a four-stroke victory and a near-flawless performance down the stretch at the Buick Invitational of California.

"I feel like a big burden has been lifted off my shoulders," Mickelson said after edging Dave Rummells for his first Tour victory as a pro. He finished 7-under-par 65.

Although he had been a pro for less than a year, Phil Mickelson felt pressure concerning his failure to win.

"I won a lot of tournaments as an amateur, but I hadn't proved myself on this level. There have been a lot of high expectations from others and a lot from myself, and I had let two victories get away," he said, referring to the previous year's B.C. Open and Northern Telecom Open.

Trailing by a shot after nine holes, he birdied four of the next six holes to take a three-shot lead.

Mickelson tied Rummells with a 3-foot birdie putt at No.10, then took the lead with a 14-footer at No.12.

"I used to come to this tournament every year when I was growing up a few miles from here," he said. "It was terrific that my family could be here to watch and I think all the local support I received was a big factor."

—*by Steve Hershey*

Scores and earnings (partial)

Player	Earnings	Scores
Phil Mickelson	$180,000	75-69-69-65–278
Dave Rummells	$108,000	77-64-71-70–282
Payne Stewart	$68,000	72-66-75-70–283
Jay Don Blake	$41,333	73-75-70-67–285
Jay Haas	$41,333	70-72-71-72–285
Greg Twiggs	$41,333	73-73-69-70–285
Keith Clearwater	$32,250	75-72-70-69–286
Joey Sindelar	$32,250	77-68-70-71–286
Mark Wiebe	$24,000	76-73-71-67–287
Hal Sutton	$24,000	73-71-74-69–287
David Peoples	$24,000	77-71-69-70–287
Len Mattiace	$24,000	76-68-71-72–287
Patrick Burke	$24,000	74-74-68-71–287
Craig Stadler	$24,000	75-68-71-73–287
Dan Pohl	$16,000	76-74-70-68–288
Tom Sieckmann	$16,000	76-72-71-692–88
Joel Edwards	$16,000	76-74-68-702–88
Tom Lehman	$16,000	79-70-68-712–88
Steve Pate	$16,000	75-76-65-722–88
Bruce Fleisher	$11,240	77-71-72-69–289
Donnie Hammond	$11,240	78-71-69-71–289
John Huston	$11,240	76-71-70-72–289
Grant Waite	$11,240	77-71-69-72–289
Jim Gallagher	$11,240	81-68-68-72–289
Jim McGovern	$7,975	76-74-70-70–290
Jodie Mudd	$7,975	74-72-73-71–290
Rick Fehr	$7,975	75-72-72-71–290
Duffy Waldorf	$7,975	74-69-75-72–290
Michael Allen	$6,088	82-67-72-70–291
Bob Estes	$6,088	76-74-71-70–291
John Ross	$6,088	77-71-73-70–291
Jim Woodward	$6,088	76-73-73-69–291
Bobby Clampett	$6,088	72-76-72-71–291
Brandel Chamblee	$6,088	76-74-70-71–291
Ronnie Black	$6,088	76-69-72-74–291
Perry Moss	$6,088	78-69-69-75–291
Gene Sauers	$4,000	78-72-71-71–292
Dillard Pruitt	$4,000	76-72-73-71–292
Scott Simpson	$4,000	77-74-69-72–292
Bill Murchison	$4,000	76-74-70-72–292
Lee Janzen	$4,000	81-68-73-70–292
Gary Hallberg	$4,000	77-72-71-72–292
Russell Beiersdorf	$4,000	64-71-77-70–292
Robert Wrenn	$4,000	79-71-73-69–292
Rocco Mediate	$4,000	78-73-73-68–292
Phil Blackmar	$4,000	75-76-73-68–292
Brad Sherfy	$2,690	75-74-72-72–293
Greg Whisman	$2,690	72-77-73-71–293
Joe Durant	$2,690	73-77-72-71–293
John Mahaffey	$2,690	74-73-76-70–293
Michael Bradley	$2,340	76-74-71-73–294
Steve Lamontagne	$2,340	75-76-69-74–294
Stan Utley	$2,340	79-69-74-72–294
Kirk Triplett	$2,340	76-70-73-75–294
Willie Wood	$2,340	78-71-70-75–294
Neal Lancaster	$2,340	76-72-77-69–294
Dennis Trixler	$2,340	77-74-74-69–294
Greg Cesario	$2,200	76-73-73-73–295
Leonard Thompson	$2,200	79-69-75-72–295
Jim Thorpe	$2,200	77-74-72-72–295
Peter Persons	$2,200	76-71-76-72–295
Morris Hatalsky	$2,200	76-75-73-71–295
John Cook	$2,090	77-73-72-74–296
Mike Standly	$2,090	74-72-73-77–296
Dave Barr	$2,090	76-74-73-73–296
Loren Roberts	$2,090	75-76-72-73–296
Mark Lye	$2,090	76-75-73-72–296
Marty Schiene	$2,090	75-76-73-72–296
Brad Fabel	$1,980	76-73-73-75–297
David Jackson	$1,980	76-75-68-78–297
Fred Funk	$1,980	76-75-75-71–297
Jaime Gomez	$1,980	74-77-75-71–297
Mark Pfeil	$1,980	80-71-77-69–297

NISSAN LOS ANGELES OPEN

AT A GLANCE

- **Course:** Riviera Country Club
- **Location:** Pacific Palisades, Calif.
- **When:** Feb. 25-28, 1993
- **Weather:** Sunny Thursday, Saturday and Sunday. Friday's round rained out and tournament shortened to 54 holes for the first time since it began in 1926.
- **Purse:** $1 million
- **Par:** 71
- **Yards:** 7,029
- **Defending champion:** Fred Couples
- **Tournament record:** 264, Lanny Wadkins, 1985

Continuing a spectacular late-career renaissance, Tom Kite birdied four of the last five holes to come from behind and win the Nissan Los Angeles Open by three strokes.

"It's been a total maturity of everything, physically and mentally," the 1992 U.S. Open winner said of his resurgence. "Also, my swing has gotten progressively better and my putting stroke has improved. I just feel very good about my game."

Confidence paid off when he fell four shots behind Jay Don Blake after a bogey at No. 9 in the final round.

"In the past, I used to be too hard on myself, I didn't have enough patience," he said. "Today, I knew I was playing well and that if I hung in, good things could happen."

As the leaders faltered, Kite birdied five of the last seven holes. He rolled in 18-footers at 12 and 14 and a 20-footer at 15. At 17 and 18, he tapped from 6 and 3 feet.

Defending champion Fred Couples marveled at Kite's ability.

"I played with him when he shot 62 and that was a great round. The conditions were a lot tougher here, but it doesn't seem to matter; he can win anywhere."

—*by Steve Hershey*

Scores and earnings

Player	Rounds–Total
Tom Kite, $180,000	73-66-67–206
Dave Barr, $66,000	71-72-66–209
Payne Stewart, $66,000	72-66-71–209
Fred Couples, $66,000	71-67-71–209
Donnie Hammond, $66,000	69-69-71–209
Howard Twitty, $28,188	70-72-68–210
Peter Jacobsen, $28,188	73-68-69–210
Jeff Maggert, $28,188	71-73-66–210
Paul Azinger, $28,188	72-68-70–210
Jodie Mudd, $28,188	71-68-71–210
Jay Don Blake, $28,188	67-72-71–210
Greg Twiggs, $28,188	72-67-71–210
Rick Fehr, $28,188	72-67-71–210
Steve Lowery, $17,000	71-72-68–211
Tom Purtzer, $17,000	73-70-68–211
Lee Janzen, $17,000	68-73-70–211
Ben Crenshaw, $17,000	72-69-70–211
Mark McCumber, $17,000	71-70-70–211
Trevor Dodds, $11,286	73-70-69–212
Chip Beck, $11,286	70-71-71–212
Hale Irwin, $11,286	72-69-71–212
Phil Mickelson, $11,286	70-71-71–212
Jeff Cook, $11,286	71-68-73–212
Jim McGovern, $11,286	67-72-73–212
Marco Dawson, $11,286	71-67-74–212
Ted Tryba, $7,400	71-71-71–213
Keith Clearwater, $7,400	73-69-71–213
Kelly Gibson, $7,400	68-76-69–213
John Daly, $7,400	70-71-72–213
David Edwards, $7,400	73-72-68–213
Rick Dalpos, $5,800	71-71-72–214
Jim Hallet, $5,800	71-71-72–214
T.C. Chen, $5,800	71-72-71–214
Dan Pohl, $5,800	73-69-72–214
Bob Tway, $5,800	73-68-73–214
Michael Allen, $5,800	72-68-74–214
Scott Gump, $4,200	70-73-72–215
David Peoples, $4,200	71-72-72–215
Mark Wiebe, $4,200	70-73-72–215
Billy Mayfair, $4,200	73-71-71–215
Paul Goydos, $4,200	72-69-74–215
Jim Woodward, $4,200	71-73-71–215
Steve Lamontagne, $4,200	72-69-74–215
Lennie Clements, $4,200	71-74-70–215
Jeff Sluman, $2,580	68-75-73–216
Steve Pate, $2,580	70-73-73–216
Fulton Allem, $2,580	73-70-73–216
Grant Waite, $2,580	71-71-74–216
Scott Simpson, $2,580	68-75-73–216
Hal Sutton, $2,580	68-75-73–216
Tad Rhyan, $2,580	71-72-73–216
Jay Haas, $2,580	70-74-72–216
Barry Cheesman, $2,580	73-71-72–216
Brian Kamm, $2,580	72-72-72–216
Yoshinori Kaneko, $2,580	73-71-72–216
Tom Sieckmann, $2,580	73-72-71–216
Marty Schiene, $2,580	72-73-71–216
Russell Beiersdorf, $2,170	67-75-75–217
John Mahaffey, $2,170	69-74-74–217
Rocco Mediate, $2,170	71-75-71–217
Gil Morgan, $2,170	73-70-74–217
Dillard Pruitt, $2,170	71-70-76–217
Gene Jones, $2,170	71-73-73–217
Bob Gilder, $2,170	76-69-72–217
Neal Lancaster, $2,170	73-72-72–217
Perry Moss, $2,010	73-70-75–218
Ronnie Black, $2,010	68-74-76–218
David Ogrin, $2,010	73-69-76–218
Robin Freeman, $2,010	72-72-74–218
Carl Cooper, $2,010	74-67-77–218
Hiroshi Makino, $2,010	74-70-74–218
Bob Estes, $2,010	75-70-73–218
Mike Hulbert, $2,010	71-74-73–218
Brian Henninger, $1,910	71-73-75–219
Dennis Trixler, $1,910	72-73-74–219
John Flannery, $1,880	71-72-77–220
Tommy Armour III, $1,860	70-71-80–221
Jeff Woodland, $1,840	69-74-80–223
John Inman, $1,820	74-71-79–224

Doral Ryder Open

AT A GLANCE

- **Course:** Doral Country Club (Blue Monster Course)
- **Location:** Miami
- **When:** March 5-8, 1993
- **Weather:** Sunny, warm, beautiful, little wind.
- **Purse:** $1.4 million
- **Par:** 72
- **Yards:** 6,939
- **Defending champion:** Fred Couples
- **Tournament record:** 23-under-par 265, Greg Norman, 1993

A rededicated Greg Norman achieved the first goal in his new seven-year plan to return to his lofty level of glories past.

"I don't want to be specific, but I've reset my goals on a seven-year plan that will take me to 45," Norman said after breezing to a four-shot win at the Doral Ryder Open.

"One of the goals was to win early. I knew I was playing well when I got here and I usually play well at Doral, so this was a great opportunity for me."

Like a man on a mission, Norman opened with a 65 and never looked back, winning wire-to-wire with a tournament-record 23-under-par 265.

A third-round, 10-under-par 62, which tied the course record he set in the final-round of his 1990 victory, gave Norman a six-shot cushion.

"I played a different game than I'm used to playing," Norman said after his final-round 70. "I was a little more conservative than I'm used to being. It's really hard to play with a big lead.

"I enjoyed this more than 1990 because I was in the lead all the way. When you're leading, it tells you you're playing extremely well."

—*by Steve Hershey*

Scores and earnings

Player		
Greg Norman, $252,000	65-68-62-70	265
Mark Mccumber, $123,200	69-67-66-67	269
Paul Azinger, $123,200	67-66-68-68	269
David Frost, $67,200	70-64-68-68	270
Sandy Lyle, $56,000	69-67-68-68	272
Nick Faldo, $48,650	72-65-70-66	273
Fred Couples, $48,650	68-67-71-67	273
Tom Kite, $43,400	66-73-69-67	275
Scott Hoch, $40,600	71-67-69-69	276
Chip Beck, $31,033	70-72-72-63	277
Lee Janzen, $31,033	71-71-70-65	277
John Adams, $31,033	72-67-70-68	277
Ed Humenik, $31,033	67-71-69-70	277
Steve Elkington, $31,033	68-72-67-70	277
Jack Nicklaus, $31,033	69-68-67-73	277
Kenny Perry, $19,005	71-69-70-68	278
Payne Stewart, $19,005	74-67-69-68	278
Kelly Gibson, $19,005	73-69-68-68	278
Andrew Magee, $19,005	71-69-69-69	278
Wayne Grady, $19,005	71-68-70-69	278
Bill Glasson, $19,005	70-69-69-70	278
Nick Price, $19,005	70-71-67-70	278
Ken Green, $19,005	69-70-68-71	278
Dave Rummells, $11,620	66-72-74-67	279
Peter Jacobsen, $11,620	68-67-74-70	279
Mark Calcavecchia, $11,620	77-65-67-70	279
Billy Mayfair, $11,620	74-67-67-71	279
Mike Standly, $11,620	70-70-66-73	279
Bruce Lietzke, $9,310	71-66-75-68	280
John Daly, $9,310	70-69-69-72	280
Rocco Mediate, $9,310	70-66-69-75	280
Keith Clearwater, $9,310	71-65-69-75	280
Billy Ray Brown, $7,560	69-72-75-65	281
Ted Tryba, $7,560	71-70-71-69	281
Brian Claar, $7,560	70-71-71-69	281
Dave Barr, $7,560	71-71-68-71	281
Ray Floyd, $7,560	72-70-68-71	281
Richard Zokol, $5,740	71-71-74-66	282
Jim Gallagher, $5,740	73-69-72-68	282
Neal Lancaster, $5,740	69-70-72-71	282
Jim Mcgovern, $5,740	70-68-73-71	282
Jay Don Blake, $5,740	69-72-70-71	282
Dillard Pruitt, $5,740	73-67-69-73	282
Tom Watson, $5,740	68-71-69-74	282
Steve Lamontagne, $4,099	73-70-70-70	283
Jeff Sluman, $4,099	72-71-70-70	283
Lanny Wadkins, $4,099	70-70-71-72	283
Tom Purtzer, $4,099	68-69-72-74	283
Brian Henninger, $4,099	69-71-69-74	283
Doug Tewell, $3,444	69-73-70-72	284
Duffy Waldorf, $3,444	73-70-69-72	284
Gil Morgan, $3,444	71-70-69-74	284
Davis Love III, $3,241	75-67-73-70	285
Dan Halldorson, $3,241	70-73-70-72	285
Eddie Pearce, $3,241	69-69-74-73	285
Curtis Strange, $3,241	71-71-70-73	285
Mark Lye, $3,122	74-68-74-70	286
John Huston, $3,122	70-72-73-71	286
David Jackson, $3,122	70-69-75-72	286
Mark Carnevale, $3,122	71-71-71-73	286
Marco Dawson, $2,996	73-68-75-71	287
Bob Lohr, $2,996	69-74-73-71	287
Ronnie Black, $2,996	72-70-73-72	287
Mike Malizia, $2,996	76-66-73-72	287
Gary Nicklaus, $2,996	72-69-73-73	287
Bob Tway, $2,870	73-70-79-66	288
Tim Crockett, $2,870	73-66-74-75	288
Larry Nelson, $2,870	71-71-71-75	288
Billy Andrade, $2,870	73-68-71-76	288
Greg Cerulli, $2,786	70-73-73-73	289
Lance Ten Broeck, $2,786	70-73-71-75	289
Tom Shaw, $2,716	74-69-75-72	290
Robert Wrenn, $2,716	68-69-76-77	290
Robin Freeman, $2,716	68-72-71-79	290
Andy Bean, $2,660	70-73-69-79	291
Paul Trittler, $2,632	72-71-79-72	294

The Honda Classic

AT A GLANCE

- **Course:** Weston Hills Country Club
- **Location:** Fort Lauderdale, Fla.
- **When:** March 11-14, 1993
- **Weather:** Sunny and warm Thursday and Friday. Saturday's round cancelled because of high winds. Sunny, mid to high 60s.
- **Purse:** $1.1 million
- **Par:** 72
- **Yards:** 7,020
- **Playoff:** Fred Couples defeated Robert Gamez par-par to par-double bogey
- **Defending champion:** Corey Pavin
- **Tournament record:** 15-under-par 273, Corey Pavin, 1992

In a long-awaited and uplifting victory, Fred Couples veered from horrible to terrific in a dramatic three-hole finale at the Honda Classic.

"I was choking like a dog," Couples said after going 5 over par in a six-hole stretch.

After playing perhaps his best front-nine of '92, Couples was nursing a one-shot lead when he sliced a 4-iron into the water on No. 16 and made double bogey to fall a shot behind.

"It was a terrible shot," Couples said. "I just fell asleep."

On No. 17, he birdied after a bunker shot near water for the lead.

"It was lucky," he said. "Not lucky I got it close to the hole, it was an easy shot, but lucky that it rolled in."

In need of a par on the par-5 18th to gain a playoff with Gamez, Couples faced a tough third shot from a bunker. With a sidehill lie, a mound in front of him, water on the right, and 158 yards to the hole, he hit a high 6-iron 30 feet behind the hole and just missed his winning birdie try. The playoff was an anticlimax.

"That's the best shot I've ever hit," Couples said upon collecting his 10th win.

—by Steve Hershey

Scores and earnings

Player	Earnings	Scores
#Fred Couples	$198,000	64-73-70–207
Robert Gamez	$118,800	68-71-68–207
Larry Mize	$74,800	69-67-72–208
Dick Mast	$52,800	68-69-72–209
Craig Parry	$44,000	67-71-72–210
Ed Dougherty	$32,136	70-74-67–211
Fuzzy Zoeller	$32,136	66-75-70–211
Mike Smith	$32,136	69-72-70–211
Rocco Mediate	$32,136	71-69-71–211
Jim McGovern	$32,136	71-69-71–211
Steve Pate	$32,136	68-71-72–211
David Frost	$32,136	68-69-74–211
Dudley Hart	$22,000	68-73-71–212
John Inman	$22,000	70-69-73–212
Don Pooley	$17,600	72-72-69–213
Corey Pavin	$17,600	70-73-70–213
Nick Faldo	$17,600	69-72-72–213
Bob Tway	$17,600	68-72-73–213
Joey Sindelar	$17,600	69-70-74–213
Bob Lohr	$11,917	72-72-70–214
Joel Edwards	$11,917	69-74-71–214
John Daly	$11,917	69-74-71–214
Gene Sauers	$11,917	66-76-72–214
Ed Humenik	$11,917	71-70-73–214
Billy Andrade	$11,917	70-68-76–214
Keith Clearwater	$7,031	71-74-70–215
David Toms	$7,031	70-75-70–215
John Flannery	$7,031	70-74-71–215
Nick Price	$7,031	70-74-71–215
Wayne Levi	$7,031	69-75-71–215
Len Mattiace	$7,031	72-72-71–215
Jeff Cook	$7,031	70-72-73–215
Andrew Magee	$7,031	66-76-73–215
Phil Blackmar	$7,031	65-77-73–215
Mark Lye	$7,031	69-73-73–215
Bobby Wadkins	$7,031	70-72-73–215
Mike Standly	$7,031	70-71-74–215
Brian Claar	$4,180	70-75-71–216
Mike Sullivan	$4,180	70-75-71–216
Bill Britton	$4,180	73-71-72–216
Gary McCord	$4,180	70-74-72–216
Skip Kendall	$4,180	71-72-73–216
Robin Freeman	$4,180	72-70-74–216
Curtis Strange	$4,180	72-70-74–216
Jim Gallagher	$4,180	68-73-75–216
Mark Calcavecchia	$4,180	68-73-75–216
Larry Rinker	$4,180	72-68-76–216
Bob Estes	$2,734	67-77-73–217
Paul Goydos	$2,734	71-73-73–217
Richard Zokol	$2,734	70-73-74–217
Dave Barr	$2,734	70-73-74–217
Bruce Fleisher	$2,734	70-72-75–217
Tim Simpson	$2,734	70-72-75–217
Steve Lamontagne	$2,734	71-71-75–217
Kelly Gibson	$2,508	70-74-74–218
Dave Peege	$2,508	68-75-75–218
Duffy Waldorf	$2,508	69-74-75–218
Gary Nicklaus	$2,431	69-76-74–219
Leonard Thompson	$2,431	73-72-74–219
Ed Fiori	$2,431	71-73-75–219
Tony Mollica	$2,431	69-72-78–219
Michael Bradley	$2,310	70-75-75–220
Rick Dalpos	$2,310	67-78-75–220
Russ Cochran	$2,310	72-73-75–220
Massy Kuramoto	$2,310	72-73-75–220
Kenny Perry	$2,310	73-71-76–220
Bob Gilder	$2,310	73-71-76–220
Bill Glasson	$2,310	67-76-77–220
Mike Hulbert	$2,222	72-70-79–221
David Jackson	$2,156	65-80-77–222
Fulton Allem	$2,156	74-71-77–222
Willie Wood	$2,156	72-73-77–222
Hal Sutton	$2,156	70-75-77–222
Scott Gump	$2,156	72-72-78–222
Brad Fabel	$2,079	73-72-78–223
Brad Faxon	$2,079	70-75-78–223
Mark Brooks	$2,046	71-74-80–225

- won on second playoff hole

The Nestlé Invitational

AT A GLANCE

- **Course:** Bay Hill Club
- **Location:** Orlando, Fla.
- **When:** March 18-21, 1993
- **Weather:** Cool, windy, rainy; high winds particularly on Friday; rain and standing water delayed play for 57 minutes on Sunday.
- **Purse:** $1 million
- **Par:** 72
- **Yards:** 7,114
- **Defending champion:** Fred Couples
- **Tournament record:** 24-under-par 264, Payne Stewart, 1987

Ben Crenshaw showed middle-aged golfers who can't keep up with long-hitting youngsters how to win during the final day of the Nestlé Invitational.

Although outdriven 25-40 yards by Davis Love III, Crenshaw used his putter, experience and course management to shoot 70 and win by two shots.

Crenshaw, 41, hit only six fairways and 10 greens but one-putted 10 times. His ability to avoid mistakes kept him in front after a birdie at the par-5 sixth.

Love, one of the game's longest hitters, had a huge advantage on the par-5s, but failed to capitalize, three-putting twice and making only one birdie.

Crenshaw laid up on the first three par-5s and birdied them all with deft pitch shots and laser putts.

"I had to play my game," Crenshaw said. "It's tough watching Davis hit irons to all the par-5s. I tried to ignore him as best I could."

Crenshaw's only top-10 finish since his victory at the previous July's Western Open, the win was a big confidence boost heading for the Masters.

—*by Steve Hershey*

Scores and earnings

Player	Scores
Ben Crenshaw, $180,000	71-70-69-70–280
Rocco Mediate, $74,667	72-72-70-68–282
Vijay Singh, $74,667	70-72-71-69–282
Davis Love III, $74,667	71-69-71-71–282
Ed Humenik, $40,000	73-69-72-70–284
Mark O'Meara, $33,500	71-72-72-70–285
Mark McCumber, $33,500	72-71-71-71–285
Bernhard Langer, $33,500	71-70-71-73–285
Joey Sindelar, $29,000	72-70-73-71–286
Billy Andrade, $21,429	72-74-70-71–287
Larry Mize, $21,429	74-72-70-71–287
Jay Haas, $21,429	71-73-71-72–287
Nick Price, $21,429	73-75-67-72–287
Greg Norman, $21,429	72-73-69-73–287
Bill Kratzert, $21,429	72-70-70-75–287
Dan Pohl, $21,429	70-72-70-75–287
Scott Simpson, $13,533	73-72-74-69–288
Bruce Fleisher, $13,533	71-75-72-70–288
John Cook, $13,533	69-77-71-71–288
Mark Lye, $13,533	73-71-72-72–288
D.A. Weibring, $13,533	72-75-67-74–288
Brad Faxon, $13,533	71-72-70-75–288
Peter Jacobsen, $8,650	76-71-71-71–289
Mike Sullivan, $8,650	74-71-72-72–289
Fuzzy Zoeller, $8,650	73-73-70-73–289
Lee Janzen, $8,650	73-72-71-73–289
Massy Kuramoto, $8,650	72-71-72-74–289
Michael Allen, $8,650	69-72-73-75–289
Curtis Strange, $6,800	70-79-70-71–290
Mike Hulbert, $6,800	75-74-68-73–290
Tom Watson, $6,800	76-68-70-76–290
Jay Delsing, $5,917	70-73-76-72–291
Brad Bryant, $5,917	70-74-75-72–291
Dan Forsman, $5,917	73-71-76-71–291
Payne Stewart, $5,038	75-70-76-71–292
Keith Clearwater, $5,038	74-72-74-72–292
Ed Dougherty, $5,038	72-73-73-74–292
John Daly, $5,038	77-71-70-74–292
Larry Rinker, $4,000	74-72-72-72–293
Steve Pate, $4,000	74-73-73-73–293
Bill Britton, $4,000	77-72-71-73–293
Scott Hoch, $4,000	71-74-73-75–293
David Peoples, $4,000	76-73-69-75–293
Kirk Triplett, $4,000	71-71-74-77–293
Brett Ogle, $2,803	77-71-74-72–294
Mike Springer, $2,803	73-73-75-73–294
Denis Watson, $2,803	74-73-74-73–294
Leonard Thompson, $2,803	72-77-72-73–294
Len Mattiace, $2,803	76-72-73-73–294
Tom Kite, $2,803	77-72-71-74–294
Billy Ray Brown, $2,803	75-70-72-77–294
Bob Lohr, $2,360	75-74-76-70–295
Corey Pavin, $2,360	74-74-73-74–295
Ian Baker-Finch, $2,360	75-70-75-75–295
Dave Rummells, $2,300	77-70-71-78–296
John Flannery, $2,250	76-72-76-73–297
Ted Schulz, $2,250	76-71-76-74–297
Steve Lowery, $2,250	75-71-75-76–297
Rick Fehr, $2,250	69-74-76-78–297
Gary Hallberg, $2,160	73-71-77-77–298
Jim Gallagher, $2,160	77-70-74-77–298
Blaine McCallister, $2,160	73-72-75-78–298
John Huston, $2,160	74-73-72-79–298
Gene Sauers, $2,160	73-73-73-79–298
Fulton Allem, $2,090	70-75-80-74–299
Robert Wrenn, $2,090	73-75-75-76–299
Kelly Gibson, $2,030	76-73-75-77–301
Nolan Henke, $2,030	74-71-78-78–301
Trevor Dodds, $2,030	76-73-73-79–301
Joe Ozaki, $2,030	72-76-74-79–301
Arnold Palmer, $1,970	73-76-78-75–302
Peter O'Malley, $1,970	75-74-75-78–302
Mark Carnevale, $1,940	71-76-80-77–304
Hal Sutton, $1,920	73-76-80-76–305
Andy Bean, $1,900	71-76-80-80–307

The Players Championship

AT A GLANCE

- **Course:** Tournament Players Club at Sawgrass
- **Location:** Ponte Vedra, Fla.
- **When:** March 25-28, 1993
- **Weather:** Sunny but cool and windy with intermittent showers Thursday, Friday and Saturday. Sunny and warm Sunday.
- **Purse:** $2.5 million
- **Par:** 72
- **Yards:** 6,896
- **Defending champion:** Davis Love III
- **Tournament record:** 18-under-par 270, Nick Price, 1993

Scores and earnings

Player	Scores
Nick Price, $450,000	64-68-71-67–270
Bernhard Langer, $270,000	65-69-70-71–275
Gil Morgan, $145,000	68-71-72-65–276
Greg Norman, $145,000	66-70-68-72–276
Mark O'Meara, $100,000	67-71-66-73–277
Joe Ozaki, $80,938	72-68-68-70–278
Rocco Mediate, $80,938	68-71-68-71–278
Ken Green, $80,938	70-67-69-72–278
Paul Azinger, $80,938	68-69-68-73–278
Tom Watson, $67,500	70-72-69-68–279
Dan Forsman, $53,000	71-67-73-69–280
Tom Lehman, $53,000	69-73-69-69–280
Mike Hulbert, $53,000	71-67-72-70–280
Joel Edwards, $53,000	66-69-72-73–280
Payne Stewart, $53,000	70-70-66-74–280
Joey Sindelar, $38,750	65-71-73-72–281
Dave Rummells, $38,750	69-65-74-73–281
Steve Elkington, $38,750	67-70-71-73–281
Corey Pavin, $38,750	69-72-67-73–281
Fulton Allem, $26,071	70-72-73-67–282
Billy Andrade, $26,071	71-70-73-68–282
Andrew Magee, $26,071	70-71-71-70–282
Bob Estes, $26,071	70-68-72-72–282
Doug Tewell, $26,071	67-67-74-74–282
Mark McCumber, $26,071	68-70-70-74–282
Jay Haas, $26,071	69-70-68-75–282
Russ Cochran, $19,250	67-72-71-73–283
Brian Claar, $16,625	72-69-74-69–284
Vijay Singh, $16,625	69-71-72-72–284
Howard Twitty, $16,625	71-70-71-72–284
Bob Lohr, $16,625	71-71-70-72–284
Bruce Lietzke, $16,625	69-69-72-74–284
Ronnie Black, $16,625	66-70-71-77–284
Fuzzy Zoeller, $12,900	67-75-74-69–285
Ted Schulz, $12,900	71-70-73-71–285
Robert Wrenn, $12,900	67-73-73-72–285
Donnie Hammond, $12,900	66-73-73-73–285
Lee Janzen, $12,900	70-71-71-73–285
Kirk Triplett, $9,750	64-78-75-69–286
Fred Funk, $9,750	68-73-72-72–286
Mike Smith, $9,750	70-69-74-73–286
Fred Couples, $9,750	68-69-75-74–286
Ian Baker-Finch, $9,750	71-71-71-73–286
Ian Woosnam, $9,750	71-70-69-76–286
Jim Gallagher, $9,750	69-69-69-79–286
Jeff Sluman, $6,800	71-65-80-71–287
Marco Dawson, $6,800	68-73-75-71–287
Gary Hallberg, $6,800	71-71-74-71–287
Larry Rinker, $6,800	70-72-72-73–287
Bruce Fleisher, $6,800	74-67-72-74–287
David Edwards, $6,800	69-70-71-77–287
Peter Persons, $5,771	73-68-73-74–288
Duffy Waldorf, $5,771	72-66-75-75–288
Billy Mayfair, $5,771	73-68-72-75–288
Denis Watson, $5,771	72-66-74-76–288
Rick Fehr, $5,771	67-71-74-76–288
Brad Bryant, $5,771	69-70-72-77–288
Tony Johnstone, $5,771	70-71-70-77–288
Dick Mast, $5,525	70-70-77-72–289
Brad Fabel, $5,525	68-68-77-76–289
Ed Dougherty, $5,375	69-71-76-74–290
Mark Wiebe, $5,375	71-70-74-75–290
D.A. Weibring, $5,375	69-73-72-76–290
Brett Ogle, $5,375	70-72-68-80–290
Kenny Perry, $5,225	70-69-76-76–291
Nolan Henke, $5,225	70-72-73-76–291
Davis Love III, $5,125	70-69-82-72–293
Mike Reid, $5,125	68-73-72-80–293
Dillard Pruitt, $5,050	70-72-72-80–294
Billy Ray Brown, $5,000	68-74-78-78–298

For years, a big question on the PGA Tour was why Nick Price didn't win.

After his performance at Sawgrass in March '93, the question became how often would he win.

Future Players Championships will be measured against Price's four-day performance, his fifth win in 22 months. (His 1992 victories included the PGA Championship and the H-E-B Texas Open.)

In his wire-to-wire romp, Price:

▶ Set a tournament record at TPC at Sawgrass, 18-under-par 270 (the previous mark was 273, held by Mark McCumber, 1988 and Davis Love III, '92).

▶ Made four bogeys, never more than one a day, despite difficult greens and strong winds.

▶ Hit 61 of 72 greens in regulation, never missing more than three a day.

▶ Hit 12 of 14 fairways every day except 9-for-14 in Saturday's wind-blown 71.

"Right now, I'd say he's the best player in the world," said Mark O'Meara, who played with Price Sunday and shot 73 to finish fifth. "(Nick) Faldo has a better record, but he hasn't played much lately.

"He was in total control of his game. He played like a machine. He did everything well."

—by Steve Hershey

Freeport-McMoran Classic

AT A GLANCE

- **Course:** English Turn Golf and Country Club
- **Location:** New Orleans
- **When:** April 1-4, 1993
- **Weather:** Windy, overcast, rainy.
- **Purse:** $1 million
- **Par:** 72
- **Yards:** 7,116
- **Defending champion:** Chip Beck
- **Tournament record:** 274, Tim Simpson, 1989

Scores and earnings (partial)

Player	Score
Mike Standly, $180,000	71-71-72-67–281
Russ Cochran, $88,000	75-68-70-69–282
Payne Stewart, $88,000	70-70-73-69–282
Greg Norman, $48,000	77-69-70-68–284
Vijay Singh, $40,000	72-73-72-68–285
Dick Mast, $32,375	76-72-70-69–287
Scott Hoch, $32,375	72-74-72-69–287
Neal Lancaster, $32,375	72-73-71-71–287
Greg Kraft, $32,375	72-71-69-75–287
Jaime Gomez, $24,000	75-70-72-71–288
Ed Fiori, $24,000	71-75-71-71–288
Duffy Waldorf, $24,000	71-73-72-72–288
Mark Brooks, $24,000	73-72-71-72–288
Kelly Gibson, $19,000	73-72-73-71–289
Brad Fabel, $17,000	75-69-75-71–290
Bill Kratzert, $17,000	71-80-68-71–290
David Toms, $17,000	74-72-71-73–290
Michael Bradley, $14,500	74-74-71-72–291
Bob Estes, $14,500	73-71-72-75–291
Greg Twiggs, $10,833	76-75-71-70–292
Steve Lowery, $10,833	75-72-74-71–292
Jc Anderson, $10,833	78-70-73-71–292
Richard Zokol, $10,833	75-74-70-73–292
Ted Schulz, $10,833	77-70-70-75–292
Steve Elkington, $10,833	73-73-71-75–292
Robin Freeman, $7,250	79-72-71-71–293
John Adams, $7,250	73-75-73-72–293
Jeff Woodland, $7,250	75-76-70-72–293
Peter O'Malley, $7,250	78-74-69-72–293
Ed Dougherty, $7,250	76-74-74-69–293
Billy Mayfair, $7,250	74-77-67-75–293
Brad Bryant, $5,414	76-70-74-74–294
Massy Kuramoto, $5,414	78-73-73-70–294
Doug Tewell, $5,414	75-76-73-70–294
Phil Blackmar, $5,414	79-70-71-74–294
Joel Edwards, $5,414	76-73-75-70–294
Fulton Allem, $5,414	78-74-73-69–294
Nick Faldo, $5,414	78-71-76-69–294
Donnie Hammond, $4,000	74-77-71-73–295
David Jackson, $4,000	78-73-72-72–295
Dave Barr, $4,000	76-74-73-72–295
Patrick Burke, $4,000	74-73-76-72–295
Eddie Pearce, $4,000	74-72-74-75–295
Jim McGovern, $4,000	77-67-81-70–295
Joe Ozaki, $2,860	76-71-74-75–296
Dudley Hart, $2,860	73-76-74-73–296
Mike Sullivan, $2,860	77-71-75-73–296
Ted Tryba, $2,860	75-74-72-75–296

Deposit Guaranty Golf Classic

AT A GLANCE

- **Course:** Hattiesburg Country Club
- **Location:** Hattiesburg, Miss.
- **When:** April 8-11, 1993
- **Weather:** Seasonable with intermittent rains.
- **Purse:** $300,000
- **Par:** 72
- **Yards:** 6,594
- **Defending champion:** Richard Zokol
- **Tournament record:** 25-under-par 263, Dan Halldorson, 1986

Scores and earnings (partial)

Player	Score
Greg Kraft, $54,000	65-70-64-68–267
Morris Hatalsky, $26,400	69-65-68-66–268
Tad Rhyan, $26,400	66-70-64-68–268
Grant Waite, $11,310	72-65-69-63–269
Doug Martin, $11,310	70-66-68-65–269
Massy Kuramoto, $11,310	69-68-66-66–269
Len Mattiace, $11,310	65-70-67-67–269
Barry Jaeckel, $11,310	68-65-66-70–269
Jeff Barlow, $8,700	69-69-65-67–270
Bill Buttner, $6,650	68-70-67-66–271
Pat Mcgowan, $6,650	70-69-66-66–271
Mike Donald, $6,650	65-70-69-67–271
Jeff Woodland, $6,650	64-68-71-68–271
Stan Utley, $6,650	68-66-69-68–271
J.P. Hayes, $6,650	68-66-68-69–271
Rex Caldwell, $4,350	69-67-69-67–272
Paul Goydos, $4,350	69-70-65-68–272
JC Anderson, $4,350	69-68-67-68–272
David Delong, $4,350	67-67-69-69–272
David Ogrin, $4,350	68-68-67-69–272
Jim Thorpe, $4,350	69-66-67-70–272
Brian Kamm, $3,000	69-68-71-65–273
John Ross, $3,000	70-66-69-68–273
Michael Bradley, $3,000	70-64-70-69–273
Chris Perry, $3,000	68-67-69-69–273
Steve Lamontagne, $2,175	68-66-72-68–274
Steve Hart, $2,175	67-68-70-69–274
Ernie Gonzalez, $2,175	70-66-69-69–274
Lennie Clements, $2,175	69-67-69-69–274
Ed Dougherty, $2,175	65-67-72-70–274
Perry Moss, $2,175	66-66-72-70–274
Mike Nicolette, $1,557	67-71-71-66–275
Brandel Chamblee, $1,557	70-70-68-67–275
Lance Ten Broeck, $1,557	71-70-65-69–275
David Canipe, $1,557	69-70-67-69–275
Jim Hallet, $1,557	71-67-68-69–275
Danny Edwards, $1,557	67-69-69-70–275
Sonny Skinner, $1,557	66-71-67-71–275
Jeff Cook, $1,557	64-68-71-72–275
Harry Taylor, $1,557	67-69-67-72–275
John Dowdall, $1,170	72-66-71-67–276
Forrest Fezler, $1,170	69-70-69-68–276
Gene Jones, $1,170	67-70-70-69–276
Skip Kendall, $885	70-69-71-67–277

MCI Heritage Classic

AT A GLANCE

- **Course:** Harbour Town Golf Links
- **Location:** Hilton Head Island, S.C.
- **When:** April 15-19, 1993
- **Weather:** Sunny and warm except for scattered showers Friday.
- **Purse:** $1.125 million
- **Par:** 71
- **Yards:** 6,657
- **Defending champion:** Davis Love III
- **Tournament record:** 16-under-par 268, Payne Stewart, 1989

To celebrate his 37th birthday—and a two-shot win at the MCI Heritage Classic—David Edwards promised to do a few loops flying his Cessna 340 to Charlotte, N.C., for a pro-am the next day.

He knew about ups and downs after his closing round of seven birdies, five bogeys and six pars for a 69 and an 11-under-par total of 273.

After an opening bogey when he drove into the trees, he was two shots behind playing partner Paul Azinger. He still was two back (of David Frost) at the turn, but despite a pair of three-putts, he reached the 18th tee with a two-shot lead on Frost.

At different times, Azinger (73), Frost (71) and Mark McCumber (71) had the lead, but all shot 1-over-par 36s on the back nine, allowing Edwards to win for the fourth time in his 15-year careeer.

Edwards had gone winless from the 1984 Los Angeles Open to the '92 Memorial.

"It was very discouraging," he said. "There are guys out here who just love to play golf, but I wouldn't put myself in that category. Golf is a job to me, and that's the way I treat it.

"When things weren't going well, I started weighing my options. But I realized I'm not really qualified for anything else. And it still beats working."

—by Steve Hershey

Scores and earnings

Player	1	2	3	4	Total
David Edwards, $202,500	68	66	70	69	273
David Frost, $121,500	67	67	70	71	275
Don Pooley, $50,738	67	70	70	70	277
Fuzzy Zoeller, $50,738	70	69	68	70	277
Ian Baker-Finch, $50,738	68	70	69	70	277
Mark McCumber, $50,738	68	68	70	71	277
Paul Azinger, $50,738	70	68	66	73	277
Gil Morgan, $31,500	71	72	69	66	278
Tom Lehman, $31,500	70	70	70	68	278
Steve Pate, $31,500	71	67	68	72	278
John Cook, $31,500	69	67	69	73	278
Bob Estes, $22,781	68	67	75	69	279
Jeff Sluman, $22,781	68	69	70	72	279
Lanny Wadkins, $22,781	66	70	70	73	279
Jodie Mudd, $22,781	69	68	69	73	279
Kelly Gibson, $17,438	74	64	72	70	280
Bernhard Langer, $17,438	69	65	74	72	280
Rick Fehr, $17,438	71	66	70	73	280
Peter Jacobsen, $17,438	70	70	67	73	280
Kenny Perry, $12,645	69	70	72	70	281
Hale Irwin, $12,645	68	70	71	72	281
Scott Hoch, $12,645	68	73	69	71	281
Billy Andrade, $12,645	70	69	70	72	281
Lee Janzen, $12,645	71	66	70	74	281
Mark O'Meara, $9,187	69	71	74	68	282
Doug Tewell, $9,187	69	71	70	72	282
Larry Nelson, $9,187	72	68	67	75	282
Phil Mickelson, $7,650	70	72	72	69	283
Corey Pavin, $7,650	67	70	74	72	283
Dick Mast, $7,650	71	72	68	72	283
Lance Ten Broeck, $7,650	70	68	72	73	283
Dillard Pruitt, $7,650	66	72	72	73	283
Dan Forsman, $6,216	69	72	71	72	284
Joel Edwards, $6,216	71	69	72	72	284
Payne Stewart, $6,216	65	70	72	77	284
Mike Standly, $6,216	66	75	67	76	284
Russ Cochran, $5,401	74	68	71	72	285
Jim McGovern, $5,401	72	69	70	74	285
Nolan Henke, $4,276	68	70	81	67	286
Jay Haas, $4,276	71	72	73	70	286
Gene Sauers, $4,276	72	71	72	71	286
Robert Gamez, $4,276	73	69	71	73	286
Mark Brooks, $4,276	71	69	72	74	286
Craig Parry, $4,276	70	69	73	74	286
Richard Zokol, $4,276	71	71	70	74	286
Howard Twitty, $4,276	70	67	74	75	286
Dan Halldorson, $2,890	71	72	73	71	287
Robert Wrenn, $2,890	73	69	72	73	287
Craig Stadler, $2,890	69	71	74	73	287
Bill Britton, $2,890	70	70	73	74	287
Rocco Mediate, $2,890	66	77	70	74	287
Vijay Singh, $2,890	73	70	70	74	287
Neal Lancaster, $2,890	71	69	71	76	287
Billy Mayfair, $2,587	71	72	73	72	288
Chip Beck, $2,587	73	69	73	73	288
Nick Price, $2,587	71	70	73	74	288
Fred Funk, $2,542	73	69	76	71	289
Dave Barr, $2,486	71	72	75	72	290
Brad Faxon, $2,486	72	67	76	75	290
Ken Green, $2,486	74	69	72	75	290
Marco Dawson, $2,486	72	71	71	76	290
Buddy Gardner, $2,396	72	71	74	74	291
D.A. Weibring, $2,396	70	73	74	74	291
Ed Fiori, $2,396	73	70	74	74	291
David Jackson, $2,396	72	71	72	76	291
Ed Humenik, $2,329	70	73	76	73	292
Mike Sullivan, $2,329	69	70	77	76	292
John Inman, $2,284	73	70	78	72	293
Barry Jaeckel, $2,284	73	70	77	73	293
Donnie Hammond, $2,250	73	69	76	76	294
Tim Simpson, $2,227	68	70	80	77	295
Tom Watson, $2,205	71	72	76	77	296
Jay Delsing, $2,182	71	71	79	76	297
Loren Roberts, $2,160	71	72	78	77	298
Wayne Grady, $2,137	71	71	75	82	299
Mike Springer, $2,115	70	73	82	76	301
John Mahaffey, $2,092	73	69	78	85	305
Jimmy Johnston, $2,070	72	71	80	84	307

K mart Greater Greensboro Open

At a Glance

- **Course:** Forest Oaks Country Club
- **Location:** Greensboro, N.C.
- **When:** April 22-25, 1993
- **Weather:** Chilly and windy, turning sunny and warm on the weekend.
- **Purse:** $1.25 million
- **Par:** 72
- **Yards:** 6,958
- **Playoff:** Rocco Mediate defeated Steve Elkington on the fourth playoff hole.
- **Defending champion:** Davis Love III
- **Tournament record:** 17-under-par 271, Sandy Lyle, 1988

Rocco Mediate outlasted a floundering field, using two superb 6-iron shots, to win the K mart Greater Greensboro Open in a playoff with Steve Elkington.

After he lost his lead with a double bogey on the par-5 15th, Mediate battled out of three bunkers before a 4-foot birdie on the fourth playoff hole sealed his victory.

On the third extra hole, the 426-yard 18th, Mediate drove in a fairway bunker and had 186 yards left. He picked a 6-iron clean and sank a 6-footer for par.

"I just missed the lip of the bunker, but I needed the 6-iron to get there," Mediate said. "I don't think I could ever hit that shot again."

Mediate's second great 6-iron came on the final hole after he hooked his drive into the light rough and had 165 yards into the wind. He hit it 4 feet below the hole and, after Elkington missed from 20 feet, sank the putt that gave him his second career victory.

—*by Steve Hershey*

Scores and earnings (partial)

Player	Rounds-Total
#Rocco Mediate, $270,000	74-67-71-69–281
Steve Elkington, $162,000	71-68-69-73–281
Dudley Hart, $78,000	72-65-74-71–282
Gil Morgan, $78,000	71-69-69-73–282
Paul Azinger, $78,000	73-67-70-72–282
Mark Wiebe, $50,250	72-73-68-70–283
Lee Janzen, $50,250	71-71-70-71–283
David Edwards, $50,250	70-71-70-72–283
Jeff Sluman, $40,500	78-65-71-70–284
Billy Andrade, $40,500	74-72-68-70–284
Vijay Singh, $40,500	72-67-72-73–284
Gene Sauers, $26,813	74-69-76-66–285
Mark Calcavecchia, $26,813	72-69-76-68–285
Tom Watson, $26,813	75-70-72-68–285
Jim McGovern, $26,813	69-72-75-69–285
Peter Jacobsen, $26,813	70-70-75-70–285
Mark O'Meara, $26,813	74-68-72-71–285
Mark Brooks, $26,813	76-68-69-72–285
Mike Sullivan, $26,813	67-68-73-77–285
Jay Haas, $16,250	69-73-74-70–286
Russell Beiersdorf, $16,250	75-71-69-71–286
John Cook, $16,250	71-73-70-72–286
Howard Twitty, $16,250	72-71-70-73–286
Donnie Hammond, $16,250	73-72-68-73–286
Lennie Clements, $16,250	70-68-72-76–286
Joel Edwards, $12,000	70-73-71-73–287
Tom Purtzer, $10,425	67-77-74-70–288
Chip Beck, $10,425	69-74-74-71–288
Tom Lehman, $10,425	72-73-71-72–288
Davis Love III, $10,425	71-74-71-72–288
John Huston, $10,425	73-70-72-73–288
John Mahaffey, $10,425	70-71-70-77–288
Brian Claar, $7,925	72-73-75-69–289
Marty Schiene, $7,925	74-71-74-70–289
Craig Parry, $7,925	71-72-74-72–289
Robert Gamez, $7,925	74-72-71-72–289
Wayne Levi, $7,925	75-72-70-72–289
Don Pooley, $7,925	74-72-70-73–289
Jim Thorpe, $6,300	75-71-72-72–290
Roger Maltbie, $6,300	70-71-76-73–290
Grant Waite, $6,300	74-73-70-73–290
Lance Ten Broeck, $6,300	72-70-72-76–290
Jim Gallagher, $4,680	73-74-76-68–291
Brian Kamm, $4,680	74-73-73-71–291
Peter Persons, $4,680	73-71-74-73–291
John Adams, $4,680	73-67-77-74–291

\# - won on fourth playoff hole

PLAYER SPOTLIGHT

Tom Sieckmann pulled off a rare feat in the third round of the Kmart Greater Greensboro Open, holing a 267-yard shot for a double eagle.

Sieckmann, who had missed eight cuts before Greensboro, hit a three-wood into the par-5, 574-yard ninth hole—the longest at Forest Oaks Country Club—for a 2.

The large gallery surrounding the bunkered green roared. There had been only two double eagles on the PGA Tour in 1992, 33 holes-in-one.

"I certainly wasn't planning to make it," said Sieckmann. "I hit it right at it, got the right bounce and it trickled up there.

"The people said it only would have gone a foot by the hole. It was rolling just like a putt."

Shell Houston Open

AT A GLANCE

- **Course:** Tournament Players Club at The Woodlands
- **Location:** The Woodlands, Texas
- **When:** April 29-May 2, 1993
- **Weather:** Rain interrupted play Thursday and Friday and washed out Saturday's scheduled third round, shortening the tournament to 54 holes.
- **Purse:** $1.3 million
- **Par:** 72
- **Yards:** 7,042
- **Playoff:** Jim McGovern defeated John Huston on the second playoff hole.
- **Defending champion:** Fred Funk
- **Tournament record:** 22-under-par 266, Curtis Strange, 1980

After two winless seasons on the PGA Tour, Jim McGovern came up with his first-ever victory.

McGovern birdied the final regulation hole of the Shell Houston Open to force a playoff, then ran in a 25-foot birdie putt on the second playoff hole to beat John Huston.

McGovern became the Houston Open's fourth consecutive first-time winner — following Fred Funk in 1992, Fulton Allem in '91 and Tony Sills in '90.

"I almost didn't come here this week," McGovern said. "I had two of my best friends get married yesterday, and they'd invited me. (They said) 'You do what you want. It's your job and who knows, you might win.'"

"They may not have known me, but they cheered on every hole," said McGovern, who tripled his year's earnings with the $234,000 paycheck. "The golf fans here are great. I felt comfortable all day."

McGovern and Huston each shot final-round 4-under-par 68s for a 199 total over 54 holes.

Scores and earnings

Player	Earnings	Scores	Total
#Jim McGovern	$234,000	67-64-68	199
John Huston	$140,400	65-66-68	199
Payne Stewart	$67,600	66-68-66	200
Donnie Hammond	$67,600	67-65-68	200
Blaine McCallister	$67,600	64-65-71	200
Larry Mize	$46,800	68-64-69	201
Mike Springer	$39,163	70-69-64	203
Fulton Allem	$39,163	66-70-67	203
Steve Elkington	$39,163	70-65-68	203
Loren Roberts	$39,163	67-67-69	203
Brian Kamm	$26,650	72-64-68	204
Andrew Magee	$26,650	68-68-68	204
Tom Byrum	$26,650	70-66-68	204
Ben Crenshaw	$26,650	67-68-69	204
Steve Pate	$26,650	67-68-69	204
Jeff Maggert	$26,650	66-68-70	204
Lance Ten Broeck	$19,500	72-67-66	205
Bill Britton	$19,500	67-69-69	205
John Daly	$19,500	69-70-66	205
Jeff Woodland	$14,083	70-68-68	206
Brian Henninger	$14,083	70-68-68	206
Gil Morgan	$14,083	67-70-69	206
Peter Persons	$14,083	69-68-69	206
Jay Haas	$14,083	68-67-71	206
Ronnie Black	$14,083	67-68-71	206
Morris Hatalsky	$9,230	68-70-69	207
Mike Sullivan	$9,230	68-71-68	207
Tom Sieckmann	$9,230	68-69-70	207
John Dowdall	$9,230	66-73-68	207
Willie Wood	$9,230	69-70-68	207
Billy Ray Brown	$9,230	67-72-68	207
Scott Hoch	$9,230	68-67-72	207
Brad Faxon	$6,581	73-65-70	208
Michael Bradley	$6,581	69-69-70	208
Jim Gallagher	$6,581	70-68-70	208
Keith Clearwater	$6,581	69-70-69	208
Dan Forsman	$6,581	69-70-69	208
Dave Barr	$6,581	68-71-69	208
Fred Funk	$6,581	69-67-72	208
John Flannery	$6,581	65-70-73	208
Perry Moss	$4,115	72-66-71	209
Trevor Dodds	$4,115	68-71-70	209
Ed Humenik	$4,115	69-69-71	209
Harry Taylor	$4,115	68-69-72	209
Rick Fehr	$4,115	70-69-70	209
Rick Dalpos	$4,115	66-73-70	209
J.L. Lewis	$4,115	69-70-70	209
Jeff Sluman	$4,115	68-68-73	209
Ted Tryba	$4,115	71-68-70	209
Kirk Triplett	$4,115	71-69-69	209
D.A. Weibring	$4,115	72-68-69	209
Tim Simpson	$3,001	72-66-72	210
Jim Woodward	$3,001	69-69-72	210
##Justin Leonard		69-68-73	210
Bobby Wadkins	$3,001	66-71-73	210
P.H. Horgan III	$3,001	69-68-73	210
Dennis Trixler	$3,001	70-69-71	210
Scott Gump	$3,001	70-69-71	210
Jaime Gomez	$3,001	71-68-71	210
Dillard Pruitt	$2,821	67-72-72	211
Michael Allen	$2,821	70-69-72	211
Brad Fabel	$2,821	71-69-71	211
John Adams	$2,821	72-68-71	211
Kelly Gibson	$2,821	69-71-71	211
Paul Goydos	$2,821	70-70-71	211
Eddie Pearce	$2,691	70-68-74	212
Neal Lancaster	$2,691	72-66-74	212
David Peoples	$2,691	71-67-74	212
JC Anderson	$2,691	71-69-72	212
Lennie Clements	$2,613	71-69-73	213
Tim Conley	$2,613	68-72-73	213
Shane Bertsch	$2,548	69-70-75	214
Ed Sneed	$2,548	66-73-75	214
David Jackson	$2,548	70-70-74	214
Steve Lowery	$2,483	68-71-76	215
David Ogrin	$2,483	67-70-78	215
Rocco Mediate	$2,431	71-69-76	216
Chip Craig	$2,431	71-69-76	216

\# - won on second playoff hole
\## - amateur

BELLSOUTH CLASSIC

AT A GLANCE

- **Course:** Atlanta Country Club
- **Location:** Marietta, Ga.
- **When:** May 6-9, 1993
- **Weather:** Sunny and warm.
- **Purse:** $1.2 million
- **Par:** 72
- **Yards:** 7,018
- **Defending champion:** Tom Kite
- **Tournament record:** 23-under-par 265, Andy Bean, 1979, and Dave Barr, 1987

Nolan Henke had considered not entering the BellSouth Classic, but as long as he made the trip, he figured he might as well give it a go.

Henke, whose earnings through his first 12 starts averaged less than $7,500 a tournament, won and bumped himself into another pay bracket.

But even entering the final round in third place, he gave himself little chance of catching the front-runners.

"I thought they would go out and pull away from everybody," Henke said of third-round leader Nick Price and Mark Calcavecchia, who began the day only one shot behind.

But Henke's bogey-free 5-under-par 67 was good enough for a two-shot victory.

"This was definitely a surprise," Henke said of his third career win and first since 1991. "I'm a streaky player. Two or three months of playing well, then I hit rock bottom. Maybe this is the start of a good streak.

"I really thought it would take 19 under to win," Henke said.

After his birdie on 14 had tied him with Price for the lead, Henke was surprised to find he held a one shot advantage when he got to the 18th green.

"I tried to block it out and just two-putt," he said.

Henke put his approach 50 feet from the hole on the par-5 18th. He rolled it within a foot and tapped in for a birdie he didn't need.

Scores and earnings

Nolan Henke, $216,000	67-69-68-67–271
Tom Sieckmann, $89,600	70-64-70-69–273
Nick Price, $89,600	69-67-64-73–273
Mark Calcavecchia, $89,600	67-67-67-72–273
Fulton Allem, $48,000	73-68-67-66–274
Mike Springer, $43,200	69-66-68-72–275
Kirk Triplett, $33,700	73-69-70-64–276
Billy Andrade, $33,700	67-66-73-70–276
Larry Mize, $33,700	69-69-68-70–276
Brian Claar, $33,700	70-68-67-71–276
Jimmy Johnston, $33,700	71-67-64-74–276
Dillard Pruitt, $33,700	66-68-68-74–276
Fred Funk, $21,840	71-69-73-64–277
Hale Irwin, $21,840	71-69-71-66–277
Corey Pavin, $21,840	69-71-70-67–277
Brandel Chamblee, $21,840	70-67-69-71–277
Russell Beiersdorf, $21,840	67-68-71-71–277
Patrick Burke, $17,400	68-72-72-66–278
Steve Lowery, $17,400	65-72-71-70–278
John Adams, $15,000	68-67-72-72–279
Davis Love III, $15,000	69-69-68-73–279
Scott Simpson, $11,520	68-71-72-69–280
Phil Blackmar, $11,520	72-69-70-69–280
David Frost, $11,520	71-68-69-72–280
Mike Hulbert, $11,520	66-70-71-73–280
John Huston, $11,520	67-71-69-73–280
Billy Mayfair, $8,520	71-68-71-71–281
Skip Kendall, $8,520	70-70-70-71–281
Morris Hatalsky, $8,520	69-72-69-71–281
David Toms, $8,520	69-70-70-72–281
Wayne Grady, $8,520	70-70-69-72–281
Mark O'Meara, $6,640	71-71-71-69–282
Payne Stewart, $6,640	69-71-72-70–282
Brad Fabel, $6,640	69-69-73-71–282
Blaine McCallister, $6,640	70-68-72-72–282
Bob Eastwood, $6,640	68-70-71-73–282
Dave Barr, $6,640	68-70-69-75–282
Neal Lancaster, $4,560	67-73-74-69–283
Joh Inman, $4,560	73-69-71-70–283
Mike Standly, $4,560	69-70-73-71–283
Grant Waite, $4,560	71-70-71-71–283
D.A. Weibring, $4,560	73-69-69-72–283
Harry Taylor, $4,560	72-70-69-72–283
Peter Persons, $4,560	70-69-71-73–283
Bill Kratzert, $4,560	68-73-69-73–283
David Ogrin, $4,560	67-75-68-73–283
Fuzzy Zoeller, $4,560	73-69-67-74–283
Mike Smith, $3,096	71-70-74-69–284
Trevor Dodds, $3,096	69-70-71-74–284
Curtis Strange, $3,096	73-69-68-74–284
Bill Britton, $3,096	71-70-68-75–284
Mark Carnevale, $2,744	66-73-76-70–285
Joel Edwards, $2,744	70-71-73-71–285
Hubert Green, $2,744	70-71-73-71–285
Brad Bryant, $2,744	72-66-75-72–285
Bria Henninger, $2,744	71-70-72-72–285
Larry Nelson, $2,744	67-72-73-73–285
Lennie Clements, $2,744	73-69-68-75–285
Willie Wood, $2,744	68-68-73-76–285
Russ Cochra, $2,744	68-67-74-76–285
John Elliott, $2,544	68-73-76-69–286
Jodie Mudd, $2,544	70-70-74-72–286
Ed Dougherty, $2,544	73-66-73-74–286
Mike Donald, $2,544	70-71-71-74–286
Tom Byrum, $2,544	72-69-71-74–286
Jim McGovern, $2,544	70-71-70-75–286
Bill Glasson, $2,544	71-69-68-78–286
Tommy Armour III, $2,436	68-74-73-72–287
Bobby Wadkins, $2,436	74-68-70-75–287
Andy Bean, $2,400	70-72-72-74–288
Ed Humenik, $2,328	72-69-75-73–289
Perry Moss, $2,328	69-72-74-74–289
Barry Cheesman, $2,328	71-69-75-74–289
Ed Fiori, $2,328	69-73-72-75–289
Paul Goydos, $2,328	69-68-75-77–289
Mark Lye, $2,244	69-73-76-72–290
Ted Tryba, $2,244	73-68-73-76–290
David Delong, $2,208	73-68-72-80–293
Lon Hinkle, $2,184	71-70-79-83–303

GTE Byron Nelson Classic

AT A GLANCE

- **Course:** TPC at Las Colinas
- **Location:** Irving, Texas
- **When:** May 13-16, 1993
- **Weather:** Sunny and warm.
- **Purse:** $1.2 million
- **Par:** 70
- **Yards:** 6,742
- **Defending champion:** Billy Ray Brown
- **Tournament record:** 15-under-par 265, Jodie Mudd, 1989

Scott Simpson staggered through the four last holes but managed to knock in a 12-foot par putt on the final hole to win the GTE Byron Nelson Classic and end a four-year victory drought.

Simpson called his grind-it-out victory "a real struggle, a struggle all the way."

After the winning putt, Simpson sank to his knees in relief and celebration. His 1-over-par 71 gave him a 270 total, a stroke ahead of Billy Mayfair.

The 1987 U.S. Open champion's sixth PGA Tour victory in 15 years was worth $216,000.

"When you're trying to win a tournament, particularly when you haven't won in so long, the money doesn't even enter into it," he said.

Simpson built a 4-shot lead with an eagle-3, blew it, rebuilt a 2-shot advantage, then made the critical 12-footer — one of 12-one-putt greens on the day — to avoid a four-man playoff.

Three one-putt pars came from 4-6 feet. An 8-footer to save bogey after he hit into the water on the third hole was very important. The 2-footer to save bogey and a 1-stroke lead on 17 was vital. The 15-footer for eagle on No.7 was critical, too.

"My putter saved me," said Simpson, who hit only four of 14 fairways and six of 18 greens. "I didn't play very well."

Scores and earnings

Player	Earnings	Scores	Total
Scott Simpson	$216,000	65-66-68-71	270
Corey Pavin	$89,600	69-68-67-67	271
D.A. Weibring	$89,600	68-65-69-69	271
Billy Mayfair	$89,600	71-61-69-70	271
Fred Couples	$43,800	71-63-70-68	272
Payne Stewart	$43,800	70-66-68-68	272
David Frost	$43,800	68-66-69-69	272
Mark Calcavecchia	$34,800	67-65-74-67	273
Ray Floyd	$34,800	66-69-70-68	273
Larry Rinker	$34,800	68-69-67-69	273
Dennis Trixler	$22,400	67-69-73-65	274
Hale Irwin	$22,400	66-72-69-67	274
Donnie Hammond	$22,400	71-64-71-68	274
Fulton Allem	$22,400	69-67-70-68	274
Larry Mize	$22,400	70-67-68-69	274
Doug Tewell	$22,400	68-66-70-70	274
Nick Price	$22,400	68-67-68-71	274
Davis Love III	$22,400	68-66-69-71	274
John Cook	$22,400	67-68-67-72	274
Dillard Pruitt	$13,000	71-69-69-66	275
Tim Simpson	$13,000	69-71-67-68	275
Gil Morgan	$13,000	73-66-66-70	275
Bob Estes	$13,000	69-69-67-70	275
Tom Watson	$13,000	68-67-68-72	275
Dan Forsman	$13,000	65-64-72-74	275
John Inman	$8,520	70-71-70-65	276
Jeff Cook	$8,520	74-66-71-65	276
Russ Cochran	$8,520	70-70-68-68	276
Jaime Gomez	$8,520	74-66-68-68	276
Loren Roberts	$8,520	68-67-70-71	276
Ed Fiori	$8,520	70-68-66-72	276
Jay Don Blake	$8,520	69-69-65-73	276
Nolan Henke	$5,820	67-74-71-65	277
Ben Crenshaw	$5,820	70-69-73-65	277
Mark Wiebe	$5,820	74-67-69-67	277
Brandel Chamblee	$5,820	70-69-70-68	277
David Peoples	$5,820	72-66-70-69	277
Russell Beiersdorf	$5,820	65-70-72-70	277
Greg Twiggs	$5,820	68-67-71-71	277
Steve Lowery	$5,820	72-67-67-71	277
Blaine McCallister	$5,820	71-66-69-71	277
Bruce Lietzke	$5,820	71-62-70-74	277
Jay Delsing	$3,744	71-70-70-67	278
John Dowdall	$3,744	69-70-72-67	278
Steve Elkington	$3,744	73-68-69-68	278
Tom Sieckmann	$3,744	71-67-72-68	278
Dudley Hart	$3,744	71-68-68-71	278
Brad Bryant	$3,744	69-66-71-72	278
Trevor Dodds	$3,744	69-67-64-78	278
Brian Kamm	$2,872	73-67-71-68	279
Gary Hallberg	$2,872	71-69-71-68	279
Mark Brooks	$2,872	70-69-71-69	279
Michael Bradley	$2,872	70-71-66-72	279
Bob Lohr	$2,872	70-69-69-71	279
Howard Twitty	$2,872	66-73-67-73	279
Lennie Clements	$2,712	67-68-77-68	280
Brian Henninger	$2,712	72-67-70-71	280
Brian Claar	$2,712	69-67-71-73	280
#Justin Leonard		70-67-68-75	280
Mike Schuchart	$2,640	71-69-71-70	281
Dave Peege	$2,640	71-64-74-72	281
Mark Hayes	$2,640	70-67-71-73	281
Mike Smith	$2,556	72-69-72-69	282
Jay Haas	$2,556	70-71-70-71	282
Harry Taylor	$2,556	71-69-70-72	282
Perry Moss	$2,556	72-66-72-72	282
Ted Schulz	$2,460	70-69-74-70	283
Jim McGovern	$2,460	72-67-72-72	283
Marco Dawson	$2,460	70-70-69-74	283
Tom Lehman	$2,460	71-67-69-76	283
John Mahaffey	$2,388	73-68-72-71	284
Steve Lamontagne	$2,388	71-70-69-74	284
Hal Sutton	$2,328	70-71-72-72	285
Tom Purtzer	$2,328	69-72-74-70	285
Neal Lancaster	$2,328	73-68-72-72	285
Paul Goydos	$2,268	72-69-75-71	287
Len Mattiace	$2,268	76-64-70-77	287

- amateur

Kemper Open

AT A GLANCE

- **Course:** TPC at Avenel
- **Location:** Potomac, Md.
- **When:** May 20-23, 1993
- **Weather:** Sunny, windy and cool Thursday. Sunny and pleasant throughout the weekend except for a 20-minute interruption of play Saturday because of lightning in the area.
- **Purse:** $1.3 million
- **Par:** 71
- **Yards:** 7,005
- **Defending champion:** Bill Glasson
- **Tournament record:** 21-under-par 263, Billy Andrade, 1991

New Zealander Grant Waite made the shot of his life to change his life by winning the Kemper Open.

After going head-to-head with Tom Kite for two days—a young non-winner against the U.S. Open champion—it came down to a bunker shot on the final hole.

Kite was on the green, looking at a 20-foot birdie attempt. Waite, with a one-shot lead, had hit a 7-iron fat into a deep green-side bunker. He blasted within 18 inches and tapped in for his first PGA Tour victory.

"That was the best bunker shot I've ever hit in my life," Waite said of the 45-foot shot. "After that, even as nervous as I was, I could wiggle it in."

For Waite, 28, his final-round 70 and 9-under-par 275 at the TPC at Avenel opened many doors—a two-year Tour exemption, invitations to the Masters and the NEC World Series of Golf.

For Kite, 43, his 1-over-par 72 was a bitter disappointment in his second tournament after returning from a back injury. But it proved that he had recovered and was primed for the defense of his U.S. Open championship.

—by Steve Hershey

Scores and earnings

Player	Earnings	Scores
Grant Waite	$234,000	66-67-72-70—275
Tom Kite	$140,400	70-65-69-72—276
Scott Hoch	$75,400	70-69-70-68—277
Michael Bradley	$75,400	69-71-69-68—277
Bob Estes	$52,000	68-70-74-66—278
J.C. Anderson	$46,800	68-73-68-70—279
Billy Mayfair	$40,517	70-69-72-69—280
Craig Parry	$40,517	71-69-71-69—280
Lee Janzen	$40,517	71-67-70-72—280
Morris Hatalsky	$31,200	72-66-75-68—281
Ed Fiori	$31,200	67-73-70-71—281
Tommy Armour III	$31,200	68-71-70-72—281
John Inman	$31,200	71-68-69-73—281
Mark Carnevale	$24,050	69-70-71-72—282
Tim Conley	$24,050	68-69-72-73—282
Bob Gilder	$21,450	71-69-72-71—283
Peter Jacobsen	$21,450	69-71-71-72—283
Jeff Maggert	$17,550	67-70-76-71—284
Howard Twitty	$17,550	70-71-72-71—284
Jim Hallet	$17,550	69-69-73-73—284
Jay Delsing	$17,550	69-71-68-76—284
Dave Barr	$10,600	69-72-74-70—285
Donnie Hammond	$10,600	70-72-73-70—285
Curtis Strange	$10,600	71-70-73-71—285
Dave DeLong	$10,600	70-72-72-71—285
Tom Sieckmann	$10,600	69-73-72-71—285
Jeff Sluman	$10,600	72-69-72-72—285
Jeff Cook	$10,600	74-65-73-73—285
Frank Conner	$10,600	69-74-69-73—285
David Toms	$10,600	67-72-72-74—285
David Ogrin	$10,600	69-68-72-76—285
Steve Lamontagne	$10,600	69-68-71-77—285
Bob Lohr	$7,020	69-70-79-68—286
Jay Haas	$7,020	71-68-75-72—286
Patrick Burke	$7,020	71-73-71-71—286
Skip Kendall	$7,020	72-70-72-72—286
Rick Dalpos	$7,020	69-71-73-73—286
Trevor Dodds	$4,940	70-73-74-70—287
Fred Funk	$4,940	71-73-73-70—287
Ian Baker-Finch	$4,940	73-71-73-70—287
Tim Simpson	$4,940	67-76-73-71—287
Dick Mast	$4,940	73-68-74-72—287
Wayne Levi	$4,940	68-74-73-72—287
John Flannery	$4,940	75-69-70-73—287
Neal Lancaster	$4,940	74-70-69-73—287
Kelly Gibson	$4,940	67-70-74-76—287
Brett Ogle	$4,940	70-71-70-76—287
Don Pooley	$3,471	72-70-73-73—288
Ronnie Black	$3,471	71-69-74-74—288
Bobby Clampett	$3,136	70-72-77-70—289
Mike Donald	$3,136	72-70-74-73—289
John Ross	$3,136	69-74-71-75—289
Russell Beiersdorf	$3,136	71-71-71-76—289
Barry Cheesman	$3,136	71-68-73-77—289
Blaine McCallister	$2,951	74-68-78-7—290
Steve Lowery	$2,951	70-73-77-70—290
Billy Andrade	$2,951	71-70-76-73—290
Ed Humenik	$2,951	72-71-74-73—290
Mark Calcavecchia	$2,886	73-69-74-75—291
Len Mattiace	$2,821	71-71-78-72—292
Ed Dougherty	$2,821	71-72-75-74—292
Mike Hulbert	$2,821	72-72-73-75—292
Brad Faxon	$2,821	68-71-76-77—292
Andy Bean	$2,730	72-71-78-72—293
Gene Jones	$2,730	70-73-77-73—293
Mike Sullivan	$2,730	73-70-73-77—293
John Elliott	$2,626	71-72-78-73—294
Robert Gamez	$2,626	69-71-78-76—294
Harry Taylor	$2,626	72-70-76-76—294
Tony Sills	$2,626	68-76-74-76—294
Marco Dawson	$2,626	72-71-75-76—294
Joey Sindelar	$2,548	73-70-77-75—295
Jay Overton	$2,522	70-74-78-76—298
Greg Kraft	$2,496	70-73-82-75—300

SOUTHWESTERN BELL COLONIAL

AT A GLANCE

- **Course:** Colonial Country Club
- **Location:** Fort Worth, Texas
- **When:** May 27-30, 1993
- **Weather:** Seasonably warm and windy.
- **Purse:** $1.3 million
- **Par:** 70
- **Yards:** 7,010
- **Defending champion:** Bruce Lietzke defeated Corey Pavin on the first playoff hole after they tied at 13-under-par 267.
- **Tournament record:** 16-under-par 264, Fulton Allem, 1993

After scattering golf balls among trees and rock walls, Fulton Allem sank pressure putts on the final three holes to defeat Greg Norman and win the Southwestern Bell Colonial.

The wisecracking South African fired a final round 3-under-par 67, nipping Norman by a shot.

"I hung in there," sighed Allem, who collected his second PGA Tour title in six years. "That's all I can say."

His record 264 total was 16 strokes under par for four trips around a Colonial Country Club course that was left defenseless by firm fairways, rain-softened greens, short rough, and uncommonly gentle breezes.

A dozen records fell, including the course record of 62. Norman's finishing 68 gave him a 265 that also bettered the tournament record of 266 shared by Corey Pavin and Keith Clearwater.

When it counted, Allem sank birdie putts of 12 and 10 feet at the 16th and 17th holes and two-putted from 65 feet at the 18th.

"How long was that putt?" someone asked.

"From here to Alabama," he replied.

Scores and earnings

Player	Earnings	Scores
Fulton Allem	$234,000	66-63-68-67–264
Greg Norman	$140,400	69-64-64-68–265
Jeff Maggert	$88,400	65-68-68-66–267
Duffy Waldorf	$57,200	65-69-69-65–268
Loren Roberts	$57,200	66-70-66-66–268
Tom Watson	$43,550	69-64-71-65–269
John Huston	$43,550	66-70-66-67–269
David Edwards	$43,550	69-67-63-70–269
Corey Pavin	$36,400	70-65-67-68–270
Keith Clearwater	$36,400	71-61-69-69–270
Lee Janzen	$26,650	70-65-75-61–271
Gil Morgan	$26,650	67-69-69-66–271
Hale Irwin	$26,650	68-66-69-68–271
D.A. Weibring	$26,650	66-68-68-69–271
Mark Calcavecchia	$26,650	69-64-69-69–271
Tom Lehman	$26,650	72-65-65-69–271
David Frost	$20,800	68-66-71-67–272
Wayne Levi	$18,850	71-68-71-63–273
Rick Fehr	$18,850	68-71-66-68–273
Russ Cochran	$16,250	66-67-77-64–274
Mark Brooks	$16,250	72-66-68-68–274
Jim Thorpe	$12,480	73-68-67-67–275
Billy Mayfair	$12,480	71-68-67-69–275
Kirk Triplett	$12,480	71-68-67-69–275
Dan Forsman	$12,480	68-69-67-71–275
Dick Mast	$12,480	64-66-69-76–275
Mike Hulbert	$9,035	68-73-72-63–276
Fred Funk	$9,035	70-71-71-64–276
Bill Glasson	$9,035	67-70-74-65–276
Craig Parry	$9,035	69-69-70-68–276
Craig Stadler	$9,035	69-68-70-69–276
Massy Kuramoto	$9,035	73-67-65-71–276
Bruce Lietzke	$6,034	69-72-70-66–277
Dudley Hart	$6,034	71-69-71-66–277
Jay Don Blake	$6,034	71-71-69-66–277
Roger Maltbie	$6,034	68-68-73-68–277
Mark Wiebe	$6,034	68-71-70-68–277
Ian Baker-Finch	$6,034	74-67-68-68–277
Bill Britton	$6,034	70-66-72-69–277
Ben Crenshaw	$6,034	72-69-68-68–277
Fuzzy Zoeller	$6,034	69-68-70-70–277
Bruce Fleisher	$6,034	71-71-65-70–277
Kenny Perry	$6,034	70-70-66-71–277
Greg Kraft	$6,034	71-66-68-72–277
Steve Elkington	$3,578	70-68-74-66–278
Ted Schulz	$3,578	71-69-70-68–278
Michael Allen	$3,578	74-68-68-68–278
Jodie Mudd	$3,578	72-68-68-70–278
Larry Mize	$3,578	68-71-69-70–278
Nick Price	$3,578	69-70-68-71–278
Gene Sauers	$3,578	68-69-69-72–278
Clark Dennis	$3,578	70-67-68-73–278
Brad Fabel	$2,995	73-69-69-68–279
Brad Faxon	$2,995	69-73-68-69–279
Blaine McCallister	$2,995	70-70-69-70–279
Russell Beiersdorf	$2,995	72-68-69-70–279
Brian Claar	$2,995	69-68-71-71–279
Tom Kite	$2,912	72-66-71-71–280
Greg Twiggs	$2,873	72-69-69-71–281
Stan Utley	$2,873	72-69-69-71–281
Phil Blackmar	$2,795	68-74-72-68–282
Steve Pate	$2,795	67-72-76-67–282
Jim Mcgovern	$2,795	72-70-70-70–282
Gary Hallberg	$2,795	71-70-70-71–282
Davis Love III	$2,678	72-70-72-69–283
Tom Byrum	$2,678	72-70-72-69–283
Dave Barr	$2,678	68-72-73-70–283
Ed Dougherty	$2,678	75-67-71-70–283
Brett Ogle	$2,678	70-71-70-72–283
Wayne Grady	$2,600	73-69-69-73–284
Mark O'Meara	$2,561	69-71-73-73–286
Justin Leonard		73-69-72-72–286
Steve Lowery	$2,561	73-68-70-75–286
Jim Gallagher	$2,522	71-68-73-75–287
Tad Rhyan	$2,496	70-71-72-75–288
Mark Hayes	$2,470	69-72-72-77–290

MEMORIAL TOURNAMENT

AT A GLANCE

- **Course:** Muirfield Village Golf Club
- **Location:** Dublin, Ohio
- **When:** June 3-6, 1993
- **Weather:** Rainy and cool the first three days with play interrupted Friday; some clearing Saturday, clear and sunny Sunday.
- **Purse:** $1.4 million
- **Par:** 72
- **Yards:** 7,104
- **Defending champion:** David Edwards
- **Tournament record:** 15-under-par 273, Kenny Perry, 1991, and David Edwards, 1992

After hitting the greatest shot of his life, Paul Azinger cried.

"I had tears in my eyes before I came out of the bunker," Azinger said after sinking a sand shot on the final hole to steal the Memorial from friend and playing partner Payne Stewart.

Try as he might, Azinger couldn't stop the tears. He remembered what he felt watching Bob Tway hole out from a bunker on the last hole of the 1986 PGA Championship to break Greg Norman's heart.

"I remember when Bob won the PGA and he was bawling and I thought, 'What a baby!'" Azinger said with a laugh. "But I couldn't help it. It was such a shock for it to go in. And then my best friend on the tour is out there and I've done it to him. It was really hard."

Azinger's shot gave him a birdie on the par-4 final hole and a 1-stroke victory over Corey Pavin. It was the most dramatic stroke of Azinger's career and left Stewart—who wound up three-putting the hole—shaken.

"It's just part of the business; you've got to take the good with the bad," Stewart said. "Hopefully, I'll learn something from this today. I don't know what it could be, but I'll think of something."

Scores and earnings

Player	Earnings	Scores	Total
Paul Azinger	$252,000	68-69-68-69	274
Corey Pavin	$151,200	69-70-69-67	275
Payne Stewart	$95,200	69-66-67-74	276
Greg Norman	$50,750	68-68-74-67	277
Jumbo Ozaki	$50,750	67-70-73-67	277
Jay Haas	$50,750	67-70-72-68	277
Brad Faxon	$50,750	69-69-70-69	277
Fred Couples	$50,750	67-68-73-69	277
Jim McGovern	$50,750	67-71-69-70	277
Bill Glasson	$36,400	69-69-68-72	278
Davis Love III	$36,400	66-72-69-71	278
Jeff Maggert	$28,350	73-72-68-67	280
John Cook	$28,350	67-73-71-69	280
Michael Allen	$28,350	70-72-70-68	280
Wayne Levi	$28,350	68-69-72-71	280
Fuzzy Zoeller	$22,400	71-69-73-68	281
Dudley Hart	$22,400	67-71-70-73	281
Vijay Singh	$22,400	71-69-68-73	281
Greg Twiggs	$18,200	70-69-71-72	282
Kenny Perry	$18,200	67-74-69-72	282
Ben Crenshaw	$18,200	70-69-71-72	282
Phil Mickelson	$14,560	73-70-72-68	283
D.A. Weibring	$14,560	72-70-72-69	283
Donnie Hammond	$14,560	66-76-69-72	283
David Frost	$10,920	75-69-71-69	284
Joey Sindelar	$10,920	70-72-73-69	284
Scott Hoch	$10,920	71-70-73-70	284
Mark Wiebe	$10,920	69-71-73-71	284
Bobby Wadkins	$10,920	68-72-72-72	284
Phil Blackmar	$8,890	69-74-72-70	285
Grant Waite	$8,890	69-72-74-70	285
Brian Claar	$8,890	70-69-74-72	285
Rocco Mediate	$8,890	69-71-73-72	285
Chip Beck	$7,070	71-73-74-68	286
Steve Pate	$7,070	70-72-74-70	286
Keith Clearwater	$7,070	70-73-72-71	286
Loren Roberts	$7,070	72-69-74-71	286
Mike Hulbert	$7,070	69-72-74-71	286
Peter Jacobsen	$7,070	72-70-71-73	286
Craig Stadler	$5,040	73-72-73-69	287
Ted Schulz	$5,040	70-71-77-69	287
Russ Cochran	$5,040	70-74-72-71	287
Dillard Pruitt	$5,040	70-74-72-71	287
Ian Baker-Finch	$5,040	75-69-72-71	287
Billy Andrade	$5,040	71-72-72-72	287
Mike Standly	$5,040	69-72-74-72	287
Brad Fabel	$5,040	70-71-73-73	287
Dave Rummells	$3,738	68-73-77-70	288
John Huston	$3,738	70-73-73-72	288
Lee Janzen	$3,328	72-69-78-70	289
David Edwards	$3,328	69-75-74-71	289
Tommy Nakajima	$3,328	70-73-74-72	289
Bob Estes	$3,328	72-71-73-73	289
Joe Ozaki	$3,328	67-73-76-73	289
Michael Bradley	$3,328	72-66-76-75	289
John Mahaffey	$3,328	71-74-69-75	289
Curtis Strange	$3,136	72-72-76-70	290
Scott Simpson	$3,136	75-70-74-71	290
Gary Hallberg	$3,136	70-72-73-75	290
Mark McCumber	$3,066	73-72-75-71	291
Larry Nelson	$3,066	71-74-72-74	291
Lanny Wadkins	$3,024	73-72-73-74	292
Jay Don Blake	$2,982	71-74-76-72	293
Dave Barr	$2,982	68-73-73-79	293
Dan Forsman	$2,940	72-71-77-74	294
Gil Morgan	$2,884	72-73-75-75	295
Mark O'Meara	$2,884	70-71-77-77	295
Robert Gamez	$2,884	70-72-76-77	295
David Peoples	$2,828	70-75-76-75	296
Don Pooley	$2,786	74-71-78-74	297
John Daly	$2,786	70-70-79-78	297
Jack Nicklaus	$2,744	70-75-81-72	298
Andrew Magee	$2,716	72-73-81-74	300

Buick Classic

AT A GLANCE

- **Course:** Westchester Country Club
- **Location:** Harrison, N.Y.
- **When:** June 10-13, 1993
- **Weather:** Hot and humid Thursday; cooler and pleasant through the weekend.
- **Purse:** $1 million
- **Par:** 71
- **Yards:** 6,779
- **Playoff:** Vijay Singh defeated Mark Wiebe on the third playoff hole.
- **Defending champion:** David Frost
- **Tournament record:** 19-under-par 261 (course then par 70), Bob Gilder, 1982

Vijay Singh, a native of Fiji who once worked as a club pro in the rain forests of Borneo, won his first PGA Tour tournament.

Singh, who previously practiced his craft on the Safari circuit and the Asian and European tours, defeated Mark Wiebe with a birdie on the third playoff hole at the Buick Classic.

Singh has won 13 other times, most recently in South Africa. But it almost certainly was his most important victory, and most welcome.

"Coming here from Europe, I thought it would be very difficult to win in America," said Singh, who began his career on the Asian circuit at age 17. "I think this came a little bit early.

"They say you have to win in the States to really make it. Now I've done that."

Singh survived a shaky finish in regulation and a first-hole playoff scare when Wiebe missed an 8-foot putt to win.

On the third extra hole, the par-4 11th, Singh's approach hit the front-left of the green, ran to the back, caught a slope and trickled within 4 feet of the flag. After Wiebe two-putted from 35 feet, Singh rapped his into the back of the cup for the biggest win of his career.

Scores and earnings

#Vijay Singh, $180,000	72-68-74-66	280
Mark Wiebe, $108,000	72-75-67-66	280
David Frost, $58,000	70-72-73-66	281
Lee Janzen, $58,000	69-72-68-72	281
Mike Smith, $38,000	72-73-69-68	282
Tom Lehman, $38,000	74-69-70-69	282
Chip Beck, $31,167	71-72-74-66	283
Payne Stewart, $31,167	74-72-68-69	283
Bob Gilder, $31,167	72-72-69-70	283
Fred Funk, $25,000	69-75-71-69	284
Tom Kite, $25,000	68-71-75-70	284
Duffy Waldorf, $25,000	69-70-70-75	284
Brad Faxon, $19,333	69-77-71-68	285
Paul Goydos, $19,333	73-73-68-71	285
Ian Baker-Finch, $19,333	71-72-69-73	285
Steve Lamontagne, $14,500	74-73-71-68	286
Andy North, $14,500	74-70-72-70	286
Doug Tewell, $14,500	74-71-69-72	286
Fred Couples, $14,500	72-69-72-73	286
Phil Blackmar, $14,500	75-71-67-73	286
Loren Roberts, $14,500	72-69-71-74	286
Bill Britton, $10,000	73-74-71-69	287
Dave Barr, $10,000	77-67-72-71	287
Willie Wood, $10,000	72-71-72-72	287
Jeff Woodland, $10,000	73-71-70-73	287
Rocco Mediate, $7,400	77-69-73-69	288
Corey Pavin, $7,400	73-74-72-69	288
Mike Standly, $7,400	74-70-72-72	288
Larry Rinker, $7,400	72-74-70-72	288
Steve Elkington, $7,400	75-72-67-74	288
Lennie Clements, $6,200	74-73-72-70	289
David Ogrin, $6,200	75-69-72-73	289
Mike Hulbert, $6,200	74-73-69-73	289
Morris Hatalsky, $5,275	75-71-73-71	290
Brandel Chamblee, $5,275	67-74-76-73	290
Mark Brooks, $5,275	76-67-73-74	290
Bob Tway, $5,275	68-74-72-76	290
Ted Schulz, $4,200	76-71-73-71	291
Brad Fabel, $4,200	72-74-73-72	291
P.H. Horgan III, $4,200	74-73-71-73	291
Mark McCumber, $4,200	73-73-71-74	291
Dudley Hart, $4,200	66-77-72-76	291
Jeff Maggert, $4,200	71-68-74-78	291
Peter Persons, $2,890	74-70-75-73	292
Hal Sutton, $2,890	75-70-74-73	292
Colin Montgomerie, $2,890	76-71-72-73	292
Skip Kendall, $2,890	73-72-72-75	292
Robin Freeman, $2,890	72-74-71-75	292
Trevor Dodds, $2,890	74-70-71-77	292
Mike Donald, $2,890	75-69-71-77	292
Bruce Fleisher, $2,890	73-72-70-77	292
Jim McGovern, $2,360	76-71-73-73	293
Michael Allen, $2,360	73-74-71-75	293
Massy Kuramoto, $2,360	70-76-70-77	293
Bill Murchison, $2,260	74-73-77-70	294
John Flannery, $2,260	73-72-77-72	294
Scott Simpson, $2,260	74-73-76-71	294
Brian Claar, $2,260	75-72-72-75	294
Marco Dawson, $2,260	71-74-73-76	294
Len Mattiace, $2,180	75-72-75-73	295
Barry Cheesman, $2,180	73-73-74-75	295
Jeff Sluman, $2,180	73-72-71-79	295
Patrick Burke, $2,100	71-74-79-73	297
Brian Kamm, $2,100	75-68-80-74	297
Jay Delsing, $2,100	70-74-76-77	297
Mark Mielke, $2,100	73-73-73-78	297
Jay Haas, $2,100	70-75-70-82	297
Roger Maltbie, $2,040	75-72-77-74	298
Wayne Levi, $2,020	71-74-78-78	301
Greg Cesario, $2,000	73-74-77-83	307
Dennis Trixler, $1,980	73-74-79-82	308

- won on third playoff hole.

Canon Greater Hartford Open

At a Glance

- **Course:** TPC at River Highlands
- **Location:** Cromwell, Conn.
- **When:** June 24-27, 1993
- **Weather:** Sunny and seasonably warm, strong winds, calming Sunday when early rain delayed play for a half-hour.
- **Purse:** $1 million
- **Par:** 70
- **Yards:** 6,820
- **Defending champion:** Lanny Wadkins
- **Tournament record:** 25-under-par 259, Tim Norris, Weathersfield (Conn.) CC, 1982

Scores and earnings (partial)

Player	Earnings	Scores
Nick Price	$180,000	67-70-69-65–271
Dan Forsman	$88,000	66-69-72-65–272
Roger Maltbie	$88,000	65-71-71-65–272
Corey Pavin	$48,000	67-65-73-69–274
Mike Springer	$38,000	69-65-73-68–275
Kenny Perry	$38,000	68-69-70-68–275
Brian Kamm	$30,125	69-75-69-64–277
John Cook	$30,125	73-68-71-65–277
Rocco Mediate	$30,125	68-70-72-67–277
Don Pooley	$30,125	70-70-66-71–277
Bruce Fleisher	$21,200	71-65-73-69–278
Davis Love III	$21,200	72-70-68-68–278
Scott Gump	$21,200	73-67-69-69–278
Frank Conner	$21,200	71-70-68-69–278
John Huston	$21,200	66-69-72-71–278
Brad Faxon	$15,500	67-71-75-66–279
Dave Peege	$15,500	71-70-72-66–279
Keith Clearwater	$15,500	66-68-73-72–279
Steve Lowery	$15,500	67-68-72-72–279
Hubert Green	$10,833	70-70-72-68–280
Patrick Burke	$10,833	68-72-72-68–280
Lance Ten Broeck	$10,833	69-68-74-69–280
Jeff Sluman	$10,833	74-68-69-69–280
Fulton Allem	$10,833	70-66-74-70–280
Chris Tucker	$10,833	70-72-68-70–280
Dudley Hart	$7,550	71-70-71-69–281
Bill Kratzert	$7,550	71-67-73-70–281
Bob Lohr	$7,550	67-73-70-71–281
Kirk Triplett	$7,550	68-69-72-72–281
Bruce Zabriski	$5,813	74-69-72-67–282
Howard Twitty	$5,813	73-66-74-69–282
Jeff Woodland	$5,813	71-71-71-69–282
Craig Stadler	$5,813	65-71-76-70–282
P.H. Horgan III	$5,813	72-71-68-71–282
Brad Bryant	$5,813	70-72-69-71–282
Ted Tryba	$5,813	75-69-67-71–282
Mark Calcavecchia	$5,813	67-71-70-74–282
Kelly Gibson	$3,800	71-70-75-67–283
David Duval	$3,800	70-72-73-68–283
David Ogrin	$3,800	72-71-72-68–283
Brian Claar	$3,800	71-69-74-69–283
Jay Haas	$3,800	70-72-71-70–283
Jay Overton	$3,800	70-69-73-71–283
Doug Tewell	$3,800	71-70-71-71–283
John Ross	$3,800	74-67-71-71–283
Harry Taylor	$3,800	71-73-68-71–283

Player Spotlight

Nick Price will be forever grateful fellow countryman Denis Watson was making a rare PGA Tour appearance at the Canon Greater Hartford Open.

Price had been in a three-month dilemma about which putter to use. After a discouraging second-round 70 at River Highlands, he still was in a quandary.

Watson, who like Price grew up in Zimbabwe, offered to loan Price a putter, and that was the difference in his one-shot victory.

Price's problems started when he signed with Ram Golf in 1992 to play its irons. But instead of using the Zebra, its popular mallet-headed putter, Price wanted to continue using his Ray Cook M1-X.

After his victory at the PGA Championship, the Cook Co. ran ads that read, "The Zebra Lost Its Stripes," referring to the fact Price rejected the Ram putter. After Price won the Players, Cook ran ads saying "Ray Cook Wins The TPC."

Price was so upset with the ad campaign he decided to stop using the Cook putter. He had another putter made, using much of the same material as the M1-X, but with a slightly different look.

The Tuesday before the U.S. Open, Price received a letter from Cook's lawyer stating if he used the new putter, there would be legal action.

A perplexed Price took the putter out of his bag and used a Pyramid putter he's had for years but rarely used. Price took 15 more putts than Janzen at the Open and lost by 8 shots, though his ball-striking was excellent.

Said a relieved Price: "I'm just glad I found another putter."

—*by Steve Hershey*

Sprint Western Open

AT A GLANCE

- **Course:** Cog Hill Golf and Country Club, Dubsdread Course
- **Location:** Lemont, Ill.
- **When:** July 1-4, 1993
- **Weather:** Cloudy Thursday and Friday, with a 2½-hour rain delay that caused the second round to be postponed overnight with 49 players still on the course. Hot and humid for the weekend; windy Sunday.
- **Purse:** $1.1 million
- **Par:** 72
- **Yards:** 7,073
- **Defending champion:** Ben Crenshaw, 12-under-par 276
- **Tournament record:** 13-under-par 275, Russ Cochran, 1991 (at Cog Hill)

Nick Price won his second PGA Tour tournament in a row and became the year's first three-time winner in a dominating wire-to-wire victory.

With six birdies and one bogey in the Western's final round, Price ended at 19-under-par 269, one stroke off the tournament record.

"I'm still trying to figure out if that was me out there," Price said. "I can honestly say I didn't have one bad break."

Greg Norman, who finished five strokes back, described Price's play succinctly.

"You'd have to put him as the best player in the world right now," Norman said. "I played like a 27-handicapper against Nicky. He blew me out of the water, simple as that."

Norman continued his inauspicious record in the Western. He was second for the third consecutive year and fifth time in nine Western starts. Even so, he still has his sense of humor.

"Maybe I shouldn't come back to (suburban) Chicago," Norman joked. "Sure, it's frustrating, but what am I going to say? 'I'm not going to come back?' I like it here."

—by Jerry Bonkowski

Scores and earnings

Player	Rounds-Total
Nick Price, $216,000	64-71-67-67–269
Greg Norman, $129,600	69-68-67-70–274
Bob Lohr, $81,600	72-69-67-69–277
Brian Henninger, $49,600	71-73-66-68–278
Mark Wiebe, $49,600	65-73-71-69–278
John Adams, $49,600	72-71-63-72–278
P.H. Horgan III, $33,700	69-74-68-68–279
Rick Fehr, $33,700	71-68-71-69–279
Michael Allen, $33,700	71-68-70-70–279
Dan Forsman, $33,700	67-73-69-70–279
Doug Tewell, $33,700	70-69-68-72–279
Curtis Strange, $33,700	69-68-69-73–279
D.A. Weibring, $21,200	68-75-70-67–280
John Huston, $21,200	70-67-74-69–280
Dillard Pruitt, $21,200	75-69-66-70–280
Mark Brooks, $21,200	69-71-69-71–280
Dudley Hart, $21,200	73-66-69-72–280
Larry Nelson, $21,200	70-70-67-73–280
Lance Ten Broeck, $14,040	71-68-72-70–281
Russ Cochran, $14,040	67-75-69-70–281
Bruce Fleisher, $14,040	74-67-69-71–281
Keith Clearwater, $14,040	67-71-71-72–281
Loren Roberts, $14,040	70-69-69-73–281
Chip Beck, $14,040	69-71-68-73–281
Mark Lye, $9,570	72-71-70-70–283
Fred Couples, $9,570	68-72-70-73–283
Mark McCumber, $9,570	69-71-70-73–283
#Justin Leonard	70-71-69-73–283
Mike Hulbert, $9,570	67-70-72-74–283
Tom Byrum, $7,466	72-72-71-69–284
Jeff Sluman, $7,466	73-68-74-69–284
Ted Schulz, $7,466	71-72-71-70–284
Jaime Gomez, $7,466	71-72-69-72–284
David Duval, $7,466	72-70-69-73–284
Tom Sieckmann, $7,466	69-72-69-74–284
Greg Kraft, $7,466	68-72-68-76–284
Trevor Dodds, $5,530	72-69-72-72–285
John Flannery, $5,530	72-69-72-72–285
Dan Pohl, $5,530	69-70-73-73–285
Brian Kamm, $5,530	67-71-73-74–285
Steve Lamontagne, $5,530	70-72-69-74–285
Don Pooley, $5,530	70-69-70-76–285
Robin Freeman, $3,967	72-72-71-71–286
Russell Beiersdorf, $3,967	67-72-76-71–286
Howard Twitty, $3,967	71-70-74-71–286
JC Anderson, $3,967	72-70-72-72–286
Tim Conley, $3,967	71-71-71-73–286
Andrew Magee, $3,967	68-75-69-74–286
Paul Goydos, $3,967	70-72-70-74–286
Dennis Trixler, $2,867	74-70-74-69–287
John Elliott, $2,867	70-73-75-69–287
Hale Irwin, $2,867	72-71-74-70–287
Kelly Gibson, $2,867	69-74-73-71–287
Ed Humenik, $2,867	70-74-71-72–287
Jeff Cook, $2,867	71-73-70-73–287
Phil Blackmar, $2,867	71-72-69-75–287
Grant Waite, $2,867	68-71-72-76–287
Mark Carnevale, $2,867	70-71-70-76–287
Scott Hoch, $2,640	71-68-76-73–288
Mark Calcavecchia, $2,640	70-73-71-74–288
Mike Springer, $2,640	72-69-73-74–288
Duffy Waldorf, $2,640	71-71-71-75–288
Tim Simpson, $2,640	73-67-72-76–288
Greg Twiggs, $2,532	75-69-73-72–289
Barry Cheesman, $2,532	70-74-71-74–289
Joel Edwards, $2,532	72-71-72-74–289
Richard Zokol, $2,532	72-70-70-77–289
Ben Crenshaw, $2,436	74-69-75-72–290
Nolan Henke, $2,436	71-70-76-73–290
Willie Wood, $2,436	73-68-74-75–290
Brian Claar, $2,436	72-71-71-76–290
Robert Gamez, $2,352	69-75-76-71–291
Skip Kendall, $2,352	72-72-75-72–291
David Ogrin, $2,352	71-71-72-77–291
Yoshinori Kaneko, $2,268	68-73-79-72–292
Fred Funk, $2,268	71-72-75-74–292
Billy Mayfair, $2,268	73-71-72-76–292
Marco Dawson, $2,268	73-70-72-77–292
Dan Halldorson, $2,208	70-74-76-73–293
Mike Schuchart, $2,172	71-73-77-73–294
Ed Fiori, $2,172	71-71-76-76–294
Eddie Pearce, $2,136	74-70-77-77–298

- amateur

Anheuser-Busch Golf Classic

AT A GLANCE

- **Course:** Kingsmill Golf Club
- **Location:** Williamsburg, Va.
- **When:** July 8-11, 1993
- **Weather:** Hot and humid.
- **Purse:** $1.1 million
- **Par:** 71
- **Yards:** 6,797
- **Defending champion:** David Peoples, 13-under-par 271
- **Tournament record:** 18-under-par 266, Lanny Wadkins, 1990, and Mike Hulbert, 1991

Jim Gallagher Jr. ended a frustrating string of second-place finishes by winning the Anheuser-Busch Golf Classic.

"Slumps end, I guess. I didn't think they ever did," Gallagher said of his first PGA Tour victory in nearly three years.

Gallagher used a 311-yard drive to set up a decisive eagle on the 506-yard par-5 15th hole.

"It was probably the longest drive I've ever hit on that hole," said the 10-year Tour veteran. "I killed my drive—absolutely murdered it. I had 195 yards left (to the green), 40 yards less than I had all week."

He closed with 6-under-par 65 for 15-under 296, two strokes ahead of Chip Beck (68).

Kingsmill resident Curtis Strange (68), Lanny Wadkins (70) and Dave Rummells (68) tied for third at 272.

Since 1990, Gallagher has been second five times. In 1992, he was second a Tour-high three times, including at Kingsmill.

"I felt like I could have won five or six tournaments," he said. "You kind of don't doubt yourself, but you do wonder when it's going to happen again."

Scores and earnings

Player	Earnings	Scores
Jim Gallagher	$198,000	66-68-70-65—269
Chip Beck	$118,800	68-68-67-68—271
Curtis Strange	$57,200	67-69-68-68—272
Dave Rummells	$57,200	67-71-66-68—272
Lanny Wadkins	$57,200	67-71-64-70—272
Jim Hallet	$38,225	70-70-68-65—273
Loren Roberts	$38,225	70-68-69-66—273
Bob Gilder	$28,600	71-69-66-68—274
Ted Tryba	$28,600	68-65-72-69—274
Lennie Clements	$28,600	70-66-69-69—274
Tom Byrum	$28,600	72-62-69-71—274
Fred Funk	$28,600	70-66-67-71—274
Dillard Pruitt	$28,600	70-68-62-74—274
Mike Hulbert	$19,800	68-72-70-65—275
Greg Lesher	$19,800	73-69-67-66—275
Hale Irwin	$19,800	70-67-68-70—275
Patrick Burke	$13,915	72-70-67-67—276
Brian Kamm	$13,915	68-68-73-67—276
Scott Hoch	$13,915	69-73-66-68—276
Jay Delsing	$13,915	70-69-68-69—276
Jeff Cook	$13,915	68-66-72-70—276
Blaine McCallister	$13,915	70-64-70-72—276
Mark McCumber	$13,915	69-65-69-73—276
John Adams	$13,915	68-65-68-75—276
Keith Clearwater	$8,773	67-70-71-69—277
Mark Brooks	$8,773	72-66-69-70—277
Kelly Gibson	$8,773	70-71-65-71—277
Kirk Triplett	$8,773	67-70-67-73—277
Mark Carnevale	$7,150	69-68-75-66—278
Jim Thorpe	$7,150	72-66-73-67—278
Robert Gamez	$7,150	71-70-69-68—278
Bobby Wadkins	$7,150	73-66-70-69—278
Hubert Green	$7,150	70-67-69-72—278
Davis Love III	$5,676	71-71-69-68—279
Roger Maltbie	$5,676	73-69-69-68—279
Bruce Zabriski	$5,676	72-68-70-69—279
Bill Kratzert	$5,676	71-69-70-69—279
Tom Sieckmann	$5,676	68-69-71-71—279
Chris van der Velde	$4,290	71-71-69-69—280
D.A. Weibring	$4,290	70-72-69-69—280
Ed Humenik	$4,290	69-70-72-69—280
Webb Heintzelman	$4,290	72-67-70-71—280
Scott Simpson	$4,290	72-67-69-72—280
Trevor Dodds	$4,290	66-70-69-75—280
Clarence Rose	$4,290	70-67-67-76—280
Bill Murchison	$2,942	68-74-70-69—281
Barry Cheesman	$2,942	71-70-71-69—281
John Inman	$2,942	71-69-71-70—281
Marco Dawson	$2,942	71-70-68-72—281
Billy Mayfair	$2,942	71-67-71-72—281
Brian Henninger	$2,942	71-70-67-73—281
Brandel Chamblee	$2,942	67-71-67-76—281
Larry Rinker	$2,547	70-70-73-69—282
Fuzzy Zoeller	$2,547	74-67-71-70—282
Russell Beiersdorf	$2,547	71-67-71-73—282
John Dowdall	$2,547	69-70-68-75—282
Jaime Gomez	$2,464	71-68-75-69—283
Lance Ten Broeck	$2,464	68-73-72-70—283
John Flannery	$2,464	66-70-76-71—283
Massy Kuramoto	$2,365	72-68-76-68—284
John Ross	$2,365	69-69-75-71—284
David Peoples	$2,365	68-70-75-71—284
Dennis Trixler	$2,365	68-69-75-72—284
Richard Zokol	$2,365	67-71-74-72—284
Mike Smith	$2,365	70-70-71-73—284
Greg Cesario	$2,233	70-72-74-69—285
Mike Schuchart	$2,233	69-72-74-70—285
Eddie Pearce	$2,233	70-71-74-70—285
P.H. Horgan III	$2,233	68-73-74-70—285
Joey Sindelar	$2,233	68-72-73-72—285
Len Mattiace	$2,233	69-73-69-74—285
Dave Peege	$2,123	72-69-73-72—286
Bob Friend	$2,123	71-69-73-73—286
Dick Mast	$2,123	73-67-73-73—286
John Elliott	$2,123	73-65-74-74—286
Rick Dalpos	$2,046	73-69-74-71—287
David Ogrin	$2,046	72-70-73-72—287
Jay Overton	$2,046	72-68-73-74—287
Barry Jaeckel	$1,991	74-68-73-74—289
Neal Lancaster	$1,991	71-69-74-75—289
Neale Smith	$1,958	73-67-78-73—291
Gary Hallberg	$1,936	69-71-72-80—292

NEW ENGLAND CLASSIC

AT A GLANCE

- **Course:** Pleasant Valley Country Club
- **Location:** Sutton, Mass.
- **When:** July 22-25, 1993
- **Weather:** Sunny and comfortable all weekend.
- **Purse:** $1 million
- **Par:** 71
- **Yards:** 7,110
- **Defending champion:** Brad Faxon, 16-under-par 268
- **Tournament record:** 17-under-par 267, George Burns, 1985

Scores and earnings

Player	Earnings	Scores
Paul Azinger	$180,000	67-69-64-68–268
Jay Delsing	$88,000	73-67-65-67–272
Bruce Fleisher	$88,000	70-67-66-69–272
Joey Sindelar	$44,000	68-67-70-69–274
Bobby Clampett	$44,000	63-71-67-73–274
Peter Jacobsen	$32,375	68-71-68-68–275
Brad Bryant	$32,375	70-65-70-70–275
Curtis Strange	$32,375	70-70-65-70–275
Willie Wood	$32,375	68-65-70-72–275
Barry Cheesman	$25,000	69-71-67-69–276
Steve Lowery	$25,000	66-69-69-72–276
David Peoples	$25,000	72-69-62-73–276
Greg Kraft	$19,333	69-70-68-70–277
John Cook	$19,333	74-67-66-70–277
Bob Estes	$19,333	70-65-68-74–277
Jim Mcgovern	$16,000	71-66-71-70–278
Nolan Henke	$16,000	71-67-69-71–278
John Adams	$16,000	70-69-68-71–278
Brian Henninger	$13,000	73-68-70-68–279
Mark Calcavecchia	$13,000	68-70-72-69–279
Jay Haas	$13,000	71-69-66-73–279
Jaime Gomez	$8,775	72-70-74-64–280
Phil Blackmar	$8,775	71-69-70-70–280
Bob Lohr	$8,775	70-72-68-70–280
Greg Twiggs	$8,775	69-72-68-71–280
Chris Perry	$8,775	71-71-67-71–280
Tim Simpson	$8,775	70-70-69-71–280
Russell Beiersdorf	$8,775	71-66-71-72–280
Bill Murchison	$8,775	71-70-67-72–280
Leonard Thompson	$5,689	69-69-73-70–281
Morris Hatalsky	$5,689	72-67-72-70–281
Kenny Perry	$5,689	72-70-69-70–281
Steve Elkington	$5,689	73-69-68-71–281
Carl Cooper	$5,689	69-73-68-71–281
Lennie Clements	$5,689	72-67-70-72–281
Hal Sutton	$5,689	71-66-71-73–281
David Jackson	$5,689	71-68-69-73–281
Rick Fehr	$5,689	67-69-71-74–281
Craig Parry	$4,400	70-70-73-69–282
David Ogrin	$4,400	69-70-72-71–282
John Ross	$3,600	71-70-75-67–283
Roger Maltbie	$3,600	72-70-71-70–283
Ted Schulz	$3,600	72-70-71-70–283
Wayne Levi	$3,600	70-71-71-71–283
Wayne Grady	$3,600	73-68-69-73–283
Jeff Cook	$3,600	70-72-68-73–283
Dudley Hart	$2,690	73-68-71-72–284
Tim Conley	$2,690	72-68-72-72–284
Chris Tucker	$2,690	74-68-70-72–284
Tom Lehman	$2,690	70-71-69-74–284
Steve Pate	$2,353	71-69-74-71–285
Robin Freeman	$2,353	73-68-72-72–285
Dana Quigley	$2,353	70-71-71-73–285
Frank Conner	$2,353	70-71-70-74–285
Massy Kuramoto	$2,353	69-67-74-75–285
Mark Wiebe	$2,353	76-66-65-78–285
Mike Donald	$2,240	70-72-71-73–286
Fred Funk	$2,240	68-74-71-73–286
Mike Smith	$2,240	71-70-70-75–286
Michael Bradley	$2,180	74-67-74-72–287
Ed Dougherty	$2,180	72-70-72-73–287
Tom Byrum	$2,180	69-67-72-79–287
Scott Gump	$2,110	73-69-72-74–288
David Duval	$2,110	75-67-72-74–288
Gene Sauers	$2,110	70-71-70-77–288
Sam Randolph	$2,110	76-66-69-77–288
Harry Taylor	$2,050	71-71-77-70–289
Lee Porter	$2,050	71-71-74-73–289
Marco Dawson	$2,020	69-72-70-79–290
Buddy Gardner	$2,000	72-70-72-78–292

The par-5s and Paul Azinger got along just fine. He birdied all three in the final round to win the New England Classic at Pleasant Valley Country Club.

Azinger's final-round 68 featured one missed fairway and his 16-under total was one shot off the tournament record.

"I hit it great. I just stayed aggressive," said Azinger. "I hit it pin-high to a good majority of the back-pin placements."

The nearest competition was four shots back, with Bruce Fleisher and Jay Delsing tied for second.

Bobby Clampett, who finished fourth, provided Azinger his stiffest challenge. He was two shots back when both players reached the 17th.

Azinger's 9-iron shot just cleared the pond fronting the green and landed safely. He later admitted his heart "skipped just a couple of beats" as the ball landed.

But a gust knocked down Clampett's 9-iron shot a foot short of the green, and it bounced back into the hazard. Clampett finished his gamble double bogey–double bogey.

"I was trying to win the tournament," Clampett said, quoting Tom Watson: "It's not the kill it's the hunt."

Azinger stopped for nothing. Even after his long blast on from the fairway on No. 5 nicked Fleisher in the next group, Azinger was not distracted. He apologized and made birdie.

—by John Bannon

PLAYER

The bounce was back in his step, the smile had returned to that magazine-cover mug, the pearly white teeth were very evident again. **Greg Norman** was one happy fella.

The easy smile wasn't just because he had won the British Open in July '93. It started almost a year before. The friendly waves, the casual backslaps, the quick needle. Norman was having fun again. And it had been a while.

"I don't know where he went, but for three or four years Greg was very distant, and I'm one of his closest friends," Nick Price said, as the two prepared for the PGA Championship at Inverness. "For a while, he was very hard to talk to.

"Last year, we were flying from Milwaukee to the Canadian Open, and I noticed a huge change in Greg. It seemed that he had come to terms with himself, that he had lost the tenseness that he had been carrying. He seemed to accept things and not fight them."

At the 1992 PGA Championship, Norman was a slump-ridden, aging 37-year-old who barely made the cut after a second-round 74. He talked of being rejuvenated after tying for 18th at the British Open, but that song had played before. There were no outward signs of the tremendous transformation about to take place.

At the Greater Milwaukee Open, Norman finished a sorry 57th. So why was he in such a good mood flying to Canada?

Price couldn't figure it out, but he knew his friend was acting like the good ol' mate of his younger days.

"I think he finally realized he wasn't having fun anymore," Price said. "Sure, he hadn't won in a long time.

"But I had been through that; I knew how it can eat at you. Plus, all those unbelievable shots made on him. Those were once in a blue moon, and he had three blue moons in a row."

At the Canadian Open, Norman finally won after 27 months of frustration.

"The way I won it, in a playoff, really helped me," Norman said. "It probably did more for my confidence than winning by three or four shots. The way I got up and down the last two holes proved to me that I was ready to start winning again."

He brought it all back at the Doral Ryder Open in 1993, tying his course record with a third-round, 10-under-par 62 and winning by four shots at a mind-boggling 23 under.

"Last year, in the middle of the year, I could have walked away from the game," Norman said that day after his smashing victory. "I have a lot of pride, and when things weren't going well, I got frustrated.

"For 20 months, I was my own worst enemy. I wasn't good to myself, I wasn't good to my friends. I got very short with everybody, and I had never been like that before.

"Then, one day, I looked at myself in the mirror and asked myself what my priorities were, what did I want to do with my life. You can never lie to yourself, and I told myself I wanted to get back to where I used to be. I wanted to be one of the best again.

"You don't just say something like that without making a commitment. I knew it would take a lot of work, and I had to make sure I was willing to work as hard as it would take. But that's what I did."

And it has payed off—with wins, top 10 finishes and a race for Player of the Year honors. Even though Norman faced another haunting playoff defeat at Inverness in 1993, Bob Tway's '86 bunker shot and the tailspin that followed seemed a long way off.

"I'm a different person than I was in '86," said Norman—that is, a most happy fella.

—*by Steve Hershey*

SPOTLIGHT

FEDERAL EXPRESS ST. JUDE CLASSIC

AT A GLANCE

- **Course:** TPC at Southwind
- **Location:** Memphis, Tenn.
- **When:** July 29-Aug. 1, 1993
- **Weather:** Hot and humid.
- **Purse:** $1.1 million
- **Par:** 71
- **Yards:** 7,006
- **Defending champion:** Jay Haas, 21-under-par 263
- **Tournament record:** 21-under-par 263, Jay Haas, 1992

The call never came, so Nick Price went out and won another tournament.

Price's wife, Sue, was expecting their second child imminently and Price said throughout the Federal Express St. Jude Classic he would leave, immediately if necessary.

After checking in at his Orlando home each day, he shot 69-65-66-66–266 to win, by three shots, his third consecutive PGA Tour tournament.

"I said all week, if she wanted me, I would be there," Price said. "Now, I'm very happy she waited."

By winning the Canon Greater Hartford Open, Sprint Western Open and in Memphis, Price became the first player to win three consecutive starts (he skipped two events) since Tom Watson in 1980.

"I'm in a zone right now," Price said. "I stand on the tee, pick out a divot in the fairway and try to roll my ball over it. I totally apply myself on every shot."

Just as he did at Hartford and the Western, Price pulled away from his challengers Sunday with a front-nine blitz that included four birdies.

"When I have pressure on me now, I seem to play better," he said. "I used to wilt like a flower."

Jay Delsing, who made the cut by a stroke, had a course-record 61 in the final round to finish eighth, seven strokes behind Price. Delsing had eagles at Nos. 5 and 16, both par-5s.

—*by Steve Hershey*

Scores and earnings

Player	Earnings	Scores
Nick Price	$198,000	69-65-66-66–266
Jeff Maggert	$96,800	67-65-71-66–269
Rick Fehr	$96,800	68-66-68-67–269
Fuzzy Zoeller	$52,800	67-68-65-70–270
Gil Morgan	$44,000	69-69-64-69–271
Tom Kite	$38,225	70-67-69-66–272
Fred Funk	$38,225	68-69-65-70–272
Jay Delsing	$33,000	72-69-71-61–273
Curtis Strange	$33,000	71-66-69-67–273
Dan Pohl	$28,600	72-68-69-65–274
Mark Brooks	$28,600	70-69-64-71–274
Dave Barr	$22,275	68-69-71-67–275
Bob Gilder	$22,275	69-69-69-68–275
John Riegger	$22,275	69-70-68-68–275
John Adams	$22,275	68-68-70-69–275
Howard Twitty	$17,600	70-68-69-69–276
Billy Mayfair	$17,600	70-67-69-70–276
John Daly	$17,600	67-66-72-71–276
Ronnie Black	$13,805	69-73-68-67–277
Bob Tway	$13,805	69-71-69-68–277
Tim Simpson	$13,805	70-70-67-70–277
David Duval	$13,805	71-68-66-72–277
Mark McCumber	$9,048	72-70-70-66–278
Doug Tewell	$9,048	67-69-73-69–278
Joel Edwards	$9,048	73-68-67-70–278
Jay Haas	$9,048	65-72-70-71–278
Lennie Clements	$9,048	70-69-68-71–278
Scott Hoch	$9,048	71-69-67-71–278
Loren Roberts	$9,048	69-67-69-73–278
Davis Love III	$9,048	65-72-66-75–278
Brandel Chamblee	$6,105	70-72-68-69–279
Jim Woodward	$6,105	71-71-68-69–279
Brad Bryant	$6,105	70-66-72-71–279
Michael Allen	$6,105	66-72-70-71–279
Jim Gallagher	$6,105	73-68-67-71–279
Jodie Mudd	$6,105	70-68-69-72–279
Neal Lancaster	$6,105	66-73-67-73–279
Kirk Triplett	$6,105	71-70-65-73–279
Dan Forsman	$4,620	67-73-73-67–280
Jeff Woodland	$4,620	67-70-73-70–280
Peter Jacobsen	$4,620	68-72-70-70–280
Bob Estes	$4,620	69-70-69-72–280
Skip Kendall	$3,432	69-72-73-67–281
Willie Wood	$3,432	69-70-73-69–281
Jeff Cook	$3,432	70-70-71-70–281
Ed Fiori	$3,432	68-72-71-70–281
Mike Hulbert	$3,432	70-69-71-71–281
Gary Hallberg	$3,432	70-70-68-73–281
Dave Rummells	$3,432	67-72-68-74–281
Gary McCord	$2,739	69-71-74-68–282
Kenny Perry	$2,739	69-70-71-72–282
John Flannery	$2,596	68-71-75-69–283
Phil Blackmar	$2,596	69-69-75-70–283
Ben Crenshaw	$2,596	69-71-69-74–283
Mark Carnevale	$2,497	70-69-77-68–284
John Cook	$2,497	70-72-71-71–284
David Toms	$2,497	72-70-68-74–284
Mark Calcavecchia	$2,497	71-69-69-75–284
Paul Goydos	$2,409	70-71-72-72–285
Jay Don Blake	$2,409	70-72-71-72–285
Hal Sutton	$2,409	72-70-71-72–285
Tom Purtzer	$2,409	67-71-72-75–285
Payne Stewart	$2,343	70-71-70-75–286
Andy Bean	$2,343	72-68-69-77–286
Bobby Clampett	$2,288	69-72-72-74–287
Ed Dougherty	$2,288	70-69-73-75–287
John Huston	$2,288	69-70-71-77–287
Jimmy Johnston	$2,233	75-67-72-74–288
Jimmy Ellis	$2,233	69-69-74-76–288
Robert Wrenn	$2,189	72-69-73-75–289
Jeff Sluman	$2,189	68-71-73-77–289
Gene Sauers	$2,145	70-72-74-74–290
Craig Lee	$2,145	71-70-71-78–290
Jim McGovern	$2,101	73-65-77-76–291
Denis Watson	$2,101	72-70-73-76–291
Ted Schulz	$2,068	71-71-75-76–293
Michael Bradley	$2,046	64-74-82-76–296

Buick Open

At a Glance

- **Course:** Warwick Hills Golf and Country Club
- **Location:** Grand Blanc, Mich.
- **When:** Aug. 5-8, 1993
- **Weather:** Sunny and warm.
- **Purse:** $1 million
- **Par:** 72
- **Yards:** 7,105
- **Defending champion:** Dan Forsman, 12-under-par 276 (withdrew in 1993 because of illness)
- **Tournament record:** 20-under-par 268, Ken Green, 1985, and Scott Verplank, 1988

Larry Mize not only won for the second time this year, he also leapfrogged six players in a last-minute drive to make the U.S. Ryder Cup team.

Though his one-shot victory over Fuzzy Zoeller moved Mize into 11th place with 555 points, Jim Gallagher Jr. held onto 10th and ultimately made the team. (The top 10, plus two captain's choices, qualify for the U.S. team.)

Zoeller, who started the day with a four-shot lead, had a chance to win for the second week in a row. At Memphis, he closed bogey–double bogey to finish fourth.

He didn't make a final-round birdie at Warwick Hills until sinking a 35-foot putt at the par-3 17th. He missed birdie putts from 5 and 6 feet on the 12th and 14th holes.

"I played terrible; I should have shot 78," Zoeller said.

Greg Norman fired a final-round 65, including seven birdies on the back nine, to finish third.

Mize birdied three of the first five holes and birdied both par-5s on the back nine, sinking putts of 20 and 10 feet. At 18, he left a 20-footer 4 feet short but sank the second try for a final-round 68 and a 16-under-par 272 total.

—by Steve Hershey

Scores and earnings

Player	Earnings	Scores	Total
Larry Mize	$180,000	64-69-71-68	272
Fuzzy Zoeller	$108,000	69-65-66-73	273
Greg Norman	$68,000	68-73-68-65	274
Corey Pavin	$44,000	71-65-71-69	276
Jay Don Blake	$44,000	69-71-67-69	276
Steve Elkington	$33,500	67-72-70-68	277
Steve Lamontagne	$33,500	67-70-70-70	277
Fred Funk	$33,500	68-71-67-71	277
Neal Lancaster	$27,000	69-71-71-67	278
David Toms	$27,000	73-67-68-70	278
Payne Stewart	$27,000	66-71-71-70	278
John Flannery	$23,000	71-70-68-70	279
Fred Couples	$20,000	72-69-67-72	280
Jim McGovern	$20,000	69-71-68-72	280
Hal Sutton	$16,500	72-70-71-68	281
Tom Watson	$16,500	70-71-70-70	281
John Huston	$16,500	66-77-66-72	281
Wayne Levi	$16,500	72-71-66-72	281
Andrew Magee	$10,875	73-69-73-67	282
Willie Wood	$10,875	72-72-70-68	282
Jay Haas	$10,875	74-70-69-69	282
Warren Schutte	$10,875	70-68-73-71	282
Rocco Mediate	$10,875	71-68-72-71	282
Dudley Hart	$10,875	69-72-70-71	282
Steve Pate	$10,875	70-72-69-71	282
Craig Stadler	$10,875	71-70-70-71	282
Jim Woodward	$5,992	71-73-72-67	283
Ed Fiori	$5,992	70-71-73-69	283
Russ Cochran	$5,992	70-74-70-69	283
Lanny Wadkins	$5,992	69-73-71-70	283
Mark Brooks	$5,992	71-71-71-70	283
Ted Tryba	$5,992	75-69-69-70	283
Peter Jacobsen	$5,992	71-69-72-71	283
Steve Lowery	$5,992	70-71-71-71	283
Skip Kendall	$5,992	70-71-71-71	283
Mark O'Meara	$5,992	69-67-75-72	283
Davis Love III	$5,992	67-73-71-72	283
John Inman	$5,992	70-69-71-73	283
Scott Gump	$5,992	68-71-71-73	283
Joel Edwards	$3,600	75-68-73-68	284
Ed Dougherty	$3,600	72-71-71-70	284
John Cook	$3,600	72-71-71-70	284
Mark McCumber	$3,600	71-70-72-71	284
Brad Bryant	$3,600	70-71-72-71	284
Lennie Clements	$3,600	70-72-70-72	284
Tom Sieckmann	$3,600	70-70-71-73	284
Paul Goydos	$3,600	66-71-72-75	284
Kirk Triplett	$2,544	73-71-71-70	285
Buddy Gardner	$2,544	75-68-71-71	285
Keith Clearwater	$2,544	69-72-72-72	285
Phil Mickelson	$2,544	70-74-69-72	285
Kenny Perry	$2,544	70-71-68-76	285
Ian Baker-Finch	$2,304	70-73-74-69	286
Peter Persons	$2,304	69-73-71-73	286
Jimmy Johnston	$2,304	72-72-70-72	286
David Ogrin	$2,304	70-72-72-72	286
David Peoples	$2,304	71-71-71-73	286
Trevor Dodds	$2,200	70-71-76-70	287
Bobby Clampett	$2,200	72-72-72-71	287
Dennis Trixler	$2,200	67-77-72-71	287
Dave Barr	$2,200	72-71-71-73	287
Jeff Sluman	$2,200	72-71-70-74	287
Gil Morgan	$2,120	72-72-71-73	288
Lance Ten Broeck	$2,120	72-72-69-75	288
Brad Faxon	$2,120	69-71-69-79	288
J.C. Anderson	$2,080	72-71-74-72	289
Kelly Gibson	$2,040	73-69-74-74	290
Michael Bradley	$2,040	71-73-72-74	290
Tim Conley	$2,040	69-73-71-77	290
Chip Beck	$1,940	70-74-74-73	291
Marco Dawson	$1,940	71-73-76-71	291
Craig Parry	$1,940	71-72-74-74	291
Bob Tway	$1,940	68-74-74-75	291
Grant Waite	$1,940	71-72-73-75	291
Mike Weir	$1,940	73-69-73-76	291
Michael Allen	$1,940	70-74-71-76	291
Dillard Pruitt	$1,860	71-72-77-72	292
Perry Moss	$1,840	71-71-75-76	293
Steve Brady	$1,820	72-71-74-79	296

The International

AT A GLANCE

- **Course:** Castle Pines Golf Club
- **Location:** Castle Rock, Colo.
- **When:** Aug. 19-22, 1993
- **Weather:** Sunny and warm with thunderstorms.
- **Purse:** $1.3 million
- **Par:** 72
- **Yards:** 7,559
- **Defending champion:** Brad Faxon, 14 points
- **Tournament record:** New format; previously, 17 points, Joey Sindelar, 1988.

Phil Mickelson's run-away victory in The International was so overwhelming he didn't even need to play the last two holes.

He did, of course, making a couple of pars that finished off an impressive 8-point victory over Mark Calcavecchia under the modified Stableford scoring system used for this unique event.

Calcavecchia finished with 37 points while Mickelson, with nine birdies in the bag, was still playing the 17th hole and holding a total of 45 points.

"He can finish 'x,' 'x' and still win," Calcavecchia noted.

But that would have deprived the 23-year-old left-hander of a standing ovation from the gallery as he marched up the 18th fairway with the victory well in hand.

"I was getting chills. The way the gallery was applauding and everything, I was getting goose-bumps," Mickelson said after breaking a mini-slump and raising again comparisons to the young Jack Nicklaus.

Mickelson was having none of that. It's happened so frequently, he has a response that seems programmed and practiced.

"It's a compliment. I appreciate it," he said. "But there'll never be another Jack Nicklaus. He's the greatest player of all time."

It was his third victory in professional competition, including one in San Diego earlier in 1993 and one in Tucson when he was still an amateur. A three-time NCAA champion, Mickelson won the 1990 U.S. Amateur and joined Nicklaus as the only men to win both the national amateur and national collegiate titles in the same year.

He became the youngest player since Nicklaus in 1962 to win three times on the PGA Tour.

This one was a rout.

"He can be very, very explosive," Calcavecchia said. "When he gets a chance to win, he knows how to do it. He's not afraid of anybody."

Scores and earnings
Under the modified Stableford scoring system, points are awarded by performance on each hole (8 points for double eagle, 5 points for eagle, 2 for birdie, zero for par, minus-1 for bogey and minus-3 for double bogey or worse).

Player	Earnings	Scores
Phil Mickelson	$234,000	11-7-11-16–45
Mark Calcavecchia	$140,400	0-4-14-19–37
Phil Blackmar	$88,400	6-15-5-7–33
Greg Norman	$57,200	11-6-5-9–31
Scott Simpson	$57,200	2-13-8-8–31
Steve Pate	$45,175	14-1-5-8–28
Brad Faxon	$45,175	13-7-2-6–28
Skip Kendall	$40,300	12-9-1-4–26
Rocco Mediate	$37,700	8-1-5-11–25
Craig Parry	$35,100	4-3-12-4–23
Hale Irwin	$31,200	4-4-7-7–22
Brian Claar	$31,200	7-9-1-5–22
Larry Rinker	$26,000	10-5-1-5–21
Mark O'Meara	$26,000	13-9-1-(-2)–21
Tommy Nakajima	$22,100	2-12-4-1–19
Steve Elkington	$22,100	5-2-10-2–19
Vijay Singh	$22,100	2-4-15-(-2)–19
Mike Hulbert	$19,500	5-1-8-4–18
Bret Ogle	$16,900	2-3-8-3–16
Peter Persons	$16,900	1-4-10-1–16
Tom Purtzer	$16,900	2-12-5-(-3)–16
Neal Lancaster	$14,560	(-2)-10-5-1–14
Perry Moss	$13,520	(-1)-10-9-(-5)–13
Marco Dawson	$12,480	4-9-0-(-4)–9

NEC World Series of Golf

AT A GLANCE

- **Course:** Firestone Country Club, South Course
- **Location:** Akron, Ohio
- **When:** Aug. 26-29, 1993
- **Weather:** Sunny, hot and humid.
- **Purse:** $2 million
- **Par:** 70
- **Yards:** 7,149
- **Defending champion:** Craig Stadler, 7-under-par 273
- **Tournament record:** 13-under-par 267, Lanny Wadkins, 1977

After a mind-boggling, final-round 62 at the NEC World Series of Golf, Fulton Allem's bags were packed again—this time for a different reason.

In 1991, the movers were on the way as Allem entered the final event of the year, the rain-delayed Houston Open. He ranked 143rd on the money list and would lose his card without a strong finish.

"My house was packed up, I was going back to South Africa," Allem recalled. "I had entered the Tour Qualifying Tournament and the European Tour school. I was wondering if I would ever play again on the U.S. tour."

Allem started the last round in Houston five shots behind Jeff Maggert and shot 6-under 66 to win and save his career.

With another come-from-behind victory at the World Series of Golf, Allem earned what he calls the ultimate reward: a 10-year exemption on the PGA Tour.

"That's like winning 10 tournaments," said Allem, 35. "It's such a great feeling."

He earned it with one of the best rounds at historic Firestone Country Club. He came within a stroke of tying Jose Maria Olazabal's record set in the first round in 1990 when the Spaniard led from start to finish.

The only round Allem could compare it to was his second-round 63 en route to a one-shot victory at the Southwestern Bell Colonial in May 1993.

"I played the same way that day," he said. "I was in a very aggressive mode and went after every putt."

Allem was struggling when he arrived at Firestone. Since the Colonial, he had missed three cuts and his best finish was 20th. The problem was his putter, and he found help in the barrel of classic clubs Guido Inna sells every year near the parking lot.

"I paid Guido $2,300 for this classic Ping putter," Allem said. "Wrote him a check on the spot. I got away from Ping putters for a while, but I guarantee you I'll keep this for a long time."

The tournament turned for Allem when he made a 25-foot par putt on the 9th hole Saturday. That kept him at par after three successive bogeys. Then, he played the back nine in 2-under par and was only a shot behind the leaders.

"Fultie's always been his own worst enemy," said Nick Price, who shot 68 and tied defending champion Craig Stadler and Jim Gallagher Jr. for second at 5-under-par 275. "He was so upset on the front nine Saturday, I didn't think he had a chance of winning. Then he just blew us away."

Allem was packing again. Now, after winning $360,000, he's buying a house in Florida.

—by Steve Hershey

SOUTH AFRICANS HAVE SERIES FIGURED OUT

Oddly, Allem became the fourth South African to win the World Series since Price started the trend with his wire-to-wire victory in 1983. Denis Watson won in '84, and David Frost beat Ben Crenshaw in a playoff in '89.

"We're all very accurate drivers," Price said. "This course is so demanding off the tee, you must keep the ball in the fairway to have a chance to position the ball on the greens."

Allem agreed: "We all grew up learning to hit the ball straight. The courses we played were very rough. If you weren't in the fairway, you needed a radar scanner to find your ball."

Allem hit 13 of 14 fairways in his career round. Price hit nine, Stadler six, Gallagher five.

"Long ago, I gave up distance for accuracy," Allem said. "It certainly paid off."

—*by Steve Hershey*

Scores and earnings

Fulton Allem, $360,000	68-68-72-62—270
Craig Stadler, $149,333	71-69-68-67—275
Nick Price, $149,333	69-67-71-68—275
Jim Gallagher, $149,333	66-75-66-68—275
Vijay Singh, $80,000	73-70-68-66—277
David Edwards, $72,000	66-69-72-72—279
Steve Elkington, $62,367	69-67-72-72—280
David Frost, $62,367	68-69-71-72—280
Greg Norman, $62,367	69-69-69-73—280
Grant Waite, $54,100	72-70-75-65—282
Fred Couples, $46,100	77-77-65-67—286
Tom Kite, $46,100	72-71-72-71—286
John Daly, $46,100	72-73-70-71—286
Lee Janzen, $37,100	75-70-73-69—287
Richard Zokol, $37,100	73-71-71-72—287
John Huston, $32,500	68-74-78-68—288
Gary Hallberg, $32,500	74-69-72-73—288
Isao Aoki, $32,500	74-72-69-73—288
Larry Mize, $28,125	75-72-70-72—289
Bradley Hughes, $28,125	73-73-69-74—289
Joe Ozaki, $26,550	76-74-68-72—290
Mike Standly, $25,150	75-72-76-68—291
Jim Mcgovern, $25,150	73-76-71-71—291
Tommy Nakajima, $25,150	71-75-71-74—291
Nolan Henke, $22,500	73-72-77-70—292
Craig Parry, $22,500	74-71-76-71—292
Davis Love III, $22,500	75-71-75-71—292
Howard Twitty, $22,500	71-76-73-72—292
Ben Crenshaw, $22,500	74-70-75-73—292
Rocco Mediate, $22,500	74-69-76-73—292
Paul Azinger, $20,900	72-72-75-75—294
Brian Watts, $20,375	70-76-73-76—295
Ron McDougal, $20,375	72-75-72-76—295
Massy Kuramoto, $19,850	68-74-81-74—297
Brett Ogle, $19,500	75-75-77-72—299
Phil Mickelson, $19,200	77-75-71-77—300
Clinton Whitelaw, $19,200	71-79-72-78—300
Peter Senior	71-73-81—DQ
John Cook	69-75-81—DQ

PLAYER

Phil Mickelson admits even 23-year-olds can suffer burnout.

Mickelson lost interest in golf last summer. What had been a riveting force for so long suddenly became trivial.

"My desire left me for a while," Mickelson said.

During one dismal stretch, he missed eight cuts in twelve starts and his best finish was a tie for 22nd at the Memorial. "Looking back, I shouldn't have played in all those tournaments," he said. "I didn't want to be there, and missing all those cuts looks bad. If I had just stayed home, nobody would have noticed."

Many fans did notice. And so did *Golf Digest*, which ran a story questioning Mickelson's desire and wondering if he ever would live up to whatever heights had been predicted.

Despite his victory at the Buick Invitational last February, Mickelson was called a disappointment. But after winning again at The International, he was suddenly having a great year: two victories and 13th on the money list.

"I had a great time when I was away. I went on a house boat for a week in Utah and even went bungee jumping," he said. "Then, I started to miss golf, started thinking about my swing. I knew it was time to come back."

At the PGA Championship, Mickelson tied for sixth, five shots out of the Paul Azinger-Greg Norman playoff.

"I started working on developing my patience," Mickelson said. "At the PGA, I tried not to force anything. I was in contention, but I needed a spurt and didn't have one. At the International, I had a couple and that was the difference."

In a pro career that is in only its 15th month, Mickelson already has made a successful comeback.

—*by Steve Hershey*

SPOTLIGHT

Greater Milwaukee Open

At a Glance

- **Course:** Tuckaway Country Club
- **Location:** Franklin, Wis.
- **When:** Sept. 2-5, 1993
- **Weather:** Cloudy and misty Thursday, sunny Friday and Saturday, sunny to partly overcast with late rain Sunday.
- **Purse:** $1 million
- **Par:** 72
- **Yards:** 7,030
- **Playoff:** Billy Mayfair won on fifth playoff hole after tying with Mark Calcavecchia and Ted Schulz at 18-under-par 270.
- **Defending champion:** Richard Zokol, 19-under-par 269
- **Tournament record:** 22-under-par 266, Bill Kratzert, 1980

Billy Mayfair, who had previously lost two PGA Tour playoffs, made a 20-foot chip shot to birdie the fourth hole of a playoff with Mark Calcavecchia and Ted Schulz, grabbing the victory in the Greater Milwaukee Open.

The three finished regulation play at 18-under-par 270.

Mayfair's playoff losses (to Jim Gallagher in the 1990 GMO and to Jodie Mudd in the 1990 Nabisco Championship) made him a stronger player, the first-time winner said.

"If there's anything I learned there, it's just don't give up on Sunday, because you never know what will happen," said Mayfair, who got his Tour card in 1988.

"This is why we hit balls for hours and hours and hours on end and practice putts for hours and hours and hours," he said. "So I said to myself, 'Don't get nervous now. Just go out and do your job.'"

Mayfair and Calcavecchia parred three playoff holes before Calcavecchia missed a 5-foot putt for birdie to share second place with Schulz, who was out of the playoff after bogeying the first hole.

Mayfair birdied six holes and bogeyed two for a final-round 68.

"They say your first victory is the sweetest," Mayfair said. "This is definitely the sweetest."

Scores and earnings

Player	Earnings	Scores
#Billy Mayfair	$180,000	67-66-69-68–270
Ted Schulz	$88,000	69-67-68-66–270
Mark Calcavecchia	$88,000	72-64-67-67–270
Bruce Lietzke	$44,000	69-66-69-67–271
Richard Zokol	$44,000	67-68-68-68–271
Ken Green	$36,000	69-66-69-68–272
Donnie Hammond	$33,500	69-65-70-69–273
Brian Kamm	$28,000	69-69-69-67–274
Hale Irwin	$28,000	70-66-70-68–274
Craig Parry	$28,000	70-66-69-69–274
Gil Morgan	$28,000	69-65-70-70–274
Harry Taylor	$20,250	67-66-76-66–275
Duffy Waldorf	$20,250	72-67-67-69–275
Ronnie Black	$20,250	69-67-68-71–275
Jim McGovern	$20,250	67-67-69-72–275
Bill Glasson	$16,000	70-69-71-66–276
David Frost	$16,000	69-68-72-67–276
Howard Twitty	$16,000	69-67-72-68–276
Ed Dougherty	$12,120	69-67-73-68–277
Jim Gallagher	$12,120	70-68-71-68–277
Rick Fehr	$12,120	71-66-71-69–277
Andrew Magee	$12,120	68-70-70-69–277
Steve Pate	$12,120	65-70-69-73–277
Scott Hoch	$8,525	67-68-76-67–278
Massy Kuramoto	$8,525	73-68-69-68–278
Blaine McCallister	$8,525	72-69-69-68–278
Russell Beiersdorf	$8,525	66-68-72-72–278
Fred Funk	$7,100	67-69-73-70–279
Corey Pavin	$7,100	67-68-71-73–279
Mark Lye	$7,100	68-68-70-73–279
Steve Lamontagne	$5,320	70-70-73-67–280
Michael Bradley	$5,320	74-66-72-68–280
Bill Kratzert	$5,320	67-73-69-71–280
Morris Hatalsky	$5,320	64-73-72-71–280
Fulton Allem	$5,320	70-69-70-71–280
Tom Sieckmann	$5,320	66-73-70-71–280
Gary Hallberg	$5,320	67-69-72-72–280
Nick Price	$5,320	68-68-71-73–280
John Adams	$5,320	67-71-69-73–280
Mark McCumber	$5,320	68-70-69-73–280
Greg Kraft	$3,405	68-68-75-70–281
Jay Haas	$3,405	66-73-72-70–281
Gene Sauers	$3,405	67-69-75-70–281
Dick Mast	$3,405	69-69-73-70–281
Chip Beck	$3,405	69-70-71-71–281
Mark Wiebe	$3,405	67-69-73-72–281
John Elliott	$3,405	69-67-71-74–281
Nolan Henke	$3,405	67-69-71-74–281
Roger Maltbie	$2,443	71-70-72-69–282
Robert Wrenn	$2,443	71-70-70-71–282
Tim Simpson	$2,443	68-72-71-71–282
David Peoples	$2,443	71-69-70-72–282
Paul Goydos	$2,443	69-70-71-72–282
Robin Freeman	$2,443	71-69-69-73–282
Kenny Perry	$2,240	71-70-73-69–283
Brad Bryant	$2,240	70-71-73-69–283
Jay Delsing	$2,240	75-65-74-69–283
John Flannery	$2,240	74-67-72-70–283
Jay Don Blake	$2,240	70-71-71-71–283
Brian Claar	$2,240	71-68-73-71–283
Dave Rummells	$2,240	68-66-74-75–283
Bob Tway	$2,130	73-68-74-69–284
Scott Gump	$2,130	72-69-73-70–284
Brandel Chamblee	$2,130	68-71-75-70–284
Bobby Clampett	$2,130	68-70-71-75–284
Dan Halldorson	$2,040	68-73-77-67–285
Steve Lowery	$2,040	69-68-77-71–285
Doug Tewell	$2,040	69-70-75-71–285
David Ogrin	$2,040	71-70-72-72–285
Jeff Cook	$2,040	69-68-73-75–285
Dan Forsman	$1,960	71-69-76-70–286
Peter Persons	$1,960	69-70-77-70–286
Keith Clearwater	$1,960	68-72-74-72–286
David Delong	$1,910	70-70-74-73–287
John Dowdall	$1,910	69-70-75-73–287
Tommy Armour III	$1,850	70-71-76-71–288
Ed Fiori	$1,850	69-72-75-72–288
Mark Carnevale	$1,850	69-71-74-74–288
Buddy Gardner	$1,850	72-67-73-76–288
JC Anderson	$1,800	69-72-79-69–289
Len Mattiace	$1,770	71-70-76-73–290
David Edwards	$1,770	69-69-78-74–290

#-won on four playoff holes

Canadian Open

AT A GLANCE

- **Course:** Glen Abbey Golf Club
- **Location:** Oakville, Ontario
- **When:** Sept. 9-12, 1993
- **Weather:** Cool, damp, Thursday morning. Wet ground caused delay in start Friday; rain caused 30-minute delay just after noon, and play was suspended because of darkness at 8 p.m. Windy and overcast Saturday and Sunday.
- **Purse:** $1 million
- **Par:** 72
- **Yards:** 7,112
- **Defending champion:** Greg Norman, 8-under-par 280
- **Tournament record:** 17-under-par 271, Steve Jones, 1989

Scores and earnings

Player, Earnings	Scores
David Frost, $180,000	72-70-69-68–279
Fred Couples, $108,000	70-71-70-69–280
Brad Bryant, $68,000	68-70-70-74–282
Craig Stadler, $41,333	71-73-71-69–284
Bruce Lietzke, $41,333	71-72-71-70–284
Steve Stricker, $41,333	66-69-74-75–284
Bill Glasson, $33,500	70-73-71-71–285
Dudley Hart, $30,000	69-71-74-72–286
Phil Blackmar, $30,000	69-71-72-74–286
P.H. Horgan III, $22,167	72-73-72-70–287
Brandel Chamblee, $22,167	70-70-76-71–287
Jim Gallagher, $22,167	73-74-68-72–287
Nick Price, $22,167	68-74-71-74–287
Ed Dougherty, $22,167	71-70-70-76–287
Kenny Perry, $22,167	70-71-70-76–287
Ian Baker-Finch, $15,500	69-75-74-70–288
Brad Faxon, $15,500	74-72-72-70–288
Scott Gump, $15,500	68-75-72-73–288
Mark McCumber, $15,500	73-72-69-74–288
Mike Hulbert, $12,500	74-71-73-71–289
Tom Lehman, $12,500	78-70-69-72–289
Steve Lowery, $8,775	75-70-74-71–290
Mark Brooks, $8,775	73-74-72-71–290
Jim McGovern, $8,775	70-73-75-72–290
Jay Don Blake, $8,775	75-72-70-73–290
John Huston, $8,775	75-72-70-73–290
Bob Lohr, $8,775	74-69-72-75–290
Paul Goydos, $8,775	71-72-71-76–290
Jimmy Johnston, $8,775	68-72-71-79–290
Russell Beiersdorf, $6,210	74-72-73-72–291
Ed Fiori, $6,210	70-76-71-74–291
Keith Clearwater, $6,210	74-72-71-74–291
Marco Dawson, $6,210	70-72-74-75–291
Denis Watson, $6,210	73-71-71-76–291
Corey Pavin, $4,930	71-76-71-74–292
Don Pooley, $4,930	73-75-70-74–292
Ed Humenik, $4,930	74-72-72-74–292
Andy Bean, $4,930	70-76-72-74–292
Rick Fehr, $4,930	74-71-71-76–292
John Flannery, $3,900	76-71-73-73–293
Billy Mayfair, $3,900	73-75-71-74–293
Bob Estes, $3,900	76-70-74-73–293
Donnie Hammond, $3,900	71-75-73-74–293
JC Anderson, $3,900	73-73-72-75–293
Brad Fabel, $2,670	70-77-78-69–294
Mark Calcavecchia, $2,670	73-72-77-72–294
Greg Twiggs, $2,670	75-73-73-73–294
Mike Standly, $2,670	74-74-73-73–294
Patrick Burke, $2,670	71-74-76-73–294
Ray Stewart, $2,670	72-75-73-74–294
Ted Tryba, $2,670	75-71-74-74–294
Jay Delsing, $2,670	73-70-76-75–294
Mark O'Meara, $2,670	76-68-73-77–294
Gary Hallberg, $2,670	72-70-74-78–294
Blaine McCallister, $2,300	72-76-72-75–295
Gene Sauers, $2,270	75-71-75-75–296
Bobby Clampett, $2,270	72-73-76-75–296
Arden Knoll, $2,230	71-74-73-79–297
Mark Wiebe, $2,230	77-68-71-81–297
Tim Conley, $2,130	72-76-78-72–298
Jim Thorpe, $2,130	71-77-77-73–298
Lee Janzen, $2,130	72-76-76-74–298
Tim Simpson, $2,130	73-72-78-75–298
Kelly Gibson, $2,130	70-78-74-76–298
D.A. Weibring, $2,130	70-71-77-80–298
Kirk Triplett, $2,130	69-78-71-80–298
Perry Moss, $2,130	69-75-74-80–298
Tom Sieckmann, $2,020	72-74-79-74–299
Skip Kendall, $2,020	75-72-77-75–299
Bob Tway, $2,020	71-74-70-84–299
John Elliott, $1,960	74-72-79-75–300
Dick Mast, $1,960	71-75-77-77–300
Massy Kuramoto, $1,960	74-74-72-80–300
Ted Schulz, $1,920	71-77-80-73–301
Len Mattiace, $1,900	73-75-77-78–303

Tied for the lead on the final hole, David Frost never gave a thought to laying up and settling for a playoff.

Instead, he boldly went for the green on the par-5 No. 18. The shot set up a 2-putt birdie that gave him his seventh PGA Tour victory.

"You don't have that many chances to win a golf tournament," Frost said. "You've worked all week to get yourself in that position. So you get there and you're going to lay up? No, I don't think so."

Frost, tied for the lead with Fred Couples and 225 yards out, grabbed his 5-wood and laced his second shot over the pond in front of the 18th green at Glen Abbey, setting up the winning 2-putt birdie from 30 feet.

"It's not a shot you want to have to win a golf tournament," Frost admitted. "But once you've done it, once you've hit it, it's a pretty big relief."

Couples, whose birdie on the final hole tied him for the lead, saluted the South African's bold play over the water.

"A perfect shot," Couples said. "I thought I was in pretty good shape, and he hit a perfect shot."

Couples played the last round without a bogey, birdied all three par-5's on the back nine and was one back at 69-280.

"Just one par-5 short," Couples said.

Hardee's Classic

AT A GLANCE

- **Course**: Oakwood Country Club
- **Location**: Coal Valley, Ill.
- **When**: Sept. 16-19, 1993
- **Weather**: Cloudy and rainy Thursday. Sunny and warm Friday; cool and cloudy Saturday and Sunday.
- **Purse**: $1 million
- **Par**: 70
- **Yards**: 6,755
- **Defending champion**: David Frost
- **Tournament record**: 21-under-par 259, David Frost, 1993

David Frost entered the upper echelon of the PGA Tour by defending his Hardee's Golf Classic championship a week after winning the Canadian Open.

Frost was called "possibly the hottest player in the world" by D.A. Weibring, who turned in a 14-under 266—but still lost by seven strokes, the widest victory margin on the Tour in 1993.

Frost's 72-hole total of 259 was also the Tour's '93 low.

"David has the whole package: driving accuracy, good iron play, nice work around the greens and great putting," Weibring said.

Frost, from South Africa, shot a final-round 6-under 64 finishing a record 21-under for 72 holes. Previous record: 19 under, Blaine McCallister, '88.

By winning the Canadian and the Hardee's in succession, Frost became the first PGA Tour player to win for a second consecutive week while repeating as a tournament winner, since Johnny Miller at Phoenix and Tucson in 1975.

"I needed a recording of 'Nice shot, David' because that's what I kept saying to him all day," Weibring said.

Frost doesn't shrink from the accolades.

"I work very hard and I'm very dedicated to what I do," Frost said. "Golf is the thing I do best and I want to take advantage of the chance to get to the top. I wouldn't say I'm there, but I feel I can compete with anyone out there on any day."

Scores and earnings

Player	Earnings	Scores	Total
David Frost	$180,000	68-63-64-64	259
Payne Stewart	$88,000	66-68-67-65	266
D.A. Weibring	$88,000	66-65-66-69	266
Bob Tway	$48,000	69-67-67-65	268
David Ogrin	$36,500	66-70-67-66	269
Mike Schuchart	$36,500	69-65-69-66	269
John Huston	$36,500	70-68-66-65	269
Tim Simpson	$26,000	70-66-68-66	270
Willie Wood	$26,000	66-69-67-68	270
Andrew Magee	$26,000	68-66-67-69	270
P.H. Horgan III	$26,000	68-68-66-68	270
Larry Rinker	$26,000	69-67-65-69	270
Kenny Perry	$26,000	65-70-64-71	270
Kelly Gibson	$16,500	69-69-67-66	271
Bob Estes	$16,500	68-69-69-65	271
Jeff Maggert	$16,500	65-70-69-67	271
Jay Delsing	$16,500	66-71-67-67	271
Brandel Chamblee	$16,500	71-64-68-68	271
David Edwards	$16,500	67-68-66-70	271
Ed Fiori	$10,429	69-68-69-66	272
Mac O'Grady	$10,429	66-68-70-68	272
Gene Jones	$10,429	69-67-68-68	272
Brian Kamm	$10,429	67-71-69-65	272
Lennie Clements	$10,429	69-69-66-68	272
Scott Hoch	$10,429	70-67-67-68	272
Dave Barr	$10,429	65-66-72-69	272
Peter Jacobsen	$7,250	69-67-69-68	273
Curtis Strange	$7,250	72-66-67-68	273
Robert Wrenn	$7,250	67-69-68-69	273
Jeff Woodland	$7,250	63-70-69-71	273
Bill Kratzert	$5,550	68-70-68-68	274
Dan Halldorson	$5,550	68-70-67-69	274
Loren Roberts	$5,550	68-68-70-68	274
David Jackson	$5,550	70-68-69-67	274
Mark Brooks	$5,550	68-70-69-67	274
Dick Mast	$5,550	68-68-72-66	274
Doug Martin	$5,550	66-68-69-71	274
Ronnie Black	$5,550	68-67-65-74	274
Harry Taylor	$3,700	70-67-68-70	275
Greg Kraft	$3,700	69-69-68-69	275
Bruce Zabriski	$3,700	67-70-69-69	275
Bill Britton	$3,700	71-65-70-69	275
Ed Dougherty	$3,700	65-67-72-71	275
Robert Gamez	$3,700	68-66-72-69	275
Lance Ten Broeck	$3,700	68-68-68-71	275
Tom Lehman	$3,700	69-69-70-67	275
Chris Perry	$3,700	68-67-68-72	275
Brad Fabel	$2,486	69-67-69-71	276
Brad Bryant	$2,486	67-70-68-71	276
Steve Elkington	$2,486	70-68-67-71	276
Tom Sieckmann	$2,486	67-69-70-70	276
David Berganio	$2,486	68-69-71-68	276
Buddy Gardner	$2,486	66-70-72-68	276
Jay Haas	$2,486	69-69-71-67	276
Neal Lancaster	$2,250	70-68-68-71	277
Bobby Clampett	$2,250	67-67-70-73	277
Dillard Pruitt	$2,250	68-69-71-69	277
Morris Hatalsky	$2,250	66-70-72-69	277
Billy Mayfair	$2,250	70-68-71-68	277
Steve Lowery	$2,250	70-68-71-68	277
Hal Sutton	$2,170	70-67-68-73	278
Robin Freeman	$2,170	69-68-72-69	278
John Elliott	$2,110	67-69-70-73	279
Russ Cochran	$2,110	69-69-69-72	279
Barry Cheesman	$2,110	66-71-71-71	279
Peter Persons	$2,110	70-68-72-69	279
Bruce Fleisher	$2,050	68-69-69-74	280
Jeff Cook	$2,050	67-70-72-71	280
Grant Waite	$2,020	66-71-72-72	281
Bill Murchison	$2,000	69-69-73-71	282
Keith Clearwater	$1,980	71-67-76-69	283
Marty Schiene	$1,940	68-70-70-76	284
Rob Sullivan	$1,940	69-67-73-75	284
Brian Henninger	$1,940	69-68-74-73	284

B. C. Open

AT A GLANCE

- **Course:** En-Joie Country Club
- **Location:** Endicott, N.Y.
- **When:** Sept. 23-26, 1993
- **Weather:** Overcast Thursday. Sunny and cool Friday and Saturday. Rain Sunday, forcing a 90-minute morning delay.
- **Purse:** $800,000
- **Par:** 71
- **Yards:** 6,966
- **Defending champion:** John Daly, 18-under-par 266
- **Tournament record:** 19-under-par 265, Calvin Peete, 1982

Scores and earnings

Player	Scores
Blaine McCallister, $144,000	68-71-65-67—271
Denis Watson, $86,400	69-70-68-65—272
Bill Glasson, $54,400	66-72-68-67—273
Greg Kraft, $33,067	70-70-68-67—275
Mark Lye, $33,067	67-71-69-68—275
David Ogrin, $33,067	71-71-64-69—275
Dick Mast, $26,800	68-72-71-65—276
Rick Fehr, $24,000	70-71-67-69—277
Chris Smith, $24,000	70-71-66-70—277
David Toms, $17,733	71-70-71-66—278
Billy Mayfair, $17,733	70-71-69-68—278
Ed Dougherty, $17,733	71-69-70-68—278
Bobby Clampett, $17,733	70-70-69-69—278
Ed Humenik, $17,733	66-75-67-70—278
Peter Jacobsen, $17,733	69-68-70-71—278
Jim Thorpe, $13,600	73-69-70-67—279
Bill Murchison, $11,600	71-69-72-68—280
Fred Funk, $11,600	69-74-69-68—280
Patrick Burke, $11,600	72-69-70-69—280
Harry Taylor, $11,600	72-69-69-70—280
Bill Britton, $7,120	68-72-72-69—281
Mark Pfeil, $7,120	69-71-72-69—281
Perry Moss, $7,120	69-72-72-68—281
Howard Twitty, $7,120	69-72-71-69—281
Lennie Clements, $7,120	68-74-70-69—281
Tom Purtzer, $7,120	70-72-70-69—281
Steve Lamontagne, $7,120	72-71-69-69—281
Nolan Henke, $7,120	68-71-72-70—281
Chris Perry, $7,120	74-67-67-73—281
Jim McGovern, $7,120	69-67-69-76—281
Bill Kratzert, $4,537	68-74-71-69—282
Jeff Woodland, $4,537	69-71-72-70—282
Ed Fiori, $4,537	69-70-72-71—282
Deane Pappas, $4,537	69-73-73-67—282
Jim Woodward, $4,537	71-70-70-71—282
Lance Ten Broeck, $4,537	70-69-71-72—282
Brad Bryant, $4,537	68-71-68-75—282
Dillard Pruitt, $3,600	70-74-69-70—283
Tom Jenkins, $3,600	70-71-71-71—283
John Inman, $3,600	72-71-69-71—283
John Elliott, $2,800	71-69-73-71—284
Brett Ogle, $2,800	70-72-72-70—284
Gene Jones, $2,800	75-69-71-69—284
Morris Hatalsky, $2,800	68-74-73-69—284
Jeff Sluman, $2,800	72-69-70-73—284
Mark Carnevale, $2,800	72-72-72-68—284
Brad Fabel, $2,800	70-73-73-68—284
Neal Lancaster, $2,011	70-70-72-73—285
Robin Freeman, $2,011	71-72-71-71—285
Mike Springer, $2,011	73-70-71-71—285
Mike McCullough, $2,011	72-69-73-71—285
Robert Wrenn, $2,011	72-68-70-75—285
Stephen Flesch, $2,011	71-73-73-68—285
Brad Faxon, $1,832	71-72-72-71—286
Dudley Hart, $1,832	69-75-72-70—286
Mark Hayes, $1,832	71-72-67-76—286
Andy Bean, $1,832	70-74-73-69—286
Paul Goydos, $1,744	72-72-70-73—287
John Daly, $1,744	71-72-71-73—287
Buddy Gardner, $1,744	72-70-72-73—287
Larry Mize, $1,744	69-74-69-75—287
Mike Schuchart, $1,744	71-73-72-71—287
Rocco Mediate, $1,744	72-71-73-71—287
Brian Kamm, $1,744	71-70-76-70—287
Lee Porter, $1,648	69-70-74-75—288
Tim Conley, $1,648	70-73-72-73—288
Marty Schiene, $1,648	72-71-72-73—288
Doug Martin, $1,648	73-71-73-71—288
Clarence Rose, $1,648	72-72-74-70—288
Neale Smith, $1,600	71-71-74-73—289
P.H. Horgan III, $1,576	71-71-73-75—290
Marco Dawson, $1,576	72-72-75-71—290
Tom Byrum, $1,520	68-73-74-76—291
Greg Lesher, $1,520	74-69-73-75—291
Brian Claar, $1,520	67-74-75-75—291
Len Mattiace, $1,520	74-70-75-72—291
Bob Lohr, $1,520	73-71-75-72—291
Jaime Gomez, $1,464	70-73-71-78—292
Richie Karl, $1,464	77-66-77-72—292
Forrest Fezler, $1,440	75-68-79-71—293
John Ross, $1,424	72-70-83-76—301

Blaine McCallister had a trying year, but things began to improve at the B.C. Open.

"It hasn't been a good year. But now it's a great year," he said after his birdie on the final hole edged Denis Watson by a stroke.

McCallister shot a final round 67 to finish at 13-under-par 271, earning his fifth PGA Tour win but his first since 1991.

McCallister, 34, started the week 107th on the PGA Tour money list and had missed the cut in six of his past 10 starts. But more serious matters also had affected him in 1993.

He moved his family from his native Texas to Florida. His wife's grandparents died. And the pseudoxanthoma elasticum (PXE) his wife, Claudia, suffers from worsened, leaving her with just peripheral vision for the rest of her life.

"It's been a tough year for us both, physically and mentally," he said.

McCallister said it was his wife's words of encouragement that improved his spirit before he arrived at En-Joie.

"When I left to come up here, she said, 'Just be yourself and put forth what you think you can and be the best you possibly can be.' That really helped me . . . She made me feel at ease, saying I could go on the road and she would be fine," he said.

"To come down the stretch and to have a chance and then hit the shot you want to hit, and then capitalize by making the putt—it was a dream come true," he said.

Buick Southern Open

AT A GLANCE

▶**Course:** Callaway Gardens Resort (Mountain View Course)
▶**Location:** Pine Mountain, Ga.
▶**When:** Sept. 30-Oct. 3, 1993
▶**Weather:** Beautiful.
▶**Purse:** $700,000
▶**Par:** 72
▶**Yards:** 7,057
▶**Playoff:** John Inman defeated Bob Estes on the second playoff hole, after they eliminated Mark Brooks, Billy Andrade and Brad Bryant on the first.
▶**Defending champion:** Gary Hallberg, 10-under-par 206 (tournament shortened to 54 holes because of rain).
▶**Tournament record:** 23-under-par 265, Kenny Knox and Jim Hallet, 1990 (Knox won with a birdie on the first playoff hole).

John Inman started the day happy he was going to make the top 10 in the Buick Southern Open and save his spot on the PGA Tour next year.

Twenty holes and two critical birdie putts later, he had his first victory since he was a rookie in 1987.

The $126,000 first prize moved him from 125th to 66th on the Tour money list. The top 125 players retain their cards for 1994.

Inman shot a 2-under 70 and finished 72 holes at 10-under-par 278, tied with Mark Brooks, Billy Andrade, Brad Bryant and Bob Estes. He sank a 7-foot birdie putt on the scond playoff hole, while Estes' 12-footer stopped short.

Inman was saved on the final hole of regulation by a 4-iron shot that stopped 12 feet from the cup.

"That was the most important shot I hit all day," he said. "I wasn't trying to hit it that close. It just happened.

"It hit in the rough shy of the green, which helped check it up a little. I was lucky, but when you are playing well, things like that happen."

Scores and earnings

Player	Scores
#John Inman, $126,000	71-73-64-70—278
Mark Brooks, $46,200	72-70-72-64—278
Billy Andrade, $46,200	68-70-73-67—278
Brad Bryant, $46,200	69-72-70-67—278
Bob Estes, $46,200	70-69-67-72—278
Tom Lehman, $24,325	70-65-76-68—279
Russ Cochran, $24,325	74-71-65-69—279
David Toms, $20,300	72-69-74-65—280
Bill Glasson, $20,300	71-73-69-67—280
Willie Wood, $20,300	69-70-71-70—280
Neal Lancaster, $16,800	68-71-73-69—281
Mike Springer, $16,800	72-69-69-71—281
Mark Calcavecchia, $13,533	73-72-69-68—282
Rick Fehr, $13,533	73-71-69-69—282
Mark Carnevale, $13,533	72-71-70-69—282
Kenny Perry, $11,200	69-77-68-69—283
Len Mattiace, $11,200	70-73-69-71—283
Jay Don Blake, $11,200	74-72-66-71—283
Mark Wiebe, $7,900	75-70-70-69—284
Kirk Triplett, $7,900	76-70-69-69—284
Ed Fiori, $7,900	70-71-72-71—284
Loren Roberts, $7,900	68-73-70-73—284
Skip Kendall, $7,900	72-71-68-73—284
Dick Mast, $7,900	69-73-69-73—284
Fred Funk, $7,900	68-71-71-74—284
Wayne Levi, $4,666	73-71-75-66—285
Jim Gallagher, $4,666	71-73-72-69—285
Mike Hulbert, $4,666	72-70-73-70—285
Patrick Burke, $4,666	69-73-73-70—285
Bobby Wadkins, $4,666	70-73-72-70—285
John Huston, $4,666	71-69-74-71—285
Lance Ten Broeck, $4,666	69-76-69-71—285
Jim Thorpe, $4,666	73-73-68-71—285
Peter Persons, $4,666	72-66-74-73—285
Scott Simpson, $4,666	69-71-72-73—285
Doug Martin, $2,873	74-71-74-67—286
Morris Hatalsky, $2,873	77-68-72-69—286
Ed Dougherty, $2,873	71-72-73-70—286
Jodie Mudd, $2,873	73-73-70-70—286
Doug Tewell, $2,873	74-70-72-70—286
Bill Kratzert, $2,873	68-73-74-71—286
Dan Pohl, $2,873	76-67-72-71—286
Jay Delsing, $2,873	72-74-69-71—286
Robin Freeman, $2,873	74-70-69-73—286
Jaime Gomez, $2,873	74-70-68-74—286
Jim Hallet, $2,873	67-72-72-75—286
Greg Lesher, $1,851	73-73-72-69—287
Gene Sauers, $1,851	73-69-75-70—287
Tom Byrum, $1,851	73-70-74-70—287
Larry Mize, $1,851	68-72-75-72—287
Perry Moss, $1,851	68-73-71-75—287
Ted Tryba, $1,608	72-74-73-69—288
Jim Woodward, $1,608	75-69-73-71—288
Mike Schuchart, $1,608	77-69-71-71—288
Phil Blackmar, $1,608	74-70-72-72—288
Tom Sieckmann, $1,608	71-74-70-73—288
Tim Simpson, $1,608	75-71-69-73—288
Scott Gump, $1,608	74-71-69-74—288
Craig Parry, $1,608	71-69-73-75—288
John Elliott, $1,519	72-74-73-70—289
Barry Cheesman, $1,519	73-72-73-71—289
Steve Lamontagne, $1,519	74-71-72-72—289
David Ogrin, $1,519	71-73-70-75—289
Brian Claar, $1,449	72-74-74-70—290
Bob Eastwood, $1,449	70-75-74-71—290
Dillard Pruitt, $1,449	74-72-73-71—290
Ronnie Black, $1,449	73-73-72-72—290
Brett Ogle, $1,449	71-75-72-72—290
Brandel Chamblee, $1,449	68-75-74-73—290
John Mahaffey, $1,393	75-71-74-71—291
P.H. Horgan III, $1,393	71-74-74-72—291
Bill Murchison, $1,365	71-74-77-70—292
Joe Durant, $1,365	74-70-76-72—292
John Flannery, $1,323	72-73-75-73—293
Blaine McCallister, $1,323	68-76-75-74—293
Neale Smith, $1,323	71-74-74-74—293
Gene Jones, $1,323	72-74-72-75—293
Marco Dawson, $1,281	72-72-74-76—294
Lon Hinkle, $1,281	72-69-76-77—294
Gary Hallberg, $1,260	72-71-77-75—295
Hubert Green, $1,246	71-75-75-75—296
Jeff Woodland, $1,211	71-75-78-73—297
Greg Twiggs, $1,211	73-73-76-75—297
Tad Rhyan, $1,211	70-73-78-76—297
Greg Cesario, $1,211	75-71-76-75—297
Fulton Allem	73-73-75-WD

#-won on second playoff hole

Walt Disney World/Oldsmobile Classic

AT A GLANCE

▸**Course:** Walt Disney World (Magnolia, Palm and Lake Buena Vista Courses)
▸**Location:** Lake Buena Vista, Fla.
▸**When:** Oct. 7-10, 1993
▸**Weather:** Partly sunny and warm Thursday. Two lightning and rain delays Friday. Rain and lightning halted play Saturday at 5 p.m., and 69 players completed the third round Sunday morning. Clear Sunday until thunderstorms suspended play for two hours. Play completed with floodlights lighting the final green.
▸**Purse:** $1.1 million
▸**Par:** each 72
▸**Yards:** Magnolia, 7,190; Palm, 6,957; Buena Vista, 6,829
▸**Defending champion:** John Huston, 26-under-par 262
▸**Tournament record:** 26-under-par 262, John Huston, 1992

After knocking on the door for three years, Jeff Maggert needed just a little light to break through and finally win his first PGA Tour tournament.

With the 18th green bathed in floodlights, Maggert completed 36 holes of the rain-marred Walt Disney World/Oldsmobile Classic in one day, shooting 66-68 for a 23-under-par 265 total.

"This is a real relief for me. I feel like I'm over a hurdle now," said Maggert, 29, who finished second twice in 1993.

Maggert also finished third twice in 1992 and had late leads at Houston, New Orleans and the 1992 PGA Championship.

"I've had a number of disappointments," he said. "Now, I don't have to answer a certain question." Like, why he hasn't won.

"I don't think we would have been able to finish without (the floodlights)," Maggert said. "I could hardly see the flag.... Most of us can probably close our eyes and hit a pretty good shot in the daytime. But when you're looking down and you can't see (the ball), it gives you a funny feeling."

—by Steve Hershey

Scores and earnings

Player	Earnings	Scores
Jeff Maggert	$198,000	66-65-66-68–265
Greg Kraft	$118,800	69-69-64-66-268
Craig Stadler	$52,800	68-67-68-67-270
Loren Roberts	$52,800	66-68-67-69-270
Ken Green	$52,800	70-68-63-69-270
Ted Tryba	$52,800	64-68-67-71-270
John Cook	$36,850	70-67-65-69-271
Tom Purtzer	$33,000	64-68-71-69-272
Billy Mayfair	$33,000	68-68-71-65-272
Keith Clearwater	$23,571	64-67-68-74-273
David Ogrin	$23,571	74-69-65-65-273
Curtis Strange	$23,571	65-70-69-69-273
Larry Mize	$23,571	66-70-66-71-273
Jay Delsing	$23,571	69-67-71-66-273
Tom Sieckmann	$23,571	69-66-69-69-273
Scott Hoch	$23,571	66-69-68-70-273
Mark Wiebe	$14,394	66-67-68-73-274
Dennis Trixler	$14,394	66-72-67-69-274
Barry Cheesman	$14,394	68-67-65-74-274
Dan Forsman	$14,394	67-70-69-68-274
Mark McCumber	$14,394	65-67-70-72-274
Skip Kendall	$14,394	65-66-68-75-274
Brian Claar	$14,394	67-67-69-71-274
Larry Rinker	$7,965	70-69-68-68-275
Robert Gamez	$7,965	71-70-66-68-275
Ronnie Black	$7,965	69-68-67-71-275
Bill Glasson	$7,965	67-68-71-69-275
Jaime Gomez	$7,965	70-65-69-71-275
Lee Janzen	$7,965	65-69-69-72-275
Perry Moss	$7,965	69-67-66-73-275
Davis Love III	$7,965	70-66-70-69-275
Jay Haas	$7,965	65-69-71-70-275
Tim Simpson	$7,965	69-68-70-68-275
JC Anderson	$7,965	65-71-66-73-275
Ed Humenik	$4,968	69-64-70-73-276
Rocco Mediate	$4,968	71-64-68-73-276
Scott Simpson	$4,968	71-69-67-69-276
Gene Sauers	$4,968	68-70-67-71-276
Andrew Magee	$4,968	71-67-68-70-276
David Jackson	$4,968	70-66-69-71-276
Phil Blackmar	$4,968	65-71-67-73-276
Dick Mast	$4,968	70-69-66-71-276
John Huston	$4,968	69-68-67-72-276
Mike Schuchart	$3,326	70-67-68-72-277
Mike Hulbert	$3,326	67-69-69-72-277
Billy Andrade	$3,326	68-68-69-72-277
Fred Funk	$3,326	66-69-69-73-277
Corey Pavin	$3,326	70-69-70-68-277
Nolan Henke	$3,326	68-67-70-72-277
Dave Barr	$2,653	69-67-71-71-278
Blaine McCallister	$2,653	73-71-65-69-278
Kirk Triplett	$2,653	68-72-69-69-278
Kenny Perry	$2,653	70-70-69-69-278
Tom Lehman	$2,653	67-67-70-74-278
John Inman	$2,486	70-71-68-70-279
Chip Beck	$2,486	68-72-68-71-279
Mike Sullivan	$2,486	67-74-68-70-279
Howard Twitty	$2,486	69-70-68-72-279
Steve Lowery	$2,486	70-70-69-70-279
Mark Carnevale	$2,387	70-71-67-72-280
Fulton Allem	$2,387	67-69-70-74-280
Paul Azinger	$2,387	70-70-67-73-280
David Peoples	$2,387	75-69-65-71-280
Robin Freeman	$2,277	70-70-69-72-281
Hubert Green	$2,277	66-71-70-74-281
D.A. Weibring	$2,277	70-69-67-75-281
Mike Smith	$2,277	70-68-69-74-281
John Mahaffey	$2,277	69-68-72-72-281
Lanny Wadkins	$2,277	74-68-67-72-281
Greg Twiggs	$2,189	70-70-67-75-282
Brad Bryant	$2,189	69-73-67-73-282
Harry Taylor	$2,145	70-67-71-76-284
Bob Lohr	$2,145	70-67-71-76-284

H-E-B Texas Open

AT A GLANCE

- **Course:** Oak Hills Country Club
- **Location:** San Antonio
- **When:** Oct. 15-18, 1993
- **Weather:** Sunny, windy and warm.
- **Purse:** $1 million
- **Par:** 71
- **Yards:** 6,650
- **Playoff:** Jay Haas birdied the second playoff hole to defeat Bob Lohr after they tied at 21-under-par 263.
- **Defending champion:** Nick Price defeated Steve Elkington on the second playoff hole after they tied at 21-under-par 263.
- **Tournament record:** 22-under-par 258, Donnie Hammond, 1989

After shooting a 64 on the last day, for a 21-under-par 263, Jay Haas birdied the second playoff hole to defeat Bob Lohr and win the $1 million H-E-B Texas Open, his first victory since June 1992.

Scores and earnings

#Jay Haas, $180,000	68-65-66-64—263
Bob Lohr, $108,000	68-64-67-64—263
Billy Andrade, $68,000	66-66-69-66—267
Bob Estes, $48,000	66-71-64-67—268
Gil Morgan, $32,750	66-66-70-67—269
Mike Standly, $32,750	66-71-65-67—269
Marco Dawson, $32,750	69-67-65-68—269
David Edwards, $32,750	68-66-66-69—269
Dan Forsman, $32,750	64-68-67-70—269
Tom Lehman, $32,750	71-63-65-70—269
John Elliott, $23,000	70-68-69-63—270
Mark Wiebe, $23,000	64-70-70-66—270
Scott Hoch, $23,000	68-66-68-68—270
Tim Conley, $17,500	67-72-67-65—271
Jim Thorpe, $17,500	69-66-68-68—271
Lanny Wadkins, $17,500	64-70-68-69—271
Tom Kite, $17,500	66-70-65-70—271
Russ Cochran, $13,500	68-69-69-66—272
Bruce Lietzke, $13,500	67-70-68-67—272
Rick Fehr, $13,500	66-69-68-69—272
Mark Lye, $13,500	69-66-66-71—272
Brad Faxon, $9,600	70-65-72-66—273
Dillard Pruitt, $9,600	74-64-69-66—273
Paul Goydos, $9,600	68-71-68-66—273
John Huston, $9,600	71-69-66-67—273
David Ogrin, $9,600	70-66-67-70—273
Brad Bryant, $7,100	69-68-71-66—274
Brandel Chamblee, $7,100	69-70-68-67—274
Willie Wood, $7,100	69-68-69-68—274
Morris Hatalsky, $7,100	71-67-68-68—274
Donnie Hammond, $7,100	72-68-65-69—274
Steve Pate, $5,660	68-69-71-67—275
Jeff Maggert, $5,660	70-67-70-68—275
Lee Porter, $5,660	69-66-70-70—275
Jim Kane, $5,660	66-70-68-71—275
Mike Schuchart, $5,660	71-68-65-71—275
Brian Claar, $3,900	68-72-71-65—276
Russell Beiersdorf, $3,900	67-70-72-67—276
D.A. Weibring, $3,900	70-68-71-67—276
Dennis Trixler, $3,900	67-69-73-67—276
Jeff Cook, $3,900	69-71-68-68—276
Gene Jones, $3,900	71-67-68-70—276
Mark O'Meara, $3,900	68-66-71-71—276
Mike Smith, $3,900	62-73-70-71—276
Corey Pavin, $3,900	70-66-69-71—276
Tim Simpson, $3,900	66-71-68-71—276
Scott Gump, $3,900	67-67-70-72—276
Blaine McCallister, $2,513	68-70-74-65—277
Jeff Woodland, $2,513	68-70-72-67—277
Barry Cheesman, $2,513	67-73-71-66—277
P.H. Horgan III, $2,513	69-69-70-69—277
Patrick Burke, $2,513	72-68-67-70—277
Ted Tryba, $2,513	67-71-67-72—277
John Flannery, $2,300	73-67-74-64—278
Brian Kamm, $2,300	70-66-71-71—278
Denis Watson, $2,300	70-68-69-71—278
Gary Hallberg, $2,230	69-71-72-67—279
Jeff Sluman, $2,230	73-65-70-71—279
Bobby Clampett, $2,230	69-71-67-72—279
Steve Elkington, $2,230	67-73-66-73—279
Ben Crenshaw, $2,170	67-73-69-71—280
Larry Nelson, $2,170	68-69-71-72—280
Howard Twitty, $2,140	74-65-76-66—281
Gary McCord, $2,110	70-70-70-72—282
Neale Smith, $2,110	69-70-69-74—282
Steve Lowery, $2,030	70-69-75-69—283
Perry Moss, $2,030	72-66-76-69—283
Leonard Thompson, $2,030	69-71-72-71—283
Bob Gilder, $2,030	70-70-72-71—283
Phil Blackmar, $2,030	70-70-71-72—283
Ed Fiori, $2,030	70-69-70-74—283
David Jackson, $1,940	69-71-74-70—284
Tom Byrum, $1,940	67-73-71-73—284
Lance Ten Broeck, $1,940	68-72-69-75—284
Dave Peege, $1,900	68-72-76-69—285
JC Anderson, $1,880	71-66-75-74—286
J.L. Lewis, $1,850	71-69-75-73—288
Chris Tucker, $1,850	68-71-76-73—288

#-won on second playoff hole

Las Vegas Invitational

AT A GLANCE

- **Course:** Las Vegas Country Club, TPC at Summerlin and Desert Inn & Country Club
- **Location:** Las Vegas
- **When:** Oct. 20-24, 1993
- **Weather:** Sunny and warm.
- **Purse:** $1.4 million
- **Par:** all 72
- **Yards:** Las Vegas CC, 7,162; TPC at Summerlin, 7,243; Desert Inn & CC, 7,111
- **Defending champion:** John Cook, 24-under-par 334
- **Tournament record:** 31-under-par 329, Andrew Magee, 1991

Davis Love III was so far ahead of the pack he started shooting for records.

The records didn't materialize, but his closing 66 gave him a 29-under-par 331 total—good enough for an eight-stroke victory at the Las Vegas Invitational.

"I got so far in front so fast I didn't know where to go or what to do or how to play," Davis said.

With a six-shot lead after four rounds, Love, who started eagle-par-eagle, played the front in 30, had a 10-shot lead at the turn and found himself out of touch with the rest of the field.

Only a meaningless double bogey from the water on the 17th kept the winning margin from double digits.

Love holed a 85-yard sand wedge shot for eagle-2 on the first hole and dropped a wide-breaking 20-foot putt for eagle-3 on the third.

Craig Stadler provided the day's only drama by dropping a double-breaking, 25-foot birdie putt on the 90th hole. That putt lifted Stadler into second place and, more importantly, qualified him for the season-ending Tour Championship in San Francisco.

(Only the top 30 money-winners are invited, and Stadler's prize vaulted him from 42nd to 27th on the money list.)

Scores and earnings

Player	Rounds
Davis Love III, $252,000	67-66-67-65-66–331
Craig Stadler, $151,200	67-66-69-72-65–339
Paul Azinger, $72,800	66-67-72-68-67–340
David Edwards, $72,800	72-66-68-67-67–340
Bob Estes, $72,800	68-68-68-67-69–340
John Huston, $46,900	69-66-69-71-67–342
Bob Tway, $46,900	71-68-68-67-68–342
Richard Zokol, $46,900	68-67-68-69-70–342
Gil Morgan, $40,600	64-68-72-70-69–343
Brian Kamm, $35,000	68-70-69-69-68–344
Dick Mast, $35,000	72-68-66-68-70–344
Robert Gamez, $35,000	66-70-68-69-71–344
Vijay Singh, $26,250	68-69-72-69-67–345
Michael Allen, $26,250	71-64-71-70-69–345
Russ Cochran, $26,250	68-70-68-69-70–345
Jay Don Blake, $26,250	71-70-66-68-70–345
Tom Lehman, $21,700	70-70-71-70-65–346
Keith Clearwater, $21,700	67-65-67-74-73–346
Kirk Triplett, $17,570	71-72-66-71-67–347
Scott Hoch, $17,570	69-70-68-72-68–347
Grant Waite, $17,570	69-69-69-68-72–347
Phil Mickelson, $17,570	65-69-68-71-74–347
John Cook, $12,460	66-73-70-73-66–348
Rick Fehr, $12,460	70-68-72-70-68–348
Brad Faxon, $12,460	66-71-71-70-70–348
Bill Murchison, $12,460	73-71-66-67-71–348
Ken Green, $12,460	69-66-68-72-73–348
Mike Sullivan, $9,310	71-75-64-72-67–349
Tim Conley, $9,310	71-68-69-72-69–349
Roger Maltbie, $9,310	69-72-68-70-70–349
Mark O'Meara, $9,310	71-69-68-71-70–349
Bill Glasson, $9,310	69-66-69-74-71–349
Mark McCumber, $9,310	68-68-71-71-71–349
Ronnie Black, $6,627	72-68-70-73-67–350
Gary Hallberg, $6,627	68-68-72-75-67–350
D.A. Weibring, $6,627	70-71-71-70-68–350
Steve Lamontagne, $6,627	71-66-71-74-68–350
Fuzzy Zoeller, $6,627	73-70-68-69-70–350
Gene Sauers, $6,627	68-71-71-69-71–350
John Inman, $6,627	67-72-70-69-72–350
Billy Mayfair, $6,627	68-68-72-69-73–350
Willie Wood, $6,627	70-70-69-68-73–350
John Mahaffey, $4,760	70-66-73-71-71–351
Paul Goydos, $4,760	69-71-71-68-72–351
Ed Dougherty, $4,760	70-65-69-74-73–351
Marco Dawson, $4,760	71-68-68-70-74–351
Scott Gump, $3,516	66-71-73-73-69–352
Blaine McCallister, $3,516	67-65-78-73-69–352
Bruce Fleisher, $3,516	67-69-70-77-69–352
JC Anderson, $3,516	72-63-75-71-71–352
Brian Claar, $3,516	68-69-72-71-72–352
Russell Beiersdorf, $3,516	75-67-67-70-73–352
Bill Britton, $3,516	73-69-65-72-73–352
Tim Simpson, $3,516	70-71-66-71-74–352
David Peoples, $3,516	70-69-64-73-76–352
Perry Moss, $3,150	68-71-72-75-67–353
Wayne Levi, $3,150	68-70-71-73-71–353
Mike Springer, $3,150	67-68-73-71-74–353
Bob Lohr, $3,150	64-68-73-71-77–353
Jeff Woodland, $3,038	64-73-69-76-72–354
Tom Sieckmann, $3,038	67-72-72-69-74–354
Harry Taylor, $3,038	71-69-68-72-74–354
Joel Edwards, $3,038	72-69-69-69-75–354
Howard Twitty, $2,940	65-73-73-77-67–355
Duffy Waldorf, $2,940	70-68-73-73-71–355
David Toms, $2,940	74-69-68-71-73–355
Jim Mcgovern, $2,884	68-71-72-75-70–356
Steve Lowery, $2,842	66-71-72-76-72–357
Steve Pate, $2,842	70-72-69-72-74–357
Kelly Gibson, $2,800	70-70-70-75-73–358
Brian Henninger, $2,758	70-72-69-73-75–359
Jay Delsing, $2,758	69-69-72-72-77–359
Tom Byrum, $2,716	69-68-71-80-73–361
John Flannery, $2,674	68-67-76-78-74–363
Ben Crenshaw, $2,674	75-68-68-75-77–363

Tour Championship

AT A GLANCE

- **Course:** The Olympic Club (Lake Course)
- **Location:** San Francisco
- **When:** Oct. 28-31, 1993
- **Weather:** Beautiful.
- **Purse:** $3 million
- **Par:** 71
- **Yards:** 6,812
- **Defending champion:** Paul Azinger, 12-under-par 276
- **Tournament record:** 20-under-par 268, Tom Watson, Oak Hills Country Club, San Antonio, 1987

Jim Gallagher stood at the 17th tee on the final day of the Tour Championship, thinking he needed a birdie to hold off Greg Norman.

His goal was realistic because the 522-yard, par-5 had given up seven birdies to the first 24 players. After a good drive, he had 238 yards to the green and never hesitated, pulling the 3-wood out of bag.

"I don't like to lay up anyway," he said. "I felt I could get it there."

The shot rolled within 20 feet of the hole. Then his problems started.

He rolled his first putt four feet past, then pulled his second and admitted later he was devastated.

"I thought, I probably let it get away there," Gallagher said. "I felt I needed a birdie and when I didn't get it, I thought it was over. I figured Greg (Norman) could par in."

So Gallagher went to the ABC-TV booth and tried to explain away his disappointment. But after Norman bogeyed the 16th and parred the 17th, Gallagher started getting edgy.

Enough of this chit-chat, it was time to warm up. He might be fortunate enough to get in a playoff. So off he went, where he couldn't see the 18th green, and got ready for a playoff that never happened.

Instead, he capped the best of his 10 PGA Tour seasons, winning for the second time to go with his 3 and 2 Ryder Cup win against Seve Ballesteros.

"This surpasses all of my goals," he said. "It's quite a turnaround from 12 years ago."

At the 1981 U.S. Amateur at San Francisco's Olympic Club, Gallagher shot 87 and was so discouraged, he said, he didn't play golf for six weeks.

"I thought, 'Maybe golf isn't for me,' " he said. "I thought I better work harder on my grades. But I'm glad I didn't give it up."

In his next competitive appearance at the Olympic Club, 12 years later, Gallagher set the course record: 8-under-par 63 in the Championship's opening round.

After three rounds, he trailed leader David Frost by three strokes.

"I wasn't discouraged," Gallagher said. "I knew I was still playing well, that I still had a chance."

Birdies on the 9th, 10th and 13th holes put Gallagher back where he finished round one—at 8-under. Even though a bunkered tee shot on No. 15 dropped him one stroke, that was enough—thanks to Norman's collapse.

"I guess I had a great year in one week," Gallagher said after he collected the $540,000 prize and more than doubled his year's earnings.

—*by Steve Hershey*

Scores and earnings
Jim Gallagher, $540,000	63-73-72-69—277
Scott Simpson, $198,750	68-70-70-70—278
John Huston, $198,750	72-68-68-70—278
David Frost, $198,750	68-68-69-73—278
Greg Norman, $198,750	72-67-68-71—278
Rick Fehr, $108,000	69-69-70-71—279
Corey Pavin, $96,000	68-73-72-67—280
Mark Calcavecchia, $96,000	69-69-75-67—280
Tom Kite, $96,000	69-68-72-71—280
Fred Couples, $83,100	74-72-70-65—281
Jay Haas, $83,100	70-69-72-70—281
Fulton Allem, $73,200	69-72-71-71—283
Chip Beck, $73,200	71-70-70-72—283
David Edwards, $73,200	71-72-68-72—283
Jeff Maggert, $66,000	71-74-69-70—284
Vijay Singh, $62,400	70-71-74-70—285
Jim McGovern, $62,400	71-70-73-71—285
Larry Mize, $58,800	69-76-71-70—286
Nick Price, $58,800	72-68-75-71—286
Gil Morgan, $58,800	70-71-71-74—286
Paul Azinger, $56,400	72-71-72-73—288
Lee Janzen, $55,200	73-68-74-74—289
Rocco Mediate, $52,800	78-70-70-72—290
Steve Elkington, $52,800	74-71-74-71—290
Nolan Henke, $52,800	69-72-74-75—290
Payne Stewart, $50,400	74-72-73-73—292
Davis Love III, $49,800	77-72-73-71—293
Phil Mickelson, $49,200	71-75-74-74—294
Craig Stadler, $48,600	71-75-73-77—296
Billy Mayfair, $48,000	77-77-74-71—299

1993 LPGA Player of the Year

LPGA Player of the Year Betsy King was first in money earned with $595,992; she had 15 top 10 finishes.

A YEAR REDEEMED ON THE FINAL HOLE

Betsy King had 17 years of experience to draw on when she stood over a 20-foot putt in the last round of the Toray Queens Cup in Yoshikawa, Japan.

It was the final putt of the final event of the LPGA's season. Hanging in the balance were a victory, Player of the Year, the Vare Trophy (for lowest 18-hole scoring average) and the money title.

"I don't think I've ever stood over a shot that had so much riding on it," says King, "but when I hit it I knew that it was in."

By making the putt for birdie she ended a season of frustration with one day of triumph. Although she won the JC Penney Skins Game in May and finished second in five events, she had no official wins when she went to Japan in early November for the final tournament of the season.

"I played well this year, but I wasn't able to win on Sunday," says King, who led eight events going into the final round before breaking through with a victory. "I went to Japan knowing that I had to win. Still, the victory was unexpected."

King won her third Rolex Player of the Year title. The other two came in 1984, the first year she won a tournament on tour, and in '89 when she won six events and earned a personal high of $654,132.

"The first time you win Player of the Year is pretty special," says King. "I consider '89 my best year because I've never played better. This year might be the most satisfying because of all the things I went through."

King finished the season with $595,992 in earnings and a scoring average of 70.85 strokes per round. Nancy Lopez had an average of 70.83, but she was not eligible for the Vare Trophy because she didn't play the required 70 rounds.

King got a personal thrill from extending her winning streak to 10 years with at least one victory. She has 29 career wins and will qualify for the LPGA's Hall of Fame with one more official victory.

"I've had two careers," says King, who played seven seasons before winning an official event. "In the first I struggled so much I thought I might never win a tournament. Obviously, I wasn't thinking about making the Hall of Fame in those years."

King credits improved putting with her breakthrough in 1984, but it was problems with putting that led to her frustrations in 1993. Time after time it disappointed her until that final round in Japan.

On that day she made par-saving putts of 25 feet on the 15th hole and 20 feet on the 17th that set up the dramatic birdie on the 18th.

"This winter I'm working on my short game," says King, "because that let me down more than anything."

King, 38, says she would have considered the season a success even if she hadn't won. But the victories she counted until the last one were psychological.

"I learned patience and perseverence," says King. "I was surprised by how many players encouraged me when I wasn't winning. Pat Bradley said to me, 'I have that card all made out to you.'"

The card is to congratulate King on joining Bradley in the Hall of Fame once she gets the 30th victory. King says she isn't looking ahead, but she adds, "I hope the 30th comes a little easier than the 29th."

—by Jerry Potter

HEALTHSOUTH PALM BEACH CLASSIC

AT A GLANCE

- **Course:** Wycliffe Golf and Country Club
- **Location:** Lake Worth, Fla.
- **When:** Feb. 5-7, 1993
- **Weather:** Sunny and windy.
- **Purse:** $400,000
- **Par:** 72
- **Yards:** 6,324
- **Playoff:** Tammie Green birdied to defeat JoAnne Carner on the first playoff hole.
- **Defending champion:** Colleen Walker defeated Dawn Coe-Jones on first playoff hole.
- **Tournament record:** 16-under-par 272, Pat Bradley, Deer Creek CC, 1983

Tammie Green could have had a perfect victory had the opponent not been her old friend JoAnne Carner. But in golf, friendship ends at the first tee.

Green was happy to win the Palm Beach Classic, beating the LPGA Hall of Famer on the first hole of a playoff.

"There's no one I'd rather see win than JoAnne," she said. "She's been a good friend since I was a rookie (1987). The first practice round I ever played at an LPGA tournament was with JoAnne."

The two tied at 8-under-par 208 after 54 holes, with Green shooting 69 on Sunday, Carner 70.

Green won with a playoff birdie, preventing Carner from becoming the oldest golfer to win a pro tour event.

Sam Snead won the 1965 Greater Greensboro Open at 52 years, 10 months.

On the playoff hole, a 380-yard par 4, Green put her 7-iron approach shot 20 feet left of the cup, while Carner's 7-iron stopped 50 feet away.

"I should have hit a hard 8-iron," Carner, 53, said. "But the ball had mud on it. I had to gamble with what the mud would make the ball do."

—by Jerry Potter

Scores and earnings

Player	Scores
#Tammie Green, $60,000	70-69-69—208
JoAnne Carner, $37,237	66-72-70—208
Brandie Burton, $27,173	66-73-70—209
Jane Geddes, $16,051	72-71-67—210
Chris Johnson, $16,051	69-73-68—210
Kelly Robbins, $16,051	70-70-70—210
Jenny Wyatt, $16,051	66-71-73—210
Kristi Albers, $7,993	70-75-66—211
Tracy Kerdyk, $7,993	71-71-69—211
Danielle Ammaccapane, $7,993	71-71-69—211
Dawn Coe-Jones, $7,993	70-72-69—211
Elaine Crosby, $7,993	71-70-70—211
Michelle McGann, $7,993	72-68-71—211
Tania Abitbol, $7,993	71-69-71—211
Patti Rizzo, $5,635	72-70-70—212
Donna Andrews, $5,635	70-72-70—212
Laura Davies, $4,456	76-69-68—213
Dottie Mochrie, $4,456	75-69-69—213
Tina Barrett, $4,456	74-70-69—213
Robin Hood, $4,456	71-73-69—213
Amy Read, $4,456	73-69-71—213
Colleen Walker, $4,456	71-70-72—213
Liselotte Neumann, $4,456	69-71-73—213
Marta Figueras-Dotti, $4,456	69-71-73—213
Alice Ritzman, $4,456	72-67-74—213
Sherri Steinhauer, $3,247	76-70-68—214
Dana Lofland-Dormann, $3,247	74-70-70—214
Lisa Walters, $3,247	73-71-70—214
Meg Mallon, $3,247	74-69-71—214
Deb Richard, $3,247	73-70-71—214
Cathy Morse, $3,247	74-68-72—214
Kris Tschetter, $3,247	70-71-73—214
Jane Crafter, $3,247	68-73-73—214
Rosie Jones, $2,404	76-70-69—215
Cindy Rarick, $2,404	72-74-69—215
Alison Nicholas, $2,404	69-77-69—215
Deborah McHaffie, $2,404	77-66-72—215
Pearl Sinn, $2,404	71-72-72—215
Michelle Estill, $2,404	73-69-73—215
Jill Briles-Hinton, $2,404	69-73-73—215
Helen Alfredsson, $2,404	68-71-76—215
Julie Larsen, $1,611	75-71-70—216
Robin Walton, $1,611	74-71-71—216
Hollis Stacy, $1,611	70-75-71—216
Vicki Fergon, $1,611	77-67-72—216
Dina Ammaccapane, $1,611	71-73-72—216
Patty Sheehan, $1,611	70-74-72—216
Joan Pitcock, $1,611	72-71-73—216
Gail Graham, $1,611	72-71-73—216
Amy Alcott, $1,611	71-72-73—216
Amy Benz, $1,611	74-68-74—216
Terry-Jo Myers, $1,116	73-73-71—217
Ellie Gibson, $1,116	73-73-71—217
Judy Dickinson, $1,116	71-75-71—217
Michele Redman, $1,116	74-70-73—217
Cathy Johnston, $875	75-71-72—218
Kathy Postlewait, $875	71-74-73—218
Muffin Spencer-Devlin, $875	74-70-74—218
Sherri Turner, $875	72-70-76—218
Beth Daniel, $640	74-72-73—219
Hiromi Kobayashi, $640	72-74-73—219
Stefania Croce, $640	74-71-74—219
Martha Nause, $640	71-74-74—219
Cindy Figg-Currier, $640	71-74-74—219
Carolyn Hill, $640	71-71-77—219
Sally Little, $640	70-71-78—219
Missie McGeorge, $476	75-71-74—220
Cindy Schreyer, $476	74-72-74—220
Dale Eggeling, $476	73-73-74—220
Juli Inkster, $476	72-74-74—220
Nancy L. Ramsbottom, $476	73-72-75—220
Pat Bradley, $476	71-74-75—220
Nancy White, $476	72-72-76—220
Michelle Mackall, $476	75-68-77—220
Kate Golden, $407	72-74-77—223
Katie Peterson-Parker, $407	74-71-78—223

- won on first hole of playoff

Itoki Hawaiian Ladies Open

At a Glance

- **Course:** Ko Olina Golf Club
- **Location:** Ewa Beach, Oahu, Hawaii
- **When:** Feb. 18-20, 1993
- **Weather:** Beautiful.
- **Purse:** $450,000
- **Par:** 72
- **Yards:** 6,244
- **Defending champion:** Lisa Walters
- **Tournament record:** 11-under-par 205, Sheri Turner, 1989

LPGA tournaments in Hawaii have become Canadian affairs.

Lisa Walters' successful defense of her Hawaiian Ladies Open title, with a one-stroke victory over Nancy Lopez, made it the fourth time in a year an LPGA player from Canada had won in Hawaii.

In addition to Walters' consecutive victories, Dawn Coe-Jones won the Women's Kemper Open and the LPGA Matchplay Championship, giving the Canadians a sweep.

It was enough for Walters to joke that she and Coe-Jones had renamed the 6,216-yard course "Coe-o-Lisa."

Walters' latest victory was much different than her 1992 triumph, when she came on with a rush, shooting a closing 65.

This time, she positioned herself for the final round with two 68s over the first two days to stay within a stroke of Lopez.

"Last year, it was one hot round," Walters said. "This year, I was a lot more consistent."

Lopez, who had eight birdies and no bogeys over the front nine the first two days, had three bogeys by the end of the first six holes Saturday.

Lopez still managed to pull even when Walters gave back two strokes with an out-of-bounds drive at the 10th and a bogey on No. 13.

But a birdie at the par-5 5,475-yard 14th put Walters ahead for good.

—by Jerry Potter

Scores and earnings

Player	Scores	Total
Lisa Walters, $67,500	68-68-74	210
Nancy Lopez, $41,891	68-67-76	211
Dottie Mochrie, $30,569	70-72-70	212
Susie Redman, $19,624	72-71-70	213
Tracy Kerdyk, $19,624	70-70-73	213
Jane Crafter, $19,624	73-66-74	213
Dawn Coe-Jones, $13,360	76-67-71	214
Kelly Robbins, $11,208	71-74-70	215
Lori Garbacz, $11,208	75-68-72	215
Patty Sheehan, $9,057	73-73-70	216
Gail Graham, $9,057	67-76-73	216
Missie Berteotti, $7,245	74-71-72	217
Ayako Okamoto, $7,245	73-71-73	217
Marta Figueras-Dotti, $7,245	73-71-73	217
Laura Davies, $7,245	70-70-77	217
Tina Barrett, $5,887	75-71-72	218
Cindy Mackey, $5,887	70-76-72	218
Caroline Keggi, $5,887	71-74-73	218
Amy Alcott, $4,796	73-76-70	219
Mary Beth Zimmerman, $4,796	71-78-70	219
Kathryn Marshall, $4,796	75-73-71	219
Michelle McGann, $4,796	75-71-73	219
Michiko Hattori, $4,796	75-71-73	219
Michele Redman, $4,796	72-72-75	219
Liselotte Neumann, $4,796	70-70-79	219
Jenny Wyatt, $3,592	77-71-72	220
Jenny Lidback, $3,592	75-73-72	220
Lynn Connelly, $3,592	72-75-73	220
Danielle Ammaccapane, $3,592	74-72-74	220
Donna Andrews, $3,592	71-75-74	220
Anne Marie Palli, $3,592	74-71-75	220
Betsy King, $3,592	72-73-75	220
Juli Inkster, $3,592	73-71-76	220
Brandie Burton, $3,592	71-73-76	220
Kris Tschetter, $2,394	74-76-71	221
Alison Nicholas, $2,394	77-72-72	221
Patti Rizzo, $2,394	75-74-72	221
Dale Eggeling, $2,394	74-75-72	221
Cathy Marino, $2,394	77-71-73	221
Jennifer Sevil, $2,394	75-72-74	221
Page Dunlap, $2,394	75-71-75	221
Cindy Rarick, $2,394	74-72-75	221
Kim Williams, $2,394	74-71-76	221
Pat Bradley, $2,394	72-73-76	221
Deb Richard, $2,394	71-72-78	221
Denise Baldwin, $2,394	71-69-81	221
Nancy L. Ramsbottom, $1,441	77-71-74	222
Pearl Sinn, $1,441	74-74-74	222
Amy Read, $1,441	74-74-74	222
Caroline Pierce, $1,441	75-72-75	222
Susie Berning, $1,441	75-72-75	222
Amy Benz, $1,441	74-73-75	222
Hollis Stacy, $1,441	73-74-75	222
Kristi Albers, $1,441	73-74-75	222
Julie Larsen, $1,441	71-73-78	222
Lori West, $954	79-70-74	223
Jane Geddes, $954	75-73-75	223
Nayoko Yoshikawa, $954	75-73-75	223
Val Skinner, $954	77-69-77	223
Jill Briles-Hinton, $954	68-77-78	223
Michele Ann Thompson, $747	77-73-74	224
Deborah McHaffie, $747	74-75-75	224
Akiko Fukushima, $747	73-75-76	224
Chris Johnson, $667	74-76-75	225
Karen Lunn, $667	72-78-75	225
Sherri Steinhauer, $599	77-73-76	226
Joan Pitcock, $599	77-73-76	226
Cindy Figg-Currier, $599	75-75-76	226
Kim Bauer, $599	76-73-77	226
Nancy Rubin, $511	78-72-77	227
Amy Fruhwirth, $511	77-72-78	227
Suzanne Strudwick, $511	76-73-78	227
Robin Walton, $511	73-75-79	227
Connie Chillemi, $459	75-75-78	228
Leigh Ann, $459 ills	71-79-78	228
Ikuyo Shiotani, $459	75-74-79	228
Lisa Kiggens, $459	74-74-80	228
Cathy Mockett, $430	76-74-79	229
Suzy Whaley, $430	73-76-80	229

PING/WELCH'S CHAMPIONSHIP

AT A GLANCE

- **Course:** Randolph Park, North Course
- **Location:** Tucson, Ariz.
- **When:** March 11-14, 1993
- **Weather:** Sunny and warm.
- **Purse:** $400,000
- **Par:** 72
- **Yards:** 6,187
- **Defending champion:** Brandie Burton
- **Tournament record:** 16-under-par 272, Meg Mallon, 1993; Chris Johnson, 1984

Meg Mallon doesn't mind knowing when she's leading an LPGA tournament. But during the final round of the Ping/Welch's Championship she was just too busy to look at a scoreboard.

"I didn't look at the leader board until Betsy was putting for eagle on 18," Mallon said, who shot 3-under-par 69 Sunday for a 272 and a one-stroke victory over King.

She started the final round one stroke behind King.

"Unless I'm a couple shots behind, I don't want to know (how the leaders are playing). I can't control the leader board, just my game."

Mallon shot her third bogey-free round of the tournament Sunday for her fifth career victory. Her last victory was in 1991, when she won the Mazda LPGA Championship and the U.S. Women's Open.

Mallon birdied No. 3 and No. 12 with 12-foot putts, then rolled in a 27-footer for birdie at No. 17 for a two-stroke lead. She saved par with chips to 3 feet at No. 5 and 2 feet at No. 14.

King, the 1987 winner, shot a 71 and was hindered by three bad tee shots, two of which resulted in bogeys.

"I drove the ball so poorly," King said. "I didn't really get anything going until the last three holes (birdie-par-birdie)."

Scores and earnings

Player	Rounds-Total
Meg Mallon, $60,000	67-66-70-69—272
Betsy King, $37,237	70-67-65-71—273
Jane Crafter, $27,173	69-67-68-70—274
Cindy Rarick, $19,121	68-70-71-66—275
Juli Inkster, $19,121	70-67-71-67—275
Pearl Sinn, $11,472	69-73-71-65—278
Alice Ritzman, $11,472	71-72-68-67—278
Nancy Lopez, $11,472	70-66-72-70—278
Hollis Stacy, $11,472	73-66-67-72—278
Kris Tschetter, $6,977	69-74-69-67—279
Kristi Albers, $6,977	69-72-71-67—279
Lisa Walters, $6,977	70-70-70-69—279
Lynn Connelly, $6,977	69-71-70-69—279
Muffin Spencer-Devlin, $6,977	69-66-73-71—279
Patti Rizzo, $6,977	69-70-66-74—279
Rosie Jones, $4,732	72-70-71-67—280
Dawn Coe-Jones, $4,732	73-71-68-68—280
Barb Bunkowsky, $4,732	69-69-74-68—280
Deborah McHaffie, $4,732	70-71-70-69—280
Marianne Morris, $4,732	68-70-73-69—280
Jill Briles-Hinton, $4,732	67-72-71-70—280
Laura Davies, $4,732	68-70-71-71—280
Dottie Mochrie, $4,732	74-67-65-74—280
Elaine Crosby, $3,662	72-69-73-67—281
Cathy Mockett, $3,662	70-70-72-69—281
Jan Stephenson, $3,662	73-69-69-70—281
Judy Dickinson, $3,662	72-70-68-71—281
Danielle Ammaccapane, $3,662	70-72-67-72—281
Anne Marie Palli, $3,124	69-73-71-69—282
Michelle Mackall, $3,124	67-75-69-71—282
Amy Benz, $3,124	70-71-70-71—282
Colleen Walker, $3,124	71-68-69-74—282
Deb Richard, $2,656	71-72-71-69—283
Ellie Gibson, $2,656	75-69-69-70—283
Donna Andrews, $2,656	75-69-69-70—283
Sherri Steinhauer, $2,656	71-70-72-70—283
Dana Lofland-Dormann, $2,656	71-72-69-71—283
JoAnne Carner, $2,070	72-72-70-70—284
Lori Garbacz, $2,070	75-68-71-70—284
Becky Pearson, $2,070	71-71-70-72—284
Annika Sorenstam, $2,070	71-70-71-72—284
Laura Baugh, $2,070	68-71-73-72—284
Helen Alfredsson, $2,070	70-70-71-73—284
Robin Walton, $2,070	70-70-70-74—284
Ayako Okamoto, $1,456	73-71-72-69—285
Amy Alcott, $1,456	72-70-73-70—285
Cathy Morse, $1,456	71-70-74-70—285
Pamela Wright, $1,456	72-68-75-70—285
Cindy Schreyer, $1,456	71-72-71-71—285
Brandie Burton, $1,456	70-70-72-73—285
Missie McGeorge, $1,456	71-70-70-74—285
Dale Eggeling, $1,456	67-72-72-74—285
Amy Read, $938	70-73-74-69—286
Kim Williams, $938	75-69-72-70—286
Lauri Merten, $938	72-69-75-70—286
Mette Hageman, $938	71-73-71-71—286
Caroline Pierce, $938	70-74-71-71—286
Nancy L. Ramsbottom, $938	70-70-73-73—286
Michele Redman, $938	72-71-68-75—286
Kelly Robbins, $938	71-69-71-75—286
Alison Nicholas, $623	73-71-73-70—287
Karen Noble, $623	73-69-74-71—287
Allison Finney, $623	72-72-71-72—287
Cathy Johnston, $623	70-74-71-72—287
Jayne Thobois, $623	71-71-73-72—287
Lenore Rittenhouse, $623	73-70-69-75—287
Patti Liscio, $492	69-72-78-69—288
Barb Thomas, $492	70-72-73-73—288
Mitzi Edge, $492	73-70-70-75—288
Beth Daniel, $492	67-74-72-75—288
Caroline Gowan, $492	69-72-70-77—288
Pat Bradley, $492	68-72-69-79—288
Joan Pitcock, $412	71-73-74-71—289
Angie Ridgeway, $412	75-68-75-71—289
Mary Beth Zimmerman, $412	69-74-75-71—289
Tania Abitbol, $412	72-72-73-72—289
Missie Berteotti, $412	72-68-77-72—289
Julie Larsen, $386	73-71-74-72—290
Dina Ammaccapane, $374	74-70-76-71—291
Penny Hammel, $374	73-70-76-72—291
Deedee Lasker, $358	73-69-74-76—292
Trish Johnson, $358	68-73-72-79—292
Alicia Dibos, $346	72-69-76-76—293
Cindy Mackey, $339	74-70-76-74—294
Jody Anschutz, $332	73-70-76-76—295

Standard Register Ping

At a Glance

- **Course:** Moon Valley Country Club
- **Location:** Phoenix, Ariz.
- **When:** March 18-21, 1993
- **Weather:** Sunny and warm; gusty winds late in the day Thursday, Friday and Saturday.
- **Purse:** $700,000
- **Par:** 73
- **Yards:** 6,483
- **Defending champion:** Danielle Ammaccapane
- **Tournament record:** 17-under-par 275, Patty Sheehan, 1993

Patty Sheehan talked about the NCAA men's basketball tournament and pro football, anything to keep her mind off the challenge of qualifying for the LPGA Hall of Fame.

"Where is Joe Montana going to play?" she asked before the final round of the Standard Register Ping. "Kansas City or Minnesota?"

Nothing could calm her nerves until she tapped in a birdie putt on the final hole to win the tournament and qualify for the Hall of Fame with her 30th victory.

"I didn't feel comfortable until the 18th hole," said Sheehan.

Sheehan finished at 70, beating Dawn Coe-Jones and Kris Tschetter by five strokes with a record 17-under-par 275.

Coe-Jones had a disappointing 75 after starting the day tied with Sheehan for the lead.

Sheehan and Jones exchanged the lead twice through 10 holes before Sheehan took control. She birdied the 11th and 13th holes, which, coupled with Coe-Jones' bogey on 11, gave Sheehan a four-stroke lead with five holes to play.

Jones missed a 3-foot birdie putt that could have kept her within three strokes.

"The turning point was the 11th hole," Coe-Jones said. "Patty hit a great shot on 13. I didn't think I was going to miss that putt."

—by Jerry Potter

Scores and earnings

Player	Earnings	Scores
Patty Sheehan	$105,000	70-70-65-70–275
Kris Tschetter	$56,359	69-71-71-69–280
Dawn Coe-Jones	$56,359	69-69-67-75–280
Annika Sorenstam	$36,985	73-66-72-70–281
Tammie Green	$29,940	73-69-67-74–283
Dottie Mochrie	$24,656	69-72-70-73–284
Helen Alfredsson	$19,549	71-72-72-70–285
Robin Walton	$19,549	69-73-69-74–285
Brandie Burton	$16,555	69-72-74-71–286
Suzanne Strudwick	$11,237	77-70-70-70–287
Trish Johnson	$11,237	70-73-74-70–287
Lisa Walters	$11,237	68-75-74-70–287
Tina Barrett	$11,237	72-72-72-71–287
Jane Crafter	$11,237	72-73-70-72–287
Hollis Stacy	$11,237	72-72-71-72–287
Nancy Ramsbottom	$11,237	71-72-72-72–287
M. Figueras-Dotti	$11,237	74-70-70-73–287
Patty Rizzo	$11,237	69-70-70-78–287
Pat Bradley	$7,973	71-72-75-70–288
Tania Abitbol	$7,973	73-73-71-71–288
Joan Pitcock	$7,973	75-70-71-72–288
Susie Berning	$7,973	77-68-67-76–288
Deb Richard	$6,358	73-72-76-68–289
Barbara Mucha	$6,358	75-71-71-72–289
Lisa Kiggens	$6,358	71-74-72-72–289
Donna Andrews	$6,358	74-73-69-73–289
Chris Johnson	$6,358	73-74-69-73–289
Florence Descampe	$6,358	73-70-73-73–289
Juli Inkster	$6,358	73-71-69-76–289
Alice Miller	$6,358	72-71-70-76–289
Michelle Mackall	$4,874	76-73-71-70–290
Sherri Steinhauer	$4,874	73-74-72-71–290
Amy Benz	$4,874	75-73-70-72–290
Cindy Rarick	$4,874	70-75-73-72–290
Nancy Scranton	$4,874	75-74-68-73–290
Susie Redman	$4,874	75-71-70-74–290
Caroline Keggi	$4,874	69-71-75-75–290
Gail Graham	$3,905	71-75-75-70–291
Lori Garbacz	$3,905	76-73-70-72–291
Rosie Jones	$3,905	73-73-72-73–291
JoAnne Carner	$3,905	74-72-72-73–291
Betsy King	$3,077	73-73-76-70–292
Dale Eggeling	$3,077	74-72-73-73–292
Judy Dickinson	$3,077	74-72-73-73–292
Sally Little	$3,077	72-77-69-74–292
Colleen Walker	$3,077	67-75-76-74–292
Hiromi Kobayashi	$3,077	68-73-76-75–292
Maggie Will	$3,077	77-67-72-76–292
Liselotte Neumann	$2,274	77-72-71-73–293
Cathy Johnston	$2,274	75-73-72-73–293
Pamela Wright	$2,274	73-75-72-73–293
Michele Redman	$2,274	76-72-70-75–293
Dana Lofland-Dormann	$2,274	72-75-71-75–293
Allison Finney	$1,739	71-77-75-71–294
Kathy Postlewait	$1,739	75-74-72-73–294
Judy Sams	$1,739	72-75-74-73–294
Judy Sams	$1,739	76-72-72-74–294
Michelle Estill	$1,739	77-71-71-75–294
Tracy Kerdyk	$1,352	72-76-75-72–295
Terry-Jo Myers	$1,352	75-72-76-72–295
Robin Hood	$1,352	74-75-72-74–295
Julie Larsen	$1,152	73-75-73-74–295
Cathy Morse	$1,152	74-73-73-75–295
Amy Read	$1,152	74-74-71-76–295
M. Spencer-Devlin	$1,035	79-70-74-73–296
Ellie Gibson	$1,035	74-73-71-78–296
Barb Bunkowsky	$1,035	75-70-72-79–296
Beth Daniel	$964	71-76-73-79–299
Michelle McGann	$911	75-74-80-71–300
Patty Jordan	$911	76-72-72-80–300
Kiernan Prechtl	$858	73-75-78-76–302

Las Vegas LPGA at Canyon Gate

AT A GLANCE

- **Course:** Canyon Gate Country Club
- **Location:** Las Vegas, Nev.
- **When:** April 2-4, 1993
- **Weather:** Sunny and warm.
- **Purse:** $450,000
- **Par:** 72
- **Yards:** 6,285
- **Defending champion:** Dana Lofland
- **Tournament record:** 7-under-par 209, Trish Johnson, 1993

Winds gusted at 40 mph, but it was Trish Johnson who blew away the competition to win the Las Vegas LPGA at Canyon Gate by four shots.

Johnson started the final round three shots behind second-round leader Brandie Burton. But she shot a 5-under-par 67, one of nine players to break par in the swirling winds.

"I could tell as soon as I got here that it was going to blow all day, which was good with the way Brandie was playing," Johnson said. "For those of us who were two or three shots behind, that was the best thing that could happen because it at least gave us a chance."

Johnson said she took advantage of knowledge she gained while playing under windy conditions in her birthplace of Bristol, England, and home of Swansea, Wales.

"It was amazing," she said. "I just hit the ball well and all of a sudden the putts started to drop."

Johnson completed 54 holes at 7-under 209 for her first victory in six seasons on the LPGA tour.

Missie McGeorge, who was paired with Johnson, shot 71 to finish second at 213.

"It was pretty tough today," McGeorge said. "I don't know if it was the toughest wind I've ever played in, but it was one of the toughest, definitely."

Scores and earnings

Player	Scores
Trish Johnson, $67,500	71-71-67–209
Missie McGeorge, $41,891	71-71-71–213
Deb Richard, $27,172	72-70-72–214
Brandie Burton, $27,172	74-65-75–214
Hollis Stacy, $16,152	73-72-70–215
Lauri Merten, $16,152	74-67-74–215
Judy Dickinson, $16,152	71-69-75–215
Caroline Pierce, $11,775	74-73-69–216
Michelle Mackall, $8,264	77-68-72–217
Shelley Hamlin, $8,264	75-70-72–217
Carolyn Hill, $8,264	74-71-72–217
Amy Benz, $8,264	73-72-72–217
Annika Sorenstam, $8,264	73-70-74–217
Patty Sheehan, $8,264	72-69-76–217
Elaine Crosby, $8,264	72-68-77–217
Alice Ritzman, $5,055	75-73-70–218
Pearl Sinn, $5,055	76-71-71–218
Jane Crafter, $5,055	76-71-71–218
Liselotte Neumann, $5,055	75-72-71–218
Penny Hammel, $5,055	75-71-72–218
Jane Geddes, $5,055	75-71-72–218
Deborah McHaffie, $5,055	73-73-72–218
Cindy Rarick, $5,055	74-71-73–218
Michelle McGann, $5,055	74-70-74–218
Cindy Figg-Currier, $5,055	73-70-75–218
Rosie Jones, $5,055	74-68-76–218
Betsy King, $3,430	73-75-71–219
Jan Stephenson, $3,430	75-72-72–219
Allison Finney, $3,430	71-76-72–219
Kathy Postlewait, $3,430	76-70-73–219
Martha Nause, $3,430	75-71-73–219
Barb Thomas, $3,430	72-73-74–219
Tammie Green, $3,430	75-69-75–219
Susie Redman, $3,430	73-71-75–219
Lynn Connelly, $3,430	72-70-77–219
Marta Figueras-Dotti, $3,430	72-69-78–219
Juli Inkster, $2,309	72-76-72–220
Karen Noble, $2,309	77-70-73–220
Michele Redman, $2,309	75-71-74–220
Terry-Jo Myers, $2,309	72-74-74–220
Lisa Walters, $2,309	73-71-76–220
Kristi Albers, $2,309	72-72-76–220
Angie Ridgeway, $2,309	76-67-77–220
Donna Wilkins, $2,309	74-69-77–220
Beth Daniel, $2,309	72-69-79–220
Pamela Wright, $2,309	70-71-79–220
Stefania Croce, $1,652	75-73-73–221
Joan Pitcock, $1,652	75-71-75–221
Nancy L. Ramsbottom, $1,652	72-74-75–221
Colleen Walker, $1,652	75-69-77–221
Lenore Rittenhouse, $1,347	74-72-76–222
Lori Garbacz, $1,347	73-73-76–222
Dale Eggeling, $1,347	78-67-77–222
Kris Monaghan, $1,347	71-73-78–222
Lisa DePaulo, $1,075	71-77-75–223
Tania Abitbol, $1,075	73-72-78–223
Kate Hughes, $1,075	73-70-80–223
Hiromi Kobayashi, $1,075	74-68-81–223
Heather Drew, $796	75-73-76–224
Jill Briles-Hinton, $796	74-74-76–224
Lisa Kiggens, $796	80-67-77–224
Tina Barrett, $796	79-68-77–224
Denise Baldwin, $796	77-69-78–224
Mary Murphy, $796	76-70-78–224
Michelle Estill, $645	75-73-77–225
Jerilyn Britz, $645	74-74-77–225
Dina Ammaccapane, $645	75-70-80–225
Meg Mallon, $645	75-68-82–225
Page Dunlap, $577	78-70-78–226
Sherri Turner, $577	77-67-82–226
Laura Davies, $543	76-70-81–227
Sandra Palmer, $520	78-70-81–229

Atlanta Women's Championship

At a Glance

- **Course:** Eagle's Landing Country Club
- **Location:** Stockbridge, Ga.
- **When:** April 15-19, 1993
- **Weather:** Partly cloudy, windy and warm, except Thursday when thunderstorms forced a 95-minute delay, leaving 18 players to complete the first round Friday.
- **Purse:** $600,000
- **Par:** 72
- **Yards:** 6,177
- **Defending champion:** Dottie Mochrie
- **Tournament record:** 11-under-par 277, Dottie Mochrie, 1992

Trish Johnson of Wales captured her second consecutive LPGA title, shooting a 2-under-par 70 to capture the Atlanta Women's Championship.

Johnson finished at 6-under-par 282, two strokes ahead of Sherri Steinhauer.

Betsy King, who shared the third-round lead with Johnson, shot 74, for a 286 total, to finish third, remaining two wins from qualifying for the LPGA Hall of Fame.

Johnson said she was boosted by a Solheim Cup victory against Patty Sheehan last year when the European team defeated the USA.

"That was a big breakthrough," she said. "Winning that cup made a lot of difference to all of us. . . . It's just confidence. That's all it is."

With Johnson's two wins, Europeans have won three consecutive LPGA events. Sweden's Helen Alfredsson won the Nabisco Dinah Shore.

Johnson took the LPGA earnings lead at $184,857 with the $90,000 first prize.

Michelle McGann was third with 71, for a 285 total. Missie Berteotti, given a two-shot penalty Saturday for slow play, had the best round of the tournament, a 7-under-par 65 Sunday to tie for fourth with King and Elaine Crosby.

Scores and earnings

Player	Earnings	Scores
Trish Johnson	$90,000	72-72-68-70—282
Sherri Steinhauer	$55,855	71-70-72-71—284
Michelle McGann	$40,759	74-68-72-71—285
Missie Berteotti	$26,166	74-69-78-65—286
Elaine Crosby	$26,166	71-72-74-69—286
Betsy King	$26,166	72-67-73-74—286
Sherri Turner	$17,813	76-67-71-73—287
Dina Ammaccapane	$14,190	77-72-71-68—288
Hiromi Kobayashi	$14,190	70-75-73-70—288
Jan Stephenson	$14,190	73-71-70-74—288
Kelly Robbins	$11,473	70-77-66-76—289
Pat Bradley	$9,359	77-72-71-70—290
Florence Descampe	$9,359	72-74-74-70—290
Nancy Lopez	$9,359	70-77-72-71—290
Judy Dickinson	$9,359	75-71-71-73—290
Kris Tschetter	$9,359	72-70-75-73—290
Michele Redman	$7,547	71-79-71-70—291
Missie McGeorge	$7,547	75-72-71-73—291
Lenore Rittenhouse	$7,547	71-74-73-73—291
Suzanne Strudwick	$6,498	73-76-73-70—292
Tina Barrett	$6,498	71-74-77-70—292
Marta Figueras-Dotti	$6,498	75-72-73-72—292
Dottie Mochrie	$6,498	67-74-77-74—292
Michelle Mackall	$5,675	70-76-74-73—293
Colleen Walker	$5,675	72-73-72-76—293
Rosie Jones	$5,675	72-70-74-77—293
Denise Baldwin	$4,951	74-73-78-69—294
Michelle Estill	$4,951	68-73-82-71—294
Jane Geddes	$4,951	76-70-76-72—294
Laura Davies	$4,951	73-74-73-74—294
Sally Little	$4,951	73-71-76-74—294
Kristi Albers	$4,287	74-71-76-74—295
Nancy Scranton	$4,287	71-72-77-75—295
Hollis Stacy	$4,287	73-70-76-76—295
Dawn Coe-Jones	$3,683	75-74-75-72—296
Robin Walton	$3,683	71-76-76-73—296
Terry-Jo Myers	$3,683	74-74-74-74—296
Ellie Gibson	$3,683	72-74-76-74—296
Helen Alfredsson	$3,683	71-72-77-76—296
Vicki Fergon	$2,903	78-71-77-71—297
Lori West	$2,903	79-69-76-73—297
Lori Garbacz	$2,903	75-75-73-74—297
Akiko Fukishima	$2,903	71-77-75-74—297
Chris Johnson	$2,903	74-72-77-74—297
Martha Nause	$2,903	74-70-76-77—297
Lisa Walters	$2,354	75-75-73-75—298
Nancy White	$2,354	73-75-74-76—298
Marianne Morris	$2,354	71-71-77-79—298
Caroline Pierce	$1,769	75-75-78-71—299
Jenny Wyatt	$1,769	77-72-77-73—299
Danielle Ammaccapane	$1,769	72-76-77-74—299
Jody Anschutz	$1,769	73-76-75-75—299
Kim Williams	$1,769	71-77-75-76—299
Alice Ritzman	$1,769	74-74-73-78—299
Ayako Okamoto	$1,769	72-75-74-78—299
Laurie Rinker-Graham	$1,769	74-68-77-80—299
Lauri Merten	$1,312	71-79-75-75—300
Carolyn Hill	$1,312	74-73-77-76—300
Loretta Alderete	$1,177	76-74-80-71—301
Penny Hammel	$1,026	76-73-79-74—302
Stephanie Farwig	$1,026	76-73-76-77—302
Pearl Sinn	$1,026	74-73-77-78—302
Nancy L. Ramsbottom	$1,026	72-77-74-79—302
Cathy Johnston	$845	75-73-81-74—303
Gail Graham	$845	75-74-76-78—303
Tina Tombs	$845	77-70-77-79—303
Martha Faulconer	$845	74-73-77-79—303
Val Skinner	$845	72-75-76-80—303
Dana Lofland-Dormann	$754	75-75-76-78—304
Nicky Le Roux	$724	77-72-79-77—305
Alicia Dibos	$679	72-72-83-79—306
Muffin Spencer-Devlin	$679	72-73-76-85—306
Barbara Mucha	$649	72-76-80-79—307
Patti Liscio	$626	78-72-81-77—308
Kate Hughes	$626	80-70-76-82—308
Michele Ann Thompson	$606	75-74-80-80—309
Beth Daniel	$593	74-75-81-81—311

SPRINT CLASSIC

AT A GLANCE

- **Course:** Killearn Country Club
- **Location:** Tallahassee, Fla.
- **When:** April 29-May 1, 1993
- **Weather:** Windy and warm.
- **Purse:** $1.2 million
- **Par:** 72
- **Yards:** 6,382
- **Defending champion:** Danielle Ammaccapane
- **Tournament record:** 17-under-par 271, Beth Daniel, 1991

Kristi Albers made a birdie that averted disaster and sealed her victory at the Sprint Classic.

"It came in at the right time," Albers said of her 5-foot birdie putt on the final hole that prevented both a playoff and one of the biggest collapses in recent LPGA history.

"I didn't know what I was going to do," added Albers, who admitted she started thinking about a playoff after her third consecutive bogey at No. 17. "I was kind of in shock. I couldn't believe I missed that putt."

Albers had six birdies, six bogeys and six pars in a par-72 finish. She avoided a playoff with Rosie Jones.

"I battled myself a lot, especially coming in," said Albers, who hung on for her first career win.

"I was out there trying to make birdies, but I guess you never know."

Albers, winless since turning pro in October 1985, earned $180,000—more than she had made in any previous year on tour.

She also catapulted from 43rd to first on the LPGA money list with $203,000 in 1993 and became the season's first wire-to-wire winner.

"She played the last hole great," said Jones, who watched Albers' game-winning putt from the gallery. "I thought she had hit it too soft."

Scores and earnings

Player	Earnings	Scores
Kristi Albers	$180,000	66-69-72-72–279
Rosie Jones	$111,711	72-70-71-67–280
Elaine Crosby	$59,629	74-69-71-68–282
Michelle McGann	$59,629	72-72-69-69–282
Deb Richard	$59,629	70-74-67-71–282
Kris Tschetter	$59,629	71-70-70-71–282
Jan Stephenson	$31,802	71-69-73-70–283
Liselotte Neumann	$31,802	69-73-68-73–283
JoAnne Carner	$31,802	72-65-71-75–283
Nancy Lopez	$21,023	73-70-71-70–284
Pat Bradley	$21,023	71-72-71-70–284
Sherri Turner	$21,023	74-68-71-71–284
Nancy L. Ramsbottom	$21,023	70-71-72-71–284
Patty Sheehan	$21,023	73-69-70-72–284
Hiromi Kobayashi	$21,023	69-70-73-72–284
Angie Ridgeway	$15,506	73-71-68-73–285
Helen Alfredsson	$15,506	72-72-68-73–285
Tina Barrett	$15,506	72-71-68-74–285
Robin Walton	$15,506	71-70-69-75–285
Missie McGeorge	$12,401	72-72-73-69–286
Judy Dickinson	$12,401	72-72-71-71–286
Barb Thomas	$12,401	71-73-71-71–286
Mary Beth Zimmerman	$12,401	71-73-69-73–286
Kris Monaghan	$12,401	70-70-71-75–286
Marta Figueras-Dotti	$12,401	71-65-74-76–286
Brandie Burton	$12,401	73-67-68-78–286
Meg Mallon	$9,675	75-67-75-70–287
Donna Andrews	$9,675	69-74-71-73–287
Florence Descampe	$9,675	72-72-69-74–287
Sherri Steinhauer	$9,675	72-68-73-74–287
Page Dunlap	$9,675	68-73-71-75–287
Shelley Hamlin	$9,675	71-69-72-75–287
Lenore Rittenhouse	$9,675	69-70-73-75–287
Tracy Kerdyk	$7,324	70-73-74-71–288
Cindy Figg-Currier	$7,324	76-70-70-72–288
Danielle Ammaccapane	$7,324	71-74-71-72–288
Ayako Okamoto	$7,324	74-71-69-74–288
Jill Briles-Hinton	$7,324	72-70-72-74–288
Martha Nause	$7,324	73-71-69-75–288
Kelly Robbins	$7,324	75-69-68-76–288
Tammie Green	$7,324	72-66-72-78–288
Beth Daniel	$5,905	74-69-70-76–289
Nancy Scranton	$5,905	69-73-71-76–289
Cindy Rarick	$5,301	74-72-69-75–290
Michele Redman	$5,301	71-71-73-75–290
Dottie Mochrie	$5,301	72-68-74-76–290
Val Skinner	$4,577	73-73-72-73–291
Lori Garbacz	$4,577	72-73-72-74–291
Vicki Fergon	$4,577	76-68-68-79–291
Barbara Mucha	$3,640	71-75-74-72–292
Denise Baldwin	$3,640	72-73-74-73–292
Lisa Walters	$3,640	73-70-76-73–292
Pearl Sinn	$3,640	70-72-75-75–292
Lynn Connelly	$3,640	71-71-74-76–292
Alicia Dibos	$3,640	76-70-68-78–292
Anne Marie Palli	$2,824	73-71-73-76–293
Karen Davies	$2,824	72-71-73-77–293
Dawn Coe-Jones	$2,824	71-71-72-79–293
Gail Graham	$2,402	69-77-74-74–294
Hollis Stacy	$2,402	69-74-73-78–294
Cindy Schreyer	$2,161	71-73-77-74–295
Ellie Gibson	$2,161	74-69-75-77–295
Patti Liscio	$1,950	72-74-73-77–296
Stefania Croce	$1,950	69-76-73-78–296
Cathy Johnston	$1,828	72-72-75-78–297
Carolyn Hill	$1,828	73-71-73-80–297
Susie Redman	$1,738	73-73-72-81–299
Cathy Mockett	$1,647	73-73-75-79–300
Debbie Massey	$1,647	71-75-75-79–300
Jayne Thobois	$1,557	72-71-77-81–301

Sara Lee Classic

AT A GLANCE

- **Course:** Hermitage Golf Club
- **Location:** Old Hickory, Tenn.
- **When:** May 7-9, 1993
- **Weather:** Sunny and warm.
- **Purse:** $525,000
- **Par:** 72
- **Yards:** 6,242
- **Playoff:** Meg Mallon defeated Tina Tombs on the third playoff hole.
- **Defending champion:** Maggie Will
- **Tournament record:** 13-under-par 203, Kathy Postlewait, 1989

For Meg Mallon, odd-numbered years are much better.

She chipped in from 30 feet on the third hole of a playoff with Tina Tombs, to win the Sara Lee Classic, her second victory of 1993. Her other four LPGA victories came in 1991.

"Maybe odd years are my years or something," she said.

"But last year I played so solid. I had 14 Top 10 finishes and didn't win a golf tournament," said Mallon, who won $400,000 in 1992.

Mallon started the final round of the Sara Lee Classic 9 under, two strokes behind second-round leader Debbie Massey, who finished 77–210 after three bogeys and a double-bogey on the last day.

Mallon played steadily and made birdies on the 3rd, 4th, 7th and 11th to go 13 under. She made bogeys on 13 and 14 to fall back into a tie with Tombs who had a final-round 64.

"I played so steadily until 13 when I missed that hole. Then my putting got a bit shaky. I'm not usually like that. That's my strength," Mallon said.

Tombs said she preferred Mallon winning the playoff with her chip.

"I don't feel like I lost it. But when she knocked it in, I had to go for the putt. Until she chipped it, I had a feeling I was going to make it," she said.

Scores and earnings

Player	Scores
#Meg Mallon, $78,750	70-71-64–205
Tina Tombs, $48,873	67-68-70–205
Dana Lofland-Dormann, $35,664	66-70-70–206
Dawn Coe-Jones, $21,068	64-76-67–207
Hiromi Kobayashi, $21,068	69-70-68–207
Brandie Burton, $21,068	70-68-69–207
Betsy King, $21,068	67-69-71–207
Barb Bunkowsky, $11,821	71-70-67–208
Val Skinner, $11,821	69-72-67–208
Dottie Mochrie, $11,821	71-67-70–208
Ayako Okamoto, $11,821	65-71-72–208
Tracy Kerdyk, $8,453	72-67-70–209
Danielle Ammaccapane, $8,453	72-67-70–209
Amy Read, $8,453	68-71-70–209
Lisa Walters, $8,453	68-68-73–209
Nancy L. Ramsbottom, $6,472	72-70-68–210
Martha Nause, $6,472	71-71-68–210
Helen Alfredsson, $6,472	69-71-70–210
Lisa Kiggens, $6,472	69-70-71–210
Trish Johnson, $6,472	66-73-71–210
Debbie Massey, $6,472	69-64-77–210
Cindy Rarick, $5,067	71-70-70–211
Pamela Wright, $5,067	70-70-71–211
Mary Beth Zimmerman, $5,067	68-72-71–211
Liselotte Neumann, $5,067	67-72-72–211
Nancy Lopez, $5,067	70-68-73–211
Jane Crafter, $5,067	69-69-73–211
Gail Graham, $3,968	69-74-69–212
Allison Finney, $3,968	72-70-70–212
Patti Rizzo, $3,968	69-73-70–212
Suzanne Strudwick, $3,968	69-73-70–212
Beth Daniel, $3,968	72-69-71–212
Tania Abitbol, $3,968	72-68-72–212
Tammie Green, $3,968	68-72-72–212
Pat Bradley, $3,968	68-71-73–212
Nancy Scranton, $2,962	72-71-70–213
Nina Foust, $2,962	71-72-70–213
Dale Eggeling, $2,962	71-72-70–213
Cindy Schreyer, $2,962	71-71-71–213
Page Dunlap, $2,962	73-68-72–213
Cindy Figg-Currier, $2,962	71-70-72–213
Marta Figueras-Dotti, $2,962	69-71-73–213
Kris Tschetter, $1,968	74-69-71–214
Ellie Gibson, $1,968	71-72-71–214
Julie Larsen, $1,968	70-73-71–214
Missie McGeorge, $1,968	74-68-72–214
Elaine Crosby, $1,968	72-70-72–214
Loretta Alderete, $1,968	72-70-72–214
Shelley Hamlin, $1,968	70-72-72–214
Jenny Wyatt, $1,968	71-70-73–214
Lauri Merten, $1,968	72-68-74–214
Deb Richard, $1,968	69-71-74–214
Angie Ridgeway, $1,968	70-69-75–214
Mitzi Edge, $1,095	73-70-72–215
Patty Sheehan, $1,095	72-71-72–215
Terry-Jo Myers, $1,095	72-71-72–215
Tina Barrett, $1,095	71-71-73–215
Melissa McNamara, $1,095	68-74-73–215
Michelle McGann, $1,095	70-71-74–215
Barb Thomas, $1,095	69-72-74–215
Jody Anschutz, $1,095	74-66-75–215
Kris Monaghan, $1,095	71-69-75–215
Jean Zedlitz, $1,095	70-69-76–215
Colleen Walker, $699	72-71-73–216
Amy Benz, $699	70-73-73–216
Michelle Mackall, $699	71-71-74–216
Michelle Estill, $699	70-72-74–216
Alison Nicholas, $699	68-74-74–216
Donna Wilkins, $699	71-70-75–216
Amy Alcott, $699	71-70-75–216
Lynn Connelly, $699	69-71-76–216
Sherri Turner, $561	73-69-75–217
Sandra Palmer, $561	72-70-75–217
Denise Baldwin, $561	68-73-76–217
Sherrl Steinhauer, $561	72-68-77–217
Kate Hughes, $524	71-72-75–218
Marianne Morris, $524	70-70-78–218
Heather Drew, $502	69-74-77–220
Karen Davies, $502	73-68-79–220
Kim Bauer, $487	72-69-82–223

 # - won on third playoff hole

McDonald's Championship

AT A GLANCE

- **Course:** DuPont Country Club
- **Location:** Wilmington, Del.
- **When:** May 13-16, 1993
- **Weather:** Seasonably warm, but windy. The final round was interrupted for an hour by thunderstorms with the leader on the 15th hole.
- **Purse:** $900,000
- **Par:** 71
- **Yards:** 6,398
- **Defending champion:** Ayako Okamoto
- **Tournament record:** 16-under-par 272, Alice Miller, 1985

Laura Davies, recognized as the longest hitter in women's golf, negotiated 7 feet to win the McDonald's Championship

A 7-foot putt for par on the final hole gave the native of England a 72-hole total of 277 and a one-stroke victory over Sherri Steinhauer.

Davies became the fifth foreign-born winner in the first 10 LPGA events of 1993.

She led by a shot with three holes to play when rain and lightning delayed play for 62 minutes.

"I was talking to the other European girls during the rain," Davies said. "They told me not to worry. But I was worrying. I thought, 'What if I go out there and blow it?'"

She came close. After parring 16 and 17, her approach on No.18 landed in deep rough 10 feet off the green.

"It was a terrible lie," Davies said. "I'd rather have been in a bunker.

"But I managed to hit a great chip. Working on the short game this year really paid off there."

And the putt?

"For a second I thought I missed it," she said. "It started drifting right and just got in. The putt hung on the edge and fell in."

Scores and earnings

Player	Earnings	Scores
Laura Davies	$135,000	66-69-73-69–277
Sherri Steinhauer	$83,783	69-72-70-67–278
Helen Alfredsson	$54,346	74-68-70-67–279
Lauri Merten	$54,346	68-69-72-70–279
Hiromi Kobayashi	$38,494	72-71-69-68–280
Pat Bradley	$25,814	73-70-71-67–281
Mary Beth Zimmerman	$25,814	72-74-65-70–281
Patty Sheehan	$25,814	68-73-70-70–281
Gail Graham	$25,814	66-69-74-72–281
Chris Johnson	$16,756	71-74-71-66–282
Nancy Lopez	$16,756	73-69-70-70–282
Val Skinner	$16,756	70-70-72-70–282
Hollis Stacy	$16,756	73-67-70-72–282
Betsy King	$12,793	71-67-78-67–283
Alison Nicholas	$12,793	73-74-67-69–283
Dale Eggeling	$12,793	70-76-68-69–283
Akiko Fukushima	$12,793	72-69-68-74–283
Judy Dickinson	$11,095	75-71-71-67–284
Tina Barrett	$11,095	73-72-71-68–284
Lisa Walters	$9,747	69-73-76-67–285
Juli Inkster	$9,747	69-74-72-70–285
Brandie Burton	$9,747	74-74-66-71–285
JoAnne Carner	$9,747	70-73-69-73–285
Pamela Wright	$8,106	75-73-70-68–286
Robin Hood	$8,106	69-71-76-70–286
Dottie Mochrie	$8,106	70-71-74-71–286
Dana Lofland-Dormann	$8,106	70-70-72-74–286
Robin Walton	$8,106	74-65-72-75–286
Alicia Dibos	$8,106	70-71-69-76–286
Pearl Sinn	$6,781	72-75-70-70–287
Barb Thomas	$6,781	72-73-71-71–287
Laurel Kean	$6,781	73-69-73-72–287
Missie Berteotti	$6,781	72-67-76-72–287
Dawn Coe-Jones	$6,090	80-68-71-69–288
Caroline Pierce	$6,090	71-72-73-72–288
Katie Peterson-Parker	$5,411	74-73-74-68–289
Kelly Robbins	$5,411	74-71-72-72–289
Liselotte Neumann	$5,411	71-75-69-74–289
Lori Garbacz	$5,411	73-69-72-75–289
Maggie Will	$4,446	77-71-71-71–290
Beth Daniel	$4,446	74-71-73-72–290
Nancy Scranton	$4,446	74-70-74-72–290
Meg Mallon	$4,446	71-71-73-75–290
Donna Wilkins	$4,446	70-69-76-75–290
Nancy Ramsbottom	$3,277	74-74-72-71–291
Muffin Spencer-Devlin	$3,277	75-73-71-72–291
Julie Larsen	$3,277	74-72-73-72–291
Amy Alcott	$3,277	73-72-73-73–291
Mary Murphy	$3,277	73-71-74-73–291
Elaine Crosby	$3,277	76-72-68-75–291
Ellie Gibson	$3,277	73-73-70-75–291
Jane Crafter	$3,277	72-71-73-75–291
Kristi Albers	$2,241	73-75-74-70–292
Denise Baldwin	$2,241	70-74-78-70–292
Jill Briles-Hinton	$2,241	76-70-75-71–292
Missie McGeorge	$2,241	75-71-74-72–292
Tracy Kerdyk	$2,241	76-72-71-73–292
Debbie Massey	$2,241	74-74-69-75–292
Tammie Green	$1,454	73-72-78-70–293
Patti Rizzo	$1,454	77-70-72-74–293
Dina Ammaccapane	$1,454	74-74-71-74–293
Joan Pitcock	$1,454	71-74-73-75–293
Terry-Jo Myers	$1,454	74-70-74-75–293
Cindy Figg-Currier	$1,454	74-70-74-75–293
Kris Tschetter	$1,454	72-71-75-75–293
Page Dunlap	$1,454	73-73-71-76–293
Laurie Rinker-Graham	$1,454	74-70-73-76–293
Shelley Hamlin	$1,109	76-72-76-70–294
Danielle Ammaccapane	$1,109	77-71-74-72–294
Kim Williams	$1,109	74-72-73-75–294
Sherri Turner	$1,109	74-72-73-75–294
Michele Redman	$973	73-74-75-73–295
Jenny Wyatt	$973	73-75-72-75–295
Trish Johnson	$973	75-71-74-75–295
Donna Andrews	$918	72-75-76-73–296
Barbara Mucha	$918	72-74-71-79–296
#Carol Semple Thompson		72-75-74-75–296
Kathy Postlewait	$881	73-73-77-74–297
Laura Baugh	$881	73-75-72-77–297
Tina Tombs	$854	76-71-78-73–298
Nancy White	$827	74-74-76-76–300
Penny Hammel	$827	72-74-74-80–300
Judy Sams	$802	71-75-77-80–303

\# - amateur

Lady Keystone Open

AT A GLANCE

- **Course:** Hershey Country Club
- **Location:** Hershey, Pa.
- **When:** May 21-23, 1993
- **Weather:** Seasonably cool.
- **Purse:** $400,000
- **Par:** 72
- **Yards:** 6,348
- **Defending champion:** Danielle Ammaccapane
- **Tournament record:** 13-under-par 203, JoAnne Carner, 1981

Val Skinner kept surging Betsy King two victories short of qualifying for the LPGA Hall of Fame by winning the Lady Keystone, her first victory in six years on the LPGA tour.

Skinner had an eagle in a final-round 5-under-par 67 and finished the 54 holes at 6-under-par 210. Her last victory had been the 1987 MasterCard International at White Plains, N.Y.

"There were a number of times when I thought I might never win again," Skinner said. "That's all behind me now.

"I was burned out the last couple of years. I had lost my confidence and it took me a long time to get it back."

King, who had 28 victories and needed 30 to qualify for the Hall of Fame, closed with a 70–212. Julie Larsen had a 72 for 213.

"When someone chips in for eagle and again for a birdie, you've got to think it's going to be their day," King said. "I'm playing better than ever. My day will come."

Brandie Burton, who had a two-stroke lead over Larsen after two rounds, faltered to a final 75, dropping into a tie at 214 with Tina Barrett, who shot a 71. Burton had previous rounds of 68 and 71.

Scores and earnings

Player	Rounds–Total
Val Skinner, $60,000	70-73-67–210
Betsy King, $37,237	70-72-70–212
Julie Larsen, $27,173	69-72-72–213
Tina Barrett, $19,121	69-74-71–214
Brandie Burton, $19,121	68-71-75–214
Cindy Figg-Currier, $14,089	73-71-71–215
Barbara Mucha, $11,170	76-72-68–216
Barb Thomas, $11,170	71-74-71–216
Dawn Coe-Jones, $8,155	72-76-69–217
Beth Daniel, $8,155	71-75-71–217
Angie Ridgeway, $8,155	71-74-72–217
Pearl Sinn, $8,155	71-72-74–217
Pat Bradley, $6,246	71-76-71–218
Shelley Hamlin, $6,246	73-73-72–218
Jennifer Myers, $6,246	69-76-73–218
Sherri Steinhauer, $5,038	78-71-70–219
Rosie Jones, $5,038	74-73-72–219
Elaine Crosby, $5,038	71-76-72–219
Donna Andrews, $5,038	72-71-76–219
Laura Davies, $5,038	76-66-77–219
Kate Rogerson, $4,015	72-80-68–220
Nancy Ramsbottom, $4,015	72-76-72–220
Robin Walton, $4,015	73-74-73–220
Sarah McGuire, $4,015	72-75-73–220
Jenny Lidback, $4,015	74-72-74–220
Hiromi Kobayashi, $4,015	74-71-75–220
Vicki Fergon, $3,368	80-71-70–221
Lynn Connelly, $3,368	75-74-72–221
Jenny Wyatt, $3,368	73-73-75–221
Marta Figueras-Dotti, $3,368	73-73-75–221
Karen Noble, $2,864	76-75-71–222
Mary Murphy, $2,864	78-71-73–222
Kathy Postlewait, $2,864	77-72-73–222
Cindy Mackey, $2,864	75-73-74–222
Chris Johnson, $2,864	73-74-75–222
Marianne Morris, $2,173	76-75-72–223
Nina Foust, $2,173	74-76-73–223
Danielle Ammaccapane, $2,173	72-78-73–223
Alison Nicholas, $2,173	77-72-74–223
Kim Shipman, $2,173	76-73-74–223
Deborah McHaffie, $2,173	73-76-74–223
Robin Hood, $2,173	72-77-74–223
Barb Bunkowsky, $2,173	73-73-77–223
Laurie Rinker-Graham, $2,173	75-70-78–223
Jane Crafter, $1,428	77-75-72–224
Lenore Rittenhouse, $1,428	76-76-72–224
Tracy Kerdyk, $1,428	78-73-73–224
Nancy Scranton, $1,428	75-76-73–224
Trish Johnson, $1,428	74-76-74–224
Sally Little, $1,428	73-77-74–224
Heather Drew, $1,428	75-74-75–224
Kim Lasken, $1,428	75-74-75–224
Caroline Pierce, $1,428	73-76-75–224
Lynn Adams, $941	76-76-73–225
Michelle Mackall, $941	75-76-74–225
Jean Zedlitz, $941	73-78-74–225
Amy Fruhwirth, $941	73-78-74–225
Pamela Wright, $941	76-74-75–225
Martha Faulconer, $941	73-72-80–225
Michelle McGann, $690	77-75-74–226
Denise Baldwin, $690	76-76-74–226
Laurel Kean, $690	74-78-74–226
Lisa Kiggens, $690	72-79-75–226
Marlene Floyd, $579	79-73-75–227
Jan Stephenson, $579	75-77-75–227
Dana Lofland-Dormann, $579	74-78-75–227
Laurie Brower, $579	75-71-81–227
Page Dunlap, $519	76-76-76–228
Deedee Lasker, $519	75-77-76–228
Kate Golden, $468	79-73-77–229
Missie McGeorge, $468	77-73-79–229
Caroline Gowan, $468	77-73-79–229
Jackie Bertsch, $433	82-70-78–230
Nancy Harvey, $433	77-75-78–230

LPGA Corning Classic

AT A GLANCE

- **Course:** Corning Country Club
- **Location:** Corning, N.Y.
- **When:** May 27-30, 1993
- **Weather:** Cool, damp.
- **Purse:** $500,000
- **Par:** 72
- **Yards:** 6,070
- **Defending champion:** Colleen Walker
- **Playoff:** Kelly Robbins parred the first playoff hole to defeat Alison Nicholas.
- **Tournament record:** 16-under-par 272, Patty Sheehan, 1983; Patty Rizzo, 1985

Kelly Robbins fended off a big back-nine run by Alison Nicholas, sinking an uphill, 6-foot par putt on the first playoff hole to win the Corning Classic.

"I'm so tired right now," Robbins, 23, said after her first LPGA victory. "It was unbelievable golf between Alison and myself."

Nicholas, from Birmingham, England, made four birdies on the back nine to erase Robbins' four-stroke lead. For the day, Nicholas shot 7-under-par 65, the best round of the tournament. Robbins shot 69, with five birdies and two bogeys.

"I enjoyed playing in the last group," Nicholas said. "We fed off each other."

But for all the great shots, Robbins' victory came on No. 8—the playoff hole—thanks to two mistakes by Nicholas.

The third-year tour veteran hooked her tee shot to the left but recovered superbly, punching her second shot under the trees and rolling it onto the back of the green. But her putt coming back rolled 7 feet past the cup, and she missed the par putt.

—by Charlie Coon, Gannett News Service

Scores and earnings

Player	Earnings	Scores	Total
#Kelly Robbins	$75,000	70-68-70-69	277
Alison Nicholas	$46,546	71-70-71-65	277
Jane Crafter	$33,966	73-70-72-67	282
Patty Sheehan	$26,418	72-70-72-69	283
Tina Barrett	$19,499	75-67-72-70	284
Hiromi Kobayashi	$19,499	71-68-73-72	284
Cindy Rarick	$13,250	73-73-71-68	285
Tammie Green	$13,250	72-70-73-70	285
Jenny Lidback	$13,250	74-69-71-71	285
Trish Johnson	$10,087	74-69-75-68	286
Rosie Jones	$10,087	75-68-71-72	286
Dawn Coe-Jones	$8,097	75-72-70-71	288
Jane Geddes	$8,097	73-70-74-71	288
JoAnne Carner	$8,097	72-71-73-72	288
Cathy Johnston-Forbes	$8,097	70-73-72-73	288
Mary Beth Zimmerman	$6,839	75-69-74-71	289
Judy Dickinson	$6,210	75-72-74-69	290
Missie Berteotti	$6,210	73-74-71-72	290
Lisa Walters	$6,210	73-72-73-72	290
Pearl Sinn	$6,210	76-68-71-75	290
Kathy Postlewait	$5,143	76-70-76-69	291
Marianne Morris	$5,143	71-73-78-69	291
Myra Blackwelder	$5,143	76-70-72-73	291
Maggie Will	$5,143	75-67-76-73	291
Michelle McGann	$5,143	72-72-73-74	291
Kris Monaghan	$4,246	74-74-76-68	292
Jan Stephenson	$4,246	77-72-73-70	292
Lisa Kiggens	$4,246	72-76-73-71	292
Katie Peterson-Parker	$4,246	75-72-73-72	292
Martha Faulconer	$4,246	79-67-73-73	292
Allison Finney	$4,246	70-74-72-76	292
Nicky Le Roux	$3,428	74-70-80-69	293
Caroline Pierce	$3,428	77-71-75-70	293
Val Skinner	$3,428	74-73-73-73	293
Alice Miller	$3,428	75-69-76-73	293
Barb Thomas	$3,428	73-70-77-73	293
Nancy Ramsbottom	$3,428	73-72-74-74	293
Helen Dobson	$2,632	73-75-75-71	294
Terry-Jo Myers	$2,632	71-76-74-73	294
Sally Little	$2,632	73-74-73-74	294
Deedee Lasker	$2,632	75-71-74-74	294
Chris Johnson	$2,632	75-73-71-75	294
Lauri Merten	$2,632	72-74-72-76	294
Amy Benz	$2,632	73-73-70-78	294
Cindy Schreyer	$2,108	74-75-73-73	295
Colleen Walker	$2,108	72-74-75-74	295
Shelley Hamlin	$2,108	75-73-72-75	295
Karen Lunn	$1,762	75-74-76-71	296
Jody Anschutz	$1,762	77-71-75-73	296
Robin Walton	$1,762	74-73-76-73	296
Kathy Guadagnino	$1,762	74-74-73-75	296
Connie Chillemi	$1,441	76-70-79-72	297
Cathy Marino	$1,441	74-73-77-73	297
Alice Ritzman	$1,441	76-71-76-74	297
Laurie Rinker-Graham	$1,441	71-76-73-77	297
Martha Nause	$1,106	74-75-74-75	298
Danielle Ammaccapane	$1,106	75-72-76-75	298
Sherri Turner	$1,106	72-74-77-75	298
Gail Graham	$1,106	74-74-74-76	298
Denise Baldwin	$1,106	73-73-73-79	298
Nancy Harvey	$900	77-72-76-74	299
Alicia Dibos	$900	73-74-76-76	299
Cathy Mockett	$799	76-73-77-74	300
Caroline Gowan	$799	75-74-77-74	300
Judy Sams	$799	76-70-73-81	300
Marci Bozarth	$711	74-74-80-73	301
Nancy White	$711	75-72-80-74	301
Leigh Ann Mills	$711	74-70-83-74	301
Kate Rogerson	$711	73-74-76-78	301
Tara Fleming	$649	79-70-80-77	306

\# - won on first playoff hole

Oldsmobile Classic

At a Glance

- **Course:** Walnut Hills Country Club
- **Location:** East Lansing, Mich.
- **When:** June 3-6, 1993
- **Weather:** Cool with gusting winds Thursday, Friday and Saturday. Sunny and warm Sunday.
- **Purse:** $550,000
- **Par:** 72
- **Yards:** 6,166
- **Defending champion:** Barb Mucha
- **Tournament record:** 12-under-par 276, Barb Mucha, 1992

Jane Geddes squeeked by with a one-stroke victory in the Oldsmobile Classic, for her first LPGA win since 1991.

Geddes' final-round 3-under-par 69 put her at 11-under 277, a shot ahead of Alice Ritzman, Trish Johnson and Tammie Green.

"It was one of those days where anybody could win," Geddes said. "I was trying not to worry about it. I just wanted to play my own game."

Betsy King, co-leader with Ritzman after the second and third rounds, tied for third with Nancy Scranton at 279.

Geddes, a shot behind and playing with King and Ritzman when the final round started, enjoyed bogey-free golf on the front nine, picking up three birdies. She birdied No. 11, a 506-yard par-5, and the 171-yard 13th, to go 12-under.

Geddes' drive and second shot on 15 went into the rough as she made her only bogey of the day. None of the challengers made a charge, so Geddes parred in for the victory.

"I think my experience served me well today," said Geddes, a 10-year veteran with 10 victories. "Even though I haven't been winning, I've been around. The times I've won, I've been real steady down the stretch."

Scores and earnings

Player	Scores
Jane Geddes, $82,500	72-68-68-69–277
Tammie Green, $39,208	69-69-71-69–278
Trish Johnson, $39,208	71-66-71-70–278
Alice Ritzman, $39,208	66-70-71-71–278
Nancy Scranton, $21,448	71-71-69-68–279
Betsy King, $21,448	68-68-71-72–279
Sherri Steinhauer, $15,359	70-71-72-67–280
Colleen Walker, $15,359	67-72-71-70–280
Beth Daniel, $12,316	72-69-70-71–282
Meg Mallon, $12,316	69-70-72-71–282
Cindy Rarick, $10,130	72-69-72-70–283
Elaine Crosby, $10,130	69-72-72-70–283
Dottie Mochrie, $7,916	75-71-71-68–285
Allison Finney, $7,916	72-72-71-70–285
Judy Dickinson, $7,916	72-72-71-70–285
Lynn Connelly, $7,916	72-70-73-70–285
Patty Sheehan, $7,916	70-71-73-71–285
Marianne Morris, $7,916	68-72-71-74–285
Kate Rogerson, $5,593	71-74-72-69–286
Kris Monaghan, $5,593	68-69-80-69–286
Kelly Robbins, $5,593	74-71-71-70–286
Kathy Guadagnino, $5,593	72-72-71-71–286
Laurel Kean, $5,593	70-71-74-71–286
Chris Johnson, $5,593	71-74-69-72–286
Alison Nicholas, $5,593	68-76-70-72–286
Jenny Lidback, $5,593	72-71-71-72–286
Nancy White, $5,593	72-69-73-72–286
Barbara Mucha, $5,593	70-71-70-75–286
Cathy Johnston-Forbes, $4,037	71-72-77-67–287
Pat Bradley, $4,037	73-73-73-68–287
Lauri Merten, $4,037	71-72-72-72–287
Angie Ridgeway, $4,037	69-73-73-72–287
Joan Pitcock, $4,037	71-72-71-73–287
Karen Lunn, $4,037	67-76-71-73–287
Helen Dobson, $4,037	67-73-74-73–287
Kristi Albers, $4,037	70-72-68-77–287
Lisa Walters, $3,000	69-74-76-69–288
Kim Williams, $3,000	73-73-72-70–288
Kim Lasken, $3,000	76-69-73-70–288
Pamela Wright, $3,000	72-73-72-71–288
Jean Zedlitz, $3,000	69-75-71-73–288
Donna Andrews, $3,000	72-73-69-74–288
Katie Peterson-Parker, $3,000	73-69-72-74–288
Lisa Kiggens, $2,518	67-76-74-72–289
Mitzi Edge, $2,816	71-75-73-71–290
Missie Berteotti, $2,816	71-75-72-72–290
Marta Figueras-Dotti, $2,816	73-72-73-72–290
Heather Drew, $2,816	72-73-73-72–290
Tracy Kerdyk, $2,816	70-76-71-73–290
Hollis Stacy, $1,563	74-72-74-71–291
Jody Anschutz, $1,563	73-73-73-72–291
Gail Graham, $1,563	73-73-71-74–291
Kathy Postlewait, $1,563	73-72-72-74–291
Alicia Dibos, $1,563	70-75-72-74–291
Kris Tschetter, $1,563	71-73-73-74–291
Deborah McHaffie, $1,563	71-71-74-75–291
Jan Stephenson, $1,563	73-72-70-76–291
Mary Beth Zimmerman, $1,086	73-70-76-73–292
Dana Lofland-Dormann, $1,086	67-74-78-73–292
Caroline Keggi, $1,086	71-74-73-74–292
Amy Benz, $1,086	72-69-75-76–292
Jenny Wyatt, $863	71-75-77-71–294
Amy Fruhwirth, $863	75-70-77-72–294
Anne Marie Palli, $863	73-72-76-73–294
Suzanne Strudwick, $863	69-72-80-73–294
Jodi Logan Stambaugh, $863	71-74-73-76–294
Laurie Brower, $747	75-71-78-71–295
Deedee Lasker, $747	69-76-79-71–295
Stefania Croce, $747	73-72-75-75–295
Susie Berning, $692	74-72-76-76–298
Kay Cockerill, $664	71-73-79-79–302
Karen Davies, $636	76-68-82-77–303

ROCHESTER INTERNATIONAL

AT A GLANCE

- **Course:** Locust Hills Country Club
- **Location:** Pittsford, N.Y.
- **When:** June 17-20, 1993
- **Weather:** Warm but scattered showers, particularly Sunday when rain delayed play 30 minutes.
- **Purse:** $500,000
- **Par:** 72
- **Yards:** 6,192
- **Defending champion:** Patty Sheehan
- **Tournament record:** 19-under-par 269, Patty Sheehan, 1992

Just after Tammie Green birdied the par-4 14th, rain delayed play at the Rochester International for 30 minutes. But that didn't stop Green's parade to victory. She dethroned defending champion Patty Sheehan in a one-stroke win. "I felt like I had some momentum going—but when the rain delay stopped play, it's like starting all over again," Green said.

Sheehan, who won the Mazda LPGA Championship a week earlier, narrowly missed her fourth Rochester title in five years.

Green waited out the rain in a maintenance building watching the U.S. Open and a NASCAR race on television.

"Somebody was running on seven cylinders," she said. "I don't know what I was running on."

When play resumed, Green saved par after missing the green on No. 15, then narrowly missed a 25-foot birdie putt after escaping a bunker two holes later.

Her 2-under-par 70 wasn't as spectacular as her career-best 63 the day before, but it was enough for her third LPGA victory.

Scores and earnings

Player	Earnings	Scores	Total
Tammie Green	$75,000	74-69-63-70	276
Patty Sheehan	$46,546	69-72-68-68	277
Helen Alfredsson	$30,192	68-75-67-68	278
Kelly Robbins	$30,192	70-71-66-71	278
Dottie Mochrie	$19,499	71-71-67-70	279
Alice Ritzman	$19,499	70-71-68-70	279
Meg Mallon	$13,963	71-67-72-70	280
Barb Bunkowsky	$13,963	69-71-69-71	280
Lynn Connelly	$10,651	70-66-74-71	281
Beth Daniel	$10,651	68-68-73-72	281
Jenny Lidback	$10,651	67-69-72-73	281
Brandie Burton	$8,806	68-72-70-72	282
Kris Monaghan	$7,799	74-66-70-73	283
Cindy Figg-Currier	$7,799	68-70-72-73	283
Nancy Lopez	$7,799	66-69-73-75	283
Sherri Steinhauer	$6,541	76-70-66-72	284
Marta Figueras-Dotti	$6,541	72-70-70-72	284
Nancy Scranton	$6,541	67-72-70-75	284
Kathy Postlewait	$5,786	70-71-75-69	285
Juli Inkster	$5,786	69-76-70-70	285
Dale Eggeling	$5,786	72-72-71-70	285
Michelle McGann	$4,906	74-73-71-68	286
Barb Thomas	$4,906	72-72-70-72	286
Missie Berteotti	$4,906	72-71-71-72	286
JoAnne Carner	$4,906	72-69-70-75	286
Lisa Walters	$4,906	69-71-71-75	286
Nancy Ramsbottom	$3,786	71-75-72-69	287
Joan Pitcock	$3,786	75-71-70-71	287
Gail Graham	$3,786	75-71-69-72	287
Karen Lunn	$3,786	70-74-71-72	287
Tina Barrett	$3,786	73-74-67-73	287
Cindy Rarick	$3,786	73-72-69-73	287
Tracy Kerdyk	$3,786	70-73-71-73	287
Pamela Wright	$3,786	73-73-67-74	287
Mary Beth Zimmerman	$3,786	75-69-69-74	287
Amy Read	$3,786	71-73-69-74	287
Allison Finney	$2,943	72-74-69-73	288
Karen Noble	$2,943	73-72-70-73	288
Lisa Kiggens	$2,943	73-70-72-73	288
Jane Crafter	$2,522	74-70-74-71	289
Alicia Dibos	$2,522	72-73-71-73	289
Rosie Jones	$2,522	73-70-73-73	289
Cathy Johnston-Forbes	$2,522	71-74-68-76	289
Stephanie Farwig	$1,962	77-68-75-70	290
Shelley Hamlin	$1,962	75-72-72-71	290
Amy Fruhwirth	$1,962	70-77-72-71	290
Anne Marie Palli	$1,962	73-72-72-73	290
Barbara Mucha	$1,962	72-72-73-73	290
Lynn Adams	$1,962	72-71-73-74	290
Sally Little	$1,962	76-71-64-79	290
Denise Baldwin	$1,396	75-71-72-73	291
Laurel Kean	$1,396	73-72-73-73	291
Cathy Morse	$1,396	76-71-70-74	291
Danielle Ammaccapane	$1,396	71-71-74-75	291
Laura Davies	$1,396	71-73-71-76	291
Lori Garbacz	$1,396	72-71-71-77	291
Lori West	$996	74-73-72-73	292
Kris Tschetter	$996	72-75-72-73	292
Patti Rizzo	$996	77-70-69-76	292
Vicki Fergon	$996	69-71-76-76	292
Tina Tombs	$996	72-74-67-79	292
Martha Faulconer	$788	73-74-73-73	293
Cathy Mockett	$788	73-74-72-74	293
Deb Richard	$788	70-72-74-77	293
Stephanie Maynor	$716	73-74-74-73	294
Donna Andrews	$716	77-70-69-78	294
Sherri Turner	$641	71-71-78-75	295
Lenore Rittenhouse	$641	75-69-73-78	295
Kristi Albers	$641	71-72-74-78	295
Muffin Spencer-Devlin	$641	72-70-75-78	295
Caroline Keggi	$557	73-72-76-75	296
Leigh Ann Mills	$557	68-78-74-76	296
Katie Peterson-Parker	$557	70-73-75-78	296
Jerilyn Britz	$528	68-72-79-78	297
Lisa Brandetsas	$516	71-74-77-77	299
Nancy Rubin	$505	71-74-74-81	300
Page Dunlap	$494	74-71-78-79	302
Caroline Gowan	$484	71-75-77-80	303
Mary Murphy	$474	78-69-78-79	304

ShopRite LPGA Classic

At A Glance

- **Course:** Greate Bay Resort & Country Club
- **Location:** Somers Point, N.J.
- **When:** June 25-27, 1993
- **Weather:** Sunny and warm with some winds.
- **Purse:** $450,000
- **Par:** 71
- **Yards:** 6,235
- **Defending champion:** Anne-Marie Palli
- **Tournament record:** 9-under-par 204, Shelly Hamlin, 1993.

Shelley Hamlin's walk on the final hole of the ShopRite Classic was something special, even after 21 LPGA seasons.

For the first time, Hamlin knew she was going to win even before putting. She had won twice before—once just seven months after breast cancer surgery—but not like this.

"I really enjoyed the walk up 18," Hamlin said. "Everyone was clapping for me. The other (victories), it wasn't quite that sensational moment walking up to the green. I still had to get up and down."

Hamlin, who had seen a three-shot lead evaporate after the 14th hole, secured a two-shot victory with birdies at 15 and 17 in a record performance. Her 9-under-par 204 total for 54 holes broke the mark of 7-under by Juli Inkster in 1988.

Hamlin downplays the courageous label people have pinned on her since her mastectomy in July 1991.

"A better description would be determined and stubborn," Hamlin said. "I think I came back to golf because I was too stubborn to let something I love get away from me. I didn't want to think cancer was going to take that away from me. I'm not courageous, just stubborn."

Scores and earnings

Player	Earnings	Score
Shelley Hamlin	$67,500	67-67-70–204
Judy Dickinson	$32,078	69-70-67–206
Amy Benz	$32,078	72-66-68–206
Beth Daniel	$32,078	70-67-69–206
Martha Faulconer	$17,548	71-68-68–207
Danielle Ammaccapane	$17,548	69-69-69–207
Brandie Burton	$12,567	67-74-67–208
Anne Marie Palli	$12,567	67-73-68–208
Angie Ridgeway	$10,076	72-70-67–209
Missie McGeorge	$10,076	71-67-71–209
Nancy Lopez	$8,023	71-72-67–210
Dale Eggeling	$8,023	70-71-69–210
Jane Geddes	$8,023	69-70-71–210
Allison Finney	$6,419	71-73-67–211
Denise Baldwin	$6,419	72-71-68–211
Laurie Brower	$6,419	71-69-71–211
Kathy Guadagnino	$6,419	70-69-72–211
Maggie Will	$4,927	72-71-69–212
Alice Ritzman	$4,927	70-73-69–212
Barb Thomas	$4,927	72-70-70–212
Sally Little	$4,927	71-71-70–212
Muffin Spencer-Devlin	$4,927	72-69-71–212
Carolyn Hill	$4,927	72-69-71–212
Sherri Steinhauer	$4,927	68-72-72–212
Sherri Turner	$4,927	71-68-73–212
Lenore Rittenhouse	$4,008	74-71-68–213
Pearl Sinn	$4,008	73-70-70–213
Cathy Johnston-Forbes	$4,008	73-68-72–213
Joan Pitcock	$3,478	69-77-68–214
Lori Garbacz	$3,478	71-73-70–214
Kate Hughes	$3,478	72-71-71–214
Mary Beth Zimmerman	$3,478	72-70-72–214
Lisa DePaulo	$3,478	69-72-73–214
Jill Briles-Hinton	$2,674	73-73-69–215
Noelle Daghe	$2,674	72-74-69–215
Marianne Morris	$2,674	72-73-70–215
Meg Mallon	$2,674	70-75-70–215
Rosie Jones	$2,674	73-71-71–215
Tina Barrett	$2,674	70-74-71–215
Missie Berteotti	$2,674	72-71-72–215
Leigh Ann Mills	$2,674	71-72-72–215
Nancy Ramsbottom	$2,674	71-70-74–215
Laurel Kean	$2,015	73-72-71–216
Marilyn Lovander	$2,015	72-73-71–216
Stephanie Farwig	$2,015	72-72-72–216
Martha Nause	$2,015	72-71-73–216
Barb Bunkowsky	$1,612	72-73-72–217
Karen Noble	$1,612	72-73-72–217
Robin Hood	$1,612	74-70-73–217
Jenny Lidback	$1,612	71-73-73–217
Jenny Wyatt	$1,612	71-71-75–217
Mary Murphy	$1,279	74-72-72–218
Betsy King	$1,279	73-73-72–218
Connie Chillemi	$1,279	70-75-73–218
Judy Sams	$1,279	71-73-74–218
Suzanne Strudwick	$899	75-71-73–219
Colleen Walker	$899	74-72-73–219
Nancy Scranton	$899	74-72-73–219
Cindy Schreyer	$899	73-73-73–219
Joal Rieder	$899	72-74-73–219
Pamela Allen	$899	71-75-73–219
Michele Redman	$899	75-70-74–219
Nancy White	$899	74-71-74–219
Nancy Harvey	$656	74-72-75–221
Page Dunlap	$656	74-72-75–221
Kathryn Marshall	$656	69-77-75–221
Caroline Gowan	$656	72-73-76–221
Jodi Logan Stambaugh	$656	71-74-76–221
Kelly Leadbetter	$577	72-73-77–222
Dina Ammaccapane	$577	70-74-78–222
Amy Fruhwirth	$543	73-71-79–223
Michele Ann Thompson	$520	70-76-80–226

Jenny Lidback's game in 1993 was the best it's ever been on the LPGA tour, thanks to help from an old mentor.

PLAYER

Jenny Lidback learned to play golf 22 years ago, but not until the summer of 1993 did she learn to compete on the LPGA tour.

"A month ago, you couldn't find me in the top 100 on the money list," said Lidback, 30, of Scottsdale, Ariz. as she prepared for the ShopRite LPGA Classic, where she aimed to clinch a spot on the 1994 tour. "I'm pretty close to being good for next year."

Most LPGA members don't think about exemption until late in the season, but Lidback, who lost her exemption in 1992, had been thinking about it since May, when she started playing the best golf of her career.

The highlight was the Mazda LPGA Championship, which she led until the final round before finishing 17th. The next week, she was tied for second through two rounds of the Rochester International and finished tied for ninth.

Over two weeks her earnings jumped to $48,545. In '92, the last qualifying player earned $50,246.

"People ask me if the LPGA Champ-ionship was a big tournament for me," Lidback said. "It was, but when you've never won, any tournament is a big event."

Lidback was a top junior player and college All-American at Texas Christian and Louisiana State, but she never reached her potential in her first four years as a pro. In 1993, she went back to her first teacher, Tommy Martty, and asked for help. Although Martty is no longer a teaching pro, he agreed to help if Lidback would follow his instruction.

"It was as if somebody brought you a Maserati," said Martty, senior vice president of Billy Casper Golf Management in Vienna, Va., "and said, 'I haven't washed it in three years and I haven't changed oil in it in three years. What's wrong with it?'"

Martty didn't say he was shocked when he saw Lidback's swing, but he did say it wasn't the one he taught her when she was a teen-ager in Baton Rouge: "She'd developed a lot of mechanical problems."

They agreed to work on a two-year program, so Lidback's performance in June was a bonus. So was her win in the Mitsubishi Motors Invitational Pro-Am Nov. 20 in Scottsdale, Ariz., where she topped off her year with an extra $25,000.

—*by Jerry Potter*

SPOTLIGHT

Jamie Farr Toledo Classic

At a Glance

- **Course:** Highland Meadows Golf Club
- **Location:** Sylvania, Ohio
- **When:** July 2-4, 1993
- **Weather:** Warm and humid.
- **Purse:** $450,000
- **Par:** 71
- **Yards:** 6,295
- **Defending champion:** Patty Sheehan, 4-under-par 209
- **Tournament record:** 11-under-par 277, Laura Davies, 1988 (at Glengarry)

Brandie Burton staved off charges from three veterans and survived sauna-like conditions with a bogey-free 67 to win the Jamie Farr Toledo Classic with a record 12-under-par 201.

In 95-degree heat with 75% humidity, Burton, 21, made up two strokes on second-round leader Jane Geddes with birdies on holes 3, 4 and 5.

Her birdie on 16 held off a late charge from runner-up Hollis Stacy, who birdied 16 and 17 but left a 15-foot birdie putt on 18 one turn short.

When the ball stopped rolling, Stacy groaned and clutched her neck in a symbolic choke-hold. If it had dropped, Stacy, playing a group ahead of Burton, would have moved into a tie for the lead.

"I knew I had to make that putt, and because of that, I don't think it was my best putting stroke," she said.

Burton iced the victory when she put her third shot on the par-five 18th 6 feet from the pin. She two-putted for par and her second title in three years.

"I saw Hollis make the the birdie (on 17) so I knew I had to make a (birdie) to go into the last hole with a one-stroke lead," Burton said. "My nerves were starting to jangle.

"This whole year I've been in the hunt and taken the gas on Sunday. I finally put three rounds together."

Burton would go on to win the du Maurier Classic, her first victory in a major championship.

Scores and earnings

Player	Earnings	Score
Brandie Burton	$67,500	68-66-67—201
Hollis Stacy	$41,891	67-67-68—202
Jane Geddes	$30,569	68-64-71—203
Patty Sheehan	$23,776	70-66-69—205
Colleen Walker	$16,152	68-71-68—207
Amy Benz	$16,152	67-71-69—207
Suzanne Strudwick	$16,152	67-70-70—207
Marianne Morris	$10,132	74-69-65—208
Michelle McGann	$10,132	70-70-68—208
Dale Eggeling	$10,132	70-70-68—208
Judy Dickinson	$10,132	69-69-70—208
Laurie Rinker-Graham	$6,509	73-71-65—209
Maggie Will	$6,509	72-72-65—209
Michele Redman	$6,509	72-71-66—209
Jenny Lidback	$6,509	72-70-67—209
Dana Lofland-Dormann	$6,509	69-71-69—209
Amy Fruhwirth	$6,509	70-69-70—209
Lori Garbacz	$6,509	72-66-71—209
Jane Crafter	$6,509	69-69-71—209
Jan Stephenson	$4,873	72-70-68—210
Lisa Kiggens	$4,873	70-72-68—210
Nancy Harvey	$4,873	72-68-70—210
Terry-Jo Myers	$4,873	72-66-72—210
Cathy Marino	$3,851	70-72-69—211
Jody Anschutz	$3,851	69-73-69—211
Ellie Gibson	$3,851	76-65-70—211
Kathy Postlewait	$3,851	73-68-70—211
Kris Tschetter	$3,851	71-70-70—211
Martha Nause	$3,851	69-72-70—211
Martha Faulconer	$3,851	70-69-72—211
Beth Daniel	$3,851	70-69-72—211
Melissa McNamara	$3,851	69-70-72—211
Barbara Mucha	$2,654	75-69-68—212
Patti Liscio	$2,654	74-69-69—212
Patty Jordan	$2,654	67-76-69—212
Betsy King	$2,654	72-70-70—212
Lori West	$2,654	70-72-70—212
Tina Tombs	$2,654	75-66-71—212
Marta Figueras-Dotti	$2,654	72-68-72—212
Nancy Scranton	$2,654	70-69-73—212
Kate Rogerson	$2,654	72-66-74—212
Robin Walton	$2,654	71-67-74—212
Jerilyn Britz	$2,654	68-70-74—212
Allison Finney	$1,682	74-70-69—213
Robin Hood	$1,682	72-71-70—213
Amy Read	$1,682	70-72-71—213
Noelle Daghe	$1,682	69-73-71—213
Tracy Kerdyk	$1,682	72-69-72—213
Laurie Brower	$1,682	72-69-72—213
Caroline Pierce	$1,682	71-70-72—213
Missie McGeorge	$1,682	71-69-73—213
Kathryn Marshall	$1,682	71-69-73—213
Cathy Reynolds	$1,120	72-73-69—214
Vicki Goetze	$1,120	74-70-70—214
Stephanie Farwig	$1,120	69-74-71—214
Kathy Guadagnino	$1,120	70-72-72—214
Joal Rieder	$1,120	70-71-73—214
Carolyn Hill	$1,120	73-67-74—214
Julie Larsen	$837	72-73-70—215
Michele Ann Thompson	$837	68-75-72—215
Chris Johnson	$837	72-67-76—215
Deborah McHaffie	$696	71-72-73—216
Barb Bunkowsky	$696	67-75-74—216
Pearl Sinn	$696	71-69-76—216
Meg Mallon	$696	70-70-76—216
Stephanie Maynor	$555	75-70-72—217
Sally Little	$555	74-71-72—217
Sue Thomas	$555	71-74-72—217
Tammie Green	$555	70-75-72—217
Susie Berning	$555	73-69-75—217
Barb Thomas	$555	69-72-76—217
Leigh Ann Mills	$555	68-72-77—217
Kelly Robbins	$555	67-73-77—217
Kate Hughes	$475	73-70-75—218
Lauri Merten	$459	75-70-74—219
Angie Ridgeway	$459	71-73-75—219
Jenny Wyatt	$439	75-70-76—221
Karin Mundinger	$439	72-73-76—221

Youngstown-Warren LPGA Classic

AT A GLANCE

- **Course:** Avalon Lakes Golf Course
- **Location:** Warren, Ohio
- **When:** July 9-11, 1993
- **Weather:** Hot and humid.
- **Purse:** $500,000
- **Par:** 72
- **Yards:** 6,188
- **Playoff:** Nancy Lopez defeated Deb Richard with a birdie on the first playoff hole.
- **Defending champion:** None (new tournament)
- **Tournament record:** 13-under 203, Nancy Lopez, 1993

Nancy Lopez proved she never gets tired of winning, not after 16½ years in the LPGA and 47 career victories.

"Winning is never dull," said Lopez after beating Deb Richard in a playoff at the inaugural Youngstown-Warren Classic.

Lopez picked up her first victory of the season in a dramatic fashion. She eagled the 18th hole with a 20-foot putt to tie Richard at 13-under-par 203 for 54 holes.

Then, in the playoff, she birdied the 18th, two-putting from 35 feet to clinch the victory.

"I have been hitting the ball so well this year that I was getting frustrated because I wasn't winning," said Lopez. "Today I told my caddie (Tom Thorpe), 'Don't let me get frustrated. Don't let me get mad.'"

Lopez three-putted the first hole for bogey, but she retained her composure and played the next eight holes 5-under par. She finished with a 67 after shooting 68s in the first two rounds.

"You always wonder if you're going to win again," said Lopez, who had won consecutive events the previous September. "I've come close this year, but I've fallen apart."

—*by Jerry Potter*

Scores and earnings

Nancy Lopez, $75,000		68-68-67–203
Deb Richard, $46,546		67-69-67–203
Pat Bradley, $24,845		73-66-65–204
Deborah McHaffie, $24,845		69-70-65–204
Hollis Stacy, $24,845		69-68-67–204
Missie McGeorge, $24,845		65-69-70–204
Donna Andrews, $12,579		70-71-65–206
Kim Williams, $12,579		70-67-69–206
Rosie Jones, $12,579		67-70-69–206
Karen Lunn, $12,579		66-68-72–206
Lori West, $7,871		72-68-67–207
Jill Briles-Hinton, $7,871		67-73-67–207
Lynn Connelly, $7,871		71-68-68–207
Ellie Gibson, $7,871		70-69-68–207
Jan Stephenson, $7,871		69-70-68–207
Kris Monaghan, $7,871		69-69-69–207
Betsy King, $7,871		67-70-70–207
Patty Sheehan, $5,912		74-65-69–208
Colleen Walker, $5,912		67-72-69–208
Ayako Okamoto, $5,912		66-72-70–208
Dottie Mochrie, $5,912		66-71-71–208
Cindy Rarick, $4,826		72-71-66–209
Karen Noble, $4,826		71-71-67–209
Michelle McGann, $4,826		70-70-69–209
Barbara Mucha, $4,826		69-68-72–209
Vicki Fergon, $4,826		66-71-72–209
Kathy Guadagnino, $4,826		67-69-73–209
Michelle Estill, $3,980		70-73-67–210
Angie Ridgeway, $3,980		71-70-69–210
Dawn Coe-Jones, $3,980		70-70-70–210
Kelly Robbins, $3,980		69-71-70–210
Susie Berning, $3,980		68-70-72–210
Lisa Walters, $3,132		69-75-67–211
Judy Dickinson, $3,132		73-70-68–211
Danielle Ammaccapane, $3,132		73-70-68–211
JoAnne Carner, $3,132		71-72-68–211
Marianne Morris, $3,132		72-69-70–211
Jane Crafter, $3,132		68-73-70–211
Dale Eggeling, $3,132		67-72-72–211
Lisa Kiggens, $3,132		68-68-75–211
Patti Liscio, $2,113		72-71-69–212
Patty Jordan, $2,113		71-72-69–212
Amy Fruhwirth, $2,113		74-68-70–212
Marta Figueras-Dotti, $2,113		72-70-70–212
Sherri Steinhauer, $2,113		71-70-71–212
Kris Tschetter, $2,113		67-74-71–212
Amy Read, $2,113		72-68-72–212
Hiromi Kobayashi, $2,113		72-68-72–212
Kathy Postlewait, $2,113		68-72-72–212
Cathy Mockett, $2,113		73-66-73–212
Shelley Hamlin, $1,471		73-71-69–213
Laurie Brower, $1,471		70-73-70–213
Kim Shipman, $1,471		68-73-72–213
Tammie Green, $1,471		67-74-72–213
Joan Pitcock, $1,131		76-66-72–214
Tina Tombs, $1,131		73-69-72–214
Lynn Adams, $1,131		72-69-73–214
Kim Bauer, $1,131		70-71-73–214
Mary Murphy, $1,131		67-73-74–214
Connie Chillemi, $729		76-68-71–215
Jenny Wyatt, $729		73-71-71–215
Cindy Schreyer, $729		73-71-71–215
Sarah McGuire, $729		73-71-71–215
Tracy Kerdyk, $729		73-71-71–215
Pamela Allen, $729		72-72-71–215
Kate Hughes, $729		71-73-71–215
Missie Berteotti, $729		72-71-72–215
Noelle Daghe, $729		71-72-72–215
Laurel Kean, $729		69-73-73–215
Stefania Croce, $729		73-68-74–215
Laurie Rinker-Graham, $729		70-71-74–215
Kristal Parker, $547		69-75-72–216
Martha Faulconer, $547		76-67-73–216
Kate Rogerson, $505		75-69-73–217
Melissa McNamara, $505		71-73-73–217
Alice Miller, $505		74-69-74–217
Eva Dahllof, $505		72-70-75–217
Val Skinner, $505		71-71-75–217
Kim Lasken, $474		73-70-75–218

JAL Big Apple Classic

At a Glance

- **Course:** Wykagyl Country Club
- **Location:** New Rochelle, N.Y.
- **When:** July 15-18, 1993
- **Weather:** Hot, dry and windy.
- **Purse:** $600,000
- **Par:** 71
- **Yards:** 6,095
- **Defending champion:** Juli Inkster, 11-under-par 273
- **Tournament record:** 15-under-par 273, Betsy King, 1990

Hiromi Kobayashi came into the JAL Big Apple Golf Classic quietly. She left loudly.

Kobayashi started the final round in second place, a stroke behind Betsy King. Shooting 69, she won by two strokes over Rosie Jones.

King, with a double bogey and four bogeys, zoomed to a 75–283 and frustratingly remained two victories shy of the 30 she needs to qualify for the LPGA Hall of Fame. King, who won this tournament in 1990 and '91, was winless in 17 tournaments this year.

As for Kobayashi, meek and mild through the first three rounds, she startled the audience at her post-victory press conference by saying: "Ayako Okamoto is my biggest target. She's the best woman player ever in my country and I'm aiming for that spot."

The 5-foot-7 Kobayashi, winner of seven titles in her native country, including the Japan Women's Open, quickly added, "I'm not just aiming to be the best Japanese player, I want to be the best on the LPGA Tour. That's why I came to this country, and someday I will be just that."

Of the two goals, taking aim at Okamoto, 42, may be more practical. Winner of 17 LPGA titles since joining in 1981, Okamoto is struggling and hasn't won since June 7, 1992 at the McDonald's Championship.

Scores and earnings

Player	Scores
Hiromi Kobayashi, $90,000	69-71-69-69–278
Rosie Jones, $55,855	72-71-68-71–282
Betsy King, $40,759	71-69-68-75–283
Danielle Ammaccapane, $28,682	72-70-73-70–285
Jan Stephenson, $28,682	72-72-68-73–285
Helen Alfredsson, $21,134	74-70-70-73–287
Barb Bunkowsky, $15,901	73-70-74-71–288
Julie Larsen, $15,901	73-68-75-72–288
Kristi Albers, $15,901	72-67-77-72–288
Nancy Lopez, $12,082	72-73-70-74–289
Tammie Green, $12,082	69-73-73-74–289
Jane Geddes, $10,275	68-77-75-70–290
Juli Inkster, $10,275	74-72-70-74–290
Michelle McGann, $8,342	73-73-74-71–291
Jill Briles-Hinton, $8,342	71-77-71-72–291
Judy Dickinson, $8,342	72-74-73-72–291
Beth Daniel, $8,342	72-73-73-73–291
JoAnne Carner, $8,342	75-67-75-74–291
Marta Figueras-Dotti, $6,293	72-77-74-69–292
Katie Peterson-Parker, $6,293	75-73-75-69–292
Chris Johnson, $6,293	75-70-77-70–292
Barb Mucha, $6,293	74-75-71-72–292
Donna Andrews, $6,293	68-76-76-72–292
Sherri Steinhauer, $6,293	71-77-70-74–292
Melissa McNamara, $6,293	72-72-74-74–292
Mary Beth Zimmerman, $6,293	70-73-69-80–292
Alice Ritzman, $5,232	74-76-71-72–293
Barb Thomas, $5,232	76-71-72-74–293
Deb Richard, $4,617	74-77-72-71–294
Amy Read, $4,617	74-73-75-72–294
Alicia Dibos, $4,617	71-73-77-73–294
Amy Alcott, $4,617	74-71-74-75–294
Tania Abitbol, $4,617	73-74-69-78–294
Jean Zedlitz, $3,768	72-78-76-69–295
Dale Eggeling, $3,768	74-75-75-71–295
Susie Berning, $3,768	71-78-74-72–295
Marilyn Lovander, $3,768	73-75-74-73–295
Alice Miller, $3,768	68-75-79-73–295
Liselotte Neumann, $3,768	71-76-73-75–295
Karen Lunn, $2,851	68-74-84-70–296
Connie Chillemi, $2,851	74-76-74-72–296
Nancy Scranton, $2,851	75-73-76-72–296
Hollis Stacy, $2,851	74-74-76-72–296
Nancy Ramsbottom, $2,851	75-74-73-74–296
Cindy Figg-Currier, $2,851	77-68-77-74–296
Vicki Fergon, $2,851	69-76-76-75–296
Caroline Keggi, $1,931	72-79-76-70–297
Angie Ridgeway, $1,931	78-72-77-70–297
Nancy White, $1,931	69-77-80-71–297
Maggie Will, $1,931	72-74-79-72–297
Dawn Coe-Jones, $1,931	76-75-73-73–297
Kate Rogerson, $1,931	76-72-76-73–297
Pat Bradley, $1,931	74-73-76-74–297
Trish Johnson, $1,931	70-80-72-75–297
Cindy Rarick, $1,931	73-75-74-75–297
Nancy Harvey, $1,321	72-76-78-72–298
Lenore Rittenhouse, $1,321	75-75-74-74–298
Brandie Burton, $1,321	72-78-74-74–298
Kris Tschetter, $1,321	74-76-73-75–298
Dottie Mochrie, $1,035	76-74-76-73–299
Carolyn Hill, $1,035	73-77-75-74–299
Ayako Okamoto, $1,035	72-73-78-76–299
Gail Graham, $1,035	75-75-72-77–299
Cindy Schreyer, $884	73-75-77-75–300
Meg Mallon, $884	72-75-76-77–300
Dina Ammaccapane, $884	73-75-74-78–300
Amy Benz, $824	73-78-74-76–301
Jodi Logan Stambaugh, $793	76-72-80-74–302
Terry-Jo Myers, $748	76-73-80-74–303
Deedee Lasker, $748	74-75-79-75–303
Patti Rizzo, $703	74-75-77-78–304
Eva Dahllof, $665	81-70-78-76–305
Amy Fruhwirth, $665	72-79-78-76–305
Kim Williams, $643	76-74-79-77–306

PLAYER SPOTLIGHT

After finishing in a tie for 60th at the JAL Big Apple Classic, Dottie Mochrie said, "I played as poorly as I probably could have played." She sought to regain her 1992 form with the help of her husband and former caddie, Doug.

Dottie Mochrie wanted to cut right through the facts about her decline as a golfer and get to the rumors.

"The newest rumor is that my husband and I are getting a divorce and I'm having an affair with Fred Couples," Mochrie said. "I've only met Fred Couples twice in my life."

Having put that rumor to rest, did Mochrie believe she was ready for the U.S. Women's Open at Crooked Stick Golf Club?

"My golf game is not what it was last year," Mochrie said. "I started screwing around with it in April, trying to fix something that wasn't broken.

"That didn't work, so now I'm trying to get back to where I was last year."

Mochrie was the best player on the LPGA tour in 1992, winning four events and leading in earnings with $693,335. In 1993 she was winless entering the Women's Open.

"A season like Dottie had last year is more difficult mentally than it is physically," said Meg Mallon, who experienced a similar fall-off after her banner 1991 tour. "You get tired. You have no time to yourself."

Mochrie says she's learned at least one thing this year: to say no to some people who want her time.

"You owe a lot to a lot of people," Mochrie said, "but you owe a lot to yourself, too. If you've never been through success before, you have to learn the hard way to handle it."

Earlier last summer, her husband, Doug, quit as her caddy and returned to Sarasota, Fla., seeking a club pro job.

He was back with her in July, not as a caddy, but as a teacher trying to get Dottie's game straightened out.

"It certainly wasn't a husband-wife conflict that sent Doug outside the gallery ropes," Dottie said. "We knew he wouldn't be my caddy forever."

—*by Jerry Potter*

PING/WELCH'S Championship

AT A GLANCE

- **Course:** Blue Hill Country Club
- **Location:** Canton, Mass.
- **When:** July 29-Aug. 1, 1993
- **Weather:** Beautiful.
- **Purse:** $450,000
- **Par:** 72
- **Yards:** 6,137
- **Playoff:** Missie Berteotti birdied the fifth playoff hole to defeat defending champion Dottie Mochrie.
- **Defending champion:** Dottie Mochrie, 6-under-par 278
- **Tournament record:** 13-under-par 275, Juli Inkster, 1991

Missie Berteotti showed unusual confidence, considering she was winless in eight years on the LPGA tour.

Berteotti never tired through the pressure-packed five-hole playoff she needed to win the PING/WELCH's Championship.

She never quivered because she was playing against last year's top money-winner and defending champion, Dottie Mochrie.

With steel nerves and steady shots, the bubbly Berteotti outlasted the serious Mochrie.

Berteotti started the day in a four-way tie for second, three strokes behind Donna Andrews. Mochrie was five strokes back; but she shot 66, Berteotti 68, and they were tied at 12-under 276 after 72 holes.

On the deciding hole, Berteotti coolly sank an 18-foot birdie putt, hitting the ball firmly without fear of leaving a tough comeback if she went long. Mochrie already had two-putted from about two inches farther.

"I just said, 'Just hit it, give it a chance.' At that point, I could have made any 3- or 4-footer coming back," Berteotti said.

Scores and earnings

Player	Scores
#Missie Berteotti, $67,500	73-66-69-68–276
Dottie Mochrie, $41,891	71-69-70-66–276
Danielle Ammaccapane, $30,569	70-72-68-68–278
Helen Alfredsson, $21,511	69-67-72-71–279
Donna Andrews, $21,511	71-68-66-74–279
Laura Davies, $14,605	72-68-71-69–280
Trish Johnson, $14,605	68-71-72-69–280
Kris Monaghan, $9,691	72-72-70-67–281
Brandie Burton, $9,691	71-71-70-69–281
Amy Benz, $9,691	71-71-70-69–281
Pat Bradley, $9,691	69-73-68-71–281
Val Skinner, $9,691	69-71-68-73–281
Dawn Coe-Jones, $7,019	74-72-67-69–282
Lori West, $7,019	70-71-70-71–282
Stefania Croce, $7,019	69-71-68-74–282
Michele Redman, $5,660	73-74-71-65–283
Barb Mucha, $5,660	72-72-72-67–283
Jane Geddes, $5,660	73-71-69-70–283
Colleen Walker, $5,660	71-74-67-71–283
Angie Ridgeway, $5,660	69-74-69-71–283
Kelly Robbins, $4,587	74-71-71-68–284
Alice Ritzman, $4,587	73-68-74-69–284
Vicki Fergon, $4,587	71-69-74-70–284
Missie McGeorge, $4,587	70-71-72-71–284
Kathy Guadagnino, $4,587	69-73-70-72–284
Alison Nicholas, $3,781	72-75-71-67–285
Meg Mallon, $3,781	70-72-75-68–285
Betsy King, $3,781	70-73-72-70–285
Carolyn Hill, $3,781	70-73-72-70–285
Maggie Will, $3,781	71-73-70-71–285
Amy Fruhwirth, $3,781	71-70-73-71–285
Sherri Steinhauer, $3,045	71-74-70-71–286
Hiromi Kobayashi, $3,045	75-68-72-71–286
Denise Baldwin, $3,045	71-72-72-71–286
Cindy Rarick, $3,045	74-68-71-73–286
Dana Lofland-Dormann, $3,045	69-73-71-73–286
Liselotte Neumann, $3,045	74-73-65-74–286
Judy Sams, $2,328	73-72-73-69–287
Patti Rizzo, $2,328	73-73-71-70–287
Pamela Wright, $2,328	74-73-66-74–287
Robin Hood, $2,328	70-72-71-74–287
Marianne Morris, $2,328	72-69-72-74–287
Deb Richard, $2,328	71-70-71-75–287
Jill Briles-Hinton, $2,328	74-67-70-76–287
Elaine Crosby, $1,765	76-70-73-69–288
Nancy Scranton, $1,765	71-74-71-72–288
Nina Foust, $1,765	74-71-69-74–288
Beth Daniel, $1,765	72-70-71-75–288
Lauri Merten, $1,765	71-73-67-77–288
Katie Peterson-Parker, $1,392	74-73-73-69–289
Barb Thomas, $1,392	71-76-72-70–289
Vicki Goetze, $1,392	68-76-71-74–289
Pearl Sinn, $1,392	73-72-68-76–289
Kathy Postlewait, $1,021	76-71-73-70–290
Laurel Kean, $1,021	73-74-73-70–290
Laurie Rinker-Graham, $1,021	73-71-75-71–290
Marci Bozarth, $1,021	75-72-71-72–290
Joan Pitcock, $1,021	74-71-73-72–290
Amy Alcott, $1,021	71-74-73-72–290
Caroline Keggi, $1,021	74-71-71-74–290
Dina Ammaccapane, $676	69-74-78-70–291
Chris Johnson, $676	71-72-76-72–291
Nancy Ramsbottom, $676	70-73-75-73–291
Robin Walton, $676	73-73-71-74–291
Julie Larsen, $676	71-75-71-74–291
Lisa Kiggens, $676	73-72-72-74–291
Tina Barrett, $676	75-70-71-75–291
Lisa Walters, $676	73-71-72-75–291
Laura Baugh, $531	75-69-75-73–292
Florence Descampe, $531	71-73-75-73–292
Jenny Lidback, $531	74-73-71-74–292
Pamela Allen, $531	74-70-72-76–292
Mitzi Edge, $480	78-69-76-70–293
Sue Thomas, $480	73-71-75-74–293
Shirley Furlong, $449	72-75-75-72–294
Deborah McHaffie, $449	75-70-76-73–294
Martha Faulconer, $449	71-75-73-75–294
Nancy Taylor, $449	75-70-74-75–294
Adele Peterson, $426	74-71-75-75–295
Mary Murphy, $412	75-71-77-73–296
Sharon Barrett, $412	76-71-73-76–296

- won on fifth playoff hole

McCall's LPGA Classic at Stratton Mtn.

AT A GLANCE

- **Course:** Stratton Mountain Country Club
- **Location:** Stratton Mountain, Vt.
- **When:** Aug. 5-8, 1993
- **Weather:** Sunny and pleasant, except for a one-hour rain delay Sunday.
- **Purse:** $500,000
- **Par:** 72
- **Yards:** 6,077
- **Defending champion:** Florence Descampe, 10-under-par 278
- **Tournament record:** 13-under-par 275, Dana Lofland-Dormann, 1993

Dana Lofland-Dormann proved a 63 goes a long way in a golf tournament.

In her case, it lasted four days, as she beat Donna Andrews by a stroke at Stratton Mountain Country Club, earning her second career victory.

Lofland-Dormann shot 69–275 but got the edge she needed by shooting 63 in Thursday's opening round. After that, she never trailed and won with a two-foot putt.

"The putt I had on 18 (in the final round) was pretty much the same putt I had on 18 Thursday to get a 63," she said. "I thought of Thursday because that 63 was pretty special to me. I said, 'Why not do it again today?'"

After shooting 9 under par Thursday, she played a total of 4 under par the next three rounds. Still, her 275 beat the old tournament record by three strokes.

Andrews, winless in four years on the LPGA tour, matched Lofland-Dormann with a final-round 69, but once again she came up a bit short. She had finished in the top seven in three of the previous four events.

"Donna really got me going," Lofland-Dormann said. "She birdied the first hole and that set the tone."

—*by Jerry Potter*

Scores and earnings

Player	Scores
Dana Lofland-Dormann, $75,000	63-73-70-69–275
Donna Andrews, $46,546	71-69-67-69–276
Deb Richard, $33,966	71-73-68-67–279
Michelle McGann, $23,902	71-73-67-70–281
Mary Beth Zimmerman, $23,902	70-68-72-71–281
Sherri Steinhauer, $15,179	74-70-70-68–282
Lisa Kiggens, $15,179	73-70-69-70–282
Patti Rizzo, $15,179	71-70-71-70–282
Kris Monaghan, $10,666	74-71-68-70–283
Nancy Lopez, $10,666	71-70-70-72–283
Brandie Burton, $10,666	73-67-69-74–283
Vicki Fergon, $8,348	72-75-70-67–284
Nancy Scranton, $8,348	73-71-71-69–284
Cindy Rarick, $8,348	72-71-71-70–284
Elaine Crosby, $6,371	71-73-72-69–285
Missie Berteotti, $6,371	74-68-74-69–285
Michele Redman, $6,371	73-73-69-70–285
Dottie Mochrie, $6,371	73-72-70-70–285
Jan Stephenson, $6,371	72-72-69-72–285
Missie McGeorge, $6,371	73-71-68-73–285
Nancy Ramsbottom, $6,371	69-69-73-74–285
Deborah McHaffie, $5,033	76-69-72-69–286
Carolyn Hill, $5,033	74-71-71-70–286
Maggie Will, $5,033	70-71-74-71–286
Tina Tombs, $5,033	71-71-68-76–286
Kathy Guadagnino, $4,246	74-71-72-70–287
Lauri Merten, $4,246	74-70-73-70–287
Shelley Hamlin, $4,246	70-70-77-70–287
Colleen Walker, $4,246	73-71-72-71–287
Joan Pitcock, $4,246	71-73-71-72–287
Laurie Rinker-Graham, $4,246	67-74-70-76–287
Cindy Figg-Currier, $3,617	67-75-74-72–288
Martha Nause, $3,617	75-70-70-73–288
Robin Walton, $3,617	73-71-70-74–288
Allison Finney, $2,988	74-73-72-70–289
Marilyn Lovander, $2,988	71-73-75-70–289
Jill Briles-Hinton, $2,988	72-75-71-71–289
Connie Chillemi, $2,988	76-71-69-73–289
Patty Sheehan, $2,988	71-73-72-73–289
Gail Graham, $2,988	73-70-73-73–289
Alice Miller, $2,988	71-71-74-73–289
Lori West, $2,309	75-71-75-69–290
Dale Eggeling, $2,309	74-72-73-71–290
Michelle Mackall, $2,309	75-70-73-72–290
Chris Johnson, $2,309	73-72-72-73–290
Alison Nicholas, $2,309	72-70-75-73–290
Kim Shipman, $1,856	74-70-75-72–291
Stefania Croce, $1,856	72-69-76-74–291
Ellie Gibson, $1,856	71-76-69-75–291
Sally Little, $1,856	73-70-71-77–291
Kate Rogerson, $1,478	76-71-74-71–292
Eva Dahllof, $1,478	74-73-73-72–292
Page Dunlap, $1,478	73-74-73-72–292
Pat Bradley, $1,478	73-74-72-73–292
Nancy Harvey, $1,478	69-76-71-76–292
Sarah McGuire, $1,176	73-73-73-74–293
Susie Berning, $1,176	71-74-74-74–293
Florence Descampe, $1,176	73-69-76-75–293
Suzanne Strudwick, $950	74-72-78-70–294
Sue Thomas, $950	75-71-74-74–294
Amy Fruhwirth, $950	73-74-72-75–294
Cathy Johnston-Forbes, $950	73-72-73-76–294
Laurel Kean, $812	74-69-78-74–295
Jenny Wyatt, $812	72-71-78-74–295
Muffin Spencer-Devlin, $761	72-75-74-75–296
Melissa McNamara, $761	75-68-76-77–296
Denise Baldwin, $711	77-70-76-74–297
Laurie Brower, $711	76-71-73-77–297
Pearl Sinn, $674	74-70-74-80–298
Karin Mundinger, $649	71-75-79-76–301

Sun-Times Challenge

At a Glance

- **Course:** White Eagle Golf Club
- **Location:** Naperville, Ill.
- **When:** Aug. 12-16, 1993
- **Weather:** Play postponed on Sunday after rain delayed play three times and forecasts called for tornadoes. Only five of 29 groups had finished play when the round was suspended. Play finished Monday.
- **Purse:** $475,000
- **Par:** 72
- **Yards:** 6,256
- **Defending champion:** Dottie Mochrie defeated Judy Dickinson and Beth Daniel on sixth playoff hole.
- **Tournament record:** 13-under-par 275, Martha Nause, 1991

Cindy Schreyer made a 3-foot putt for par on the final hole to earn her first career victory, a one-stroke triumph over Betsy King in the rain-delayed Sun-Times Challenge.

For King, it was another disappointment: her fourth runner-up finish of 1993, her 20th consecutive tournament without a victory.

Schreyer, the NCAA champion at Georgia in 1984, faltered down the stretch but pulled ahead on No. 16, where King three-putted.

Schreyer and King were tied at 14-under when they got to the par-3 16th. Schreyer chipped to within eight feet and made the par putt.

King's tee shot went over the green, and she three-putted from the fringe—her second putt missing from only three feet. After that, King "only" managed to match Schreyer's birdie on the 451 yard No. 17, a hole she had eagled in each of the first three rounds.

Schreyer, whose previous best showing in 1993 was a 24th-place finish at the Nabisco Dinah Shore Open, three-putted both the 11th and 15th greens to drop back into a tie with King before her rally.

Scores and earnings

Player	Scores
Cindy Schreyer, $71,250	67-68-66-71—272
Betsy King, $44,219	67-67-67-72—273
Gail Graham, $32,268	67-73-67-68—275
Dale Eggeling, $20,714	68-71-67-70—276
Kris Monaghan, $20,714	66-69-70-71—276
Marta Figueras-Dotti, $20,714	69-65-71-71—276
Allison Finney, $13,265	67-71-71-69—278
Dottie Mochrie, $13,265	69-66-71-72—278
Colleen Walker, $10,132	73-69-69-68—279
Page Dunlap, $10,132	71-71-67-70—279
Danielle Ammaccapane, $10,132	68-69-72-70—279
Alice Ritzman, $7,076	69-69-72-70—280
Judy Dickinson, $7,076	72-68-69-71—280
Sherri Steinhauer, $7,076	69-70-70-71—280
Michele Redman, $7,076	72-66-71-71—280
Sally Little, $7,076	69-68-72-71—280
Marianne Morris, $7,076	71-70-67-72—280
Patti Rizzo, $7,076	71-68-69-72—280
Barb Mucha, $5,106	71-71-68-71—281
Michelle McGann, $5,106	72-70-70-69—281
Angie Ridgeway, $5,106	68-71-73-69—281
Terry-Jo Myers, $5,106	70-68-73-70—281
Nancy Scranton, $5,106	68-72-69-72—281
Nancy Lopez, $5,106	70-70-68-73—281
Laurel Kean, $5,106	69-70-69-73—281
Kristi Albers, $3,966	70-72-70-70—282
Vicki Fergon, $3,966	70-71-70-71—282
Deborah McHaffie, $3,966	69-71-71-71—282
Melissa McNamara, $3,966	68-69-74-71—282
Michele Ann Thompson, $3,966	72-69-69-72—282
Denise Baldwin, $3,966	71-70-68-73—282
Julie Larsen, $3,966	67-71-70-74—282
Kris Tschetter, $2,958	71-70-72-70—283
Lisa Kiggens, $2,958	72-68-73-70—283
Dawn Coe-Jones, $2,958	69-71-73-70—283
Eva Dahllof, $2,958	73-68-71-71—283
Elaine Crosby, $2,958	70-71-71-71—283
Hiromi Kobayashi, $2,958	71-69-72-71—283
Kelly Robbins, $2,958	72-71-68-72—283
Martha Nause, $2,958	69-72-70-72—283
Stephanie Maynor, $2,958	71-71-65-76—283
Mary Beth Zimmerman, $2,289	71-70-71-73—285
Karen Noble, $2,289	74-66-71-74—285
Nancy Harvey, $2,289	71-68-71-75—285
Cathy Johnston-Forbes, $1,858	71-71-72-72—286
Lenore Rittenhouse, $1,858	74-66-74-72—286
Tina Barrett, $1,858	72-69-72-73—286
Jenny Wyatt, $1,858	69-71-73-73—286
Shelley Hamlin, $1,858	71-71-69-75—286
Kim Bauer, $1,858	70-71-70-75—286
Tina Tombs, $1,476	72-70-73-72—287
Susan Smith, $1,476	70-72-72-73—287
Val Skinner, $1,476	70-72-71-74—287
Nancy White, $1,225	70-72-74-72—288
Donna Wilkins, $1,225	72-69-75-72—288
Noelle Daghe, $1,225	70-67-78-73—288
Joan Pitcock, $1,225	70-72-70-76—288
Sue Thomas, $1,010	69-73-74-73—289
Maggie Will, $1,010	74-68-73-74—289
Nancy Rubin, $879	72-71-72-75—290
Cindy Mackey, $879	72-71-72-75—290
Lynn Adams, $879	70-68-77-75—290
Pamela Wright, $784	68-70-75-78—291
Kiernan Prechtl, $724	71-70-78-75—294
Marilyn Lovander, $724	73-70-75-76—294
Liz Rogers, $724	71-71-75-77—294
Mary Murphy, $724	70-72-73-79—294
Michelle Mackall, $652	67-74-79-75—295
Margie Muzik-Curtis, $652	71-72-75-77—295
Pamela Allen, $615	71-72-75-78—296

Minnesota LPGA Classic

AT A GLANCE

- **Course:** Edinburgh USA
- **Location:** Brooklyn Park, Minn.
- **When:** Aug. 20-22, 1993
- **Weather:** Overcast Friday; sunny Saturday; overcast and rainy on Sunday.
- **Purse:** $450,000
- **Par:** 72
- **Yards:** 6,141
- **Defending champion:** Kris Tschetter, 5-under-par 211
- **Tournament record:** 13-under-par 203, Beth Daniel, 1990

Japan's Hiromi Kobayashi didn't need to change a thing.

After matching the Minnesota LPGA Classic tournament record with a final-round 65 that included eight birdies, she headed into a playoff with Cindy Rarick with the same even-headed approach she had used all day.

The mind-set worked as Kobayashi made a 3-foot par putt and then watched Rarick push a 5-foot try wide. The 30-year-old had her second victory of the year.

"I knew 18 is not an easy hole to make a birdie, so I just tried to make par," Kobayashi said of the playoff hole. "But I was on kind of a good run, so I just tried to play the same as before."

Kobayashi wielded a hot putter, making birdie putts of 36 feet on No. 11 and 30 feet on No. 9, as well as six others between 1 and 18 feet long. She equalled the tournament record set by Barb Bunkowsky in 1990.

"All I was thinking about today was making a good score, I wasn't thinking about 65," Kobayashi said.

Kobayashi and Rarick, the second-round leader, finished 54 holes at 11-under 205. Both played most of the back nine in a constant drizzle which gave the greens the consistency of wet cement but never threatened play.

Scores and earnings

Player	Earnings	Scores
Hiromi Kobayashi	$67,500	73-67-65–205
Cindy Rarick	$41,891	67-69-69–205
Tina Barrett	$30,569	68-72-66–206
Dana Lofland-Dormann	$23,776	66-72-69–207
Jill Briles-Hinton	$17,548	70-70-68–208
Jane Crafter	$17,548	72-66-70–208
Amy Alcott	$12,567	70-72-68–210
Jody Anschutz	$12,567	71-66-73–210
Noelle Daghe	$9,599	71-73-67–211
Brandie Burton	$9,599	71-69-71–211
Stephanie Farwig	$9,599	68-70-73–211
Nancy Rubin	$7,739	71-72-69–212
Alice Ritzman	$7,739	71-70-71–212
Tammie Green	$5,899	74-70-69–213
Judy Dickinson	$5,899	71-71-71–213
Missie Berteotti	$5,899	71-71-71–213
Beth Daniel	$5,899	67-75-71–213
Nina Foust	$5,899	72-69-72–213
Angie Ridgeway	$5,899	70-71-72–213
Val Skinner	$5,899	74-66-73–213
Gail Graham	$5,899	69-71-73–213
Kelly Robbins	$4,456	76-69-69–214
Pearl Sinn	$4,456	71-74-69–214
Martha Faulconer	$4,456	74-70-70–214
Kim Williams	$4,456	73-68-73–214
Lisa Kiggens	$4,456	72-69-73–214
Patty Jordan	$3,890	74-72-69–215
Martha Nause	$3,890	71-73-71–215
Betsy King	$3,890	71-72-72–215
Robin Walton	$3,088	72-74-70–216
Kathy Guadagnino	$3,088	70-76-70–216
Carolyn Hill	$3,088	76-69-71–216
Kim Bauer	$3,088	72-73-71–216
Kathryn Marshall	$3,088	71-74-71–216
Missie McGeorge	$3,088	75-69-72–216
Julie Larsen	$3,088	73-71-72–216
Dawn Coe-Jones	$3,088	72-71-73–216
Eva Dahllof	$3,088	72-69-75–216
Melissa McNamara	$3,088	68-73-75–216
Colleen Walker	$2,172	76-70-71–217
Tina Tombs	$2,172	73-73-71–217
Sally Little	$2,172	74-70-73–217
Mary Beth Zimmerman	$2,172	72-72-73–217
Suzanne Strudwick	$2,172	70-73-74–217
Rosie Jones	$2,172	74-68-75–217
Jan Stephenson	$2,172	68-73-76–217
Nancy White	$1,517	75-71-72–218
Barb Mucha	$1,517	75-70-73–218
Lenore Rittenhouse	$1,517	71-74-73–218
Karin Mundinger	$1,517	71-74-73–218
Nancy Ramsbottom	$1,517	72-71-75–218
Robin Hood	$1,517	71-72-75–218
Katie Peterson-Parker	$1,517	73-69-76–218
Kris Tschetter	$1,517	72-68-78–218
Judy Sams	$1,028	74-72-73–219
Lori Garbacz	$1,028	73-73-73–219
Maggie Will	$1,028	72-74-73–219
Dina Ammaccapane	$1,028	72-73-74–219
Cathy Mockett	$1,028	70-74-75–219
Page Dunlap	$1,028	71-70-78–219
Susie Berning	$741	73-72-75–220
Sue Fogleman	$741	73-71-76–220
Marilyn Lovander	$741	73-71-76–220
Mitzi Edge	$741	72-72-76–220
Jerilyn Britz	$741	71-73-76–220
Tracy Kerdyk	$741	72-71-77–220
Kathy Postlewait	$651	70-74-77–221
Michelle Mackall	$628	71-74-77–222
Deb Richard	$606	69-77-77–223
Sue Thomas	$583	70-73-81–224
Kristi Albers		72-69-DQ

STATE FARM RAIL CLASSIC

AT A GLANCE

- **Course:** Rail Golf Club
- **Location:** Springfield, Ill.
- **When:** Sept. 4-6, 1993
- **Weather:** Sunny, breezy and pleasant Saturday and Sunday; rainy Monday morning, delaying start of play, but partly sunny in the afternoon.
- **Purse:** $500,000
- **Par:** 72
- **Yards:** 6,403
- **Playoff:** Helen Dobson defeated Dottie Mochrie on the fifth playoff hole after they tied at 13-under-par 203.
- **Defending champion:** Nancy Lopez defeated Laura Davies on the first playoff hole after they tied at 17-under-par 199.
- **Tournament record:** 19-under-par 197, Pat Bradley, 1991

An hour after losing to Helen Dobson at the State Farm Rail Classic, Dottie Mochrie still didn't know much about the woman who had defeated her on the fifth playoff hole.

Dobson, who lives in Skegness, England, earned $75,000 and her first victory on the LPGA tour. In June 1993 she won the BMW European Masters in Brussels, Belgium.

"When I got over here I couldn't believe how good everyone was," said Dobson, 22. "I'm quite surprised that I could have won so soon."

Dobson shot 71–203, while Mochrie posted her second consecutive 68 to tie Dobson in regulation at 13-under par for 54 holes at the Rail Golf Club in Springfield, Ill.

Before winning the Rail Classic, Dobson's best finish this year was a tie for 29th at the Oldsmobile Classic in East Lansing, Mich.

"I putted well most of the week and I think that was the difference," said Dobson, who shot a commanding 7-under-par 65 in the second round after Mochrie and Jane Crafter shared the first-round lead.

—*by Jerry Potter*

Scores and earnings

Player	Scores
#Helen Dobson, $75,000	67-65-71–203
Dottie Mochrie, $46,546	67-68-68–203
Jean Zedlitz, $33,966	68-69-68–205
Nancy Lopez, $23,902	70-70-67–207
Page Dunlap, $23,902	69-69-69–207
Lynn Connelly, $11,825	73-68-67–208
Hollis Stacy, $11,825	72-68-68–208
Rosie Jones, $11,825	73-66-69–208
Lauri Merten, $11,825	70-69-69–208
Tammie Green, $11,825	68-71-69–208
D. Ammaccapane, $11,825	67-71-70–208
Betsy King, $11,825	71-66-71–208
Amy Alcott, $11,825	69-67-72–208
Tania Abitbol, $7,547	70-69-70–209
Sherri Steinhauer, $7,547	68-71-70–209
Kris Tschetter, $5,800	72-70-68–210
Pat Bradley, $5,800	73-68-69–210
Stefania Croce, $5,800	71-70-69–210
Michelle McGann, $5,800	71-69-70–210
Kim Williams, $5,800	67-73-70–210
Helen Alfredsson, $5,800	69-70-71–210
Missie McGeorge, $5,800	69-68-73–210
Lori West, $5,800	66-71-73–210
Jane Crafter, $5,800	66-69-75–210
Florence Descampe, $4,654	71-69-71–211
Mary Beth Zimmerman, $4,654	68-72-71–211
Donna Andrews, $3,918	71-71-70–212
Nancy Scranton, $3,918	74-67-71–212
Marianne Morris, $3,918	72-69-71–212
Michele Ann Thompson, $3,918	69-72-71–212
Barb Bunkowsky, $3,918	72-68-72–212
Cindy Rarick, $3,918	69-70-73–212
Vicki Fergon, $3,918	69-69-74–212
Deborah McHaffie, $3,918	70-66-76–212
Dina Ammaccapane, $2,826	73-71-69–213
Elaine Crosby, $2,826	69-73-71–213
Martha Faulconer, $2,826	68-74-71–213
Meg Mallon, $2,826	74-67-72–213
Sally Little, $2,826	70-71-72–213
Kathy Postlewait, $2,826	70-70-73–213
Dale Eggeling, $2,826	69-71-73–213
Kristi Albers, $2,826	69-71-73–213
Kate Rogerson, $2,826	70-68-75–213
Dana Lofland-Dormann, $1,962	72-71-71–214
Kelly Leadbetter, $1,962	73-69-72–214
Muffin Spencer-Devlin, $1,962	71-70-73–214
Missie Berteotti, $1,962	71-70-73–214
Sarah McGuire, $1,962	70-70-74–214
Kathryn Marshall, $1,962	70-70-74–214
Melissa McNamara, $1,962	70-69-75–214
Pearl Sinn, $1,433	71-73-71–215
Kim Shipman, $1,433	70-74-71–215
Chris Johnson, $1,433	73-70-72–215
Nancy Ramsbottom, $1,433	72-71-72–215
Karen Lunn, $1,433	69-70-76–215
Connie Chillemi, $1,031	71-73-72–216
Ellie Gibson, $1,031	71-72-73–216
Alicia Dibos, $1,031	70-73-73–216
Eva Dahllof, $1,031	74-68-74–216
Mary Murphy, $1,031	73-69-74–216
Laurie Brower, $1,031	72-70-74–216
Adele Peterson, $746	73-71-73–217
Allison Finney, $746	71-73-73–217
Jill Briles-Hinton, $746	71-73-73–217
Robin Hood, $746	69-74-74–217
Nina Foust, $746	72-70-75–217
Judy Dickinson, $746	71-71-75–217
##Emilee Klein	70-72-75–217
Pamela Allen, $629	72-72-74–218
Sue Fogleman, $629	73-69-76–218
Jenny Lidback, $629	71-70-77–218
Suzy Whaley, $565	75-69-75–219
Patti Rizzo, $565	72-71-76–219
Marilyn Lovander, $534	76-68-76–220
Kris Monaghan, $534	70-72-78–220
Pamela Wright, $510	73-71-77–221
Nancy Harvey, $510	71-73-77–221

#-won on fifth playoff hole
##-amateur

Ping-Cellular One LPGA Golf Championship

AT A GLANCE

▸**Course:** Columbia-Edgewater Country Club
▸**Location:** Portland, Ore.
▸**When:** Sept. 10-12, 1993
▸**Weather:** Partly cloudy to sunny with light breezes all weekend.
▸**Purse:** $450,000
▸**Par:** 72
▸**Yards:** 6,319
▸**Defending champion:** Nancy Lopez defeated Jane Crafter on the second playoff hole after they tied at 7-under-par 209.
▸**Tournament record:** 9-under-par 207, Ayako Okamoto, 1986

Tina Barrett's 18th hole nightmare was a rerun.

For the second year in a row, Barrett failed to make par on the final hole at the Ping-Cellular One golf tournament and, for the second year in a row, she lost.

Instead, Donna Andrews came from four strokes back in the final five holes to pick up her first LPGA victory.

Barrett, who began the final round in a tie with Betsy King and Brandie Burton, was 10-under par through 13 holes; then things started falling apart.

"I feel bad about the way I played coming in," she said. "I mean, I bogeyed 14, 16 and 18. Maybe I'll handle it better next time."

Andrews, 26, of Pinehurst, N.C., took advantage of the opening with birdies on 14 and 15, then parred the final three.

She shot a 2-under-par 70 in the final round for a 54-hole, 8-under-par 208 total.

Andrews was second at the McCall's Classic and tied for second at the U.S. Women's Open this year. She had four top-10 finishes in her previous seven tournaments. Finally, she got the victory many expected of her.

"Now," she said, "maybe people will quit asking me when it's going to be my time."

Scores and earnings

Player	Scores
Donna Andrews $67,500	69-69-70–208
Missie McGeorge $36,230	69-69-71–209
Tina Barrett $36,230	66-70-73–209
Meg Mallon $23,776	69-69-72–210
Betsy King $19,247	71-65-75–211
Barb Mucha $14,605	70-73-69–212
Danielle Ammaccapane $14,605	67-71-74–212
Dottie Mochrie $8,689	74-72-67–213
Lenore Rittenhouse $8,689	71-74-68–213
Jane Crafter $8,689	70-75-68–213
Rosie Jones $8,689	73-70-70–213
Lisa Kiggens $8,689	70-72-71–213
Nina Foust $8,689	70-70-73–213
Katie Peterson-Parker $8,689	68-72-73–213
Brandie Burton $8,689	66-70-77–213
Judy Dickinson $5,547	76-69-69–214
Cindy Figg-Currier $5,547	73-72-69–214
Muffin Spencer-Devlin $5,547	72-71-71–214
Kristi Albers $5,547	69-74-71–214
Kelly Robbins $5,547	68-74-72–214
Karen Lunn $5,547	71-70-73–214
Lori West $4,415	74-73-68–215
Michele Redman $4,415	72-71-72–215
Pearl Sinn $4,415	70-72-73–215
Robin Walton $4,415	69-73-73–215
Nancy Harvey $4,415	69-71-75–215
Jenny Wyatt $3,466	73-73-70–216
Elaine Crosby $3,466	72-73-71–216
Lori Garbacz $3,466	71-74-71–216
Beth Daniel $3,466	73-71-72–216
Amy Fruhwirth $3,466	71-72-73–216
Mary Beth Zimmerman $3,466	71-71-74–216
Colleen Walker $3,466	71-71-74–216
Juli Inkster $3,466	71-71-74–216
Dawn Coe-Jones $3,466	69-72-75–216
Shelley Hamlin $2,437	73-73-71–217
Patti Rizzo $2,437	72-74-71–217
Maggie Will $2,437	75-69-73–217
Stephanie Farwig $2,437	75-69-73–217
Jan Stephenson $2,437	71-73-73–217
Kate Hughes $2,437	71-73-73–217
Helen Alfredsson $2,437	71-73-73–217
Jane Geddes $2,437	70-74-73–217
Nancy Scranton $2,437	71-72-74–217
Page Dunlap $1,765	75-71-72–218
Joan Pitcock $1,765	74-72-72–218
Sherri Steinhauer $1,765	71-74-73–218
Kris Monaghan $1,765	68-77-73–218
Mary Murphy $1,765	68-76-74–218
Hollis Stacy $1,324	71-75-73–219
Tammie Green $1,324	70-76-73–219
Dale Eggeling $1,324	73-71-75–219
Robin Hood $1,324	72-72-75–219
Sharon Barrett $1,324	73-69-77–219
Kathy Postlewait $1,324	72-69-78–219
Melissa McNamara $927	75-72-73–220
Lynn Adams $927	73-74-73–220
Amy Read $927	72-73-75–220
Kathryn Marshall $927	69-76-75–220
Dina Ammaccapane $927	76-67-77–220
Michelle Mackall $927	66-75-79–220
Patty Sheehan $683	73-74-74–221
Cindy Schreyer $683	73-74-74–221
Judy Sams $683	73-74-74–221
Tina Tombs $683	73-73-75–221
Marta Figueras-Dotti $683	72-72-77–221
Caroline Keggi $611	76-71-75–222
Amy Alcott $533	76-71-76–223
Angie Ridgeway $533	74-73-76–223
Carolyn Hill $533	73-74-76–223
Pat Bradley $533	72-75-76–223
Marilyn Lovander $533	74-71-78–223
Patti Liscio $533	69-75-79–223
Nancy Kessler $469	73-74-78–225
Cindy Mackey $469	72-67-86–225
Karen Noble $454	77-69-81–227
Jerilyn Britz $444	69-78-82–229
Donna Wilkins $435	76-71-83–230

SAFECO CLASSIC

AT A GLANCE

- **Course:** Meridian Valley Country Club
- **Location:** Kent, Wash.
- **When:** Sept. 16-19, 1993
- **Weather:** Fog delay Thursday morning but sunny later. Sunny and warm Friday; partly cloudy Saturday, cloudy with light rain Sunday.
- **Purse:** $450,000
- **Par:** 72
- **Yards:** 6,222
- **Defending champion:** Colleen Walker, 11-under-par 277
- **Tournament record:** 15-under-par 273, Beth Daniel, 1989

Brandie Burton left Arizona State University in 1990 after one year for a career in professional golf that is becoming extremely successful.

"I knew what I wanted to do, and my family knew what I wanted to do," Burton said after winning the Safeco Classic for her fourth victory in three years on the LPGA tour.

She fired a 7-under-par 65 to come from five strokes behind leader Rosie Jones and win by one shot (14-under-par 274).

Jones closed 71–275 for her third runner-up finish of 1993 and third in a row in the Safeco Classic.

"When I left school I was a little cautious," said Burton. "If you can grind through the first year, the sky is the limit. It makes you respect the tour that much more."

Burton, 21, from Rialto, Calif., has drawn plenty of respect. She set an LPGA record by reaching $1 million in winnings in two years, 180 days.

Scores and earnings

Player	Earnings	Scores
Brandie Burton	$67,500	68-68-73-65–274
Rosie Jones	$41,891	70-67-67-71–275
Patty Sheehan	$30,569	73-70-67-69–279
Kris Monaghan	$21,511	69-71-68-72–280
Lauri Merten	$21,511	72-66-70-72–280
Dottie Mochrie	$12,906	72-70-72-67–281
Nancy Scranton	$12,906	72-70-70-69–281
Jenny Lidback	$12,906	68-76-66-71–281
Amy Benz	$12,906	72-65-73-71–281
Tammie Green	$9,510	72-67-70-73–282
Liselotte Neumann	$8,619	72-69-72-70–283
Lori West	$7,713	76-65-71-72–284
Helen Alfredsson	$7,713	70-67-72-75–284
Dale Eggeling	$6,411	71-74-71-69–285
Elaine Crosby	$6,411	72-70-74-69–285
Lenore Rittenhouse	$6,411	71-71-70-73–285
Judy Dickinson	$6,411	71-67-72-75–285
Michelle McGann	$5,449	73-70-72-71–286
Beth Daniel	$5,449	73-70-72-71–286
Hollis Stacy	$5,449	76-66-73-71–286
Julie Larsen	$4,602	73-71-72-71–287
Muffin Spencer-Devlin	$4,602	75-71-69-72–287
Missie McGeorge	$4,602	73-71-71-72–287
Barb Mucha	$4,602	70-74-70-73–287
Cindy Figg-Currier	$4,602	72-71-71-73–287
Juli Inkster	$3,932	74-72-72-70–288
Pearl Sinn	$3,932	71-74-71-72–288
Donna Andrews	$3,932	70-75-71-72–288
Kathy Guadagnino	$3,932	74-69-72-73–288
Susie Redman	$3,290	70-74-74-71–289
Karen Lunn	$3,290	74-70-73-72–289
Helen Dobson	$3,290	71-73-73-72–289
Hiromi Kobayashi	$3,290	70-69-78-72–289
Joan Pitcock	$3,290	75-72-69-73–289
Kathy Postlewait	$3,290	74-71-71-73–289
Barb Bunkowsky	$2,607	76-70-71-73–290
Jody Anschutz	$2,607	70-73-74-73–290
Maggie Will	$2,607	72-72-72-74–290
Jenny Wyatt	$2,607	75-68-73-74–290
Amy Alcott	$2,607	71-73-69-77–290
Suzanne Strudwick	$2,607	68-72-73-77–290
Jan Stephenson	$2,052	74-73-75-69–291
Lynn Adams	$2,052	73-72-73-73–291
Missie Berteotti	$2,052	77-67-74-73–291
Sherri Steinhauer	$2,052	71-72-75-73–291
JoAnne Carner	$2,052	73-70-73-75–291
Cindy Rarick	$1,604	77-68-73-74–292
Pat Bradley	$1,604	71-72-75-74–292
Denise Baldwin	$1,604	73-72-72-75–292
Jane Crafter	$1,604	68-74-75-75–292
Dawn Coe-Jones	$1,604	70-75-71-76–292
Michelle Mackall	$1,305	75-70-75-73–293
Heather Drew	$1,305	74-73-72-74–293
Cathy Mockett	$1,305	72-73-73-75–293
Vicki Fergon	$1,033	73-74-76-71–294
Florence Descampe	$1,033	73-74-73-74–294
Robin Walton	$1,033	74-72-74-74–294
Martha Faulconer	$1,033	73-72-73-76–294
Ellie Gibson	$1,033	77-70-70-77–294
Penny Hammel	$766	74-72-77-72–295
Kris Tschetter	$766	72-74-75-74–295
Kim Shipman	$766	72-75-73-75–295
Cathy Johnston-Forbes	$766	74-71-74-76–295
Lisa Walters	$766	72-72-74-77–295
Martha Nause	$660	74-73-77-72–296
Sharon Barrett	$660	74-71-73-78–296
Amy Read	$626	73-74-76-74–297
Patty Jordan	$602	76-69-75-78–298
Dina Ammaccapane	$580	76-71-74-78–299
Angie Ridgeway	$534	75-72-79-75–301
Kate Hughes	$534	75-72-78-76–301
Karen Davies	$534	74-73-78-76–301
Tracy Kerdyk	$500	75-71-73-83–302

KYOCERA INAMORI CLASSIC

AT A GLANCE
▸**Course:** Stardust Country Club
▸**Location:** San Diego
▸**When:** Sept. 23-26, 1993
▸**Weather:** Perfect.
▸**Purse:** $425,000
▸**Par:** 72
▸**Yards:** 6,200
▸**Defending champion:** Judy Dickinson, 11-under-par 277
▸**Tournament record:** 13-under-par 275, Ayako Okamoto, 1987, and Kris Monaghan, 1993

After picking up the winner's check, Kris Monaghan felt there was even a bigger payoff at the Kyocera Inamori Classic.

Those rewards became clear after she entered the final round with a one-stroke lead and then shot 1-under-par 71 to edge Julie Inkster by a stroke.

It was Monaghan's second LPGA victory and second at the Kyocera Inamori Classic—though it was switched in 1993 both to a new course and from spring to fall.

When she won in 1990, Monaghan acknowledged a dire need for the money. This time, she felt richer in ways beyond the $63,750 first prize.

"It's quite a bit different," Monaghan said. "Money is one of the reasons that we're out here, but I'm also here for the glory. I want to win. I want to be in the hunt."

Monaghan, 33, credited this victory to age and wisdom. In 1990, she said, she simply capitalized on a hot day. Last year, she said she was better able to put aside the pressure faced by third-round leaders in the end game.

"I seem to be maturing," she said. "With that comes patience and maybe the acceptance that things will out. So, win or lose, I knew that I had a good tournament going."

Monaghan shot 13-under-par 275 to hold off Inkster and Patty Sheehan, who twice tied for the lead. Sheehan faded after consecutive bogeys on Nos. 8 and 9, closing at 73, three shots off the pace.

Scores and earnings

Player	Scores
Kris Monaghan, $63,750	66-69-69-71–275
Juli Inkster, $39,564	69-68-69-70–276
Patty Sheehan, $28,871	69-66-70-73–278
Dawn Coe-Jones, $22,455	70-72-72-65–279
Lauri Merten, $16,574	70-72-71-68–281
Pat Bradley, $16,574	69-77-66-69–281
Jane Geddes, $10,692	72-71-70-69–282
Meg Mallon, $10,692	69-72-71-70–282
Michelle McGann, $10,692	74-70-67-71–282
Donna Andrews, $10,692	66-72-68-76–282
Kristi Albers, $7,099	72-74-69-68–283
Joan Pitcock, $7,099	69-72-71-71–283
Dale Eggeling, $7,099	72-71-68-72–283
Laura Davies, $7,099	68-70-73-72–283
Florence Descampe, $7,099	70-74-66-73–283
Nancy Scranton, $5,239	75-71-69-69–284
Caroline Keggi, $5,239	72-71-72-69–284
Jan Stephenson, $5,239	70-73-69-72–284
Michelle Mackall, $5,239	69-71-72-72–284
Gail Graham, $5,239	67-68-77-72–284
Sherri Steinhauer, $5,239	75-69-67-73–284
Tina Barrett, $4,101	67-74-75-69–285
Kim Williams, $4,101	70-76-67-72–285
Carolyn Hill, $4,101	72-72-68-73–285
Helen Alfredsson, $4,101	68-74-70-73–285
Judy Dickinson, $4,101	71-70-71-73–285
Missie McGeorge, $4,101	69-70-73-73–285
Lisa Walters, $3,102	71-75-73-67–286
Barb Bunkowsky, $3,102	72-71-74-69–286
Sue Thomas, $3,102	71-71-75-69–286
Dana Lofland-Dormann, $3,102	71-73-72-70–286
Missie Berteotti, $3,102	74-70-71-71–286
Amy Benz, $3,102	70-72-73-71–286
Beth Daniel, $3,102	72-72-70-72–286
Jenny Lidback, $3,102	72-71-71-72–286
Nancy Harvey, $3,102	70-70-73-73–286
Barb Mucha, $3,102	70-69-71-76–286
Susie Redman, $2,502	70-72-72-73–287
Marta Figueras-Dotti, $2,017	72-74-76-66–288
Brandie Burton, $2,017	72-69-77-70–288
Karen Lunn, $2,017	77-69-71-71–288
Stephanie Farwig, $2,017	69-73-74-72–288
Page Dunlap, $2,017	69-71-76-72–288
Hiromi Kobayashi, $2,017	72-73-70-73–288
Elaine Crosby, $2,017	74-70-71-73–288
Denise Baldwin, $2,017	71-70-74-73–288
Shelley Hamlin, $2,017	71-69-75-73–288
Liselotte Neumann, $1,289	73-73-72-71–289
Cathy Johnston-Forbes, $1,289	75-69-73-72–289
Julie Larsen, $1,289	70-73-74-72–289
Marianne Morris, $1,289	72-72-73-72–289
Suzanne Strudwick, $1,289	74-69-72-74–289
Sharon Barrett, $1,289	71-72-72-74–289
Betsy King, $1,289	73-70-71-75–289
Stefania Croce, $1,289	70-73-70-76–289
Judy Sams, $1,289	70-72-71-76–289
Katie Peterson-Parker, $846	71-75-74-70–290
Deborah McHaffie, $846	69-75-75-71–290
Pamela Wright, $846	71-71-74-74–290
Sally Little, $846	71-71-74-74–290
Patty Jordan, $846	71-75-69-75–290
Eva Dahllof, $645	71-74-75-71–291
Leigh Ann Mills, $645	69-77-73-72–291
Jean Zedlitz, $645	73-73-72-73–291
Amy Fruhwirth, $645	70-70-76-75–291
Colleen Walker, $645	73-72-69-77–291
Lori West, $534	76-70-75-71–292
Angie Ridgeway, $534	73-73-75-71–292
Robin Walton, $534	72-71-78-71–292
Tracy Kerdyk, $534	73-73-73-72–292
Ellie Gibson, $534	72-73-72-75–292
Kim Lasken, $454	76-70-76-72–294
Muffin Spencer-Devlin, $454	71-75-75-73–294
Christy Erb, $454	72-74-74-74–294
Sarah McGuire, $454	72-74-72-76–294
Cindy Mackey, $424	73-73-76-73–295
Tania Abitbol, $424	72-74-74-75–295
Lisa Kiggens, $406	74-72-77-73–296
Karen Noble, $406	72-70-78-76–296
Kiernan Prechtl, $393	73-72-78-76–299
Anne-Marie Palli, $381	77-69-78-76–300
Janet Anderson, $381	75-71-78-76–300
Michele Ann Thompson, $369	73-70-82-77–302

World Championship of Women's Golf

AT A GLANCE

- **Course:** Naples National Country Club
- **Location:** Naples, Fla.
- **When:** Oct.14-17, 1993
- **Weather:** Mostly sunny and warm.
- **Purse:** $400,000
- **Par:** 72
- **Yards:** 6,390
- **Defending champion:** Meg Mallon, 3-under-par 216 in 1991, at Paradise Palms Golf Course in Cairns, Australia. (Not played in 1992.)
- **Tournament record:** 14-under-par 274, Amy Alcott, 1985, Stouffer's Pine Isle Resort, Lake Lanier Island, Ga.

Dottie Mochrie capped a six-month comeback with a two-stroke victory at the World Championship of Women's Golf.

At New Rochelle, N.Y., mid-July, 1993, Mochrie thought her world had collapsed. Seven months after being named LPGA Player of the Year, she hit rock bottom, tying for 60th at the JAL Big Apple Classic.

"I had lost distance, was hitting it sideways and didn't have any confidence over 4-foot putts," she said. "I was miserable, my scores looked like football scores, lots of sixes and sevens. I finally told myself, 'Enough of this mediocrity.'"

The next week, before the U.S. Women's Open, Mochrie refocused and tried to regain the swing that produced four wins and the 1992 Vare Trophy (low scoring average).

"Doug (her husband and former caddy) came out, and I beat golf balls for three days," she said. "He helped me a lot to just get four key thoughts and repeat them every swing. Slowly, it started coming around."

Mochrie won after Donna Andrews put a 4-iron shot in the water on the last hole, made double bogey and finished in a four-way tie for second.

Said Mochrie: "I've given away a couple this year, maybe it was my turn."

—by Steve Hershey

Scores and earnings

Player	Earnings	Scores
Dottie Mochrie	$102,500	72-71-68-72–283
Donna Andrews	$31,600	72-74-70-69–285
Michelle McGann	$31,600	69-74-73-69–285
Sherri Steinhauer	$31,600	78-69-67-71–285
Meg Mallon	$31,600	67-74-73-71–285
Nancy Lopez	$14,100	70-75-69-72–286
Lauri Merten	$13,800	70-71-72-74–287
Betsy King	$13,600	73-71-73-73–290
Brandie Burton	$13,400	77-73-70-71–291
Trish Johnson	$13,100	70-76-75-71–292
Helen Alfredsson	$13,100	78-67-73-74–292
Hiromi Kobayashi	$12,800	70-75-71-77–293
Tammie Green	$12,600	76-74-71-74–295
Rosie Jones	$12,300	76-73-71-77–297
Laura Davies	$12,300	72-72-72-81–297
Patty Sheehan	$12,000	78-77-72-72–299

Nichirei International

AT A GLANCE

- **Course:** Ami Golf Club
- **Location:** Japan
- **When:** Oct. 29-31, 1993
- **Weather:** Cool and rainy.
- **Purse:** $500,000
- **Par:** 72
- **Yards:** 6,337
- **Defending champion:** USA

The U.S. LPGA team, led by Laura Davies' 67, won 12 of 16 final-day matches for its ninth consecutive victory (and 13th in 15 years) in the Nichirei International.

"One stroke costs 10 to 15 places in our tour. We usually try our best on the last nine, and that may be the reason for the victory," U.S. captain Helen Alfredsson said.

After two rounds of four-ball stroke play, the USA led 11-5, and finished with a 23-9 victory.

"I had expected to narrow the U.S. team's lead on the final day but, I was disappointed," said Japanese captain Mayumi Hirase, who lost 67-76 to Davies, a British golfer playing the U.S. tour.

Hirase, 24, was the Japanese team's youngest player but was the 1993 Japan LPGA leading money winner.

Alfredsson beat Japan's Fusako Nagata 72-76.

PLAYER

Helen Alfredsson believes most things in life are determined by effort and destiny: "My motto is that I try to give 100 percent. If I've done that, I have to accept what happens."

In a year that saw her go from 1992 Rookie of the Year to one of the LPGA's top players, Alfredsson prepared for the du Maurier Classic with a close loss in the U.S. Women's Open fresh in her mind.

Alfredsson led the Open entering the final round but tied for second, a stroke behind Lauri Merten. A victory would have given Alfredsson two major championships in 1993. In March, she won the Nabisco Dinah Shore by two strokes after entering the final round tied with Betsy King.

"Obviously, I have some flashbacks about the Open," said Alfredsson, 28. "You have to be honest with yourself and accept that you did what you could do and it wasn't good enough."

Alfredsson shot 74 in the final round of the Open, to Merten's 68. Said the former Swedish model: "That haunts me. But Lauri played extremely well and she had luck on her side. At the Dinah Shore I had the luck on my side. I made the putts I needed and Betsy King didn't."

Before joining the LPGA, she was a star on the European tour (where she was Rookie of the Year in 1989, making her the only player to win that award on both tours), but her LPGA debut was delayed when she forgot to register for the qualifying school in '89.

She flew from Sweden to Houston, site of the qualifying tournament, before she discovered the oversight.

"I had to go back to Europe and play," she said. "But I won the Women's British Open in 1990, and I qualified for the Solheim Cup in '91. None of that would have happened had I qualified for the LPGA."

—by Jerry Potter

SPOTLIGHT

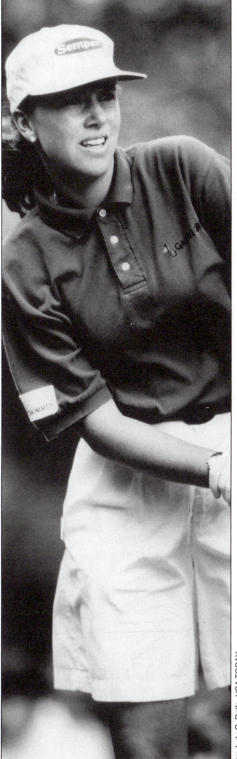

Helen Alfredsson won the Nabisco Dinah Shore and came close to winning a second major in 1993.

by Judy G. Rolfe, USA TODAY

Toray Queens Cup

AT A GLANCE

- **Course:** Lions Country Club
- **Location:** Yokawa, Japan
- **When:** Nov. 5-7, 1993
- **Weather:** Cool.
- **Purse:** $650,000
- **Par:** 72
- **Yards:** 6,336
- **Defending champion:** Betsy King, 9-under-par 205
- **Tournament record:** 11-under-par 277, Amy Alcott, 1979

Scores and earnings

Player	Score
Betsy King, USA $97,500	68-70-67–205
Jane Geddes, USA $60,510	70-70-66–206
Trish Johnson, Britain $35,433	70-68-69–207
Dana Lofland-Dormann, USA $35,433	69-68-70–207
Dale Eggeling, USA $35,433	70-66-71–207
Brandie Burton, USA $21,096	70-68-72–210
Jan Stephenson, Australia $21,096	68-69-73–210
Laura Davies, Britain $14,645	67-72-72–211
Deb Richard, USA $14,645	67-71-73–211
Alison Nicholas, Britain $14,645	67-71-73–211
Tina Barrett, USA $14,645	69-67-75–211
Toshimi Kimura, Japan $10,827	76-67-69–212
Chris Johnson, USA $10,827	70-72-70–212
Suzuko Maeda, Japan $10,827	67-70-75–212
Val Skinner, USA $8,973	68-73-72–213
Barb Bunkowsky, Canada $8,973	68-72-73–213
Hollis Stacy, USA $8,973	68-68-77–213
Kris Tschetter, USA $7,119	72-72-70–214
Jennifer Sevil, Australia $7,119	74-69-71–214
Julie Larsen, USA $7,119	70-72-72–214
Patti Rizzo, USA $7,119	71-70-73–214
Michelle McGann, USA $7,119	70-71-73–214
Amy Benz, USA $7,119	69-72-73–214
Kristi Albers, USA $7,119	72-68-74–214
Elaine Crosby, USA $7,119	69-71-74–214
Mayumi Murai, Japan $5,310	73-71-71–215
Ku Ok-hee, South Korea $5,310	76-68-71–215
Lynn Connelly, USA $5,310	73-71-71–215
Sherri Steinhauer, USA $5,310	73-70-72–215
Missie Berteotti, USA $5,310	71-72-72–215
Helen Alfredsson, Sweden $5,310	74-68-73–215
Tammie Greens, USA $5,310	71-71-73–215
Dawn Coe-Jones, Canada $5,310	72-69-74–215
Kumiko Hiyoshi, Japan $4,023	74-71-71–216
Cindy Schreyer, USA $4,023	72-70-74–216
Chieko Nishida, Japan $4,023	70-72-74–216
Ikuyo Shiotani, Japan $4,023	72-69-75–216
Pat Bradley, USA $4,023	71-70-75–216
Hiromi Kobayashi, Japan $4,023	69-72-75–216
Vicki Fergon, USA $4,023	69-71-76–216
Norimi Terasawa, Japan $3,303	74-72-71–217
Won Jae-sook, South Korea $3,303	74-67-76–217
Aiko Takasu, Japan $2,910	74-75-69–218
Cindy Rarick, USA $2,910	74-71-73–218
Gail Graham, Colombia $2,910	73-72-73–218
Shelley Hamlin, USA $2,910	73-68-77–218
Dottie Mochrie, USA $2,219	73-75-71–219
Fuki Kido, Japan $2,219	77-70-72–219
Nancy Ramsbottom, USA $2,219	72-74-73–219
Rosie Jones, USA $2,219	73-72-74–219
Huang Bie-shyun, Taiwan $2,219	72-73-74–219
Nayoko Yoshikawa, Japan $2,219	73-71-75–219
Kaori Harada, Japan $2,219	68-75-76–219
Fumiko Maraguchi, $1,553	79-70-71–220

Betsy King waited all year to win an official LPGA tournament. On the final hole of the regular season, she hit the jackpot and took the Queens Cup in Yokawa, Japan.

King birdied the last hole to win the tournament, the LPGA money title, the Vare Trophy for lowest 18-hole scoring average and the Rolex Player of the Year award.

"I would say it was worth the wait," said the 38-year-old King. "My season was very trying but it had a happy ending."

By winning the Queens Cup, King moved within one victory of qualifying for the LPGA Hall of Fame.

She started the season with 28. Though she won the JCPenney Skins Game in May, it didn't count toward the Hall of Fame. However, the prize money helped her win the money title with $595,992.

"I don't think I've ever had a tournament where so much was riding on my performance," said King. "Really, it came down to the last hole."

King made birdie on the 18th hole for a final-round 67. She totalled 11-under-par 205 and beat Jane Geddes by a stroke.

King planned to skip some specialty events in the fall to rest for 1994 when she goes after her 30th victory and the Hall of Fame.

—by Jerry Potter

Senior PGA Player of the Year

Dave Stockton won five events and earned $1,115,944, the best in both categories on the '93 Senior Tour.

Dave Stockton Enjoyed a Banner Year

Dave Stockton never considered himself a premiere player in golf because in his younger days there was always a Lee Trevino or Jack Nicklaus to get the glory.

That has not been the case since Stockton graduated to the Senior PGA Tour.

Trevino is around most of the time and Nicklaus is around some times, but in 1993 Stockton walked away with the big prizes on the Senior Tour.

He won five events and earned $1,115,944, the best in both categories on the Senior Tour.

"Golf has never been easier for me. I was just playing and enjoying myself, trying to make birdies," said Stockton, 52, of Mentone, Calif.

"The year was 10 times better than it could have been. There's no question it was the best year I've ever had in golf."

Stockton, who turned pro in 1964, had his best year on the PGA Tour in 1974 when he won three events and earned $160,000.

He played the PGA Tour regularly from 1964 through 1991, earning $1,275,453 with 11 victories, including the PGA Championship in 1970 and '76.

In two years of senior golf, Stockton has won six events, including one major in the 1992 PGA Senior Players Championship. That major helped Stockton be the Rookie of the Year in '92.

"It has been easier for me to play the Senior Tour because I'm more focused than I was on the PGA Tour," Stockton said. "I had young children, and I was doing corporate outings all over the country to make money.

"To be a good golfer you have to concentrate on playing golf. It's a 12-month a year job. You don't realize how much you're hurting your golf until you get on the Senior Tour and see what you can accomplish when you're focused."

Stockton played the final 14 events without a break, in an all-out assault on the money title and Player of the Year awards. From Aug. 15 to Oct. 31 he won three times, finished second three times and earned $640,244.

"Winning five tournaments this year was more significant than winning a million dollars," said Stockton. "When I joined the Senior Tour my goal was to surpass my accomplishments on the PGA Tour—11 victories and two major championships."

Stockton believes he can break those personal records in 1994, but he knows it will be a critical year for his career.

"I'll be trying to prove that 1993 was not a fluke," said Stockton. "When I played 14 straight events I was playing as well at the end of the streak as I was at the beginning. I had just as much fun at the start as I had at the end."

Stockton will have one little distraction in 1994. His son, David Jr., qualified for the PGA Tour, so Dave Sr. will be keeping watch over both tours.

In other tour highlights, Bob Charles also broke the million dollar barrier in '93—earning it in a record 26 events. Stockton won his million in 6 months, 10 days, also a Senior Tour record.

But perhaps the biggest triumph of the year was Illinois club professional Tom Wargo's win at the PGA Seniors' Championship.

Wargo didn't win again, but he established himself on the Senior Tour and will be a gallery favorite in 1994.

A former assembly line worker in the auto industry, Wargo didn't even know about agents when he beat Bruce Crampton in a playoff at Palm Beach Gardens, Fla.

"I've heard of such critters," he said, when asked if he had an agent, "but I don't know any of them."

—by Jerry Potter

Sr. Infiniti Tournament of Champions

AT A GLANCE

- **Course:** LaCosta Country Club
- **Location:** Carlsbad, Calif.
- **When:** Jan. 7-10, 1993
- **Weather:** Rainy and overcast. Thursday's round rained out. Two rounds played Friday.
- **Purse:** $350,000
- **Par:** 72
- **Yards:** 6,935
- **Defending champion:** Al Geiberger
- **Tournament record:** 9-under-par 279, Bruce Crampton, 1991
- **Field:** Winners of all 1992 Senior PGA Tour events

After ringing in the new year with an old tradition, Al Geiberger made a new resolution.

For the second year in a row, Geiberger started his season by winning the Infiniti Senior Tournament of Champions. He was determined to build on the win this time around.

Geiberger pulled away to beat long-hitting Jim Dent by two shots with a final-round 71 at rain-soaked La Costa.

In 1992, after finishing 1-3-5 in his first three starts, Geiberger eased up. He wound up playing only 26 tournaments and was 19th on the money list, his worst since joining the Senior PGA Tour in 1987.

"I don't know why, but after I have a win or a hot streak, I have a tendency to lay," Geiberger said. "My wife calls it laziness. This year I'm going to try not to do that."

Geiberger's success at La Costa doesn't surprise him because he likes the long course.

"This course is pretty straight away, not a lot of dog legs and it plays to my length," he said.

In four days, Geiberger only missed 10 fairways while shooting a steady 70-70-69-71—280. If he had competed against the regular tour, he would have finished eighth, beating 22 players.

— *by Steve Hershey*

Al Geiberger won the Senior Infiniti Tournament of Champions for the second year in a row.

Scores and earnings

Player	Earnings	Scores
Al Geiberger	$52,500	70-70-69-71—280
Jim Dent	$35,000	70-69-70-73—282
Dave Stockton	$28,000	72-71-69-73—285
George Archer	$28,000	71-69-72-73—285
Mike Hill	$23,000	72-70-70-74—286
Isao Aoki	$20,500	72-74-70-71—287
Ray Floyd	$17,500	71-72-73-73—289
Dale Douglass	$17,500	69-75-72-73—289
Tommy Aaron	$15,000	71-72-76-73—292
Bob Charles	$12,750	70-73-73-77—293
Chi Chi Rodriguez	$12,750	77-70-71-75—293
Don Bies	$11,000	75-75-71-75—296
Terry Dill	$10,000	75-72-76-74—297
Larry Laoretti	$9,400	74-73-72-79—298
Orville Moody	$8,800	77-72-74-76—299
Mike Joyce	$8,800	76-74-73-76—299
Gibby Gilbert	$8,200	76-72-76-76—300
Bruce Crampton	$8,200	71-79-75-75—300
Jim Colbert	$7,900	75-74-77-79—305
Jimmy Powell	$7,700	77-74-81-74—306
Don Massengale	$7,500	80-74-81-80—315

Royal Caribbean Classic

AT A GLANCE

- **Course:** The Links at Key Biscayne
- **Location:** Key Biscayne, Fla.
- **When:** Feb. 5-7, 1993
- **Weather:** Sunny and windy.
- **Purse:** $750,000
- **Par:** 71
- **Yards:** 6,725
- **Defending champion:** Don Massengale
- **Tournament record:** 14-under par 199, Jim Colbert, 1993

Jim Colbert and Ray Floyd used to play practice rounds against each other for $5. This time the stakes were a little higher: $112,500.

Colbert, who began the final round of the Royal Caribbean Classic with a five-shot lead, managed a 1-under-par 70 Sunday to edge playing partners Floyd and Al Geiberger by one stroke.

Floyd made a late charge with a string of three consecutive birdies beginning at No. 15 and finished at 65, the best final-round score, but Colbert held off his old rival.

Though he squandered most of his lead with three bogeys, Colbert made the critical shots, including a 5-foot putt at No. 17 that saved par and preserved his two-shot edge.

His 54-hole 14-under 199 broke Gary Player's tournament record of 200 set in 1991.

Colbert maintained a lead of at least three shots on the front nine, thanks partly to birdies on the first two par-3s, where his tee shots came to rest within a foot of the cup.

"Those were two fantastic iron shots," Floyd said.

Final-round collapses are almost a tradition on The Links at Key Biscayne—Player and Jim Dent both blew big back-nine leads in recent years.

"If you're not careful, you can panic," Colbert said. "I kept telling myself, 'Make 'em come and get you.'"

Scores and earnings

Player	Earnings	Scores
Jim Colbert	$112,500	65-64-70–199
Al Geiberger	$60,000	65-69-66–200
Ray Floyd	$60,000	67-68-65–200
J.C. Snead	$40,500	66-69-69–204
Don January	$40,500	69-67-68–204
George Archer	$30,000	69-68-68–205
Simon Hobday	$24,000	70-69-68–207
Bob Charles	$24,000	71-69-67–207
Mike Hill	$24,000	73-64-70–207
Kermit Zarley	$18,750	69-71-68–208
Jim Albus	$18,750	71-67-70–208
Gary Player	$14,813	71-69-69–209
Dave Hill	$14,813	71-68-70–209
Butch Baird	$14,813	70-69-70–209
Larry Ziegler	$14,813	66-72-71–209
Tom Wargo	$12,000	73-69-68–210
Al Kelley	$12,000	72-69-69–210
Gibby Gilbert	$12,000	69-70-71–210
Jim Dent	$9,925	73-69-69–211
Jimmy Powell	$9,925	71-68-72–211
Chi Chi Rodriguez	$9,925	68-70-73–211
Bruce Crampton	$8,275	70-71-71–212
Lee Elder	$8,275	70-71-71–212
Terry Dill	$8,275	70-68-74–212
Tommy Aaron	$6,258	73-70-70–213
Harold Henning	$6,258	72-70-71–213
Don Bies	$6,258	73-71-69–213
Larry Laoretti	$6,258	69-72-72–213
Walter Zembriski	$6,258	71-70-72–213
Dewitt Weaver	$6,258	73-68-72–213
Bob Goalby	$6,258	70-70-73–213
Larry Gilbert	$6,258	71-69-73–213
Larry Mowry	$6,258	69-68-76–213
Dave Stockton	$4,725	71-71-72–214
Tom Shaw	$4,725	74-68-72–214
Doug Dalziel	$4,725	71-70-73–214
Miller Barber	$4,125	72-71-72–215
Dick Hendrickson	$4,125	73-71-71–215
Jim Ferree	$4,125	73-72-70–215
Gay Brewer	$3,375	74-69-73–216
Bob Wynn	$3,375	73-70-73–216
Bobby Nichols	$3,375	76-68-72–216
Mike Joyce	$3,375	72-73-71–216
Orville Moody	$3,375	72-69-75–216
Bob Reith	$3,375	69-71-76–216
Gene Littler	$3,375	71-69-76–216
Rafe Botts	$2,625	73-72-72–217
Frank Beard	$2,625	72-73-72–217
Harry Toscano	$2,625	70-77-70–217
Joe Jimenez	$2,325	78-69-71–218
Bruce Lehnhard	$1,920	70-73-76–219
Roger Kennedy	$1,920	73-71-75–219
Billy Casper	$1,920	76-70-73–219
Dick Lotz	$1,920	74-72-73–219
Charlie Owens	$1,920	70-77-72–219
Rives Mcbee	$1,650	70-74-76–220
John Brodie	$1,463	71-74-76–221
Bob Brue	$1,463	71-74-76–221
Don Massengale	$1,463	73-76-72–221
Leon Rowland	$1,463	75-75-71–221
Charlie Sifford	$1,125	73-71-78–222
Howie Johnson	$1,125	74-73-75–222
Marion Heck	$1,125	78-70-74–222
Bruce Devlin	$1,125	75-73-74–222
Steve Spray	$1,125	71-78-73–222
Dick Rhyan	$863	76-72-75–223
Bert Yancey	$863	76-72-75–223
Dave Ragan	$750	75-76-73–224
Ben Smith	$705	77-72-76–225
Charles Coody	$638	74-75-77–226
Billy Maxwell	$638	78-74-74–226
Phil Rodgers	$570	77-74-78–229
Rocky Thompson	$525	76-74-80–230
Jack Kiefer	$495	80-75-76–231
Frankie Jones	$465	77-76-79–232
Ken Still	$435	76-77-81–234
Doug Ford	$405	81-78-77–236

The Challenge

AT A GLANCE

- **Course:** The Vineyards
- **Location:** Naples, Fla.
- **When:** Feb. 12-14, 1993
- **Weather:** Sunny, windy, cool.
- **Purse:** $500,000
- **Par:** 72
- **Yards:** 6,682
- **Defending champion:** Jimmy Powell
- **Tournament record:** 19-under-par 197, Jimmy Powell, 1992

Mike Hill began the last day ahead six shots and ended up holding on for a victory after a roller coaster finish at the Challenge.

Hill's 2-under-par 70 in the final round at the Vineyards kept him just ahead of Dave Stockton, who shot a 66 and closed within two shots at the end.

Hill had been up eight shots at one point in the afternoon.

"I think the turning point came for me at 10, when I missed a 3-foot putt," he said. "I think if I would've made that shot, I would've shot 2- or 3-under on the backside, instead of struggling after that.

"I've never had a six-stroke lead, so I didn't know how to act with it. It's almost like the ball starts snowballing, and you don't know whether you're able to stop it or not."

Hill shot 32 on the front nine, eagling the par-5 second hole and registering a birdie on the first and ninth holes. But some tentative play on the back nine yielded a 2-over 38. He saved himself by closing with three straight pars.

Stockton, meanwhile, was shooting duplicate 33s on the front and back nines. He birdied the first, seventh and eighth holes on the front side, then got birdies on the 10th, 13th and 15th holes.

"If I would've sunk that putt at the 16th hole, it wouldn't have brought me to within one shot, and then I think (Hill) would've taken notice," Stockton said.

Scores and earnings

Player	Rounds–Total
Mike Hill, $75,000	67-65-70–202
Dave Stockton, $44,000	67-71-66–204
Bob Charles, $36,000	69-71-66–206
Lee Elder, $24,667	69-71-67–207
J.C. Snead, $24,667	70-70-67–207
Gibby Gilbert, $24,667	71-67-69–207
Dewitt Weaver, $17,000	72-68-68–208
Jim Dent, $17,000	70-68-70–208
Miller Barber, $12,000	69-71-69–209
Don January, $12,000	71-69-69–209
Harry Toscano, $12,000	70-69-70–209
Jim Albus, $12,000	72-68-69–209
Larry Gilbert, $12,000	70-68-71–209
Dick Rhyan, $8,750	72-71-67–210
Jim O'Hern, $8,750	68-72-70–210
Bruce Crampton, $8,750	69-71-70–210
Butch Baird, $8,750	72-68-70–210
George Archer, $6,838	71-72-68–211
Chi Chi Rodriguez, $6,838	70-73-68–211
Bob Reith, $6,838	70-72-69–211
Bruce Lehnhard, $6,838	69-71-71–211
Kermit Zarley, $5,142	70-72-70–212
Simon Hobday, $5,142	70-71-71–212
Dave Hill, $5,142	72-70-70–212
Jimmy Powell, $5,142	70-70-72–212
Walter Zembriski, $5,142	71-69-72–212
Mike Joyce, $5,142	69-69-74–212
Bob Thatcher, $3,960	72-74-67–213
Tommy Aaron, $3,960	71-74-68–213
Rocky Thompson, $3,960	68-76-69–213
Jim Colbert, $3,960	72-70-71–213
Orville Moody, $3,960	72-68-73–213
Dick Lotz, $3,225	73-73-68–214
Dale Douglass, $3,225	70-74-70–214
Jack Kiefer, $3,225	69-73-72–214
Gay Brewer, $3,225	74-68-72–214
Gary Player, $2,800	69-74-72–215
Larry Ziegler, $2,800	74-70-71–215
Harold Henning, $2,500	71-75-70–216
Roger Kennedy, $2,500	73-73-70–216
Bill Kennedy, $2,500	72-73-71–216
Walter Morgan, $2,500	73-70-73–216
Dick Hendrickson, $2,100	76-71-70–217
Billy Casper, $2,100	74-71-72–217
Bob Brue, $2,100	74-71-72–217
Al Kelley, $2,100	73-71-73–217
Terry Dill, $1,750	71-76-71–218
Bob Wynn, $1,750	75-71-72–218
Joe Jimenez, $1,750	75-70-73–218
Howie Johnson, $1,325	74-74-71–219
Phil Rodgers, $1,325	75-73-71–219
Bobby Nichols, $1,325	76-71-72–219
Doug Dalziel, $1,325	75-72-72–219
Charles Coody, $1,325	73-73-73–219
Tom Shaw, $1,325	72-71-76–219
Frank Beard, $1,100	75-72-73–220
Jim Ferree, $975	77-74-70–221
Robert Gaona, $975	71-75-75–221
Don Bies, $975	73-73-75–221
Bruce Devlin, $975	72-72-77–221
Bert Yancey, $825	75-76-71–222
Charlie Sifford, $825	75-73-74–222
Gene Littler, $675	74-74-75–223
Rives Mcbee, $675	75-73-75–223
Ralph Terry, $675	73-74-76–223
Bob Goalby, $675	72-75-76–223
Billy Maxwell, $507	75-74-75–224
Larry Laoretti, $507	73-76-75–224
Larry Mowry, $507	71-75-78–224
Mike Fetchick, $410	75-75-75–225
Ken Still, $410	76-75-74–225
Tom Nieporte, $410	75-74-76–225
Doug Sanders, $350	74-75-77–226
Don Massengale, $330	79-76-74–229
Doug Ford, $310	77-77-80–234

GTE Suncoast Classic

AT A GLANCE

- **Course:** TPC of Tampa Bay at Cheval
- **Location:** Lutz, Fla.
- **When:** Feb. 19-21, 1993
- **Weather:** Sunny, cold Friday morning. Warm Saturday, Sunday.
- **Purse:** $500,000
- **Par:** 72
- **Yards:** 6,631
- **Defending champion:** Jim Colbert
- **Tournament record:** 16-under-par 200, Jim Colbert, 1992

Despite the two-stroke margin of victory, Jim Albus' second Senior PGA Tour win of his career was not assured until the final hole.

Albus went to the 18th hole, a 415-yard dogleg left par-4, with a one-stroke lead in the final round of the GTE Suncoast Classic. Despite a narrow landing area and water stretching along the entire right side, he hit driver.

The ball rolled into the rough, just 5 feet from the hazard.

"I probably should have laid up, but if you hit a good drive it makes the hole pretty easy," Albus said. "I'd thought ahead of time what I would do if I had the lead and driving is what I do best."

Albus said he wasn't sure his tee shot was dry until walking up the fairway, but once he found it, a wedge to 3 feet produced a birdie and a victory.

Albus, who never played the PGA Tour, won with a 1-under-par 70. His 54-hole total of 7-under 206 was good for a two-stroke victory over Don Bies and second-round leader Gibby Gilbert.

Albus, who began Sunday one stroke behind Gilbert, bogeyed his second hole of the day and double-bogeyed his third. But he regrouped and took the lead on the par-5 14th with a wedge to 15 feet and a birdie putt.

"Jim Albus played a great round," Gilbert said. "He got off to a bad start, then fought back really well. He deserved to win."

Scores and earnings

Player	Scores
Jim Albus, $75,000	68-68-70—206
Don Bies, $40,000	70-69-69—208
Gibby Gilbert, $40,000	69-66-73—208
Gary Player, $24,667	73-68-68—209
Tom Wargo, $24,667	72-68-69—209
Jim Ferree, $24,667	73-66-70—209
Al Geiberger, $16,000	67-72-71—210
Miller Barber, $16,000	69-68-73—210
Bob Charles, $16,000	71-66-73—210
George Archer, $11,500	69-72-70—211
Don January, $11,500	72-70-69—211
Ray Floyd, $11,500	71-69-71—211
Dick Rhyan, $11,500	73-67-71—211
Harry Toscano, $9,500	73-71-68—212
Kermit Zarley, $8,750	70-73-70—213
Rives McBee, $8,750	73-68-72—213
Simon Hobday, $8,000	74-72-68—214
Walter Zembriski, $7,050	74-72-69—215
Don Massengale, $7,050	73-72-70—215
Dave Hill, $7,050	69-73-73—215
Bob Wynn, $5,833	71-72-73—216
Larry Gilbert, $5,833	73-70-73—216
Jim Colbert, $5,833	72-71-73—216
Dewitt Weaver, $4,571	72-76-69—217
Al Kelley, $4,571	71-76-70—217
Orville Moody, $4,571	74-72-71—217
Harold Henning, $4,571	73-72-72—217
Tommy Aaron, $4,571	71-74-72—217
Terry Dill, $4,571	69-74-74—217
Mike Hill, $4,571	73-68-76—217
Dave Stockton, $3,600	78-71-69—218
Jim Dent, $3,600	78-66-74—218
J.C. Snead, $3,600	75-70-73—218
Joe Jimenez, $3,010	76-73-70—219
Tom Shaw, $3,010	70-78-71—219
Billy Casper, $3,010	72-75-72—219
Bobby Nichols, $3,010	72-73-74—219
Chi Chi Rodriguez, $3,010	75-69-75—219
Jimmy Powell, $2,450	70-79-71—220
Bob Murphy, $2,450	73-76-71—220
Bruce Crampton, $2,450	78-70-72—220
Arnold Palmer, $2,450	76-71-73—220
Rocky Thompson, $2,450	74-73-73—220
Mike Joyce, $2,150	80-70-71—221
Larry Laoretti, $2,000	77-73-72—222
Dick Lotz, $2,000	76-71-75—222
Bob Reith, $1,700	79-74-70—223
Bob Goalby, $1,700	76-71-76—223
Butch Baird, $1,700	73-73-77—223
Charles Coody, $1,700	77-67-79—223
Gay Brewer, $1,400	78-74-72—224
Dale Douglass, $1,400	81-69-74—224
Roger Kennedy, $1,200	74-76-75—225
Frank Beard, $1,200	74-74-77—225
Bert Yancey, $1,200	75-72-78—225
Larry Ziegler, $1,100	77-78-71—226
Dick Hendrickson, $975	78-76-73—227
Phil Rodgers, $975	76-75-76—227
Bob Brue, $975	74-75-78—227
Doug Dalziel, $975	74-75-78—227
Bill McDonough, $850	83-72-73—228
Bruce Devlin, $800	77-74-78—229
Jack Kiefer, $725	79-80-71—230
Billy Maxwell, $725	76-76-78—230
Howie Johnson, $650	79-77-75—231
Billy Farrell, $575	77-79-76—232
Ken Still, $575	77-78-77—232
Ben Smith, $500	78-77-78—233
Gene Littler, $455	83-83-70—236
Bruce Lehnhard, $455	75-81-80—236
Tom Nieporte, $410	78-79-80—237
Doug Ford, $380	82-77-81—240
R. Stuart Chancellor, $350	81-80-81—242

THE CHRYSLER CUP

AT A GLANCE

- **Course:** TPC at Prestancia
- **Location:** Sarasota, Fla.
- **When:** Feb. 26-28, 1993
- **Weather:** Sunny and mild.
- **Purse:** $600,000 (unofficial money)
- **Par:** 72
- **Yards:** 6,765
- **Defending champion:** USA
- **Format:** Individual and team competition.
- **Field:** 16 U.S. and international senior players.

Tom Weiskopf, holding off self-described "little demons," won his first golf tournament in more than 10 years, capturing the Chrysler Cup at the TPC at Prestancia.

A non-winner since his PGA Tour victory at the Western Open in 1982, Weiskopf shot a final-round 69 in his first Senior Tour event. In doing so, he helped the USA to its sixth consecutive title in the team competition.

Weiskopf, 50, overcame his anxiousness at being rusty. He had not played competitively since last year's British Open and had recently began practicing after knee surgery.

"Even with a lot of confidence, there were little demons popping their heads up out there," he said.

The U.S. team beat the International Team by nine strokes, led by Weiskopf's 54-hole 14-under 202. New Zealand's Bob Charles, who shot 71 Sunday, and George Archer of the U.S., who had a 68, tied for second at 206.

Scores and earnings

United States

Player	Scores
Tom Weiskopf, $55,000	66-67-69–202
George Archer, $33,500	65-73-68–206
Chi Chi Rodriguez, $24,000	67-72-69–208
Jim Colbert, $18,000	70-73-67–210
Al Geiberger, $14,333	70-71-72–213
Miller Barber, $12,000	72-72-70–214
Mike Hill, $8,500	71-78-71–220
Dale Douglass, $6,000	73-disqualified
Total	338-355-343–1,036 (-44)

International

Player	Scores
Bob Charles, $33,500	68-67-71–206
Isao Aoki, $20,000	69-71-69–209
Gary Player, $17,000	71-71-69–211
Tommy Horton, $14,333	69-72-72–213
Bruce Crampton, $14,333	70-68-75–213
Harold Henning, $11,000	74-72-69–215
Simon Hobday, $10,000	73-73-71–217
Bruce Devlin, $8,500	71-72-77–220
Total	347-349-349–1,045 (-35)

(U.S. members received additional $25,000 for the team victory; international received additional $12,000.)

By H. Darr Beiser, USA TODAY

In his first year on the Senior Tour, Tom Weiskopf led the U.S. team to victory at the Chrysler Cup.

GTE West Classic

AT A GLANCE

- **Course:** Ojai Valley Inn & Country Club
- **Location:** Ojai, Calif.
- **When:** March 6-8, 1993
- **Weather:** Sunny, warm, some wind.
- **Purse:** $500,000
- **Par:** 72
- **Yards:** 6,190
- **Defending champion:** Bruce Crampton
- **Tournament record:** 21-under-par 195, Bruce Crampton, 1992

Al Geiberger survived Isao Aoki's front-nine birdie barrage to win the GTE West Classic by two strokes.

Geiberger finished the 54-hole event at 12-under 198, outlasting Aoki and third-round leader George Archer.

Aoki trailed Archer by four shots and Geiberger by three after two rounds. He burned up the front nine of the Ojai Valley Inn & Country Club course with a record 7-under 29 to take the lead.

With an eagle on the ninth hole and another birdie on 10, Aoki built a two-stroke lead before Geiberger birdied the eighth to cut the lead to a stroke.

Then Aoki bogied the 15th and 16th and dropped to second.

"I was trying to win," he said, "but I choked. I hit my only bad drive on 15, and that was when the trouble started."

Geiberger, who was suffering from allergies, shot a final-round 4-under 66.

"I was so busy getting up and down from bunkers on 11, 12 and 14, I didn't notice that Aoki (two groups ahead) had made two bogeys and I was ahead," Geiberger said. "Watch out for a sick golfer. They usually win."

Scores and earnings

Player	Earnings	Scores
Al Geiberger	$75,000	67-65-66–198
Isao Aoki	$40,000	68-67-65–200
George Archer	$40,000	63-68-69–200
Chi Chi Rodriguez	$30,000	68-70-63–201
Tom Weiskopf	$24,000	70-65-67–202
Dewitt Weaver	$16,200	65-71-67–203
Bruce Crampton	$16,200	67-68-68–203
Mike Joyce	$16,200	72-64-67–203
Walter Zembriski	$16,200	64-70-69–203
Gary Player	$16,200	63-69-71–203
Tom Wargo	$9,714	71-69-64–204
Don January	$9,714	71-69-64–204
Simon Hobday	$9,714	71-69-64–204
Jim Colbert	$9,714	69-69-66–204
Arnold Palmer	$9,714	66-70-68–204
Jack Kiefer	$9,714	64-69-71–204
Kermit Zarley	$9,714	67-67-70–204
Dave Stockton	$7,050	69-71-65–205
Dave Hill	$7,050	69-69-67–205
Don Bies	$7,050	68-66-71–205
Dale Douglass	$5,550	71-70-66–207
Dick Hendrickson	$5,550	69-71-67–207
Rocky Thompson	$5,550	68-71-68–207
Larry Gilbert	$5,550	67-71-69–207
Harold Henning	$5,550	67-69-71–207
Orville Moody	$4,450	70-70-68–208
Tommy Aaron	$4,450	68-71-69–208
Jimmy Powell	$4,450	70-69-69–208
Al Kelley	$4,450	71-68-69–208
Bob Wynn	$3,850	67-73-69–209
Jim Ferree	$3,850	70-68-71–209
Larry Laoretti	$3,375	71-72-67–210
Dick Rhyan	$3,375	71-70-69–210
Tommy Aycock	$3,375	72-69-69–210
Bob Betley	$3,375	67-72-71–210
Lee Elder	$2,813	69-72-70–211
Doug Dalziel	$2,813	69-70-72–211
Dick Lotz	$2,813	72-66-73–211
John Paul Cain	$2,813	70-68-73–211
Billy Maxwell	$2,150	70-74-68–212
Bob Thatcher	$2,150	71-72-69–212
Bruce Devlin	$2,150	68-75-69–212
Jim O'Hern	$2,150	72-71-69–212
Roger Kennedy	$2,150	71-72-69–212
Harry Toscano	$2,150	71-71-70–212
Terry Dill	$2,150	74-69-69–212
Jim Albus	$2,150	74-68-70–212
Rives McBee	$2,150	68-69-75–212
Frank Beard	$1,500	72-73-68–213
Walter Morgan	$1,500	73-72-68–213
Joe Jimenez	$1,500	72-70-71–213
Larry Ziegler	$1,500	69-70-74–213
Bruce Lehnhard	$1,175	74-69-71–214
Miller Barber	$1,175	71-70-73–214
Fred Ruiz	$1,175	69-71-74–214
Jesse Vaughn	$1,175	71-68-75–214
Bob Brue	$1,025	74-74-67–215
Michel Damiano	$1,025	75-68-72–215
Butch Baird	$925	75-70-71–216
Bert Yancey	$925	76-68-72–216
Ken Still	$825	74-72-71–217
Gene Littler	$825	74-72-71–217
Bob Reith	$700	73-74-71–218
Gary Longfellow	$700	77-70-71–218
Mike Fetchick	$700	76-71-71–218
Richard Bassett	$550	74-76-69–219
Ben Smith	$550	68-79-72–219
Jim Jones	$550	72-72-75–219
Homero Blancas	$470	75-73-72–220
Jerry Barber	$440	73-73-75–221
Phil Rodgers	$368	76-73-73–222
Billy Farrell	$368	75-73-74–222
Bob Goalby	$368	71-77-74–222
Tom Barber	$368	74-71-77–222
Howie Johnson	$310	76-75-73–224
Doug Ford	$290	76-75-75–226
R. Stuart Chancellor	$270	78-74-80–232
William Hetzell	$250	80-77-78–235

The Vantage at the Dominion

AT A GLANCE

- **Course:** Dominion Country Club
- **Location:** San Antonio
- **When:** March 12-14, 1993
- **Weather:** Cool and windy.
- **Purse:** $400,000
- **Par:** 72
- **Yards:** 6,814
- **Defending champion:** Lee Trevino
- **Tournament record:** 15-under-par 201, Larry Mowry 1989 and Lee Trevino, 1992

Scores and earnings

Player	Scores	Total
J.C. Snead, $97,500	71-73-70	214
Gary Player, $52,000	75-71-69	215
Bobby Nichols, $52,000	74-68-73	215
Dave Stockton, $39,000	70-74-72	216
Ray Floyd, $31,200	73-73-71	217
Gibby Gilbert, $26,000	71-73-74	218
Dale Douglass, $20,800	74-76-69	219
Charles Coody, $20,800	73-72-74	219
Bob Murphy, $20,800	72-70-77	219
Jack Kiefer, $13,975	75-75-70	220
Dick Lotz, $13,975	77-72-71	220
Tom Weiskopf, $13,975	72-76-72	220
Rives McBee, $13,975	75-73-72	220
Chi Chi Rodriguez, $13,975	76-72-72	220
Tom Wargo, $13,975	73-73-74	220
Isao Aoki, $10,725	75-76-70	221
Larry Mowry, $10,725	73-75-73	221
Orville Moody, $8,374	74-78-70	222
Jim Ferree, $8,374	79-72-71	222
Jim Albus, $8,374	76-75-71	222
Kermit Zarley, $8,374	74-75-73	222
Roger Kennedy, $8,374	77-71-74	222
Mike Joyce, $8,374	75-73-74	222
Simon Hobday, $6,214	75-76-72	223
Gay Brewer, $6,214	72-78-73	223
Walter Zembriski, $6,214	74-75-74	223
Tommy Aaron, $6,214	75-73-75	223
Snell Lancaster, $6,214	74-74-75	223
Jim Dent, $4,810	78-74-72	224
Bruce Crampton, $4,810	77-75-72	224
Harry Toscano, $4,810	77-76-71	224
Dick Rhyan, $4,810	78-72-74	224
Bob Menne, $4,810	76-74-74	224
Al Kelley, $4,810	74-74-76	224
Don Massengale, $3,819	77-75-73	225
Terry Dill, $3,819	78-75-72	225
Dick Hendrickson, $3,819	77-77-71	225
Michel Damiano, $3,819	77-72-76	225
Bruce Lehnhard, $3,120	78-74-74	226
Billy Casper, $3,120	77-76-73	226
Doug Dalziel, $3,120	75-76-75	226
Butch Baird, $3,120	79-74-73	226
Tom Shaw, $3,120	80-73-73	226
Larry Ziegler, $3,120	75-75-76	226
Phil Rodgers, $2,405	77-75-75	227
Rocky Thompson, $2,405	79-74-74	227
Jimmy Powell, $2,405	77-77-73	227
Dewitt Weaver, $2,405	78-78-71	227
Bob Rawlins, $2,405	81-75-71	227
Steve Wilkinson, $1,885	76-77-75	228
George Archer, $1,885	77-77-74	228
Larry Gilbert, $1,885	80-76-72	228
Howie Johnson, $1,235	77-75-77	229
Joe Jimenez, $1,528	77-76-76	229
Gene Littler, $1,528	82-72-75	229
Bob Wynn, $1,528	81-76-72	229
Larry Laoretti, $1,528	81-76-72	229
Bob Brue, $1,235	82-70-78	230
Mike Fetchick, $1,235	78-76-76	230
Don January, $1,235	80-76-74	230
Ben Smith, $1,235	82-75-73	230
Harold Henning, $1,040	79-78-74	231
John Paul Cain, $943	84-74-74	232
Bert Yancey, $943	85-74-73	232
Ken Still, $845	77-80-76	233
Terry Forcum, $715	77-76-81	234
Charlie Sifford, $715	80-77-77	234
Miller Barber, $715	82-78-74	234
Lou Graham, $611	85-76-75	236
Doug Ford, $572	76-81-80	237
Bob Goalby, $514	79-81-78	238
Bob Reith, $514	81-79-78	238
Reginald Golden, $442	76-85-78	239
Billy Maxwell, $442	85-77-77	239
Bill Johnston, $403	85-83-84	252

J.C. Snead usually likes playing in the wind.

On a windy and chilly day during the final round of the Vantage at the Dominion, Snead struggled but still handled the conditions better than anyone else. He played the only bogeyless final round to edge Gary Player and Bobby Nichols by one stroke.

"This weather came and really threw everything out of kilter," Snead said. "I felt that I wasn't in control like I should have been."

Snead started the final round two strokes off the lead. He birdied No. 9 to close within a stroke, then went in front on the leaders' bogies.

"It was just one of those days I felt like I had to keep plugging along," Snead said.

Snead went for a big shot late in the round, thinking he was still trailing Player. The gamble produced a birdie at No. 16 that gave him the lead.

"I looked at the board a couple times. All the time I was thinking I was two shots behind going to 16. I was tied for the lead. It worked out all right," Snead said.

Nichols, the second-round leader, had a 25-foot birdie putt on the 18th hole that would have created a playoff, but left it short.

Player had six birdies on the day and briefly held a one-stroke lead at two under before bogeying No. 16.

Gulfstream Aerospace Invitational

At a Glance

- **Course:** Indian Wells Golf Resort, West Course
- **Location:** Indian Wells, Calif.
- **When:** March 19-21, 1993
- **Weather:** Sunny, warm and mild; breezes all weekend.
- **Purse:** $550,000
- **Par:** 72
- **Yards:** 6,476
- **Defending champion:** Mike Hill
- **Tournament record:** 22-under-par 194, Ray Floyd, 1993

Scores and earnings

Player	Scores	Total
Ray Floyd, $82,500	65-65-64	194
George Archer, $49,500	63-67-69	199
Isao Aoki, $40,700	67-67-66	200
Miller Barber, $33,550	69-62-70	201
Al Geiberger, $24,750	67-68-67	202
Bob Charles, $24,750	66-68-68	202
Chi Chi Rodriguez, $17,325	72-66-67	205
Dave Stockton, $17,325	69-69-67	205
Jim Albus, $17,325	70-67-68	205
Dick Lotz, $17,325	69-68-68	205
Charles Coody, $12,650	69-68-69	206
Dave Hill, $12,650	68-69-69	206
Bruce Crampton, $12,650	67-65-74	206
Jim Colbert, $10,725	71-70-66	207
Gibby Gilbert, $10,725	70-69-68	207
Tom Shaw, $9,900	71-68-69	208
Tommy Aaron, $8,525	70-73-66	209
Jim Dent, $8,525	69-71-69	209
Dale Douglass, $8,525	67-71-71	209
Terry Dill, $8,525	70-68-71	209
Rocky Thompson, $6,728	73-68-69	210
J.C. Snead, $6,728	71-70-69	210
Walter Zembriski, $6,728	68-71-71	210
Mike Joyce, $5,555	70-74-67	211
Tom Weiskopf, $5,555	73-71-67	211
Orville Moody, $5,555	72-70-69	211
Mike Hill, $5,555	72-70-69	211
Don Massengale, $4,620	72-72-68	212
Don January, $4,620	70-72-70	212
Bruce Devlin, $4,620	71-71-70	212
Butch Baird, $4,620	69-68-75	212
Don Bies, $3,658	66-78-69	213
Larry Laoretti, $3,658	67-75-71	213
Billy Casper, $3,658	73-70-70	213
Larry Mowry, $3,658	71-71-71	213
Dewitt Weaver, $3,658	67-74-72	213
Lee Trevino, $3,658	69-71-73	213
Lee Elder, $3,080	73-71-70	214
Simon Hobday, $3,080	71-69-74	214
Harold Henning, $2,915	69-72-74	215
Bobby Nichols, $2,585	72-75-69	216
Bob Brue, $2,585	75-70-71	216
Jimmy Powell, $2,585	73-73-70	216
Jim O'Hern, $2,585	72-72-72	216
Frank Beard, $2,585	71-71-74	216
Lou Graham, $2,200	71-72-74	217
Gay Brewer, $2,200	70-71-76	217
Larry Ziegler, $2,035	68-75-75	218
Bob Goalby, $1,925	71-75-75	221
John Brodie, $1,815	71-79-72	222
John Joseph, $1,705	72-75-76	223
Gene Littler, $1,650	76-71-77	224
Kyle Burton, $1,606	81-76-75	232
Mike Reasor, $1,584	78-78-78	234

In a tight race, Ray Floyd finally broke away from George Archer on the final nine holes of the Gulfstream Aerospace Invitational to win by five strokes.

Floyd, who started 65-65, shot an 8-under-par 64 in the last round and was 22 under par for 54 holes at Indian Wells Golf Resort.

Floyd and Archer were tied for the lead at 14-under after 36 holes and were tied again at 16-under through 45 holes. Archer had birdies at the second and eighth holes, Floyd birdied the fifth and sixth.

Floyd took the lead for good when he birdied the par-3 10th hole with a 20-foot putt.

"That putt on 10 was really a key," Floyd said. "It was coming downhill and then, my goodness, it went in the hole. The same thing happened at 11 and 12. Both were downhill breaking putts and they went in."

Floyd birdied the 11th, sinking a putt from 15 feet, and then birdied the 12th with an 8-foot putt.

Archer drew within two shots of the lead when he birdied the 13th. But Floyd answered with a 3-foot birdie putt at the 14th to regain his 3-shot lead.

Archer lost any chance when he double-bogeyed the 15th by hitting his tee shot into the water.

"I'm the bridesmaid," he said. "Is there an easier tour I can go to?"

Doug Sanders Kingwood Celebrity Classic

AT A GLANCE

- **Course:** Deerwood Country Club
- **Location:** Kingwood, Texas
- **When:** March 26-29, 1993
- **Weather:** Sunny, warm and windy.
- **Purse:** $500,000
- **Par:** 72
- **Yards:** 6,659
- **Defending champion:** Mike Hill
- **Tournament record:** 13-under-par 203, Lee Trevino, 1990, and Mike Hill, 1991

Scores and earnings (partial)

Bob Charles, $75,000		69-70-69–208
Jim Ferree, $45,000		70-71-68–209
Mike Hill, $30,733		70-73-67–210
Harold Henning, $30,733		72-68-70–210
Bob Murphy, $30,733		68-72-70–210
Kermit Zarley, $20,600		71-69-71–211
Dewitt Weaver, $17,600		69-73-70–212
Bobby Nichols, $17,600		71-69-72–212
Dick Rhyan, $13,100		70-72-71–213
Rocky Thompson, $13,100		70-71-72–213
Jim Albus, $13,100		66-74-73–213
Walter Zembriski, $13,100		74-73-67–214
John Paul Cain, $9,300		74-71-70–215
Mike Joyce, $9,300		71-73-71–215
Terry Dill, $9,300		70-74-71–215
Al Geiberger, $9,300		71-72-72–215
Tom Shaw, $7,800		74-73-69–216
Miller Barber, $7,800		69-73-74–216
Tommy Aycock, $6,042		74-75-68–217
Jack Kiefer, $6,042		74-72-71–217
Rives McBee, $6,042		74-70-73–217
Chi Chi Rodriguez, $6,042		71-72-74–217
Dick Hendrickson, $6,042		74-69-74–217
Jimmy Powell, $6,042		71-72-74–217
Bob Brue, $4,850		74-73-71–218
Joe Jimenez, $4,850		72-75-71–218
Homero Blancas, $4,350		73-78-68–219
Babe Hiskey, $4,350		75-75-69–219
Ben Smith, $4,350		74-70-75–219
Dale Douglass, $3,767		73-76-71–220
Larry Laoretti, $3,767		74-74-72–220
Larry Mowry, $3,767		68-77-75–220
Don Massengale, $3,450		74-74-73–221
Larry Ziegler, $3,088		73-77-72–222
Butch Baird, $3,088		72-77-73–222
Gibby Gilbert, $3,088		72-77-73–222
Simon Hobday, $3,088		73-74-75–222
Bruce Devlin, $2,800		74-74-76–224
Gene Littler, $2,700		76-77-72–225
Doug Sanders, $2,500		73-77-76–226
Bert Yancey, $2,500		76-75-75–226
Bob Betley, $2,500		75-74-77–226
Dow Finsterwald, $2,300		75-76-76–227
Charles Coody, $2,100		75-79-75–229
Bob Goalby, $2,100		75-78-76–229
Frank Beard, $2,100		75-79-75–229
Charlie Sifford, $1,900		76-78-76–230

Muratec Reunion Pro-Am

AT A GLANCE

- **Course:** Stonebriar Country Club
- **Location:** Frisco, Texas
- **When:** April 22-25, 1993
- **Weather:** Windy.
- **Purse:** $450,000
- **Par:** 72
- **Yards:** 6,737
- **Defending Champion:** George Archer defeated Tommy Aaron on fourth playoff hole.
- **Tournament Record:** 207, Frank Beard, 1990

Scores and earnings (partial)

Dave Stockton, $75,000		73-72-66–211
Harold Henning, $44,000		74-69-72–215
Ben Smith, $36,000		74-72-70–216
Lee Trevino, $27,000		74-73-70–217
Bob Murphy, $27,000		74-74-69–217
Don January, $20,000		72-74-72–218
Larry Mowry, $17,000		76-73-70–219
Simon Hobday, $17,000		78-70-71–219
George Archer, $14,000		77-74-69–220
Charles Coody, $12,500		77-71-73–221
Walter Zembriski, $12,500		73-74-74–221
Jack Kiefer, $10,500		74-80-68–222
Tommy Aycock, $10,500		78-75-69–222
Dewitt Weaver, $9,000		75-76-72–223
Chi Chi Rodriguez, $9,000		73-74-76–223
Tommy Aaron, $9,000		74-74-75–223
Homero Blancas, $6,858		78-76-70–224
Joe Jimenez, $6,858		76-75-73–224
Orville Moody, $6,858		76-75-73–224
J.C. Snead, $6,858		76-77-71–224
Rives McBee, $6,858		76-76-72–224
Larry Laoretti, $6,858		70-76-78–224
Rocky Thompson, $5,010		81-72-72–225
Harry Toscano, $5,010		83-70-72–225
Bruce Devlin, $5,010		74-74-77–225
Mike Hill, $5,010		77-73-75–225
Gene Littler, $5,010		72-75-78–225
Dick Lotz, $3,713		79-76-71–226
Jim Ferree, $3,713		77-78-71–226
Richard Bassett, $3,713		77-78-71–226
Tom Shaw, $3,713		79-75-72–226
Jim Dent, $3,713		77-77-72–226
Bob Wynn, $3,713		82-72-72–226
Don Massengale, $3,713		77-75-74–226
Jimmy Powell, $3,713		76-74-76–226
Larry Gilbert, $2,708		74-86-67–227
Jesus Rodriguez, $2,708		77-73-77–227
Dick Hendrickson, $2,708		75-75-77–227
Jim Hardy, $2,708		76-77-74–227
Bob Reith, $2,708		73-76-78–227
Kermit Zarley, $2,708		78-73-76–227
Bob Goalby, $2,100		79-78-71–228
John Paul Cain, $2,100		79-77-72–228
Walter Morgan, $2,100		78-78-72–228
Terry Dill, $2,100		79-74-75–228
Phil Rodgers, $2,100		77-74-77–228
Bob Betley, $2,100		77-72-79–228
Dick Rhyan, $1,500		86-74-69–229

Las Vegas Senior Classic

AT A GLANCE

- **Course:** Desert Inn and Country Club
- **Location:** Las Vegas
- **When:** April 30-May 2, 1993
- **Weather:** Warm and windy.
- **Purse:** $700,000
- **Par:** 72
- **Yards:** 6,810
- **Defending champion:** Lee Trevino
- **Tournament record:** 13-under-par 203, Al Geiberger, 1987

Scores and earnings

Player	Earnings	Scores
Gibby Gilbert	$105,000	70-63-71–204
Mike Hill	$62,300	68-69-68–205
Bob Charles	$51,100	70-67-69–206
Rocky Thompson	$42,560	66-73-68–207
Tom Wargo	$34,160	70-66-72–208
Miller Barber	$24,395	68-74-68–210
Mike Joyce	$24,395	71-70-69–210
George Archer	$24,395	73-68-69–210
Simon Hobday	$24,395	71-66-73–210
Chi Chi Rodriguez	$16,240	72-72-67–211
Dick Hendrickson	$16,240	69-73-69–211
Harold Henning	$16,240	71-71-69–211
Larry Ziegler	$16,240	72-65-74–211
Kermit Zarley	$16,240	62-74-75–211
Larry Laoretti	$12,250	74-73-65–212
Jim Colbert	$12,250	71-72-69–212
Tommy Aaron	$12,250	70-72-70–212
Don Massengale	$12,250	68-72-72–212
Jim Ferree	$9,800	69-76-68–213
Larry Mowry	$9,800	71-73-69–213
Gay Brewer	$9,800	71-73-69–213
Dale Douglass	$7,735	73-70-71–214
Frank Beard	$7,735	70-72-72–214
Dewitt Weaver	$7,735	72-70-72–214
Jimmy Powell	$7,735	69-70-75–214
Tom Shaw	$6,230	74-73-68–215
Charles Coody	$6,230	70-75-70–215
Al Geiberger	$6,230	75-70-70–215
Lee Elder	$6,230	69-75-71–215
J.C. Snead	$6,230	69-73-73–215
Don January	$5,180	74-73-70–217
Jim Albus	$5,180	74-70-73–217
Orville Moody	$5,180	71-70-76–217
Terry Dill	$4,445	74-72-72–218
Bobby Nichols	$4,445	72-73-73–218
Dave Stockton	$4,445	73-72-73–218
Charlie Sifford	$4,445	72-73-73–218
Don Bies	$3,710	73-75-71–219
Rives McBee	$3,710	69-78-72–219
Dave Hill	$3,710	79-69-71–219
Ken Still	$3,710	73-73-73–219
Martin Roesink	$3,710	71-74-74–219
Lee Trevino	$3,290	76-72-72–220
Walter Zembriski	$3,150	72-74-75–221
John Brodie	$2,870	75-75-72–222
Roberto De Vicenzo	$2,870	75-73-74–222
Bruce Crampton	$2,870	75-73-74–222
Butch Baird	$2,520	81-72-72–225
Gene Littler	$2,520	73-77-75–225
Dow Finsterwald	$2,240	75-78-73–226
Bruce Devlin	$2,240	75-77-74–226
Homero Blancas	$2,030	79-76-72–227
Billy Casper	$1,890	77-74-78–229
Doug Sanders	$1,820	80-74-76–230
Lou Graham	$1,750	78-76-77–231
Bob Goalby	$1,680	76-78-79–233

Gibby Gilbert's bid for a tournament record nearly cost him the Las Vegas Senior Classic.

Gilbert needed a 5-foot bogey putt on the final hole to avoid a playoff with Mike Hill.

The winning putt came after Gilbert, in chase of a birdie that would have set a tournament record, declined to play safe with a 2-shot lead and pulled out a driver on the par-4 18th hole at Desert Inn and Country Club.

The tournament record was worth an extra $5,000. It nearly cost Gilbert $42,700, the difference between first prize and second.

"I never dreamed double bogey. It never entered my mind," Gilbert said. "I figured I could make bogey from anywhere out there."

Gilbert drove into a fairway trap, hit the lip with an 8-iron, then hit a 9-iron fat short of the green. He chipped to 5 feet, setting up the winning putt.

"I told my son, Mark, that this is like a sudden death playoff," Gilbert said of the final putt. "I had a shot to win it with the putt and let's start here."

Told that Gilbert still was short of the green after three shots on the par-4 final hole, Hill left the interview room to get his golf shoes.

Liberty Mutual Legends of Golf

AT A GLANCE

- **Course:** Barton Creek Country Club
- **Location:** Austin, Texas
- **When:** May 7-9, 1993
- **Weather:** Sunny, warm, windy with intermittent showers and thunderstorms. Playoff interrupted between holes by thunderstorm.
- **Purse:** $1,000,000 (unofficial money)
- **Par:** 72
- **Yards:** 6,777
- **Playoff:** Harold Henning defeated Don January and Tom Weiskopf.
- **Defending champion:** No defending champion; format changed from two-man teams to 54-hole individual stroke play.
- **Tournament record:** New format began this year.

Scores and earnings

Player	Earnings	Scores
#Harold Henning	$250,000	69-70-65–204
Don January	$83,000	70-68-66–204
Tom Weiskopf	$83,000	65-72-67–204
Bob Charles	$43,500	70-69-66–205
Gibby Gilbert	$43,500	65-71-69–205
Bobby Nichols	$24,000	73-69-64–206
Chi Chi Rodriguez	$24,000	71-70-75–206
Dale Douglass	$24,000	75-63-68–206
George Archer	$24,000	66-66-74–206
Tommy Aaron	$24,000	70-66-70–206
Mike Fetchick	$17,000	76-65-68–209
Al Geiberger	$16,000	66-74-70–210
Jim Albus	$14,000	71-71-69–211
J.C. Snead	$14,000	66-75-70–211
Mike Hill	$14,000	72-68-71–211
Ray Floyd	$10,625	68-74-70–212
Orville Moody	$10,625	71-70-71–212
Gay Brewer	$10,625	71-69-72–212
Jim Dent	$10,625	69-71-72–212
Charles Coody	$8,800	74-70-69–213
Arnold Palmer	$8,800	68-73-72–213
Larry Laoretti	$8,000	70-66-77–213
Tom Shaw	$8,000	70-73-71–214
Don Bies	$7,033	71-72-72–215
Lee Trevino	$7,033	68-73-74–215
R. DeVicenzo	$7,033	69-71-75–215
Howie Johnson	$6,400	70-72-74–216
Billy Maxwell	$5,950	74-72-71–217
Larry Mowry	$5,950	71-71-75–217
Bruce Devlin	$5,300	72-77-69–218
Lee Elder	$5,300	75-71-72–218
Bob Goalby	$5,300	72-73-73–218
Dave Hill	$4,900	72-73-74–219
Billy Casper	$4,600	72-75-73–220
Peter Thomson	$4,600	73-75-72–220
Paul Harney	$4,300	73-79-79–221
Gene Littler	$4,300	70-78-73–221
Bob Toski	$4,300	75-72-74–221
Jim Ferree	$4,100	79-73-71–223
Dow Finsterwald	$3,950	78-74-72–224
Bruce Crampton	$3,950	78-72-74–224
Joe Jimenez	$3,800	74-75-76–225
Jack Fleck	$3,650	77-76-74–227
Bob Rosberg	$3,650	76-75-76–227
Charles Sifford	$3,500	77-74-78–229
Frank Beard	$3,400	75-80-75–230
Lou Graham	$3,300	76-78-79–233
Lionel Herbert	$3,200	81-77-80–238
Mike Souchak	$3,100	77-82-84–243

- won on second playoff hole

Harold Henning had to overcome rain, lightning, a seven-shot deficit and a playoff to win the Liberty Mutual Legends of Golf.

He earned $250,000—the richest senior golf prize outside skins games. The earnings are considered "unofficial money," but Henning's bank won't care.

"This is a major as far as I'm concerned," Henning said of the event that began the senior golf boom as a two-man tournament. "This is the most prestigious tournament I've ever won. I've already been through two or three fortunes and I'll try to keep this one."

Henning, who hadn't won since 1991, began the final round seven shots behind George Archer. But the Australian shot 7-under-par 65 and defeated Tom Weiskopf and Don January in a playoff.

Henning made par from a bunker on the 191-yard, par-3 No. 17 to beat January, who bogeyed on the second hole of the playoff after he skulled his second shot into a bunker.

Henning and January birdied the first hole but Weiskopf parred and was eliminated.

PaineWebber Invitational

AT A GLANCE

- **Course:** TPC at Piper Glen
- **Location:** Charlotte, N.C.
- **When:** May 14-16, 1993
- **Weather:** Windy and warm.
- **Purse:** $550,000
- **Par:** 72
- **Yards:** 6,774
- **Defending champion:** Don Bies
- **Tournament record:** 13-under-par 203, Don Bies, 1992

After losing to him by two strokes in the PaineWebber Invitational, Tom Weiskopf called Mike Hill the Senior PGA Tour's best player over the past three years.

"Week in and week out, he's probably the best," Weiskopf said after being outputted by Hill when it mattered most.

Hill immodestly seconded Weiskopf's motion.

"I think he's right," Hill said. "Go look at the book."

Hill's 12-under-par 204 total was two better than Weiskopf and three up on J.C. Snead (who closed with a course-record 64), Bobby Nichols and Dave Stockton.

The victory was Hill's second of 1993 and 15th of his four-year senior career. He retained the Senior PGA Tour earnings lead, picking up $82,500 and pushing his '93 total to $427,470.

Hill's career senior earnings, $3,593,332, stood within $400,000 of Chi Chi Rodriguez and Bob Charles, who led the seniors career list.

Adding three unofficial senior wins, 14 second-place finishes and 23 top-10 finishes in 29 starts during 1992, Hill had a solid case for himself.

"I don't think that's bragging or being out of line. . . . Go look at the money list. I've made more in four years than anyone out here," he said.

Scores and earnings

Player	Scores
Mike Hill, $82,500	69-67-68–204
Tom Weiskopf, $48,400	67-70-69–206
J.C. Snead, $33,000	72-71-64–207
Bobby Nichols, $33,000	68-71-68–207
Dave Stockton, $33,000	68-69-70–207
Jack Kiefer, $18,700	70-73-66–209
Don Bies, $18,700	71-69-69–209
Simon Hobday, $18,700	68-70-71–209
Jimmy Powell, $18,700	69-67-73–209
Walter Zembriski, $12,210	72-71-67–210
Dick Lotz, $12,210	70-72-68–210
Rocky Thompson, $12,210	73-68-69–210
Tom Wargo, $12,210	72-69-69–210
Larry Gilbert, $12,210	69-69-72–210
Isao Aoki, $9,900	73-69-69–211
Rives McBee, $9,350	72-67-73–212
Al Kelley, $8,268	71-70-72–213
Babe Hiskey, $8,268	71-69-73–213
Kermit Zarley, $8,268	67-69-77–213
Dick Hendrickson, $6,298	69-75-70–214
Mike Fetchick, $6,298	73-71-70–214
Don Massengale, $6,298	70-73-71–214
Bert Yancey, $6,298	70-73-71–214
Tom Shaw, $6,298	72-70-72–214
Dewitt Weaver, $6,298	70-70-74–214
Arnold Palmer, $4,675	72-75-68–215
Walter Morgan, $4,675	73-72-70–215
Larry Ziegler, $4,675	71-74-70–215
Jim Dent, $4,675	69-74-72–215
Bob Betley, $4,675	71-72-72–215
Gibby Gilbert, $4,675	73-70-72–215
Gary Cowan, $3,630	70-76-70–216
Bob Murphy, $3,630	70-76-70–216
Terry Dill, $3,630	75-70-71–216
Bruce Crampton, $3,630	73-71-72–216
Jim O'Hern, $3,630	71-71-74–216
Mike Joyce, $3,080	74-73-70–217
Bob Verwey, $3,080	70-74-73–217
Jim Colbert, $3,080	70-73-74–217
Harry Toscano, $2,585	71-78-69–218
Bob Reith, $2,585	75-72-71–218
Larry Mowry, $2,585	74-72-72–218
Tommy Aycock, $2,585	71-75-72–218
Ken Still, $2,585	76-69-73–218
Tommy Horton, $2,585	72-71-75–218
Miller Barber, $2,145	74-70-75–219
Agim Bardha, $2,145	73-68-78–219
Michel Damiano, $1,980	68-74-78–220
Bob Thatcher, $1,604	75-75-71–221
Harold Henning, $1,604	72-77-72–221
Charlie Sifford, $1,604	73-74-74–221
Dick Rhyan, $1,604	77-71-73–221
Orville Moody, $1,604	75-72-74–221
Roger Kennedy, $1,604	72-72-77–221
Rod Curl, $1,320	73-75-74–222
Snell Lancaster, $1,210	71-80-72–223
Bruce Devlin, $1,210	75-76-72–223
Bob Wynn, $1,210	72-76-75–223
Bob Menne, $1,100	74-73-77–224
Bruce Lehnhard, $990	74-75-76–225
Gay Brewer, $990	74-75-76–225
Quinton Gray, $990	76-70-79–225
Bob Toski, $853	74-79-74–227
Doug Dalziel, $853	75-76-76–227
John Brodie, $715	77-80-72–229
Phil Rodgers, $715	77-77-75–229
Bob Brue, $715	72-80-77–229
Lou Graham, $605	78-78-75–231
Jesus Rodriguez, $556	77-76-80–233
Howie Johnson, $556	78-75-80–233
Ben Smith, $506	74-73-88–235
Doug Ford, $473	77-82-82–241

Bell Atlantic Classic

At a Glance

- **Course:** Chester Valley Country Club
- **Location:** Malvern, Pa.
- **When:** May 21-23
- **Weather:** Overcast Friday; pleasant for the weekend.
- **Purse:** $650,000
- **Par:** 70
- **Yards:** 6,608
- **Defending champion:** Lee Trevino, 5-under-par 205
- **Tournament record:** 8-under-par 202, Chi Chi Rodriguez, 1987

Quiet, efficient Bob Charles almost silently became the first player to win $4 million on the Senior PGA Tour with his victory in the Bell Atlantic Classic.

He matched par 70 in the final round for a 6-under-par 204 total and finished one stroke ahead of Dave Stockton.

"I just go with the flow, or whatever," Charles said of his second victory in 1993 and 19th since joining the Senior Tour in 1986. The $97,500 first prize put his career earnings at $4,039,195.

"It's enough to say I remain calm on the outside, and on the inside I'm fighting it all the way with everyone else," he said.

"I try not to get too disappointed with the way I'm putting. I say to myself, 'Well, you're missing putts, you'll have to hit it closer to the hole.'"

Charles called it "a win for consistency and steadiness and not for brilliance."

Others challenged and fell back.

Stockton birdied three holes on the front nine and had a two-stroke lead at 8-under through No. 5, then bogeyed the next three holes, which "took the wind out of my sails," he said.

"It seems like every time I took a step, I got knocked down again."

"Bob Charles never changes," Stockton said. "He just goes his merry way."

Scores and earnings

Player	Earnings	Score
Bob Charles	$97,500	67-67-70—204
Dave Stockton	$57,200	69-66-70—205
Bob Murphy	$35,750	73-67-66—206
Mike Hill	$35,750	72-68-66—206
Jim Colbert	$35,750	68-68-70—206
Lee Trevino	$35,750	68-66-72—206
Rocky Thompson	$22,100	65-73-72—210
George Archer	$22,100	70-69-71—210
Tommy Aaron	$18,200	72-69-71—212
Larry Laoretti	$14,430	71-73-69—213
Larry Gilbert	$14,430	71-72-70—213
Bobby Nichols	$14,430	71-70-72—213
Jim Albus	$14,430	69-71-73—213
Dick Lotz	$14,430	72-68-73—213
Kermit Zarley	$11,375	70-75-69—214
Jack Kiefer	$11,375	72-71-71—214
Gibby Gilbert	$9,474	70-75-70—215
Mike Joyce	$9,474	73-72-70—215
Jim Dent	$9,474	74-70-71—215
Jim Ferree	$9,474	73-71-71—215
Al Kelley	$7,583	74-74-68—216
Billy Casper	$7,583	74-70-72—216
Bob Wynn	$7,583	72-69-75—216
Simon Hobday	$6,354	75-73-69—217
Dick Hendrickson	$6,354	72-75-70—217
Al Geiberger	$6,354	69-75-73—217
Jimmy Powell	$6,354	72-71-74—217
Isao Aoki	$4,931	77-72-69—218
Chi Chi Rodriguez	$4,931	75-73-70—218
Charles Coody	$4,931	70-76-72—218
Rives Mcbee	$4,931	74-72-72—218
Joe Jimenez	$4,931	71-74-73—218
Walter Zembriski	$4,931	69-75-74—218
Jack Nicklaus	$4,931	72-71-75—218
Tommy Aycock	$3,534	72-75-72—219
Dick Smith	$3,534	73-74-72—219
Bob Reith	$3,534	73-74-72—219
Tom Shaw	$3,534	73-72-74—219
Bob Brue	$3,534	72-73-74—219
Ken Still	$3,534	71-72-76—219
Butch Baird	$3,534	72-71-76—219
Dave Hill	$3,534	72-69-78—219
Gene Littler	$2,275	77-74-69—220
Bob Thatcher	$2,275	74-75-71—220
Don January	$2,275	71-78-71—220
Harry Toscano	$2,275	77-72-71—220
John Paul Cain	$2,275	70-78-72—220
Don Massengale	$2,275	74-74-72—220
Dick Rhyan	$2,275	77-70-73—220
Larry Ziegler	$2,275	73-74-73—220
Bert Yancey	$2,275	74-72-74—220
Homero Blancas	$2,275	73-73-74—220
Bruce Crampton	$2,275	72-71-77—220
Babe Hiskey	$1,528	72-75-74—221
Tom Wargo	$1,528	73-73-75—221
Ben Smith	$1,430	75-73-74—222
Miller Barber	$1,268	74-77-72—223
Don Bies	$1,268	74-76-73—223
Jim Stefanich	$1,268	74-72-77—223
Doug Dalziel	$1,268	74-72-77—223
Mike Fetchick	$1,008	75-77-72—224
Bruce Lehnhard	$1,008	76-74-74—224
Frank Beard	$1,008	71-78-75—224
Gay Brewer	$1,008	78-71-75—224
Roger Kennedy	$813	76-79-70—225
Arnold Palmer	$813	76-74-75—225
Terry Dill	$683	75-78-73—226
Bob Goalby	$683	74-79-73—226
Dan Morgan	$611	82-71-74—227
Dale Douglass	$572	72-76-80—228
Billy Maxwell	$533	76-79-74—229
Charlie Sifford	$494	78-78-74—230
Phil Rodgers	$442	80-74-78—232
Howie Johnson	$442	78-77-77—232
Robert Pfister	$390	80-76-77—233
Lou Graham	$390	82-78-73—233
Doug Ford	$351	77-78-81—236

Cadillac/NFL Golf Classic

AT A GLANCE

- **Course:** Upper Montclair Country Club
- **Location:** Clifton, N.J.
- **When:** May 28-30, 1993
- **Weather:** Cool, damp and threatening.
- **Purse:** $850,000
- **Par:** 72
- **Yards:** 6,486
- **Defending champion:** New tournament.

Lee Trevino never questioned whether he would win again after thumb surgery in December 1992. The question was when.

Trevino answered that by winning the Cadillac/NFL Golf Classic by two strokes over ailing Raymond Floyd and Bruce Crampton.

Trevino, 53, had last won May 24, 1992. But this victory didn't surprise the man who had dominated the Senior PGA Tour the previous three years.

He had a good feeling after coming within a stroke of winning the Bell Atlantic Classic the weekend before in Pennsylvania.

"I wasn't playing well going into last week and I didn't expect to win," Trevino said. "I got in the lead and probably was as surprised as anybody. I came in here playing extremely well. I was very confident. I expected to win."

Trevino expected a tough battle coming into the final round at the Upper Montclair Country Club with a two-stroke lead over Floyd.

Though they both shot par 72s, the showdown never materialized as Floyd struggled while waging a battle with food poisoning.

"With a healthy Raymond, 72 would not have been beaten him," Trevino said. "I've got to take my hat off to Raymond. He was very ill."

Scores and earnings

Player	Scores
Lee Trevino, $127,500	67-70-72—209
Bruce Crampton, $68,000	69-72-70—211
Ray Floyd, $68,000	69-70-72—211
Miller Barber, $45,900	74-73-66—213
Jim Albus, $45,900	72-72-69—213
Bob Charles, $34,000	71-74-69—214
Tommy Aaron, $27,200	69-73-73—215
Larry Gilbert, $27,200	68-73-74—215
Don Bies, $27,200	67-73-75—215
J.C. Snead, $17,729	70-77-69—216
Simon Hobday, $17,729	75-72-69—216
Larry Mowry, $17,729	74-72-70—216
Dave Stockton, $17,729	69-75-72—216
Tom Wargo, $17,729	74-70-72—216
Mike Hill, $17,729	70-73-73—216
Rocky Thompson, $17,729	67-75-74—216
Jim Dent, $12,019	70-77-70—217
Walter Zembriski, $12,019	69-75-73—217
Bob Wynn, $12,019	71-71-75—217
Gene Littler, $12,019	70-72-75—217
Gary Player, $12,019	70-71-76—217
Al Geiberger, $9,378	71-76-71—218
Charles Coody, $9,378	74-71-73—218
Tommy Aycock, $9,378	69-75-74—218
Charlie Sifford, $7,579	71-76-72—219
Jim O'Hern, $7,579	72-74-73—219
Butch Baird, $7,579	74-72-73—219
Dick Lotz, $7,579	69-74-76—219
Roger Kennedy, $7,579	68-74-77—219
Gary Cowan, $7,579	72-71-76—219
Dale Douglass, $5,865	77-74-69—220
Gibby Gilbert, $5,865	71-77-72—220
Al Kelley, $5,865	76-72-72—220
Bob Reith, $5,865	76-71-73—220
George Archer, $5,865	70-73-77—220
Ben Smith, $4,781	74-74-73—221
Harry Toscano, $4,781	73-75-73—221
Jim Colbert, $4,781	72-75-74—221
Bruce Devlin, $4,781	68-75-78—221
Dick Rhyan, $3,995	69-80-73—222
Isao Aoki, $3,995	74-75-73—222
Bob Murphy, $3,995	73-76-73—222
Dewitt Weaver, $3,995	73-74-75—222
Bruce Lehnhard, $3,995	73-74-75—222
Larry Laoretti, $3,485	77-72-74—223
Rives McBee, $3,145	74-75-75—224
Chi Chi Rodriguez, $3,145	74-72-78—224
Orville Moody, $3,145	70-75-79—224
Bob Betley, $2,331	75-76-74—225
Don January, $2,331	74-77-74—225
Jack Kiefer, $2,331	75-76-74—225
Chuck Thorpe, $2,331	71-79-75—225
Kermit Zarley, $2,331	73-76-76—225
Dick Hendrickson, $2,331	73-76-76—225
Larry Ziegler, $2,331	73-73-79—225
Gay Brewer, $1,743	73-80-73—226
Dave Hill, $1,743	73-79-74—226
Doug Dalziel, $1,743	78-72-76—226
Jimmy Powell, $1,743	74-76-76—226
Billy Casper, $1,403	75-78-74—227
Bobby Nichols, $1,403	70-81-76—227
Homero Blancas, $1,403	75-74-78—227
Don Massengale, $1,403	73-74-80—227
Lou Graham, $1,190	73-76-80—229
Terry Dill, $1,105	76-77-77—230
Bob Brue, $901	78-78-75—231
Lee Elder, $901	79-75-77—231
Joe Jimenez, $901	76-77-78—231
Mike Joyce, $901	73-74-84—231
Tom Shaw, $723	76-80-76—232
Bert Yancey, $723	76-75-81—232
Arnold Palmer, $621	78-79-76—233
Harold Henning, $621	77-79-77—233
John Brodie, $561	74-81-79—234
Phil Rodgers, $527	75-81-81—237
Howie Johnson, $476	80-80-78—238
Chuck Workman, $476	76-80-82—238
Doug Ford, $425	77-84-82—243

NYNEX Commemorative

AT A GLANCE

- **Course:** Sleepy Hollow Country Club
- **Location:** Scarborough, N.Y.
- **When:** June 4-6, 1993
- **Weather:** Cool all weekend. Rainy Friday morning but clearing later; rain all day Saturday, overcast Sunday.
- **Purse:** $550,000
- **Par:** 70
- **Yards:** 6,505
- **Defending champion:** Dale Douglass (tournament shortened to 54 holes because of bad weather)
- **Tournament record:** 17-under par 193, Bob Charles, 1989, and Charles Coody, 1991

Bob Wynn sank a 22-foot birdie putt on the final hole to win his first Senior PGA Tour victory.

Wynn's final-round 4-under-par 66 put him at 7-under 203, a stroke better than Bob Charles, Chi Chi Rodriguez and Larry Gilbert.

Wynn became the third first-time winner on the senior tour in 1993, joining J.C. Snead and Tom Wargo.

"I didn't expect to win at all, especially after the way I was driving on Tuesday, Wednesday and Thursday," Wynn said. "It was just horrible.

"On my last putt I played it 14 inches outside the hole and it went dead center. Even after that I never thought it was my tournament."

Wynn, 53, from LaQuinta, Calif., earned $82,500, his largest payday and roughly one-fifth his career earnings.

Charles, 57, who won the Commemorative in 1988 and '89, shot a closing 68 on the Sleepy Hollow Country Club course, with Rodriguez and Gilbert also at 68.

Scores and earnings

Player	Scores
Bob Wynn, $82,500	69-68-66–203
Chi Chi Rodriguez, $40,333	66-70-68–204
Bob Charles, $40,333	70-66-68–204
Larry Gilbert, $40,333	69-67-68–204
Tom Joyce, $22,733	67-71-68–206
Isao Aoki, $22,733	68-69-69–206
Simon Hobday, $22,733	69-68-69–206
Dick Rhyan, $15,767	65-72-70–207
Gary Player, $15,767	69-68-70–207
Tommy Aycock, $15,767	67-69-71–207
Lou Graham, $12,650	69-71-68–208
Jim Dent, $12,650	66-71-71–208
Tommy Aaron, $10,725	68-72-69–209
Ben Smith, $10,725	69-70-70–209
Jack Kiefer, $8,811	75-70-65–210
Mike Joyce, $8,811	68-73-69–210
Mike Fetchick, $8,811	69-72-69–210
Lloyd Monroe, $8,811	70-69-71–210
John Brodie, $8,811	69-69-72–210
Charles Coody, $7,040	68-75-68–211
Bruce Crampton, $7,040	72-70-69–211
Dick Lotz, $5,531	70-74-68–212
Dick Hendrickson, $5,531	74-69-69–212
Rocky Thompson, $5,531	70-71-71–212
Jim Ferree, $5,531	69-72-71–212
Robert Gaona, $5,531	65-75-72–212
Terry Dill, $5,531	70-70-72–212
Roger Kennedy, $5,531	70-70-72–212
Jim Albus, $4,345	69-75-69–213
Bob Thatcher, $4,345	72-71-70–213
Tom Wargo, $4,345	68-71-74–213
Dale Douglass, $3,795	68-76-70–214
Ted Hayes, $3,795	70-73-71–214
Bob Betley, $3,795	71-68-75–214
Jimmy Powell, $3,168	71-77-67–215
Bob Reith, $3,168	68-75-72–215
Walter Zembriski, $3,168	69-73-73–215
Harry Toscano, $3,168	68-72-75–215
Bruce Lehnhard, $3,168	69-70-76–215
Miller Barber, $2,805	71-72-73–216
Michel Damiano, $2,530	74-73-70–217
Dewitt Weaver, $2,530	73-73-71–217
Tom Storey, $2,530	71-74-72–217
Larry Laoretti, $2,530	73-68-76–217
Jerry Barber, $2,035	73-74-71–218
Rod Curl, $2,035	71-74-73–218
Al Kelley, $2,035	74-71-73–218
Orville Moody, $2,035	71-72-75–218
Jim O'Hern, $2,035	73-70-75–218
Bob Menne, $1,458	73-76-70–219
Don Massengale, $1,458	71-75-73–219
Gary Cowan, $1,458	74-73-72–219
Billy Casper, $1,458	71-75-73–219
Bert Yancey, $1,458	73-72-74–219
Babe Hiskey, $1,458	73-70-76–219
John Paul Cain, $1,155	73-77-70–220
Ralph Terry, $1,155	69-76-75–220
John Joseph, $1,155	67-75-78–220
Steve Reid, $990	74-73-74–221
Marty Bohen, $990	74-71-76–221
Walter Morgan, $990	70-74-77–221
Doug Dalziel, $880	70-75-77–222
Jacky Cupit, $798	78-75-70–223
Richard Bassett, $798	73-74-76–223
George Johnson, $715	75-74-75–224
Lee Elder, $660	71-77-77–225
Labron Harris, $578	69-81-76–226
Fred Ruiz, $578	81-70-75–226
Howie Johnson, $501	76-75-76–227
Tom Nieporte, $501	70-79-78–227
Billy Farrell, $451	74-80-75–229
Bill Johnston, $418	75-82-76–233
Doug Ford, $385	78-78-80–236
Al Besselink, $363	84-76-80–240
Bob Walter, $341	84-82-80–246

Southwestern Bell Classic

At A Glance

- **Course:** Loch Lloyd Country Club
- **Location:** Beldon, Mo.
- **When:** June 11-13, 1993
- **Weather:** Sunny and warm.
- **Purse:** $700,000
- **Par:** 70
- **Yards:** 6,539
- **Defending champion:** Gibby Gilbert
- **Tournament record:** 17-under-par 193, Gibby Gilbert, 1992

Dave Stockton's 4-foot par putt on the final hole let him win the Southwestern Bell Classic when, from almost the same spot, Walt Zembriski pushed his par putt to the right.

Stockton finished at 1-over-par 71 for a 54-hole, 6-under 204 total. Zembriski, who a week earlier switched to a cross-handed putting grip, had a 72–205.

"I knocked it in and he stepped up and didn't make it," said Stockton. "I wish to hell I could have made my birdie putt. Then he would have made his. But it wasn't meant to be. My ball rolled right over the top of his coin."

Zembriski, a former iron worker who never qualified to play the PGA Tour, made an 8-footer for a par on the 17th after Stockton chipped to within 2 feet to save par.

"The putts Walt and I had at 17 were harder than the ones we had on 18," Stockton said. "I really thought that was going to be the deciding hole."

Said Zembriski, "He made his. I missed mine. That's golf."

Scores and earnings

Player	Earnings	Scores
Dave Stockton	$105,000	65-68-71–204
Larry Mowry	$56,000	68-71-66–205
Walter Zembriski	$56,000	67-66-72–205
Gibby Gilbert	$37,800	66-73-67–206
George Archer	$37,800	65-70-71–206
Lee Trevino	$28,000	71-68-68–207
Bob Brue	$21,350	72-68-68–208
Larry Ziegler	$21,350	71-67-70–208
Rocky Thompson	$21,350	68-69-71–208
Dick Rhyan	$21,350	69-65-74–208
Agim Bardha	$15,400	73-68-68–209
Larry Gilbert	$15,400	69-69-71–209
Isao Aoki	$15,400	69-65-75–209
Jim Albus	$11,230	71-72-67–210
Jim Colbert	$11,230	69-72-69–210
Dick Hendrickson	$11,230	69-72-69–210
Simon Hobday	$11,230	71-70-69–210
Harry Toscano	$11,230	71-69-70–210
Bob Murphy	$11,230	73-67-70–210
Miller Barber	$11,230	70-67-73–210
Butch Baird	$8,167	70-71-70–211
Gary Player	$8,167	69-72-70–211
Kermit Zarley	$8,167	65-72-74–211
Jim Ferree	$7,000	70-72-70–212
Gay Brewer	$7,000	70-69-73–212
Ben Smith	$7,000	67-69-76–212
Tom Wargo	$5,810	70-73-70–213
Bert Yancey	$5,810	69-72-72–213
Bob Reith	$5,810	69-71-73–213
Tommy Aycock	$5,810	68-72-73–213
Michel Damiano	$5,810	68-68-77–213
Mike Joyce	$4,515	71-74-69–214
Jim Stefanich	$4,515	72-73-69–214
Dick Lotz	$4,515	69-73-72–214
Bob Rawlins	$4,515	71-70-73–214
Charles Coody	$4,515	70-70-74–214
Bob Betley	$4,515	70-70-74–214
Bob Wynn	$3,640	75-70-70–215
Bruce Crampton	$3,640	72-71-72–215
Bruce Lehnhard	$3,640	77-66-72–215
Larry Laoretti	$3,640	72-71-72–215
Jack Kiefer	$3,080	71-74-71–216
Doug Dalziel	$3,080	72-72-72–216
Rod Curl	$3,080	74-69-73–216
Bob Charles	$3,080	70-72-74–216
Bobby Nichols	$2,450	75-71-71–217
Labron Harris	$2,450	73-71-73–217
Dewitt Weaver	$2,450	73-69-75–217
Bob Goalby	$2,450	70-71-76–217
J.C. Snead	$2,450	73-67-77–217
Lou Graham	$1,750	75-74-69–218
Don Massengale	$1,750	77-72-69–218
Leon Chapman	$1,750	73-73-72–218
John Brodie	$1,750	74-70-74–218
Dow Finsterwald	$1,750	71-71-76–218
Ken Still	$1,750	70-70-78–218
Jimmy Powell	$1,225	76-73-70–219
Orville Moody	$1,225	73-74-72–219
Art Proctor	$1,225	73-74-72–219
Walter Morgan	$1,225	70-77-72–219
Al Kelley	$1,225	76-69-74–219
Richard Bassett	$1,225	73-69-77–219
Billy Casper	$1,225	70-69-80–219
Charlie Sifford	$1,225	68-70-81–219
Fred Ruiz	$910	76-73-71–220
Joe Jimenez	$805	74-72-75–221
Bruce Devlin	$805	73-73-75–221
Bob Thatcher	$700	68-76-78–222
Howie Johnson	$658	75-75-73–223
John Paul Cain	$574	79-72-73–224
Mike Fetchick	$574	72-73-79–224
Roger Kennedy	$574	71-72-81–224
Billy Maxwell	$490	74-74-77–225
Bud Williamson	$448	75-78-74–227
Don January	$448	77-74-76–227
Wayne Morris	$392	77-77-77–231
Larry Fryer	$392	74-76-81–231
Doug Ford	$350	72-77-85–234

Burnet Senior Classic

AT A GLANCE

- **Course:** Bunker Hills Golf Club
- **Location:** Coon Rapids, Minn.
- **When:** June 18-20, 1993
- **Weather:** Cool and sunny.
- **Purse:** $1,050,000
- **Par:** 72
- **Yards:** 6,894
- **Defending champion:** New event.

Chi Chi Rodriguez, for a time a dominant Senior PGA Tour player but more recently just another frustrated golfer, shot a 7-under-par 65 to win the inaugural Burnet Senior Classic by two strokes over Bob Murphy and Jim Colbert.

"I could tell a lot of guys thought I was washed up because I've been playing so bad lately," said Rodriguez, 57, who is second on the Senior Tour career earnings money list but had won only once the previous two years. "I was doubting, too."

Both Murphy and Colbert felt happy for Rodriguez.

"If I can't win, I want Chi Chi to win," said Murphy, who was tied with Rodriguez at 8 under after two rounds.

Said Colbert: "There's no question about it, he's a great asset to the human race as well as the Senior PGA Tour. He does an awful lot of good for an awful lot of people. It's great to have him for your champion."

Scores and earnings

Player	Earnings	Scores
Chi Chi Rodriguez	$157,500	69-67-65–201
Bob Murphy	$84,000	67-69-67–203
Jim Colbert	$84,000	68-69-66–203
Jack Kiefer	$63,000	64-70-70–204
Larry Gilbert	$40,950	70-68-67–205
Jim Ferree	$40,950	67-68-70–205
Rocky Thompson	$40,950	67-69-69–205
Jim Dent	$40,950	68-67-70–205
Bob Charles	$27,300	69-70-67–206
Jim Albus	$27,300	70-69-67–206
Simon Hobday	$27,300	66-68-72–206
Mike Hill	$23,100	70-68-69–207
Joe Jimenez	$20,475	68-71-69–208
Tommy Aycock	$20,475	69-70-69–208
Don January	$17,325	72-71-66–209
Babe Hiskey	$17,325	72-71-66–209
Larry Ziegler	$17,325	68-72-69–209
Dick Hendrickson	$17,325	65-74-70–209
Dale Douglass	$13,466	72-72-66–210
Kermit Zarley	$13,466	72-69-69–210
Dave Stockton	$13,466	71-69-70–210
Terry Dill	$13,466	70-69-71–210
Bruce Lehnhard	$10,521	70-73-68–211
Al Geiberger	$10,521	73-68-70–211
Isao Aoki	$10,521	68-73-70–211
Gibby Gilbert	$10,521	68-73-70–211
Dave Hill	$10,521	69-71-71–211
Gary Player	$7,965	72-71-69–212
Lee Trevino	$7,965	69-74-69–212
Harold Henning	$7,965	72-70-70–212
Gay Brewer	$7,965	69-73-70–212
George Archer	$7,965	72-68-72–212
Rives McBee	$7,965	70-70-72–212
Dewitt Weaver	$7,965	69-71-72–212
Charles Coody	$6,048	72-71-70–213
J.C. Snead	$6,048	69-74-70–213
Don Bies	$6,048	71-72-70–213
Dick Lotz	$6,048	71-72-70–213
Tom Weiskopf	$6,048	70-71-72–213
Bob Reith	$5,145	73-70-71–214
John Brodie	$5,145	69-74-71–214
Bobby Nichols	$5,145	70-69-75–214
Larry Laoretti	$4,410	73-73-69–215
Bruce Crampton	$4,410	71-73-71–215
Mike Joyce	$4,410	71-72-72–215
Al Kelley	$4,410	68-74-73–215
Don Massengale	$3,675	71-75-70–216
Frank Beard	$3,675	73-71-72–216
Miller Barber	$3,675	73-69-74–216
Walter Zembriski	$3,045	75-73-69–217
Larry Mowry	$3,045	74-74-69–217
Butch Baird	$3,045	73-73-71–217
Tom Wargo	$2,310	75-74-69–218
Doug Dalziel	$2,310	73-73-72–218
Tommy Aaron	$2,310	73-72-73–218
Orville Moody	$2,310	72-72-74–218
Lee Elder	$2,310	75-70-73–218
Ben Smith	$2,310	72-72-74–218
Bob Wynn	$2,310	72-71-75–218
Tom Shaw	$1,890	72-76-71–219
Bob Brue	$1,732	73-75-72–220
Bert Yancey	$1,732	71-76-73–220
Bruce Devlin	$1,522	74-73-74–221
Bob Goalby	$1,522	73-72-76–221
Harry Toscano	$1,260	74-75-73–222
Jimmy Powell	$1,260	76-73-73–222
Roger Kennedy	$1,260	74-72-76–222
Homero Blancas	$1,018	74-76-75–225
George Johnson	$1,018	72-78-75–225
Dick Rhyan	$892	73-76-77–226
Ken Still	$892	76-74-76–226
Lou Graham	$798	77-75-75–227
Charlie Sifford	$714	75-79-75–229
Doug Sanders	$714	77-76-76–229
Robert Zimmerman	$630	78-74-80–232
Billy Maxwell	$630	77-75-80–232
Howie Johnson	$567	79-79-79–237
Dow Finsterwald	$525	75-84-81–240

Kroger Senior Classic

AT A GLANCE

- **Course:** Jack Nicklaus Sports Center
- **Location:** Mason, Ohio
- **When:** July 2-4, 1993
- **Weather:** Hot and humid, with thunderstorms late Friday and Saturday. Sunny Sunday.
- **Purse:** $850,000
- **Par:** 71
- **Yards:** 6,628
- **Defending champion:** Gibby Gilbert, 10-under-par 203, defeated J.C. Snead on second playoff hole.
- **Tournament record:** 15-under-par 198, Gibby Gilbert, 1992

Simon Hobday, a former cattle farmer and car salesman in Zambia is kicking himself for not trying the U.S. tour 25 years ago.

"When I was younger and my time came to come over here and play—I was playing in Europe—I chickened out," said Hobday, who shot a 5-under-par 66–202 to win the Kroger Classic.

He stayed in Europe because he saw no future playing the U.S. tour.

"Over the years I thought, 'Hang on, you made a mistake.' So when the Senior Tour came up again, I didn't even hesitate. I was here like a shot," he said.

Hobday has won more than $1 million since joining the Senior Tour in 1991. In retrospect, even the thought of facing the PGA Tour regulars is less daunting.

"After you'd played with them a few times in Europe . . . I knew they were good, but they weren't miles ahead," Hobday said.

Hobday won the Zambian Amateur five consecutive years, won twice on the PGA European tour between 1969 and '86 and won four times on the South African tour.

Said Hobday, "The biggest check I ever won was $8,000 in the old days." His Kroger take-home: $127,500.

Scores and earnings

Player	Earnings	Score
Simon Hobday	$127,500	67-69-66–202
Gibby Gilbert	$62,333	69-69-65–203
Mike Hill	$62,333	66-69-68–203
Bob Reith	$62,333	67-67-69–203
Chi Chi Rodriguez	$35,133	71-66-67–204
Kermit Zarley	$35,133	69-67-68–204
Tommy Aycock	$35,133	68-67-69–204
Larry Gilbert	$24,367	67-73-65–205
George Archer	$24,367	72-68-65–205
Bob Charles	$24,367	68-66-71–205
Bob Murphy	$18,700	70-68-68–206
Isao Aoki	$18,700	71-66-69–206
Dick Rhyan	$18,700	67-68-71–206
Dewitt Weaver	$14,875	66-73-68–207
Al Geiberger	$14,875	72-67-68–207
Rocky Thompson	$14,875	68-69-70–207
Lee Trevino	$14,875	67-69-71–207
Gary Player	$12,368	70-69-69–208
Jim Dent	$12,368	69-68-71–208
Rives McBee	$10,540	68-72-69–209
Larry Mowry	$10,540	68-70-71–209
Tom Shaw	$10,540	68-70-71–209
Dick Hendrickson	$8,148	72-68-70–210
Jim Colbert	$8,148	70-70-70–210
Jim Albus	$8,148	70-69-71–210
Don Bies	$8,148	69-70-71–210
Larry Laoretti	$8,148	67-71-72–210
Billy Casper	$8,148	70-68-72–210
Don January	$8,148	69-68-73–210
Miller Barber	$5,748	70-73-68–211
Al Kelley	$5,748	73-68-70–211
Larry Ziegler	$5,748	68-72-71–211
Robert Zimmerman	$5,748	68-72-71–211
J.C. Snead	$5,748	72-68-71–211
Butch Baird	$5,748	72-68-71–211
Dick Lotz	$5,748	68-70-73–211
Joe Jimenez	$5,748	68-67-76–211
Bob Brue	$4,250	73-70-69–212
Jack Kiefer	$4,250	72-70-70–212
Harry Toscano	$4,250	71-70-71–212
Tom Wargo	$4,250	73-69-70–212
Gay Brewer	$4,250	73-68-71–212
Walter Zembriski	$4,250	71-68-73–212
Terry Dill	$3,570	75-70-68–213
Charles Coody	$3,570	72-70-71–213
Jim Ferree	$3,145	72-72-70–214
Mike Joyce	$3,145	70-74-70–214
Harold Henning	$3,145	69-71-74–214
Dale Douglass	$2,465	72-74-69–215
Ted Hayes	$2,465	70-74-71–215
Bobby Nichols	$2,465	70-73-72–215
Ken Still	$2,465	74-69-72–215
Ben Smith	$2,465	69-72-74–215
Bob Wynn	$1,998	73-75-68–216
Orville Moody	$1,998	73-73-70–216
Liam Higgins	$1,785	73-75-69–217
John Paul Cain	$1,785	73-73-71–217
Roger Kennedy	$1,785	73-73-71–217
Tommy Aaron	$1,615	75-73-70–218
Bert Yancey	$1,445	72-78-69–219
Jimmy Powell	$1,445	80-71-68–219
Bob Hauer	$1,445	67-82-70–219
Bruce Devlin	$1,190	79-73-68–220
Doug Dalziel	$1,190	70-76-74–220
Homero Blancas	$1,190	70-73-77–220
Bob Goalby	$935	75-75-71–221
Bruce Lehnhard	$935	73-74-74–221
Billy Maxwell	$935	72-73-76–221
Lou Graham	$799	73-73-76–222
Mike Fetchick	$723	74-75-74–223
Fred Ruiz	$723	69-76-78–223
Ron Skiles	$646	76-80-69–225
Lee Elder	$595	73-77-76–226
Howie Johnson	$561	76-78-73–227
Charlie Sifford	$527	73-78-80–231
Dow Finsterwald	$493	81-78-77–236
Bill Lowry	$459	77-77-83–237
Doug Ford	$425	82-80-84–246

Jack Nicklaus and K mart Greater Greensboro Open-winner Rocco Mediate are among many top golfers who have benefited from the sure eye of teacher Rick Smith.

TEACHER

Just when **Jack Nicklaus** was ready to end his legendary playing career, he won the 1993 U.S. Senior Open. Some credit for that victory must to go to Rick Smith.

Smith, one of golf's hottest gurus, helps Nicklaus when problems arise in his swing. Smith also coached '93 U.S. Open champion Lee Janzen, making it two major titles in four weeks for his pupils.

When he isn't teaching Tour pros, Smith is golf director at Treetops Sylvan Resort in Gaylord, Mich.

Smith also worked with '93 Greater Greensboro (N.C.) Open champion Rocco Mediate, Hawaiian Open runner-up Joey Sindelar and Billy Andrade, a two-time winner in 1991.

"I've studied the golf swing all my life," Smith says. "I've got a pretty good eye. I've used these eyes for so long. I used to study Jack Nicklaus' swing when I was 16 years old."

Smith, 35, fits golfers into two categories: rotators and swingers. Paul Azinger is a rotator. Payne Stewart and Fred Couples are swingers.

"The thing is, there is no thing," says Smith. "The method is, there is no method."

Nicklaus, who has authored as many articles and videotapes on the golf swing as any man alive, still turns to Smith.

At the Senior Players championship in June '93, Smith noticed Nicklaus was standing more erect than usual. After adjustments, Nicklaus played better.

"You can't talk back to a videotape," Nicklaus says. "Sometimes I'll just use Rick as a sounding board. . . . He knows my swing, he knows what I'm talking about."

Smith helped Janzen with a few problems the week of the Open and says, "I'll be there anytime they ask me."

"We're always working on something," says Janzen, who calls Smith about every two weeks.

"I just think Rick's the best teacher in the world."

Janzen, 29, was 14 when he and Smith met in Lakeland, Fla. Smith was visiting his brother, Andy, at Florida Southern College. Janzen and Mediate are FSC alumni.

"I would have no chance on the Tour without Rick," Mediate says. "I wouldn't have done anything without him."

—*by Jerry Potter*

SPOTLIGHT

AMERITECH SENIOR OPEN

AT A GLANCE

▶ **Course:** Stonebridge Country Club
▶ **Location:** Aurora, Ill.
▶ **When:** July 16-18, 1993
▶ **Weather:** Partly cloudy and windy Friday and Saturday, with a light shower Saturday afternoon. Rain suspended play Sunday at 1:40 p.m. An attempt was made to resume at 3 p.m., but more rain delayed play until the tournament was halted at about 5 p.m.
▶ **Purse:** $600,000
▶ **Par:** 72
▶ **Yards:** 6,840
▶ **Defending champion:** Dale Douglass, 15-under-par 201
▶ **Tournament record:** 16-under-par 200, Mike Hill, 1991

George Archer took advantage of lightning, a rainstorm and, finally, cancellation of the final round to win the Ameritech Open.

Archer, third, fourth and second in the Ameritech the last three years, was declared the winner after two suspensions of play and delays of more than three hours.

The winner by two strokes on the basis of his 11-under-par 67-66–133 in the first two rounds, Archer had reached the fifth hole when play was halted. After a delay of one hour and twenty minutes, players were sent out again, but before they could hit a shot, rain again suspended play.

"Last year, I was in contention in several tournaments that were cancelled," Archer said. "So everything comes out evenly."

Archer has had a history of back problems and has two steel rods in his back.

"My back was bothering me and the wind had kicked up," said Archer, "and I'm not a good wind player. The dice rolled my way today. If I had to go out there again, I don't think I could have done it physically."

Scores and earnings

Player	Score
George Archer, $90,000	67-66–133
Dick Rhyan, $44,000	71-64–135
Jim Colbert, $44,000	70-65–135
Simon Hobday, $44,000	69-66–135
Rocky Thompson, $23,400	71-65–136
Walter Zembriski, $23,400	70-66–136
Bob Charles, $23,400	68-68–136
Jim Albus, $23,400	65-71–136
Mike Hill, $13,900	70-67–137
Bob Murphy, $13,900	69-68–137
Walter Morgan, $13,900	69-68–137
Dewitt Weaver, $13,900	68-69–137
Dick Hendrickson, $13,900	68-69–137
Dave Hill, $13,900	68-69–137
Jim Dent, $10,200	70-68–138
Harold Henning, $10,200	69-69–138
Al Geiberger, $10,200	68-70–138
Bruce Lehnhard, $7,153	73-66–139
Orville Moody, $7,153	72-67–139
Tom Shaw, $7,153	72-67–139
Kermit Zarley, $7,153	71-68–139
Arnold Palmer, $7,153	70-69–139
Jim O'Hern, $7,153	68-71–139
J.C. Snead, $7,153	68-71–139
Chi Chi Rodriguez, $7,153	67-72–139
Bill McDonough, $7,153	67-72–139
Roger Kennedy, $5,220	70-70–140
Jack Kiefer, $5,220	69-71–140
Dave Stockton, $5,220	69-71–140
Rives McBee, $4,332	73-68–141
Dale Douglass, $4,332	73-68–141
Larry Laoretti, $4,332	72-69–141
Butch Baird, $4,332	70-71–141
Dick Lotz, $4,332	68-73–141
Al Kelley, $3,456	76-66–142
Rod Curl, $3,456	73-69–142
Mike Fetchick, $3,456	71-71–142
Bob Reith, $3,456	70-72–142
Gay Brewer, $3,456	70-72–142
Joe Jimenez, $2,640	75-68–143
Larry Ziegler, $2,640	73-70–143
Ben Smith, $2,640	73-70–143
Harry Toscano, $2,640	73-70–143
Billy Casper, $2,640	71-72–143
Tommy Aycock, $2,640	71-72–143
Bob Thatcher, $2,640	71-72–143
Larry Gilbert, $2,640	69-74–143
Bert Yancey, $1,920	75-69–144
Tom Wargo, $1,920	71-73–144
Agim Bardha, $1,920	71-73–144
John Paul Cain, $1,920	70-74–144
Babe Hiskey, $1,620	71-74–145
Robert Gaona, $1,320	76-70–146
Lou Graham, $1,320	76-70–146
Tom Weiskopf, $1,320	74-72–146
Jim Stefanich, $1,320	74-72–146
Ken Still, $1,320	74-72–146
Bob Brue, $1,320	73-73–146
Richard Bassett, $1,320	72-74–146
Tommy Aaron, $990	77-70–147
John Brodie, $990	77-70–147
Bruce Crampton, $990	76-71–147
Lee Elder, $990	74-73–147
Jerry Barber, $810	74-74–148
Larry Mowry, $810	73-75–148
Charlie Sifford, $720	78-71–149
Labron Harris, $608	76-75–151
Mike Joyce, $608	76-75–151
John Joseph, $608	75-76–151
Bob Menne, $492	81-71–152
Bruce Devlin, $492	81-71–152
Bob Betley, $492	76-76–152
Jesse Vaughn, $408	78-75–153
Jacky Cupit, $408	77-76–153
Dudley Wysong, $372	80-75–155
Fred Ruiz, $348	78-78–156
Tony Holguin, $324	75-82–157
Bill Johnston, $300	78-80–158
Doug Ford, $300	79-80–159
Howie Johnson, $300	81-79–160

First of America Classic

AT A GLANCE

- **Course:** The Highlands
- **Location:** Grand Rapids, Mich.
- **When:** July 23-25, 1993
- **Weather:** Sunny and comfortable Friday and Saturday. Thunderstorms delayed play for four hours Sunday; sunny thereafter.
- **Purse:** $550,000
- **Par:** 71
- **Yards:** 6,419
- **Playoff:** George Archer parred the third extra hole to defeat Jim Colbert after Chi Chi Rodriguez dropped out with a bogey on the first playoff hole.
- **Defending champion:** Gibby Gilbert, 11-under-par 202
- **Tournament record:** 13-under-par 200, Billy Casper, 1987

George Archer became the first back-to-back winner on the Senior Tour in 1993, riding a record-tying 8-under-par 63 in the final round to a playoff victory.

After Chi Chi Rodriguez fell out with a bogey on the first playoff hole, Archer defeated Jim Colbert on the third. The three had tied with course record 14-under 199 totals, while both Rodriguez and Archer shot record-tying 63s at the Highlands.

On the third extra hole, the 398-yard par-4 18th, Archer hit his tee shot under a tree on the left side of the fairway but made a daring second shot and was able to scramble for a par.

"I had a little opening through there," said Archer. "I'm pretty good hitting out of the trees, though. I get in them a lot. If you are going to get in the trees, you've got to learn to get out of them."

Scores and earnings

Player	Scores	Total
#George Archer, $82,500	67-69-63	199
Chi Chi Rodriguez, $44,000	68-68-63	199
Jim Colbert, $44,000	65-67-67	199
Lee Trevino, $33,000	67-67-66	200
Bob Murphy, $26,400	66-68-67	201
Dave Stockton, $22,000	71-66-65	202
Jim Dent, $16,775	66-76-64	206
Dick Hendrickson, $16,775	69-69-68	206
Jack Kiefer, $16,775	68-69-69	206
Jesse Vaughn, $16,775	71-65-70	206
Tommy Aaron, $12,650	70-68-69	207
Butch Baird, $12,650	63-72-72	207
Dick Lotz, $9,625	71-70-67	208
Roger Kennedy, $9,625	68-73-67	208
Joe Jimenez, $9,625	72-68-68	208
Gibby Gilbert, $9,625	69-70-69	208
Bob E. Smith, $9,625	70-69-69	208
Ken Still, $9,625	69-66-73	208
Jim Stefanich, $7,508	67-73-69	209
Jim Ferree, $7,508	69-74-66	209
Tom Wargo, $5,822	69-73-68	210
Bob Reith, $5,822	67-73-70	210
Gay Brewer, $5,822	68-72-70	210
Rocky Thompson, $5,822	70-70-70	210
Lou Graham, $5,822	66-73-71	210
Agim Bardha, $5,822	68-71-71	210
Ben Smith, $5,822	73-71-66	210
Harold Henning, $4,455	70-72-69	211
Dave Hill, $4,455	68-73-70	211
Richard Bassett, $4,455	74-68-69	211
Mike Hill, $4,455	71-74-66	211
Snell Lancaster, $3,713	69-73-70	212
Rives Mcbee, $3,713	73-67-72	212
Don January, $3,713	73-67-72	212
Bruce Devlin, $3,713	67-72-73	212
Bob Brue, $3,218	72-70-71	213
Harry Toscano, $3,218	69-71-73	213
Lee Elder, $2,860	70-72-72	214
Orville Moody, $2,860	70-70-74	214
Al Kelley, $2,860	76-70-68	214
Doug Dalziel, $2,860	72-71-71	214
Bob Goalby, $2,420	71-71-73	215
Calvin Peete, $2,420	77-70-68	215
Miller Barber, $2,420	69-75-71	215
Thomas Schafer, $2,420	71-72-72	215
Babe Hiskey, $1,870	69-71-76	216
Bob Thatcher, $1,870	74-73-69	216
Jimmy Powell, $1,870	69-76-71	216
Bob Betley, $1,870	69-70-77	216
John Paul Cain, $1,870	72-72-72	216
Labron Harris, $1,870	71-72-73	216
Jerry Mcgee, $1,393	73-73-71	217
John Brodie, $1,393	68-76-73	217
John Joseph, $1,393	73-71-73	217
Mike Fetchick, $1,183	72-73-73	218
Tommy Aycock, $1,183	70-75-73	218
Rod Curl, $1,183	70-73-75	218
Walter Morgan, $1,183	76-68-74	218
Charlie Sifford, $963	74-75-70	219
Steve Wilkinson, $963	75-72-72	219
Dow Finsterwald, $963	70-76-73	219
Bob Menne, $963	70-74-75	219
Bruce Lehnhard, $798	72-77-71	220
Billy Maxwell, $798	76-73-71	220
Dudley Wysong, $660	77-75-70	222
Jerry Barber, $660	72-75-75	222
Howie Johnson, $660	75-72-75	222
Jack Fleck, $550	76-75-72	223
Tony Holguin, $468	76-74-74	224
Bert Yancey, $468	78-73-73	224
Don Massengale, $468	76-74-74	224
Mike Joyce, $468	74-75-75	224
Terry Dill, $363	78-74-73	225
Freddie Haas, $363	75-77-73	225
Randy Glover, $363	72-76-77	225
Jacky Cupit, $319	77-77-75	229
Doug Ford, $297	80-76-75	231
Al Besselink, $275	80-78-79	237
Bill Johnston, $275	79-82-80	241
Fred Ruiz	73-79-DQ	

 # - won on third playoff hole

Northville Long Island Classic

AT A GLANCE

- **Course:** Meadow Brook Country Club
- **Location:** Jericho, N.Y.
- **When:** July 30-Aug. 1, 1993
- **Weather:** Hot and humid Friday; sunny and pleasant Saturday and Sunday.
- **Purse:** $550,000
- **Par:** 72
- **Yards:** 6,775
- **Defending champion:** George Archer, 11-under-par 205
- **Tournament record:** 14-under-par 202, Don Bies, 1988

With the electronic scoreboards malfunctioning, it was hard for golfers to know Raymond Floyd was closing on the leaders.

"I wanted the guys to feel the heat," said Floyd, who began the final round of the Northville Long Island Classic five strokes back.

"I figured after three birdies and being 3-under that they would know I was in serious contention."

Was he ever.

Floyd sank a 30-foot birdie putt on the 17th hole in a tournament record-tying 7-under-par 65, and won by two strokes with an 8-under 208 total.

"When you're trailing by as much as I was going into the last round, it's important to shoot a low score," said Floyd. "The only way you can do that is by getting off to a fast start."

He made birdie putts from 8 feet on the par-5 first hole, 2 feet on the third, and 15 feet on the par-3 fourth.

On No. 10, a 506-yard par-5, he used his driver and 3-wood, but made a bad pitch. He recovered with a 22-foot putt for the fourth of his seven birdies.

"If I didn't make birdie there," Floyd said, "the game is all over. No question, 17 was a big hole, but without the 10th I was dead."

Scores and earnings

Player	Scores
Ray Floyd, $82,500	73-70-65–208
Bob Betley, $33,880	73-70-67–210
Bob Charles, $33,880	74-69-67–210
Bruce Lehnhard, $33,880	70-72-68–210
Harold Henning, $33,880	68-74-68–210
Walter Zembriski, $33,880	70-68-72–210
Larry Gilbert, $18,700	72-70-69–211
Bob Murphy, $18,700	71-69-71–211
Dave Stockton, $15,400	71-68-73–212
Tom Wargo, $14,300	75-70-68–213
Jim Colbert, $11,688	77-71-66–214
Doug Dalziel, $11,688	74-72-68–214
George Archer, $11,688	69-71-74–214
Terry Dill, $11,688	72-70-72–214
Gibby Gilbert, $9,075	73-72-70–215
Ben Smith, $9,075	73-70-72–215
Gay Brewer, $9,075	74-70-71–215
Joe Jimenez, $9,075	75-68-72–215
Jimmy Powell, $7,054	73-73-70–216
Larry Ziegler, $7,054	74-72-70–216
Lee Trevino, $7,054	73-72-71–216
Dewitt Weaver, $7,054	75-70-71–216
Mike Joyce, $5,390	74-74-69–217
Rives McBee, $5,390	73-74-70–217
Rocky Thompson, $5,390	77-70-70–217
Miller Barber, $5,390	74-72-71–217
Dick Hendrickson, $5,390	74-72-71–217
Orville Moody, $5,390	69-75-73–217
Don Bies, $4,565	74-75-69–218
Bob Reith, $4,235	77-71-71–219
Jim Albus, $4,235	75-70-74–219
Carl Lohren, $3,795	72-75-73–220
Jim Stefanich, $3,795	73-73-74–220
J.C. Goosie, $3,795	71-70-79–220
Jim Ferree, $3,049	73-77-71–221
Robert Gaona, $3,049	73-76-72–221
Jack Kiefer, $3,049	73-75-73–221
Bruce Crampton, $3,049	76-73-72–221
John Paul Cain, $3,049	78-70-73–221
Walter Morgan, $3,049	75-70-76–221
Charlie Sifford, $3,049	71-73-77–221
Bobby Nichols, $2,530	74-73-75–222
Bob Brue, $2,530	75-71-76–222
Dick Lotz, $1,980	74-79-70–223
Bert Yancey, $1,980	81-72-70–223
Tom Joyce, $1,980	72-80-71–223
Al Kelley, $1,980	75-76-72–223
Charles Coody, $1,980	68-83-72–223
Jim Brown, $1,980	81-69-73–223
Jim O'Hern, $1,980	74-75-74–223
Michel Damiano, $1,980	75-74-74–223
Larry Laoretti, $1,430	80-74-70–224
Jerry McGee, $1,430	72-74-78–224
Ted Hayes, $1,238	74-78-73–225
Mike Fetchick, $1,238	75-76-74–225
Bob Goalby, $1,238	79-72-74–225
Labron Harris, $1,238	78-73-74–225
Richard Bassett, $1,018	76-77-73–226
Austin Straub, $1,018	78-75-73–226
Roger Kennedy, $1,018	76-74-76–226
Dick Rhyan, $1,018	73-76-77–226
Billy Maxwell, $853	79-76-72–227
Bob Menne, $853	75-77-75–227
Babe Hiskey, $770	76-77-75–228
Don Massengale, $633	80-76-73–229
Fred Ruiz, $633	77-77-75–229
Lou Graham, $633	77-77-75–229
Ken Still, $633	75-79-75–229
Jesus Rodriguez, $517	81-74-75–230
Jack Fleck, $484	80-77-74–231
Simon Hobday, $435	78-76-78–232
Homero Blancas, $435	77-76-79–232
Jerry Barber, $363	79-77-77–233
Doug Ford, $363	78-80-75–233
Roger Stern, $363	80-74-79–233
Jacky Cupit, $319	82-79-75–236
Bill Johnston, $297	85-77-77–239
Chuck Huckaby, $275	82-80-78–240
Al Besselink, $275	82-81-77–240
Tony Holguin, $275	81-81-82–244

Bank of Boston Classic

At a Glance

- **Course:** Nashawtuc Country Club
- **Location:** Concord, Mass.
- **When:** Aug. 6-8, 1993
- **Weather:** Sunny and pleasant.
- **Purse:** $750,000
- **Par:** 72
- **Yards:** 6,742
- **Defending champion:** Mike Hill, 8-under-par 136 in rain-shortened tournament (Hill was disqualified this year for missing his tee time for the pro-am).
- **Tournament record:** 18-under-par 198, Chi Chi Rodriguez, 1987

Bob Betley, a one-time Utah motorcycle policeman who began playing golf at age 28, shot 3-under-par 69 for a one-stroke victory in the Bank of Boston Classic.

He finished at 204 for his biggest payday ($112,500) in three years on the Senior Tour. Runner-up Bob Murphy closed 69–205.

Betley went from one stroke behind to three strokes ahead with final-round birdies on Nos. 5 and 6. He held off challengers with pars over the next 12 holes.

Chi Chi Rodriguez, who tied the Nashawtuc Country Club course record with a 64 for the second time in three years, Gibby Gilbert (66) and Jim Albus (70) shared third at 206.

Betley's check more than doubled his 1993 earnings. Before joining the Senior Tour, his biggest victories included the PGA Rocky Mountain Section championship and various state titles.

Murphy, who joined the tour after turning 50 in February 1993, earned $66,800 to surpass $2 million in combined winnings on the PGA Tour and Senior PGA Tour.

Scores and earnings

Player	Earnings	Scores
Bob Betley	$112,500	66-69-69–204
Bob Murphy	$66,000	67-69-69–205
Chi Chi Rodriguez	$45,000	71-71-64–206
Gibby Gilbert	$45,000	70-70-66–206
Jim Albus	$45,000	69-67-70–206
Larry Gilbert	$30,000	69-68-70–207
Ken Still	$27,000	69-70-69–208
Lee Trevino	$22,500	74-67-68–209
George Archer	$22,500	68-71-70–209
Rocky Thompson	$16,125	72-70-68–210
Larry Ziegler	$16,125	71-70-69–210
Jim Colbert	$16,125	71-70-69–210
Dewitt Weaver	$16,125	68-72-70–210
Tom Wargo	$16,125	70-70-70–210
Bob Charles	$16,125	70-68-72–210
Joe Carr	$10,639	70-74-67–211
Al Geiberger	$10,639	71-73-67–211
Harry Toscano	$10,639	70-72-69–211
Tommy Aaron	$10,639	72-69-70–211
Jim Ferree	$10,639	69-70-72–211
Jerry McGee	$10,639	69-70-72–211
Kermit Zarley	$10,639	71-64-76–211
Gary Cowan	$7,875	70-70-72–212
Bruce Lehnhard	$7,875	72-68-72–212
Lee Elder	$7,875	71-69-72–212
Miller Barber	$5,727	73-73-67–213
Simon Hobday	$5,727	75-71-67–213
Bob Brue	$5,727	72-73-68–213
Homero Blancas	$5,727	74-70-69–213
Ben Smith	$5,727	74-69-70–213
Walter Zembriski	$5,727	70-72-71–213
Michel Damiano	$5,727	68-73-72–213
Dale Douglass	$5,727	69-72-72–213
David Philo	$5,727	68-72-73–213
J.C. Snead	$5,727	70-69-74–213
Tommy Aycock	$5,727	66-71-76–213
Dick Hendrickson	$3,975	71-73-70–214
Terry Dill	$3,975	77-67-70–214
Bert Yancey	$3,975	69-72-73–214
Al Kelley	$3,975	68-73-73–214
Dick Rhyan	$3,975	68-70-76–214
Bob Wynn	$3,450	73-73-69–215
Jack Kiefer	$3,450	71-69-75–215
Calvin Peete	$2,550	71-76-69–216
Walter Morgan	$2,550	71-74-71–216
Gay Brewer	$2,550	72-73-71–216
Mike Joyce	$2,550	72-73-71–216
Bruce Crampton	$2,550	74-71-71–216
Dick Lotz	$2,550	71-73-72–216
John Paul Cain	$2,550	72-71-73–216
Charles Coody	$2,550	75-67-74–216
J.C. Goosie	$2,550	73-69-74–216
Bob Menne	$2,550	70-71-75–216
Butch Baird	$1,688	74-74-69–217
Billy Maxwell	$1,688	75-73-69–217
Rives McBee	$1,688	71-73-73–217
Tom Shaw	$1,688	73-71-73–217
Larry Laoretti	$1,425	76-72-70–218
Roger Kennedy	$1,425	71-75-72–218
Fred Ruiz	$1,425	72-72-74–218
Lou Graham	$1,200	75-76-68–219
Charlie Sifford	$1,200	75-73-71–219
Jesus Rodriguez	$1,200	76-71-72–219
Joe Jimenez	$938	75-73-72–220
Larry Mowry	$938	75-74-71–220
Doug Dalziel	$938	75-72-73–220
Jim Stefanich	$938	71-75-74–220
Jimmy Powell	$705	76-76-69–221
Richard Bassett	$705	76-73-72–221
Tony Morosco	$705	76-70-75–221
Harold Henning	$615	72-73-77–222
Bobby Nichols	$548	75-75-73–223
Don Massengale	$548	72-74-77–223
Jim Brown	$480	80-76-68–224
Bob Goalby	$480	74-77-73–224
Doug Ford	$435	79-74-76–229
Joe Bernat	$405	78-78-82–238
Ted Libernini	$375	88-85-83–256

Franklin Quest Championship

AT A GLANCE

- **Course:** Park Meadows Golf Club
- **Location:** Park City, Utah
- **When:** Aug. 12-15, 1993
- **Weather:** Clear on Friday and Saturday; partly cloudy on Sunday
- **Purse:** $500,000
- **Par:** 72
- **Yards:** 6,881
- **Defending champion:** Orville Moody birdied the eighth playoff hole to defeat Bob Betley.
- **Tournament record:** 14-under-par 202, Rives McBee, 1990

Dave Stockton shot a near-perfect game, firing a 9-under-par 63 to win the Franklin Quest Championship by nine shots over Al Geiberger.

Stockton, who began the day at 10-under, carded eight birdies, one eagle and a lone bogey over the mountain course. He finished the 54-hole, tournament at 19-under, while Geiberger, who closed with a 68, wound up with a 10-under 206.

"My goal was to make seven birdies on the day," said Stockton, who won PGA Championships in 1970 and 1976.

"I am not surprised by winning by nine strokes. My long game is stronger now than when I was on the regular tour, and my putting is as good as ever. When I was younger, I tended to get a lead and just hang on," he said.

Stockton became the first Senior PGA Tour player to win three events in 1993.

Stockton's winning margin tied the all-time Senior PGA Tour record set in 1992 by Gibby Gilbert at the Southwestern Bell Classic, and his closing 63 set a course record at Park Meadows.

Stockton's 54-hole total was the second lowest of the year. Raymond Floyd had the year's best score thus far at 22-under at the Gulfstream Invitational.

Scores and earnings

Player	Earnings	Score
Dave Stockton	$75,000	68-66-63–197
Al Geiberger	$44,000	71-67-68–206
Rocky Thompson	$36,000	72-65-70–207
Dale Douglass	$23,000	69-71-68–208
Charles Coody	$23,000	71-68-69–208
Jack Kiefer	$23,000	70-67-71–208
Bob Betley	$23,000	68-68-72–208
Dewitt Weaver	$15,000	72-67-71–210
Tom Weiskopf	$15,000	67-70-73–210
Walter Morgan	$13,000	70-70-71–211
Tommy Aycock	$11,000	76-65-71–212
Jim Ferree	$11,000	74-66-72–212
Bruce Crampton	$11,000	72-67-73–212
Don Bies	$9,000	72-74-68–214
Tom Storey	$9,000	72-70-72–214
Tom Shaw	$9,000	68-68-78–214
Jim Albus	$7,750	71-74-70–215
J.C. Snead	$7,750	67-74-74–215
Ben Smith	$6,067	74-74-68–216
Harry Toscano	$6,067	75-70-71–216
Bobby Nichols	$6,067	72-71-73–216
Larry Laoretti	$6,067	69-74-73–216
Larry Ziegler	$6,067	73-70-73–216
Richard Bassett	$6,067	70-70-76–216
Orville Moody	$4,458	70-76-71–217
Joe Jimenez	$4,458	76-71-70–217
Simon Hobday	$4,458	71-75-71–217
John Paul Cain	$4,458	73-73-71–217
Doug Dalziel	$4,458	70-75-72–217
Billy Casper	$4,458	72-71-74–217
Bruce Lehnhard	$3,525	77-72-69–218
Jerry Mcgee	$3,525	70-76-72–218
Babe Hiskey	$3,525	73-73-72–218
Dick Lotz	$3,525	74-71-73–218
Gay Brewer	$2,938	73-75-71–219
Butch Baird	$2,938	72-74-73–219
Bert Yancey	$2,938	75-70-74–219
Rives Mcbee	$2,938	71-73-75–219
Bruce Devlin	$2,400	71-76-73–220
Kermit Zarley	$2,400	76-71-73–220
Roger Kennedy	$2,400	73-73-74–220
Frank Beard	$2,400	75-71-74–220
Gary Longfellow	$2,400	75-69-76–220
Tommy Aaron	$2,400	73-69-78–220
Mike Joyce	$1,950	79-72-70–221
Jim Allred	$1,950	75-69-77–221
Bill Viele	$1,950	71-71-79–221
Dick Rhyan	$1,550	78-75-69–222
Al Kelley	$1,550	73-75-74–222
Al Cotton	$1,550	72-75-75–222
Dick Hendrickson	$1,550	73-73-76–222
Larry Gilbert	$1,550	73-72-77–222
Jimmy Powell	$1,175	71-81-71–223
Jim Stefanich	$1,175	74-78-71–223
Bob Menne	$1,175	78-73-72–223
Bob Thatcher	$1,175	73-77-73–223
Mike Fetchick	$1,025	79-74-71–224
Terry Dill	$1,025	76-71-77–224
Bob Wynn	$950	68-76-81–225
J.C. Goosie	$900	73-75-79–227
Michel Damiano	$775	77-77-74–228
Bob Reith	$775	77-77-74–228
John Brodie	$775	73-79-76–228
Dow Finsterwald	$775	76-74-78–228
Dudley Wysong	$650	71-78-80–229
Labron Harris	$550	78-76-76–230
Rod Curl	$550	77-75-78–230
Bob Goalby	$550	75-74-81–230
Billy Maxwell	$470	74-77-80–231
Fred Ruiz	$410	78-77-77–232
Jack Fleck	$410	81-74-77–232
Lanny Nielsen	$410	78-73-81–232
Jacky Cupit	$350	78-80-76–234
George Bayer	$330	81-79-76–236
Leon Chapman	$300	81-77-79–237
Jerry Barber	$300	71-83-83–237
Bill Johnston	$270	79-81-79–239
Doug Ford	$250	81-83-77–241
Al Besselink	$250	81-79-81–241
Tony Holguin	$250	81-90-89–260
Bob Rosburg		84-84-WD

GTE Northwest Classic

AT A GLANCE

- **Course:** Inglewood Country Club
- **Location:** Kenmore, Wash.
- **When:** Aug. 19-22, 1993
- **Weather:** Sunny on Friday; rain on Saturday and Sunday.
- **Purse:** $500,000
- **Par:** 72
- **Yards:** 6,440
- **Defending champion:** Mike Joyce, 12-under-par-204
- **Tournament record:** 18-under-par 198, Mike Hill, 1991

Dave Stockton was having a good time making life miserable for the rest of the Senior PGA Tour.

He took a one-stroke lead into the final round of the GTE Northwest Classic and built it into a five-shot lead by the 11th hole. He led by as many as eight strokes before settling for a four-shot victory, his second consecutive win on the Senior PGA Tour and his fourth of the year.

"This is as good as it's gotten," said Stockton. "My attitude's good. I'm having a good time, and I'm enjoying the people."

Finishing at 16-under 200, Stockton had shot six consecutive rounds in the 60's and stayed under par in 13 of his last 14.

"Last week was still fresh in my mind," Stockton said. "I thought since I did it last week, there was no reason I couldn't do it again this week."

Stockton, runner-up Dale Douglass and Bert Yancey were all tied at 11-under after the first hole, a 457-yard par-5, as Yancey and Douglass made birdies.

Stockton regained his one-shot lead on the next hole, making an impressive birdie after his tee shot landed under a tree. He followed with a low 4-iron that bounced in front of the green and rolled within 20 feet. Stockton drained the putt and took some momentum away from Yancey and Douglass.

Scores and earnings

Player	Rounds–Total
Dave Stockton, $75,000	65-68-67–200
Dale Douglass, $44,000	67-67-70–204
Tom Wargo, $36,000	70-68-67–205
Bob Betley, $30,000	67-70-69–206
George Archer, $22,000	73-67-67–207
Butch Baird, $22,000	71-67-69–207
Don Bies, $16,000	73-68-67–208
Larry Laoretti, $16,000	69-69-70–208
Dick Hendrickson, $16,000	68-70-70–208
Al Geiberger, $12,500	73-69-67–209
Bert Yancey, $12,500	69-65-75–209
Tom Weiskopf, $11,000	73-69-68–210
Tommy Aycock, $9,250	72-71-68–211
J.C. Snead, $9,250	69-71-71–211
Bob Brue, $9,250	68-72-71–211
Kermit Zarley, $9,250	73-67-71–211
Chi Chi Rodriguez, $8,000	70-72-70–212
Walter Morgan, $6,630	74-73-66–213
Rives McBee, $6,630	71-71-71–213
Rocky Thompson, $6,630	72-69-72–213
Harry Toscano, $6,630	72-69-72–213
Doug Dalziel, $6,630	68-72-73–213
Bruce Lehnhard, $5,010	76-70-68–214
J.C. Goosie, $5,010	73-73-68–214
Ben Smith, $5,010	73-72-69–214
Jack Kiefer, $5,010	70-74-70–214
Jerry McGee, $5,010	72-70-72–214
Mike Joyce, $4,050	72-72-71–215
Richard Bassett, $4,050	70-73-72–215
Jim O'Hern, $4,050	70-73-72–215
Billy Casper, $4,050	70-72-73–215
Bruce Crampton, $3,375	73-75-68–216
John Paul Cain, $3,375	76-69-71–216
Mike Fetchick, $3,375	72-71-73–216
Dick Rhyan, $3,375	67-73-76–216
Ted Wurtz, $2,925	77-68-72–217
Jim Albus, $2,925	74-70-73–217
Al Kelley, $2,650	72-77-69–218
Babe Hiskey, $2,650	78-71-69–218
Rod Curl, $2,650	74-69-75–218
Fred Ruiz, $2,250	73-76-70–219
Lee Elder, $2,250	73-74-72–219
Roger Kennedy, $2,250	75-72-72–219
Bob Thatcher, $2,250	74-72-73–219
Ken Still, $2,250	70-75-74–219
Tom Shaw, $1,800	73-74-73–220
Bob Wynn, $1,800	75-73-72–220
Michel Damiano, $1,800	76-71-73–220
Bill McDonough, $1,800	69-73-78–220
John Joseph, $1,500	75-72-74–221
Jim Stefanich, $1,500	70-76-75–221
Bill Tindall, $1,238	76-77-69–222
Simon Hobday, $1,238	75-77-70–222
Arnold Palmer, $1,238	76-74-72–222
Bob Reith, $1,238	76-72-74–222
Orville Moody, $1,075	73-79-71–223
Dudley Wysong, $1,075	76-73-74–223
Billy Maxwell, $975	75-75-74–224
Steve Reid, $975	74-76-74–224
Jack Fleck, $850	77-77-71–225
Bob Menne, $850	72-77-76–225
Charlie Sifford, $850	77-73-75–225
Dow Finsterwald, $725	80-73-75–228
Doug Ford, $725	73-75-80–228
Fred Hawkins, $650	76-76-77–229
Douglas MacDonald, $575	77-78-75–230
Quinton Gray, $575	78-74-78–230
Skip Whittet, $500	80-76-75–231
Jacky Cupit, $470	74-78-80–232
R. Stuart Chancellor, $425	79-78-76–233
Jerry Barber, $425	82-72-79–233
Tony Holguin, $365	82-82-74–238
Billy Derickson, $365	78-80-80–238
Bill Johnston, $330	83-77-79–239
Al Besselink, $310	86-76-81–243
George Bayer, $290	86-87-79–252

Bruno's Memorial Classic

AT A GLANCE

- **Course:** Greystone Golf Club
- **Location:** Birmingham, Ala.
- **When:** Aug. 27-29, 1993
- **Weather:** Hot and humid.
- **Purse:** $850,000
- **Par:** 72
- **Yards:** 7,027
- **Defending champion:** George Archer, 8-under-par 208
- **Tournament record:** 8-under-par 208, George Archer, 1992

Bob Murphy appeared to have the Bruno's Memorial Classic won with his 12-foot birdie putt on the final hole.

But his first Senior PGA Tour victory may have been decided by a 2-foot miss earlier in the round.

Murphy decided to have a little talk with himself as he walked away from the 11th hole, where he blew a birdie putt from that distance.

"Here I was with a 2-footer, and I was torn between where to play the putt. I missed it," he said after the one-shot victory over Bob Charles and Lee Trevino. "I told myself, 'You can't allow yourself to have those little arguments.' That's not the way I usually putt. I've always been an aggressive putter."

After scolding himself, Murphy birdied three of the last seven holes, making the 12-footer to finish with a 13-under-par 203 total, including a final-round 5-under 67.

Charles bogeyed 17 to open the door for Murphy, then missed a chance on 18 to force a playoff when his 27-foot birdie putt on 18 skidded wide right on one of the unsteady greens, which had been painted to cover up bare patches left by scorching heat.

Trevino also had a chance to tie with a birdie, but pulled his 22-footer to the right. That left Murphy with his first victory since the 1986 PGA Tour Canadian Open.

Scores and earnings

Player	Scores
Bob Murphy, $127,500	69-67-67–203
Bob Charles, $68,000	68-67-69–204
Lee Trevino, $68,000	70-66-68–204
Gibby Gilbert, $51,000	71-66-68–205
Dewitt Weaver, $40,800	67-68-71–206
Dave Stockton, $32,300	67-71-69–207
Jim Albus, $32,300	70-67-70–207
Harold Henning, $22,440	75-68-66–209
Tom Wargo, $22,440	69-73-67–209
George Archer, $22,440	72-69-68–209
Kermit Zarley, $22,440	67-70-72–209
Walter Morgan, $22,440	68-68-73–209
Larry Laoretti, $14,462	71-73-66–210
Terry Dill, $14,462	68-74-68–210
Don January, $14,462	70-71-69–210
Jim Ferree, $14,462	73-68-69–210
Tommy Aaron, $14,462	71-69-70–210
Tom Shaw, $14,462	68-71-71–210
Chi Chi Rodriguez, $14,462	68-70-72–210
Joe Jimenez, $10,540	73-71-67–211
Rives McBee, $10,540	70-73-68–211
Mike Hill, $10,540	72-70-69–211
Orville Moody, $8,330	69-72-71–212
Bruce Devlin, $8,330	73-69-70–212
Bob Brue, $8,330	72-69-71–212
Dick Hendrickson, $8,330	69-71-72–212
Bruce Lehnhard, $8,330	70-70-72–212
John Paul Cain, $8,330	74-66-72–212
J.C. Snead, $6,426	71-73-69–213
Jim Colbert, $6,426	69-73-71–213
Miller Barber, $6,426	71-71-71–213
Dale Douglass, $6,426	72-68-73–213
Simon Hobday, $6,426	70-69-74–213
Arnold Palmer, $5,228	75-70-69–214
Walter Zembriski, $5,228	72-71-71–214
Don Bies, $5,228	69-72-73–214
Rocky Thompson, $5,228	69-69-76–214
Larry Ziegler, $4,165	70-75-70–215
Bert Yancey, $4,165	74-71-70–215
Richard Bassett, $4,165	71-73-71–215
Al Kelley, $4,165	67-76-72–215
Bob Reith, $4,165	73-70-72–215
Jack Kiefer, $4,165	69-73-73–215
Butch Baird, $4,165	73-69-73–215
Bob Wynn, $3,060	71-75-70–216
Bob Goalby, $3,060	73-72-71–216
Bob Betley, $3,060	75-70-71–216
Ben Smith, $3,060	72-71-73–216
Michel Damiano, $3,060	73-70-73–216
Billy Casper, $3,060	72-69-75–216
Charlie Sifford, $2,295	72-73-72–217
Mike Joyce, $2,295	72-72-73–217
Jerry McGee, $2,295	69-73-75–217
Jimmy Powell, $1,955	73-76-69–218
Robert Gaona, $1,955	72-71-75–218
Tommy Aycock, $1,955	74-69-75–218
Roger Kennedy, $1,785	76-74-69–219
Bobby Nichols, $1,615	72-77-71–220
Wayne Morris, $1,615	73-74-73–220
Billy Maxwell, $1,615	75-71-74–220
Doug Dalziel, $1,360	74-73-74–221
Fred Ruiz, $1,360	74-73-74–221
Jim Dent, $1,360	70-75-76–221
Harry Toscano, $1,148	74-74-74–222
Larry Gilbert, $1,148	72-73-77–222
Gary Cowan, $901	72-76-75–223
Lee Elder, $901	76-73-74–223
Bob Thatcher, $901	70-73-80–223
Dick Rhyan, $901	72-71-80–223
Hank Johnson, $723	79-75-70–224
Gay Brewer, $723	72-80-72–224
Lloyd Moody, $646	76-75-74–225
Jim Stefanich, $595	76-77-74–227
Ken Still, $561	78-74-76–228
Lou Graham, $527	73-74-82–229
Doug Ford, $476	76-79-75–230
Chuck Jones, $476	76-75-79–230
Larry Mowry	68-69-WD

Quicksilver Classic

AT A GLANCE

- **Course:** Quicksilver Country Club
- **Location:** Midway, Pa.
- **When:** Sept. 3-5, 1993
- **Weather:** Lightning suspended play Friday with 33 players on the course; clear and sunny Saturday and Sunday.
- **Purse:** $1.05 million
- **Par:** 72
- **Yards:** 6,907
- **Defending champion:** New event.

Ten holes into his final round at the $1.05 million Quicksilver Classic, Bob Charles had the rest of the field gasping for air.

Having set a course record the day before with a 7-under-par 65, Charles was 4-under after 10 holes of the final round, building a five-stroke lead.

"Charles was going to have to do something bad to give someone else a chance, and he doesn't do many things bad," third-place finisher Harry Toscano said.

There was a glimmer of hope when Charles bogeyed No. 14, a 189-yard par 3. He three-putted after leaving his tee shot 60 feet from the pin.

But he birdied the next hole, a 529-yard par 5, with an 18-foot putt to move back to 9-under for the tournament.

Toscano, Dave Stockton and Raymond Floyd could do nothing but watch as Charles won a career-high $157,500 and became the sixth Senior PGA Tour player to pass $5 million in career earnings.

"My putter certainly was hot the first 10 holes," Charles said. The New Zealand left-hander's four, early, final-round birdies included putts from 40 and 20 feet.

"That gave me a jump on the field. I managed to par the rest of the way in and that was enough."

Scores and earnings

Player	Scores	Total
Bob Charles, $157,500	74-65-68	207
Dave Stockton, $92,400	72-70-69	211
Harry Toscano, $69,300	70-73-69	212
Ray Floyd, $69,300	70-71-71	212
Bob Murphy, $35,100	79-68-67	214
Jack Kiefer, $35,100	75-72-67	214
Dewitt Weaver, $35,100	73-73-68	214
Jim Dent, $35,100	72-74-68	214
J.C. Snead, $35,100	71-72-71	214
Jim Colbert, $35,100	72-70-72	214
George Archer, $35,100	70-71-73	214
Rocky Thompson, $20,160	72-73-70	215
Dave Hill, $20,160	75-69-71	215
Gibby Gilbert, $20,160	74-70-71	215
Mike Hill, $20,160	74-69-72	215
Simon Hobday, $20,160	73-70-72	215
Larry Gilbert, $14,403	74-74-68	216
Al Geiberger, $14,403	74-74-68	216
Orville Moody, $14,403	78-69-69	216
Larry Laoretti, $14,403	74-70-72	216
Kermit Zarley, $14,403	71-72-73	216
Chi Chi Rodriguez, $14,403	73-69-74	216
Tommy Aaron, $10,763	75-72-70	217
Bruce Crampton, $10,763	74-72-71	217
Miller Barber, $10,763	76-68-73	217
Tom Wargo, $10,763	72-70-75	217
Bobby Nichols, $9,135	77-70-71	218
Doug Dalziel, $9,135	74-72-72	218
Gary Player, $9,135	75-71-72	218
Bruce Devlin, $7,420	76-74-69	219
Dale Douglass, $7,420	77-71-71	219
Charles Coody, $7,420	74-74-71	219
Don January, $7,420	74-74-71	219
Bruce Lehnhard, $7,420	76-70-73	219
Arnold Palmer, $7,420	75-71-73	219
Jim Albus, $5,906	75-74-71	220
Dick Hendrickson, $5,906	74-75-71	220
Harold Henning, $5,906	73-75-72	220
Bert Yancey, $5,906	74-74-72	220
Butch Baird, $4,935	77-71-73	221
Dick Rhyan, $4,935	73-74-74	221
Walter Zembriski, $4,935	75-72-74	221
Jerry Mcgee, $4,935	75-71-75	221
Bob Reith, $4,935	72-73-76	221
Jimmy Powell, $3,885	77-73-72	222
Al Kelley, $3,885	77-73-72	222
Isao Aoki, $3,885	72-76-74	222
Terry Dill, $3,885	77-71-74	222
Joe Jimenez, $3,885	72-74-76	222
Dick Lotz, $3,150	79-70-74	223
Tom Shaw, $3,150	75-73-75	223
Jim Ferree, $2,599	72-79-73	224
Rives Mcbee, $2,599	75-77-72	224
Lee Trevino, $2,599	77-73-74	224
Bob Betley, $2,599	75-75-74	224
Lou Graham, $2,205	75-78-72	225
Ken Still, $2,205	79-72-74	225
Roger Kennedy, $2,205	78-70-77	225
Ben Smith, $1,943	78-75-73	226
Don Bies, $1,943	73-76-77	226
Thomas Schafer, $1,785	75-78-74	227
Gay Brewer, $1,628	79-73-76	228
Bob Brue, $1,628	78-73-77	228
Bob Goalby, $1,418	73-80-76	229
Agim Bardha, $1,418	76-76-77	229
Mike Joyce, $1,260	79-76-75	230
Ralph Terry, $1,103	79-76-76	231
Bob Wynn, $1,103	77-80-74	231
Lee Elder, $987	80-77-75	232
Billy Maxwell, $924	75-78-80	233
Don Massengale, $861	80-80-74	234
Charlie Sifford, $798	82-73-82	237
Denny Spencer, $735	79-75-86	240
Chuck Scally, $672	83-79-80	242
Doug Ford, $672	78-82-82	242
Dow Finsterwald, $609	82-86-76	244
Larry Mowry	79-71	WD

GTE North Classic

AT A GLANCE

- **Course:** Broadmoor Country Club
- **Location:** Indianapolis
- **When:** Sept. 10-12, 1993
- **Weather:** Sunny and windy Friday; cool and sunny Saturday. Rain suspended play Sunday morning; then tournament was called at 1:10 p.m. when a second thunderstorm hit.
- **Purse:** $500,000
- **Par:** 72
- **Yards:** 6,670
- **Defending champion:** Ray Floyd, 17-under-par 199
- **Tournament record:** 17-under-par 199, George Archer, 1991, and Ray Floyd, 1992

In 1992, Bob Murphy wasn't sure he'd ever be able to play the Senior PGA Tour. After his second '93 win, he was a leading contender for rookie of the year honors.

Arthritis limited Murphy to only four tournaments and eight rounds on the regular PGA Tour in 1992, and he hadn't earned a penny in PGA competition since 1988.

"I have overcome the arthritis and it is in remission right now. Goodness knows how long it will remain that way and we're trying to take advantage of that," Murphy said after rain and lightning forced officials to cancel the final round of the scheduled 54-hole GTE North Classic.

Murphy, who never started his final round, was declared the winner at 10-under 134 for 36 holes. It was his second victory of '93 and the $75,000 prize gave him a rookie-record $635,563.

Jim Ferree, who shared second place with Chi Chi Rodriguez and Dave Hill, recalled what Murphy went through.

"I can remember when his hands were just so bad he couldn't do anything," Ferree said. "To come back and to get back into top form, which he's certainly in, is very nice. He was a very, very good player on the other tour and not to have the chance to play out here would have been a shame."

Scores and earnings

Player	Score
Bob Murphy, $75,000	68-66—134
Jim Ferree, $36,667	68-68—136
Chi Chi Rodriguez, $36,667	70-66—136
Dave Hill, $36,667	69-67—136
Dave Stockton, $24,000	66-71—137
Rocky Thompson, $18,000	67-71—138
Bob Betley, $18,000	67-71—138
Dewitt Weaver, $18,000	69-69—138
Al Geiberger, $13,500	72-67—139
Richard Bassett, $13,500	72-67—139
Mike Hill, $10,000	69-71—140
Tom Wargo, $10,000	71-69—140
Don January, $10,000	70-70—140
Gibby Gilbert, $10,000	69-71—140
Arnold Palmer, $10,000	73-67—140
Bert Yancey, $10,000	71-69—140
Bobby Nichols, $6,858	70-71—141
Ray Floyd, $6,858	72-69—141
Dale Douglass, $6,858	72-69—141
Gay Brewer, $6,858	70-71—141
Bruce Crampton, $6,858	73-68—141
Jim Albus, $6,858	73-68—141
Lee Trevino, $5,010	73-69—142
Ben Smith, $5,010	72-70—142
Dick Lotz, $5,010	71-71—142
Tommy Aycock, $5,010	76-66—142
Kermit Zarley, $5,010	75-67—142
Art Proctor, $3,713	70-73—143
Rives McBee, $3,713	69-74—143
Joe Jimenez, $3,713	72-71—143
Mike Fetchick, $3,713	71-72—143
Pat O'Brien, $3,713	70-73—143
Bob Menne, $3,713	75-68—143
Larry Gilbert, $3,713	75-68—143
Miller Barber, $3,713	72-71—143
Jerry McGee, $2,760	71-73—144
Larry Laoretti, $2,760	73-71—144
Isao Aoki, $2,760	73-71—144
Dick Hendrickson, $2,760	72-72—144
Harry Toscano, $2,760	73-71—144
Jim Dent, $2,300	73-72—145
Simon Hobday, $2,300	70-75—145
Michel Damiano, $2,300	78-67—145
Terry Dill, $2,300	74-71—145
Bruce Lehnhard, $1,850	69-77—146
Roger Kennedy, $1,850	75-71—146
Charles Coody, $1,850	73-73—146
Bill Hall, $1,850	70-76—146
Al Kelley, $1,850	78-68—146
Larry Ziegler, $1,450	70-77—147
Bob Thatcher, $1,450	77-70—147
Dave Eichelberger, $1,450	75-72—147
Dick Rhyan, $1,025	71-77—148
Walter Morgan, $1,025	71-77—148
Gary Player, $1,025	74-74—148
Walter Zembriski, $1,025	72-76—148
Fred Ruiz, $1,025	72-76—148
John Paul Cain, $1,025	76-72—148
Bob Hauer, $1,025	75-73—148
Dow Finsterwald, $1,025	74-74—148
Jim Stefanich, $1,025	81-67—148
Bob Rosburg, $1,025	78-70—148
Homero Blancas, $750	77-72—149
Bob Brue, $625	73-77—150
Tommy Aaron, $625	78-72—150
Thomas Deaton, $625	74-76—150
Lou Graham, $625	74-76—150
Bob Carson, $485	76-75—151
Charlie Sifford, $485	75-76—151
Jerry Barber, $440	75-77—152
Doug Ford, $380	76-77—153
Charlie Owens, $380	78-75—153
Labron Harris, $380	77-76—153
R. Stuart Chancellor, $320	78-76—154
Mike Joyce, $320	78-76—154
Bob Goalby, $290	75-80—155
Jimmy Powell, $260	80-76—156
Don Massengale, $260	75-81—156
Freddie Haas, $250	83-81—164
Alva Hall, $250	80-88—168

Bank One Classic

At A Glance

- **Course:** Kearney Hills Links
- **Location:** Lexington, Ky.
- **When:** Sept. 17-19, 1993
- **Weather:** Cool and cloudy Friday; sunny and cool Saturday and Sunday.
- **Purse:** $550,000
- **Par:** 72
- **Yards:** 6,768
- **Defending champion:** Terry Dill, 13-under-par 203
- **Tournament record:** 15-under-par 201, Rives McBee, 1990

Gary Player won his 17th Senior PGA Tour title by starting the final round with five consecutive birdies. He finished with a 6-under-par 66 for a 54-hole, 14-under, 202 total and a three-stroke victory in the Bank One Classic.

"What a start!" said Player, who hadn't won since the 1991 Royal Caribbean Classic. "I phoned my son (Wayne) last night. He gave me a little tip and J.C. Snead did, too. Those two gave significant help in what I did."

Snead, who finished seven strokes back at 209, told Player he was moving forward too much on his swing while Wayne reminded him to make a complete backswing.

But it was Player's putting on the first five holes that drew attention.

"He did so well at the start it kind of froze the rest of us out," said Dale Douglass, who closed 69–205.

Player, Douglass and Jim Albus, the final threesome, got off to a rousing start with birdies at No. 1.

On the par-3 second, Player sank a 15-foot birdie putt and Douglass made a 12-footer. Albus missed a 6-footer.

Player followed with a 12-foot birdie on the par-5 third, a 10-footer at No. 4 and a 40-foot putt from the fringe on No. 5.

At 58, Player became the oldest Senior Tour winner in 1993.

"You have to have patience," Player said of winning. "These things happen."

Scores and earnings

Player	Scores	Total
Gary Player, $82,500	68-68-66	202
Dale Douglass, $48,400	66-70-69	205
Jerry McGee, $36,300	70-72-66	208
Jim Albus, $36,300	71-66-71	208
Mike Hill, $22,733	72-67-70	209
Bruce Crampton, $22,733	68-69-72	209
J.C. Snead, $22,733	68-69-72	209
Larry Gilbert, $16,500	71-68-71	210
Dave Stockton, $16,500	69-68-73	210
Gibby Gilbert, $13,200	71-72-68	211
George Archer, $13,200	71-68-72	211
Jim Colbert, $13,200	69-70-72	211
Rives McBee, $10,450	71-72-69	212
Robert Gaona, $10,450	69-72-71	212
Jack Kiefer, $10,450	71-69-72	212
Lee Trevino, $8,800	70-70-73	213
Roger Kennedy, $8,800	71-69-73	213
Walter Morgan, $8,800	69-69-75	213
Bert Yancey, $7,508	69-73-72	214
Bruce Lehnhard, $7,508	71-70-73	214
Jim Ferree, $6,105	72-75-68	215
Mike Joyce, $6,105	75-71-69	215
Bruce Devlin, $6,105	76-68-71	215
Dick Hendrickson, $6,105	67-74-74	215
Jim Dent, $6,105	71-70-74	215
Jimmy Powell, $4,573	70-76-70	216
Gay Brewer, $4,573	76-69-71	216
Larry Laoretti, $4,573	73-71-72	216
Dave Hill, $4,573	73-71-72	216
Dick Lotz, $4,573	71-72-73	216
Rocky Thompson, $4,573	73-68-75	216
Bobby Nichols, $4,573	70-70-76	216
Michel Damiano, $3,465	73-75-69	217
Snell Lancaster, $3,465	75-73-69	217
Bob Wynn, $3,465	74-71-72	217
Tommy Aycock, $3,465	72-73-72	217
Robert Zimmerman, $3,465	72-72-73	217
Terry Dill, $2,970	72-74-72	218
Dick Rhyan, $2,970	67-77-74	218
Dewitt Weaver, $2,695	75-76-68	219
Bob Betley, $2,695	76-73-70	219
Frank Beard, $2,695	72-72-75	219
Kermit Zarley, $2,365	77-71-72	220
Joe Jimenez, $2,365	73-73-74	220
Bob Thatcher, $2,365	73-71-76	220
Rod Curl, $2,035	77-75-69	221
Richard Bassett, $2,035	73-77-71	221
Bob Verwey, $2,035	74-75-72	221
Dave Eichelberger, $1,76	73-74-75	222
Walter Zembriski, $1,760	74-72-76	222
James Benning, $1,595	77-73-73	223
Jim Stefanich, $1,302	75-75-74	224
Doug Dalziel, $1,302	75-75-74	224
Jim O'Hern, $1,302	76-74-74	224
Simon Hobday, $1,302	74-74-76	224
Lou Graham, $1,302	72-75-77	224
Bob Goalby, $1,302	73-74-77	224
Al Kelley, $990	75-78-73	226
Ben Smith, $990	80-73-73	226
Fred Ruiz, $990	77-76-73	226
Don Massengale, $990	74-78-74	226
Labron Harris, $990	74-74-78	226
Miller Barber, $798	75-76-76	227
John Paul Cain, $798	76-74-77	227
Mike Fetchick, $633	79-75-75	229
Bob Menne, $633	76-77-76	229
Harold Henning, $633	76-74-79	229
Billy Maxwell, $633	74-75-80	229
Harry Toscano, $517	77-76-77	230
Dow Finsterwald, $451	76-79-76	231
Bob Rosburg, $451	77-77-77	231
Jesse Vaughn, $451	78-75-78	231
Jerry Barber, $374	77-78-77	232
Jacky Cupit, $374	75-78-79	232
Jack Fleck, $341	78-78-78	234
Randy Glover, $319	83-78-74	235
Doug Ford, $297	82-79-78	239
Buddy Demling, $275	79-80-82	241
Al Besselink, $275	79-81-81	241
Tony Holguin, $275	84-79-80	243
Freddie Haas, $275	80-83-83	246
Marty Furgol, $275	92-89-93	274

NATIONWIDE CHAMPIONSHIP

AT A GLANCE

- **Course:** Country Club of the South
- **Location:** Alpharetta, Ga.
- **When:** Sept. 24-26, 1993
- **Weather:** Warm and pleasant all weekend.
- **Purse:** $950,000
- **Par:** 72
- **Yards:** 6,856
- **Defending champion:** Isao Aoki, 8-under-par 208
- **Tournament record:** 11-under-par 205, Lee Trevino, 1993

Lee Trevino couldn't believe he was so calm.

"Generally I get to spitting cotton," he said. "You could knit a sweater.

"(But) I was about as relaxed as I've ever been."

Trevino never lost the lead he took in the second round of the Nationwide Championship, despite a final-round 1-over-par 73.

"Seventy-three shouldn't have won," Trevino said after his first victory in four months. "I just wanted to go out and see what would happen. I didn't get upset after the double bogey at 11 and the only real mental mistake I made was the tee shot at 15."

His double-bogey 6 on No. 11 came after he drove into water. He missed the green on 15 and missed an 8-foot par putt.

Trevino, the first player to reach $7 million in combined earnings on the Senior Tour and PGA Tour, completed 54 holes in 11-under-par 205.

Finishing in a five-way tie for second, Dave Stockton won $58,520, enough to lift him into the Senior Tour earnings lead with $924,419. Bob Charles, the leader entering the tournament, dropped to second with $905,346.

It was the 17th Seniors victory for Trevino, who has 27 triumphs on the regular Tour.

"I probably shouldn't have won, but I caught a couple of players who weren't playing very well," Trevino said.

Scores and earnings

Player	Scores
Lee Trevino, $142,500	66-66-73–205
Jim Ferree, $58,520	73-68-66–207
Rocky Thompson, $58,520	71-67-69–207
Mike Hill, $58,520	65-73-69–207
Dave Stockton, $58,520	71-66-70–207
George Archer, $58,520	70-66-71–207
Bob Murphy, $30,400	69-71-68–208
Tom Wargo, $30,400	67-69-72–208
Isao Aoki, $30,400	70-65-73–208
Jim Dent, $22,800	71-66-72–209
Kermit Zarley, $22,800	70-67-72–209
Al Geiberger, $22,800	67-68-74–209
Bob Charles, $19,000	69-71-70–210
Bob Betley, $17,575	74-68-69–211
Larry Gilbert, $17,575	71-65-75–211
Simon Hobday, $14,749	73-72-68–213
Gibby Gilbert, $14,749	72-71-70–213
Larry Ziegler, $14,749	72-70-71–213
Jack Nicklaus, $14,749	68-73-72–213
Orville Moody, $11,448	72-72-70–214
Billy Casper, $11,448	72-71-71–214
Dick Hendrickson, $11,448	72-70-72–214
Chi Chi Rodriguez, $11,448	72-69-73–214
Don Bies, $9,738	74-69-72–215
Charles Coody, $9,738	72-70-73–215
Tommy Aaron, $7,899	73-76-67–216
Tom Shaw, $7,899	73-76-67–216
Jerry McGee, $7,899	71-74-71–216
Bruce Crampton, $7,899	71-72-73–216
Walter Zembriski, $7,899	76-67-73–216
Gary Player, $7,899	71-71-74–216
Arnold Palmer, $7,899	71-68-77–216
Mike Joyce, $6,413	67-79-71–217
Doug Dalziel, $6,413	72-71-74–217
Miller Barber, $5,368	74-74-70–218
Gay Brewer, $5,368	71-75-72–218
Rives McBee, $5,368	72-72-74–218
Dale Douglass, $5,368	73-71-74–218
Don January, $5,368	72-71-75–218
Bert Yancey, $5,368	72-67-79–218
Ken Still, $4,560	73-71-75–219
Walter Morgan, $4,560	67-74-78–219
Harry Toscano, $4,085	74-73-73–220
Dewitt Weaver, $4,085	72-73-75–220
Dick Rhyan, $4,085	72-73-75–220
Butch Baird, $3,610	73-74-74–221
Jim Albus, $3,610	71-76-74–221
Jimmy Powell, $3,135	74-77-71–222
Snell Lancaster, $3,135	73-77-72–222
Bob Brue, $3,135	73-75-74–222
Charlie Sifford, $2,755	74-71-79–224
Dick Lotz, $2,248	78-74-73–225
Homero Blancas, $2,248	73-77-75–225
Ben Smith, $2,248	75-75-75–225
Ted Hayes, $2,248	79-71-75–225
John Joseph, $2,248	74-75-76–225
Joe Jimenez, $2,248	78-67-80–225
Jim O'Hern, $1,710	73-82-71–226
Lou Graham, $1,710	81-75-70–226
Lee Elder, $1,710	76-76-74–226
Jim Colbert, $1,710	75-75-76–226
Terry Dill, $1,710	73-74-79–226
Dave Hill, $1,378	79-75-73–227
Bill Hall, $1,378	74-76-77–227
Kenneth Scott, $1,188	80-74-74–228
Dave Eichelberger, $1,188	79-75-74–228
Larry Laoretti, $1,045	76-74-79–229
Billy Maxwell, $922	76-74-80–230
Bob Goalby, $922	74-75-81–230
Calvin Peete, $836	80-77-74–231
Bruce Lehnhard, $779	75-76-81–232
Doug Sanders, $722	79-74-80–233
Bob Wynn, $665	78-79-79–236
Fred Ruiz, $608	85-76-76–237
Bobby Nichols, $608	79-82-76–237

Vantage Championship

AT A GLANCE

- **Course:** Tanglewood Park
- **Location:** Clemmons, N.C.
- **When:** Oct. 1-3, 1993
- **Weather:** Beautiful.
- **Purse:** $1.5 million
- **Par:** 72
- **Yards:** 6,680
- **Defending champion:** Jim Colbert, 12-under-par 132 (tournament shortened to 36 holes because of rain).
- **Tournament record:** 18-under-par 198, Lee Trevino, 1993

When Lee Trevino left the 1992 Senior PGA Tour Vantage Championship in pain, he said he didn't know if his career was over. After winning his second tournament in a row (and third of the year) last October, he was talking about another money title.

Trevino had to withdraw after six holes in 1992 because of a recurring thumb injury. After surgery in December, he didn't play until the Gulfstream Aerospace Invitational March 15, 1993, at Indian Wells, Calif.

Even though he won the Cadillac NFL Classic, he had a difficult year—until suddenly his putting touch returned.

"This gives me a chance to win the money title," Trevino said after his final-round 6-under-par 66 gave him a tournament-record 18-under-par 198 and his 18th Senior Tour victory.

"I knew coming in, I had to squeeze another win in before Puerto Rico (Senior Tour Championship) to have a chance."

With his $225,000 prize, largest on the Senior Tour, Trevino moved within striking distance ($810,124) of money-leaders Bob Charles ($956,346) and Dave Stockton ($951,633).

Runner-up DeWitt Weaver eagled the fourth hole and matched Trevino's 4-under 32 on the front nine. But he lost his chance when he hit an iron off the tee on the 395-yard, water-guarded 13th, which Trevino birdied after hitting driver, sand wedge.

—*by Steve Hershey*

Scores and earnings

Player	Earnings	Scores
Lee Trevino	$225,000	65-67-66–198
Dewitt Weaver	$132,000	71-64-68–203
Jim Dent	$108,000	65-66-73–204
Chi Chi Rodriguez	$90,000	69-67-69–205
Isao Aoki	$66,000	68-69-70–207
Ben Smith	$66,000	70-65-72–207
Bob Betley	$51,000	73-66-69–208
Bob Charles	$51,000	72-66-70–208
Harold Henning	$39,000	70-72-67–209
Don January	$39,000	69-69-71–209
Jim Albus	$39,000	67-70-72–209
Dave Stockton	$27,214	72-71-68–211
Dick Lotz	$27,214	73-70-68–211
Miller Barber	$27,214	71-70-70–211
Kermit Zarley	$27,214	73-67-71–211
Jerry McGee	$27,214	70-68-73–211
Mike Hill	$27,214	72-65-74–211
Jim Colbert	$27,214	73-64-74–211
Jim Ferree	$18,690	73-72-67–212
George Archer	$18,690	72-71-69–212
J.C. Snead	$18,690	72-68-72–212
Rocky Thompson	$18,690	75-66-71–212
Al Geiberger	$18,690	70-69-73–212
Larry Gilbert	$15,750	71-71-72–214
Arnold Palmer	$12,255	77-69-69–215
Bruce Crampton	$12,255	71-74-70–215
Harry Toscano	$12,255	71-73-71–215
Gary Player	$12,255	74-70-71–215
Bob Brue	$12,255	76-68-71–215
Dave Hill	$12,255	75-69-71–215
Charles Coody	$12,255	73-70-72–215
Butch Baird	$12,255	72-71-72–215
Orville Moody	$12,255	74-67-74–215
John Paul Cain	$12,255	74-68-73–215
Jim O'Hern	$7,845	77-70-69–216
Terry Dill	$7,845	74-71-71–216
Mike Fetchick	$7,845	72-72-72–216
Dick Hendrickson	$7,845	72-72-72–216
Tom Shaw	$7,845	73-71-72–216
Jimmy Powell	$7,845	73-71-72–216
Dale Douglass	$7,845	75-69-72–216
Walter Zembriski	$7,845	75-69-72–216
Rives McBee	$7,845	70-72-74–216
Tommy Aaron	$7,845	72-68-76–216
Walter Morgan	$5,700	70-74-73–217
Gibby Gilbert	$5,700	71-72-74–217
Bob Wynn	$5,700	72-71-74–217
Simon Hobday	$5,700	71-71-75–217
Tom Wargo	$4,500	73-75-70–218
Joe Jimenez	$4,500	70-76-72–218
Bob Murphy	$4,500	73-73-72–218
Richard Bassett	$4,500	73-71-74–218
Gay Brewer	$3,675	77-70-72–219
Don Bies	$3,675	72-71-76–219
Roger Kennedy	$3,225	75-75-70–220
Mike Joyce	$3,225	75-73-72–220
Charlie Sifford	$3,225	74-73-73–220
Billy Casper	$3,225	71-72-77–220
Bruce Lehnhard	$2,700	73-75-73–221
Lee Elder	$2,700	70-76-75–221
Doug Dalziel	$2,700	73-73-75–221
Jack Kiefer	$2,250	75-74-73–222
Larry Ziegler	$2,250	70-77-75–222
Babe Hiskey	$2,250	74-69-79–222
Al Kelley	$1,875	74-75-75–224
Bert Yancey	$1,875	76-73-75–224
Larry Laoretti	$1,650	80-70-75–225
Bobby Nichols	$1,500	74-76-76–226
Dick Rhyan	$1,320	83-70-74–227
Bob Goalby	$1,320	70-77-80–227
Ken Still	$1,320	72-73-82–227
Tommy Aycock	$1,140	74-78-76–228
Homero Blancas	$1,050	77-75-77–229
Don Massengale	$990	76-76-78–230
Dow Finsterwald	$930	82-75-78–235
Billy Maxwell	$870	81-75-82–238
Doug Ford	$810	80-77-83–240

Transamerica Senior Golf Championship

AT A GLANCE

- **Course:** Silverado Country Club (South Course)
- **Location:** Napa, Calif.
- **When:** Oct. 8-10, 1993
- **Weather:** Sunny Friday; scattered showers to partly sunny Saturday and Sunday.
- **Purse:** $600,000
- **Par:** 72
- **Yards:** 6,632
- **Defending champion:** Bob Charles, 16-under-par 200
- **Tournament record:** 16-under-par 200, Bob Charles, 1992

Dave Stockton began the final round of the 1992 Transamerica with a two-stroke lead, only to have Bob Charles fire a tournament record-tying 63 and win by one stroke.

In 1993, Stockton began the day three strokes behind leader Tom Shaw, but said he figured it was his turn.

"I was going to try to shoot 63, since it was done to me last year," Stockton said.

He came close, posting a final-round 64 for a one-stroke victory—his fifth of the year. It placed him firmly atop the 1993 earnings list with $1,041,634.

Lee Trevino and Simon Hobday missed putts on the 18th hole that could have tied Stockton.

Stockton birdied the final three holes to edge the South African Hobday and Trevino, who narrowly missed his third victory in three weeks.

Trevino reached the green at the 500-yard par-5 18th in two and needed to sink his 40-foot eagle putt to win. Trevino left his first putt 3½ feet short; then his birdie attempt slid past the hole.

Also reaching the 18th in two, Hobday left his 25-foot, downhill eagle attempt 2 inches short of the cup.

Scores and earnings

Player	Earnings	Scores
Dave Stockton	$90,000	68-71-64–203
Lee Trevino	$48,000	68-70-66–204
Simon Hobday	$48,000	71-66-67–204
Isao Aoki	$29,600	70-69-67–206
J.C. Snead	$29,600	71-68-67–206
Gary Player	$29,600	69-69-68–206
Arnold Palmer	$19,200	70-70-67–207
Tom Shaw	$19,200	68-68-71–207
Chi Chi Rodriguez	$19,200	69-69-69–207
Jim Albus	$15,600	73-71-64–208
Tommy Aycock	$12,360	73-70-66–209
Gibby Gilbert	$12,360	67-73-69–209
Dale Douglass	$12,360	71-69-69–209
Tom Wargo	$12,360	72-67-70–209
Al Geiberger	$12,360	69-69-71–209
Don Bies	$8,770	73-71-66–210
Bob Murphy	$8,770	71-73-66–210
Tommy Aaron	$8,770	71-70-69–210
Dewitt Weaver	$8,770	73-68-69–210
Rives McBee	$8,770	72-68-70–210
Charles Coody	$8,770	70-69-71–210
John Paul Cain	$6,465	73-70-68–211
Walter Zembriski	$6,465	70-72-69–211
Larry Gilbert	$6,465	72-70-69–211
Bob Betley	$6,465	70-71-70–211
Larry Laoretti	$5,220	74-71-67–212
Dick Hendrickson	$5,220	72-72-68–212
Bob Charles	$5,220	71-72-69–212
Mike Hill	$5,220	72-70-70–212
Kermit Zarley	$5,220	74-67-71–212
Dave Eichelberger	$4,230	72-73-68–213
George Archer	$4,230	72-73-68–213
Jimmy Powell	$4,230	72-70-71–213
Orville Moody	$4,230	72-67-74–213
Terry Dill	$3,690	74-72-68–214
Jack Kiefer	$3,690	74-69-71–214
Don January	$3,420	75-70-70–215
Bruce Crampton	$3,060	72-73-71–216
Bill Viele	$3,060	72-73-71–216
Harold Henning	$3,060	70-71-75–216
Ben Smith	$3,060	75-74-67–216
Jim Colbert	$3,060	76-75-65–216
Miller Barber	$2,400	74-71-72–217
Bruce Devlin	$2,400	72-71-74–217
Bob Wynn	$2,400	68-74-75–217
Dick Lotz	$2,400	74-68-75–217
Walter Morgan	$2,400	75-72-70–217
Rocky Thompson	$2,400	77-73-67–217
Mike Joyce	$1,860	74-73-71–218
Robert Zimmerman	$1,860	74-75-69–218
Doug Dalziel	$1,860	76-73-69–218
Larry Ziegler	$1,420	73-73-73–219
Ken Still	$1,420	74-72-73–219
Bert Yancey	$1,420	73-74-72–219
Dick Rhyan	$1,420	74-74-71–219
Bob Brue	$1,420	75-73-71–219
Bruce Lehnhard	$1,420	77-72-70–219
Richard Bassett	$1,140	76-70-74–220
Butch Baird	$1,140	73-74-73–220
Billy Casper	$1,140	77-72-71–220
Phillip Fezler	$900	74-73-74–221
Roger Kennedy	$900	72-75-74–221
Al Kelley	$900	76-73-72–221
Lou Graham	$900	77-73-71–221
Harry Toscano	$900	79-71-71–221
Charlie Sifford	$660	74-73-75–222
Michel Damiano	$660	79-71-72–222
John Brodie	$660	77-75-70–222
Agim Bardha	$546	75-72-76–223
Jerry McGee	$546	73-76-74–223
Doug Sanders	$492	76-75-74–225
Bob Rosburg	$456	80-72-74–226
Fred Ruiz	$420	75-74-78–227
Billy Maxwell	$396	77-75-77–229
Mike Higgins	$372	79-77-76–232
Don Massengale	$348	78-75-80–233
Howie Johnson	$324	82-75-78–235
Dow Finsterwald	$300	80-84-73–237

RALEY'S SENIOR CLASSIC

AT A GLANCE

- **Course:** Rancho Murieta Country Club (North Course)
- **Location:** Rancho Murieta, Calif.
- **When:** Oct. 16-18, 1993
- **Weather:** Beautiful.
- **Purse:** $600,000
- **Par:** 72
- **Yards:** 6,685
- **Defending champion:** Bob Charles, 15-under-par 201
- **Tournament record:** 15-under-par 201, Bob Charles, 1992

George Archer birdied the final hole for a one-stroke win over Bob Charles and Chi Chi Rodriguez in the Senior PGA Tour Raley's Classic. Archer's 14-under-par 202 was one stroke off the tournament record, set by Charles the previous year.

Scores and earnings

George Archer, $90,000	68-66-68–202
Bob Charles, $48,000	66-69-68–203
Chi Chi Rodriguez, $48,000	65-71-67–203
Bob Betley, $29,600	72-69-68–209
Tom Wargo, $29,600	69-70-70–209
Walter Morgan, $29,600	67-70-72–209
Larry Gilbert, $19,200	69-73-68–210
Larry Ziegler, $19,200	71-69-70–210
J.C. Snead, $19,200	71-69-70–210
Isao Aoki, $15,000	72-70-69–211
Orville Moody, $15,000	71-68-72–211
Walter Zembriski, $11,520	70-72-70–212
John Paul Cain, $11,520	72-69-71–212
Tom Shaw, $11,520	77-64-71–212
Rives McBee, $11,520	70-70-72–212
Jim Colbert, $11,520	73-65-74–212
Don Bies, $7,997	71-74-68–213
Charles Coody, $7,997	75-70-68–213
Mike Hill, $7,997	69-73-71–213
Rod Curl, $7,997	68-73-72–213
Gary Player, $7,997	73-68-72–213
Simon Hobday, $7,997	72-69-72–213
Gay Brewer, $7,997	69-70-74–213
Fred Ruiz, $5,610	72-72-70–214
Dick Lotz, $5,610	72-71-71–214
Gibby Gilbert, $5,610	75-68-71–214
Bob Murphy, $5,610	74-69-71–214
Dave Stockton, $5,610	68-72-74–214
Dale Douglass, $5,610	69-71-74–214
Bruce Crampton, $4,740	73-72-70–215
Jerry McGee, $4,320	72-74-70–216
Jack Kiefer, $4,320	73-72-71–216
Richard Bassett, $4,320	66-74-76–216
Dick Hendrickson, $3,612	77-71-69–217
Homero Blancas, $3,612	74-71-72–217
Rocky Thompson, $3,612	69-74-74–217
Butch Baird, $3,612	71-72-74–217
Tommy Aycock, $3,612	68-72-77–217
Ben Smith, $3,180	72-72-74–218
Dewitt Weaver, $2,940	75-74-70–219
Bert Yancey, $2,940	74-73-72–219
Bob Goalby, $2,940	70-73-76–219
Jimmy Powell, $2,400	72-77-71–220
Bob Thatcher, $2,400	75-74-71–220
Miller Barber, $2,400	77-71-72–220
Dick Rhyan, $2,400	73-74-73–220
Jim Ferree, $2,400	70-76-74–220
Al Kelley, $2,400	71-74-75–220
Jim Albus, $1,740	77-73-71–221
Lou Graham, $1,740	74-75-72–221
Roger Kennedy, $1,740	70-76-75–221
Bob Brue, $1,740	76-71-74–221
Tommy Aaron, $1,740	71-75-75–221
Billy Casper, $1,380	75-74-73–222
Jim Hardy, $1,380	70-78-74–222
Kermit Zarley, $1,380	75-71-76–222
Charlie Sifford, $1,140	75-74-74–223
Joe Jimenez, $1,140	72-75-76–223
Bruce Devlin, $1,140	70-76-77–223
Ken Still, $1,140	74-72-77–223
Doug Dalziel, $1,140	75-70-78–223
Jesus Rodriguez, $930	75-75-74–224
Bruce Lehnhard, $930	78-72-74–224
Harry Toscano, $750	78-77-71–226
Bob E. Smith, $750	75-77-74–226
John Brodie, $750	79-74-73–226
Gary Longfellow, $750	75-75-76–226
Larry Laoretti, $582	79-76-72–227
Dave Eichelberger, $582	74-75-78–227
Michel Damiano, $528	76-75-77–228
Robert Dominguez, $492	75-77-77–229
Doug Sanders, $456	78-73-79–230
Lee Elder, $396	82-75-74–231
Mike Joyce, $396	75-78-78–231
Don Massengale, $396	76-75-80–231
Howie Johnson, $348	81-75-79–235
Billy Maxwell	77-77-WD
Bob Wynn	76-80-WD

Ralph's Senior Classic

AT A GLANCE

- **Course:** Rancho Park Golf Course
- **Location:** Los Angeles
- **When:** Oct. 22-24, 1993
- **Weather:** Beautiful.
- **Purse:** $650,000
- **Par:** 71
- **Yards:** 6,307
- **Playoff:** Dale Douglass birdied the first playoff hole to defeat Jim Dent after they tied at 17-under-par 196.
- **Defending champion:** Ray Floyd, 18-under-par 195
- **Tournament record:** 18-under-par 195, Ray Floyd, 1992

Dale Douglass won the Ralph's Senior Classic with a birdie on the first playoff hole, but a 20-foot putt on the 17th was the key to victory.

Jim Dent led Douglass by two strokes going into the final two holes of regulation. He bogeyed No. 17, whereupon Douglass, who had holed a 25-foot putt on the 14th hole, sank his birdie-putt, closing the gap.

"The 17th hole was just amazing," said Douglass, who had a chance to win on the 18th but missed a 9-foot birdie putt.

Douglass and Dent closed with 7-under-par 64s to finish the three-day tournament at 17-under 196 at the Rancho Park course. Jim Albus, George Archer and Isao Aoki tied for third at 14-under.

Douglass and Dent began the day in a three-way tie for fourth, trailing Aoki, Archer and Larry Ziegler by a stroke.

"We waited on quite a few holes," Douglass said. "But it didn't bother me at all. I didn't have anything else to do today."

The victory, worth $97,500, gave Douglass his first Senior Tour victory of the year and 10th of his career.

"This was a thrill for me," he said.

Scores and earnings

Player	Scores
#Dale Douglass, $97,500	66-66-64—196
Jim Dent, $57,200	66-66-64—196
Jim Albus, $39,000	63-70-66—199
Isao Aoki, $39,000	68-63-68—199
George Archer, $39,000	64-67-68—199
Chi Chi Rodriguez, $24,700	68-67-65—200
Dave Stockton, $24,700	67-68-65—200
Harold Henning, $16,467	67-68-66—201
Lee Trevino, $16,467	68-67-66—201
Tom Wargo, $16,467	68-67-66—201
Jim Ferree, $16,467	67-67-67—201
Al Geiberger, $16,467	65-67-69—201
Larry Ziegler, $16,467	63-68-70—201
Dick Lotz, $11,700	66-70-66—202
Tommy Aaron, $11,700	67-69-66—202
Bob Murphy, $11,700	67-69-66—202
Don Bies, $10,400	67-69-67—203
Walter Zembriski, $8,889	68-72-64—204
Jack Kiefer, $8,889	68-71-65—204
Miller Barber, $8,889	70-66-68—204
Jim Colbert, $8,889	63-72-69—204
Rives McBee, $6,684	70-68-67—205
Larry Gilbert, $6,684	69-69-67—205
John Paul Cain, $6,684	66-70-69—205
Bob Betley, $6,684	69-67-69—205
Tom Shaw, $6,684	69-66-70—205
Bruce Crampton, $6,684	69-66-70—205
Bob Wynn, $5,395	69-70-67—206
Mike Hill, $5,395	69-69-68—206
Bert Yancey, $5,395	68-67-71—206
Harry Toscano, $4,583	69-70-68—207
Orville Moody, $4,583	68-70-69—207
J.C. Snead, $4,583	67-71-69—207
Bob Charles, $4,583	67-69-71—207
Mike Joyce, $3,673	71-70-67—208
Homero Blancas, $3,673	69-70-69—208
Don January, $3,673	68-70-70—208
Gibby Gilbert, $3,673	69-69-70—208
Doug Dalziel, $3,673	71-67-70—208
Tommy Aycock, $3,673	70-66-72—208
Rocky Thompson, $2,860	69-72-68—209
Bob Goalby, $2,860	72-70-67—209
Al Kelley, $2,860	68-72-69—209
Kermit Zarley, $2,860	67-72-70—209
Bob Brue, $2,860	71-69-69—209
Charles Coody, $2,860	72-67-70—209
Bob Thatcher, $2,340	72-69-69—210
Terry Dill, $2,340	68-69-73—210
Gay Brewer, $1,831	76-68-67—211
Curtis Sifford, $1,831	73-70-68—211
Gary Player, $1,831	68-74-69—211
Gaylord Burrows, $1,831	69-72-70—211
Butch Baird, $1,831	70-70-71—211
Jerry McGee, $1,831	72-67-72—211
Larry Laoretti, $1,398	72-72-68—212
Dave Eichelberger, $1,398	69-74-69—212
Bruce Lehnhard, $1,398	69-73-70—212
Joe Jimenez, $1,398	70-68-74—212
Ben Smith, $1,170	68-74-71—213
Calvin Peete, $1,170	69-73-71—213
Dick Rhyan, $1,170	69-70-74—213
Jim O'Hern, $975	73-71-70—214
Roger Kennedy, $975	72-71-71—214
Don Massengale, $975	71-72-71—214
Richard Bassett, $780	71-74-70—215
Jimmy Powell, $780	75-69-71—215
Jerry Barber, $780	70-71-74—215
Charlie Sifford, $592	76-70-70—216
Dick Hendrickson, $592	73-71-72—216
Lee Elder, $592	70-73-73—216
Ken Still, $592	73-70-73—216
Michel Damiano, $494	76-71-70—217
Arnold Palmer, $455	72-75-72—219
John Brodie, $429	71-74-75—220
Doug Sanders, $403	77-72-72—221
Dow Finsterwald, $377	73-73-76—222
Fred Ruiz, $338	74-74-75—223
Howie Johnson, $338	77-72-74—223

- won with birdie on first playoff hole

Kaanapali Classic

AT A GLANCE

- **Course:** Royal Kaanapali Golf Club (North Course)
- **Location:** Maui, Hawaii
- **When:** Oct. 29-31, 1993
- **Weather:** Couldn't be better.
- **Purse:** $550,000
- **Par:** 71
- **Yards:** 6,439
- **Playoff:** George Archer birdied the first playoff hole to defeat Dave Stockton and Lee Trevino after they tied at 14-under-par 199.
- **Defending champion:** Tommy Aaron, 15-under-par 198
- **Tournament record:** 18-under-par 195, Jim Colbert, 1991

George Archer didn't think much of his chances when he teed off in the final round of the Kaanapali Classic.

Archer trailed leader Dave Stockton by four shots and 10 other golfers were either ahead of or tied with him. The absence of the usual blustery trade winds guaranteed low scores.

But as Archer would say later, "When you shoot a 63, you have a chance to do something."

Archer's 8-under-par 63 propelled him into a playoff with Stockton and Lee Trevino. Stockton closed with a 67, Trevino with a 64. Trevino, who never held or shared the lead until the final hole, snuck into the playoff by making a 20-foot birdie putt from the collar of the 18th green.

Archer put matters to a quick end, sinking a 25-foot birdie putt on the first extra hole.

It was Archer's fourth victory of the year and his third in four tries. Before Kaanapali, he was fourth on the money list.

"I've had a lot of fun this year," Archer said. "Life's real good for me right now. My wife lets me do a little hunting and she gets to play with grandkids so we're having a ball."

Scores and earnings

#George Archer, $82,500	67-69-63–199
Lee Trevino, $44,000	68-67-64–199
Dave Stockton, $44,000	66-66-67–199
Don January, $33,000	69-67-65–201
Jimmy Powell, $24,200	69-68-65–202
Bob Murphy, $24,200	65-69-68–202
Jim Colbert, $18,700	70-67-66–203
Tom Wargo, $18,700	65-68-70–203
Rocky Thompson, $13,200	71-68-66–205
Tommy Aaron, $13,200	68-69-68–205
Terry Dill, $13,200	69-67-69–205
Bruce Crampton, $13,200	66-69-70–205
Mike Hill, $13,200	68-66-71–205
Bob Charles, $10,175	70-68-68–206
Jim Albus, $10,175	69-68-69–206
Gary Cowan, $7,802	71-69-67–207
Tom Shaw, $7,802	70-69-68–207
Dale Douglass, $7,802	70-68-69–207
Charles Coody, $7,802	66-71-70–207
Doug Dalziel, $7,802	69-68-70–207
Walter Morgan, $7,802	69-68-70–207
Dewitt Weaver, $7,802	71-66-70–207
Bob Betley, $5,272	69-71-68–208
Bert Yancey, $5,272	69-70-69–208
Babe Hiskey, $5,272	70-69-69–208
Harold Henning, $5,272	71-67-70–208
John Paul Cain, $5,272	69-68-71–208
Gibby Gilbert, $5,272	69-68-71–208
Larry Laoretti, $5,272	68-68-72–208
Don Bies, $4,143	70-72-67–209
Tommy Aycock, $4,143	72-69-68–209
Bob Brue, $4,143	69-67-73–209
Jack Kiefer, $3,630	72-70-68–210
Dick Lotz, $3,630	67-71-72–210
Dick Rhyan, $3,630	70-67-73–210
Gay Brewer, $3,094	72-71-68–211
Jerry McGee, $3,094	74-67-70–211
Al Kelley, $3,094	75-69-67–211
Al Geiberger, $3,094	71-68-72–211
Mike Joyce, $2,640	71-71-70–212
Jim Dent, $2,640	72-68-72–212
Jim Ferree, $2,640	78-67-67–212
Miller Barber, $2,640	74-72-66–212
Keith Alexander, $2,145	69-73-71–213
Jack Fleck, $2,145	71-70-72–213
Kermit Zarley, $2,145	74-69-70–213
Ken Still, $2,145	75-69-69–213
Ben Smith, $2,145	76-69-68–213
Butch Baird, $1,705	73-70-71–214
Larry Gilbert, $1,705	74-71-69–214
Bruce Lehnhard, $1,705	67-69-78–214
Bob Menne, $1,485	77-69-69–215
Bob Rawlins, $1,320	74-69-73–216
Dave Eichelberger, $1,320	74-71-71–216
Richard Bassett, $1,320	74-74-68–216
Dick Hendrickson, $1,210	75-73-69–217
Charlie Sifford, $1,073	73-74-71–218
Dean Prince, $1,073	76-71-71–218
Fred Ruiz, $1,073	77-70-71–218
Lou Graham, $1,073	79-70-69–218
Bob Wynn, $853	74-69-76–219
Orville Moody, $853	74-71-74–219
Lee Elder, $853	72-74-73–219
Michel Damiano, $853	78-68-73–219
Harry Toscano, $688	80-69-71–220
Mike Fetchick, $688	74-78-68–220
Jerry Barber, $605	71-73-77–221
Bob Thatcher, $550	76-73-73–222
Joe Jimenez, $501	73-73-78–224
Roger Kennedy, $501	76-75-73–224
Doug Sanders, $435	73-76-77–226
Tom Matthews, $435	83-73-70–226
Bob Rosburg, $385	74-78-75–227
Randy Glover, $363	77-76-75–228
Jim Stefanich, $341	73-76-81–230
Ray Demello, $308	78-76-79–233
Dow Finsterwald, $308	77-78-78–233
Howie Johnson, $275	77-79-79–235
Doug Ford, $275	79-80-78–237
Masa Kaya, $275	80-80-82–242
Tony Holguin, $275	81-83-80–244

- won on first playoff hole

Senior Tour Championship

At a Glance

- **Course:** Hyatt Dorado Beach (East Course)
- **Location:** Dorado, Puerto Rico
- **When:** Dec. 10-12, 1993
- **Weather:** Windy and warm.
- **Purse:** $1 million
- **Par:** 72
- **Yards:** 6,740
- **Defending champion:** Ray Floyd, 19-under-par 197
- **Tournament record:** 19-under-par 197, Ray Floyd, 1992

Simon Hobday, a free-spirited South African, took a night off from carousing and turned it into his biggest career payday.

"I ducked out on my mates before they could get me into a bar," Hobday said after his bogey-free final-round 67 gave him a two-stroke victory in the Senior Tour Championship.

He was referring to the night before his triumph, when he took a break from his usual routine and got a good night's sleep before the final round of the season-ending event.

Mistakes by Dave Stockton and Larry Gilbert, Hobday's playing partners, paved the way for his second victory of the year. The three had entered the final round tied for the lead.

First Stockton knocked himself out of the lead when he popped up a 4-wood second shot into the water and made a bogey-6 at No. 13 while Hobday made birdie and Gilbert eagle.

Then, on the final hole and in a tie with Hobday for the lead, Gilbert got his 7-iron approach into an awkward position in the left bunker, came out long and then three-putted for double bogey, running his 20-foot par putt 5 feet past the hole.

"It's a cruel game sometimes," Gilbert said.

Gilbert, a rookie on the over-50 circuit and not yet a winner, shot 69 and tied for second with defending champion Ray Floyd at 201.

Floyd, who never got closer than two shots, had an eagle in his 66.

Stockton slipped to a 70 and was fourth at 202. He led the seniors with five victories this season and also completed the season as the top money-winner at $1,175,944. But he needed to at least tie for second to achieve his goal, beating Trevino's single-season money-winning record of $1,190,518.

He won $60,000 but admitted "I'm disappointed in that. I really wanted to catch Lee (Trevino) and I missed by a shot."

Hobday, who played most of his golf in South Africa and on the PGA European Tour before joining the Senior PGA Tour three seasons ago, acknowledged the mistakes of Stockton on 13 and Gilbert on 18 were crucial.

But he also quickly pointed out that both played with more confidence and control than he did.

"Larry gave it a full run and Stockton got a little unlucky there on the back," Hobday said.

"They weren't choking," Hobday said. "I was choking.

"I was shaking like a dog out there. But I'll tell you this: it couldn't have happened to a nicer guy."

Scores and earnings

Player	Rounds–Total
Simon Hobday, $150,000	64-68-67–199
Ray Floyd, $95,000	71-64-66–201
Larry Gilbert, $95,000	66-66-69–201
Dave Stockton, $60,000	66-66-70–202
Bob Murphy, $48,000	66-71-66–203
Kermit Zarley, $38,000	70-70-65–205
Lee Trevino, $38,000	68-70-67–205
George Archer, $28,750	72-69-66–207
Tom Wargo, $28,750	72-67-68–207
Dale Douglass, $28,750	70-68-69–207
Jim Albus, $28,750	68-68-71–207
J.C. Snead, $24,500	72-69-67–208
Bob Charles, $22,500	69-69-71–209
Jack Kiefer, $22,500	69-68-72–209
Jim Dent, $20,500	69-73-68–210
Gibby Gilbert, $20,500	71-69-70–210
Isao Aoki, $20,500	73-68-69–210
Al Geiberger, $19,500	72-69-70–211
Mike Hill, $19,000	72-73-67–212
Jim Colbert, $18,000	75-71-67–213
Rocky Thompson, $18,000	74-72-67–213
Tom Shaw, $18,000	72-68-73–213
Dewitt Weaver, $17,000	72-73-69–214
Walter Zembriski, $16,000	70-73-72–215
Miller Barber, $16,000	72-72-71–215
Chi Chi Rodriguez, $16,000	72-69-74–215
Harold Henning, $15,000	73-74-69–216
Jim Ferree, $14,750	73-71-74–218
Bruce Crampton, $14,500	70-72-77–219
Bob Betley, $14,250	73-73-75–221

1993 Skins Games

Senior Skins Game

▸**Course:** Mauna Lani Resort
▸**Location:** Kohala Coast, Hawaii
▸**When:** Jan. 30-31, 1993
▸**Par:** 72
▸**Yards:** 6,763
▸**Defending champion:** Arnold Palmer

Nothing compares to his historic successes at Augusta National or Cherry Hills, but these days Arnold Palmer gladly settles for the Mauna Lani Resort.

At 63, Palmer doesn't dream of more Masters wins or shooting 65 to pass 14 players and win the U.S. Open as he did at Cherry Hills in Denver in 1960.

What he still seeks are Senior Skins titles at the lava-bordered Mauna Lani course—not only seeks, but wins.

After dropping a 22-foot birdie putt worth $140,000 to clinch his third Skins title in four years, Palmer romped around and slapped high-fives with the gallery.

Palmer won $190,000 from the purse of $450,000. Chi Chi Rodriguez, who got into the field as a replacement for Lee Trevino, won $145,000, including $70,000 in a playoff. Jack Nicklaus won $55,000 and Ray Floyd $60,000.

"Sometimes, I forget just how fortunate I've been," Palmer said before the 18-hole event.

The crowds never have left him. As Lee Trevino pointed out, "more people go watch Arnie load his clubs in his car than watch the leaders at some tournaments."

—*by Steve Hershey*

JCPenney/LPGA Skins Game

▸**Course:** Stonebriar Country Club
▸**Location:** Frisco, Texas
▸**When:** May 29-30, 1993
▸**Par:** 72
▸**Yards:** 6,070
▸**Defending champion:** Pat Bradley

Betsy King was thinking only of making the 3-foot putt on the 17th hole, worth $70,000. Others had to tell her the putt clinched the JCPenney/LPGA Skins Game.

"I didn't realize it," King said. "What a nice surprise."

King added a birdie at No. 18 to win the final skin and increase her earnings to $185,000. Nancy Lopez earned $110,000, all the first-day.

Defending champion Pat Bradley earned $85,000. Dottie Mochrie averted a shutout by knocking a nine-iron to 2 feet on the par-four 15th and tapping in the birdie for $70,000.

All four players stood on the 17th tee with a shot at the championship.

King, Mochrie and Bradley put their tee shots close to the cup as rain began. After a two hour delay due to the threat of lightning, Bradley and Mochrie missed from 10 and 6 feet, but King made her short putt to claim the two skins and $70,000.

"It was worth the wait," King said. "But I really thought Dottie was going to make her putt."

SKINS GAME

- **Course:** Bighorn Golf Club
- **Location:** La Quinta, Calif.
- **When:** Nov. 27-28, 1993
- **Par:** 72
- **Yards:** 6,848
- **Defending champion:** Payne Stewart

Fred Couples stopped Arnold Palmer but not Payne Stewart.

Couples twice made long putts to keep Palmer from winning skins, but he missed two putts that could have kept Stewart from a third consecutive Skins Game title.

Stewart sank putts worth $100,000 and $120,000 in becoming the only player to win three consecutive Skins titles and be the career money leader in the made-for-TV event, with $760,000.

Couples, runner-up in 1992, earned $260,000. Palmer, who replaced the suspended John Daly, and Paul Azinger were shut out.

"I just couldn't make the putts against Payne," Couples said.

Said Stewart: "I'm fortunate the couple of putts I did make were very big. If I miss the putt at 13 and Freddie makes his, he wins the whole thing."

Instead, Stewart made his 15-foot birdie, then watched Couples miss from 12 feet for the halve. The hole was worth $100,000, since the previous two holes were halved.

Stewart, Couples and Azinger all said they wished Palmer, 64, had won a skin.

"I haven't felt that bad all year," Couples said about taking the skin on 18 from Palmer.

By Russell Beeker, USA TODAY

George Archer won four seniors tournaments and finished third on the money list with $963,124 in 1993.

USGA REPORT

U.S. AMATEUR ...191

IN PURSUIT OF BOBBY JONES...192

U.S. JUNIOR AMATEUR...193

AND MUCH MORE...

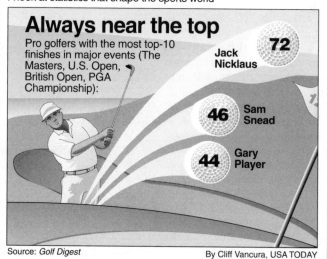

1993 USGA: Harris won two, Tiger won third

Few surprises were expected in 1993 U.S. Golf Association tournaments. But one name seemed sure to dominate headlines: Eldrick (Tiger) Woods.

Would Woods, the 17-year-old Californian, win his third consecutive U.S. Junior Amateur?

Only the annual spectacle of watching the world's best golfers hack their way through the rough and struggle to putt the formica-fast greens of the U.S. Open would rate close to Woods' bid for a three-peat.

But along came John.

John Harris, 41, an insurance executive from Edina, Minn., had the golf experience most players can't imagine. In a stretch of 12 days, Harris twice sat atop the world of amateur golf.

On Aug. 19, Harris clinched the USA's Walker Cup victory, sinking a putt to defeat reigning British Amateur champion Iain Pyman 3 and 2. Harris' son, Chris, 15, served as his caddy, and the matches were played in his hometown (Interlachen Country Club, Edina, Minn.), as the USA walked over Britain-Ireland 19-5.

On Aug. 30, Harris, again with Chris as his caddy, defeated 22-year-old Danny Ellis 5 and 3 in their 36-hole final to win the U.S. Amateur championship.

Harris was a popular winner in both matches. At the Walker Cup, many friends and relatives walked the course with him in each match.

At the Amateur at Champions Golf Club in Houston, Harris defeated U.S. Public Links champion David Berganio 3 and 2 and defending Amateur champion Justin Leonard 2 and 1—the same day.

"If I was going to lose, I wanted it to be to John Harris," Leonard, a University of Texas golfer, said after their match. "He is a great player and a great gentleman."

Harris, named Minnesota Golfer of the Year seven consecutive times, is part of a family that shares 38 state championships. John has 14 with the other 24 shared by his father, Dr. Bob Harris, brothers Rob, Mark and Scott and sister Nancy Harris Blanchard.

Tiger Woods won his third straight U.S. Jr. Amateur.

For his U.S. Amateur victory, Harris received invitations to play in The Masters, U.S. Open, British Open and British Amateur. He also will be invited to play several PGA Tour events.

Woods? He moves on to college golf at Stanford and the adult amateur ranks, undoubtedly preparing for a pro career.

But he grabbed his third consecutive junior title in dramatic fashion.

Deep in trouble in the championship match against Ryan Armour, 17, of Silver Lake, Ohio, all Woods did was birdie both the 17th and 18th holes to square the match, then made par on the first extra hole to win.

Woods played the third consecutive championship low-key.

"The only thing special about it was my comeback," he said. "I had to play the best two holes of my life—birdie on 17, birdie on 18. I did it."

—by Don Cronin

United States Amateur

AT A GLANCE

▶ **Course:** Champions Golf Club (Cypress Creek Course)
▶ **Location:** Houston, Texas
▶ **When:** Aug. 24-29, 1993
▶ **Weather:** Hot and very humid.
▶ **Par:** 71
▶ **Yards:** 7,148
▶ **Defending champion:** Justin Leonard

John Harris skipped lunch on Aug. 29, then feasted at a late-afternoon victory party.

During a midmatch break in the U.S. Amateur finals, Danny Ellis ate lunch and played cards. Harris went straight to the putting green and got some advice from his son, and caddy, Chris, 15.

When play resumed, Harris birdied the 19th hole. He didn't miss a green the rest of the match, defeating Ellis 5 and 3 for the championship.

Asked to describe his feelings at winning the tournament after several narrow misses, Harris said, "I grew up playing on sandy greens in . . ." before he became too choked with emotion to speak.

With the victory, Harris, 41, picked up invitations to play in The Masters and U.S. and British Opens.

He was qualifying medalist in the 1991 U.S. Amateur and reached the quarterfinals last year. He tried to make it on the pro tour in the late 1970s but fell short.

Harris continued to work on his game and play amateur events. Finally, his moment came.

Harris took a 3-hole lead early in the scheduled 36-hole final. But near the end of the first 18 holes, Ellis went 1 up. Harris began worrying that his dream was fading.

"I worked so hard over the break to get myself mentally ready for the afternoon round," Harris said. "I was confused. There was a virus in my game. I went out and hit 50-60 balls and putted for 30 minutes."

Chris caddied for his father throughout the tournament and gave him pointed advice.

"He knows the four or five things that usually go wrong with my game and he watches for those things," Harris said. "He was really good out there today."

In the afternoon round, Harris had a par on the 10th hole and ran in a 24-foot birdie on the 11th hole to take control of the match.

He missed a 4-foot putt for a bogey at No. 12, giving Ellis another chance to get back into the match.

"But then I hit it to the right and made a bogey," Ellis said. "If I could have birdied that hole, it could have been different."

Instead, Harris won the final three holes. Ellis conceded on the 33rd hole before either golfer holed out.

Harris said his son suggested he alter his putting stance.

"I tend to get conservative out there," Harris said. "Chris is very aggressive. His big thing is to remind me to trust myself and let it happen. He's a big help."

Ellis, who played at Clemson (S.C.) University, never solved his putting woes although he remained close until the start of the back nine in the afternoon.

"I didn't putt real well and I didn't hit my driver too well either," Ellis said. "The putter didn't do anything."

REVENGE: Qualifying medalist Brian Gay, 22, of Daleville, Ala., avenged a loss to England's Van Phillips in the Walker Cup the week before. Gay made a 12-foot birdie putt on the final hole of first-round match play, defeating Phillips 1 up.

"I figured I'd have to make birdie to win, or else we'd go extra holes," said Gay, who had built a 2-up lead through nine holes before Phillips pulled even with a par on the 15th. Gay was a University of Florida senior.

In Pursuit of Jones

Jack Nicklaus and Anne Sander—one name recognizable to even the least interested observer of golf and the other comparably unknown—continued their climb toward golf immortality in 1993.

Both closed in on the legendary Bobby Jones' record of nine U.S. Golf Association national championships. Nicklaus took his eighth title with his victory at the U.S. Senior Open. Sander, a life-long amateur, collected her seventh—winning the USGA Senior Women's Amateur for the fourth time.

Nicklaus' first USGA championship came in the U.S. Amateur as a 19-year-old Ohio State University freshman. He later added another Amateur, four U.S. Opens and two Senior Open titles.

Sander, a longtime Seattle resident who now lives in Santa Barbara, Calif., began her run with the 1958 U.S. Women's Amateur, won that two more times and has added four Senior Women's titles.

LEADERS IN USGA TITLES

- **Bobby Jones—9:** ('23, '26, '29-'30 Open; '24-'25, '27-'28, '30 Amateur)
- **Jack Nicklaus—8:** ('59, '61 Amateur; '62, '67, '72, '80 Open; '91, '93 Senior Open)
- **JoAnne Carner—8:** ('56 Girls Junior; '57, '60, '62, '66, '68 Women's Amateur; '71, '76 Women's Open)
- **Anne Sander—7:** ('58, '61, '63 Women's Amateur; '87, '89-'90, '93 Senior Women's Amateur)
- **Hollis Stacy—6:** ('69-'70-'71 Girls Junior; '77-'78, '84 Women's Open)
- **Glenna Collett Vare—6:** ('22, '25, '28-'29, '30, '35 Women's Amateur)
- **Jerome Travers—5:** ('07-'08, '12-'13 Amateur; '15 Open)
- **Mickey Wright—5:** ('52 Girls Junior; '58-'59, '61, '64 Women's Open)
- **Carolyn Cudone—5:** ('68-'69-'70-'71-'72 Senior Women's Amateur)
- **Dorothy Porter—5:** ('49 Women's Amateur; '77, '80-'81, '83 Senior Women's Amateur)
- **Jay Sigel—5:** ('82-'83 Amateur; '83, '85, '87 Mid-Amateur)

Source: U.S. Golf Association

Women's Amateur Public Links

- **Course:** Jackson Hole Golf & Tennis Club
- **Location:** Jackson, Wyo.
- **When:** June 23-27, 1993
- **Weather:** Cool and comfortable.
- **Par:** 72
- **Yards:** 6,112
- **Defending champion:** Amy Fruhwirth

Connie Masterson did not lead the final match until she birdied the 14th hole. But she managed to hang on for a 1-up victory against Holly Reynolds to win the U.S. Women's Amateur Public Links Championship.

"I'm a battler; I don't let anything get me down," Masterson, a senior at Central Florida University, said. "I just kept telling myself, 'You can win this.' I felt like I was in control because I came from 2 down. I haven't won a golf tournament since junior golf. I can't even remember back that far. I must have been 15 or 16, somewhere in there."

Masterson started shakily, losing three consecutive holes to go 2 down after four holes. But Reynolds, 21, of Morrisville, Vt., didn't win another hole.

Masterson came back with pars on the seventh and ninth holes to tie the match.

The deciding hole was the 372-yard, par-4 14th, where Masterson, 21, of Sorrento, Fla., holed a 12-footer for birdie. They halved the next four holes, three with pars and each with a birdie-3 on 17.

Masterson reached the final with a 4 and 2 win over Jill McGill, 21, of Denver. Reynolds advanced with a 3 and 2 win over Missy Arthur, 21, of Ames, Iowa.

Amateur Public Links

▸**Course:** Riverdale Dunes Golf Club (Dunes Course)
▸**Location:** Brighton, Colo.
▸**When:** July 12-17, 1993
▸**Weather:** Cloudy and cool.
▸**Par:** 71
▸**Yards:** 6,922
▸**Defending champion:** Warren Schutte

David Berganio of Sylmar, Calif., took a commanding 5-up lead after 27 holes and went on to defeat Brandon Knight of Argyle, Texas, 2 and 1 in the scheduled 36-hole final of the U.S. Amateur Public Links Championship.

Berganio, who won the 1991 publinx title and was qualifying medalist this year, had a 1-up lead after 18 holes. He had four birdies on the front nine in the afternoon to take a 5-up lead and was in control thereafter.

U.S. Junior Amateur

▸**Course:** Waverly Country Club
▸**Location:** Portland, Ore.
▸**When:** July 27-31, 1993
▸**Weather:** Warm and humid.
▸**Par:** 70
▸**Yards:** 6,465
▸**Defending champion:** Eldrick "Tiger" Woods

Golf historians might as well put the name Eldrick "Tiger" Woods in the books.

When he won his second consecutive U.S. Junior Amateur championship in '92, he became the first to win two titles. Now, he has the triple crown.

Woods won his third junior championship at Waverly Country Club in Portland, Ore., defeating Ryan Armour on the first playoff hole.

The Cypress, Calif. resident rolled in a 4-foot par putt on the 19th hole of their scheduled 18-hole match leaving Armour, 17, of Silver Lake, Ohio, heartbroken. Armour made quite a comeback after being trounced 8 and 6 by Woods in the '92 quarterfinals.

Armour had Woods 2 down with two holes to play after Woods missed a short putt on No. 16. All Armour needed was to halve one of the final two holes. But Woods' birdie-birdie finish forced the extra hole.

"If I parred 17, I thought I'd win this match," said Armour.

Woods has won 18 consecutive Junior Amateur matches and is 22-1 in four years.

Four players have finished 1-2 in the Junior Amateur: Tim Straub won in 1983 after being runner-up in '82; Mike Brannan won in '71 and was runner-up two years later; Eddie Pearce won in '68 and was runner-up the following year, and Mason Rudolph won in '50 after finishing second in '49.

In the semifinals a day earlier, Woods beat U.S. Open qualifier Ted Oh, 16, of Torrance, Calif., 4 and 3. Armour ousted 94-pound Charles Howell, 14, of Augusta, Ga., 4 and 3.

"I started out bad and gave him some quick, easy ones," Oh said. "I had a couple of lip-outs that I should have made. That's golf."

Said Woods, "I played extremely solid against Ted. On the back side, I went and took the match."

Girls' Junior Championship

▸**Course:** Mesa Verde Country Club
▸**Location:** Costa Mesa, Calif.
▸**When:** Aug. 2-7, 1993
▸**Weather:** Hot and breezy.
▸**Par:** 72
▸**Yards:** 5,934
▸**Defending champion:** Jamie Koizumi

Kellee Booth of Coto de Caza, Calif., chipped in from 20 feet on the 18th hole to win the 45th U.S. Girls Junior Championship 1 up against Erika Hayashida of Peru.

Booth was 1 up as they went to the 18th tee at Costa Mesa (Calif.) Country Club. Her tee shot on the 159-yard par-3 just missed the green. Hayashida nearly holed her 3-iron tee shot, but Booth then made her chip for the victory.

Women's Amateur

▸**Course:** San Diego Country Club
▸**Location:** Chula Vista, Calif.
▸**When:** Aug. 9-14, 1993
▸**Weather:** Warm and windy early in the week; calm the last three days.
▸**Par:** 73
▸**Yards:** 6,330
▸**Defending champion:** Vicki Goetze

Jill McGill, of Denver, Colo., made a 45-foot birdie putt on the third hole and led the rest of the way to defeat Sarah Ingram, of Nashville, Tenn., 1 up for the U.S. Women's Amateur title.

McGill, a senior at Southern California, increased her margin to 4 up through 17 holes before Ingram rallied to cut the margin to 1 up on the 34th hole of the 36-hole final match.

"I think having no expectations coming into this week helped me," said McGill, who, along with Ingram, failed to qualify for match play a year ago. "Or maybe it was the Broncos cap, I don't know. But I'm really excited because it shows a lot of progress in my game."

Ingram was the more experienced of the two, having played on the 1992 U.S. Curtis Cup and World Amateur teams. She also won the 1991 U.S. Women's Mid-Amateur title and has played in nine Amateurs, compared to McGill's three.

"If I could have just gotten it to 1-up a little earlier," said Ingram, who just missed a chip for birdie that would have tied the match on the final hole. "If I hadn't 3-putted that 13th hole. That probably was the killer right there."

U.S. Women's Mid-Amateur

▸**Course:** Rochester Golf & Country Club
▸**Location:** Rochester, Minn.
▸**When:** Sept. 11-16, 1993
▸**Weather:** Weekend was sunny and warm. Rain postponed Monday play to Tuesday. Overcast, damp and cool Tuesday, Wednesday and early Thursday, with warming Thursday afternoon.
▸**Par:** 72
▸**Yards:** 5,930
▸**Defending champion:** Marion Maney-McInerney parred the first extra hole to defeat Carol Semple Thompson.

Sarah Labrun Ingram rolled past six match-play opponents—including Mary Burkhardt of St. Augustine, Fla., who she defeated 2 and 1 in the 18-hole final—to win her second U.S. Women's Mid-Amateur Championship.

Ingram, 27, from Nashville, Tenn., won the title 33 days after she lost the U.S. Women's Amateur final to University of Southern California golfer Jill McGill. She was trying to join Carol Semple Thompson as the only player to win both titles.

"Winning here doesn't make up for not winning the Amateur," Ingram said. "But I couldn't be happier. This makes a good finish for the year. I started the summer by winning (the Broadmoor, Colorado Invitational) and ended with a win."

Ingram, a former Duke University All-American, was 6-under par through her first five match victories, but struggled and was 6-over in the final. Burkhardt, from the University of Alabama Birmingham, was 7-over.

Burkhardt chipped in at No. 12 to pull even but gave it back with a bogey at 13. Ingram won the match with her third consecutive bogey, at 17.

In the semifinals, Ingram defeated Wendy Kaupp of Los Altos, Calif., 5 and 4 and Burkhardt defeated Andrea Gaston of Canoga Park, Calif., in 20 holes.

Ingram won the 1991 championship in Scottsdale, Ariz.

Mid-Amateur

▸**Course:** Eugene Country Club
▸**Location:** Eugene, Ore.
▸**When:** Sept. 18-23, 1993
▸**Weather:** Beautiful.
▸**Par:** 72
▸**Yards:** 6,713
▸**Defending champion:** Danny Yates, of Atlanta, defeated David Lind, of Burr Ridge, Ill., 1 up.

Just a few months after switching to a long-shafted putter with a split grip, Jeff

Thomas of South Plainfield, N.J., rolled in a 2-foot par putt on the final hole to defeat Joey Ferrari of Lodi, Calif., 1 up and win the U.S. Men's Mid-Amateur Championship.

Thomas, 34, said he "never would have made (the winning putt) with a short putter. I could make more 20-footers than I could 3- or 4-footers with a regular putter. The long putter takes my nerves out of the game."

Thomas took an early 2-up lead, but Ferrari made a charge, as he had on the back nine to win his quarterfinal and semifinal matches. Ferrari won the 15th with a par, then pulled within one at the 17th with a birdie from 3 feet.

Ferrari earlier was runner-up for both the California Amateur and Northern California Amateur championships.

Jay Coatta of Hopkins, Minn., was qualifying medalist at 69-70–139, a stroke ahead of Paul Murphy of Arlington, Mass.

Defending champion Danny Yates of Atlanta was eliminated 2 and 1 in the first round by Jerry Courville of Norwalk, Conn.

SENIOR AMATEUR

▸**Course:** Farmington Country Club
▸**Location:** Charlottesville, Va.
▸**When:** Sept. 20-25, 1993
▸**Weather:** Overcast and rainy.
▸**Par:** 70
▸**Yards:** 6,354
▸**Defending champion:** Clarence Moore

Joe Ungvary, 55, of Cuyahoga Falls, Ohio, won three of the first four holes and went on to a record-setting 7 and 6 victory against Jerry Nelson, 55, of Warsaw, Ind., to win the U.S. Senior Amateur Championship at Farmington Country Club.

Ungvary, an employee of the Summit County Treasurer's Office, finished 4-under par and didn't allow Nelson to win a hole. He closed out the match with a 7-foot birdie putt on the 13th hole for the largest margin of victory ever in a Senior Amateur championship.

"I just had it inside me that I knew I could do it," said Ungvary, who sports a license plate that reads 'Even Par.' "Something like this only happens once. I put everything into it I had."

Of Ungvary's two birdies in the first three holes, Nelson said, "I was stunned. I don't remember anyone coming at me that hard before. Now I know how Custer must have felt."

To reach the final, Ungvary shot four birdies and never trailed in a 3 and 2 victory against Robert Housen, 55, of Brielle, N.J. Nelson won holes 12 and 13 with pars, then hung on for a 1 up semifinal victory against Jim McMurtrey, 61, of Danville, Calif.

SENIOR WOMEN'S AMATEUR

▸**Course:** Preakness Hills Country Club
▸**Location:** Wayne, N.J.
▸**When:** Sept. 29-Oct. 1, 1993
▸**Weather:** Sunny and clear except for scattered rain Thursday.
▸**Par:** 72
▸**Yards:** 5,843
▸**Defending champion:** Rosemary Thompson, 50, of Albuquerque, N.M.

Anne Sander of Santa Barbara, Calif., trailed by four strokes starting the final round, but shot a 1-over-par 73 for a three-stroke victory and her fourth U.S. Senior Women's Amateur championship. She finished at 2-over 230.

Sander, 57, has played in more U.S. Golf Association competitions than any other comer.

"This is the most gratifying of the four (titles)," Sander said. "This course is the most difficult of the four. I've never struggled so hard to win."

Sander, winner in 1987, '89 and '90, is one off Carolyn Cudone's record five titles. A three-time U.S. Women's Amateur champion, she trails only Robert T. Jones Jr. (nine), JoAnne Gunderson Carner and Jack Nicklaus (eight each) in USGA championships.

PGA Championship winner Paul Azinger finished second to Bernhard Langer in the PGA Grand Slam of Golf, a made-for-television showdown involving the year's four majors winners.

GOLF ALMANAC 1994

PGA OF AMERICA

PGA OF AMERICA TOURNAMENTS ...198

USA SNAPSHOTS®
A look at statistics that shape the sports world

Counting golf's champions
In the past 11 years, golfers who won their first major championship at:

- PGA — 8
- Masters — 5
- British Open — 5
- U. S. Open — 4

Source: USA TODAY research By Elys A. McLean, USA TODAY

1993 PGA OF AMERICA TOURNAMENTS

MAXFLI PGA JUNIOR CHAMPIONSHIP

▶**Course:** Pinehurst Golf Resort & Country Club (No. 4)
▶**Location:** Pinehurst, N.C.
▶**When:** Aug. 24-27, 1993
▶**Weather:** Very hot and humid.
▶**Par:** 72
▶**Yards:** Boys—6,618; Girls—5,679
▶**Defending champions:** D.A. Points, Pekin, Ill. (boy's division), and Kellee Booth, Coto de Caza, Calif. (girl's division).

Pat Perez obliterated the tournament record at the Maxfli PGA Junior Championship, winning by seven strokes.

Perez, from San Diego, blistered Pinehurst Resort and Country Club's No. 4 course with a 17-under-par 271 (70-69-63-69), 17 strokes better than the previous record by Chris Couch of North Lauderdale, Fla., set in 1990. Included in Perez's record total was a front-nine 7-under-par 29 during his third-round 63.

Robert Floyd of Miami Beach, Fla., son of veteran PGA Tour and Senior PGA Tour star Ray Floyd, finished second with a 278 total—which would have tied Couch's previous record.

Erika Hayashida of Lima, Peru, made a shambles of the girls competition in a nine-stroke victory. Hayashida, 17, became the first foreign-born winner of the tournament with a 7-under-par 65 in the final round. Her 279 total set a tournament record, one stroke better than LPGA tour rookie Vicki Goetz's 1990 total.

Boys' scores (partial)	
Pat Perez, San Diego	70-69-63-69–271
Robert Floyd, Miami Beach, Fla.	74-65-67-72–278
Steve Scott, Coral Springs, Fla.	71-68-73-70–282
Al Hromulak, Johnstown, Pa.	75-71-68-73–287
Michael Henderson, Raleigh, N.C.	67-72-75-73–287
Jeremy Anderson, Lake Mary, Fla.	70-76-74-69–289
Brian Wright, Mobile, Ala.	70-73-73-73–289
Jason Semelsberger, Newhall, Calif.	73-74-68-74–289
Ted Oh, Torrance, Calif.	70-77-70-73–290
D.A. Points, Pekin, Ill.	78-71-71-70–290
Girls' scores (partial)	
Erika Hayashida, Lima, Peru	71-69-74-65–279
Betty Chen, La Quinta, Calif.	71-75-72-70–288
Kellee Booth, Coto De Caza, Calif.	74-71-72-72–289
Cristie Kerr, Miami	78-69-69-74–290
Alicia Allison, Santa Ana, Calif.	73-75-73-71–292
Jody Niemann, Rigby, Idaho	78-73-73-69–293
Shauna Estes, Orangeburg, S.C.	74-73-73-73–293

NATIONAL OLDSMOBILE SCRAMBLE CHAMPIONSHIP

▶**Course:** Walt Disney World Golf Resort
▶**Location:** Lake Buena Vista, Fla.
▶**When:** Sept. 30-Oct. 4, 1993
▶**Weather:** Couldn't have been better.
▶**Purse:** $250,000 approx., for pros.
▶**Par:** 72, all three courses.
▶**Yards:** Lake Buena Vista, 6800; Palm, 6957; Magnolia, 7190.
▶**Defending champions:** Karsten Golf Club, Tempe, Ariz. (net division) and Jaycee Golf Club, Chillicothe, Ohio (gross division).

Led by the first woman to play on a winning team, PGA West of La Quinta, Calif.—joined by PGA Tour pro Tommy Armour III—won the 10th annual Oldsmobile Scramble National Championship's Gross Division.

Sue Gilstrap joined her husband, Jim, PGA West pro John O'Neill, John Test, Chuck Shubin and Armour to post a 70-under-par 218 total (54-56-54-54), breaking the gross division scoring record by two strokes.

Pompano Beach (Fla.) Country Club was runner-up, four strokes back.

In the Net Division, Valley Wood Golf Club of Swanton, Ohio, came from three strokes back in the final round to win. Team members were club pro Mike Thompson, John Zieler, Drew McNeill, Hugh Snyder and Mark Heintschel with PGA Tour pro Bill Britton. They shot a handicap-assisted 74-under-par 218 (56-51-56-51).

Gross Division scores (partial)	
218–PGA West, La Quinta, CA	54-56-54-54
222–Pompano Beach, FL CC	59-56-55-52
226–Wedgewood G&CC, Powell, OH	59-58-57-52
226–Baywood CC, Pasadena, TX	55-58-56-57
227–Crawfordsville (Ind.) GC	59-54-57-57
228–Quail Hollow Resort, Painesville, OH	59-56-57-56
230–Jaycee GC, Chillicothe, OH	60-56-59-55
231–Hidden Valley CC, Salem, VA	59-59-58-55
231–Kailleen (Texas) Muni GC	58-57-59-57
231–Shoal Creek (Ala.)	56-58-60-57
Net Division scores (partial)	
214–Valleywood GC, Swanton, OH	56-56-51-51
215–Oregon GC, West Linn, OR	52-54-54-55
217–Commonwealth CC, Horsham, PA	56-56-55-50
218–Pines Of Grand View, Nisswa, MN	56-54-58-50
218–Shaker Run GC, Lebanon, OH	56-56-55-51

Taylor Made PGA Club Professional Championship

▸**Course:** PGA National Resort & Spa
▸**Location:** Palm Beach Gardens, Fla.
▸**When:** Oct. 7-10, 1993
▸**Weather:** Sunny, hot and humid Thursday until lightning and rain suspended play for 90 minutes at 2:15 p.m., causing 171 players to not finish the first round. Again, sunny, hot and humid Friday until lightning suspended play at 3:48 p.m. with 231 players still on the course. Restarted Saturday at 7:45 a.m. under partly cloudy and humid conditions; play suspended at 2:10 p.m., restarted at 5 p.m. then suspended because of darkness at 6:10 p.m. with 168 players yet to complete the third round. After it was finished early Sunday, the final round began at 11:45 a.m. with play in foursomes.
▸**Purse:** $400,000
▸**Par:** 72, all three courses
▸**Yards:** Champion Course, 7,022 yards; Estate Course, 6,784 yards; Haig Course, 6,806 yards
▸**Defending champion:** Ron McDougal

Jeff Roth, pro at Flint (Mich.) Golf Club, outlasted the rain, storms and weird weather to win the 26th PGA Club Pro Championship.

His 13-under-par 275 was two strokes ahead of John Lee of Naples, Fla. Lee sank a 40-foot putt on the final hole to escape a large group and take second alone at 277.

Defending champion Ron McDougal of Purchase, N.Y., Todd Smith of Rochester, Ind., Delaware's Pete Oakley, Michigan's George Bowman and Tennessee's Walt Chapman tied for third at 278.

Scores and earnings (partial)

Jeffrey R. Roth	68-69-66-72–275	$32,000.00
John D. Lee	65-71-69-72–277	$22,000.00
Todd M. Smith	71-68-70-69–278	$12,800.00
Pete Oakley	68-70-71-69–278	$12,800.00
George Bowman	69-70-69-70–278	$12,800.00
Walt Chapman	67-69-71-71–278	$12,800.00
Ronald McDougal	68-66-71-73–278	$12,800.00
Rick Acton	68-75-68-68–279	$ 8,500.00
Tom Cleaver	69-68-73-69–279	$ 8,500.00
Brad Sherfy	71-72-70-67–280	$ 6,620.00

PGA Senior Club Professional Championship

▸**Course:** BallenIsles Country Club of JDM
▸**Location:** Palm Beach Gardens, Fla.
▸**When:** Oct. 26-29, 1993
▸**Weather:** Beautiful.
▸**Purse:** $185,000
▸**Par:** 72
▸**Yards:** 6,780
▸**Defending champion:** Roger Kennedy, Pompano Beach, Fla.

Both an owner and operator of a golf course, Bob Carson joined another group—tournament winners—at the PGA Senior Club Pro Championship.

Carson fired a final-round 2-under-par 70, after opening 69-69-69, for an 11-under 277. Carson finished eight strokes ahead of runner-up Tom Joyce, pro at Glen Oaks Golf Club in Old Westbury, N.Y.

Carson is owner and head professional at Bent Oak Country Club in Titusville, Fla., about 125 miles north of BallenIsles CC of JDM, the tournament site for the past four years.

Carson's 11-under-par total and his eight-stroke victory margin set tournament records.

With the victory, Carson earned an exemption for regional qualifying for the Senior PGA Tour and moved directly to the finals. Carson made good use of the exemption, tying at 6-over-par 294.

In addition to gaining a conditional Senior PGA Tour card for 1994 (he can play in several events but isn't exempt for the entire schedule of tournaments), Carson took home $2,450 at the seniors Q-School.

Scores and earnings (partial)

277–Bob Carson	69-69-69-70	$14,000
285–Tom Joyce	73-72-69-71	$11,000
287–Bill Garrett	78-71-72-66	$ 9,000
288–Pat O'Brien	68-75-73-72	$ 7,500
289–Al Krueger	73-70-76-70	$ 6,000
289–Mike O'Sullivan	72-74-70-73	$ 6,000
290–Austin Straub	74-72-72-72	$ 4,500
290–Larry Mancour	74-71-70-75	$ 4,500
291–Dave Philo	73-74-70-74	$ 3,875
291–Tom Deaton	69-75-72-75	$ 3,875
292–Martin Roesink	73-76-72-71	$ 3,137
292–Tom Storey	75-75-70-72	$ 3,137
292–Bill Kennedy	73-71-76-72	$ 3,137
292--Dick Goetz	74-72-72-74	$ 3,137

PGA Grand Slam of Golf

▶**Course:** PGA West (Jack Nicklaus Resort Course)
▶**Location:** La Quinta, Calif.
▶**When:** Nov. 16-17, 1993
▶**Weather:** Sunny and warm.
▶**Purse:** $1 million
▶**Par:** 72
▶**Yards:** 7,261
▶**Defending champion:** Nick Price

No one could have imagined the problems the winners of golf's four 1993 major championships would encounter in the PGA Grand Slam of Golf, a 36-hole stroke-play, made-for-television event.

British Open champion Greg Norman won—if it can be called that—with a 1-over-par 145. PGA Championship winner Paul Azinger shot 75-72–147. U.S. Open winner Lee Janzen (74-74–148) and Masters champion Bernhard Langer (78-70–148) tied for third.

All told, the group needed nearly six hours to complete the round. Along the way, they whacked 10 golf balls into various bodies of water. Langer was assessed six penalty strokes for violations, including grounding his club in a hazard.

The "worst-ball" score of the foursome was 21-over par.

Norman birdied four of the first five holes on the first day to build a three-stroke lead over Janzen and six over Azinger and Langer. But he crashed to earth the second day—from a seven-stroke lead over Janzen with 13 holes to play down to a one-stroke lead going into the final hole.

Then Janzen hit one last shot into a lake beside the final green and took double bogey.

"Sometimes you win pretty and sometimes you win ugly; this was winning ugly," Norman admitted. "It was like a mackerel in the moonlight—shiny one minute, smelly the next."

Scores and earnings

Greg Norman, $400,000	71-71–145
Paul Azinger, $250,000	75-72–147
Bernhard Langer, $200,000	78-70–148
Lee Janzen, $150,000	74-74–148

Titleist and Foot-Joy PGA Assistant Pro Championship

▶**Course:** PGA West (Jack Nicklaus Private Course)
▶**Location:** La Quinta, Calif.
▶**When:** Dec. 14-17, 1993
▶**Weather:** Glorious.
▶**Purse:** $75,000
▶**Par:** 72
▶**Yards:** 6,762
▶**Defending champion:** Bill Loeffler, Littleton, Colo.
▶**Tournament record (72 holes):** 278, Kim Thompson, American Fork, Utah, 1991

Steve Brady of Rochester Hills, Mich., fired a final-round 1-under-par 71 and cruised to victory in the Titleist and Foot-Joy PGA Assistant Professional Championship.

Brady, 35, led over the final 24 holes and his four-stroke victory margin was a record for 72 holes in the tournament.

Rob McNamara of Gainesville, Fla., was runner-up with a final-round 73 and a 288 total.

Brady birdied five holes to overcome a double bogey on the par-4, 404-yard sixth hole, where he dumped his tee shot into a pond. McNamara, playing in the final group with Brady, saw his hopes wane on the same hole. His approach shot also found the water, and he took double bogey.

Brady, the first Titleist winner from the Michigan PGA Section, closed his impressive week with a 6-foot par putt on the 18th green.

"Everything fell into place this week," said Brady, who has attempted to qualify for the PGA Tour 14 times.

Said McNamara: "I think anyone who has tried to qualify for the Tour 14 times ought to be given a free ride to heaven."

Scores and earnings

S. Brady, Rochester Hills, Mich., $6,000	71-73-69-71–284
Rob McNamara, Gainesville, Fla., $4,500	68-75-72-73–288
J. Dal Corobbo, Countryside, Ill., $3,500	73-72-71-74–290
John Mazza, Beaver Falls, Pa., $3,250	72-76-74-69–291
Joe Meade, Chuckey, Tenn., $2,758	74-75-75-72–296
Dan Hornig, Walnut, Calif., $2,758	76-74-74-72–296
Mike Taylor, Charlotte, N.C., $2,758	70-74-74-78–296
Rod Pampling, Brisbane, Australia, $2,225	74-74-80-69–297
Greg Hemann, Evans, Ga., $2,225	73-80-73-71–297
Craig Everett, Glasgow, Scotland, $2,000	77-74-75-72–298

GOLF ALMANAC 1994

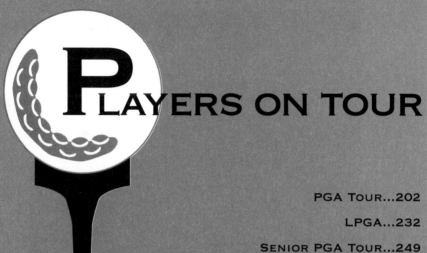

PLAYERS ON TOUR

PGA TOUR...202

LPGA...232

SENIOR PGA TOUR...249

GOLF ALMANAC 1994

PGA Tour players

JOHN ADAMS
Height: 6'3"
Birth date: May 5, 1954
College: Arizona State University
Career earnings: $1,166,234 (144)
Weight: 220
Residence: Scottsdale, Ariz.
Turned professional: 1976

Annual earnings and rank:
1978—$2,025—196	1983—$59,287—87	1988—$64,341—140
1979—$1,785—224	1984—$73,567—80	1989—$104,824—120
1980—$19,895—123	1985—$9,613—181	1990—$126,733—122
1981—$17,898—138	1986—$64,906—124	1991—$117,549—125
1982—$54,014—85	1987—$51,976—149	1992—$173,069—89
		1993—$221,753—78

FULTON ALLEM
Height: 5'11"
Birth date: Sept. 15, 1957
Turned professional: 1976
Career earnings: $1,810,872 (86)
Weight: 215
Residence: Heathrow, Fla.

Tour victories: 1991 Independent Insurance Agent Open. * 1993 The Colonial, World Series. (TOTAL: 3)

Annual earnings and rank:
1987—$88,734—105	1989—$134,706—104	1991—$229,702—71
1988—$163,911—73	1990—$134,493—116	1992—$209,982—74
		1993—$851,345—9

MICHAEL ALLEN
Height: 6'
Birth date: Jan. 31, 1959
College: University of Nevada-Reno
Career earnings: $385,472 (255)
Weight: 185
Residence: Scottsdale, Ariz.
Turned professional: 1984

Annual earnings and rank:
1990—$95,319—140	1992—$11,455—233
1991—$47,626—177	1993—$231,072—73

BILLY ANDRADE
Height: 5'8"
Residence: Bristol, R.I. and Atlanta
College: Wake Forest University
Career earnings: $1,692,587 (95)
Weight: 155
Birth date: Jan. 25, 1964
Turned professional: 1987

Tour victories: 1991 Kemper Open, Buick Classic. (TOTAL: 2)

Annual earnings and rank:
1988—$74,950—134	1990—$231,362—64	1992—$202,509—76
1989—$202,242—69	1991—$615,765—14	1993—$365,759—40

PAUL AZINGER

Height: 6'2"
Birth date: Jan. 6, 1960
College: Brevard JC and Florida State Univ.
Weight: 175
Residence: Bradenton, Fla.
Turned professional: 1981
Career earnings: $6,761,307 (2)
Tour victories: 1987 Phoenix Open, Panasonic-Las Vegas Invitational, Canon-Sammy Davis Jr.- Greater Hartford Open. ✱ 1988 Hertz Bay Hill Classic. ✱ 1989 Canon Greater Hartford Open. ✱ 1990 MONY Tournament of Champions. ✱ 1991 AT&T Pebble Beach National Pro-Am. ✱ 1992 TOUR Championship. ✱ 1993 Memorial Tournament, New England Classic, PGA Championship. (TOTAL: 11)
Annual earnings and rank:

1982—$10,655—171	1987—$822,481—2	1991—$685,603—9
1984—$27,821—144	1988—$594,850—11	1992—$929,863—7
1985—$81,179—93	1989—$951,649—3	1993—$1,458,456—2
1986—$254,019—29	1990—$944,731—4	

IAN BAKER-FINCH

Height: 6'4"
Residence: Sanctuary Cove, Queensland, Australia
Turned professional: 1979
Weight: 190
Birth date: Oct. 24, 1960
Career earnings: $1,916,751 (77)
Tour victories: 1989 Southwestern Bell Colonial. (TOTAL: 1)
Annual earnings and rank:

1988—$75,840—133	1990—$611,492—16	1992—$261,817—58
1989—$253,309—53	1991—$649,513—13	1993—$140,621—114

SEVE BALLESTEROS

Height: 6'
Residence: Pedrena, Santander, Spain
Turned professional: 1974
Weight: 175
Birth date: April 9, 1957
Career earnings: NA
Tour victories: 1978 Greater Greensboro Open. ✱ 1980 Masters Tournament. ✱ 1983 Masters Tournament, Manufacturers Hanover Westchester Classic. ✱ 1985 USF&G Classic. ✱ 1988 Manufacturers Hanover Westchester Classic. (TOTAL: 6)
Also won British Open in 1979, 1984, 1988.
Annual earnings and rank:

1983—$210,933—18	1987—$305,058—32	1991—$64,320—160
1984—$132,660—52	1988—$165,202—71	1992—$39,206—184
1985—$206,638—18	1989—$138,094—101	1993—$34,850—193
1986—$45,877—141	1990—$84,584—144	

DAVE BARR

Height: 6'1"
Birth date: March 1, 1952
College: Oral Roberts University
Weight: 200
Residence: Richmond, B.C.
Turned professional: 1974
Career earnings: $1,837,220 (82)
Tour victories: 1981 Quad Cities Open. ✱ 1987 Georgia Pacific Atlanta Golf Classic. (TOTAL: 2)

Annual earnings and rank:
1978—$11,897—133	1983—$52,800—96	1988—$291,244—33
1979—$13,022—142	1984—$113,336—62	1989—$190,480—75
1980—$14,664—141	1985—$126,177—65	1990—$197,979—80
1981—$46,214—90	1986—$122,181—70	1991—$144,389—108
1982—$12,474—166	1987—$202,241—54	1992—$118,859—119
		1993—$179,264—96

CHIP BECK

Height: 5'10" **Weight:** 170
Birth date: Sept. 12, 1956 **Residence:** Highland Park, Ill.
College: University of Georgia **Turned professional:** 1978
Career earnings: $5,304,632 (11)
Tour victories: 1988 Los Angeles Open, USF&G Classic. * 1990 Buick Open. * 1992 Freeport-McMoRan Classic. (TOTAL: 4)
Annual earnings and rank:
1979—$4,166—194	1984—$177,289—34	1989—$694,087—9
1980—$17,109—131	1985—$76,038—97	1990—$571,816—17
1981—$30,034—110	1986—$215,140—39	1991—$578,535—16
1982—$57,608—76	1987—$523,003—9	1992—$689,704—17
1983—$149,909—33	1988—$916,818—2	1993—$603,376—25

JAY DON BLAKE

Height: 6'2" **Weight:** 180
Birth date: Oct. 28, 1958 **Residence:** St. George, Utah
College: Utah State **Turned professional:** 1981
Career earnings: $1,634,087 (101)
Tour victories: 1991 Shearson Lehman Brothers Open. (TOTAL: 1)
Annual earnings and rank:
1987—$87,634—10	1989—$200,499—71	1991—$563,854—21
1988—$131,937—90	1990—$148,384—106	1992—$299,298—51
		1993—$202,482—86

MICHAEL BRADLEY

Height: 6' **Weight:** 180
Birth date: July 16, 1966 **Residence:** Valrico, Fla.
College: Oklahoma State **Turned Professional:** 1988
Career earnings: $126,160 (338)
Annual earnings and rank:
1993—$126,160—121

MARK BROOKS

Height: 5'9" **Weight:** 150
Birth date: March 25, 1961 **Residence:** Fort Worth
College: University of Texas **Turned professional:** 1983
Career earnings: $2,410,031 (57)
Tour victories: 1988 Canon Sammy Davis Jr.-Greater Hartford Open. * 1991 Kmart Greater Greensboro Open, Greater Milwaukee Open. (TOTAL: 3)

Annual earnings and rank:
1984—$40,438—122	1987—$42,100—16	1990—$307,948—45
1985—$32,094—141	1988—$280,636—36	1991—$667,263—11
1986—$47,264—140	1989—$112,834—115	1992—$629,754—21
		1993—$249,696—66

BILLY RAY BROWN

Height: 6'3" **Weight:** 205
Birth date: April 5, 1963 **Residence:** Missouri City, Texas
College: University of Houston **Turned professional:** 1986
Career earnings: $1,565,916 (112)
Tour victories: 1991 Canon Greater Hartford Open. * 1992 GTE Byron Nelson Classic. (TOTAL: 2)

Annual earnings and rank:
1988—$83,590—125	1990—$312,466—44	1992—$485,151—29
1989—$162,964—85	1991—$348,082—46	1993—$173,622—97

MARK CALCAVECCHIA

Height: 6' **Weight:** 200
Birth date: June 12, 1960 **Residence:** West Palm Beach, Fla.
College: University of Florida **Turned professional:** 1981
Career earnings: $4,489,962 (19)
Tour victories: 1986 Southwest Golf Classic. * 1987 Honda Classic. * 1988 Bank of Boston Classic. * 1989 Phoenix Open, Nissan Los Angeles Open. * 1992 Phoenix Open. (TOTAL: 6)
Also won British Open in 1989.

Annual earnings and rank:
1981—$404—253	1985—$15,957—162	1989—$807,741—5
1982—$25,064—134	1986—$155,012—58	1990—$834,281—7
1983—$16,313—161	1987—$522,423—10	1991—$323,621—50
1984—$29,660—140	1988—$751,912—6	1992—$377,234—39
		1993—$630,366—21

BRIAN CLAAR

Height: 5'8" **Weight:** 145
Birth date: July 29, 1959 **Residence:** Palm Harbor, Fla.
College: University of Tampa **Turned professional:** 1981
Career earnings: $1,056,018 (153)

Annual earnings and rank:
1986—$117,355—75	1989—$88,010—133	1992—$192,255—78
1987—$43,111—162	1990—$161,356—98	1993—$202,624—85
1988—$30,276—172	1991—$251,309—67	

KEITH CLEARWATER

Height: 6' **Weight:** 180
Birth date: Sept. 1, 1959 **Residence:** Orem, Utah
College: Brigham Young University **Turned professional:** 1982
Career earnings: $1,818,238 (83)
Tour victories: 1987 Colonial National Invitation, Centel Classic. (TOTAL: 2)

Annual earnings and rank:
1987—$320,007—3   1989—$87,490—136   1991—$239,727—69
1988—$82,876—127   1990—$130,103—118   1992—$609,273—22
                                               1993—$348,763—44

LENNIE CLEMENTS

Height: 5'8"   **Weight:** 160
Birth date: Jan. 20, 1957   **Residence:** San Diego
College: San Diego State University   **Turned professional:** 1980
Career earnings: $880,045 (178)
Annual earnings and rank:
1981—$7,766—178   1985—$49,383—120   1989—$69,399—147
1982—$44,796—97   1986—$112,642—79   1990—$80,095—146
1983—$44,455—110   1987—$124,989—83   1991—$62,827—163
1984—$25,712—146   1988—$86,332—120   1992—$30,121—198
                                               1993—$141,526—113

RUSS COCHRAN

Height: 6'   **Weight:** 160
Birth date: Oct. 31, 1958   **Residence:** Paducah, Ky.
College: University of Kentucky   **Turned professional:** 1979
Career earnings: $2,283,493 (63)
Tour victories: 1991 Centel Western Open. (TOTAL: 1)
Annual earnings and rank:
1983—$7,968—188   1987—$148,110—74   1991—$684,851—10
1984—$133,342—51   1988—$148,960—80   1992—$326,290—46
1985—$87,331—87   1989—$132,678—107   1993—$293,868—59
1986—$89,817—92   1990—$230,278—65

JOHN COOK

Height: 6'   **Weight:** 175
Birth date: Oct. 2, 1957   **Residence:** Rancho Mirage, Calif.
College: Ohio State University   **Turned professional:** 1979
Career earnings: $3,845,252 (27)
Tour victories: 1981 Bing Crosby National Pro-Am. * 1983 Canadian Open. * 1987 International. * 1992 Bob Hope Chrysler Classic, United Airlines Hawaiian Open, Las Vegas Invitational. (TOTAL: 6)
Annual earnings and rank:
1980—$43,316—78   1985—$63,573—106   1989—$39,445—172
1981—$127,608—25   1986—$255,126—27   1990—$448,112—28
1982—$57,483—77   1987—$333,184—29   1991—$546,984—26
1983—$216,868—16   1988—$139,916—84   1992—$1,165,606—3
1984—$65,710—89   1993—$342,321—45

FRED COUPLES

Height: 5'11"   **Weight:** 185
Birth date: Oct. 3, 1959   **Residence:** South Andros, Bahamas
College: University of Houston   **Turned professional:** 1980
Career earnings: $6,263,494 (6)

Tour victories: 1983 Kemper Open. ✶ 1984 Tournament Players Championship. ✶ 1987 Byron Nelson Golf Classic. ✶ 1990 Nissan Los Angeles Open. ✶ 1991 Federal Express St. Jude Classic, B.C. Open. ✶ 1992 Nissan Los Angeles Open, Nestlé Invitational, Masters. ✶ 1993 Honda Classic, Kapalua International (TOTAL: 11)
Annual earnings and rank:

1981—$78,939—53	1985—$171,272—38	1989—$693,944—11
1982—$77,606—53	1986—$116,065—76	1990—$757,999—9
1983—$209,733—19	1987—$441,025—19	1991—$791,749—3
1984—$334,573—7	1988—$489,822—21	1992—$1,344,188—1
		1993—$796,579—10

BEN CRENSHAW

Height: 5'9" **Weight:** 170
Birth date: Jan. 11, 1952 **Residence:** Austin, Texas
College: University of Texas **Turned professional:** 1973
Career earnings: $5,448,507 (9)
Tour victories: 1973 San Antonio-Texas Open. ✶ 1976 Bing Crosby National Pro-Am, Hawaiian Open, Ohio Kings Island Open. ✶ 1977 Colonial National Invitation. ✶ 1979 Phoenix Open, Walt Disney World Team Championship (with George Burns). ✶ 1980 Anheuser-Busch Classic. ✶ 1983 Byron Nelson Classic. ✶ 1984 Masters Tournament. ✶ 1986 Buick Open, Vantage Championship. ✶ 1987 USF&G Classic. ✶ 1988 Doral Ryder Open. ✶ 1990 Southwestern Bell Colonial. ✶ 1992 Centel Western Open. ✶ 1993 Nestlé Invitational. (TOTAL: 17)
Annual earnings and rank:

1973—$76,749—34	1980—$237,727—5	1987—$638,194—3
1974—$71,065—31	1981—$151,038—20	1988—$696,895—8
1975—$63,528—32	1982—$54,277—83	1989—$433,095—21
1976—$257,759—2	1983—$275,474—7	1990—$351,193—33
1977—$123,841—16	1984—$270,989—16	1991—$224,563—75
1978—$108,305—21	1985—$25,814—149	1992—$439,071—31
1979—$236,769—5	1986—$388,169—8	1993—$318,605—51

JOHN DALY

Height: 5'11" **Weight:** 175
Birth date: April 28, 1966 **Residence:** Orlando, Fla.
College: University of Arkansas **Turned professional:** 1987
Career earnings: $1,187,828 (142)
Tour victories: 1991 PGA Championship. ✶ 1992 B.C. Open. (TOTAL: 2)
Annual earnings and rank:
1991—$574,783—17   1992—$387,455—37   1993—$225,591—76

TREVOR DODDS

Height: 6'1" **Weight:** 195
Birth date: Sept. 26, 1959 **Residence:** Namibia
College: Lamar **Turned professional:** 1985
Career earnings: $287,748 (288)
Annual earnings and rank:

1986—$15,738—190	1989—$47,086—166	1993—$119,436—126
1987—$48,933—155	1990—$74,544—153	
1988—$17,404—202	1991—$57,786—167	

ED DOUGHERTY

Height: 6'1"
Birth date: Nov. 4, 1947
Turned professional: 1969
Career earnings: $978,429 (168)
Weight: 215
Residence: Linwood, Penn.

Annual earnings and rank:
1975—$9,374—129	1980—$9,113—168	1989—$1,800—267
1976—$17,333—113	1982—$27,948—128	1990—$124,505—123
1977—$17,606—113	1987—$76,705—115	1991—$201,958—82
1978—$9,936—141	1988—$22,455—195	1992—$237,525—66
1979—$24,802—115		1993—$167,651—99

DAVID EDWARDS

Height: 5'8"
Birth date: April 18, 1956
College: Oklahoma State University
Career earnings: $2,961,573 (44)
Weight: 155
Residence: Edmond, Okla.
Turned professional: 1978

Tour victories: 1980 Walt Disney World National Team Championship (with Danny Edwards). * 1984 Los Angeles Open. * 1992 Memorial Tournament. * 1993 Heritage Classic. (TOTAL: 4)

Annual earnings and rank:
1979—$44,456—88	1984—$236,061—23	1989—$239,908—57
1980—$35,810—93	1985—$21,506—157	1990—$166,028—95
1981—$68,211—65	1986—$122,079—71	1991—$396,695—38
1982—$49,896—91	1987—$148,217—73	1992—$515,070—27
1983—$114,037—48	1988—$151,513—76	1993—$653,086—20

JOEL EDWARDS

Height: 6'
Birth date: Nov. 22, 1961
College: North Texas State
Career earnings: $521,366 (228)
Weight: 165
Residence: Irving, Texas
Turned professional: 1984

Annual earnings and rank:
1989—$46,851—167	1991—$106,820—131	1993—$150,623—106
1990—$109,808—132	1992—$107,264—126	

STEVE ELKINGTON

Height: 6'2"
Birth date: Dec. 8, 1962
College: University of Houston
Career earnings: $2,976,192 (43)
Weight: 190
Residence: Sydney, Australia
Turned professional: 1985

Tour victories: 1990 Kmart Greater Greensboro Open. * 1991 THE PLAYERS Championship. * 1992 Infiniti Tournament of Champions. (TOTAL: 3)

Annual earnings and rank:
1987—$75,738—118	1989—$231,062—61	1991—$549,120—25
1988—$149,972—79	1990—$548,564—18	1992—$746,352—12
		1993—$675,383—17

BOB ESTES

Height: 6'1"
Birth date: Feb. 2, 1966
College: University of Texas
Career earnings: $1,133,047 (147)
Weight: 175
Residence: Austin, Texas
Turned professional: 1988

Annual earnings and rank:
1988—$5,968—237	1990—$212,090—69	1992—$190,778—80
1989—$135,628—102	1991—$147,364—105	1993—$447,187—32

NICK FALDO

Height: 6'3"
Birth date: July 18, 1957
Turned professional: 1976
Career earnings: NA
Weight: 195
Residence: Surrey, England

Tour victories: 1984 Sea Pines Heritage Classic. * 1989 Masters Tournament. * 1990 Masters Tournament. (TOTAL: 3) Also won British Open in 1987, 1990, 1992.

Annual earnings and rank:
1981—$23,320—119	1986—$52,965—135	1991—$127,156—117
1982—$56,667—79	1987—$36,281—169	1992—$345,168—41
1983—$67,851—79	1988—$179,120—64	1993—$188,886—91
1984—$116,845—38	1989—$327,981—31	
1985—$54,060—117	1990—$345,262—37	

BRAD FAXON

Height: 6'1"
Birth date: Aug. 1, 1961
College: Furman University
Career earnings: $2,452,804 (55)
Weight: 170
Residence: Orlando, Fla.
Turned professional: 1983

Tour victories: 1986 Provident Classic. * 1991 Buick Open. * 1992 New England Classic, International. (TOTAL: 4)

Annual earnings and rank:
1984—$71,688—82	1987—$113,534—90	1990—$197,118—81
1985—$46,813—124	1988—$162,656—74	1991—$422,088—34
1986—$92,716—90	1989—$222,076—63	1992—$812,093—8
		1993—$312,023—55

RICK FEHR

Height: 5'11"
Birth date: Aug. 28, 1962
College: Brigham Young University
Career earnings: $1,898,467 (79)
Weight: 160
Residence: Redmond, Wash.
Turned professional: 1984

Tour victories: 1986 B.C. Open. (TOTAL: 1)

Annual earnings and rank:
1985—$40,101—133	1988—$79,080—130	1991—$288,983—55
1986—$151,162—61	1989—$93,142—131	1992—$433,003—33
1987—$106,808—94	1990—$149,867—105	1993—$556,322—28

ED FIORI

Height: 5'7"
Birth date: April 21, 1953
College: Houston
Career earnings: $1,723,564 (92)
Weight: 190
Residence: Stafford, Texas
Turned professional: 1977

Tour victories: 1979 Southern Open. * 1981 Western Open. * 1982 Bob Hope Desert Classic. (TOTAL: 3)

Annual earnings and rank:
1978—$19,846—109	1983—$175,619—26	1988—$193,765—58
1979—$64,428—65	1984—$41,582—119	1989—$188,637—77
1980—$79,488—52	1985—$116,002—71	1990—$108,816—133
1981—$105,510—48	1986—$70,828—119	1991—$120,722—123
1982—$91,599—45	1987—$104,570—95	1992—$124,537—115
		1993—$117,617—127

JOHN FLANNERY

Height: 6'1"
Birth date: April 11, 1962
College: University of Southern California
Career earnings: $161,233 (323)
Weight: 170
Residence: La Quinta, Calif.
Turned professional: 1985

Annual earnings and rank:
1993—$161,234—102

DAN FORSMAN

Height: 6'4"
Birth date: July 15, 1958
College: Arizona State University
Career earnings: $2,684,806 (51)
Weight: 195
Residence: Provo, Utah
Turned professional: 1982

Tour victories: 1985 Lite Quad Cities Open. * 1986 Hertz Bay Hill Classic. * 1990 Shearson Lehman Hutton Open. * 1992 Buick Open. (TOTAL: 4)

Annual earnings and rank:
1983—$37,859—118	1987—$157,727—63	1991—$214,175—78
1984—$52,152—105	1988—$269,440—40	1992—$763,190—10
1985—$150,334—53	1989—$141,174—99	1993—$410,150—36
1986—$169,445—54	1990—$319,160—43	

ROBIN FREEMAN

Height: 6'
Birth date: May 7, 1959
College: Central State U.
Career Earnings: $220,255 (306)
Weight: 180
Residence: Rancho Mirage, Calif.
Turned professional: 1983

Annual earnings and rank:
1989—$26,517—188	1992—$101,642—128	1993—$92,096—148

DAVID FROST

Height: 5'11"
Weight: 172
Birth date: Sept. 11, 1959
Residence: Dallas
Turned professional: 1981
Career earnings: $4,428,831 (20)
Tour victories: 1988 Southern Open, Northern Telecom Tucson Open. * 1989 NEC World Series of Golf. * 1990 USF&G Classic. * 1992 Buick Classic, Hardee's Golf Classic. * 1993 Canadian Open, Hardee's Classic. (TOTAL: 8)
Annual earnings and rank:
1985—$118,537—70	1988—$691,500—9	1991—$171,262—93
1986—$187,944—46	1989—$620,430—11	1992—$717,883—15
1987—$518,072—11	1990—$372,485—32	1993—$1,030,717—5

FRED FUNK

Height: 5'8"
Weight: 165
Birth date: June 14, 1956
Residence: Ponte Vedra Beach, Fla.
College: University of Maryland
Turned professional: 1981
Career earnings: $1,192,321 (141)
Tour victories: 1992 Shell Houston Open. (TOTAL:1)
Annual earnings and rank:
1989—$59,695—157	1991—$226,915—73	1993—$309,435—56
1990—$179,346—91	1992—$416,930—34	

JIM GALLAGHER JR.

Height: 6'
Weight: 180
Birth date: March 24, 1961
Residence: Greenwood, Miss.
College: University of Tennessee
Turned professional: 1983
Career earnings: $3,200,722 (40)
Tour victories: 1990 Greater Milwaukee Open. * 1993 Anheuser-Busch Classic, TOUR Championship. (TOTAL: 3)
Annual earnings and rank:
1984—$22,249—148	1987—$39,402—166	1990—$476,706—25
1985—$19,061—159	1988—$83,766—124	1991—$570,627—18
1986—$79,967—107	1989—$265,809—50	1992—$638,314—19
		1993—$1,078,870—4

ROBERT GAMEZ

Height: 5'9"
Weight: 170
Birth date: July 21, 1968
Residence: Las Vegas
College: University of Arizona
Turned professional: 1989
Career earnings: $1,193,861 (140)
Tour victories: 1990 Northern Telecom Tucson Open, Nestlé Invitational. (TOTAL: 2)
Annual earnings and rank:
1989—$4,827—237	1991—$280,349—59	1993—$236,458—70
1990—$461,407—27	1992—$215,648—72	

KELLY GIBSON

Height: 5'10"
Birth date: May 2, 1964
College: Lamar University
Career earnings: $285,987 (290)
Annual earnings and rank:
1992—$137,984—105   1993—$148,003—110

Weight: 170
Residence: New Orleans
Turned professional: 1986

BILL GLASSON

Height: 5'11"
Birthdate: April 29, 1960
College: Oral Roberts University
Career earnings: $2,129,022 (70)
Weight: 165
Residence: Oldsmar, Fla.
Turned professional: 1983

Tour victories: 1985 Kemper Open. * 1988 B.C. Open, Centel Classic. * 1989 Doral Ryder Open. * 1992 Kemper Open. (TOTAL: 5)
Annual earnings and rank:
1984—$17,845—162   1987—$151,701—69   1990—$156,791—100
1985—$195,449—29   1988—$380,651—30   1991—$46,995—178
1986—$121,516—72   1989—$474,511—19   1992—$283,765—54
                                         1993—$299,799—57

KEN GREEN

Height: 5'10"
Birth date: July 23, 1958
College: Palm Beach JC
Career earnings: $3,019,069 (41)
Weight: 175
Residence: West Palm Beach, Fla.
Turned professional: 1979

Tour victories: 1985 Buick Open. * 1986 International. * 1988 Canadian Open, Greater Milwaukee Open. * 1989 Kmart Greater Greensboro Open. (TOTAL: 5)
Annual earnings and rank:
1982—$11,899—167   1986—$317,835—16   1990—$267,172—54
1983—$40,263—114   1987—$237,271—36   1991—$263,034—65
1984—$20,160—156   1988—$779,181—4   1992—$360,397—41
1985—$151,355—52   1989—$304,754—37   1993—$229,750—75

JAY HAAS

Height: 5'10"
Birth date: Dec. 2, 1953
College: Wake Forest
Career earnings: $4,011,175 (23)
Weight: 170
Residence: Greenville, S.C.
Turned professional: 1976

Tour victories: 1978 Andy Williams-San Diego Open. * 1981 Greater Milwaukee Open, B.C. Open. * 1982 Hall of Fame Classic, Texas Open. * 1987 Big "I" Houston Open. * 1988 Bob Hope Chrysler Classic. * 1992 Federal Express St. Jude Classic. * 1993 Texas Open. (TOTAL: 9)

Annual earnings and rank:

1977—$32,326—77	1983—$191,735—23	1988—$490,409—20
1978—$77,176—31	1984—$146,514—45	1989—$248,830—54
1979—$102,515—34	1985—$121,488—69	1990—$180,023—89
1980—$114,102—35	1986—$189,204—45	1991—$200,637—84
1981—$181,894—15	1987—$270,347—37	1992—$632,628—20
1982—$229,746—13		1993—$601,603—26

DONNIE HAMMOND

Height: 5'10"
Birth date: April 1, 1957
College: Jacksonville University
Career earnings: $2,131,142 (69)
Weight: 170
Residence: Winter Park, Fla.
Turned professional: 1979

Tour victories: 1986 Bob Hope Chrysler Classic. * 1989 Texas Open presented by Nabisco. (TOTAL: 2)

Annual earnings and rank:

1983—$41,336—112	1987—$157,480—64	1990—$151,811—104
1984—$67,874—86	1988—$256,010—44	1991—$102,668—135
1985—$102,719—77	1989—$458,741—20	1992—$197,085—77
1986—$254,987—28		1993—$340,432—47

DUDLEY HART

Height: 5'10"
Birth date: Aug. 4, 1968
College: University of Florida
Career earnings: $697,870 (198)
Weight: 170
Residence: West Palm Beach, Fla.
Turned professional: 1990

Annual earnings and rank:

1991—$126,217—120	1992—$254,903—61	1993—$316,750—52

MORRIS HATALSKY

Height: 6'
Birth date: Nov. 10, 1951
College: United States International University
Career earnings: $1,611,544 (103)
Weight: 165
Residence: Ormond Beach, Fla.
Turned Professional: 1973

Tour victories: 1981 Hall of Fame Classic. * 1983 Greater Milwaukee Open. * 1988 Kemper Open. * 1990 Bank of Boston Classic. (TOTAL: 4)

Annual earnings and rank:

1976—$249—288	1982—$66,128—65	1988—$239,019—47
1977—$32,193—79	1983—$102,567—56	1989—$66,577—149
1978—$43,062—114	1984—$50,957—107	1990—$253,639—59
1979—$61,625—69	1985—$76,059—96	1991—$106,265—132
1980—$47,107—74	1986—$105,543—83	1992—$55,042—170
1981—$70,186—63	1987—$150,654—70	1993—$111,057—135

NOLAN HENKE

Height: 6'
Birth date: Nov. 25, 1964
College: Florida State University
Career earnings: $1,699,629 (93)
Weight: 165
Residence: Fort Myers, Fla.
Turned professional: 1987

Tour victories: 1990 B.C. Open. * 1991 Phoenix Open. * 1993 BellSouth Classic. (TOTAL: 3)
Annual earnings and rank:
1989—$59,465—159   1991—$518,811—28   1992—$326,387—45
1990—$294,592—48   1993—$502,375—31

SCOTT HOCH

Height: 5'11"
Birth date: Nov. 24, 1955
College: Wake Forest University
Career earnings: $3,868,695 (26)
Weight: 160
Residence: Orlando, Fla.
Turned professional: 1979

Tour victories: 1980 Quad Cities Open. * 1982 USF&G Classic. * 1984 Lite Quad Cities Open. * 1989 Las Vegas Invitational. (TOTAL: 4)
Annual earnings and rank:
1980—$45,600—75   1985—$186,020—35   1989—$670,680—10
1981—$49,606—85   1986—$222,077—36   1990—$333,978—40
1982—$193,862—16   1987—$391,747—20   1991—$520,038—27
1983—$144,605—37   1988—$397,599—26   1992—$84,798—146
1984—$224,345—27   1993—$403,742—37

MIKE HULBERT

Height: 6'
Birth date: April 14, 1958
College: East Tennessee State
Career earnings: $2,345,965 (60)
Weight: 175
Residence: Orlando, Fla.
Turned professional: 1981

Tour victories: 1986 Federal Express St. Jude Classic. * 1989 B.C. Open. * 1991 Anheuser-Busch Golf Classic. (TOTAL: 3)
Annual earnings and rank:
1985—$18,368—161   1988—$127,752—94   1991—$551,750—24
1986—$276,687—21   1989—$477,621—16   1992—$279,577—55
1987—$204,375—49   1990—$216,002—67   1993—$193,833—89

ED HUMENIK

Height: 5'11"
Birth date: June 29, 1959
College: Michigan
Career earnings: $472,779 (235)
Weight: 210
Residence: Hobe Sound, Fla.
Turned professional: 1984

Annual earnings and rank:
1989—$46,384—168   1992—$149,337—100   1993—$152,562—105
1991—$124,497—121

JOHN HUSTON

Height: 5'10"
Birth date: June 1, 1961
College: Auburn University
Career earnings: $2,381,943 (59)
Weight: 155
Residence: Palm Harbor, Fla.
Turned professional: 1983

Tour victories: 1990 Honda Classic. * 1992 Walt Disney World/Oldsmobile Classic. (TOTAL: 2)
Annual earnings and rank:
1988—$150,301—78   1990—$435,690—30   1992—$515,453—26
1989—$203,207—68   1991—$395,853—40   1993—$681,441—15

JOHN INMAN

Height: 5'10" **Weight:** 155
Birth date: Nov. 26, 1962 **Residence:** Roswell, Ga.
College: University of North Carolina **Turned professional:** 1985
Career earnings: $899,826 (175)
Tour victories: 1987 Provident Classic. * 1993 Southern Open. (TOTAL: 2)
Annual earnings and rank:
1987—$148,386—72   1989—$99,378—178   1991—$84,501—167
1988—$66,305—137   1990—$85,289—143   1992—$173,828—87
                                      1993—$242,140—69

HALE IRWIN

Height: 6' **Weight:** 175
Birth date: June 3, 1945 **Residence:** Frontenac, Mo.
College: University of Colorado **Turned professional:** 1968
Career earnings: $4,839,626 (18)
Tour victories: 1971 Heritage Classic. * 1973 Heritage Classic. * 1974 U. S. Open. * 1975 Western Open, Atlanta Classic. * 1976 Glen Campbell-Los Angeles Open, Florida Citrus Open. * 1977 Atlanta Classic, Hall of Fame Classic, San Antonio-Texas Open. * 1979 U.S. Open. * 1981 Hawaiian Open, Buick Open. * 1982 Honda-Inverrary Classic. * 1983 Memorial Tournament. * 1984 Bing Crosby Pro-Am. * 1985 Memorial Tournament. * 1990 U.S. Open, Buick Classic. (TOTAL: 19)
Annual earnings and rank:
1968—$9,093—117   1977—$221,456—4   1985—$195,007—31
1969—$18,571—88   1978—$191,666—7   1986—$59,983—128
1970—$46,870—49   1979—$154,168—19   1987—$100,825—96
1971—$99,473—13   1980—$109,810—38   1988—$164,996—72
1972—$111,539—13   1981—$276,499—7   1989—$150,977—93
1973—$130,388—7   1982—$173,719—19   1990—$838,249—6
1974—$152,529—7   1983—$232,567—13   1991—$422,652—33
1975—$205,380—4   1984—$183,384—31   1992—$98,208—131
1976—$252,718—3   1993—$252,685—65

PETER JACOBSEN

Height: 6'3" **Weight:** 200
Birth date: March 4, 1954 **Residence:** Portland, Ore.
College: University of Oregon **Turned professional:** 1976
Career earnings: $3,260,745 (34)
Tour victories: 1980 Buick-Goodwrench Open. * 1984 Colonial National Invitation, Sammy Davis Jr.-Greater Hartford Open. * 1990 Bob Hope Chrysler Classic. (TOTAL: 4)

Annual earnings and rank:

1977—$12,608—129	1983—$158,765—29	1989—$267,241—48
1978—$34,188—82	1984—$295,025—10	1990—$547,279—19
1979—$49,439—44	1985—$214,959—23	1991—$263,180—64
1980—$138,562—8	1986—$112,964—78	1992—$106,100—127
1981—$85,624—44	1987—$79,924—111	1993—$222,291—77
1982—$145,832—25	1988—$526,765—16	

LEE JANZEN

Height: 6'
Birth date: Aug. 28, 1964
College: Florida Southern College
Weight: 175
Residence: Kissimmee, Fla.
Turned professional: 1986
Career earnings: $2,088,842 (73)
Tour victories: 1992 Northern Telecom Open. * 1993 Phoenix Open, The U.S. Open. (TOTAL: 3)
Annual earnings and rank:

1990—$132,986—115	1991—$228,242—72	1992—$795,279—9
		1993—$932,335—7

TOM KITE

Height: 5'8"
Birth date: Dec. 9, 1949
College: University of Texas
Weight: 155
Residence: Austin, Texas
Turned professional: 1972
Career earnings: $8,500,729 (1)
Tour victories: 1976 IVB-Bicentennial Golf Classic. * 1978 B.C. Open. * 1981 American Motors-Inverrary Classic. * 1982 Bay Hill Classic. * 1983 Bing Crosby National Pro-Am. * 1984 Doral-Eastern Open, Georgia-Pacific Atlanta Classic. * 1985 MONY Tournament of Champions. * 1986 Western Open. * 1987 Kemper Open. * 1989 Nestlé Invitational, THE PLAYERS Championship, Nabisco Championships. * 1990 Federal Express St. Jude Classic. * 1991 Infiniti Tournament of Champions. * 1992 BellSouth Classic, U.S. Open. * 1993 Bob Hope Classic, Los Angeles Open. (TOTAL: 19)
Annual earnings and rank:

1972—$2,582—233	1979—$166,878—17	1986—$394,164—7
1973—$54,270—56	1980—$152,490—20	1987—$525,516—8
1974—$82,055—26	1981—$375,699—1	1988—$760,405—5
1975—$87,045—18	1982—$341,081—3	1989—$1,395,278—1
1976—$116,180—21	1983—$257,066—9	1990—$658,202—15
1977—$125,204—14	1984—$348,640—5	1991—$396,580—39
1978—$161,370—11	1985—$258,793—14	1992—$957,445—6
		1993—$887,811—8

GREG KRAFT

Height: 5'11"
Birth date: April 4, 1964
College: Tampa
Weight: 170
Residence: Clearwater, Fla.
Turned professional: 1986
Career earnings: $379,404 (259)
Tour Victories: 1993 Deposit Guaranty Classic. (TOTAL 1)
Annual earnings and rank:
1992—$88,824—140   1993—$290,581—60

NEAL LANCASTER

Height: 6'
Birth date: Sept. 13, 1960
Turned professional: 1985
Career earnings: $562,053 (217)
Weight: 170
Residence: Smithfield, N.C.

Annual earnings and rank:
1990—$85,769—142	1992—$146,967—103	1993—$149,381—107
1991—$180,037—90		

BERNHARD LANGER

Height: 5'9"
Birth date: Aug. 27, 1957
Turned professional: 1972
Career earnings: NA
Weight: 155
Residence: Anhausen, Germany

Tour victories: 1985 Masters Tournament, Sea Pines Heritage Classic. * 1993 Masters Tournament. * 1993 Masters. (TOTAL: 4)

Annual earnings and rank:
1984—$82,465—75	1987—$366,430—23	1990—$35,150—187
1985—$271,044—13	1988—$100,635—111	1991—$112,539—129
1986—$379,800—10	1989—$195,973—73	1992—$41,211—181
		1993—$626,938—23

TOM LEHMAN

Height: 6'2"
Birth date: March 7, 1959
College: University of Minnesota
Career earnings: $1,040,881 (155)
Weight: 190
Residence: Scottsdale, Ariz.
Turned professional: 1982

Annual earnings and rank:
1983—$9,413—183	1992—$579,093—24	1993—$422,761—33
1984—$9,382—184		

WAYNE LEVI

Height: 5'9"
Birth date: Feb. 22, 1952
College: Oswego State (NY)
Career earnings: $3,990,815 (24)
Weight: 165
Residence: New Hartford, N.Y.
Turned professional: 1973

Tour victories: 1978 Walt Disney World National Team Play (with Bob Mann). * 1979 Houston Open. * 1980 Pleasant Valley-Jimmy Fund Classic. * 1982 Hawaiian Open, LaJet Classic. * 1983 Buick Open. * 1984 B.C. Open. * 1985 Georgia-Pacific Atlanta Classic. * 1990 BellSouth Atlanta Classic, Centel Western Open, Canon Greater Hartford Open, Canadian Open. (TOTAL: 12)

Annual earnings and rank:
1977—$8,136—159	1983—$193,252—22	1989—$499,292—16
1978—$25,039—99	1984—$252,921—20	1990—$1,024,647—2
1979—$141,612—20	1985—$221,425—22	1991—$195,861—87
1980—$120,145—32	1986—$154,777—59	1992—$237,935—65
1981—$62,177—69	1987—$203,322—53	1993—$179,521—95
1982—$280,681—8	1988—$190,073—61	

ROBERT LOHR

Height: 6'1"
Birth date: Nov. 2, 1960
College: Miami University of Ohio
Weight: 185
Residence: Orlando, Fla.
Turned professional: 1983

Career earnings: $1,747,794 (90)
Tour victories: 1988 Walt Disney World/Oldsmobile Classic. (TOTAL: 1)
Annual earnings and rank:
1985—$93,651—81	1988—$315,536—32	1991—$386,759—41
1986—$85,949—99	1989—$144,242—98	1992—$128,307—112
1987—$137,108—80	1990—$141,260—109	1993—$314,982—54

DAVIS LOVE III

Height: 6'3"
Birth date: April 13, 1964
College: University of North Carolina
Weight: 175
Residence: Sea Island, Ga.
Turned professional: 1985

Career earnings: $4,037,672 (22)
Tour victories: 1987 MCI Heritage Classic. * 1990 International. * 1991 MCI Heritage Classic. * 1992 THE PLAYERS Championship, MCI Heritage Classic, Kmart Greater Greensboro Open. * 1993 Tournament of Champions, Las Vegas Invitational. (TOTAL: 8)
Annual earnings and rank:
1986—$113,245—77	1989—$278,760—44	1992—$1,191,630—2
1987—$297,378—33	1990—$537,172—20	1993—$777,059—12
1988—$156,068—75	1991—$686,361—8	

STEVE LOWERY

Height: 6'2"
Birth date: Oct. 12, 1960
College: University of Alabama
Weight: 210
Residence: Orlando, Fla.
Turned professional: 1983

Career earnings: $411,343 (246)
Annual earnings and rank:
1988—$44,327—157	1990—$68,524—159	1992—$22,608—207
1989—$38,699—174	1991—$87,597—143	1993—$188,287—92

ANDREW MAGEE

Height: 6'
Birth date: May 22, 1962
College: University of Oklahoma
Weight: 180
Residence: Scottsdale, Ariz.
Turned professional: 1984

Career earnings: $2,144,914 (68)
Tour victories: 1988 Pensacola Open. * 1991 Nestlé Invitational, Las Vegas Invitational. (TOTAL: 3)
Annual earnings and rank:
1985—$75,593—99	1988—$261,954—43	1991—$750,082—5
1986—$69,478—120	1989—$126,770—109	1992—$285,946—53
1987—$94,598—99	1990—$210,507—71	1993—$269,986—62

JEFF MAGGERT

Height: 5'9"
Birth date: Feb. 20, 1964
College: Texas A&M
Career earnings: $1,411,371 (123)
Weight: 165
Residence: The Woodlands, Texas
Turned professional: 1986
Tour Victories: 1993 Disney World Classic. (TOTAL: 1)
Annual earnings and rank:
1990—$2,060—277   1992—$377,408—38   1993—$793,023—11
1991—$240,940—68

DICK MAST

Height: 5'11"
Birth date: March 23, 1951
College: St. Petersburg Junior College
Career earnings: $736,302 (194)
Weight: 180
Residence: Orlando, Fla.
Turned professional: 1972
Annual earnings and rank:
1974—$7,108—156   1985—$2,887—219   1989—$38,955—65
1975—$280—276   1986—$79,389—109   1990—$4,200—252
1977—$4,387—182   1987—$90,768—103   1992—$150,847—98
1979—$5,715—180   1988—$128,568—56   1993—$210,125—82

BILLY MAYFAIR

Height: 5'8"
Birth date: Aug. 6, 1966
College: Arizona State
Career earnings: $1,696,274 (94)
Weight: 155
Residence: Phoenix
Turned professional: 1988
Tour Victories: 1993 Greater Milwaukee Open. (TOTAL: 1)
Annual earnings and rank:
1989—$111,998—116   1991—$185,668—89   1993—$513,072—30
1990—$693,658—12   1992—$191,878—79

BLAINE MCCALLISTER

Height: 5'9"
Birth date: Oct. 17, 1958
College: University of Houston
Career earnings: $2,088,043 (74)
Weight: 175
Residence: Houston, Texas
Turned professional: 1981
Tour victories: 1988 Hardee's Golf Classic. * 1989 Honda Classic, Bank of Boston Classic. * 1991 H-E-B. Texas Open. * 1993 B.C. Open. (TOTAL: 5)
Annual earnings and rank:
1982—$7,894—180   1987—$120,005—87   1990—$152,048—103
1983—$5,218—201   1988—$225,660—49   1991—$412,974—36
1986—$88,732—94   1989—$593,891—15   1992—$261,187—59
                                            1993—$290,434—61

MARK MCCUMBER

Height: 5'8"
Birth date: Sept. 7, 1951
Turned professional: 1974
Career earnings: $3,215,569 (38)
Weight: 170
Residence: Jacksonville, Fla.

Tour victories: 1979 Doral-Eastern Open. * 1983 Western Open, Pensacola Open. * 1985 Doral-Eastern Open. * 1987 Anheuser-Busch Classic. * 1988 THE PLAYERS Championship. * 1989 Beatrice Western Open. (TOTAL: 7)

Annual earnings and rank:
1978—$6,948—160	1983—$268,294—8	1988—$559,111—13
1979—$67,886—60	1984—$133,445—50	1989—$546,587—14
1980—$36,985—88	1985—$192,752—32	1990—$163,413—97
1981—$33,363—103	1986—$110,442—80	1991—$173,852—92
1982—$31,684—119	1987—$390,885—22	1992—$136,653—106
		1993—$363,269—41

JIM MCGOVERN

Height: 6'2"
Birth date: Feb. 5, 1965
College: Old Dominion
Career earnings: $846,251 (181)
Weight: 195
Residence: River Edge, N.J.
Turned professional: 1988

Tour Victories: Houston Open. (TOTAL: 1)

Annual earnings and rank:
1991—$88,869—141   1992—$169,889—92   1993—$587,495—27

ROCCO MEDIATE

Height: 6'1"
Birth date: Dec. 17, 1962
College: Florida Southern
Career earnings: $2,215,680 (66)
Weight: 200
Residence: Ponte Vedra, Fla.
Turned professional: 1985

Tour victories: 1991 Doral Ryder Open. * 1993 Greater Greensboro Open. (TOTAL: 2)

Annual earnings and rank:
1986—$20,670—174	1989—$132,501—108	1992—$301,896—49
1987—$112,099—91	1990—$240,625—62	1993—$680,623—16
1988—$129,829—92	1991—$597,438—15	

PHIL MICKELSON

Height: 6'2"
Birth date: June 16, 1970
College: Arizona State University
Career earnings: $800,448 (188)
Weight: 190
Residence: Scottsdale, Ariz.
Turned professional: 1992

Tour victories: 1991 Northern Telecom Open. * 1993 Buick Invitational, The International. (TOTAL: 3)

Annual earnings and rank:
1992—$171,713—90   1993—$628,735—22

LARRY MIZE

Height: 6'
Birth date: Sept. 23, 1958
College: Georgia Tech
Career earnings: $3,908,681 (25)
Weight: 165
Residence: Columbus, Ga.
Turned professional: 1980

Tour victories: 1983 Danny Thomas-Memphis Classic. * 1987 Masters. * 1993 Northern Telecom Open, Buick Open. (TOTAL: 4)

Annual earnings and rank:

1982—$28,787—124	1986—$314,051—17	1990—$668,198—14
1983—$146,325—35	1987—$561,407—6	1991—$279,061—60
1984—$172,513—36	1988—$187,823—62	1992—$316,428—47
1985—$231,041—17	1989—$278,388—45	1993—$724,660—13

GIL MORGAN

Height: 5'9"
Birth date: Sept. 25, 1946
College: East Central State College
Career earnings: $4,426,178 (21)
Weight: 175
Residence: Edmond, Okla.
Turned professional: 1972

Tour victories: 1977 B.C. Open. * 1978 Glen Campbell-Los Angeles Open, World Series of Golf. * 1979 Danny Thomas-Memphis Classic. * 1983 Joe Garagiola-Tucson Open, Glen Campbell-Los Angeles Open. * 1990 Kemper Open. (TOTAL: 7)

Annual earnings and rank:

1973—$3,800—204	1980—$135,308—28	1987—$133,980—81
1974—$23,880—94	1981—$171,184—18	1988—$288,002—34
1975—$42,772—60	1982—$139,652—26	1989—$300,395—39
1976—$61,372—42	1983—$306,133—5	1990—$702,629—11
1977—$104,817—24	1984—$281,948—13	1991—$232,913—70
1978—$267,459—2	1985—$133,941—62	1992—$272,959—56
1979—$115,857—29	1986—$98,770—84	1993—$610,312—24

JODIE MUDD

Height: 5'11"
Birth date: April 23, 1960
College: Georgia Southern University
Career earnings: $2,735,887 (49)
Weight: 150
Residence: Louisville
Turned professional: 1982

Tour victories: 1988 Federal Express St. Jude Classic. * 1989 GTE Byron Nelson Golf Classic. * 1990 THE PLAYERS Championship, Nabisco Championships. (TOTAL: 4)

Annual earnings and rank:

1982—$34,216—114	1986—$182,812—48	1990—$911,746—5
1983—$21,515—145	1987—$203,923—51	1991—$148,453—102
1984—$42,244—114	1988—$422,022—23	1992—$88,081—141
1985—$186,648—34	1989—$404,860—26	1993—$89,366—150

GREG NORMAN

Height: 6'1"
Birth date: Feb. 10, 1955
Turned professional: 1976
Career earnings: $6,607,562 (3)
Weight: 185
Residence: Hobe Sound, Fla.

Tour victories: 1984 Kemper Open, Canadian Open. ∗ 1986 Panasonic-Las Vegas Invitational, Kemper Open. ∗ 1988 MCI Heritage Classic. ∗ 1990 Doral Ryder Open, Memorial Tournament. ∗ 1992 Canadian Open. ∗ 1993 Doral Open. (TOTAL: 10) Also won British Open in 1986 and 1993.
Annual earnings and rank:
1983—$71,411—74
1984—$310,230—9
1985—$165,458—42
1986—$653,296—1
1987—$535,450—7
1988—$514,854—17
1989—$835,096—4
1990—$1,165,477—1
1991—$320,196—53
1992—$676,443—18
1993—$1,359,653—3

BRETT OGLE
Height: 6'2"
Birth date: July 14, 1964
Turned professional: 1985
Career earnings: $337,373 (270)
Weight: 165
Residence: London
Tour victories: 1993 Pebble Beach National Pro-Am. (TOTAL: 1)
Annual earnings and rank:
1993—$337,374—48

JOSE MARIA OLAZBAL
Height: 5'10"
Birth date: Feb. 5, 1966
Turned professional: 1985
Career earnings: NA
Weight: 160
Residence: Fuenterrabia, Spain
Tour victories: 1990 NEC World Series of Golf. ∗ 1991 International. (TOTAL: 2)
Annual earnings and rank:
1987—$7,470—215
1989—$56,039—160
1990—$337,837—38
1991—$382,124—43
1992—$63,429—161
1993—$60,160—174

MARK O'MEARA
Height: 6'
Birth date: Jan. 13, 1957
College: Long Beach State
Career earnings: $4,998,267 (15)
Weight: 180
Residence: Orlando, Fla.
Turned professional: 1980
Tour victories: 1984 Greater Milwaukee Open. ∗ 1985 Bing Crosby Pro-Am, Hawaiian Open. ∗ 1989 AT&T Pebble Beach National Pro-Am. ∗ 1990 AT&T Pebble Beach National Pro-Am, H.E.B. Texas Open. ∗ 1991 Walt Disney World/Oldsmobile Classic. ∗ 1992 AT&T Pebble Beach National Pro-Am. (TOTAL: 8)
Annual earnings and rank:
1981—$76,063—55
1982—$31,711—118
1983—$69,354—76
1984—$465,873—2
1985—$340,840—10
1986—$252,827—30
1987—$327,250—30
1988—$438,311—22
1989—$615,804—13
1990—$707,175—10
1991—$563,896—20
1992—$759,648—11
1993—$349,516—43

NAOMICHI "JOE" OZAKI
Height: 5'9"
Birth date: May 18, 1956
Turned professional: 1977
Weight: 150
Residence: Chiba, Japan

Career earnings: $294,395 (285)
Annual earnings and rank:
1989—$1,605—274   1991—$38,850—185   1993—$139,784—115
1990—$37,330—185 1992—$75,946—151

CRAIG PARRY

Height: 5'6"
Birth date: Dec. 1, 1966
Turned professional: 1985
Weight: 170
Residence: Kardinya, W. Australia
Career earnings: $564,968 (215)
Annual earnings and rank:
1989—$1,650—282   1991—$63,767—218   1993—$323,068—50
1990—$43,351—181 1992—$241,901—64

STEVE PATE

Height: 6'
Birth date: May 26, 1961
College: UCLA
Weight: 175
Residence: Orlando, Fla.
Turned professional: 1983
Career earnings: $3,280,181 (33)
Tour victories: 1987 Southwest Classic. * 1988 MONY Tournament of Champions, Shearson Lehman Hutton-Andy Williams Open. * 1991 Honda Classic. * 1992 Buick Invitational of California. (TOTAL: 5)
Annual earnings and rank:
1985—$89,358—86   1988—$582,473—12   1991—$727,997—6
1986—$176,100—51   1989—$306,554—35   1992—$472,626—30
1987—$335,728—26   1990—$334,505—39   1993—$254,841—64

COREY PAVIN

Height: 5'9"
Birth date: Nov. 16, 1959
College: UCLA
Weight: 140
Residence: Orlando, Fla.
Turned professional: 1982
Career earnings: $4,929,138 (16)
Tour victories: 1984 Houston Coca-Cola Open. * 1985 Colonial National Invitation. * 1986 Hawaiian Open, Greater Milwaukee Open. * 1987 Bob Hope Chrysler Classic, Hawaiian Open. * 1988 Texas Open presented by Nabisco. * 1991 Bob Hope Chrysler Classic, BellSouth Atlanta Classic. * 1992 Honda Classic. (TOTAL: 10)
Annual earnings and rank:
1984—$260,536—18   1987—$498,406—15   1990—$468,830—26
1985—$367,506—6   1988—$216,768—50   1991—$979,430—1
1986—$304,558—19   1989—$177,084—82   1992—$980,934—5
                                       1993—$675,087—18

DON POOLEY

Height: 6'2"
Birth date: Aug. 27, 1951
College: University of Arizona
Weight: 185
Residence: Tucson, Ariz.
Turned professional: 1973
Career earnings: $2,507,341 (54)
Tour victories: 1980 B.C. Open. * 1987 Memorial Tournament. (TOTAL: 2)

Annual earnings and rank:
1976—$2,139—208
1977—$24,507—94
1978—$31,945—84
1979—$6,932—170
1980—$157,973—18
1981—$75,730—57
1982—$87,962—48
1983—$145,979—36
1984—$120,699—54
1985—$162,094—46
1986—$268,274—22
1987—$450,005—18
1988—$239,534—46
1989—$214,662—66
1990—$192,570—83
1991—$67,549—156
1992—$135,683—107
1993—$123,105—122

NICK PRICE

Height: 6'
Birth date: Jan. 28, 1957
Turned professional: 1977
Career earnings: $5,226,491 (12)
Weight: 190
Residence: Orlando, Fla.

Tour victories: 1983 World Series of Golf. * 1991 GTE Byron Nelson Classic, Canadian Open. * 1992 PGA Championship, H-E-B Texas Open. * 1993 The Players Championship, Greater Hartford Open, Western Open, St. Jude Classic. (TOTAL: 9)

Annual earnings and rank:
1983—$49,435—103
1984—$109,480—66
1985—$96,069—80
1986—$225,373—35
1987—$334,169—28
1988—$266,300—42
1989—$296,170—42
1990—$520,777—22
1991—$714,389—7
1992—$1,135,773—4
1993—$1,478,557—1

DILLARD PRUITT

Height: 5'11"
Birth date: Sept. 24, 1961
College: Clemson
Career earnings: $739,758 (192)
Weight: 180
Residence: Greenville, S.C.
Turned professional: 1985

Tour victories: 1990 Chattanooga Classic. (TOTAL: 1)

Annual earnings and rank:
1988—$33,889—164
1990—$76,352—150
1991—$271,861—63
1992—$189,604—82
1993—$168,053—98

LOREN ROBERTS

Height: 6'2"
Birth date: June 24, 1955
College: Cal Poly San Luis Obispo
Career earnings: $2,115,727 (72)
Weight: 190
Residence: Memphis
Turned professional: 1975

Annual earnings and rank:
1981—$8,935—172
1983—$7,724—189
1984—$67,515—87
1985—$92,761—83
1986—$53,655—133
1987—$57,489—138
1988—$136,890—89
1989—$275,882—46
1990—$478,522—24
1991—$281,174—58
1992—$338,673—43
1993—$316,506—53

DAVE RUMMELLS

Height: 6'
Birth date: Jan. 26, 1958
College: Iowa
Career earnings: $1,601,058 (107)
Weight: 160
Residence: West Branch, Iowa
Turned professional: 1981

Annual earnings and rank:
1986—$83,227—103
1987—$154,720—189
1988—$274,800—38
1989—$419,979—24
1990—$111,539—131
1991—$213,627—79
1992—$95,203—134
1993—$247,963—67

GENE SAUERS

Height: 5'8"
Birth date: Aug. 22, 1962
College: Georgia Southern
Career earnings: $2,440,343 (56)
Weight: 150
Residence: Savannah, Ga.
Turned professional: 1984
Tour victories: 1986 Bank of Boston Classic. * 1989 Hawaiian Open. (TOTAL: 2)
Annual earnings and rank:
1984—$36,537—128
1985—$48,526—121
1986—$199,044—42
1987—$244,655—38
1988—$280,719—35
1989—$303,669—38
1990—$374,485—31
1991—$400,535—37
1992—$434,566—32
1993—$117,608—128

TOM SIECKMANN

Height: 6'5"
Birth date: Jan. 14, 1955
College: Oklahoma State University
Career earnings: $1,247,353 (136)
Weight: 220
Residence: Omaha
Turned professional: 1977
Tour victories: 1988 Anheuser-Busch Classic. (TOTAL: 1)
Annual earnings and rank:
1985—$30,052—143
1986—$63,395—125
1987—$52,259—146
1988—$209,151—54
1989—$97,465—128
1990—$141,241—110
1991—$278,598—61
1992—$173,424—88
1993—$201,429—87

SCOTT SIMPSON

Height: 6'2"
Birth date: Sept. 17, 1955
College: Univ. of Southern California
Career earnings: $3,665,272 (29)
Weight: 180
Residence: Kailua, Hawaii
Turned professional: 1977
Tour victories: 1980 Western Open. * 1984 Manufacturers Hanover Westchester Classic. * 1987 Greater Greensboro Open, U.S. Open. * 1989 BellSouth Atlanta Classic. * 1993 Byron Nelson Classic. (TOTAL: 6)
Annual earnings and rank:
1979—$53,084—74
1980—$141,323—24
1981—$108,793—34
1982—$146,903—24
1983—$144,172—38
1984—$248,581—22
1985—$171,245—39
1986—$202,223—41
1987—$621,032—4
1988—$108,301—106
1989—$298,920—40
1990—$235,309—63
1991—$322,936—51
1992—$155,284—97
1993—$707,166—14

JOEY SINDELAR

Height: 5'10"
Birth date: March 30, 1958
College: Ohio State University
Career earnings: $3,247,940 (35)
Weight: 200
Residence: Horseheads, N.Y.
Turned professional: 1981

Tour victories: 1985 Greater Greensboro Open, B.C.Open. * 1987 B.C. Open. * 1988 Honda Classic, International. * 1990 Hardee's Golf Classic. (TOTAL: 6)
Annual earnings and rank:
1984—$116,528—59
1985—$282,762—12
1986—$341,231—14
1987—$235,033—40
1988—$813,732—3
1989—$196,092—72
1990—$307,207—46
1991—$168,352—94
1992—$396,354—35
1993—$391,649—38

VIJAY SINGH

Height: 6'2"
Birth date: Feb. 22, 1963
College: NA
Weight: NA
Residence: Fiji
Turned professional: 1982
PGA Tour victories: 1993 Buick Classic. (TOTAL: 1)
Career earnings: $657,831 (205)
Joined Tour: 1993
Annual earnings and rank:
1993—$657,831—19

JEFF SLUMAN

Height: 5'7"
Birth date: Sept. 11, 1957
College: Florida State University
Weight: 140
Residence: Naples, Fla.
Turned professional: 1980
Career earnings: $2,995,571 (42)
Tour victories: 1988 PGA Championship. (TOTAL: 1)
Annual earnings and rank:
1983—$13,643—171
1984—$603—281
1985—$100,523—78
1986—$154,129—60
1987—$335,590—27
1988—$503,321—18
1989—$154,507—89
1990—$264,012—56
1991—$552,979—23
1992—$729,027—14
1993—$187,841—93

MIKE SPRINGER

Height: 5'11"
Birth date: Nov. 3, 1965
College: Arizona
Weight: 210
Residence: Fresno, Calif.
Turned professional: 1988
Career earnings: $537,632 (221)
Annual earnings and rank:
1991—$178,587—91
1992—$144,316—104
1993—$214,729—79

CRAIG STADLER

Height: 5'10"
Birth date: June 2, 1953
College: University of Southern California
Weight: 210
Residence: San Diego
Turned professional: 1975
Career earnings: $5,131,605 (13)
Tour victories: 1980 Bob Hope Desert Classic, Greater Greensboro Open. * 1981 Kemper Open. * 1982 Joe Garagiola-Tucson Open, Masters Tournament, Kemper Open, World Series of Golf. * 1984 Byron Nelson Classic. * 1991 THE TOUR Championship. * 1992 NEC World Series of Golf. (TOTAL: 10)

Annual earnings and rank:
1976—$2,702—196	1982—$446,462—1	1988—$278,313—37
1977—$42,949—66	1983—$214,496—17	1989—$409,419—25
1978—$63,486—48	1984—$324,241—8	1990—$278,482—52
1979—$73,392—55	1985—$297,926—11	1991—$827,628—2
1980—$206,291—8	1986—$170,076—53	1992—$487,460—28
1981—$218,829—8	1987—$235,831—39	1993—$553,623—29

MIKE STANDLY

Height: 6'
Birth date: May 19, 1964
College: Houston
Career earnings: $593,444 (212)
Weight: 200
Residence: Houston, Texas
Turned professional: 1986
Tour Victories: 1993 Freeport-McMoRan Classic. (TOTAL: 1)
Annual earnings and rank:
1991—$55,846—171   1992—$213,712—73   1993—$323,886—49

PAYNE STEWART

Height: 6'1"
Birth date: Jan. 30, 1957
College: Southern Methodist University
Career earnings: $6,377,573 (4)
Weight: 175
Residence: Orlando, Fla.
Turned professional: 1979
Tour victories: 1982 Quad Cities Open. * 1983 Walt Disney World Classic. * 1987 Hertz Bay Hill Classic. * 1989 MCI Heritage Classic, PGA Championship. * 1990 MCI Heritage Classic, GTE Byron Nelson Classic. (TOTAL: 7)
Annual earnings and rank:
1981—$13,400—157	1985—$225,729—19	1989—$1,201,301—2
1982—$98,686—38	1986—$535,389—3	1990—$976,281—3
1983—$178,809—25	1987—$511,026—12	1991—$476,971—31
1984—$288,795—11	1988—$553,571—14	1992—$334,738—44
		1993—$982,875—6

CURTIS STRANGE

Height: 5'11"
Birth date: Jan. 30, 1955
College: Wake Forest University
Career earnings: $6,042,561 (7)
Weight: 170
Residence: Kingsmill, Va.
Turned professional: 1976
Tour victories: 1979 Pensacola Open. * 1980 Michelob-Houston Open, Manufacturers Hanover Westchester Classic. * 1983 Sammy Davis, Jr.-Greater Hartford Open. * 1984 LaJet Classic. * 1985 Honda Classic, Panasonic-Las Vegas Invitational, Canadian Open. * 1986 Houston Open. * 1987 Canadian Open, Federal Express St. Jude Classic, NEC World Series of Golf. * 1988 Independent Insurance Agent Open, Memorial Tournament, U.S. Open, Nabisco Championships. * 1989 U.S. Open. (TOTAL: 17)
Annual earnings and rank:
1977—$28,144—87	1983—$200,116—21	1989—$752,587—7
1978—$29,346—88	1984—$276,773—14	1990—$277,172—53
1979—$138,368—21	1985—$542,321—1	1991—$336,333—48
1980—$271,888—3	1986—$237,700—32	1992—$150,639—99
1981—$201,513—9	1987—$925,941—1	1993—$262,697—63
1982—$263,378—10	1988—$1,147,644—1	

KIRK TRIPLETT

Height: 6'3"
Birth date: March 29, 1962
College: University of Nevada
Career earnings: $686,051 (200)
Weight: 190
Residence: Cave Creek, Ariz.
Turned professional: 1985

Annual earnings and rank:
1990—$183,464—88
1991—$137,302—112
1992—$175,868—85
1993—$189,418—90

GREG TWIGGS

Height: 6'2"
Birth date: Oct. 30, 1960
College: San Diego State University
Career earnings: $672,082 (203)
Weight: 235
Residence: Greensboro, N.C.
Turned professional: 1982

Tour victories: 1989 Shearson Lehman Hutton Open. (TOTAL: 1)

Annual earnings and rank:
1985—$33,559—139
1986—$41,418—147
1987—$21,443—186
1988—$2,999—262
1989—$154,302—90
1990—$49,696—178
1991—$65,080—158
1992—$74,761—153
1993—$231,823—72

HOWARD TWITTY

Height: 6'5"
Birth date: Jan. 15, 1949
College: Arizona State University
Career earnings: $2,393,070 (58)
Weight: 210
Residence: Paradise Valley, Ariz.
Turned professional: 1974

Tour victories: 1979 B.C. Open. * 1980 Sammy Davis, Jr.-Greater Hartford Open. * 1993 Hawaiian Open. (TOTAL: 3)

Annual earnings and rank:
1975—$8,211—139
1976—$54,268—51
1977—$60,091—49
1978—$92,409—25
1979—$179,619—15
1980—$166,190—14
1981—$52,183—79
1982—$57,355—78
1983—$20,000—150
1984—$51,971—106
1985—$92,958—82
1986—$156,119—57
1987—$169,442—61
1988—$87,985—119
1989—$107,200—119
1990—$129,444—120
1991—$226,426—74
1992—$264,042—57
1993—$416,833—34

BOBBY WADKINS

Height: 6'1"
Birth date: July 26, 1951
College: East Tennessee State
Career earnings: $2,073,328 (75)
Weight: 185
Residence: Richmond, Va.
Turned professional: 1973

Annual earnings and rank:
1975—$23,330—90
1976—$23,510—93
1977—$20,867—103
1978—$70,426—41
1979—$121,373—28
1980—$56,728—67
1981—$58,346—73
1982—$69,400—59
1983—$56,363—92
1984—$108,335—67
1985—$84,542—90
1986—$226,079—33
1987—$342,173—25
1988—$193,022—59
1989—$152,184—91
1990—$190,613—85
1991—$206,503—81
1992—$30,382—197
1993—$39,153—189

LANNY WADKINS

Height: 5'9"
Birth date: Dec. 5, 1949
College: Wake Forest University
Career earnings: $5,877,256 (8)
Weight: 170
Residence: Dallas
Turned professional: 1971

Tour victories: 1972 Sahara Invitational. ∗ 1973 Byron Nelson Classic, USI Classic. ∗ 1977 PGA Championship, World Series of Golf. ∗ 1979 Glen Campbell-Los Angeles Open, Tournament Players Championship. ∗ 1982 Phoenix Open, MONY Tournament of Champions, Buick Open. ∗ 1983 Greater Greensboro Open, MONY Tournament of Champions. ∗ 1985 Bob Hope Classic, Los Angeles Open, Walt Disney World/Olds-mobile Classic. ∗ 1987 Doral Ryder Open. ∗ 1988 Hawaiian Open, Colonial National Invitation. ∗ 1990 Anheuser-Busch Golf Classic. ∗ 1991 United Hawaiian Open. ∗ 1992 Canon Greater Hartford Open. (TOTAL: 21)

Annual earnings and rank:

1971—$15,291—111	1979—$195,710—10	1987—$501,727—13
1972—$116,616—10	1980—$67,778—58	1988—$616,596—10
1973—$200,455—5	1981—$51,704—81	1989—$233,363—60
1974—$51,124—54	1982—$306,827—7	1990—$673,433—13
1975—$23,582—88	1983—$319,271—3	1991—$651,495—12
1976—$42,849—64	1984—$198,996—29	1992—$366,837—40
1977—$244,882—3	1985—$446,893—2	1993—$244,544—68
1978—$53,811—61	1986—$264,931—23	

GRANT WAITE

Height: 6'
Birth date: Aug. 11, 1964
College: Oklahoma
Career earnings: $461,481 (237)
Weight: 185
Residence: Salt Lake City
Turned professional: 1987

Tour Victories: 1993 Kemper Open. (TOTAL: 1)
Annual earnings and rank:
1990—$50,076—177   1993—$411,405—35

DUFFY WALDORF

Height: 5'11"
Birth date: Aug. 20, 1962
College: UCLA
Career earnings: $1,312,853 (129)
Weight: 225
Residence: Valencia, Calif.
Turned professional: 1985

Annual earnings and rank:

1987—$53,175—148	1989—$149,945—94	1991—$196,081—86
1988—$55,221—143	1990—$71,673—157	1992—$582,120—23
		1993—$202,638—84

TOM WATSON

Height: 5'9"
Birth date: Sept. 4, 1949
College: Stanford University
Career earnings: $6,370,949 (5)
Weight: 160
Residence: Mission Hills, Kan.
Turned professional: 1971

Tour victories: 1974 Western Open. ∗ 1975 Byron Nelson Golf Classic. ∗ 1977 Bing Crosby National Pro-Am, Wickes-Andy Williams San Diego Open, Masters, Western Open. ∗ 1978 Joe Garagiola-Tucson Open, Bing Crosby National Pro-Am, Byron Nelson Golf Classic, Colgate Hall of Fame Classic, Anheuser-Busch Classic. ∗ 1979 Sea Pines Heritage Classic, Tournament of Champions, Byron Nelson Golf Classic, Memorial Tournament, Colgate Hall of Fame Classic. ∗ 1980 Andy Williams-San Diego Open, Glen Campbell-Los Angeles Open, MONY Tournament of Champions, New Orleans Open, Byron Nelson Classic, World Series of Golf. ∗ 1981 Masters, USF&G-New Orleans Open, Atlanta Classic. ∗ 1982 Glen Campbell-Los Angeles Open, Sea Pines Heritage Classic, U.S. Open. ∗ 1984 Seiko-Tucson Match Play, MONY Tournament of Champions, Western Open. ∗ 1987 Nabisco Championships of Golf. (TOTAL: 32)
Also won British Open in 1975, 1977, 1980, 1982 and 1983.

Annual earnings and rank:
1971—$2,185—224
1972—$31,081—79
1973—$74,973—35
1974—$135,474—10
1975—$153,795—7
1976—$138,202—12
1977—$310,653—1
1978—$362,429—1
1979—$462,636—1
1980—$530,808—1
1981—$347,660—3
1982—$316,483—5
1983—$237,519—12
1984—$476,260—1
1985—$226,778—18
1986—$278,338—20
1987—$616,351—5
1988—$273,216—39
1989—$185,398—80
1990—$213,988—68
1991—$354,877—45
1992—$299,818—50
1993—$342,023—46

D.A. WEIBRING

Height: 6'1"
Birth date: May 25, 1953
College: Illinois State
Weight: 180
Residence: Plano, Texas
Turned professional: 1975
Career earnings: $2,839,550 (48)
Tour victories: 1979 Quad Cities Open. ∗ 1987 Beatrice Western Open. ∗ 1991 Hardee's Golf Classic. (TOTAL: 3)

Annual earnings and rank:
1977—$1,681—215
1978—$41,052—75
1979—$71,343—57
1980—$78,611—53
1981—$92,365—45
1982—$117,941—31
1983—$61,631—84
1984—$110,325—65
1985—$153,079—50
1986—$167,602—55
1987—$391,363—21
1988—$186,677—63
1989—$98,686—127
1990—$156,235—101
1991—$558,648—22
1992—$253,018—62
1993—$299,293—58

MARK WIEBE

Height: 6'2"
Birth date: Sept. 13, 1957
College: San Jose State
Weight: 210
Residence: Denver
Turned professional: 1980
Career earnings: $2,120,874 (71)
Tour victories: 1985 Anheuser-Busch Classic, 1986 Hardee's Golf Classic. (TOTAL: 2)

Annual earnings and rank:
1984—$16,257—166
1985—$181,894—36
1986—$260,180—25
1987—$128,651—82
1988—$392,166—28
1989—$296,269—41
1990—$210,435—72
1991—$100,046—136
1992—$174,763—86
1993—$360,213—42

IAN WOOSNAM

Height: 5'4"
Birth date: March 2, 1958
Turned professional: 1976
Career earnings: NA
Weight: 161
Residence: Oswestry, Wales

Tour victories: 1991 USF&G Classic, Masters Tournament. (TOTAL: 2)
Annual earnings and rank:

1986—$4,000—233	1989—$146,323—97	1992—$52,046—171
1987—$3,980—236	1990—$72,138—156	1993—$55,426—176
1988—$8,464—219	1991—$485,023—23	

ROBERT WRENN

Height: 5'10"
Birth date: Sept. 11, 1959
College: Wake Forest
Career earnings: $1,263,084 (135)
Weight: 170
Residence: Richmond, Va.
Turned professional: 1981

Tour victories: 1987 Buick Open. (TOTAL: 1)
Annual earnings and rank:

1985—$36,396—135	1988—$209,404—52	1991—$141,255—109
1986—$22,869—171	1989—$243,638—55	1992—$127,729—113
1987—$203,557—52	1990—$174,308—92	1993—$103,928—143

FUZZY ZOELLER

Height: 5'10"
Birth date: Nov. 11, 1951
Weight: 190
Residence: New Albany, Ind.

College: Edison Junior College in Ft. Myers, Fla., and University of Houston
Turned professional: 1973
Career earnings: $3,731,261 (28)
Tour victories: 1979 Wickes-Andy Williams San Diego Open, Masters. * 1981 Colonial National Invitation. * 1983 Sea Pines Heritage Classic, Las Vegas Pro-Celebrity Classic. * 1984 U.S. Open. * 1985 Hertz Bay Hill Classic. * 1986 AT&T Pebble Beach National Pro-Am, Sea Pines Heritage Golf Classic, Anheuser-Busch Golf Classic. (TOTAL: 10)
Annual earnings and rank:

1975—$7,318—146	1981—$151,571—19	1987—$222,921—44
1976—$52,557—56	1982—$126,512—28	1988—$209,564—51
1977—$76,417—40	1983—$417,597—2	1989—$217,742—65
1978—$109,055—20	1984—$157,460—40	1990—$199,629—79
1979—$196,951—9	1985—$244,003—15	1991—$385,139—42
1980—$95,531—46	1986—$358,115—13	1992—$125,003—114
		1993—$378,175—39

LPGA Tour players

KRISTI ALBERS
Height: 5'7"
Birth date: Dec. 7, 1963
College: University of New Mexico
Residence: El Paso
Joined LPGA: October 1985
Career earnings: $815,477 (57)
LPGA Tour victories: 1993 Centel Classic. (TOTAL: 1)
Annual earnings and rank:
1986—$9,230—122   1990—$111,515—35
1987—$17,569—104   1991—$139,982—31
1988—$27,609—81   1992—$173,189—30
1989—$72,900—44   1993—$263,483—17

AMY ALCOTT
Height: 5'6"
Birth date: Feb. 22, 1956
Joined LPGA: 1975
Residence: Princeville, Hawaii
Career earnings: $2,910,706 (6)
LPGA Tour victories: 1975 Orange Blossom Classic. ∗ 1976 LPGA Classic, Colgate Far East Open. ∗ 1977 Houston Exchange Clubs Classic. ∗ 1978 American Defender Classic. ∗ 1979 Elizabeth Arden Classic, Peter Jackson Classic, United Virginia Bank Classic, Mizuno Japan Classic. ∗ 1980 American Defender/WRAL Classic, Mayflower Classic, U.S. Women's Open, Inamori Classic. ∗ 1981 Bent Tree Ladies Classic, Lady Michelob. ∗ 1982 Women's Kemper Open. ∗ 1983 Nabisco Dinah Shore Invitational. ∗ 1984 United Virginia Bank Classic, Lady Keystone Open, Portland Ping Championship, San Jose Classic. ∗ 1985 Circle K Tuscon Open, Moss Creek Women's Invitational, Nestlé World Championship of Women's Golf. ∗ 1986 Mazda Hall of Fame Championship, LPGA National Pro-Am. ∗ 1988 Nabisco Dinah Shore. ∗ 1989 Boston Five Classic. ∗ 1991 Nabisco Dinah Shore. (TOTAL: 29)
Annual earnings and rank:
1975—$26,798—15   1985—$283,111—4
1976—$71,122—7   1986—$244,410—4
1977—$47,637—14   1987—$125,831—17
1978—$75,516—9   1988—$292,349—7
1979—$144,838—3   1989—$168,089—18
1980—$219,887—3   1990—$99,208—42
1981—$149,089—7   1991—$258,270—13
1982—$169,581—6   1992—$100,064—55
1983—$153,721—8   1993—$60,518—77
1984—$220,412—5

HELEN ALFREDSSON
Height: 5'10"
Birth date: April 9, 1965
College: United States International University in San Diego
Residence: Sweden
Joined LPGA: October 1991
Career earnings: $664,800 (67)
LPGA Tour victories: 1993 Dinah Shore. (TOTAL: 1)

Annual earnings and rank:
1992—$262,115—16   1993—$402,685—5

DANIELLE AMMACCAPANE

Height: 5'5"
Birth date: Nov. 27, 1965
Residence: Phoenix
College: Arizona State University
Joined LPGA: October 1987
Career earnings: $1,569,872 (18)
LPGA Tour victories: 1991 Standard Register Ping. * 1992 Standard Register Ping, Centel Classic, Lady Keystone Open. (TOTAL: 4)
Annual earnings and rank:
1988—$71,106—44   1991—$361,925—6
1989—$135,109—23   1992—$513,639—3
1990—$300,231—9   1993—$187,862—28

DONNA ANDREWS

Height: 5'8"
Birth date: April 12, 1967
Residence: Pinehurst, N.C.
College: University of North Carolina
Joined LPGA: October 1989
Career earnings: $760,026 (59)
LPGA Tour victories: 1993 Ping-Cellular One Championship. (TOTAL: 1)
Annual earnings and rank:
1990—$52,430—75   1992—$299,839—13
1991—$73,472—65   1993—$334,285—9

TINA BARRETT

Height: 5'4"
Birth date: June 5, 1966
Residence: Phoenix
College: Longwood College
Joined LPGA: October 1988
Career earnings: $641,726 (72)
LPGA Tour victories: 1989 Mitsubishi Motors Ocean State Open. (TOTAL: 1)
Annual earnings and rank:
1989—$39,776—69   1992—$184,719—28
1990—$17,867—121   1993—$261,491—19
1991—$138,232—32

AMY BENZ

Height: 5'5"
Birth date: May 12, 1962
Residence: Boca Raton, Fla.
Joined LPGA: August 1983
Career earnings: $979,987 (41)
Annual earnings and rank:
1983—$13,143—95   1989—$98,129—35
1984—$41,014—54   1990—$128,216—29
1985—$62,260—31   1991—$96,248—51
1986—$72,407—31   1992—$141,673—40
1987—$42,870—57   1993—$166,968—35
1988—$117,059—24

MISSIE BERTEOTTI

Height: 5'10"
Birth date: Sept. 22, 1963
College: University of Miami
Residence: Pittsburgh
Joined LPGA: October 1985
Career earnings: $816,234 (56)
LPGA Tour victories: 1993 Ping-Welch's Championship.(TOTAL: 1)
(Annual earnings and rank:
1986—$34,092—65   1990—$107,030—38
1987—$62,446—45   1991—$106,459—47
1988—$69,441—45   1992—$213,720—22
1989—$38,493—71   1993—$184,553—31

PAT BRADLEY

Height: 5'6"
Birth date: March 24, 1951
College: Florida International University
Residence: Marco Island, Fla.
Joined LPGA: January 1974
Career earnings: $4,535,841 (1)
LPGA Tour victories: 1976 Girl Talk Classic. * 1977 Bankers Trust Classic. * 1978 Lady Keystone, Hoosier Classic, Rail Charity Classic. * 1980 Greater Baltimore Classic, Peter Jackson Classic. * 1981 Women's Kemper Open, U.S. Women's Open. * 1983 Mazda Classic of Deer Creek, Chrysler-Plymouth Charity Classic, Columbia Savings Classic, Mazda Japan Classic. * 1985 Rochester International, du Maurier Classic, LPGA National Pro-Am. * 1986 Nabisco Dinah Shore, S&H Golf Classic, LPGA Championship, du Maurier Classic, Nestlé World Championship. * 1987 Standard Register Turquoise Classic. * 1989 AI-Star/Centinela Hospital Classic. * 1990 Oldsmobile LPGA Classic, Standard Register Turquoise Classic, LPGA Corning Classic. * 1991 Centel Classic, Rail Charity Golf Classic, Safeco Classic, MBS LPGA Classic. (TOTAL: 30)
Annual earnings and rank:
1974—$10,839—39   1984—$220,478—4
1975—$28,293—14   1985—$387,378—2
1976—$84,288—6   1986—$492,021—1
1977—$78,709—8   1987—$140,132—15
1978—$118,057—2   1988—$15,965—109
1979—$132,428—4   1989—$423,714—4
1980—$183,377—6   1990—$480,018—5
1981—$197,050—3   1991—$763,118—1
1982—$113,089—11   1992—$238,541—19
1983—$240,207—3   1993—$188,135—27

BRANDIE BURTON

Height: 5'7"
Birth date: Jan. 8, 1972
College: Arizona State University
Residence: Rialto, Calif.
Joined LPGA: October 1990
Career earnings: $1,113,724 (32)
LPGA victories: 1992 Ping/Welch's Championship. *1993 Jamie Farr Toledo Classic, du Maurier Classic, Safeco Classic. (TOTAL: 4)
Annual earnings and rank:
1991—$176,412—22   1993—$517,741—3
1992—$419,571—4

JOANNE CARNER

Height: 5'7"
Birth date: April 4, 1939
Joined LPGA: 1970
Residence: Palm Beach, Fla.
Career earnings: $2,784,598 (7)
LPGA Tour victories: 1970 Wendell West Open. * 1971 U.S. Women's Open, Bluegrass Invitational. * 1974 Bluegrass Invitational, Hoosier Classic, Desert Inn Classic, St. Paul Open, Dallas Civitan, Portland Classic. * 1975 American Defender Classic, All-American Classic, Peter Jackson Classic. * 1976 Orange Blossom Classic, Lady Tara Classic, Hoosier Classic, U.S. Women's Open. * 1977 Talk Tournament, Borden Classic, National Jewish Hospital Open. * 1978 Peter Jackson Classic, Borden Classic. * 1979 Honda Civic Classic, Women's Kemper Open. * 1980 Whirlpool Championship of Deer Creek, Bent Tree Ladies Classic, Sunstar '80, Honda Civic Classic, Lady Keystone Open. * 1981 S&H Golf Classic, Lady Keystone Open, Columbia Savings LPGA Classic, Rail Charity Golf Classic. * 1982 Elizabeth Arden Classic, McDonald's LPGA Kids' Classic, Chevrolet World Championship of Women's Golf, Henredon Classic, Rail Charity Golf Classic. * 1983 Chevrolet World Championship of Women's Golf, Portland Ping Championship. * 1984 Corning Classic. * 1985 Elizabeth Arden Classic, Safeco Classic. (TOTAL: 42)

Annual earnings and rank:

1970—$14,551—11
1971—$21,604—6
1972—$18,902—15
1973—$19,688—25
1974—$87,094—1
1975—$64,843—2
1976—$103,275—3
1977—$113,712—2
1978—$108,093—4
1979—$98,219—9
1980—$185,916—5
1981—$206,648—2
1982—$310,399—1
1983—$291,404—1
1984—$144,900—9
1985—$141,941—11
1986—$82,802—26
1987—$66,601—41
1988—$121,218—21
1989—$97,888—36
1990—$87,218—48
1991—$86,874—56
1992—$175,880—29
1993—$134,956—41

DAWN COE-JONES

Height: 5'7"
Birth date: Oct. 19, 1960
College: Lamar University
Residence: Tampa
Joined LPGA: October 1983
Career earnings: $1,298,788 (26)
LPGA Tour victories: 1992 Women's Kemper Open. (TOTAL: 1)

Annual earnings and rank:

1984—$19,603—91
1985—$34,864—68
1986—$54,332—47
1987—$72,045—33
1988—$52,659—58
1989—$143,423—19
1990—$240,478—11
1991—$158,013—25
1992—$251,392—17
1993—$271,978—16

JANE CRAFTER

Height: 5'4"
Birth date: Dec. 14, 1955
Joined LPGA: July 1981
Residence: Adelaide, Australia

Career earnings: $852,329 (51)
LPGA Tour victories: 1990 Phar-Mor at Inverrary. (TOTAL: 1)
Annual earnings and rank:
1981—$1,617—135   1988—$32,733—73
1982—$7,472—108   1989—$35,086—77
1983—$37,433—43   1990—$112,840—34
1984—$48,729—46   1991—$34,168—101
1985—$60,884—32   1992—$155,485—35
1986—$79,431—28   1993—$187,190—29
1987—$59,876—48

ELAINE CROSBY

Height: 5'8"
Birth date: June 6, 1958   **Residence:** Ft. Myers, Fla.
College: University of Michigan   **Joined LPGA:** October 1984
Career earnings: $827,248 (53)
LPGA Tour victories: 1989 Mazda Japan Classic. (TOTAL: 1)
Annual earnings and rank:
1985—$10,133—122   1990—$169,543—18
1986—$5,533—146   1991—$181,610—21
1987—$31,024—74   1992—$109,125—50
1988—$15,655—112   1993—$177,726—33
1989—$126,899—28

LAURA DAVIES

Height: 5'10"
Birth date: Oct. 5, 1963   **Residence:** West Byfleet, England
Joined LPGA: October 1987
Career earnings: $998,456 (40)
LPGA Tour victories: 1988 Circle K LPGA Tucson Open, Jamie Farr Toledo Classic. * 1989 Lady Keystone Open. * 1991 Inamori Classic. * 1993 McDonald's Championship. (TOTAL: 5)
Annual earnings and rank:
1988—$160,382—15   1991—$200,831—20
1989—$181,574—13   1992—$150,163—39
1990—$64,863—64   1993—240,643—20

JUDY DICKINSON

Height: 5'4"
Birth date: March 4, 1950   **Residence:** Tequesta, Fla.
College: Glassboro State College   **Joined LPGA:** January 1978
Career earnings: $1,743,929 (16)
LPGA Tour victories: 1985 Boston Five Classic. * 1986 Rochester International, Safeco Classic. * 1992 Inamori Classic. (TOTAL: 4)
Annual earnings and rank:
1978—$5,330—83   1986—$195,834—10
1979—$24,561—48   1987—$19,602—96
1980—$30,648—46   1988—$160,440—14
1981—$42,570—36   1989—$23,460—96
1982—$47,187—29   1990—$80,784—52

1983—$69,091—23
1984—$85,479—18
1985—$167,809—9
1991—$251,018—14
1992—$351,559—10
1993—$186,317—30

HELEN DOBSON

Height 5'7"
Birth date: Feb. 25, 1971
Residence: Skegness, England
Joined LPGA: October 1992
Career earnings: $84,959 (239)
LPGA Tour victories: 1993 Rail Charity Classic. (TOTAL: 1)
Annual earnings and rank:
1993—$84,959—58

MARTA FIGUERAS-DOTTI

Height 5'8"
Birth date: Nov. 12, 1957
College: University of Southern California
Residence: Madrid, Spain
Joined LPGA: October 1983
Career earnings: $920,962 (44)
Annual earnings and rank:
1984—$96,655—15
1985—$53,094—43
1986—$68,081—34
1987—$70,616—36
1988—$156,065—16
1989—$77,790—40
1990—$64,874—63
1991—$104,896—48
1992—$127,789—45
1993—$101,102—52

LORI GARBACZ

Height: 5'6"
Birth date: Aug. 11, 1958
College: University of Florida
Residence: Boca Raton, Fla.
Joined LPGA: January 1979
Career earnings: $878,217 (49)
LPGA Tour victories: 1989 Circle K LPGA Tucson Open. (TOTAL: 1)
Annual earnings and rank:
1979—$32,457—34
1980—$61,120—16
1981—$24,016—58
1982—$28,255—55
1983—$40,552—38
1984—$55,540—32
1985—$126,631—15
1986—$61,160—39
1987—$85,269—27
1988—$28,869—76
1989—$138,124—22
1990—$9,582—146
1991—$70,884—68
1992—$56,448—83
1993—$59,308—78

JANE GEDDES

Height: 5'5"
Birth date: Feb. 5, 1960
College: Florida State University
Residence: Miami
Joined LPGA: August 1983
Career earnings: $1,995,654 (12)
LPGA Tour victories: 1993 Oldsmobile Classic. (TOTAL: 1)
Annual earnings and rank:
1993—$263,149—18

TAMMIE GREEN

Height: 5'8"
Birth date: Dec. 17, 1959
College: Marshall University
Career earnings: $1,296,894 (27)

Residence: Somerset, Ohio
Joined LPGA: October 1986

LPGA Tour victories: 1989 du Maurier Ltd. Classic. * 1993 Palm Beach Classic, Rochester International. (TOTAL: 3)

Annual earnings and rank:
1987—$68,346—39   1991—$237,073—15
1988—$120,271—22   1992—$154,717—37
1989—$204,143—8   1993—$356,579—7
1990—$155,756—22

SHELLEY HAMLIN

Height: 5'5"
Birth date: May 28, 1949
Joined LPGA: 1972
Career earnings: $849,596 (52)

Residence: Phoenix

LPGA Tour victories: 1993 ShopRite Classic.
1993—$129,447—44

JULI INKSTER

Height: 5'7"
Birth date: June 24, 1960
Joined LPGA: August 1983
Career earnings: $1,956,589 (13)

Residence: Los Altos, Calif.

LPGA Tour victories: 1983 Safeco Classic. * 1984 Nabisco Dinah Shore, du Maurier Classic. * 1985 Lady Keystone Open. * 1986 Women's Kemper Open, McDonald's Championship, Lady Keystone Open, Atlantic City Classic. * 1988 Crestar Classic, Atlantic City Classic, Safeco Classic. * 1989 Nabisco Dinah Shore, Crestar Classic. * 1991 LPGA Bay State Classic. * 1992 JAL Big Apple Classic. (TOTAL: 15)

Annual earnings and rank:
1983—$52,220—30   1989—$180,848—1
1984—$186,501—6   1990—$54,251—73
1985—$99,651—19   1991—$213,096—1
1986—$285,293—3   1992—$392,063—7
1987—$140,739—14   1993—$116,583—47
1988—$235,344—1

CHRIS JOHNSON

Height: 5'11"
Birth date: April 25, 1958
College: University of Arizona
Career earnings: $1,345,438 (24)

Residence: Tucson, Ariz.
Joined LPGA: July 1980

LPGA Tour victories: 1984 Samaritan Turquoise Classic, Tucson Conquistadores Open. * 1986 GNA/Glendale Federal Classic. * 1987 Columbia Savings LPGA National Pro-Am. * 1990 Atlantic City Classic. * 1991 Ping/Welch's Championship. (TOTAL: 6)

Annual earnings and rank:

1980—$2,827—123	1987—$197,722—8
1981—$25,182—55	1988—$46,219—61
1982—$60,449—24	1989—$97,195—3
1983—$37,967—42	1990—$187,486—14
1984—$70,979—25	1991—$135,416—33
1985—$67,123—29	1992—$105,197—53
1986—$200,648—8	1993—$111,027—50

TRISH JOHNSON

Height: 5'10"
Birth date: Jan. 17, 1966   **Residence:** Swansea, Wales
Joined LPGA: October 1987
Career earnings: $550,403 (83)
LPGA Tour victories: 1993 LPGA at Canyon Gate, Atlanta Women's Championship. (TOTAL: 2)
Annual earnings and rank:

1988—$23,972—89	1991—$85,639—57
1989—$17,215—115	1992—$33,103—112
1990—$58,729—71	1993—$331,745—10

ROSIE JONES

Height: 5'7"
Birth date: Nov. 13, 1959   **Residence:** Atlanta
College: Ohio State University   **Joined LPGA:** July 1982
Career earnings: $2,069,366 (11)
LPGA Tour victories: 1987 Rail Charity Golf Classic. ∗ 1988 USX Golf Classic, Nestlé World Championship, Santa Barbara Open. ∗ 1991 Rochester International. (TOTAL: 5)
Annual earnings and rank:

1982—$2,869—127	1988—$323,392—3
1983—$64,955—27	1989—$110,671—32
1984—$81,793—19	1990—$353,832—6
1985—$66,665—30	1991—$281,089—12
1986—$71,399—33	1992—$204,096—25
1987—$188,000—10	1993—$320,964—11

TRACY KERDYK

Height: 5'8"
Birth date: March 5, 1966   **Residence:** Coral Gables, Fla.
College: University of Miami   **Joined LPGA:** October 1988
Career earnings: $287,605 (132)
Annual earnings and rank:

1989—$64,644—51	1992—$63,732—72
1990—$35,199—96	1993—$64,908—71
1991—$59,122—78	

BETSY KING

Height: 5'6"
Birth date: Aug. 13, 1955
College: Furman University
Career earnings: $4,502,634 (2)
Residence: Limekiln, Pa.
Joined LPGA: July 1977

LPGA Tour victories: 1984 Women's Kemper Open, Freedom Orlando Classic, Columbia Savings Classic. * 1985 Samaritan Turquoise Classic, Rail Charity Classic. * 1986 Henredon Classic, Rail Charity Classic. * 1987 Circle K LPGA Tucson Open, Nabisco Dinah Shore, McDonald's Championship, Atlantic City Classic. * 1988 Women's Kemper Open, Rail Charity Golf Classic, Cellular One-Ping Golf Championship. * 1989 Jamaica Classic, Women's Kemper Open, USX Golf Classic, McDonald's Championship, U.S. Women's Open, Nestlé World Championship.* 1990 Nabisco Dinah Shore, U.S. Women's Open, JAL Big Apple Classic. * 1991 LPGA Corning Classic, JAL Big Apple Classic. * 1992 Mazda LPGA Championship, Phar-Mor in Youngstown, Mazda Japan Classic * 1993 LPGA Skins Game, Japan Classic. (TOTAL: 30)

Annual earnings and rank:
1977—$4,008—83
1978—$44,092—20
1979—$53,900—19
1980—$28,480—50
1981—$51,029—22
1982—$50,563—28
1983—$94,767—14
1984—$266,771—1
1985—$214,411—6
1986—$290,195—2
1987—$460,385—2
1988—$256,957—8
1989—$654,132—1
1990—$543,844—3
1991—$341,784—9
1992—$551,320—2
1993—$595,992—1

HIROMI KOBAYASHI

Height: 5'8"
Birth date: Jan. 8, 1963
Joined LPGA tour: 1989
Residence: Ibaraki, Japan

LPGA Tour victories: 1993 Big Apple Classic, Minnesota Classic.. (TOTAL: 2)
Annual earnings and rank:
1990—$66,325—60
1991—$76,582—63
1992—$58,851—80
1993—$347,060—8

DANA LOFLAND-DORMANN

Height: 5'9"
Birth date: Sept. 16, 1967
College: San Jose University
Career earnings: $595,202 (78)
Residence: Pleasanton, Calif.
Joined LPGA: October 1990

LPGA Tour victories: 1992 Las Vegas LPGA International. * 1993 Stratton Mountain Classic. (TOTAL: 2)
Annual earnings and rank:
1991—$90,374—52
1992—$270,413—14
1993—$234,415—21

NANCY LOPEZ

Height: 5'5"
Birth date: Jan. 6, 1957
College: Tulsa University
Career earnings: $3,866,851 (4)
Residence: Albany, Ga.
Joined LPGA: 1977

LPGA Tour victories: 1978 Bent Tree Ladies Classic, Sunstar Classic, Greater Baltimore Classic, Coca-Cola Classic, Golden Lights Championship, LPGA Championship, Bankers Trust Classic, Colgate European Open, Colgate Far East Open. * 1979 Sunstar Classic, Sahara National Pro-Am, Women's International, Coca-Cola Classic, Golden Lights Championship, Lady Keystone Open, Colgate European Open, Mary Kay Classic. * 1980 Women's Kemper Open, Sarah Coventry, Rail Charity Classic. * 1981 Arizona Copper Classic, Colgate Dinah Shore, Sarah Coventry. * 1982 J&B Scotch Pro-Am, Mazda Japan Classic. * 1983 Elizabeth Arden Classic, J&B Scotch Pro-Am. * 1984 Uniden LPGA Invitational, Chevrolet World Championship of Women's Golf. * 1985 Chrysler-Plymouth Charity Classic, LPGA Championship, Mazda Hall of Fame Championship, Henredon Classic, Portland Ping Championship. * 1987 Sarasota Classic, Cellular One-Ping Golf Championship. * 1988 Mazda Classic, AI-Star/Centinela Hospital Classic, Chrysler-Plymouth Classic. * 1989 Mazda LPGA Championship, Atlantic City Classic, Nippon Travel-MBS Classic. * 1990 MBS LPGA Classic. * 1991 Sara Lee Classic. * 1992 Rail Charity Golf Classic, Ping-Cellular One LPGA Golf Championship * 1993 Youngstown-Warren Classic. (TOTAL: 47)

Annual earnings and rank:

1977—$23,138—31	1986—$67,700—35
1978—$189,813—1	1987—$204,823—7
1979—$197,488—1	1988—$322,154—4
1980—$209,078—4	1989—$487,153—3
1981—$165,679—6	1990—$301,262—8
1982—$166,474—6	1991—$153,772—26
1983—$91,477—15	1992—$382,128—8
1984—$183,756—7	1993—$304,480—14
1985—$416,472—1	

MEG MALLON

Height: 5'6"
Birth date: April 14, 1963
College: Ohio State University
Career earnings: $1,508,674 (20)
Residence: Ramona, Calif.
Joined LPGA: October 1986

LPGA Tour victories: 1991 Oldsmobile LPGA Classic, Mazda LPGA Championship, U.S. Women's Open, Daikyo World Championship * 1993 Ping-Welch's Championship, Sara Lee Classic. (TOTAL: 6)

Annual earnings and rank:

1987—$1,572—175	1991—$633,802—2
1988—$25,002—87	1992—$400,052—6
1989—$42,574—67	1993—$276,291—15
1990—$129,381—27	

MICHELLE MCGANN

Height: 5'11"
Birth date: Dec. 30, 1969
Joined LPGA: October 1988
Residence: Riviera Beach, Fla.

Career earnings: $723,171 (63)
Annual earnings and rank:
1989—$11,679—130
1990—$34,846—98
1991—$121,663—40
1992—$239,062—18
1993—$315,921—12

MISSIE MCGEORGE
Height: 5'7"
Birth date: Aug. 20, 1959
College: Southern Methodist University
Career earnings: $713,100 (64)
Residence: Southlake, Texas
Joined LPGA: August 1983
Annual earnings and rank:
1983—$4,596—133
1984—$20,117—89
1985—$21,563—87
1986—$23,436—83
1987—$63,259—44
1988—$93,397—31
1989—$68,493—48
1990—$93,721—45
1991—$113,959—46
1992—$30,248—118
1993—180,311—32

LAURI MERTEN
Height: 5'5"
Birth date: July 6, 1960
College: Arizona State University
Residence: Greenville, Del.
Joined LPGA: January 1983
Career earnings: $910,216 (45)
LPGA Tour victories: 1983 Rail Charity Golf Classic. * 1984 Jamie Farr Toledo Classic * 1993 U.S. Women's Open. (TOTAL: 3)
Annual earnings and rank:
1983—$51,930—31
1984—$108,920—13
1985—$39,597—55
1986—$45,967—55
1987—$63,492—43
1988—$36,772—70
1989—$42,832—66
1990—$47,263—82
1991—$25,494—112
1992—$53,204—86
1993—$394,744—6

DOTTIE MOCHRIE
Height: 5'6"
Birth date: Aug. 17, 1965
College: Furman University
Residence: Osprey, Fla.
Joined LPGA: October 1987
Career earnings: $2,099,753 (10)
LPGA Tour victories: 1989 Oldsmobile LPGA Classic. * 1990 Crestar Classic. * 1992 Nabisco Dinah Shore, Sega Women's Championship, Welch's Classic, Sun-Times Challenge * 1993 World Championship of Women's Golf. (TOTAL: 7)
Annual earnings and rank:
1988—$137,293—20
1989—$130,830—27
1990—$231,410—12
1991—$477,767—3
1992—$693,335—1
1993—$429,118—4

KRIS MONAGHAN

Height: 5'6"
Birth date: Aug. 24, 1960
College: University of New Mexico
Residence: Albuquerque
Joined LPGA: October 1984
Career earnings: $546,434 (86)
LPGA Tour victories: 1993 Inamori Classic. (TOTAL: 1)
Annual earnings and rank:
1985—$17,942—96
1986—$19,756—94
1987—$21,937—91
1988—$19,670—101
1989—$17,639—112
1990—$65,725—61
1991—$134,753—36
1992—$40,025—102
1993—$208,987—23

LISELOTTE NEUMANN

Height: 5'6"
Birth date: May 20, 1966
Joined LPGA: October 1987
Residence: Finspang, Sweden
Career earnings: $858,777 (50)
LPGA Tour victories: 1988 U.S. Women's Open. * 1991 Mazda Japan Classic. (TOTAL: 2)
Annual earnings and rank:
1988—$188,729—12
1989—$119,915—30
1990—$82,323—51
1991—$151,367—27
1992—$225,667—21
1993—$90,776—57

NANCY RAMSBOTTOM

Height: 5'5"
Birth date: Aug. 19, 1962
College: University of Texas
Residence: Tampa
Joined LPGA: October 1984
Career earnings: $297,121 (126)
Annual earnings and rank:
1985—$16,997—97
1986—$17,300—98
1987—$24,490—83
1988—$10,834—131
1989—$16,493—116
1990—$31,974—101
1991—$22,294—120
1992—$63,385—73
1993—$93,354—55

CINDY RARICK

Height: 5'8"
Birth date: Sept. 12, 1959
College: University of Hawaii
Residence: Tucson, Ariz.
Joined LPGA: October 1984
Career earnings: $1,263,785 (29)
LPGA Tour victories: 1987 Tsumura Hawaiian Ladies Open, LPGA Corning Classic. * 1989 Chrysler-Plymouth Classic. * 1990 Planters Pat Bradley International. * 1991 Northgate Computer Classic. (TOTAL: 5)

Annual earnings and rank:
1985—$22,094—86
1986—$29,093—72
1987—$162,073—11
1988—$63,699—49
1989—$196,611—11
1990—$259,163—10
1991—$201,342—19
1992—$155,303—36
1993—$174,407—34

DEB RICHARD

Height: 5'6"
Birth date: June 3, 1963
College: University of Florida
Residence: Ponte Vedra Beach, Fla.
Joined LPGA: October 1985
Career earnings: $1,417,730 (21)
LPGA Tour victories: 1987 Rochester International. * 1991 Women's Kemper Open, Phar-Mor in Youngstown. (TOTAL: 3)
Annual earnings and rank:
1986—$98,451—22
1987—$83,225—30
1988—$112,647—26
1989—$70,594—47
1990—$186,464—15
1991—$376,640—5
1992—$266,427—15
1993—$223,282—22

PATTI RIZZO

Height: 5'7"
Birth date: June 19, 1960
College: University of Miami
Residence: Miami
Joined LPGA: January 1982
Career Earnings: $1,072,651 (34)
LPGA Tour victories: 1983 Boston Five Classic. * 1985 LPGA Corning Classic. * 1988 Sara Lee Classic. * 1989 Red Robin Kyocera Inamori Classic. (TOTAL: 4)
Annual earnings and rank:
1982—$46,441—31
1983—$78,731—1
1984—$69,613—27
1985—$86,465—24
1986—$88,936—23
1987—$98,456—22
1988—$108,960—28
1989—$198,868—9
1990—$145,377—25
1991—$39,432—95
1992—DNP
1993—$111,371—49

KELLY ROBBINS

Height: 5'9"
Birth date: Sept. 29, 1969
College: University of Tulsa
Residence: Naples, Fla.
Joined LPGA: October, 1991
Career Earnings: $291,149 (129)
LPGA Tour victories: 1993 Corning Classic. (TOTAL: 1)
Annual earnings and rank:
1992—$90,405—59
1993—$200,744—24

CINDY SCHREYER

Height: 5"7"
Birth date: Jan. 21, 1963
College: University of Georgia
Residence: Peachtree City, Ga.
Joined LPGA: 1988
LPGA Tour victories: 1993 Sun-Times Challenge. (TOTAL: 1)

Career earnings: $244,609 (149)
Annual earnings and rank:
1989—$14,984—120   1992—$50,513—89
1990—$20,156—114   1993—$95,343—54
1991—$63,613—73

PATTY SHEEHAN

Height: 5'3"
Birth date: Oct. 27, 1956   **Residence:** Reno
Joined LPGA: July 1980
Career earnings: $4,131,837 (3)
LPGA Tour victories: 1981 Mazda Japan Classic. * 1982 Orlando Lady Classic, Safeco Classic, Inamori Classic.* 1983 Corning Classic, LPGA Championship, Henredon Classic, Inamori Classic. * 1984 Elizabeth Arden Classic, LPGA Championship, McDonald's Kids Classic, Henredon Classic. * 1985 Sarasota Classic, J&B Scotch Pro-Am.* 1986 Sarasota Classic, Kyocera Inamori Classic, Konica San Jose Classic. * 1988 Sarasota Classic, Mazda Japan Classic. * 1989 Rochester International. * 1990 The Jamaica Classic, McDonald's Championship, Rochester International, Ping-Cellular One Golf Championship, Safeco Classic. * 1991 Orix Hawaiian Ladies Open. * 1992 Rochester International, Jamie Farr Toledo Classic, U.S. Women's Open * 1993 Standard Register Ping, LPGA Championship. (TOTAL: 31)

Annual earnings and rank:
1980—$17,139—63   1987—$208,107—6
1981—$118,463—11   1988—$326,171—2
1982—$225,022—4   1989—$253,605—5
1983—$250,399—2   1990—$732,618—2
1984—$255,185—2   1991—$342,204—8
1985—$227,908—5   1992—$418,622—5
1986—$214,281—7   1993—$540,547—2

PEARL SINN

Height: 5'3"
Birth date: July 17, 1967   **Residence:** Bellflower, Calif.
College: Arizona State University **Joined LPGA:** October 1990
Career earnings: $169,790 (177)
Annual earnings and rank:
1991—$41,318—92   1993—$69,393—65
1992—$59,079—78

VAL SKINNER

Height: 5'6"
Birth date: Oct. 16, 1960   **Residence:** La Quinta, Calif.
College: Oklahoma State University **Joined LPGA:** January 1983
Career earnings: $934,335 (43)
LPGA Tour victories: 1985 Konica San Jose Classic. * 1986 Mazda Classic. * 1987 MasterCard International * 1993 Lady Keystone Open. (TOTAL: 4)
Annual earnings and rank:
1983—$29,485—57   1989—$102,089—34
1984—$23,021—79   1990—$66,577—59

1985—$132,307—14
1986—$165,243—11
1987—$122,039—18
1988—$60,334—52
1991—$61,923—74
1992—$41,651—100
1993—$129,665—43

HOLLIS STACY

Height: 5'5"
Birth date: March 16, 1954
College: Rollins College
Career earnings: $1,908,964 (14)
Residence: La Quinta, Calif.
Joined LPGA: July 1974

LPGA Tour victories: *1977 Rail Charity Golf Classic, Lady Tara Classic, U.S. Women's Open. * 1978 U.S. Women's Open, Birmingham Classic. * 1979 Mayflower Classic. * 1980 CPC International. * 1981 West Virginia LPGA Classic, Inamori Classic. * 1982 Whirlpool Championship of Deer Creek, S&H Golf Classic, West Virginia LPGA Classic. * 1983 S&H Golf Classic, CPC International, Peter Jackson Classic. * 1984 U.S. Women's Open. * 1985 Mazda Classic of Deer Creek. * 1991 Crester-Farm Fresh Classic. (TOTAL: 18)

Annual earnings and rank:
1974—$5,071—60
1975—$14,409—33
1976—$34,842—16
1977—$89,155—5
1978—$95,800—6
1979—$81,265—11
1980—$89,913—11
1981—$138,908—9
1982—$161,379—8
1983—$149,036—9
1984—$87,106—17
1985—$100,592—18
1986—$104,286—19
1987—$86,261—24
1988—$34,091—72
1989—$134,460—24
1990—$64,074—65
1991—$114,731—45
1992—$132,323—44
1993—$191,257—26

SHERRI STEINHAUER

Height: 5'7"
Birth date: Dec. 27, 1962
College: University of Texas
Career earnings: $1,054,648 (36)
Residence: Madison, Wis.
Joined LPGA: October 1985

LPGA Tour victories: 1992 du Maurier Ltd. Classic. (TOTAL: 1)

Annual earnings and rank:
1986—$7,733—1
1987—$45,741—54
1988—$54,262—57
1989—$44,825—64
1990—$109,407—37
1991—$165,568—24
1992—$315,145—12
1993—$311,967—13

JAN STEPHENSON

Height: 5'5"
Birth date: Dec. 22, 1951
Joined LPGA: July 1974
Career earnings: $2,175,309 (9)
Residence: Fort Worth

LPGA Tour victories: 1976 Sarah Coventry Naples Classic, Birmingham Classic. * 1978 Women's International. * 1980 Sun City Classic. * 1981 Peter Jackson Classic, Mary Kay Classic, United Virginia Bank Classic. * 1982 LPGA Championship, Lady Keystone. * 1983 Tucson Conquistadores LPGA Open, Lady Keystone Open, U.S.

Women's Open. * 1985 GNA Classic. * 1987 Santa Barbara Open, Safeco Classic, Konica San Jose Classic. (TOTAL: 16)

Annual earnings and rank:

1974—$16,270—28	1984—$101,215—14
1975—$20,066—21	1985—$148,030—10
1976—$64,827—8	1986—$165,238—12
1977—$65,820—1	1987—$227,303—4
1978—$66,033—1	1988—$236,739—9
1979—$69,519—1	1989—$71,550—45
1980—$41,318—34	1990—$31,070—105
1981—$180,528—5	1991—$49,467—88
1982—$133,212—1	1992—$132,634—42
1983—$193,364—4	1993—$161,123—36

KRIS TSCHETTER

Height: 5'7"
Birth date: Dec. 30, 1964
College: Texas Christian University
Career earnings: $549,255 (84)
Residence: Sioux Falls, S.D.
Joined LPGA: October 1987
LPGA Tour victories: 1992 Northgate Computer Classic. (TOTAL: 1)

Annual earnings and rank:

1988—$7,590—145	1991—$129,532—38
1989—$18,315—109	1992—$157,436—33
1990—$39,469—91	1993—$196,913—25

SHERRI TURNER

Height: 5'5"
Birth date: Oct. 4, 1956
College: Furman University
Career earnings: $1,088,120 (33)
Residence: Oak Ridge, N.C.
Joined LPGA: October 1983
LPGA Tour victories: 1988 Mazda LPGA Championship, LPGA Corning Classic. * 1989 Orix Hawaiian Ladies Open. (TOTAL: 3)

Annual earnings and rank:

1984—$52,644—38	1989—$198,353—10
1985—$56,562—38	1990—$122,937—30
1986—$56,773—41	1991—$25,153—115
1987—$118,708—20	1992—$52,767—87
1988—$350,851—1	1993—$53,372—85

LISA WALTERS

Height: 5'7"
Birth date: Jan. 9, 1960
College: Florida State University
Career earnings: $565,571 (80)
Residence: Tampa
Joined LPGA: October 1983
LPGA Tour victories: 1992 Itoki Hawaiian Ladies Open * 1993 Hawaiian Ladies Open. (TOTAL: 2)

Annual earnings and rank:

1984—$37,568—56	1989—$21,979—100
1985—$32,080—70	1990—$36,047—94
1986—$53,411—48	1991—$32,380—105

1987—$72,024—34
1988—$22,665—94
1992—$108,157—51
1993—$149,260—37

ROBIN WALTON

Height: 5'8"
Birth date: Jan. 7, 1956
College: University of Washington
Career earnings: $628,082 (76)
Residence: Scottsdale, Ariz.
Joined LPGA: July 1979

Annual earnings and rank:
1979—$402—129
1980—$6,281—102
1981—$8,447—104
1982—$12,230—87
1983—$14,507—92
1984—$51,232—44
1985—$35,947—62
1986—$52,784—49
1987—$59,304—49
1988—$84,501—34
1989—$45,283—63
1990—$72,519—55
1991—$61,130—76
1992—$49,185—92
1993—$74,329—63

MARY BETH ZIMMERMAN

Height: 5'4"
Birth date: Dec. 11, 1960
College: Florida International University
Career earnings: $643,613 (70)
Residence: Charlotte, N.C.
Joined LPGA: August 1983

LPGA Tour victories: 1986 Standard Register/Samaritan Turquoise Classic, Uniden LPGA Invitational. * 1987 Henredon Classic. (TOTAL: 3)

Annual earnings and rank:
1983—$3,239—141
1984—$34,306—59
1985—$89,088—22
1986—$221,072—6
1987—$82,346—31
1988—$42,339—66
1989—$2,047—170
1990—$14,376—131
1991—$10,776—152
1992—$25,398—125
1993—$118,626—46

Senior PGA Tour players

TOMMY AARON
Height: 6'1" **Weight:** 185
Birth date: Feb. 22, 1937 **Residence:** Gainesville, Ga.
College: University of Florida **Turned professional:** 1960
PGA Tour victories: 1970 Atlanta Classic. * 1973 Masters. (TOTAL: 2)
PGA Tour career earnings: $902,760
Joined senior tour: 1987
Sr. PGA Tour victories: 1992 Kaanapali Classic. (TOTAL: 1)
Sr. PGA Tour career earnings: $1,217,805 (39)
Annual earnings and rank:
1987—$98,421—29	1989—$ 51,800—60	1991—$152,443—43
1988—$81,829—41	1990—$107,651—46	1992—$459,230—12
		1993—$266,611—34

JIM ALBUS
Height: 6'2" **Weight:** 200
Birth date: June 18, 1940 **Residence:** Oyster Bay, N.Y.
College: Bucknell, UCLA **Turned professional:** 1968
PGA Tour career earnings: $3,750
Joined senior tour: 1990
Sr. PGA Tour victories: 1991 MAZDA Presents THE SENIOR PLAYERS Championship.* 1993 Suncoast Classic. (TOTAL: 2)
Sr. PGA Tour career earnings: $1,348,415 (33)
Annual earnings and rank:
1990—$14,433—95	1991—$301,406—20	1992—$404,693—16
		1993—$627,883—12

ISAO AOKI
Height: 6' **Weight:** 170
Birth date: Aug. 31, 1942 **Residence:** Tokyo
Turned professional: 1964
PGA Tour victories: 1983 Hawaiian Open. (TOTAL: 1)
PGA Tour career earnings: $872,456 (179)
Sr. PGA Tour victories: 1992 Nationwide Championship. (TOTAL: 1)
Sr. PGA Tour career earnings: $882,317 (51)
Annual earnings and rank:
1992—$324,650—26   1993—$557,667—15

GEORGE ARCHER
Height: 6'5" **Weight:** 195
Birth date: Oct. 1, 1939 **Residence:** Incline Village, Nev.
Turned professional: 1964
PGA Tour victories: 1965 Lucky International. * 1967 Greensboro. * 1968 Pensacola, New Orleans. * 1969 Masters, Bing Crosby National. * 1971 Andy Williams-San Diego, Hartford. * 1972 Glen Campbell-Los Angeles, Greensboro. * 1976 Del Webb Sahara Invitational. * 1984 Bank of Boston Classic. (TOTAL: 12)

PGA Tour career earnings: $1,882,242
Joined senior tour: 1989
Sr. PGA Tour victories: 1989 Gatlin Brothers Southwest Classic. * 1990 MONY Tournament of Champions, Northville Long Island Classic, GTE Northwest Classic, Gold Rush at Rancho Murieta. * 1991 Northville Long Island Classic, GTE North Classic, Raley's Senior Gold Rush. * 1992 Murata Reunion Pro-Am, Northville Long Island Classic, Bruno's Memorial Classic. *1993 Ameritech Open, First of America Classic, Gold Rush, Kaanapali Classic.(TOTAL: 15)
Sr. PGA Tour career earnings: $3,634,508 (5)
Annual earnings and rank:

1989—$ 98,063—45	1991—$963,455—2	1993—$963,124—3
1990—$749,691—4	1992—$860,175—2	

MILLER BARBER

Height: 5'11"
Birth date: March 31, 1931
College: Arkansas
Weight: 210
Residence: Sherman, Texas
Turned professional: 1959
PGA Tour victories: 1964 Cajun Classic. * 1967 Oklahoma City Open. * 1968 Byron Nelson Classic. * 1969 Kaiser International. * 1970 New Orleans Open. * 1971 Phoenix Open. * 1972 Tucson Open. * 1973 World Open. * 1974 Ohio Kings Island Open. * 1977 Anheuser-Busch Classic. * 1978 Phoenix Open. (TOTAL: 11)
PGA Tour career earnings: $1,602,408 (106)
Joined senior tour: 1981
Sr. PGA Tour victories: 1981 Peter Jackson Champions, Suntree Senior Classic, PGA Seniors Championship. * 1982 U.S. Senior Open, Suntree Senior Classic, Hilton Head Seniors International. * 1983 Senior TPC, Merrill Lynch/Golf Digest Commemorative, United Virginia Bank, Hilton Head Seniors International. * 1984 Roy Clark Senior Challenge, U.S. Senior Open, Greater Syracuse Seniors, Denver Post Champions. * 1985 Sunrise Senior Classic, U.S. Senior Open, PaineWebber World Seniors Invitational. * 1986 MONY Tournament of Champions. * 1987 Showdown Classic, Newport Cup. * 1988 Showdown Classic, Fairfield-Barnett Classic. * 1989 MONY Tournament of Champions, Vintage Chrysler Invitational. (TOTAL: 24)
Sr. PGA Tour career earnings: $3,267,325 (8)
Annual earnings and rank:

1981—$83,136—1	1985—$241,999—4	1989—$370,229—11
1982—$106,890—1	1986—$204,837—9	1990—$274,184—21
1983—$231,008—2	1987—$347,571—5	1991—$288,753—21
1984—$299,099—2	1988—$329,833—9	1992—$170,798—40
		1993—$318,986—30

BOB BETLEY

Height: 6'
Birth date: Feb. 1, 1940
College: Weber State University
Weight: 195
Residence: Fish Haven, Idaho
Turned professional: 1970
PGA Tour career earnings: $4,938
Senior PGA Tour victories: 1993 Bank of Boston Classic. (TOTAL: 1)
Senior PGA Tour career earnings: $2,241,688
Joined senior tour: 1970
Sr. PGA Tour career earnings: $669,077 (65)

Annual earnings and rank:
1990—$99,503—50   1991—$84,262—59   1992—$78,012—70
                                      1993—$407,300—24

DON BIES
Height: 6'1"   **Weight:** 170
Birth date: Dec. 10, 1937   **Residence:** Seattle
Turned professional: 1957
PGA Tour victories: 1975 Sammy Davis, Jr.-Greater Hartford Open. (TOTAL: 1)
PGA Tour career earnings: $538,209
Joined senior tour: 1988
Sr. PGA Tour victories: 1988 Northville Invitational, GTE Kaanapali Classic. *
1989 Murata Seniors Reunion, Tradition at Desert Mountain, GTE Kaanapali Classic.
* 1992 PaineWebber Invitational. (TOTAL: 6)
Sr. PGA Tour career earnings: $1,764,168 (23)
Annual earnings and rank:
1988—$293,552—11   1990—$265,275—23   1992—$352,618—21
1989—$421,769—8   1991—$191,174—33   1993—$239,781—36

BOB CHARLES
Height: 6'1"   **Weight:** 170
Birth date: March 14, 1936
Residence: New Zealand and Palm Beach Gardens, Fla.
Turned professional: 1960
PGA Tour victories: 1963 Houston Open. * 1965 Tucson Open. * 1967 Atlanta
Classic. * 1968 Canadian Open. * 1974 Greater Greensboro Open. (TOTAL: 5)
PGA Tour career earnings: $539,118
Joined senior tour: 1986
Sr. PGA Tour victories: 1987 Vintage Chrysler Invitational, GTE Classic, Sunwest
Bank/Charley Pride Golf Classic. * 1988 NYNEX/Golf Digest Commemorative,
Sunwest Bank/Charley Pride Classic, Rancho Murieta Senior Gold Rush, Vantage
Presents Bank One Classic, Pepsi Senior Challenge. * 1989 GTE Suncoast Classic,
NYNEX/Golf Digest Commemorative, Digital Seniors Classic, Sunwest Bank/Charley
Pride Classic, Fairfield Barnett Space Coast Classic * 1990 Digital Seniors Classic,
GTE Kaanapali Classic. * 1991 GTE Suncoast Classsic. * 1992 Raley's Senior Gold
Rush, Transamerica Senior Golf Classic. * 1993 Doug Sanders Classic, Bell Atlantic
Classic, Quicksilver Classic. (TOTAL: 21)
Sr. PGA Tour career earnings: $4,689,368 (1)
Annual earnings and rank:
1986—$261,160—7   1989—$725,887—1   1992—$473,903—10
1987—$389,437—3   1990—$584,318—7   1993—1,046,823—2
1988—$533,929—1   1991—$673,910—6

JIM COLBERT
Height: 5'9"   **Weight:** 165
Birth date: March 9, 1941   **Residence:** Las Vegas
College: Kansas State   **Turned professional:** 1965

PGA Tour victories: 1969 Monsanto Open. ✷ 1972 Greater Milwaukee Open. ✷ 1973 Greater Jacksonville Open. ✷ 1974 American Golf Classic. ✷ 1975 Walt Disney World Team Championship (with Dean Refram). ✷ 1980 Joe Garagiola-Tucson Open. ✷ 1983 Colonial National Invitation, Texas Open. (TOTAL: 8)
PGA Tour career earnings: $1,553,135 (113)
Joined senior tour: 1991
Sr. PGA Tour victories: 1991 Southwestern Bell Classic, Vantage Championship, First Development Kaanapali Classic. ✷ 1992 GTE Suncoast Classic, Vantage Championship. ✷ 1993 Royal Caribbean Classic, Senior Players Championship. (TOTAL: 7)
Sr. PGA Tour career earnings: $2,486,406 (15)
Annual earnings and rank:
1991—$880,749—3   1992—$825,768—3   1993—$779,889—7

CHARLES COODY

Height: 6'2"
Birth date: July 13, 1937
College: Texas Christian
Weight: 195
Residence: Abilene, Texas
Turned professional: 1963
PGA Tour victories: 1964 Dallas Open. ✷ 1969 Cleveland Open. ✷ 1971 Masters. (TOTAL: 3)
PGA Tour career earnings: $1,211,989 (137)
Joined senior tour: 1987
Sr. PGA Tour victories: 1989 General Tire Las Vegas Classic. ✷ 1990 Vantage Championship. ✷ 1991 NYNEX Commemorative, Transamerica Senior Golf Championship. (TOTAL: 4)
Sr. PGA Tour career earnings: $2,472,733 (16)
Annual earnings and rank:
1987—$93,064—31   1989—$403,880—10   1991—$543,326—8
1988—$161,286—20   1990—$762,901—3   1992—$286,294—28
                                         1993—$221,982—37

BRUCE CRAMPTON

Height: 5'9"
Birth date: Sept. 28, 1935
Turned professional: 1953
Weight: 178
Residence: Tapatio Springs, Texas
PGA Tour victories: 1961 Milwaukee Open. ✷ 1962 Motor City Open. ✷ 1964 Texas Open. ✷ 1965 Bing Crosby National Pro-Am, Colonial NIT, "500" Festival Open. ✷ 1969 Hawaiian Open. ✷ 1970 Westchester Classic. ✷ 1971 Western Open. ✷ 1973 Phoenix Open, Tucson Open, Houston Open, American Golf Classic. ✷ 1975 Houston Open. (TOTAL: 14)
PGA Tour career earnings: $1,376,194 (125)
Joined senior tour: 1985
Sr. PGA Tour victories: 1986 Benson & Hedges Invitational at the Dominion, MONY Syracuse Senior Classic, GTE Northwest Classic, PaineWebber World Seniors Invitational, Pepsi Senior Challenge, Las Vegas Senior Classic, Shearson Lehman Brothers Seniors. ✷ 1987 Denver Champions of Golf, Greenbrier/American Express Championship, MONY Syracuse Seniors Classic, Vantage Presents Bank One Seniors. ✷ 1988 United Hospitals Classic, GTE Northwest Classic. ✷ 1989 MONY Arizona Classic, Ameritech Senior Open. ✷ 1990 PaineWebber Invitational, Gatlin Brothers Southwest Senior Classic. ✷ 1991 Infiniti Senior Tournament of Champions. ✷ 1992 GTE West Classic. (TOTAL: 19)

Sr. PGA Tour career earnings: $3,500,675 (7)
Annual earnings and rank:
1985—$14,250—57 1988—$332,927—8 1991—$514,509—11
1986—$454,299—1 1989—$443,582—7 1992—$471,873—11
1987—$437,904—2 1990—$464,569—11 1993—$366,762—25

JIM DENT

Height: 6'3"   **Weight:** 224
Birth date: May 9, 1939   **Residence:** Tampa
College: Paine College   **Turned professional:** 1966
PGA Tour career earnings: $565,244 (214)
Joined senior tour: 1989
Sr. PGA Tour victories: 1989 MONY Syracuse Senior Classic, Newport Cup. * 1990 Vantage at the Dominion, MONY Syracuse Senior Classic, Kroger Senior Classic, Crester Classic * 1992 Newport Cup. (TOTAL: 7)
Sr. PGA Tour career earnings: $2,667,715 (14)
Annual earnings and rank:
1989—$337,691—12   1991—$529,315—9   1992—$593,979—9
1990—$693,214—6   1993—$513,515—18

TERRY DILL

Height: 6'3"   **Weight:** 195
Birth date: May 13, 1939   **Residence:** Tapatio Springs, Texas
College: University of Texas, University of Texas Law School
Turned professional: 1962
PGA Tour career earnings: $255,049 (299)
Joined senior tour: 1989
Sr. PGA Tour victories: 1992 Bank One Senior Classic. (TOTAL: 1)
Sr. PGA Tour career earnings: $994,869 (48)
Annual earnings and rank:
1989—$82,332—50   1991—$242,191—31   1993—$179,976—50
1990—$278,372—19   1992—$211,998—34

DALE DOUGLASS

Height: 6'2"   **Weight:** 160
Birth date: March 5, 1936   **Residence:** Castle Rock, Colo.
College: University of Colorado   **Turned professional:** 1960
PGA Tour victories: 1969 Azalea Open, Kemper Open. * 1970 Phoenix Open. (TOTAL: 3)
PGA Tour career earnings: $577,950 (213)
Joined senior tour: 1986
Sr. PGA Tour victories: 1986 Vintage Invitational, Johnny Mathis Senior Classic, U.S. Senior Open, Fairfield-Barnett Senior Classic. * 1988 GTE Suncoast Classic. * 1990 Bell Atlantic Classic. * 1991 Showdown Classic. * 1992 NYNEX Commemorative, Ameritech Senior Open. * 1993 Ralph's Classic. (TOTAL: 10)
Sr. PGA Tour career earnings: $3,569,491 (6)

Annual earnings and rank:
1986—$309,760—3 1989—$313,275—14 1992—$694,564—6
1987—$296,429—7 1990—$568,198—8 1993—$499,858—19
1988—$280,457—12 1991—$606,949—7

JIM FERREE

Height: 5'9" **Weight:** 165
Birth date: June 10, 1931 **Residence:** Hilton Head Island, S.C.
College: North Carolina **Turned professional:** 1955
PGA Tour victories: 1958 Vancouver Centennial. (TOTAL: 1)
PGA Tour career earnings: $107,719 (354)
Joined senior tour: 1981
Sr. PGA Tour victories: 1986 Greater Grand Rapids Open. * 1991 Bell Atlantic Classic. (TOTAL: 2)
Sr. PGA Tour career earnings: $2,009,502 (19)
Annual earnings and rank:
1981—$16,694—15 1985—$153,087—9 1989—$194,992—24
1982—$16,455—30 1986—$184,667—11 1990—$144,680—40
1983—$69,547—11 1987—$111,858—23 1991—$279,384—23
1984—$103,717—13 1988—$112,137—30 1992—$194,633—37
           1993—$424,333—22

RAYMOND FLOYD

Height: 6'1" **Weight:** 200
Birth date: Sept. 4, 1942 **Residence:** Miami
Turned professional: 1961
PGA Tour victories: 1963 St. Petersburg Open. *1965 St. Paul Open. * 1969 Jacksonville Open, American Golf Classic, PGA Championship. * 1975 Kemper Open. * 1976 Masters, World Open. * 1977 Byron Nelson Classic, Pleasant Valley Classic. * 1979 Greensboro Open. * 1980 Doral-Eastern Open. * 1981 Doral-Eastern Open, Tournament Players Championship, Manufacturers Hanover-Westchester Classic. * 1982 Memorial Tournament, Danny Thomas-Memphis Classic, PGA Championship. * 1985 Houston Open. * 1986 U.S. Open, Walt Disney/Oldsmobile Classic * 1992 Doral Ryder Open. (TOTAL: 22)
PGA Tour career earnings: $5,033,996 (14)
Joined senior tour: 1992
Sr. PGA Tour victories: 1992 GTE North Classic, Ralphs Senior Classic, Senior TOUR Championship. * 1993 Gulfstream Invitational, Long Island Classic. (TOTAL: 5)
Sr PGA Tour career earnings: $1,150,158 (43)
Annual earnings and rank:
1992—$436,991—14 1993—$713,168—9

AL GEIBERGER

Height: 6'2" **Weight:** 185
Birth date: Sept. 1, 1937 **Residence:** Solvang, Calif.
College: Southern California **Turned professional:** 1959
PGA Tour victories: 1962 Ontario Open. * 1963 Almaden Open. * 1965 American Golf Classic. * 1966 PGA Championship. * 1974 Sahara Invitational. * 1975 Tournament of Champions, Tournament Players Championship. * 1976 Greater

Greensboro Open, Western Open. * 1977 Danny Thomas-Memphis Classic. * 1979 Colonial National Invitation. (TOTAL: 11)
PGA Tour career earnings: $1,265,187 (134)
Joined senior tour: 1987
Sr. PGA Tour victories: 1987 Vantage Championship, Hilton Head Seniors International, Las Vegas Senior Classic. * 1988 Pointe/Del E Webb Arizona Classic. * 1989 GTE Northwest Classic. * 1991 Kroger Senior Classic. * 1992 Infiniti Tournament of Champions. * 1993 Tournament of Champions, West Classic. (TOTAL: 9)
Sr. PGA Tour career earnings: $3,028,331 (10)
Annual earnings and rank:

1987—$264,798—9	1989—$527,033—3	1991—$519,926—10
1988—$348,735—6	1990—$373,624—13	1992—$385,339—19
		1993—$608,877—13

GIBBY GILBERT

Height: 5'9" **Weight:** 175
Birth date: Jan. 14, 1941 **Residence:** Chattanooga, Tenn.
College: University of Chattanooga **Turned professional:** 1963
PGA Tour victories: 1970 Houston Champion International. * 1976 Danny Thomas-Memphis Classic. * 1977 Walt Disney World National Team Championship (with Grier Jones). (TOTAL: 3)
PGA Tour career earnings: $1,055,472 (154)
Joined senior tour: 1991
Sr. PGA Tour victories: 1992 Southwestern Bell Classic, First of America Classic, Kroger Senior Classic. * 1993 Las Vegas Classic. (TOTAL: 4)
Sr. PGA Tour career earnings: $1,657,360 (24)
Annual earnings and rank:
1991—$392,351—14   1992—$603,630—8   1993—$661,378—11

LARRY GILBERT

Height: 6' **Weight:** 192
Birth date: Nov. 19, 1942 **Residence:** Lexington, Ky.
College: Middle Tennessee St. **Turned professional:** 1967
Joined senior tour: 1992
Sr. PGA Tour career earnings: $515,790 (74)
Annual earnings and rank:
1993—$515,790—17

DICK HENDRICKSON

Height: 6'7" **Weight:** 270
Birth date: Jan. 22, 1935 **Residence:** Malvern, Pa.
Turned professional: 1957
PGA Tour career earnings: $14,605
Joined senior tour: 1985
Sr. PGA Tour career earnings: $1,192,480 (40)
Annual earnings and rank:

1985—$1,463—114	1988—$83,076—38	1991—$281,863—22
1986—$5,069—79	1989—$144,739—31	1992—$270,025—31
1987—$3,915—103	1990—$159,070—34	1993—$243,262—35

HAROLD HENNING

Height: 6'
Birth date: Oct. 3, 1934
Turned professional: 1953
Weight: 175
Residence: Lake Worth, Fla.
PGA Tour victories: 1966 Texas Open. (TOTAL: 1)
PGA Tour career earnings: $217,047
Joined senior tour: 1984
Sr. PGA Tour victories: 1985 Seiko/Tucson Match Play Championship. * 1988 GTE Classic. * 1991 First of America Classic. * 1993 Legends of Golf. (TOTAL: 4)
Sr. PGA Tour career earnings: $2,815,179 (12)
Annual earnings and rank:

1984—$ 6,500—72	1987—$151,986—17	1990—$409,879—12
1985—$197,624—6	1988—$366,230—5	1991—$394,803—13
1986—$173,034—12	1989—$453,163—6	1992—$347,857—22
		1993—$314,104—31

DAVE HILL

Height: 5'11"
Birth date: May 20, 1937
Turned professional: 1958
Weight: 152
Residence: Jackson, Mich.
PGA Tour victories: 1961 Home of the Sun Open, Denver. * 1963 Hot Springs. * 1967 Memphis. * 1969 Memphis, Buick, IVB-Philadelphia. * 1970 Danny Thomas-Memphis. * 1972 Monsanto. * 1973 Danny Thomas-Memphis. * 1974 Houston. * 1975 Sahara Invitational. * 1976 Greater Milwaukee. (TOTAL: 13)
PGA Tour career earnings: $1,130,429 (149)
Joined senior tour: 1987
Sr. PGA Tour victories: 1987 Fairfield Barnett Senior Golf Classic. * 1988 MONY Senior Tournament of Champions, MONY Syracuse Senior Classic, PaineWebber Invitational. * 1989 Bell Atlantic Classic, Rancho Murieta Senior Gold Rush. (TOTAL: 6)
Sr. PGA Tour career earnings: $2,009,502 (18)
Annual earnings and rank:

1987—$232,189—11	1989—$488,541—5	1991—$251,467—30
1988—$415,594—3	1990—$354,046—14	1992—$ 94,297—64
		1993—$173,368—51

MIKE HILL

Height: 5'10"
Birth date: Jan. 27, 1939
College: Arizona State University
Weight: 170
Residence: Brooklyn, Mich.
Turned professional: 1967
PGA Tour victories: 1970 Doral-Eastern Open. * 1972 San Antonio-Texas Open. * 1977 Ohio Kings Island Open. (TOTAL: 3)
PGA Tour career earnings: $573,724
Joined senior tour: 1989
Sr. PGA Tour victories: 1990 GTE Suncoast Classic, GTE North Classic, Fairfield Barnett Space Coast Classic, Security Pacific Senior Classic, New York Life Champions. * 1991 Doug Sanders Kingwood Celebrity Classic, Ameritech Senior Open, GTE Northwest Classic, Nationwide Championship, New York Life Champions. * 1992 Vintage ARCO Invitational, Doug Sanders Kingwood Celebrity Classic, Digital Senior Classic. * 1993 The Challenge, PaineWebber Invitational. (TOTAL: 15)
Sr. PGA Tour career earnings: $3,973,978 (3)

Annual earnings and rank:
1989—$412,104—9   1991—$1,065,657—1   1993—$798,116—6
1990—$895,678—2   1992—$802,423—4

SIMON HOBDAY

Height: 5'11"
Birth date: June 23, 1940
College: Bishops College, South Africa
Joined senior tour: 1991
Weight: 170
Residence: Pretoria, South Africa
Turned professional: 1969
Sr. PGA Tour victories: 1993 Kroger Classic, Senior Tour Championship. (TOTAL:2)
Sr. PGA Tour career earnings: $1,421,454 (30)
Annual earnings and rank:
1991—$353,654—16   1992—$397,382—18   1993—$670,417—10

DON JANUARY

Height: 6'
Birth date: Nov. 20, 1929
College: North Texas State University
Weight: 175
Residence: Dallas
Turned professional: 1955
PGA Tour victories: 1956 Dallas Centennial Open. * 1960 Tucson Open. * 1961 St. Paul Open. * 1963 Tucson Open. * 1966 Philadelphia Classic. * 1967 PGA Championship. * 1968 Tournament of Champions. * 1970 Jacksonville Open. * 1975 San Antonio-Texas Open. * 1976 MONY Tournament of Champions. (TOTAL: 10)
PGA Tour career earnings: $1,140,925 (146)
Joined senior tour: 1980
Sr. PGA Tour victories: 1980 Atlantic City Senior International. * 1981 Michelob-Egypt Temple, Eureka Federal Savings. * 1982 Michelob Classic, PGA Seniors Championship. * 1983 Gatlin Brothers Senior Classic, Peter Jackson Champions, Marlboro Classic, Denver Post Champions, Citizens Union Senior Classic, Suntree Seniors Classic. * 1984 Vintage Invitational, du Maurier Champions, Digital Middlesex Classic. * 1985 Senior TOUR Roundup, Dominion Seniors, United Hospitals Senior Golf Championship, Greenbrier/American Express Championship. * 1986 Senior Players Reunion Pro-Am, Greenbrier/American Express Championship, Seiko/Tucson Match Play Championship. * 1987 MONY Senior Tournament of Champions. (TOTAL: 22)
Sr. PGA Tour career earnings: $2,679,215 (13)
Annual earnings and rank:
1981—$68,075—2   1985—$247,006—3   1989—$59,813—58
1982—$99,508—2   1986—$299,795—4   1990—$216,243—28
1983—$237,571—1   1987—$116,685—21   1991—$262,437—28
1984—$328,597—1   1988—$82,013—40   1992—$328,896—25
                                      1993—$274,338—33

MIKE JOYCE

Height: 5'10"
Birth date: May 2, 1939
College: University of Colorado
Joined senior tour: 1989
Weight: 190
Residence: Huntington, N.Y.
Turned professional: 1961
Sr. PGA Tour victories: 1992 GTE Northwest Classic. (TOTAL: 1)
Sr. PGA Tour career earnings: $469,268 (77)

Annual earnings and rank:
1989—$5,705—100 1991—$31,480—78 1993—$171,308—52
1990—$52,050—73 1992—$208,725—35

AL KELLEY

Height: 6'
Birth date: Feb. 9, 1935
College: University of Florida
Weight: 175
Residence: Eustis, Fla.
Turned professional: 1962
PGA Tour career earnings: $7,448
Joined senior tour: 1986
Sr. PGA Tour victories: 1990 Newport Cup. (TOTAL: 1)
Senior PGA Tour career earnings: $806,968 (53)
Annual earnings and rank:
1986—$1,463—111 1989—$76,824—54 1992—$104,777—58
1987—$43,204—52 1990—$263,011—24 1993—$119,553—60
1988—$36,253—61 1991—$161,884—40

JACK KIEFER

Height: 5'10"
Birth date: Jan. 1, 1940
College: Millersville State
Weight: 175
Residence: Andover, N.J.
Turned professional: 1967
Joined senior tour: 1990
Sr. PGA Tour career earnings: $677,989 (62)
Annual earnings and rank:
1990—$21,930—87 1991—$119,453—54 1992—$203,095—18
                                    1993—$333,511—27

LARRY LAORETTI

Height: 5'11"
Birth date: July 11, 1939
Turned professional: 1960
Weight: 185
Residence: Stuart, Fla.
Joined senior tour: 1989
Sr. PGA Tour victories: 1992 U.S. Senior Open. (TOTAL: 1)
Sr. PGA Tour career earnings: $1,167,539 (42)
Annual earnings and rank:
1989—$3,025—110 1991—$371,097—15 1993—$183,694—46
1990—$165,339—32 1992—$444,385—13

DICK LOTZ

Height: 5'8"
Birth date: Oct. 15, 1942
College: San Mateo Junior College
Weight: 180
Residence: Phoenix
Turned professional: 1963
PGA Tour victories: 1969 Alameda Open. * 1970 Kemper Open, Pensacola Open. (TOTAL: 3)
PGA Tour career earnings: $282,981
Joined senior tour: 1992
Sr. PGA Tour career earnings: $201,919 (114)
Annual earnings and rank:
1992—$2,675—140 1993—$199,244—44

DON MASSENGALE

Height: 6'1"
Birth date: April 23, 1937
Turned professional: 1960
Weight: 195
Residence: Conroe, Texas
PGA Tour victories: 1966 Bing Crosby Celebrity Pro-Am, Canadian Open. (TOTAL: 2)
PGA Tour career earnings: $206,663 (309)
Joined senior tour: 1987
Sr. PGA Tour victories: 1990 Greater Grand Rapids Open. * 1992 Royal Caribbean Classic. (TOTAL: 2)
Sr. PGA Tour career earnings: $1,140,359 (44)
Annual earnings and rank:
1987—$100,191—28   1989—$134,297—33   1991—$271,835—25
1988—$161,047—21   1990—$229,184—27   1992—$168,014—42
                                     1993—$75,792—72

RIVES MCBEE

Height: 5'11"
Birth date: Oct. 31, 1938
College: North Texas State
Weight: 218
Residence: Irving, Texas
Turned professional: 1965
PGA Tour career earnings: $68,245
Joined senior tour: 1989
Sr. PGA Tour victories: 1989 RJR Bank One Classic. * 1990 Showdown Classic, Vantage Bank One Classic. (TOTAL: 3)
Sr. PGA Tour career earnings: $1,191,226 (41)
Annual earnings and rank:
1989—$258,487—18   1991—$141,745—47   1993—$181,803—47
1990—$480,329—10   1992—$128,862—49

ORVILLE MOODY

Height: 5'10"
Birth date: Dec. 9, 1933
College: University of Oklahoma
Weight: 210
Residence: Sulphur Springs, Texas
Turned professional: 1967
PGA Tour victories: 1969 U.S. Open. (TOTAL: 1)
PGA Tour career earnings: $389,915 (253)
Joined senior tour: 1984
Sr. PGA Tour victories: 1984 Daytona Beach Seniors Classic, MONY Tournament of Champions. * 1987 Rancho Murieta Senior Gold Rush, GTE Kaanapali Classic. * 1988 Vintage Chrysler Invitational, Senior Players Reunion, Greater Grand Rapids Open. * 1989 Mazda Senior TPC, U.S. Senior Open. * 1991 PaineWebber Invitational. * 1992 Franklin Showdown Classic. (TOTAL: 11)
Sr. PGA Tour career earnings: $2,848,834 (11)
Annual earnings and rank:
1984—$183,920—5   1987—$355,793—4   1990—$273,224—22
1985—$134,643—12   1988—$411,859—4   1991—$227,826—32
1986—$128,755—16   1989—$647,985—2   1992—$288,263—27
                                     1993—$196,565—45

LARRY MOWRY

Height: 6'2"
Weight: 194
Birth date: Oct. 20, 1936
Residence: Magnolia Point, Fla.
Turned professional: 1959
PGA Tour career earnings: $87,715
Joined senior tour: 1986
Sr. PGA Tour victories: 1987 Crestar Classic, Pepsi Senior Challenge. * 1988 General Tire Las Vegas Classic. * 1989 General Foods PGA Seniors Championship, RJR at the Dominion. (TOTAL: 5)
Sr. PGA Tour career earnings: $1,460,547 (29)
Annual earnings and rank:

1986—$2,563—96	1989—$322,788—13	1992—$96,322—60
1987—$200,151—13	1990—$314,657—17	1993—$180,703—49
1988—$275,466—13	1991—$67,899—62	

BOB MURPHY

Height: 5'10"
Weight: 200
Birth date: Feb. 14, 1943
Residence: Boynton Beach, Fla.
College: University of Florida
Turned professional: 1967
PGA Tour victories: 1968 Philadelphia Classic, Thunderbird Classic. * 1970 Greater Hartford Open. * 1975 Jackie Gleason-Inverrary Classic. * 1986 Canadian Open. (TOTAL: 5)
PGA Tour career earnings: $1,642,861 (100)
Joined senior tour: 1993
Sr. PGA Tour victories: 1993 Bruno's Classic, North Classic. (TOTAL: 2)
Sr. PGA Tour career earnings: $768,743 (56)
Annual earnings and rank:
1993—$768,743—8

BOBBY NICHOLS

Height: 6'2"
Weight: 190
Birth date: April 14, 1936
Residence: Ft. Pierce, Fla.
College: Texas A&M
Turned professional: 1960
PGA Tour victories: 1962 St. Petersburg Open, Houston Classic. * 1963 Seattle Open. * 1964 PGA Championship, Carling World Open. * 1965 Houston Classic. * 1966 Minnesota Classic. * 1970 Dow Jones Open. * 1973 Westchester Classic. * 1974 Andy Williams-San Diego Open, Canadian Open. (TOTAL: 11)
PGA Tour career earnings: $993,005 (166)
Joined senior tour: 1986
Sr. PGA Tour victories: 1989 Southwestern Bell Classic. (TOTAL: 1)
Sr. PGA Tour career earnings: $1,505,966 (26)
Annual earnings and rank:

1986—$56,676—36	1989—$210,097—22	1991—$252,764—29
1987—$196,698—14	1990—$158,144—35	1992—$223,218—32
1988—$226,936—14		1993—$181,433—48

JACK NICKLAUS

Height: 5'11" **Weight:** 185
Birth date: Jan. 21, 1940
Residence: North Palm Beach, Fla., and Muirfield Village, Ohio
College: Ohio State University **Turned professional:** 1961
PGA Tour victories: 1962 U.S. Open, Seattle World's Fair, Portland. * 1963 Palm Springs, Masters, Tournament of Champions, PGA Championship, Sahara. * 1964 Portland, Tournament of Champions, Phoenix, Whitemarsh. * 1965 Portland, Masters, Memphis, Thunderbird, Philadelphia. * 1966 Masters, Sahara. * 1967 U.S. Open, Sahara, Bing Crosby, Western, Westchester. * 1968 Western, American Golf Classic. * 1969 Sahara, Kaiser, San Diego. * 1970 Byron Nelson, National Four-Ball (w/ Arnold Palmer). * 1971 PGA Championship, Tournament of Champions, Byron Nelson, National Team (w/ Arnold Palmer), Disney World. * 1972 Bing Crosby, Doral- Eastern, Masters, U.S. Open, Westchester, Match Play, Disney. * 1973 Bing Crosby, New Orleans, Tournament of Champions, Atlanta, PGA Championship, Ohio Kings Island, Walt Disney. * 1974 Hawaii, Tournament Players Championship. * 1975 Doral- Eastern, Heritage, Masters, PGA Championship, World Open. * 1976 Tournament Players Championship, World Series of Golf. * 1977 Gleason Inverrary, Tournament Players Championship, Memorial. * 1978 Gleason Inverrary, Tournament Players Championship, IVB Philadelphia. * 1980 U.S. Open, PGA Championship. * 1982 Colonial National Invitation. * 1984 Memorial. * 1986 Masters. (TOTAL: 70) Also won British Open in 1966, 1970 and 1978.
PGA Tour career earnings: $5,360,662 (10)
Joined Sr. Tour: 1990
Sr. PGA Tour victories: 1990 Tradition at Desert Mtn., Mazda Senior TPC. * 1991 Tradition at Desert Mtn., PGA Seniors Championship, U.S. Senior Open. * 1993 U.S. Senior Open. (TOTAL: 16)
Sr. PGA Tour career earnings: $1,004,310 (47)
Annual earnings and rank:
1990—$340,000—15   1992—$114,548—53
1991—$343,734—17   1993—$206,028—42

ARNOLD PALMER

Height: 5'10" **Weight:** 185
Birth date: Sept. 10, 1929 **Residence:** Bay Hill, Fla.
College: Wake Forest University **Turned professional:** 1954
PGA Tour victories: 1955 Canadian. * 1956 Insurance City, Eastern. * 1957 Houston, Azalea, Rubber City, San Diego. * 1958 St Petersburg, Masters, Pepsi. * 1959 Thunderbird Invitational, Oklahoma City, West Palm Beach. * 1960 Palm Springs Classic, Texas Open, Baton Rouge, Pensacola, Masters, U.S. Open, Insurance City, Mobile Sertoma. * 1961 San Diego, Phoenix, Baton Rouge, Texas, Western. * 1962 Palm Springs Classic, Phoenix, Masters, Texas, Tournament of Champions, Colonial National, American Golf Classic. * 1963 Los Angeles, Phoenix, Pensacola, Thunderbird, Cleveland, Western, Whitemarsh. * 1964 Masters, Oklahoma City. * 1967 Los Angeles, Tucson, American Golf Classic, Thunderbird Classic. * 1968 Bob Hope Desert Classic, Kemper. * 1969 Heritage, Danny Thomas-Diplomat. * 1970 National Four-Ball (w/ Jack Nicklaus). * 1971 Bob Hope Desert Classic, Florida Citrus, Westchester, National Team (w/ Jack Nicklaus). * 1973 Bob Hope Desert Classic. (TOTAL: 60)
PGA Tour career earnings: $1,904,667 (78)
Joined senior tour: 1980

Sr. PGA Tour victories: 1980 PGA Seniors Championship. * 1981 U.S. Senior Open. * 1982 Marlboro Classic, Denver Post Champions. * 1983 Boca Grove Senior Classic. * 1984 PGA Seniors Championship, Senior TPC, Quadel Senior Classic. * 1985 Senior TPC. * 1988 Crestar Classic. * 1993 Senior Skins. (TOTAL:11)
Sr. PGA Tour career earnings: $1,500,776 (27)
Annual earnings and rank:

1981—$55,100—4	1985—$137,024—11	1989—$119,907—38
1982—$73,848—4	1986—$99,056—21	1990—$66,519—65
1983—$106,590—6	1987—$128,910—19	1991—$143,967—46
1984—$184,582—4	1988—$185,373—17	1992—$70,815—72
		1993—$106,232—64

GARY PLAYER

Height: 5'7" **Weight:** 147
Birth date: Nov. 1, 1935 **Residence:** Alaqua, Fla.
Turned professional: 1953
PGA Tour victories: 1958 Kentucky Derby Open. * 1961 Lucky International, Sunshine, Masters. * 1962 PGA Championship. * 1963 San Diego. * 1964 "500" Festival, Pensacola. * 1965 U.S. Open. * 1969 Tournament of Champions. * 1970 Greater Greensboro. * 1971 Jacksonville, National Airlines. * 1972 New Orleans, PGA Championship. * 1973 Southern. * 1974 Masters, Danny Thomas-Memphis. * 1978 Masters, Tournament of Champions, Houston Open. (TOTAL: 21)
PGA Tour career earnings: $1,814,950 (84)
Joined senior tour: 1985
Sr. PGA Tour victories: 1985 Quadel Seniors Classic. * 1986 General Foods PGA Seniors Championship, United Hospital Classic, Denver Post Champions. * 1987 Mazda Senior TPC, U.S. Senior Open, PaineWebber World Seniors Invitational. * 1988 General Foods PGA Seniors Championship, Aetna Challenge, Southwestern Bell Classic, U.S. Senior Open, GTE North Classic. * 1989 GTE North Classic, RJR Championship. * 1990 PGA Seniors Championship. * 1991 Royal Caribbean Classic. * 1993 Bank One Classic. (TOTAL: 17)
Also won British Open in 1959, 1968 and 1974.
Sr. PGA Tour career earnings: $3,156,251 (9)
Annual earnings and rank:

1985—$30,000—44	1988—$435,914—2	1991—$337,253—18
1986—$291,190—5	1989—$514,116—4	1992—$346,798—23
1987—$333,439—6	1990—$507,268—9	1993—$360,272—26

JIMMY POWELL

Height: 6'1" **Weight:** 200
Birth date: Jan. 17, 1935 **Residence:** La Quinta, Calif.
College: North Texas State University **Turned professional:** 1959
PGA Tour career earnings: $27,796
Joined senior tour: 1985
Sr. PGA Tour victories: 1990 Southwestern Bell Classic. * 1992 Aetna Challenge. (TOTAL: 2)
Sr. PGA Tour career earnings: $1,234,095 (37)
Annual earnings and rank:

1985—$45,465—36	1988—$106,300—31	1991—$153,605—42
1986—$44,211—43	1989—$178,998—26	1992—$274,371—29
1987—$58,707—41	1990—$208,183—30	1993—$164,255—54

DICK RHYAN

Height: 5'8"
Birth date: Nov. 28, 1934
College: Ohio State
PGA Tour career earnings: $100,481
Joined senior tour: 1987
Sr. PGA Tour career earnings: $934,398 (50)
Weight: 185
Residence: Sarasota, Fla.
Turned professional: 1964

Annual earnings and rank:
1987—$1,300—150	1989—$109,933—41	1991—$179,486—36
1988—$147,423—23	1990—$156,868—37	1992—$131,013—48
		1993—$208,374—41

CHI CHI RODRIGUEZ

Height: 5'7"
Birth date: Oct. 23, 1935
Turned professional: 1960
Weight: 132
Residence: Naples, Fla.

PGA Tour victories: 1963 Denver Open. * 1964 Lucky International, Western Open. * 1967 Texas Open. * 1968 Sahara Invitational. * 1972 Byron Nelson Classic. * 1973 Greater Greensboro Open. * 1979 Tallahassee Open. (TOTAL: 8)
PGA Tour career earnings: $1,037,105 (157)
Joined senior tour: 1985
Sr. PGA Tour victories: 1986 Senior TPC, Digital Seniors Classic, United Virginia Bank Seniors. * 1987 General Foods PGA Seniors Championship, Vantage at the Dominion, United Hospitals Classic, Silver Pages Classic, Senior Players Reunion, Digital Seniors Classic, GTE Northwest Classic. * 1988 Doug Sanders Kingwood Classic, Digital Seniors Classic. * 1989 Crestar Classic. * 1990 Las Vegas Senior Classic, Ameritech Senior Open, Sunwest Bank/Charley Pride Senior Goff Classic. * 1991 GTE West Classic, Vintage ARCO Invitational, Las Vegas Senior Classic, Murata Reunion Pro-Am. * 1992 Ko Olina Senior Invitational. * 1993 Burnet Classic. (TOTAL: 22)
Sr. PGA Tour career earnings: $4,539,124 (2)

Annual earnings and rank:
1985—$7,700—71	1988—$313,940—10	1991—$794,013—4
1986—$399,172—2	1989—$275,414—17	1992—$711,095—5
1987—$509,145—1	1990—$729,788—5	1993—$798,857—5

TOM SHAW

Height: 5'10"
Birth date: Dec. 13, 1938
College: University of Oregon
Weight: 180
Residence: Ft. Lauderdale, Fla.
Turned professional: 1963

PGA Tour victories: 1969 Doral Open, AVCO Golf Classic. * 1971 Bing Crosby National Pro-Am, Hawaiian Open. (TOTAL: 4)
PGA Tour career earnings: $422,009 (244)
Joined senior tour: 1989
Sr. PGA Tour victories: 1989 Showdown Classic. * 1993 The Tradition. (TOTAL: 2)
Sr. PGA Tour career earnings: $1,264,385 (35)

Annual earnings and rank:
1989—$281,393—16	1991—$278,103—24	1993—$324,385—29
1990—$235,683—26	1992—$144,821—45	

J.C. SNEAD
Height: 6'2" **Weight:** 200
Birth date: Oct. 14, 1940
Residence: Hot Springs, Va., and Ponte Vedra Beach, Fla.
College: East Tennessee State University **Turned professional:** 1964
PGA Tour victories: 1971 Tucson Open, Doral-Eastern Open. * 1972 Philadelphia Classic. * 1975 Wickes-Andy Williams San Diego Open. * 1976 Andy Williams San Diego Open, Kaiser International. * 1981 Southern Open. * 1987 Manufacturers Hanover-Westchester Classic. (TOTAL: 8)
PGA Tour career earnings: $2,219,171 (65)
Joined senior tour: 1990
Sr. PGA Tour victories: 1993 The Dominion. (TOTAL: 1)
Sr. PGA Tour career earnings: $1,220,979 (38)
Annual earnings and rank:
1990—$47,494—74   1991—$302,287—19   1992—$383,698—20
                                         1993—$487,500—20

DAVE STOCKTON
Height: 5'11" **Weight:** 180
Birth date: Nov. 2, 1941 **Residence:** Mentone, Calif.
College: Southern California **Turned professional:** 1964
PGA Tour victories: 1967 Colonial National Invitation, Haig Scotch Foursome (with Laude Hammer). * 1968 Cleveland Open, Greater Milwaukee Open. * 1970 PGA Championship. * 1971 Massachusetts Classic. * 1973 Greater Milwaukee Open. * 1974 Glen Campbell-Los Angeles Open, Quad Cities Open, Sammy Davis, Jr.-Greater Hartford Open. * 1976 PGA Championship. (TOTAL: 11)
PGA Tour career earnings: $1,275,453 (131)
Joined senior tour: 1991
Sr. PGA Tour victories: 1992 MAZDA Presents THE SENIOR PLAYERS Championship. * 1993 Reunion Pro-Am, Southwestern Bell Classic, Franklin Showdown Classic, Northwest Classic, Transamerica Championship. (TOTAL: 6)
Sr. PGA Tour career earnings: $1,845,366 (21)
Annual earnings and rank:
1991—$12,965—94   1992—$656,458—7   1993—$1,175,944—1

ROCKY THOMPSON
Height: 5'11" **Weight:** 172
Birth date: Oct. 14, 1939 **Residence:** Toco, Texas
College: University of Houston **Turned professional:** 1964
PGA Tour career earnings: $144,429 (333)
Joined senior tour: 1989
Sr. PGA Tour victories: 1991 MONY Syracuse Senior Classic, Digital Seniors Classic. (TOTAL: 2)
Sr. PGA Tour career earnings: $1,766,631 (22)
Annual earnings and rank:
1989—$17,300—84   1991—$435,794—12   1993—$571,844—14
1990—$308,915—18   1992—$432,778—15

LEE TREVINO

Height: 5'7"
Birth date: Dec. 1, 1939
Turned professional: 1960
Weight: 180
Residence: Jupiter Island, Fla.

PGA Tour victories: 1968 U.S. Open, Hawaiian Open. * 1969 Tucson Open. * 1970 Tucson Open, National Airlines Open. * 1971 Tallahassee Open, Danny Thomas-Memphis Classic, U.S. Open, Canadian Open, Sahara Invitational. * 1972 Danny Thomas-Memphis Classic, Greater Hartford Open, Greater St. Louis Classic. * 1973 Jackie Gleason-Inverrary, Doral-Eastern Open. * 1974 New Orleans Open, PGA Championship. * 1975 Florida Citrus Open. * 1976 Colonial National Invitation. * 1977 Canadian Open. * 1978 Colonial National Invitation. * 1979 Canadian Open. * 1980 Tournament Players Championship, Danny Thomas-Memphis Classic, San Antonio-Texas Open. * 1981 MONY Tournament of Champions. * 1984 PGA Championship. (TOTAL: 27)
Also won British Open in 1971 and 1972.
PGA Tour career earnings: $3,478,449 (31)
Joined senior tour: 1989
Sr. PGA Tour victories: 1990 Royal Caribbean Classic, Aetna Challenge, Vintage Chrysler Invitational, Doug Sanders Kingwood Celebrity Classic, NYNEX Commemorative, U.S. Senior Open, Transamerica Senior Golf Championship. * 1991 Aetna Challenge, Vantage at the Dominion, Sunwest Bank/Charley Pride Senior Classic. * 1992 Vantage at the Dominion, The Tradition, PGA Seniors Championship, Las Vegas Senior Classic, Bell Atlantic Classic. * 1993 Cadillac NFL Classic, Nationwide Championship, Vantage Championship. (TOTAL: 18)
Sr. PGA Tour career earnings: $3,906,533 (4)
Annual earnings and rank:
1989—$9,258—93   1991—$723,163—5   1993—$956,591—4
1990—$1,190,518—1   1992—$1,027,002—1

TOM WARGO

Height: 6'0"
Birth date: Sept. 16, 1942
Turned professional: 1976
Weight: 200
Residence: Centralia, Ill.

PGA Tour career earnings: $9,000
Joined senior tour: 1993
Sr. PGA Tour victories: 1993 PGA Seniors Championship. (TOTAL: 1)
Sr. PGA Tour career earnings: $557,270 (71)
Annual earnings and rank:
1993—$557,270—16

DEWITT WEAVER

Height: 5'10"
Birth date: Sept. 14, 1939
College: Southern Methodist University
Weight: 185
Residence: Helen, Ga.
Turned professional: 1963

PGA Tour victories: 1971 U.S. Professional Match Play. * 1972 Southern Open. (TOTAL: 2)
PGA Tour career earnings: $272,500 (293)
Joined senior tour: 1989
Sr. PGA Tour victories: 1991 Bank One Senior Classic. (TOTAL: 1)
Sr. PGA Tour career earnings: $1,258,632 (36)

Annual earnings and rank:
1989—$4,133—105   1991—$264,569—27   1993—$472,220—21
1990—$118,555—45   1992—$399,155—17

TOM WEISKOPF
Height: 6'3"   **Weight:** 190
Birth date: Nov. 9, 1942   **Residence:** Paradise Valley, Ariz.
College: Ohio State University   **Turned professional:** 1964
PGA Tour victories: 1968 Andy Williams-San Diego Open, Buick Open. ∗ 1971 Kemper Open, IVB-Philadelphia Classic. ∗ 1972 Jackie Gleason-Inverarry Classic. ∗ 1973 Colonial National Invitation, Kemper Open, IVB-Philadelphia Classic, Canadian Open. ∗ 1975 Greater Greensboro Open, Canadian Open. ∗ 1977 Kemper Open. ∗ 1978 Doral-Eastern Open. ∗ 1981 LaJet Classic. ∗ 1982 Western Open. (TOTAL: 15) Also won British Open in 1974.
PGA Tour career earnings: $2,241,687 (64)
Joined senior tour: 1993
Sr. PGA Tour victories: 1993 Chrysler Cup. (TOTAL: 1)
Sr. PGA Tour career earnings: $296,528 (94)
Annual earnings and rank:
1993—$296,528—32

BOB WYNN
Height: 6'1"   **Weight:** 185
Birth date: Jan. 27, 1940   **Residence:** La Quinta, Calif.
College: Ohio University   **Turned professional:** 1959
PGA Tour victories: 1976 B.C. Open. (TOTAL: 1)
PGA Tour career earnings: $262,059 (297)
Joined senior tour: 1990
Sr. PGA Tour career earnings: $449,243 (78)
Annual earnings and rank:
1990—$59,660—70   1992—$95,497—62   1993—$168,692—53
1991—$125,394—53

KERMIT ZARLEY
Height: 6'   **Weight:** 175
Birth date: Sept. 29, 1941   **Residence:** Friendswood, Texas
College: University of Houston   **Turned professional:** 1963
PGA Tour victories: 1968 Kaiser International. ∗ 1970 Canadian Open. (TOTAL: 2)
PGA Tour career earnings: $715,721 (197)
Joined senior tour: 1991
Sr. PGA Tour career earnings: $763,220 (57)
Annual earnings and rank:
1991—$6,858—113   1992—$341,647—24   1993—$414,715—23

WALT ZEMBRISKI
Height: 5'8"   **Weight:** 160
Birth date: May 24, 1935   **Residence:** Orlando, Fla.
Turned professional: 1965
Joined senior tour: 1985

Sr. PGA Tour victories: 1988 Newport Cup, Vantage Championship. ✶ 1989 GTE West Classic. (TOTAL: 3)
Sr. PGA Tour career earnings: $2,127,658 (17)
Annual earnings and rank:

1985—$47,023—35	1988—$348,531—7	1991—$265,951—26
1986—$103,551—19	1989—$291,861—15	1992—$273,087—30
1987—$189,403—15	1990—$276,292—20	1993—$331,960—28

LARRY ZIEGLER

Height: 6' **Weight:** 185
Birth date: Aug. 12, 1939 **Residence:** Amana, Iowa
Turned professional: 1959
PGA Tour victories: 1969 Michigan Classic. ✶ 1975 Greater Jacksonville Open. ✶ 1976 First NBC New Orleans Open. (TOTAL: 3)
PGA Tour career earnings: $733,277
Joined senior tour: 1989
Sr. PGA Tour victories: 1991 Newport Cup. (TOTAL: 1)
Sr. PGA Tour career earnings: $756,266 (58)
Annual earnings and rank:

1989—$133,339—35	1991—$169,686—38	1992—$135,015—47
1990—$102,152—49		1993—$216,073—38

Bernhard Langer won his second green jacket at The Masters in 1993 and earned $626,938 in six tour events.

GOLF ALMANAC 1994

Final Player Statistics

PGA Tour...270

LPGA...277

Senior PGA Tour...281

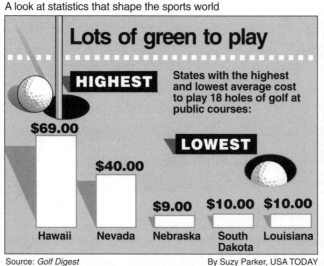

GOLF ALMANAC 1994

PGA Tour final statistics

	Driving distance	Driving accuracy (%)	Greens in regulation (%)	Putting average	Total eagles	Total birdies	Sand saves (%)	Scoring average	All-around	Tournaments entered	Top 10 finishes	Official money
ADAMS, JOHN	277.6(5)	61.9(174)	65.9(79)	1.808(119)	7(37)	297(61)	45.6(166)	71.30	818	29	2	221,753
ALLEN, FULTON	257.1(116)	77.6(7)	67.7(47)	1.777(39)	5(67)	322(30)	54.2(61)	70.80	439	28	4	851,345
ALLEN, MICHAEL	264.2(58)	65.3(141)	62.8(154)	1.791(74)	8(25)	267(99)	45.0(169)	71.10	907	27	3	231,072
ALLENBY, ROBERT#										6		11,052
ANDERSON, JC	270.6(18)	62.9(166)	65.5(89)	1.854(183)	8(25)	236(133)	49.6(123)	72.12	992	27	1	89,782
ANDRADE, BILLY	258.8(97)	67.9(98)	63.6(137)	1.777(39)	5(67)	316(33)	48.9(133)	70.97	776	29	7	365,759
AOKI, ISAO										1		32,500
ARMOUR, TOMMY	263.0(64)	66.1(129)	65.2(101)	1.842(175)	4(89)	161(177)	45.8(164)	72.11	1164	20	1	52,011
AUBREY, EMLYN#										1		18,125
AZINGER, PAUL	273.3(12)	70.9(66)	70.6(12)	1.770(26)	5(67)	301(55)	56.8(34)	69.75	286	24	12	1,458,456
BAKER-FINCH, IAN	252.3(159)	73.1(43)	63.1(148)	1.820(148)	1(164)	182(163)	53.0(75)	71.19	1105	20	1	140,621
BALLESTEROS, SEVE#										3		34,850
BARLOW, JEFF#										1	1	8,700
BARR, DAVE	258.5(98)	70.9(66)	70.7(11)	1.832(168)	7(37)	280(83)	49.3(129)	71.17	735	28	1	179,264
BEAN, ANDY	265.2(47)	58.0(184)	58.3(186)	1.823(154)	2(144)	173(168)	45.9(163)	72.77	1383	21		37,292
BECK, CHIP	258.2(101)	67.9(98)	64.7(117)	1.797(92)	8(25)	284(76)	62.6(7)	70.77	677	27	5	603,376
BEIERSDORF, RUSS				1.770(26)	7(37)	350(13)	47.7(146)	71.32	624	30		111,750
BERGANIO, DAVID#										4		2,486
BERTSCH, SHANE#										1		2,548
BLACK, RONNIE	263.5(61)	64.7(151)	65.4(92)	1.800(100)	6(50)	291(67)	50.6(111)	71.26	863	28		120,041
BLACKMAR, PHIL	271.4(16)	60.9(178)	63.5(139)	1.781(52)	8(25)	287(72)	50.0(116)	71.62	829	30	2	207,310
BLAKE, JAY DON	257.8(111)	66.9(121)	67.0(60)	1.787(61)	3(116)	275(89)	46.2(159)	71.24	964	26	3	202,482
BOROWICZ, BOB#										1		2,475
BRADLEY, MICHAEL	268.8(29)	55.2(188)	63.4(142)	1.780(47)	6(50)	263(107)	61.7(10)	71.67	843	26	1	126,160
BRADY, STEVE#										1		1,820
BRITTON, BILL	256.3(123)	70.8(68)	64.7(117)	1.789(69)	0(183)	290(69)	56.8(34)	71.32	865	30		74,748
BROOKS, MARK	257.2(115)	73.0(46)	67.0(60)	1.815(135)	4(89)	305(53)	51.0(104)	70.58	690	31	3	249,696
BROWN, BILLY RAY										15	1	173,662
BROWNE, OLIN										2		2,738
BRYANT, BRAD	268.1(34)	65.0(147)	66.3(71)	1.786(60)	7(37)	353(12)	52.1(89)	71.12	613	31	3	230,139
BURKE, PATRICK	258.0(105)	72.5(51)	64.3(126)	1.811(127)	3(116)	167(173)	56.2(40)	70.75	830	17	1	100,717
BURNS, GEORGE										9		2,550
BURTON, KEVIN#										2		2,513
BUTTNER, BILL#										1	1	6,650
BYRUM, TOM	249.5(178)	76.9(10)	63.4(142)	1.817(142)	3(116)	211(145)	48.3(138)	72.01	1123	26	1	82,355
CALCAVECCHIA, MARK	265.2(47)	62.7(167)	65.3(97)	1.780(47)	10(9)	333(24)	56.0(42)	70.66	610	30	6	630,366
CALDWELL, REX										2		4,350
CANIPE, DAVID#										2		1,557
CARNEVALE, MARK	257.1(116)	74.6(29)	65.3(97)	1.863(184)	5(67)	249(123)	52.5(83)	72.28	907	32		100,046
CARTER, JIM#										1		2,753
CERULLI, GREG#										2		2,786
CESARIO, GREG	251.4(167)	60.2(180)	52.3(189)	1.829(166)	1(164)	146(183)	56.3(39)	72.91		25		15,333
CHAMBLEE, BRANDEL	256.6(122)	70.1(76)	66.8(66)	1.799(97)	4(89)	266(103)	46.2(159)	71.09	896	29	2	126,940
CHEESMAN, BARRY	278.6(4)	61.2(176)	65.3(97)	1.841(173)	4(89)	271(96)	41.8(183)	71.80	1042	30	1	66,748
CHEN, T.C.										1		5,800
CHRISTIE, MICHAEL#										1		6,526
CLAAR, BRIAN	255.1(137)	73.6(40)	67.0(60)	1.777(39)	1(164)	364(9)	55.9(43)	71.05	638	32	1	202,624
CLAMPETT, BOBBY	260.7(80)	63.0(164)	64.6(121)	1.806(112)	2(144)	169(170)	51.2(102)	70.85	1106	16	3	112,293
CLEARWATER, KEITH	257.9(108)	70.2(73)	67.5(51)	1.788(65)	11(6)	384(4)	59.9(16)	70.53	440	31	6	348,763
CLEMENTS, LENNIE	254.4(146)	73.9(32)	68.8(27)	1.781(52)	4(89)	279(85)	58.1(26)	70.73	579	26	2	141,526
COCHRAN, RUSS	260.7(80)	70.2(73)	68.1(40)	1.760(11)	7(37)	344(15)	54.5(59)	70.76	405	27	2	293,868

FINAL PLAYER STATISTICS

	Driving distance	Driving accuracy (%)	Greens in regulation (%)	Putting average	Total eagles	Total birdies	Sand saves (%)	Scoring average	All-around	Tournaments entered	Top 10 finishes	Official money
CONLEY, TIM	249.9(173)	73.4(41)	63.9(133)	1.789(69)	3(116)	198(152)	48.0(143)	71.79	1104	22		66,593
CONNER, FRANK										7		34,154
COODY, CHARLES										1		3,800
COOK, JEFF	255.8(130)	67.0(119)	61.6(165)	1.808(119)	2(144)	249(123)	50.8(108)	71.66	1199	29		72,398
COOK, JOHN	256.2(124)	73.7(38)	71.7(4)	1.790(73)	2(144)	286(75)	42.7(181)	70.45	723	23	5	342,321
COOPER, CARL										19		10,774
COUPLES, FRED	275.0(7)	60.4(179)	68.3(37)	1.774(31)	8(25)	273(92)	58.6(23)	69.85	495	19	9	796,579
CRAIG, CHIP#										1		2,431
CRENSHAW, BEN	259.0(95)	63.0(164)	61.0(170)	1.755(8)	6(50)	222(140)	58.0(27)	71.15	902	22	1	318,605
CROCKETT, TIM#										1		2,870
CROWDER, RETT#										1		702
DALPOS, RICK	252.2(161)	56.7(187)	58.8(182)	1.815(135)	4(89)	181(164)	51.5(95)	72.62	1382	28		31,585
DALY, JOHN	288.9(1)	59.1(182)	61.7(164)	1.837(171)	12(3)	205(150)	55.2(49)	71.70	942	24	1	225,591
DAWSON, MARCO	267.8(36)	59.6(181)	65.3(97)	1.825(161)	9(16)	311(38)	46.7(153)	71.70	954	32	1	120,462
DELONG, DAVID	240.7(189)	67.4(106)	56.3(188)	1.844(177)	0(183)	122(189)	43.6(178)	73.53		22		21,059
DELSING, JAY	274.8(8)	62.0(173)	64.9(112)	1.803(107)	13(2)	314(36)	51.3(100)	71.10	698	29	3	233,484
DENNIS, CLARK#										2		6,050
DODDS, TREVOR	257.9(108)	63.1(161)	61.8(162)	1.832(168)	4(89)	243(129)	39.2(187)	71.87	1322	30	1	119,436
DONALD, MIKE	253.7(149)	67.4(106)	64.3(126)	1.823(154)	6(50)	253(117)	53.6(68)	71.74	1072	34	1	51,313
DOUGHERTY, ED	256.8(120)	69.9(79)	65.9(79)	1.827(164)	5(67)	341(18)	46.5(155)	71.42	906	35	3	167,651
DOWDALL, JOHN	247.9(181)	75.2(21)	59.3(181)	1.851(180)	1(164)	128(188)	52.6(81)	72.80	1298	22		20,381
DURANT, JOE										18		4,055
DUVAL, DAVID#										5		27,181
EAKS, R.W.#										1		5,414
EASTWOOD, BOB										17		24,289
EDWARDS, DANNY										3		1,557
EDWARDS, DAVID	252.0(163)	78.3(5)	72.1(3)	1.787(61)	0(183)	288(70)	57.0(31)	70.32	603	21	6	653,086
EDWARDS, JOEL	253.2(153)	71.6(61)	65.7(86)	1.820(148)	2(144)	270(98)	50.3(113)	71.61	1064	30		150,623
EICHELBERGER, DAVE										5		1,640
ELKINGTON, STEVE	267.5(37)	68.6(92)	69.0(24)	1.780(47)	6(50)	317(31)	53.4(69)	69.97	384	23	8	675,383
ELLIOTT, JOHN	274.2(10)	57.1(185)	61.0(170)	1.821(153)	3(116)	246(127)	44.6(174)	72.30	1214	28		60,378
ELLIS, JIM#										1		2,233
ELS, ERNIE#										6	1	38,185
ESTES, BOB	262.3(67)	71.8(60)	67.9(41)	1.783(57)	8(25)	343(16)	46.4(156)	70.25	463	28	5	447,187
FABEL, BRAD	252.8(157)	64.7(151)	64.3(126)	1.831(167)	7(37)	221(141)	50.9(106)	71.78	1208	27		59,672
FALDO, NICK#										6	2	188,886
FAXON, BRAD	254.5(145)	64.9(149)	61.9(161)	1.741(2)	5(67)	310(40)	58.3(25)	70.68	810	25	4	312,023
FEHR, RICK	260.4(86)	72.6(49)	68.5(31)	1.775(33)	5(67)	343(16)	44.9(170)	70.09	491	26	6	556,322
FEZLER, FORREST										7		2,610
FIORI, ED	244.7(187)	77.3(8)	65.4(92)	1.833(170)	3(116)	253(117)	59.2(18)	71.41	924	31	2	117,617
FLANNERY, JOHN	256.2(124)	63.5(158)	64.0(132)	1.753(6)	5(67)	370(7)	51.3(100)	71.38	879	31	1	161,234
FLEISHER, BRUCE	249.8(175)	75.6(18)	66.1(72)	1.789(69)	0(183)	298(60)	48.4(137)	71.01	886	28	1	214,279
FLESCH, STEPHEN#										3		6,786
FLOYD, RAY										6	2	126,516
FORD, BOB#										1		2,588
FORSBRAND, ANDERS#										5		34,850
FORSMAN, DAN	260.5(84)	69.5(85)	67.8(45)	1.769(24)	5(67)	309(42)	51.5(95)	70.38	537	25	6	410,150
FREEMAN, ROBIN	261.9(71)	63.1(161)	63.2(145)	1.805(110)	5(67)	280(83)	51.5(95)	71.97	1039	30	1	92,096
FRIEND, ROBERT										10		5,647
FROST, DAVID	260.8(77)	67.7(102)	66.7(67)	1.739(1)	2(144)	287(72)	57.4(29)	69.48	573	22	9	1,030,717
FUNK, FRED	251.2(170)	80.6(3)	68.2(39)	1.793(77)	3(116)	394(3)	54.6(58)	70.86	593	34	5	309,435
GALLAGHER, JR., JIM	268.7(30)	64.5(154)	67.7(47)	1.794(82)	4(89)	312(37)	44.9(170)	71.05	771	27	6	1,078,870
GAMEZ, ROBERT	259.1(93)	72.7(48)	65.9(79)	1.810(125)	3(116)	299(59)	48.1(142)	71.66	825	25	3	236,458
GARDNER, BUDDY	258.0(105)	53.0(189)	61.3(168)	1.816(141)	1(164)	197(154)	56.5(36)	72.55	1314	27		13,722
GIBSON, KELLY	270.9(17)	67.0(119)	64.9(112)	1.813(129)	10(9)	325(26)	58.8(21)	71.56	585	33		148,003

	Driving distance	Driving accuracy (%)	Greens in regulation (%)	Putting average	Total eagles	Total birdies	Sand saves (%)	Scoring average	All-around	Tournaments entered	Top 10 finishes	Official money
GILDER, BOB	257.8(111)	71.0(64)	65.2(101)	1.805(110)	2(144)	256(113)	60.6(13)	71.21	819	27	2	148,496
GLASSON, BILL	267.9(35)	73.7(38)	72.3(2)	1.791(74)	4(89)	291(67)	51.9(92)	70.49	434	22	6	299,799
GOMEZ, JAIME	252.3(159)	73.1(43)	63.5(139)	1.793(77)	4(89)	263(107)	53.3(70)	71.73	937	30	1	77,495
GONZALEZ, ERNIE										2		2,175
GOTSCHE, STEVE#										1		5,657
GOYDOS, PAUL	256.1(127)	74.5(30)	64.4(124)	1.793(77)	6(50)	301(55)	50.9(106)	71.60	740	30		87,804
GRADY, WAYNE	251.1(172)	67.8(100)	62.9(151)	1.815(135)	1(164)	147(182)	49.4(127)	72.17	1372	20		45,959
GREEN, HUBERT	245.8(185)	74.7(27)	58.6(183)	1.809(123)	1(164)	145(184)	54.2(61)	72.87	1247	19		29,786
GREEN, KEN	257.7(113)	66.0(132)	64.7(117)	1.750(3)	2(144)	216(144)	64.4(1)	71.90	961	22	3	229,750
GUMP, SCOTT	261.4(72)	72.1(57)	66.9(64)	1.811(127)	3(116)	279(85)	46.3(157)	71.65	831	31		96,822
HAAS, JAY	260.3(87)	69.3(88)	69.7(19)	1.806(112)	8(25)	374(5)	55.3(48)	70.32	478	29	6	601,603
HALLBERG, GARY	265.0(51)	62.3(171)	59.9(176)	1.771(29)	8(25)	308(44)	63.3(5)	71.60	765	27		147,706
HALLDORSON, DAN	260.7(80)	65.2(143)	63.0(150)	1.868(186)	3(116)	208(147)	43.0(180)	72.69	1327	30		24,284
HALLET, JIM	248.7(179)	65.1(145)	62.8(154)	1.848(179)	4(89)	251(121)	53.9(65)	72.21	1288	34	1	80,366
HAMMOND, DONNIE	259.5(92)	74.9(25)	68.4(35)	1.758(9)	2(144)	309(42)	47.3(149)	70.51	544	23	3	340,432
HART, DUDLEY	265.2(47)	65.5(136)	66.6(69)	1.815(135)	6(50)	267(99)	60.4(15)	70.93	702	30	4	316,750
HART, STEVE#										1		2,175
HATALSKY, MORRIS	243.2(188)	76.0(17)	62.7(156)	1.777(39)	2(144)	196(156)	63.7(2)	70.55	861	18	2	111,057
HAYES, J.P.#										1	1	6,650
HAYES, MARK										9		6,942
HEAFNER, VANCE										3		6,526
HEINTZELMAN, WEBB#										2		4,290
HENKE, NOLAN	265.5(45)	67.7(102)	65.2(101)	1.774(31)	3(116)	339(20)	52.5(83)	71.01	604	26	4	502,375
HENNINGER, BRIAN	264.0(59)	68.7(91)	64.8(114)	1.801(104)	9(16)	284(76)	54.7(57)	71.92	706	31	1	112,811
HINKLE, LON										13		8,621
HOCH, SCOTT	258.0(105)	72.1(57)	71.2(7)	1.780(47)	3(116)	347(14)	51.7(94)	70.36	521	28	6	403,742
HORGAN III, P.H.	257.6(114)	67.2(113)	63.7(135)	1.801(104)	5(67)	272(95)	47.4(147)	72.06	1082	31	3	105,571
HUGHES, BRADLEY#										2		28,125
HULBERT, MIKE	253.0(155)	66.6(124)	65.2(101)	1.787(61)	9(16)	315(35)	54.8(54)	71.20	810	31		193,833
HUMENIK, ED	272.7(15)	66.4(125)	67.8(45)	1.820(148)	12(3)	300(58)	49.3(129)	71.24	649	31	3	152,562
HUSTON, JOHN	270.6(18)	63.1(161)	68.4(35)	1.768(21)	6(50)	426(1)	48.3(138)	70.60	539	30	6	681,441
INGRAHAM, STU#										2		7,058
INMAN, JOHN	245.0(186)	75.1(22)	62.2(158)	1.775(33)	4(89)	306(52)	56.5(36)	71.41	817	32	2	242,140
IRWIN, HALE	253.7(149)	79.8(4)	68.3(37)	1.782(55)	1(164)	232(135)	47.8(144)	70.30	751	21	2	252,686
JACKSON, DAVID	278.7(3)	58.9(183)	64.8(114)	1.844(177)	3(116)	287(72)	52.9(77)	72.19	1006	31		53,563
JACOBSEN, PETER	262.1(68)	73.9(32)	68.5(31)	1.796(90)	9(16)	256(113)	51.9(92)	70.38	480	23	3	222,291
JAECKEL, BARRY										11	1	15,585
JANZEN, LEE	257.1(116)	71.0(64)	66.1(72)	1.766(18)	7(37)	340(19)	53.3(70)	70.21	494	26	7	932,335
JENKINS, TOM										4		4,302
JOHNSON, ERIC#										2		1,880
JOHNSTON, JIMMY	253.9(148)	67.6(104)	60.0(175)	1.826(162)	3(116)	198(152)	63.6(3)	72.42	1199	28	1	54,419
JOHNSTONE, TONY#										4		10,893
JONES, GENE				1.813(129)	3(116)	171(169)	38.4(188)	72.12	1276	20		24,522
JORDAN, PETER#										1		5,405
KAMM, BRIAN	264.8(56)	66.4(125)	66.1(72)	1.775(33)	5(67)	307(46)	58.7(22)	70.88	563	27	3	183,185
KANE, JIM#										2		5,660
KANEKO, YOSHINORI#										3		4,848
KARL, RICHIE										1		1,464
KENDALL, SKIP	258.1(103)	72.3(54)	65.1(107)	1.826(162)	2(144)	293(66)	53.1(72)	71.75	894	32	1	115,189
KIRBY, EDWARD#										2		6,526
KITE, TOM	263.3(62)	72.0(59)	69.4(21)	1.768(21)	2(144)	267(99)	45.3(167)	69.74	596	20	8	887,811
KNOLL, ARDEN#										2		8,171
KNOX, KENNY										21		3,630
KOCH, GARY										4		702
KRAFT, GREG	257.0(119)	65.2(143)	63.1(148)	1.760(11)	5(67)	241(132)	47.0(151)	71.17	1024	24	4	290,581

	Driving distance	Driving accuracy (%)	Greens in regulation (%)	Putting average	Total eagles	Total birdies	Sand saves (%)	Scoring average	All-around	Tournaments entered	Top 10 finishes	Official money
KRATZERT, BILL	261.0(75)	67.1(115)	69.2(23)	1.824(156)	4(89)	156(179)	55.7(44)	70.32	802	15	1	78,993
KURAMOTO, MASSY	254.1(147)	61.1(177)	57.8(187)	1.808(119)	7(37)	176(166)	53.7(67)	71.81	1228	21	1	74,133
LAMONTAGNE, STEVE	270.3(21)	62.3(171)	65.4(92)	1.818(144)	10(9)	301(55)	48.3(138)	71.50	849	33	1	107,077
LANCASTER, NEAL	266.2(42)	62.7(167)	67.0(60)	1.793(77)	12(3)	335(23)	51.2(102)	71.25	702	32	2	149,381
LANE, BARRY#										2		24,089
LANGER, BERNARD#										6	3	626,938
LEE, CRAIG#										1		2,145
LEHMAN, TOM	269.5(23)	67.3(111)	68.6(29)	1.794(82)	11(6)	324(27)	49.3(129)	70.18	448	28	6	422,761
LESHER, GREG										14		23,171
LEVI, WAYNE	260.8(77)	73.1(43)	67.4(54)	1.758(9)	7(37)	276(88)	46.6(154)	70.83	534	25	2	179,521
LEWALLEN, RICK#										1		2,610
LEWIS, J.L.#										3		5,965
LIETZKE, BRUCE	259.9(89)	76.6(12)	69.9(17)	1.817(142)	6(50)	169(170)	60.6(13)	70.95	568	16	2	163,241
LOHR, BOB	249.8(175)	76.8(11)	65.9(79)	1.765(16)	1(164)	284(76)	57.0(31)	70.76	694	26	3	314,982
LOUSTALOT, TIM#										1		2,550
LOVE III, DAVIS	280.2(2)	63.2(160)	67.7(47)	1.778(45)	15(1)	361(10)	56.1(41)	70.28	381	26	5	777,059
LOWERY, STEVE	267.0(40)	66.3(128)	67.3(55)	1.776(37)	10(9)	372(6)	48.5(136)	70.99	544	32	1	188,287
LYE, MARK	263.3(62)	62.4(170)	64.4(124)	1.824(156)	4(89)	195(158)	50.0(116)	71.47	1144	23	1	106,936
LYLE, SANDY#										7	1	86,121
MAGEE, ANDREW	262.6(65)	70.3(70)	67.9(41)	1.797(92)	10(9)	243(129)	52.7(80)	71.31	616	25	2	269,986
MAGGERT, JEFF	264.5(57)	76.3(14)	69.0(24)	1.800(100)	7(37)	337(21)	55.1(52)	70.24	328	28	6	793,023
MAHAFFEY, JOHN	251.7(166)	74.8(26)	67.9(41)	1.863(184)	1(164)	196(156)	39.3(186)	72.42	1200	28		36,913
MAKINO, HIROSHI#										1		2,010
MALIZIA, MIKE#										1		2,996
MALTBIE, ROGER	255.1(137)	68.5(93)	65.6(87)	1.801(104)	5(67)	185(161)	46.2(159)	71.09	1034	20	2	155,454
MARTIN, DOUG										5	1	21,381
MARTIN, MIGUEL#										1		6,019
MAST, DICK	252.1(162)	66.7(123)	60.6(173)	1.754(7)	2(144)	311(38)	61.7(10)	71.16	916	28	4	210,125
MATTIACE, LEN	256.1(127)	65.7(134)	58.6(183)	1.818(144)	4(89)	207(148)	53.9(65)	72.04	1214	26	2	74,521
MAYFAIR, BILLY	253.0(155)	76.2(15)	70.1(15)	1.807(117)	4(89)	356(11)	46.3(157)	70.95	691	32	5	513,072
MCCALLISTER, BLAINE	265.0(51)	75.5(19)	70.3(13)	1.793(77)	2(144)	328(25)	48.9(133)	70.90	526	27	2	290,434
MCCORD, GARY										8		16,456
MCCULLOUGH, MIKE										3		2,011
MCCUMBER, MARK	264.9(55)	72.4(52)	69.5(20)	1.795(86)	5(67)	283(80)	49.6(123)	70.27	515	21	3	363,269
MCDOUGAL, RON#										5		20,375
MCGOVERN, JIM	267.1(38)	73.2(42)	65.8(83)	1.777(39)	10(9)	412(2)	49.7(122)	70.71	389	34	3	587,495
MCGOWAN, PAT										4	1	6,650
MEDIATE, ROCCO	261.3(73)	73.8(36)	68.5(31)	1.824(156)	3(116)	284(76)	53.1(72)	70.59	611	24	6	680,623
MICKELSON, PHIL	269.2(25)	65.4(138)	66.1(72)	1.800(100)	6(50)	246(127)	50.4(112)	71.20	772	24	4	628,735
MIELKE, MARK#										3		2,100
MIZE, LARRY	259.0(95)	74.7(27)	67.3(55)	1.768(21)	6(50)	261(110)	62.7(6)	70.18	397	22	7	724,660
MIZUMAKI, YOSHINORI#										2		1,710
MOLLICA, TONY#										1		2,431
MONTGOMERIE, COLIN#										4		17,992
MORGAN, GIL	265.4(46)	76.1(16)	71.1(8)	1.781(52)	9(16)	295(64)	56.5(36)	70.12	252	24	9	610,312
MOSS, PERRY	257.9(108)	67.1(115)	64.7(117)	1.814(132)	4(89)	253(117)	50.0(116)	72.04	1092	29		63,565
MUDD, JODIE	273.3(12)	65.4(138)	63.3(144)	1.788(65)	3(116)	197(154)	61.4(12)	71.75	817	20	1	89,366
MURCHISON, BILL	252.0(163)	64.6(153)	62.1(160)	1.815(135)	3(116)	153(181)	50.0(116)	71.51	1327	19		45,402
MUROTA, KIYOSHI#										1		2,472
NAKAJIMA, TOMMY#										4		50,578
NELSON, LARRY	256.2(124)	69.8(80)	65.6(87)	1.795(86)	4(89)	178(165)	52.3(86)	71.87	985	18		54,870
NICKLAUS, GARY#										6		5,427
NICKLAUS, JACK										10	1	51,532
NICOLETTE, MIKE										2		1,557
NOBILO, FRANK#										1		14,500

	Driving distance	Driving accuracy (%)	Greens in regulation (%)	Putting average	Total eagles	Total birdies	Sand saves (%)	Scoring average	All-around	Tournaments entered	Top 10 finishes	Official money
NORMAN, GREG	274.4(9)	73.9(32)	70.0(16)	1.751(4)	1(164)	224(139)	62.4(8)	68.90	374	15	12	1,359,653
NORTH, ANDY										4		14,500
O'GRADY, MAC										4		10,429
O'MALLEY, PETER#										3		9,220
O'MEARA, MARK	262.1(68)	68.9(89)	67.5(51)	1.799(97)	4(89)	305(53)	54.8(54)	71.10	625	26	4	349,516
OGLE, BRETT	276.9(6)	63.3(159)	66.0(77)	1.824(156)	8(25)	184(162)	52.0(90)	71.95	891	18	2	337,374
OGRIN, DAVID	249.6(177)	75.0(23)	68.5(31)	1.807(117)	1(164)	307(46)	50.0(116)	71.16	869	28	3	155,016
OLAZABAL, JOSE MARIA#										6	1	60,160
OVERTON, JAY										13		8,368
OZAKI, JOE										12	1	139,784
OZAKI, JUMBO#										4	1	66,742
PALMER, ARNOLD										5		1,970
PAPPAS, DEANE#										3		4,537
PARRY, CRAIG	260.2(88)	69.4(86)	63.8(134)	1.770(26)	2(144)	254(115)	48.8(135)	70.82	851	23	6	323,068
PATE, STEVE	258.3(100)	66.1(129)	66.1(72)	1.797(92)	4(89)	288(70)	61.9(9)	71.07	784	28	4	254,841
PAVIN, COREY	251.9(165)	76.6(12)	70.9(10)	1.760(11)	2(144)	337(21)	55.6(46)	70.00	493	24	6	675,087
PEARCE, EDDIE	258.1(103)	64.5(154)	60.6(173)	1.880(188)	3(116)	165(175)	51.0(104)	73.02	1367	27		18,741
PEEGE, DAVE	247.4(183)	75.0(23)	58.5(185)	1.870(187)	1(164)	136(186)	57.3(30)	72.12	1249	22		33,531
PEOPLES, DAVID	265.1(50)	70.0(77)	70.2(14)	1.852(181)	3(116)	249(123)	50.0(116)	71.81	843	29	2	105,309
PERRY, CHRIS										9		25,333
PERRY, KENNY	269.1(26)	69.7(82)	67.9(41)	1.806(112)	3(116)	307(46)	41.8(183)	70.82	672	29	3	196,863
PERSONS, PETER	248.7(179)	73.0(46)	65.1(107)	1.814(132)	2(144)	252(120)	52.0(90)	71.90	1112	30		73,092
PFEIL, MARK										5		9,100
PLAYER, GARY										1		3,700
POHL, DAN	270.5(20)	67.4(106)	71.5(5)	1.840(172)	4(89)	169(170)	41.9(182)	71.48	882	20	2	97,830
POOLEY, DON										15	2	123,105
PORTER, LEE	255.2(136)	68.8(90)	59.6(179)	1.843(176)	0(183)	132(187)	55.6(46)	72.32	1319	19		14,908
PRICE, NICK	273.9(11)	73.9(32)	71.3(6)	1.766(18)	3(116)	264(106)	63.6(3)	69.11	296	18	8	1,478,557
PRUITT, DILLARD	254.8(141)	81.7(2)	71.1(8)	1.818(144)	5(67)	267(99)	44.7(173)	70.91	730	26	2	168,053
PURTZER, TOM	268.4(32)	66.4(125)	65.8(83)	1.796(90)	8(25)	175(167)	52.8(78)	71.59	770	21	1	107,570
QUIGLEY, DANA#										2		2,353
RANDOLPH, SAM										4		4,460
REID, MIKE										5		5,125
RHYAN, TAD	247.1(184)	70.3(70)	61.0(170)	1.819(147)	9(16)	207(148)	47.1(150)	72.56	1228	32	1	50,524
RIEGGER, JOHN#										1		22,275
RINKER, LARRY	251.3(168)	70.0(77)	63.7(135)	1.795(86)	5(67)	235(134)	49.2(132)	71.33	1062	28	2	130,613
RINKER, LEE#										1		11,052
ROBERTS, LOREN	249.9(173)	77.2(9)	68.9(26)	1.789(69)	4(89)	307(46)	57.0(31)	70.61	570	28	4	316,506
ROMERO, EDUARDO#										1		18,500
ROSE, CLARENCE										4		6,823
ROSS, JOHN										15		23,412
RUMMELLS, DAVE	266.4(41)	67.1(115)	67.1(58)	1.784(59)	11(6)	262(109)	47.8(144)	71.49	695	28	2	247,963
SANDER, BILL										1		582
SAUERS, GENE	261.0(75)	67.8(100)	64.1(130)	1.788(65)	9(16)	316(33)	52.8(78)	71.36	674	28		117,608
SCHIENE, MARTY	255.0(140)	71.1(62)	59.4(180)	1.885(189)	0(183)	155(180)	45.1(168)	72.40	1394	25		20,857
SCHUCHART, MIKE	260.5(84)	69.8(80)	65.5(89)	1.820(148)	3(116)	227(138)	47.4(147)	71.91	1012	24	1	61,492
SCHULZ, TED	260.8(77)	66.0(132)	63.2(145)	1.824(156)	2(144)	273(92)	50.8(108)	71.86	1131	31	1	164,260
SCHUTTE, WARREN#										6		10,875
SELSER, ED#										1		624
SENIOR, PETER#										3		3,600
SHAW, TOM										2		2,716
SHERFY, BRAD#										2		2,690
SHIREY, JR., DON#										3		597
SIECKMANN, TOM	262.5(66)	65.4(138)	64.5(123)	1.775(33)	9(16)	324(27)	51.4(98)	71.41	733	31	2	201,429
SILLS, TONY										5		11,686

	Driving distance	Driving accuracy (%)	Greens in regulation (%)	Putting average	Total eagles	Total birdies	Sand saves (%)	Scoring average	All-around	Tournaments entered	Top 10 finishes	Official money
SIMPSON, SCOTT	255.4(134)	70.8(68)	65.4(92)	1.752(5)	1(164)	278(87)	58.9(19)	70.33	711	22	5	707,166
SIMPSON, TIM	255.1(137)	74.3(31)	69.8(18)	1.808(119)	3(116)	282(81)	55.7(44)	71.18	697	28	1	111,436
SINDELAR, JOEY	267.1(38)	67.2(113)	67.5(51)	1.798(95)	6(50)	220(142)	43.8(177)	70.65	746	22	5	391,649
SINGH, VIJAY										14	6	657,831
SKINNER, SONNY#										1		1,557
SLUMAN, JEFF	260.7(80)	66.9(121)	64.1(130)	1.800(100)	4(89)	296(63)	55.2(49)	71.17	831	27	1	187,841
SMITH, CHRIS#										3	1	24,000
SMITH, MIKE	255.6(132)	70.2(73)	64.6(121)	1.809(123)	3(116)	260(111)	45.8(164)	71.72	1100	33	2	107,375
SMITH, NEALE	265.7(44)	64.3(156)	61.6(165)	1.852(181)	7(37)	145(184)	44.8(172)	72.71	1236	22		11,413
SNEED, ED										3		3,124
SPRINGER, MIKE	266.1(43)	65.3(141)	64.8(114)	1.782(55)	5(67)	275(89)	51.4(98)	71.36	803	30	4	214,729
STADLER, CRAIG	268.2(33)	68.4(94)	68.6(29)	1.813(129)	5(67)	265(104)	50.8(108)	70.60	624	24	5	553,623
STANDLY, MIKE	269.9(22)	64.1(157)	65.2(101)	1.803(107)	8(25)	297(61)	50.3(113)	71.40	773	30	2	323,886
STEWART, PAYNE	269.1(26)	69.6(83)	69.4(21)	1.765(16)	5(67)	365(8)	58.4(24)	69.82	266	26	12	982,875
STEWART, RAY#										1		2,670
STRANGE, CURTIS	254.7(142)	75.5(19)	67.2(57)	1.769(24)	3(116)	271(96)	49.5(125)	70.51	663	24	5	262,697
STRECK, RON										2		885
STRICKER, STEVE#										6	1	46,171
SULLIVAN, MIKE										15		68,587
SULLIVAN, ROB#										1		1,940
SUTTON, HAL	256.0(129)	64.8(150)	64.2(129)	1.798(95)	3(116)	273(92)	35.8(189)	72.12	1239	29	1	74,144
TAYLOR, HARRY	251.3(168)	73.8(36)	68.7(28)	1.806(112)	4(89)	281(82)	52.3(86)	71.22	815	30		105,845
TEN BROECK, LANCE				1.771(29)	4(89)	307(46)	54.2(61)	71.53	916	32		88,262
TEWELL, DOUG	253.4(151)	82.5(1)	66.7(67)	1.820(148)	0(183)	189(160)	52.6(81)	70.95	895	21	1	132,478
THOMAS, STEVE#										1		597
THOMPSON, BARNEY#										1		5,122
THOMPSON, LEONARD										12		15,153
THORPE, JIM	255.4(134)	67.4(106)	65.5(89)	1.841(173)	1(164)	164(176)	46.1(162)	71.30	1260	19		70,376
TOMS, DAVID	259.1(93)	65.5(136)	63.6(137)	1.799(97)	6(50)	274(91)	40.6(185)	72.11	1101	32	3	120,952
TRIPLETT, KIRK	255.6(132)	72.3(54)	67.6(50)	1.780(47)	9(16)	310(40)	54.9(53)	70.98	553	27	2	189,418
TRITTLER, PAUL#										2		2,632
TRIXLER, DENNIS	254.6(144)	71.1(62)	62.9(151)	1.814(132)	7(37)	242(131)	44.6(174)	72.17	1126	29		75,032
TRYBA, TED	262.1(68)	68.0(96)	65.0(110)	1.794(82)	4(89)	317(31)	54.3(60)	71.69	728	33	2	136,670
TUCKER, CHRIS										14		17,473
TWAY, BOB	253.3(152)	56.9(186)	61.2(169)	1.788(65)	1(164)	211(145)	53.0(75)	72.05	1300	25	2	148,120
TWIGGS, GREG	265.0(51)	65.1(145)	66.9(64)	1.791(74)	8(25)	308(44)	52.5(83)	71.24	688	29	3	231,823
TWITTY, HOWARD	268.7(30)	67.4(106)	65.0(110)	1.779(46)	6(50)	323(29)	49.4(127)	70.70	572	29	2	416,833
UTLEY, STAN										5	1	17,371
VAN DER VELDE, CHRIS#										2		6,854
WADKINS, BOBBY	259.7(91)	67.1(115)	62.6(157)	1.827(164)	5(67)	167(173)	48.3(138)	72.06	1190	24		39,153
WADKINS, LANNY	251.2(170)	72.4(52)	67.1(58)	1.764(14)	6(50)	248(126)	44.2(176)	71.28	885	22	2	244,544
WADSWORTH, FRED										3		609
WAITE, GRANT	264.0(59)	68.0(96)	65.4(92)	1.804(109)	1(164)	294(65)	53.1(72)	71.18	788	30	4	411,405
WALDORF, DUFFY	269.3(24)	66.1(129)	66.0(77)	1.815(135)	6(50)	259(112)	43.2(179)	71.46	862	25	4	202,638
WARGO, TOM#										1		7,058
WATSON, DENIS	256.8(120)	61.5(175)	59.7(178)	1.764(14)	6(50)	195(158)	49.5(125)	72.62	1181	25	1	111,977
WATSON, TOM	269.1(26)	72.6(49)	65.2(101)	1.766(18)	5(67)	205(150)	59.3(17)	70.19	451	16	4	342,023
WATTS, BRIAN#										3		23,235
WEAVER, DOUG#										1		4,681
WEIBRING, D.A.	252.5(158)	77.9(6)	66.4(70)	1.777(39)	1(164)	254(115)	58.9(19)	70.75	677	22	2	299,293
WEIR, MIKE#										2		1,940
WHISMAN, GREG										2		3,392
WHITELAW, CLINTON#										1		19,200
WIEBE, MARK	261.1(74)	69.4(86)	65.1(107)	1.776(37)	7(37)	307(46)	46.9(152)	70.90	650	27	5	360,213
WILSON, JEFF#										3		5,508

	Driving distance	Driving accuracy (%)	Greens in regulation (%)	Putting average	Total eagles	Total birdies	Sand saves (%)	Scoring average	All-around	Tournaments entered	Top 10 finishes	Official money
WOLCOTT, BOB#										3		702
WOOD, WILLIE	255.8(130)	65.7(134)	63.2(145)	1.810(125)	4(89)	229(137)	54.8(54)	70.85	1040	25	3	146,206
WOODLAND, JEFF	247.5(182)	68.4(94)	59.9(176)	1.783(57)	2(144)	231(136)	57.8(28)	71.65	1118	27	1	73,367
WOODWARD, JIM	259.8(90)	62.7(167)	62.2(158)	1.795(86)	1(164)	161(177)	52.2(88)	72.10	1257	19		52,731
WOOSNAM, IAN#										6		55,426
WRENN, ROBERT	258.2(101)	67.5(105)	61.8(162)	1.806(112)	2(144)	250(122)	50.3(113)	72.06	1144	28	1	103,928
YOUNG, KIM										17		2,343
ZABRISKI, BRUCE										8		16,829
ZOELLER, FUZZY	273.3(12)	72.2(56)	73.6(1)	1.794(82)	10(9)	265(104)	55.2(49)	70.14	329	18	4	378,175
ZOKOL, RICHARD	253.2(153)	70.3(70)	62.9(151)	1.787(61)	3(116)	220(142)	54.0(64)	71.36	1005	25	2	214,419

= Non-PGA Tour members

Minimum of 50 rounds played for players to qualify for complete statistical analysis.

Statistics courtesy of PGA Tour.

LPGA TOUR FINAL STATISTICS

Player	Driving distance	Driving accuracy (%)	Greens in regulation (%)	Putting average	Total eagles	Total birdies	Sand saves (%)	Scoring average	Rounds under par	Total rounds	Tournaments entered	Top 10 finishes	Official money
ABITBOL, TANIA	237.2(19)	63.6(124)	62.8(80)	31.06(152)	1(129)	132(123)	28.3(164)	73.39	12	49	18	1	35,417
ADAMS, LYNN	223.0(125)	61.2(143)	57.0(143)	30.04(41)	4(44)	109(136)	52.7(9)	74.02	4	47	18		8,860
ALBERS, KRISTI	237.1(21)	62.8(132)	64.1(64)	30.09(45)	8(2)	241(25)	37.5(110)	72.17	30	78	25	4	263,483
ALCOTT, AMY	221.6(131)	69.2(67)	67.7(22)	31.17(159)	1(129)	191(68)	37.5(109)	72.91	19	66	22	2	60,518
ALDERETE, LORETTA	229.0(65)	70.3(56)	54.8(166)	30.19(56)		40(184)	29.0(162)	75.48	3	21	10		3,145
ALFREDSSON, HELEN	243.1(6)	66.7(99)	69.5(7)	30.32(74)	6(16)	265(10)	37.7(106)	71.40	43	77	22	9	402,685
ALLEN, PAMELA	220.0(144)	69.4(64)	55.6(161)	30.63(110)	2(92)	65(169)	38.7(98)	74.55	3	31	12		3,403
AMBROSE, JAYNE	225.2(103)	62.6(133)	53.0(170)	30.21(59)		52(177)	58.5(1)	75.17	3	29	15		2,180
AMMACCAPANE, D.	220.4(140)	77.5(9)	64.9(51)	30.65(113)	2(92)	249(21)	45.5(38)	71.88	33	80	23	8	187,862
AMMACCAPANE, DINA	226.7(85)	63.3(127)	58.0(135)	30.26(65)	2(92)	195(60)	40.7(80)	73.97	21	72	24	1	37,188
ANDERSON, JANET	212.2(175)	64.6(114)	48.8(180)	30.30(71)		42(183)	45.2(40)	75.96	1	24	11		381
ANDREWS, DONNA	223.9(113)	82.4(2)	67.9(21)	30.14(52)	5(25)	284(7)	34.2(139)	71.54	43	84	23	7	334,285
ANSCHUTZ, JODY	214.2(171)	79.5(6)	59.9(120)	30.19(55)	3(62)	151(105)	47.2(26)	73.68	13	59	21	1	34,105
BALDWIN, DENISE	235.3(29)	64.3(117)	63.1(74)	30.69(119)	5(25)	201(54)	39.8(87)	73.36	20	77	24		39,328
BARRETT, SHARON					1(129)	62(171)			6	27	8		11,665
BARRETT, TINA	222.2(127)	81.2(3)	66.1(37)	30.12(47)	7(8)	236(29)	52.4(10)	71.87	38	83	25	7	261,491
BAUER, KIM	223.0(124)	66.5(100)	55.6(160)	30.66(115)	1(129)	89(152)	44.4(48)	74.58	9	38	16		7,163
BAUGH, LAURA						52(177)			3	24	9		3,482
BENZ, AMY	227.3(77)	67.5(91)	66.7(28)	30.63(111)	1(129)	196(59)	38.9(94)	72.25	29	75	23	6	166,968
BERNING, SUSIE	214.6(168)	76.6(12)	59.5(125)	29.76(20)	2(92)	102(143)	41.1(77)	73.50	7	42	15		20,326
BERTEOTTI, MISSIE	233.2(35)	59.4(154)	66.1(38)	30.51(96)	8(2)	242(23)	36.0(125)	72.29	30	86	27	3	184,553
BERTSCH, JACKIE	231.0(45)	53.0(176)	54.9(165)	32(176)		31(189)	33.3(144)	76.17	1	18	10		433
BLACKWELDER, MYRA						16(198)			1	8	3		5,143
BOZARTH, MARCI	219.3(150)	53.3(175)	55.8(155)	30.81(131)		66(168)	25.0(173)	76.27	2	26	11		1,732
BRADLEY, PAT	228.1(72)	74.0(23)	68.6(15)	30.64(112)	3(62)	244(22)	32.3(153)	71.96	35	82	24	6	188,135
BRILES-HINTON, JILL	242.0(8)	56.3(162)	64.8(53)	30.93(139)	5(25)	202(51)	27.8(165)	72.78	23	72	26	1	65,668
BRITZ, JERILYN	212.3(174)	73.8(27)	55.0(163)	30.67(116)	1(129)	82(159)	43.4(54)	75.13	6	40	17		5,012
BROWER, LAURIE	234.5(32)	60.7(147)	66.7(32)	31.21(162)	2(92)	117(132)	35.8(126)	73.56	10	43	16		19,534
BUNKOWSKY, BARB	217.4(162)	74.8(18)	60.5(113)	29.66(15)	2(92)	181(78)	46.3(33)	72.32	25	68	22	4	142,907
BURTON, BRANDIE	245.3(5)	64.2(118)	69.3(8)	29.83(22)	4(44)	334(1)	35.1(131)	71.02	51	91	26	16	517,741
CARNER, JOANNE	231.6(43)	60.4(149)	61.7(100)	29.85(25)	6(16)	186(73)	51.9(11)	72.46	24	61	18	2	134,956
CHILLEMI, CONNIE	227.7(75)	52.9(177)	60.1(115)	31.55(173)	2(92)	89(152)	43.1(58)	73.85	8	40	15		10,778
COCKERILL, KAY	217.6(160)	63.6(125)	50.4(176)	30.68(118)		88(155)	25.7(171)	76.30	3	47	23		664
COE-JONES, DAWN	237.6(18)	69.5(63)	69.0(11)	30.37(83)	5(25)	272(9)	46.2(34)	71.71	38	86	25	8	271,978
CONNELLY, LYNN	220.9(133)	77.7(8)	63.9(68)	30.61(107)	3(62)	176(81)	42.4(65)	72.88	26	69	25	3	71,564
CRAFTER, JANE	221.9(129)	74.0(22)	64.2(61)	29.45(8)	2(92)	226(37)	41.9(67)	71.71	34	72	22	7	187,190
CROCE, STEFANIA	230.5(50)	65.5(108)	59.8(122)	29.95(31)	2(92)	137(120)	46.8(29)	73.41	14	56	19		25,401
CROSBY, ELAINE	224.7(110)	76.5(13)	68.1(17)	30.47(92)	1(129)	292(6)	37.5(110)	72.20	39	89	27	4	177,726
DAGHE, NOELLE	226.3(90)	58.8(156)	60.1(116)	31.26(164)	2(92)	88(155)	27.7(166)	74.39	9	38	16	1	15,909
DAHLLOF, EVA	236.3(26)	59.3(155)	61.8(99)	31.26(163)	3(62)	100(145)	44.6(43)	74.28	11	43	16		10,370
DANIEL, BETH	234.5(31)	55.0(169)	67.6(23)	30.28(68)	6(16)	250(20)	41.1(75)	72.25	33	84	23	4	140,001
DAVIES, KAREN	214.5(169)	49.6(179)	52.1(174)	30.34(77)		105(141)	31.9(156)	76	5	53	24		4,496
DAVIES, LAURA	253.9(1)	55.8(164)	64.0(66)	29.52(10)	6(16)	203(50)	45.1(41)	72	24	57	16	3	240,643
DELK, JOAN	211.9(177)	72.5(39)	50.2(177)	30.71(120)		32(188)	40.4(81)	76.63	1	24	12		
DESCAMPE, F.	246.2(3)	60.1(150)	64.2(59)	31.06(151)	4(44)	162(97)	49.3(15)	73.58	12	55	18		46,414
DIBOS, ALICIA	226.5(89)	79.3(7)	66.2(36)	31.49(172)	1(129)	159(100)	36.4(123)	73.75	12	69	25		28,721
DICKINSON, JUDY	234.0(33)	70.1(60)	68.0(19)	30.31(72)	5(25)	255(15)	46.1(35)	71.59	45	86	24	4	186,317
DOBSON, HELEN					1(129)	67(166)			6	25	9	1	84,959
DREW, HEATHER	220.5(138)	71.2(50)	57.6(138)	30.76(126)		93(151)	42.9(59)	74.32	3	47	19		10,957
DUNLAP, PAGE	225.2(104)	59.5(153)	60.0(118)	30.26(66)	4(44)	175(82)	39.5(91)	73.46	19	70	25	2	59,053
EDGE, MITZI	219.6(147)	58.6(157)	55.8(156)	30.07(43)		124(129)	31.9(155)	73.25	11	55	24		4,994

Name	Driving distance	Driving accuracy (%)	Greens in regulation (%)	Putting average	Total eagles	Total birdies	Sand saves (%)	Scoring average	Rounds under par	Total rounds	Tournaments entered	Top 10 finishes	Official money
EGGELING, DALE	227.2(79)	72.2(40)	69.1(10)	30.80(129)	4(44)	227(35)	46.7(31)	71.93	35	82	26	3	145,789
ESTILL, MICHELLE	239.5(11)	63.5(126)	61.6(101)	31.29(165)	3(62)	143(115)	33.9(142)	74.48	15	58	24		21,428
FARWIG, STEPHANIE	228.5(69)	68.3(79)	65.4(45)	31.48(171)	1(129)	147(110)	54.8(4)	73.84	11	64	24	1	29,192
FAULCONER, .	223.9(113)	70.3(55)	59.4(127)	30.51(97)	2(92)	154(104)	34.1(140)	74.05	12	66	24	1	38,421
FERGON, VICKI	233.1(36)	59.7(151)	63.5(71)	30.39(86)	6(16)	227(35)	25.3(172)	72.98	33	81	28	1	79,308
FIGG-CURRIER, C.	219.5(151)	71.9(43)	62.2(93)	30.04(40)	1(129)	189(71)	31.6(158)	72.99	20	70	23	1	66,440
FIGUERAS-DOTTI, M.	218.1(158)	81.1(4)	64.6(56)	29.84(24)	4(44)	207(47)	39.7(88)	72.32	22	71	23	2	101,102
FINNEY, ALLISON	230.2(56)	65.7(107)	66.3(35)	31(143)	4(44)	199(56)	37.1(115)	72.77	23	71	23		66,263
FLEMING, TARA	225.6(98)	52.2(178)	52.6(172)	31.20(160)	2(92)	75(162)	22.2(178)	76.43	3	40	19		649
FOGLEMAN, SUE	219.9(145)	66.5(101)	57.6(139)	31.37(168)	1(129)	67(166)	23.1(176)	75.37	3	30	14		1,370
FOUST, NINA	225.5(99)	64.0(119)	59.2(128)	30.55(104)		141(116)	47.3(24)	73.83	14	63	24	1	39,893
FRUHWIRTH, AMY	217.3(163)	77.4(10)	61.3(103)	30.52(98)	2(92)	138(118)	40.3(82)	73.50	15	54	18		22,949
FURLONG, SHIRLEY	218.2(157)	39.3(180)	50.9(175)	30.38(84)	1(129)	94(150)	43.2(57)	76.50	2	48	22		1,099
GARBACZ, LORI	232.5(39)	65.2(111)	61.1(106)	29.84(23)	2(92)	184(75)	48.9(16)	72.66	20	68	23	1	59,308
GEDDES, JANE	237.0(23)	63.1(131)	64.1(62)	29.41(6)	3(62)	235(30)	32.0(154)	71.93	33	71	23	5	263,149
GIBSON, ELLIE	231.8(41)	64.8(113)	64.9(52)	31(144)	1(129)	192(66)	48.1(19)	73.15	24	71	24		34,124
GOLDEN, KATE	225.0(106)	62.5(134)	52.1(173)	30.91(138)	1(129)	79(160)	36.4(122)	76.16			22		875
GOWAN, CAROLINE	220.8(134)	55.6(166)	55.1(162)	30.98(142)	2(92)	86(157)	36.8(119)	75.50	5	50	21		2,899
GRAHAM, GAIL	227.8(74)	73.4(31)	65.8(41)	29.96(32)	5(25)	242(23)	42.9(60)	72.49	24	79	24	3	126,048
GREEN, TAMMIE	232.5(37)	74.1(21)	66.7(30)	29.74(17)	5(25)	265(10)	37.5(107)	71.46	37	79	23	9	356,579
GUADAGNINO, K.	222.2(128)	73.7(28)	68.0(18)	30.96(141)	2(92)	145(112)	37.7(105)	72.69	18	54	18	1	58,661
HAGGE, MARLENE						24(194)			2	16	7		722
HAMLIN, SHELLEY	225.0(108)	73.6(30)	64.8(54)	30.71(122)	4(44)	221(39)	38.6(99)	72.73	24	77	25	2	129,447
HAMMEL, PENNY	221.9(130)	67.8(87)	53.0(169)	30.11(46)	3(62)	110(135)	41.6(70)	75.09	3	55	24		8,048
HARVEY, NANCY	216.4(166)	61.4(140)	56.6(149)	29.51(9)		130(124)	28.3(163)	73.37	16	49	16		28,279
HESSION, THERESE						3(212)					1		
HILL, CAROLYN	218.4(155)	70.4(54)	59.2(129)	29.90(26)	1(129)	138(118)	45.5(39)	73.39	15	59	21	1	35,662
HOOD, ROBIN	240.5(10)	53.9(174)	61.3(104)	30.17(53)	5(25)	182(77)	29.6(161)	73.84	13	61	23		30,513
HUGHES, KATE	220.1(142)	67.8(85)	56.7(147)	30.74(125)	1(129)	136(121)	34.8(134)	75.03	8	58	24		9,878
HULL, GINA	217.4(161)	54.8(171)	52.8(171)	31.04(150)	1(129)	52(177)	35.4(130)	76.50			12		
HURLBUT, LAURA						3(212)					1		
INKSTER, JULI	238.1(16)	67.8(84)	63.2(73)	30.29(69)	5(25)	194(62)	47.3(25)	72.50	25	68	21	2	116,583
JOHNSON, CHRIS	242.0(9)	61.3(142)	65.2(47)	30.36(81)	4(44)	218(43)	26.7(169)	72.66	24	76	23	3	111,027
JOHNSON, TRISH	230.2(57)	72.7(36)	62.9(76)	29.35(3)	3(62)	189(71)	42.6(62)	71.64	29	58	16	10	331,745
JOHNSTON-FORBES,C.	219.4(149)	68.9(73)	55.7(157)	29.36(4)	3(62)	205(48)	41.2(74)	73.43	20	76	25	1	53,623
JONES, ROSIE	223.3(119)	73.4(32)	64.5(58)	29.41(5)	3(62)	254(17)	41.8(68)	71.85	33	81	24	7	320,964
JORDAN, PATTY	226.3(91)	62.2(136)	60.3(114)	31.11(157)		146(111)	33.3(146)	74.57	13	63	25		13,133
JOYCE, JOAN						21(197)					8		
KEAN, LAUREL	229.2(64)	65.3(110)	58.7(131)	30.35(79)	5(25)	173(84)	40.0(83)	73.91	12	66	27		24,143
KEGGI, CAROLINE	228.8(67)	61.6(139)	56.7(148)	29.97(34)	3(62)	159(100)	38.8(95)	74.04	12	68	25		29,411
KELLY, ANNE						8(204)					3		
KERDYK, TRACY	223.8(116)	72.6(37)	66.8(26)	30.59(106)	1(129)	186(73)	48.3(18)	72.97	23	73	24	2	64,908
KIGGENS, LISA	236.0(27)	65.9(106)	64.1(63)	30.40(88)	7(8)	199(56)	37.1(115)	72.78	23	72	24	2	64,851
KING, BETSY	237.0(22)	71.9(42)	71.1(4)	29.92(28)	8(2)	320(2)	44.6(47)	70.85	51	93	27	15	595,992
KLEIMAN, JAN	224.0(112)	60.9(144)	49.4(178)	31.38(169)	1(129)	53(176)	31.3(160)	77.40			15		
KOBAYASHI, HIROMI	220.9(132)	80.8(5)	64.6(57)	29.43(7)	4(44)	257(13)	42.7(61)	71.78	37	83	24	8	347,060
KU, OK-HEE						9(203)			2	3	1		5,310
LARSEN, JULIE	228.3(70)	67.8(86)	63.7(70)	30.62(109)	5(25)	192(66)	33.3(148)	72.85	24	79	26	2	83,532
LARSON, BECKY						2(217)					1		
LASKEN, KIM	211.7(178)	67.0(96)	57.6(139)	30.23(61)	1(129)	69(164)	34.7(136)	74.37	5	30	12		5,356
LASKER, DEEDEE	217.3(164)	68.9(72)	57.5(141)	31.31(166)	1(129)	113(134)	22.6(177)	74.88	4	51	21		5,004
LE ROUX, NICKY						34(187)			2	16	7		4,152
LEADBETTER, KELLY						16(198)			1	8	3		2,539
LIDBACK, JENNY	216.6(165)	73.0(35)	66.7(31)	29.93(29)	3(62)	168(88)	44.6(44)	72.02	22	55	17	3	82,136
LISCIO, PATTI	218.0(159)	75.3(15)	56.0(152)	30.76(127)	2(92)	128(125)	38.8(97)	75.07	9	57	25		8,368

	Driving distance	Driving accuracy (%)	Greens in regulation (%)	Putting average	Total eagles	Total birdies	Sand saves (%)	Scoring average	Rounds under par	Total rounds	Tournaments entered	Top 10 finishes	Official money
LITTLE, SALLY	223.1(123)	69.0(70)	62.2(95)	30.26(64)	2(92)	195(60)	39.6(90)	73.12	23	78	26		49,658
LOFLAND-DORMANN,D.	225.3(102)	69.1(69)	65.2(48)	30.37(82)	2(92)	240(26)	44.3(49)	72.31	34	81	26	5	234,415
LOPEZ, NANCY	243.0(7)	70.1(59)	69.8(6)	30.02(37)	7(8)	220(42)	37.3(112)	70.83	40	65	18	11	304,480
LOVANDER, MARILYN	225.4(101)	70.1(58)	57.2(142)	30.71(121)	3(62)	101(144)	44.6(44)	74.70	6	40	15		11,303
LUNN, KAREN	238.2(15)	55.7(165)	63.8(69)	30.27(67)	6(16)	119(131)	43.9(52)	72.66	18	44	13	1	40,021
MACKALL, MICHELLE	220.2(141)	73.1(33)	62.4(92)	30.80(130)	1(129)	191(68)	33.3(149)	73.64	17	70	24	1	35,896
MACKEY, CINDY	226.0(93)	54.4(173)	55.9(153)	30.57(105)	3(62)	96(147)	36.4(120)	74.51	5	45	18		10,862
MALLON, MEG	226.6(88)	73.9(25)	68.0(20)	30.09(44)	6(16)	233(31)	39.1(86)	71.82	35	78	23	7	276,291
MANT, CATHY						1(219)					1		
MARINO, CATHY						26(192)			3	12	4		7,686
MARSHALL, KATHRYN	231.7(42)	68.2(82)	62.6(88)	31.09(155)	4(44)	83(158)	34.0(141)	73.88	10	34	14		13,111
MASSEY, DEBBIE	227.2(80)	66.9(97)	58.3(134)	30.12(48)	1(129)	73(163)	48.6(17)	73.41	6	27	10		20,985
MAYNOR, STEPHANIE					1(129)	63(170)			6	23	9		4,229
MCALLISTER, SUSIE						6(207)					5		
MCGANN, MICHELLE	251.3(2)	66.5(102)	70.3(5)	31.02(146)	8(2)	298(3)	48.1(20)	71.63	46	91	27	9	315,921
MCGEORGE, MISSIE	229.0(65)	71.3(48)	66.6(33)	29.99(35)	5(25)	230(33)	44.3(49)	72.17	31	81	25	4	180,311
MCGUIRE, SARAH	229.9(59)	62.4(135)	61.6(102)	31.40(170)	5(25)	106(138)	34.7(137)	74.68	6	57	25		8,336
MCHAFFIE, DEBORAH	232.5(38)	65.4(109)	62.6(87)	30.36(80)	3(62)	168(88)	46.8(30)	72.70	22	63	22	1	56,427
MCNAMARA, MELISSA	220.6(136)	68.2(81)	59.5(126)	30.02(38)	3(62)	165(94)	37.9(103)	73.86	15	64	24		29,089
MERTEN, LAURI	224.9(109)	63.7(122)	62.8(82)	29.33(2)	2(92)	239(27)	53.4(8)	72.03	34	78	23	8	394,744
MILLER, ALICE	227.9(73)	64.5(115)	60.9(110)	30.74(124)	2(92)	145(112)	55.7(3)	73.95	14	59	23		25,472
MILLS, LEIGH ANN	227.7(76)	64.0(120)	62.8(81)	31.78(175)	1(129)	106(138)	35.0(132)	74.62	6	45	18		5,601
MOCHRIE, DOTTIE	230.3(54)	77.0(11)	74.1(1)	30.24(62)	2(92)	293(5)	38.2(102)	71.09	53	91	25	11	429,118
MOCKETT, CATHY	225.7(97)	73.9(26)	66.4(34)	32.56(179)	3(62)	127(126)	45.6(37)	74.42	6	59	23		11,772
MONAGHAN, KRIS	225.8(96)	70.2(57)	69.0(12)	30.79(128)	3(62)	252(19)	41.1(76)	72	39	75	24	6	208,987
MORRIS, MARIANNE	239.3(12)	60.8(146)	65.2(49)	30.48(93)	8(2)	177(80)	37.5(108)	72.53	24	64	22	1	56,615
MORSE, CATHY					1(129)	43(182)			6	18	6		7,351
MOXNESS, BARBARA						12(201)					2		
MUCHA, BARB	225.4(100)	72.6(38)	64.9(50)	30.38(85)	2(92)	221(39)	49.5(14)	72.56	28	77	23	2	91,806
MUNDINGER, KARIN	218.7(152)	57.6(160)	55.0(164)	31(145)		60(172)	32.7(150)	75.07	3	28	12		2,605
MURPHY, MARY	230.7(49)	60.7(148)	65.9(39)	32.02(177)	3(62)	133(122)	32.4(152)	74.60	11	60	23		13,753
MYERS, TERRY-JO	227.1(82)	71.4(46)	60.7(112)	30.31(73)	4(44)	159(100)	31.5(159)	73.43	13	61	21		46,176
NAUSE, MARTHA	228.2(71)	69.0(71)	62.8(83)	30.53(101)	1(129)	173(84)	46.9(28)	73.14	19	66	23		42,090
NEUMANN, LISELOTTE	224.1(111)	67.7(88)	62.7(86)	29.17(1)	5(25)	161(98)	39.7(89)	72.54	18	56	16	1	90,776
NICHOLAS, ALISON	228.8(68)	73.6(29)	63.9(67)	30.13(50)	1(129)	148(109)	41.3(71)	72.25	20	51	16	2	101,203
NOBLE, KAREN	230.8(48)	66.3(104)	60.1(117)	30.81(132)	7(8)	165(94)	45.7(36)	73.94	16	69	26		28,630
OKAMOTO, AYAKO	230.2(55)	71.2(51)	60.7(111)	29.63(14)	2(92)	125(128)	43.3(56)	72.78	14	46	15	2	61,504
ORLEY, EVELYN	212.0(176)	58.5(159)	49.1(179)	30.12(49)		78(161)	41.0(78)	76	1	42	20		1,499
PALLI, ANNE-MARIE	223.3(120)	58.5(158)	57.6(137)	30.07(42)	3(62)	145(112)	40.0(83)	74.02	12	59	24	1	31,617
PALMER, SANDRA						35(186)			2	18	7		1,773
PEARSON, BECKY	218.2(156)	59.6(152)	55.7(158)	32.32(178)	2(92)	69(164)	37.3(113)	76.53	3	38	18		2,762
PETERSON, ADELE						39(185)			3	19	8		1,172
PETERSON-PARKER,K.	223.2(121)	68.4(78)	62.7(85)	30.50(94)	2(92)	175(82)	37.2(114)	73.52	13	64	23	1	33,485
PIERCE, CAROLINE	214.3(170)	73.0(34)	56.8(146)	29.97(33)	3(62)	140(117)	56.1(2)	73.79	10	66	25	1	33,978
PITCOCK, JOAN	220.6(135)	69.2(68)	63.3(72)	30.40(87)	3(62)	223(38)	51.8(12)	72.70	29	80	24		66,622
PORTER-KING, M.						28(190)					8		
POSTLEWAIT, KATHY	210.7(180)	75.4(14)	62.4(91)	30.14(51)	4(44)	172(86)	36.1(124)	73.01	20	72	24		40,530
PRECHTL, KIERNAN	229.2(63)	55.5(168)	56.8(145)	31.33(167)	2(92)	98(146)	54.5(7)	75.81	3	52	23		1,975
PULZ, PENNY						3(212)					1		
RAMSBOTTOM, .	220.4(139)	83.4(1)	67.3(24)	30.42(90)	3(62)	215(45)	47.8(22)	72.64	25	83	24	2	93,354
RARICK, CINDY	222.7(126)	74.0(24)	65.8(40)	30.02(39)	4(44)	261(12)	42.4(64)	72.08	37	88	26	3	174,407
READ, AMY	234.8(30)	68.8(74)	65.3(46)	30.87(135)	3(62)	166(92)	24.3(174)	73.51	15	68	25		33,733
REDMAN, MICHELE	230.4(51)	69.5(62)	65.4(43)	30.54(103)	4(44)	184(75)	37.9(103)	72.61	23	72	24		64,518
REDMAN, SUSIE	226.7(85)	68.3(80)	61.2(105)	30.61(108)	2(92)	103(142)	47.8(21)	73.77	11	44	16	1	36,426
REYNOLDS, CATHY						27(191)			1	16	8		1,120

FINAL PLAYER STATISTICS

Player	Driving distance	Driving accuracy (%)	Greens in regulation (%)	Putting average	Total eagles	Total birdies	Sand saves (%)	Scoring average	Rounds under par	Total rounds	Tournaments entered	Top 10 finishes	Official money
RICHARD, DEB	230.8(47)	63.8(121)	65.4(42)	30.21(58)	5(25)	208(46)	43.6(53)	72.25	31	71	23	5	223,282
RIDGEWAY, ANGIE	225.9(94)	72.1(41)	62.4(90)	30.22(60)	5(25)	202(51)	41.2(73)	72.85	26	79	26	2	75,290
RIEDER, JOAL	223.4(118)	69.3(65)	59.8(121)	33.06(180)	1(129)	55(175)	23.8(175)	76.74	1	34	16		2,019
RINKER-GRAHAM, L.	223.1(122)	61.8(138)	58.5(133)	30.18(54)	4(44)	150(106)	40.0(85)	73.90	11	61	24		19,342
RITTENHOUSE, L.	230.9(46)	66.3(105)	61.9(97)	31.04(148)	5(25)	205(48)	34.5(138)	73.99	16	77	28	1	49,477
RITZMAN, ALICE	235.9(28)	71.7(44)	66.8(25)	30.50(95)	6(16)	193(65)	34.8(135)	72.34	25	62	21	3	113,992
RIZZO, PATTI	236.5(24)	61.9(137)	68.6(14)	30.73(123)	8(2)	197(58)	25.8(170)	72.32	30	66	20	4	111,371
ROBBINS, KELLY	245.5(4)	67.4(94)	68.2(16)	30.33(75)	11(1)	221(39)	44.6(46)	71.59	43	73	22	4	200,744
ROGERS, LIZ	220.0(143)	67.4(95)	53.3(168)	30.52(99)		52(177)	35.7(129)	76.21	3	28	13		724
ROGERSON, KATE	227.0(83)	55.5(167)	59.6(123)	30.82(133)		106(138)	31.7(157)	73.53	11	38	13		19,713
RUBIN, NANCY	213.3(173)	67.9(83)	60.0(119)	30.65(114)	1(129)	96(147)	20.4(179)	74.59	6	34	14		9,634
SAMS, JUDY	220.5(137)	63.1(130)	61.0(107)	31.08(153)	2(92)	126(127)	35.8(127)	74.64	7	64	25		10,730
SANDERS, SUSAN					2(92)	6(207)					2		
SCHREYER, CINDY	213.4(172)	74.9(17)	59.5(124)	30.35(78)	2(92)	163(96)	38.6(99)	73.74	18	74	27	1	95,343
SCRANTON, NANCY	233.6(34)	68.6(75)	71.4(3)	31.21(161)	7(8)	257(13)	33.3(145)	72.35	35	88	27	3	129,766
SHEEHAN, PATTY	229.5(61)	70.8(53)	69.2(9)	29.57(12)	3(62)	253(18)	51.4(13)	71.04	42	75	21	12	540,547
SHERK, CATHY						1(219)					1		
SHIPMAN, KIM	230.0(58)	54.9(170)	56.2(150)	30.42(89)	2(92)	108(137)	27.0(168)	74.76	4	41	17		7,699
SINN, PEARL	218.5(153)	71.3(49)	62.9(77)	30.20(57)	4(44)	202(51)	39.8(86)	72.84	26	77	25	2	69,393
SKINNER, VAL	238.5(14)	54.8(172)	65.4(44)	31.11(156)	5(25)	194(62)	46.6(32)	73.10	18	69	25	4	129,665
SMITH, SUSAN						24(194)				2	10	4	1,476
SMYERS, SHERRIN						24(194)					5		
SOLOMON, BETH						2(217)					1		
SPENCER-DEVLIN, M.	227.1(81)	68.4(77)	62.9(78)	30.89(136)	2(92)	169(87)	36.4(121)	73.59	16	66	21	1	35,730
SPUZICH, SANDRA					1(129)	25(193)					8		
STACY, HOLLIS	227.3(78)	67.5(92)	62.5(89)	29.62(13)	2(92)	216(44)	44.7(42)	71.87	30	70	21	8	191,257
STAMBAUGH, JODI					2(92)	56(173)			1	23	9		2,312
STEINBACH, DEBRA						4(211)					2		
STEINHAUER, SHERRI	231.5(44)	74.3(20)	71.8(2)	30.91(137)	6(16)	296(4)	40.9(79)	71.64	53	99	28	6	311,967
STEPHENSON, JAN	225.1(105)	69.9(61)	62.9(75)	29.83(21)	1(129)	238(28)	39.4(92)	72.19	28	79	24	4	161,123
STRUDWICK, S.	219.4(148)	75.1(16)	57.8(136)	29.94(30)		156(103)	41.3(72)	73.24	15	63	22	2	51,161
STUBBLEFIELD, M.						1(219)					1		
TAYLOR, NANCY	219.8(146)	68.5(76)	58.5(132)	31.62(174)	1(129)	56(173)	27.6(167)	75.77	3	26	12		449
THOMAS, BARB	229.3(62)	67.7(89)	61.8(98)	29.74(18)	3(62)	149(108)	47.2(27)	72.48	19	61	20	1	63,052
THOMAS, SUE	218.4(154)	71.3(47)	56.9(144)	30.29(70)		89(152)	34.9(133)	74	7	38	14		6,680
THOMPSON, M.	230.4(52)	56.5(161)	55.7(159)	30.95(140)	3(62)	96(147)	38.6(101)	74.85	7	41	16		10,963
TOMBS, TINA	230.4(53)	63.2(128)	58.9(130)	29.73(16)	7(8)	160(99)	42.5(63)	73.38	14	58	20	1	68,592
TSCHETTER, KRIS	238.6(13)	63.1(129)	64.2(60)	29.92(27)	7(8)	282(8)	47.4(23)	72.29	33	86	26	3	196,913
TURNER, SHERRI	238.0(17)	66.9(98)	64.0(65)	31.09(154)	5(25)	121(130)	32.7(150)	73.43	11	46	15	2	53,372
WALKER, COLLEEN	226.6(87)	66.4(103)	62.9(79)	29.56(11)	1(129)	232(32)	54.7(6)	72.16	32	80	24	3	96,384
WALTERS, LISA	236.5(25)	60.8(145)	66.7(29)	30.53(102)	7(8)	255(15)	43.9(51)	72.43	30	84	24	3	149,260
WALTON, ROBIN	232.3(40)	71.6(45)	66.8(27)	30.82(134)	4(44)	201(54)	41.7(69)	72.82	22	74	23	1	74,329
WEST, LORI	226.9(84)	69.2(66)	62.2(94)	30.33(76)		194(62)	43.3(55)	71.93	22	68	23		61,736
WHALEY, SUZY	223.6(117)	61.4(141)	56.2(151)	31.04(149)	1(129)	48(181)	14.6(180)	75.19	1	26	13		995
WHITE, NANCY	226.2(92)	63.6(123)	55.8(154)	30.52(100)	2(92)	167(91)	35.7(128)	74.52	6	63	25		15,533
WHITWORTH, KATHY						11(202)					2		
WILKINS, DONNA	210.9(179)	67.6(90)	54.2(167)	29.75(19)		117(132)	38.8(96)	74.56	8	55	24		9,114
WILL, MAGGIE	223.9(115)	64.5(116)	61.0(108)	30.01(36)	3(62)	190(70)	37.0(117)	72.79	20	72	23		49,770
WILLIAMS, KIM	225.8(95)	65.2(112)	60.9(109)	30.25(63)	2(92)	168(88)	36.8(118)	73.41	18	70	25	1	51,053
WRIGHT, PAMELA	225.0(107)	70.9(52)	64.7(55)	30.68(117)	3(62)	180(79)	33.3(147)	73.01	21	72	23		57,888
WYATT, JENNIFER	215.3(167)	74.5(19)	62.7(84)	30.46(91)	1(129)	166(92)	42.1(66)	73.37	16	67	25		40,107
ZEDLITZ, JEAN	237.1(20)	56.1(163)	61.9(96)	31.16(158)	3(62)	150(106)	54.7(5)	74.11	11	61	25	1	44,241
ZIMMERMANN, M. B.	229.7(60)	67.4(93)	68.9(13)	31.04(147)	1(129)	228(34)	33.7(143)	72.45	34	78	25	2	118,626

Minimum of 10 events played for all listed players.
Statistics courtesy of LPGA.

SENIOR PGA TOUR FINAL STATISTICS

FINAL PLAYER STATISTICS

	Driving distance	Driving accuracy (%)	Greens in regulation (%)	Putting average	Total eagles	Total birdies	Sand saves (%)	Scoring average	All-around	Consecutive cuts	Official money
AARON, TOMMY	251.7(44)	67.4(43)	64.9(45)	1.805(23)	6(22T)	301(24)	46.9(34)	71.73	319	107(21T)	266,611
ALBUS, JIM	262.1(18)	73.5(9T)	71.3(12)	1.798(18)	6(22T)	387(4)	48.1(25T)	70.82	125	92(26)	627,883
AOKI, ISAO	262.9(14T)	71.7(16T)	71.7(9)	1.762(5T)	10(5T)	285(36)	47.7(28T)	70.21	124	31(66T)	557,667
ARCHER, GEORGE	253.6(43)	65.0(54)	71.5(11)	1.748(2)	4(40T)	397(3)	64.2(1)	69.86	217	127(19T)	963,124
AYCOCK, TOMMY	272.9(4)	64.4(57T)	69.0(25)	1.810(29T)	2(55T)	269(38)	43.4(47T)	71.54	308	57(40)	211,826
BAIRD, BUTCH	248.0(54)	66.6(46)	64.8(46)	1.826(44T)	9(7T)	234(53)	49.0(24)	72.38	378	107(21T)	150,038
BARBER, MILLER	257.9(30)	72.5(14T)	67.5(34)	1.803(22)	10(5T)	337(12)	38.0(64T)	71.92	227	11(116)	318,986
BETLEY, BOB	261.1(20)	66.4(48)	66.2(42T)	1.789(15)	6(22T)	268(39T)	45.5(38T)	71.55	283	52(45)	407,300
BIES, DON	256.3(37T)	68.8(35)	69.5(22)	1.818(37)	9(7T)	258(45)	49.6(21T)	71.49	268	74(35)	239,781
BREWER, GAY	246.3(60)	64.6(56)	59.2(64)	1.812(31)	1(64T)	252(48)	57.9(3)	72.64	438	278(1)	117,650
BRUE, BOB	249.6(48)	63.0(66)	60.3(62)	1.841(52T)	4(40T)	254(46T)	52.2(15)	73.20	455	14(105T)	114,496
CAIN, JOHN PAUL	249.4(50T)	72.5(14T)	67.4(35)	1.844(57T)	0(68T)	209(59)	34.0(70)	72.96	437	14(105T)	92,873
CASPER, BILLY	241.6(64T)	68.6(36)	57.1(66)	1.841(52T)	0(68T)	174(66)	54.9(8)	73.04	478	219(4)	81,544
CHARLES, BOB	249.5(49)	76.1(3)	75.9(1)	1.768(7)	7(18T)	349(9)	54.8(9)	69.59	111	43(53T)	1,046,823
COLBERT, JIM	247.3(56)	75.0(4)	70.9(14)	1.778(10)	6(22T)	343(10)	57.8(4)	70.57	153	83(31)	779,889
COODY, CHARLES	257.6(33)	67.0(44)	69.4(23)	1.843(55T)	5(35T)	254(46T)	40.5(60)	72.13	377	153(12)	221,982
CRAMPTON, BRUCE	242.5(62)	70.5(24)	67.1(39)	1.807(25)	4(40T)	294(29T)	51.1(17)	71.60	315	37(56)	366,762
DALZIEL, DOUG	247.1(58)	65.1(53)	63.7(51)	1.884(68)	6(22T)	228(54)	43.4(47T)	73.56	482	14(105T)	90,637
DENT, JIM	277.8(1)	66.1(49)	70.2(16T)	1.797(17)	9(7T)	330(14)	47.7(28T)	70.84	160	145(14T)	513,515
DEVLIN, BRUCE	246.9(59)	70.8(22T)	61.8(59)	1.827(46)	2(55T)	181(64)	37.5(67)	73.53	482	90(28)	65,383
DILL, TERRY	275.1(2)	56.7(70)	62.7(56T)	1.802(20T)	6(22T)	316(21)	38.4(62)	72.50	336	59(39)	179,976
DOUGLASS, DALE	256.3(37T)	71.7(16T)	69.8(20)	1.806(24)	6(22T)	326(17T)	50.3(18)	71.06	190	87(29)	499,858
ELDER, LEE	229.3(70)	73.9(7)	53.0(70)	1.852(61)	2(55T)	150(69)	53.4(11)	73.75	451	16(93T)	75,761
FERREE, JIM	268.7(7)	72.9(13)	72.9(7)	1.841(52T)	6(22T)	291(34T)	43.0(49T)	71.18	207	171(7)	424,333
FORD, DOUG	202.3(72)	73.5(9T)	31.9(72)	1.941(72)	1(64T)	84(72)	42.1(54)	78.82	534	19(84)	10,381
GEIBERGER, AL	255.2(40)	71.5(18)	74.1(3)	1.762(5T)	8(11T)	300(25T)	46.8(35)	69.89	161	137(18)	608,877
GILBERT, GIBBY	259.0(26T)	69.3(34)	70.2(16T)	1.775(8)	8(11T)	365(7)	50.0(19T)	70.72	156	95(24)	661,378
GILBERT, LARRY	267.5(8)	74.9(5)	69.7(21)	1.813(32)	8(11T)	327(16)	46.7(36)	70.98	147	32(61T)	515,790
GOALBY, BOB	241.2(66)	69.4(30T)	60.8(61)	1.910(69)	2(55T)	154(68)	47.3(31T)	74.59	506	28(70)	42,506
GRAHAM, LOU	241.6(64T)	52.7(72)	56.7(67)	1.874(66)	3(48T)	160(67)	49.3(23)	74.91	549	3(153)	44,045
HENDRICKSON, DICK	266.2(9)	66.0(50)	66.9(40)	1.808(26)	12(3)	326(17T)	37.7(66)	71.77	264	51(46)	243,262
HENNING, HAROLD	244.8(61)	69.6(27T)	64.1(50)	1.814(33)	2(55T)	265(41T)	61.3(2)	72.02	359	5(139)	314,104
HILL, MIKE	257.7(31T)	73.0(12)	73.4(5)	1.780(12T)	8(11T)	328(15)	39.4(61)	69.97	162	157(11)	798,116
HOBDAY, SIMON	259.1(25)	68.0(40)	69.1(24)	1.809(27T)	5(35T)	353(8)	43.6(46)	71.40	259	101(23)	670,417
JANUARY, DON	255.3(39)	68.5(37)	67.7(33)	1.792(16)	7(18T)	248(52)	44.3(44)	71.44	305	201(6)	274,338
JIMENEZ, JOE	262.6(16)	66.5(47)	68.2(29)	1.844(57T)	5(35T)	250(49)	34.6(69)	72.88	382	43(53T)	121,780
JOYCE, MIKE	256.6(35T)	70.3(25)	64.3(48)	1.864(64)	3(48T)	292(33)	44.8(41)	72.76	367	16(93T)	171,308
KELLEY, AL	249.8(47)	64.2(59)	62.9(54)	1.823(40T)	2(55T)	249(50T)	42.4(52)	72.70	468	15(98T)	119,553
KENNEDY, ROGER	247.7(55)	69.5(29)	63.3(52T)	1.883(67)	1(64T)	215(57)	43.0(49T)	73.40	485	15(98T)	81,178
KIEFER, JACK	258.5(29)	73.7(8)	70.1(18)	1.825(43)	6(22T)	300(25T)	40.9(58)	71.60	238	50(47)	333,511
LAORETTI, LARRY	256.6(35T)	63.9(60T)	62.8(55)	1.835(50)	2(55T)	294(29T)	41.5(56)	72.70	444	141(17)	183,694
LEHNHARD, BRUCE	259.0(26T)	63.9(60T)	65.4(44)	1.843(55T)	8(11T)	249(50T)	47.3(31T)	72.81	379	30(68)	137,409
LOTZ, DICK	254.9(41)	69.4(30T)	68.1(30T)	1.836(51)	3(48T)	268(39T)	49.6(21T)	71.77	330	32(61T)	199,244
MASSENGALE, DON	231.6(68)	63.6(62T)	53.6(69)	1.868(65)	0(68T)	180(65)	53.0(12)	74.48	546	34(58)	75,792
MAXWELL, BILLY	227.6(71)	68.4(38)	52.1(71)	1.927(71)	0(68T)	96(71)	47.4(30)	75.87	555	21(70)	17,531
MCBEE, RIVES	248.7(52)	70.0(26)	64.6(47)	1.830(48)	7(18T)	265(41T)	50.0(19T)	72.20	337	15(98T)	181,803
MOODY, ORVILLE	250.1(46)	70.8(22T)	64.2(49)	1.822(39)	5(35T)	293(32)	53.8(10)	72.23	306	158(10)	196,565
MORGAN, WALTER	265.5(11T)	71.2(19T)	68.1(30T)	1.824(42)	4(40T)	182(63)	42.2(53)	72.05	299	55(42)	138,700
MOWRY, LARRY	257.3(34)	68.2(39)	68.7(26T)	1.834(49)	2(55T)	194(61)	48.1(25T)	72.23	371	1(208)	180,703
MURPHY, BOB	257.7(31T)	73.3(11)	73.8(4)	1.780(12T)	8(11T)	313(22)	52.8(13)	70.24	120	27(71)	768,743
NICHOLS, BOBBY	259.3(24)	56.4(71)	59.8(63)	1.816(35)	4(40T)	202(60)	44.4(43)	73.19	451	9(121)	181,433

	Driving distance	Driving accuracy (%)	Greens in regulation (%)	Putting average	Total eagles	Total birdies	Sand saves (%)	Scoring average	All-around	Consecutive cuts	Official money
PLAYER, GARY	241.9(63)	69.4(30T)	68.6(28)	1.779(11)	4(40T)	227(55)	51.6(16)	70.81	311	165(8)	360,272
POWELL, JIMMY	249.4(50T)	56.8(69)	61.6(60)	1.815(34)	1(64T)	300(25T)	45.5(38T)	73.00	464	14(105T)	164,255
REITH, BOB	259.9(22)	69.4(30T)	66.2(42T)	1.862(62)	4(40T)	183(62)	27.7(72)	72.97	399	56(41)	142,173
RHYAN, RICHARD	248.4(53)	74.4(6)	67.3(36)	1.846(59T)	3(48T)	271(37)	31.8(71)	72.67	377	15(98T)	208,374
RODRIGUEZ, CHI CHI	260.5(21)	71.1(21)	73.3(6)	1.785(14)	6(22T)	378(5)	55.2(6T)	70.41	112	42(55)	798,857
SHAW, TOM	259.4(23)	66.9(45)	68.0(32)	1.802(20T)	3(48T)	320(19)	36.8(68)	71.89	321	91(27)	324,385
SIFFORD, CHARLES	236.2(67)	78.2(1)	56.2(68)	1.926(70)	0(68T)	146(70)	38.0(64T)	74.76	509	22(78)	42,177
SMITH, BEN	258.8(28)	61.9(68)	62.4(58)	1.800(19)	3(48T)	300(25T)	47.2(33)	72.91	390	31(66T)	209,427
SNEAD, J.C.	269.0(5)	64.8(55)	70.5(15)	1.817(36)	9(7T)	303(23)	55.2(6T)	70.91	186	82(32T)	487,500
STILL, KEN	231.3(69)	63.2(65)	57.5(65)	1.826(44T)	3(48T)	211(58)	44.1(45)	73.90	531	48(48)	86,982
STOCKTON, DAVE	254.0(42)	69.6(27T)	71.6(10)	1.742(1)	8(11T)	419(2)	57.4(5)	69.71	137	68(37)	1175,944
THOMPSON, ROCKY	268.9(6)	64.4(57T)	68.7(26T)	1.755(4)	11(4)	420(1)	44.6(42)	71.00	186	145(14T)	571,844
TOSCANO, HARRY	262.9(14T)	67.8(41T)	66.3(41)	1.863(63)	6(22T)	260(44)	41.1(57)	72.69	347	15(98T)	201,150
TREVINO, LEE	265.5(11T)	71.2(19T)	74.4(2)	1.750(3)	6(22T)	319(20)	52.6(14)	70.00	101	82(32T)	956,591
WARGO, TOM	263.5(13)	67.8(41T)	72.1(8)	1.776(9)	7(18T)	371(6)	48.1(25T)	70.60	148	32(61T)	557,270
WEAVER, DEWITT	274.3(3)	65.5(52)	69.9(19)	1.820(38)	17(1)	332(13)	45.7(37)	71.34	203	127(19T)	472,220
WYNN, BOB	247.2(57)	63.6(62T)	62.7(56T)	1.823(40T)	5(35T)	222(56)	44.9(40)	73.18	472	2(167)	168,692
YANCEY, BERT	261.8(19)	63.4(64)	63.3(52T)	1.846(59T)	2(55T)	265(41T)	43.0(49T)	73.24	449	162(9)	104,218
ZARLEY, KERMIT	262.5(17)	65.6(51)	71.2(13)	1.809(27T)	13(2)	338(11)	41.6(55)	71.05	227	62(38)	414,715
ZEMBRISKI, WALTER	250.3(45)	77.0(2)	67.2(37T)	1.828(47)	6(22T)	291(34T)	40.6(59)	71.70	288	261(1)	331,960
ZIEGLER, LARRY	266.1(10)	62.3(67)	67.2(37T)	1.810(29T)	4(40T)	294(29T)	38.2(63)	72.18	357	46(49)	216,073

Minimum of 61 rounds played for all listed players.
Statistics courtesy of Senior PGA Tour.

GOLF ALMANAC 1994

For the Record

ALL-TIME TOUR RECORDS...284

TOURNAMENT HISTORIES...299

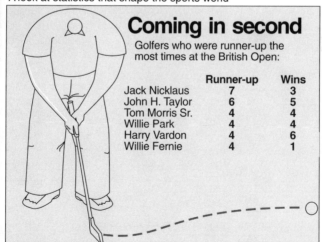

USA SNAPSHOTS®
A look at statistics that shape the sports world

Coming in second
Golfers who were runner-up the most times at the British Open:

	Runner-up	Wins
Jack Nicklaus	7	3
John H. Taylor	6	5
Tom Morris Sr.	4	4
Willie Park	4	4
Harry Vardon	4	6
Willie Fernie	4	1

Source: USA TODAY research   By Julie Stacey, USA TODAY

PGA TOUR ALL-TIME RECORDS

THE VARDON TROPHY

YEAR	PLAYER	POINTS
1937	Harry Cooper	*500
1938	Sam Snead	*520
1939	Byron Nelson	*473
1940	Ben Hogan	*432
1941	Ben Hogan	*494
1942-1946	No Award— World War II	
1947	Jimmy Demaret	69.90
1948	Ben Hogan	69.30
1949	Sam Snead	69.37
1950	Sam Snead	69.23
1951	Lloyd Mangrum	70.05
1952	Jack Burke	70.54
1953	Lloyd Mangrum	70.22
1954	E. J. Harrison	70.41
1955	Sam Snead	69.86
1956	Cary Middlecoff	70.35
1957	Dow Finsterwald	70.30
1958	Bob Rosburg	70.11
1959	Art Wall	70.35
1960	Billy Casper	69.95
1961	Arnold Palmer	69.95
1962	Arnold Palmer	70.27
1963	Billy Casper	70.58
1964	Arnold Palmer	70.01
1965	Billy Casper	70.85
1966	Billy Casper	70.27
1967	Arnold Palmer	70.18
1968	Billy Casper	69.82
1969	Dave Hill	70.34
1970	Lee Trevino	70.64
1971	Lee Trevino	70.27
1972	Lee Trevino	70.89
1973	Bruce Crampton	70.57
1974	Lee Trevino	70.64
1975	Bruce Crampton	70.51
1976	Don January	70.56
1977	Tom Watson	70.32
1978	Tom Watson	70.16
1979	Tom Watson	70.27
1980	Lee Trevino	69.73
1981	Tom Kite	69.80
1982	Tom Kite	70.21
1983	Raymond Floyd	70.61
1984	Calvin Peete	70.56
1985	Don Pooley	70.36
1986	Scott Hoch	70.08
1987	Dan Pohl	70.25
1988	Chip Beck	69.46
1989	Greg Norman	69.49
1990	Greg Norman	69.10
1991	Fred Couples	69.59
1992	Fred Couples	69.38
1993	Nick Price	69.11

*Point system used 1937-41.

PGA PLAYER OF THE YEAR AWARD

1948	Ben Hogan
1949	Sam Snead
1950	Ben Hogan
1951	Ben Hogan
1952	Julius Boros
1953	Ben Hogan
1954	Ed Furgol
1955	Doug Ford
1956	Jack Burke
1957	Dick Mayer
1958	Dow Finsterwald
1959	Art Wall
1960	Arnold Palmer
1961	Jerry Barber
1962	Arnold Palmer
1963	Julius Boros
1964	Ken Venturi
1965	Dave Marr
1966	Billy Casper
1967	Jack Nicklaus
1968	*Not awarded*
1969	Orville Moody
1970	Billy Casper
1971	Lee Trevino
1972	Jack Nicklaus
1973	Jack Nicklaus
1974	Johnny Miller
1975	Jack Nicklaus
1976	Jack Nicklaus
1977	Tom Watson
1978	Tom Watson
1979	Tom Watson
1980	Tom Watson
1981	Bill Rogers
1982	Tom Watson
1983	Hal Sutton
1984	Tom Watson
1985	Lanny Watson
1986	Bob Tway
1987	Paul Azinger
1988	Curtis Strange
1989	Tom Kite
1990	Nick Faldo
1991	Corey Pavin
1992	Fred Couples
1993	Nick Price

PGA TOUR PLAYER OF THE YEAR

1990	Wayne Levi
1991	Fred Couples
1992	Fred Couples
1993	Nick Price

PGA TOUR ROOKIE OF THE YEAR

1990	Robert Gamez
1991	John Daly
1992	Mark Carnevale
1993	Vijay Singh

SCORING RECORDS

Low scores

72 holes:

257 (60-68-64-65) by Mike Souchak, at Brackenridge Park Golf Course, San Antonio, in 1955 Texas Open (27-under-par).

258 (65-64-65-64) by Donnie Hammond, at Oak Hills CC, San Antonio, in 1989 Texas Open Presented by Nabisco (22-under-par).

259 (62-68-63-66) by Byron Nelson, at Broadmoor Golf Club, Seattle, in 1945 Seattle Open (21-under-par).

259 (70-63-63-63) by Chandler Harper, at Brackenridge Park Golf Course, San Antonio, in 1954 Texas Open (25-under-par).

259 (63-64-66-66) by Tim Norris, at Wethersfield CC, Hartford, Conn., in 1982 Sammy Davis Greater Hartford Open (25-under-par)

259 (64-63-66-66) by Corey Pavin, at Oak Hills CC, San Antonio, in 1988 Texas Open Presented by Nabisco (21-under-par).

90 holes:

325 (67-67-64-65-62) by Tom Kite at four courses, La Quinta, Calif., in the 1993 Bob Hope Chyrsler Classic (35-under-par).

329 (69-65-67-62-66) by Andrew Magee, at three courses, Las Vegas, in the 1991 Las Vegas Invitational (31-under-par).

329 (70-64-65-64-66) by D.A.

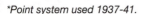

Most shots under par

72 holes:

- 27 Mike Souchak in winning the 1955 Texas Open with 257.
- 27 Ben Hogan in winning the 1945 Portland Invitational with 261.
- 26 Gay Brewer in winning the 1967 Pensacola Open with 262.
- 26 Robert Wrenn in winning the 1987 Buick Open with 262.
- 26 Chip Beck in winning the 1988 USF&G Classic with 262.
- 26 John Huston in winning the 1992 Walt Disney World/Oldsmobile Classic with 262.

90 holes:

- 31 Andrew Magee in winning the 1991 Las Vegas Invitational with 329.
- 31 D.A. Weibring in finishing second in the 1991 Las Vegas Invitational with 329 (lost playoff).
- 29 Corey Pavin in winning the 1991 Bob Hope Chrysler Classic with 331.
- 29 Mark O'Meara in finishing second in the 1991 Bob Hope Chrysler Classic with 331 (lost playoff).
- 29 Chip Beck in finishing third in the 1991 Las Vegas Invitational with 331.
- 29 Jim Gallagher, Jr. in finishing third in the 1991 Las Vegas Invitational with 331.
- 29 Ted Schulz in finishing third in the 1991 Las Vegas Invitational with 331.
- 331 (65-69-66-66-65) by Corey Pavin, at four courses, Palm Springs, Calif., in the 1991 Bob Hope Chrysler Classic (29-under-par).
- 331 (66-65-66-67-67) by Mark O'Meara, at four courses, Palm Springs, Calif., in the 1991 Bob Hope Chrysler Classic (29-under-par).
- 331 (65-72-59-68-67) by Chip Beck, at three courses, Las Vegas, in the 1991 Las Vegas Invitational (29-under-par).
- 331 (69-65-69-61-67) by Jim Gallagher, Jr., at three courses, Las Vegas, in the 1991 Las Vegas Invitational (29-under-par).
- 331 (65-68-67-66-65) by Ted Schulz., at three courses, Las Vegas, in the 1991 Las Vegas Invitational (29-under-par).

54 holes:

Opening rounds

- 191 (66-64-61) by Gay Brewer, at Pensacola CC, Pensacola, Fla., in winning 1967 Pensacola Open (22-under-par).
- 192 (60-68-64) by Mike Souchak, at Brackenridge Park Golf Course. San Antonio, in 1955 Texas Open (21-under-par).
- 192 (64-63-65) by Bob Gilder, at Westchester CC, Harrison, N.Y., in 1982 Manufacturers Hanover Westchester Classic (18-under-par).

Consecutive rounds

- 189 (63-63-63) by Chandler Harper in the last three rounds of the 1954 Texas Open at Brackenridge (24-under-par).

36 holes:

Opening rounds

- 126 (64-62) by Tommy Bolt, at Cavalier Yacht & Country Club, Virginia Beach, Va., in 1954 Virginia Beach Open 12-under-par).
- 126 (64-62) by Paul Azinger, at Oak Hills CC, San Antonio, in 1989 Texas Open Presented by Nabisco (14-under-par).

Consecutive rounds

- 125 (63-62) by Ron Streck in the last two rounds of the 1978 Texas Open at Oak Hills Country Club, San Antonio, 5-under-par).
- 125 (62-63) by Blaine McCallister in the middle two rounds of the 1988 Hardee's Golf Classic at Oakwood CC, Coal Valley, Ill. (15-under-par).
- 126 (62-64) by Johnny Palmer in the last two rounds of the 1948 Tucson Open at El Rio Country Club, Tucson, Ariz. (14-under-par).
- 126 (63-63) by Sam Snead in the last two rounds of the 1950 Texas Open at Brackenridge Park GC, San Antonio (16-under-par).
- 126 (63-63) by Chandler Harper in the middle rounds and last two rounds of the 1954 Texas Open at Brackenridge Park GC, San Antonio (16-under-par).
- 126 (60-66) by Sam Snead in the middle rounds of the 1957 Dallas Open at Glen Lakes Country Club, Dallas (16-under-par).
- 126 (61-65) by Jack Rule, Jr. in the middle rounds of the 1963 St. Paul Open at Keller Golf Club, St. Paul, Minn. (18-under-par).
- 126 (63-63) by Mark Pfeil, in the middle rounds of the 1983 Texas Open at Oak Hills CC, San Antonio (14-under-par).

18 holes:

- 59 by Al Geiberger, at Colonial Country Club, Memphis, in second round of 1977 Memphis Classic (13-under-par).
- 59 by Chip Beck, at Sunrise Golf Club, Las Vegas, in third round of 1991 Las Vegas Invitational (13-under-par).
- 60 by Al Brosch, at Brackenridge Park Golf Course, San Antonio, in third round of 1951 Texas Open (11-under-par).
- 60 by Bill Nary, at El Paso Country Club, El Paso, in third round of 1952 El Paso Open (11-under-par).

60 by Ted Kroll, at Brackenridge Park Golf Course, San Antonio, in third round of 1954 Texas Open (11-under-par).
60 by Wally Ulrich, at Cavalier Yacht and Country Club, Virginia Beach, Va., in second round of 1954 Virginia Beach Open (9-under-par).
60 by Tommy Bolt, at Wethersfield Country Club, Hartford, Conn., in second round of 1954 Insurance City Open (11-under-par).
60 by Mike Souchak at Brackenridge Park Golf Course, San Antonio, in first round of 1955 Texas Open (11-under-par).
60 by Sam Snead, at Glen Lakes Country Club, Dallas, in second round of 1957 Dallas Open (11-under-par).
60 by David Frost, at Randolph Park Golf Course, Tucson, Ariz., in second round of 1990 Northern Telecom Tucson Open (12-under-par).

9 holes:

27 by Mike Souchak, at Brackenridge Park Golf Course, San Antonio, on par-35 second nine of first round in 1955 Texas Open.
27 by Andy North at En-Joie Golf Club, Endicott, N.Y., on par-34 second nine of first round in 1975 B.C. Open.

Best Vardon Trophy scoring average

69.23   Sam Snead in 1950 (6646 strokes, 96 rounds).
69.30   Ben Hogan in 1948 (5267 strokes, 76 rounds).
69.37   Sam Snead in 1949 (5064 strokes, 73 rounds).

Most consecutive rounds under 70

19   Byron Nelson in 1945.

Most birdies in a row

8   Bob Goalby at Pasadena Golf Club, St. Petersburg Fla., during fourth round of 1961 St. Petersburg Open.
8   Fuzzy Zoeller, at Oakwood Country Club, Coal Valley, Ill., during first round of 1976 QuadCities Open.
8   Dewey Arnette, Warwick Hills GC, Grand Blanc, Mich., during first round of the 1987 Buick Open.

Best birdie-eagle streak

6   birdies and 1 eagle by Al Geiberger, at Colonial Country Club, Memphis, during second round of 1977 Danny Thomas Memphis Classic.

Most birdies in a row to win

5   by Jack Nicklaus to win 1978 Jackie Gleason Inverrary Classic (last 5 holes).

VICTORY RECORDS

Most tour victories, career

1.	Sam Snead	81
2.	Jack Nicklaus	70
3.	Ben Hogan	63
4.	Arnold Palmer	60
5.	Byron Nelson	52
6.	Billy Casper	51
T7.	Walter Hagen	40
	Cary Middlecoff	40
9.	Gene Sarazen	38
10.	Lloyd Mangrum	36
T11.	Horton Smith	32
	Tom Watson	32
T13.	Harry Cooper	31
	Jimmy Demaret	31
15.	Leo Diegel	30
T16.	Gene Littler	29
	Paul Runyan	29
18.	Lee Trevino	27
19.	Henry Picard	26
T20.	Tommy Armour	24
	Macdonald Smith	24
22.	Johnny Miller	23
T23.	Johnny Farrell	22
	Gary Player	22
	Ray Floyd	22
T26.	Willie Macfarlane	21
	Bill Mehlhorn	21
	Craig Wood	21
	Lanny Wadkins	21
T30.	James Barnes	20
	Doug Sanders	20
T32.	Doug Ford	19
	Tom Kite	19
	Hubert Green	19
	Hale Irwin	19
T36.	Julius Boros	18
	Jim Ferrier	18
	Johnny Revolta	18
T39.	Jack Burke	17
	Bobby Cruickshank	17
	Ben Crenshaw	17
	Harold McSpaden	17
	Curtis Strange	17
44.	Ralph Guldahl	16
T45.	Tommy Bolt	15
	Ed Dudley	15
	Denny Shute	15
	Mike Souchak	15
	Tom Weiskopf	15
T50.	Bruce Crampton	14
	Dave Hill	14
	Joe Turnesa	14
	Ken Venturi	14

Most tour victories, year by year

1916	James Barnes	3
	Walter Hagen	3
1917	James Barnes	2
	Mike Brady	2
1918	Jock Hutchison	1
	Walter Hagen	1
	Patrick Doyle	1
1919	James Barnes	5
1920	Jock Hutchison	4
1921	James Barnes	4
1922	Gene Sarazen	3
	Walter Hagen	3
1923	Walter Hagen	5
	Joe Kirkwood, Sr	5
1924	Joe Kirkwood, Sr	4
	Walter Hagen	4
1925	Leo Diegel	5
1926	Bill Mehlhorn	5
	Macdonald Smith	5
1927	Johnny Farrell	7
1928	Bil Mehlhorn	7
1929	Horton Smith	8
1930	Gene Sarazen	8
1931	Wiffy Cox	4
1932	Craig Wood	3
	Gene Sarazen	3
	Olin Dutra	3
	Mike Turnesa	3
	Tommy Armour	3
1933	Paul Runyan	9
1934	Paul Runyan	7

Year	Player	Wins
1935	Johnny Revolta	5
	Henry Picard	5
1936	Ralph Guldahl	3
	Henry Picard	3
	Jimmy Hines	3
1937	Harry Cooper	8
1938	Sam Snead	8
1939	Henry Picard	8
1940	Jimmy Demaret	6
1941	Sam Snead	7
1942	Ben Hogan	6
1943	Sam Byrd	1
	Harold McSpaden	1
	Steve Warga	1
1944	Byron Nelson	8
1945	Byron Nelson	18
1946	Ben Hogan	13
1947	Ben Hogan	7
1948	Ben Hogan	10
1949	Cary Middlecoff	7
1950	Sam Snead	11
1951	Cary Middlecoff	6
1952	Jack Burke, Jr	5
	Sam Snead	5
1953	Ben Hogan	4
	Lloyd Mangrum	4
1954	Bob Toski	4
1955	Cary Middlecoff	6
1956	Mike Souchak	4
1957	Arnold Palmer	4
1958	Ken Venturi	4
1959	Gene Littler	5
1960	Arnold Palmer	8
1961	Arnold Palmer	5
	Doug Sanders	5
1962	Arnold Palmer	7
1963	Arnold Palmer	7
1964	Jack Nicklaus	4
	Billy Casper	4
	Tony Lema	4
1965	Jack Nicklaus	5
1966	Billy Casper	4
1967	Jack Nicklaus	5
1968	Billy Casper	6
1969	Dave Hill	3
	Billy Casper	3
	Jack Nicklaus	3
	Ray Floyd	3
1970	Billy Casper	4
1971	Jack Nicklaus	5
	Lee Trevino	5
1972	Jack Nicklaus	7
1973	Jack Nicklaus	7
1974	Johnny Miller	8
1975	Jack Nicklaus	5
1976	Ben Crenshaw	3
	Hubert Green	3
1977	Tom Watson	4
1978	Tom Watson	5
1979	Tom Watson	5
1980	Tom Watson	6
1981	Tom Watson	3
	Bruce Lietzke	3
	Ray Floyd	3
	Bill Rogers	3
1982	Craig Stadler	4
	Calvin Peete	4
1983	Fuzzy Zoeller	2
	Lanny Wadkins	2
	Calvin Peete	2
	Hal Sutton	2
	Gil Morgan	2
	Mark McCumber	2
	Jim Colbert	2
	Seve Ballesteros	2
1984	Tom Watson	3
	Denis Watson	3
1985	Lanny Wadkins	3
	Curtis Strange	3
1986	Bob Tway	4
1987	Curtis Strange	3
	Paul Azinger	3
1988	Curtis Strange	4
1989	Tom Kite	3
	Steve Jones	3
1990	Wayne Levi	4
1991	Ian Woosnam	2
	Corey Pavin	2
	Billy Andrade	2
	Tom Purizer	2
	Mark Brooks	2
	Nick Price	2
	Fred Couples	2
	Andrew Magee	2
1992	Fred Couples	3
	Davis Love III	3
	John Cook	3
1993	Nick Price	4

Most victories during career (PGA Tour co-sponsored and/or approved tournaments only)

81	Sam Snead	
70	Jack Nicklaus	
63	Ben Hogan	
60	Arnold Palmer	
52	Byron Nelson	
51	Billy Casper	

Most consecutive years winning at least one tournament

17	Jack Nicklaus	(1962-78)
17	Arnold Palmer	(1955-71)
16	Billy Casper	(1956-71)

Most consecutive victories

11 Byron Nelson, from March 8-11, 1945, through August 2-4, 1945: Miami Four Ball, Miami Springs Course, Miami, March 8-11, won 8-6, $1,500; Charlotte Open, Myers Park Golf Club, Charlotte, N.C., March 16-19, 272, $2000; Greensboro Open, Starmount Country Club, Greensboro, N.C., March 23-25, 271, $1,000; Durham Open, Hope Valley Country Club, Durham, N.C., March 30-April 1, 276, $1,000; Atlanta Open, Capital City Course, Atlanta, April 5-8, 263, $2000; Montreal Open, Islemere Golf and Country Club, Montreal, June 7-10, 268, $2000; Philadelphia Inquirer Invitational, Llanerch Country Club, Philadelphia, June 14-17, 269, $3000; Chicago Victory National Open, Calumet Country Club, Chicago, Ill., June 29-July 1, 275, $2000; PGA Championship, Moraine Country Club, Dayton, Ohio, July 9-15,4-3, $3750; Tam O'Shanter Open, Tam O'Shanter Country Club, Chicago, July 26-29 269, $10,000; Canadian Open,Thornhill Country Club, Toronto, August 2-4, 280, $2000; Total winnings for streak $30,250.

NOTE: Nelson won a 12th event in Spring Lake, N.J., which is not accounted as official as its $2,500 purse was below the PGA Tour's $3000 minimum.

4	Jackie Burke, Jr., from February 14, 1952 to March 9, 1952: Texas Open, Houston Open, Baton Rouge Open, St. Petersburg Open.	
3	Byron Nelson in 1944, 1945-46.	
3	Sam Snead in 1945.	
3	Ben Hogan in 1946.	
3	Bobby Locke in 1947.	
3	Jim Ferrier in 1951.	
3	Billy Casper in 1960.	
3	Arnold Palmer in 1960, 1962.	
3	Johnny Miller in 1974.	

3 Hubert Green in 1976.
3 Gary Player in 1978.

Most victories in a single event

8 Sam Snead, Greater Greensboro Open: 1938, 1946, 1949, 1950, 1955, 1956, 1960, and 1965
6 Sam Snead, Miami Open: 1937, 1939, 1946, 1950, 1951, and 1955.
6 Jack Nicklaus, Masters: 1963, 1965, 1966, 1972, 1975 and 1986.
5 Walter Hagen, PGA Championship: 1921, 1924 1925, 1926, and 1927.
5 Ben Hogan Colonial NIT: 1946 1947, 1952, 1953, and 1959.
5 Arnold Palmer, Bob Hope Desert Classic: 1960, 1962, 1968, 1971, and 1973.
5 Jack Nicklaus Tournament of Champions: 1963, 1964, 1971, 1973, and 1977.
5 Jack Nicklaus, PGA Championship: 1963, 1971, 1973, 1975, and 1980.
5 Walter Hagen, Western Open: 1916, 1921, 1926, 1927, 1932.

Most consecutive victories in a single event

4 Walter Hagen, PGA Championship, 1924-1927.
3 Willie Anderson, U.S. Open, 1903-1905.
3 Ralph Guidahl, Western Open, 1936-1938.
3 Gene Littler, Tournament of Champions, 1955-1957.
3 Billy Casper, Portland Open, 1959-1961.
3 Arnold Palmer, Texas Open, 1960-1962, Phoenix Open, 1961-1963.
3 Jack Nicklaus, Disney World Golf Classic, 1971-1973.
3 Johnny Miller, Tucson Open, 1974-1976.
3 Tom Watson, Byron Nelson Classic, 1978-1980.

Most victories in a calendar year

18 Byron Nelson (1945)
13 Ben Hogan (1946)
11 Sam Snead (1950)
10 Ben Hogan (1948)
8 Byron Nelson (1944)
8 Lloyd Mangrum (1948)
8 Arnold Palmer (1960)
8 Johnny Miller (1974)
8 Sam Snead (1938)
7 11 times

Most first-time winners during one calendar year

14 1991
12 1979, 1980, 1986
11 1977, 1985, 1988
10 1968, 1969, 1971, 1974, 1983, 1987, 1990

Most years between victories

12 Leonard Thompson (1977-1989)
11 Bob Murphy (1975-1986)

Most years from first victory to last

29 by Sam Snead (1936-65)
29 by Ray Floyd (1963-92)
24 by Jack Nicklaus (1962-86)
23 by Gene Littler (1954-77)
22 by Art Wall (1953-75)

Youngest winners

Johnny McDermott, 19 years and 10 months, 1911 U.S. Open.
Gene Sarazen, 20 years and 4 months, 1922 U.S. Open.
Horton Smith, 20 years and 5 months, 1928 Oklahoma City Open.
Ray Floyd, 20 years and 6 months, 1963 St. Petersburg Open.
Phil Mickelson, 20 years and 6 months, 1991 Northern Telecom Open.
Seve Ballesteros, 20 years and 11 months, 1978 Greater Greensboro Open.

Oldest winners

Sam Snead, 52 years and 10 months, 1965 Greater Greensboro Open.
Art Wall, 51 years and 10 months, 1975 Greater Milwaukee Open.
John Barnum, 51 years and 1 month, 1962 Cajun Classic.
Jim Barnes, 50 years, 1937 Long Island Open.
Ray Floyd, 49 years and 6 months, 1992 Doral-Ryder Open.

Widest winning margin, strokes

16 Bobby Locke, 1948 Chicago Victory National Championship.
14 Ben Hogan, 1945 Portland Invitational.
14 Johnny Miller, 1975 Phoenix Open.
13 Byron Nelson 1945 Seattle Open.
12 Arnold Palmer, 1962 Phoenix Open.
12 Jose Maria Olazabal, 1990 NEC World Series of Golf.

MISCELLANEOUS RECORDS

Most consecutive events without missing cut

113 Byron Nelson, during the 1940's.
105 Jack Nicklaus, from Sahara Open, November 1970, through World Series of Golf, September 1976 (missed cut in 1976 World Open).
86 Hale Irwin, from Tucson Open, February 1975, through conclusion of 1978 season.
72 Dow Finsterwaid, from Carling Golf Classic, September 1955, through Houston Invitational, February, 1958.

Youngest pro shooting age

66 (4 under), Sam Snead (age 67), 1979 Quad Cities Open.

MONEY WINNING RECORDS

Past leading money-winners, year by year

Year	Player	Amount
1934	Paul Runyan	$6,767
1935	Johnny Revolta	9,543
1936	Horton Smith	7,682
1937	Harry Cooper	14,139
1938	Sam Snead	19,534
1939	Henry Picard	10,303
1940	Ben Hogan	10,655
1941	Ben Hogan	18,358
1942	Ben Hogan	13,143
1943	*No Statistics Compiled*	
1944	Byron Nelson (War Bonds)	37,968
1945	Byron Nelson (War Bonds)	63,336
1946	Ben Hogan	42,556
1947	Jimmy Demaret	27,937
1948	Ben Hogan	32,112
1949	Sam Snead	31,594
1950	Sam Snead	35,759
1951	Lloyd Mangrum	26,089
1952	Julius Boros	37,033
1953	Lew Worsham	34,002
1954	Bob Toski	65,820
1955	Julius Boros	63,122
1956	Ted Kroll	72,836
1957	Dick Mayer	65,835
1958	Arnold Palmer	42,607
1959	Art Wall	53,168
1960	Arnold Palmer	75,263
1961	Gary Player	64,540
1962	Arnold Palmer	81,448
1963	Arnold Palmer	128,230
1964	Jack Nicklaus	113,284
1965	Jack Nicklaus	140,752
1966	Billy Casper	121,945
1967	Jack Nicklaus	188,998
1968	Billy Casper	205,169
1969	Frank Beard	164,707
1970	Lee Trevino	157,038
1971	Jack Nicklaus	244,490
1972	Jack Nicklaus	320,542
1973	Jack Nicklaus	308,362
1974	Johnny Miller	353,022
1975	Jack Nicklaus	298,149
1976	Jack Nicklaus	266,439
1977	Tom Watson	310,653
1978	Tom Watson	362,429
1979	Tom Watson	462,636
1980	Tom Watson	530,808
1981	Tom Kite	375,699
1982	Craig Stadler	446,462
1983	Hal Sutton	426,668
1984	Tom Watson	476,260
1985	Curtis Strange	542,321
1986	Greg Norman	653,296
1987	Curtis Strange	925,941
1988	Curtis Strange	1,147,644
1989	Tom Kite	1,395,278
1990	Greg Norman	1,165,477
1991	Corey Pavin	979,430
1992	Fred Couples	1,344,188
1993	Nick Price	1,478,557

Most money won in a single season

Amount	Player	Year
$1,478,557	Nick Price	1993
$1,458,456	Paul Azinger	1993
$1,395,278	Tom Kite	1989
$1,359,653	Greg Norman	1993
$1,344,188	Fred Couples	1992
$1,201,301	Payne Stewart	1989
$1,191,630	Davis Love III	1992
$1,165,606	John Cook	1992

Most money won by a rookie

Amount	Player	Year
$657,831	Vijay Singh	1993
$574,783	John Daly	1991
$461,407	Robert Gamez	1990
$411,405	Grant Waite	1993
$337,374	Brett Ogla	1993
$320,007	Keith Clearwater	1987
$260,536	Corey Pavin	1984
$240,940	Jeff Maggert	1991

Most money won in first two seasons

- $962,238 by John Daly (1991-1992)
- $818,804 by Bob Tway (1985-1986)
- $805,650 by Billy Mayfair (1989-1990)
- $800,448 by Phil Mickelson (1992-1993)
- $741,755 by Robert Gamez (1990-1991)
- $664,102 by Hal Sutton (1982-1983)

Most consecutive years $100,000 or more

- 20 Tom Watson (1974-present)
- 18 Tom Kite (1976-present)
- 16 Jack Nicklaus (1963-1978)
- 15 Curtis Strange (1979-present)

Most consecutive years $200,000 or more

- 13 Tom Kite (1981-present)
- 12 Curtis Strange (1980-1991)
- 12 Tom Watson (1977-1988)
- 10 Payne Stewart (1984-present)
- 8 Jack Nicklaus (1971-1978)
- 8 Paul Azinger (1986-present)

Most consecutive years $300,000 or more

- 8 Payne Stewart (1986-present)
- 8 Greg Norman (1986-present)
- 7 Fred Couples (1987-present)
- 7 Paul Azinger (1987-present)
- 6 Tom Watson (1977-1982)

Most consecutive years $400,000 or more

- 7 Paul Azinger (1987-present)
- 6 Payne Stewart (1986-1991)

Most consecutive years $500,000 or more

- 7 Paul Azinger (1987-present)
- 7 Chip Beck (1987-present)
- 5 Payne Stewart (1986-1990)
- 5 Greg Norman (1986-1990)

Most consecutive years $600,000 or more

- 5 Fred Couples (1989-present)
- 5 Paul Azinger (1989-present)

Most consecutive years Top 10 Money List

- 17 Jack Nicklaus (1962-1978)
- 15 Arnold Palmer (1957-1971)

Most years Top 10 Money List

- 18 Jack Nicklaus
- 15 Arnold Palmer
- 15 Sam Snead

Most years leading Money List

- 8 Jack Nicklaus

Most consecutive years leading Money List

- 4 Tom Watson (1977-1980)

Most money won in a single season without a victory

- $982,875 by Payne Stewart in 1993
- $834,281 by Mark Calcavecchia in 1990.
- $760,405 by Tom Kite in 1988.
- $729,027 by Jeff Sluman in 1992.

$694,087 by Chip Beck in 1989.
$693,658 by Billy Mayfair in 1990.

YEAR BY YEAR STATISTICAL LEADERS (1980-PRESENT)

SCORING AVERAGE

1980	Lee Trevino	69.73
1981	Tom Kite	69.80
1982	Tom Kite	70.21
1983	Raymond Floyd	70.61
1984	Calvin Peete	70.56
1985	Don Pooley	70.36
1986	Scott Hoch	70.08
1987	David Frost	70.09
1988	Greg Norman	69.38
1989	Payne Stewart	*69.485
1990	Greg Norman	69.10
1991	Fred Couples	69.59
1992	Fred Couples	69.38
1993	Nick Price	69.11

DRIVING DISTANCE

1980	Dan Pohl	274.3
1981	Dan Pohl	280.1
1982	Bill Calfee	275.3
1983	John McComish	277.4
1984	Bill Glasson	276.5
1985	Andy Bean	278.2
1986	Davis Love III	285.7
1987	John McComish	283.9
1988	Steve Thomas	284.6
1989	Ed Humenik	280.9
1990	Tom Purizer	279.6
1991	John Daly	288.9
1992	John Daly	283.4
1993	John Daly	288.9

DRIVING ACCURACY

1980	Mike Reid	79.5%
1981	Calvin Peete	81.9
1982	Calvin Peete	84.6
1983	Calvin Peete	81.3
1984	Calvin Peete	77.5
1985	Calvin Peete	80.6
1986	Calvin Peete	81.7
1987	Calvin Peete	83.0
1988	Calvin Peete	82.5
1989	Calvin Peete	82.6
1990	Calvin Peete	83.7
1991	Hale Irwin	78.3
1992	Doug Tewell	82.3
1993	Doug Tewell	82.5

GREENS IN REGULATION

1980	Jack Nicklaus	72.1%
1981	Calvin Peete	73.1
1982	Calvin Peete	72.4
1983	Calvin Peete	71.4
1984	Andy Bean	72.1
1985	John Mahaffey	71.9
1986	John Mahaffey	72.0
1987	Gil Morgan	73.3
1988	John Adams	73.9
1989	Bruce Lietzke	72.6
1990	Doug Tewell	70.9
1991	Bruce Lietzke	73.3
1992	Tim Simpson	74.0
1993	Fuzzy Zoeller	73.6

PUTTING

1980	Jerry Pate	28.81
1981	Alan Tapie	28.70
1982	Ben Crenshaw	28.65
1983	Morris Hatalsky	27.96
1984	Gary McCord	28.57
1985	Craig Stadler	28.627
1986	Greg Norman	1.736
1987	Ben Crenshaw	1.743
1988	Don Pooley	1.729
1989	Steve Jones	1.734
1990	Larry Rinker	*1.7467
1991	Jay Don Blake	*1.7326
1992	Mirk O'Meara	1.731
1993	David Frost	1.739

ALL-AROUND

1987	Dan Pohl	170
1988	Payne Stewart	170
1989	Paul Azinger	250
1990	Paul Azinger	162
1991	Scott Hoch	283
1992	Fred Couples	256
1993	Gil Morgan	252

SAND SAVES

1980	Bob Eastwood	65.4%
1981	Tom Watson	60.1
1982	Isao Aoki	60.2
1983	Isao Aoki	62.3
1984	Peter Oosterhuis	64.7
1985	Tom Purizer	60.8
1986	Paul Azinger	63.8
1987	Paul Azinger	63.2
1988	Greg Powers	63.5
1989	Mike Sullivan	66.0
1990	Paul Azinger	67.2
1991	Ben Crenshaw	64.9
1992	Mitch Adcock	66.9
1993	Ken Green	64.4

PAR BREAKERS (category discontinued)

1980	Tom Watson	.213
1981	Bruce Lietzke	.225
1982	Tom Kite	*.2154
1983	Tom Watson	.211
1984	Craig Stadler	.220
1985	Craig Stadler	.218
1986	Greg Norman	.248
1987	Mark Calcavecchia	.221
1988	Ken Green	.236
1989	Greg Norman	.224
1990	Greg Norman	.219

TOTAL DRIVING

1991	Bruce Lietzke	42
1992	Bruce Lietzke	50
1993	Greg Norman	41

EAGLES

1980	Dave Eichelberger	16
1981	Bruce Lietzke	12
1982	Tom Weiskopf	10
	J.C. Snead	10
	Andy Bean	10
1983	Chip Beck	15
1984	Gary Hallberg	5
1985	Larry Rinker	1
1986	Joey Sindelar	16
1987	Phil Blackmar	20
1988	Ken Green	21
1989	Lon Hinkle	14
	Duffy Waldorf	14
1990	Paul Azinger	14
1991	Andy Bean	15
	John Huston	15
1992	Dan Forsman	18
1993	Davis Love III	15

BIRDIES

1980	Andy Bean	388
1981	Vance Heafner	388
1982	Andy Bean	392
1983	Hal Sutton	399
1984	Mark O'Meara	419
1985	Joey Sindelar	411
1986	Joey Sindelar	415
1987	Dan Forsman	409
1988	Dan Forsman	465
1989	Ted Schulz	415
1990	Mike Donald	401
1991	Scott Hoch	446
1992	Jeff Sluman	417
1993	John Huston	426

Key: *had to be carried a decimal further

LPGA ALL-TIME RECORDS

Rolex player of the year

YEAR	PLAYER	POINTS
1966	Kathy Whitworth	131
1967	Kathy Whitworth	116
1968	Kathy Whitworth	141
1969	Kathy Whitworth	102
1970	Sandra Haynie	41
1971	Kathy Whitworth	57
1972	Kathy Whitworth	91
1973	Kathy Whitworth	83
1974	JoAnne Carner	82
1975	Sandra Palmer	40
1976	Judy Rankin	79
1977	Judy Rankin	66
1978	Nancy Lopez	92
1979	Nancy Lopez	88
1980	Beth Daniel	78
1981	JoAnne Carner	60
1982	JoAnne Carner	75
1983	Patty Sheehan	61
1984	Betsy King	55
1985	Nancy Lopez	85
1986	Pat Bradley	78
1987	Ayako Okamoto	68
1988	Nancy Lopez	49
1989	Betsy King	76
1990	Beth Daniel	82
1991	Pat Bradley	59
1992	Dottie Mochrie	54
1993	Betsy King	54

Vare trophy: scoring average

1953	Patty Berg	75.00
1954	Babe Zaharias	75.48
1955	Patty Berg	74.47
1956	Patty Berg	74.57
1957	Louise Suggs	74.64
1958	Beverly Hanson	74.921
1959	Betsy Rawls	74.03
1960	Mickey Wright	73.25
1961	Mickey Wright	73.55
1962	Mickey Wright	73.67
1963	Mickey Wright	72.81
1964	Mickey Wright	72.46
1965	Kathy Whitworth	72.61
1966	Kathy Whitworth	72.60
1967	Kathy Whitworth	72.74
1968	Carol Mann	72.04
1969	Kathy Whitworth	72.38
1970	Kathy Whitworth	72.26
1971	Kathy Whitworth	72.88
1972	Kathy Whitworth	72.38
1973	Judy Rankin	73.08
1974	JoAnne Carner	72.87
1975	JoAnne Carner	72.40
1976	Judy Rankin	72.25
1977	Judy Rankin	72.16
1978	Nancy Lopez	71.76
1979	Nancy Lopez	71.20
1980	Amy Alcott	71.51
1981	JoAnne Carner	71.75
1982	JoAnne Carner	71.49
1983	JoAnne Carner	71.41
1984	Patty Sheehan	71.40
1985	Nancy Lopez	70.73
1986	Pat Bradley	71.10
1987	Betsy King	71.14
1988	Colleen Walker	71.26
1989	Beth Daniel	70.38
1990	Beth Daniel	70.54
1991	Pat Bradley	70.66
1992	Dottie Mochrie	70.80
1993	Nancy Lopez	70.83

Gatorade rookie of the year

1962	Mary Mills
1963	Clifford Ann Creed
1964	Susie Berning
1965	Margie Masters
1966	Jan Ferraris
1967	Sharron Moran
1968	Sandra Post
1969	Jane Blalock
1970	JoAnne Carner
1971	Sally Little
1972	Jocelyne Bourassa
1973	Laura Baugh
1974	Jan Stephenson
1975	Amy Alcott
1976	Bonnie Laer
1977	Debbie Massey
1978	Nancy Lopez
1979	Beth Daniel
1980	Myra Van Hoose
1981	Patty Sheehan
1982	Patti Rizzo
1983	Stephanie Faig
1984	Juli Inkster
1985	Penny Hammel
1986	Jody Rosenthal
1987	Tammie Green
1988	Liselotte Neumann
1989	Pamela Wright
1990	Hiromi Kobayashi
1991	Brandie Burton
1992	Helen Alfredsson
1993	Suzanne Strudwick

SCORING RECORDS

(Official LPGA Tournaments Only)

72 holes:

268 (66-67-69-66) by Nancy Lopez at the Willow Creek GC, High Point, N.C., in the 1985 Henredon Classic. Par 72.

54 holes:

197 (67-65-65) by Pat Bradley at the Rail Golf Club, Springfield, Ill., in the 1991 Rail Charity Golf Classic. Par 72.

36 holes:

129 (64-65) by Judy Dickinson at Pasadena Yacht & CC, St. Petersburg, Fla., in the 1985 S&H Golf Classic. Par 72.

18 holes:

62 (30-32) by Mickey Wright at Hogan Park GC, Midland, Texas, in the first round of the 1964 Tall City Open. Par 71.

62 (32-30) by Vicki Fergon at Almaden G&CC, San Jose, Calif., in the second round of the 1984 San Jose Classic. Par 73.

62 (32-30) by Laura Davies at the Rail Golf Club, Springfield, Ill., in the first round of the 1991 Rail Charity Golf Classic. Par 72.

62 (30-32) by Hollis Stacy at Meridian Valley Country Club, Seattle, in the second round of the 1992 Safeco Classic. Par 72.

9 holes:

28 Mary Beth Zimmerman at the Rail Golf Club, Springfield, Ill., 1984 Rail Charity Golf Classic. Par 36. Zimmerman shot 64.

28 Pat Bradley at Green Gables CC, Denver, 1984 Columbia Savings Classic. Par 35. Bradley shot 65.
28 Muffin Spencer-Deviin at Knollwood CC, Elmsford, N.Y., 1985 MasterCard International Pro-Am. Par 35. Spencer-Deviin shot 64.
28 Peggy Kirsch at Squaw Creek CC, Vienna, Ohio, 1991 Phar-Mor in Youngstown. Par 35. Kirsch shot 67.

Low 36-Hole Cut

144 1989 Sara Lee Classic, Old Hickory, Tenn. 74 players. Par 72. 1992 Rail Charity Golf Classic, Springfield, Ill. 71 players. Par 72.

Largest winning margin

14 strokes by Louise Suggs at Prince George's CC, Landover, Md., in 1949 U.S. Women's Open; by Cindy Mackey at Knollwood CC, Westchester County, N.Y., in 1986 MasterCard International Pro-Am.

Most birdies in one round

11 by Vicki Fergon at Almaden G&CC in San Jose, Calif., in the second round of the 1984 San Jose Classic. She shot 62, 11-under-par. 10, by Sherri Turner at Corning CC in Corning, N.Y., in the second round of the 1988 LPGA Corning Classic. She shot 63, 9-under-par.

Most consecutive birdies

8 Mary Beth Zimmerman at Rail GC in Springfield, Ill., in the second round of the 1984 Rail Charity Golf Classic. She shot 36-28–64, 8-underpar.

Most consecutive rounds in 60's

9 Beth Daniel , 1990 JAL Big Apple Classic, final two rounds 68-68, Northgate Classic the next week, 66-69-68, Rail Charity Golf Classic the next week, 67-69-67, and the Safeco Classic first round of 69.

Most rounds in the 60's in one calendar year

33 by Betsy King in 1989.

Most sub-par holes in a single event

25 Nancy Lopez, 1985 Henredon Classic, 66-67-69-66.

Most sub-par rounds in a season

61 Pat Bradley 1991
59 Pat Bradley 1985
58 Nancy Lopez 1985
57 Pat Bradley 1986
Record is unofficial.

Most top 10 finishes in one calendar year

25 by Judy Rankin in 1973.

Three eagles in one round

Alice Ritzman, holes 10, 12 and 16 at Sunningdale GC near London, second round,1979 Colgate European Open. Ritzman also had 15 pars for a 6-under-par 68.

Holes-in-one, tour

25 1985

Holes-in-one, season

3 Tracy Kerdyk 1991
2 Missie Berteotti 1990
2 Dale Eggering 1990
2 Sherri Turner 1990
2 Betsy King 1990
2 Alice Ritzman 1989
2 Heather Drew 1988
2 Mei-Chi Cheng 1988
2 Sharon Barrett 1985
2 Kyle O'Brien 1982
2 Jo Ann Washam 1979
2 Bonnie Bryant 1977
2 Sandra Haynie 1976.

Holes-in-one, career

11 Kathy Whitworth
6 Marlene Hagge
6 Sandra Spuzich
5 Pat Bradley
5 Jan Stephenson
4 Murie Breer
4 Kathy Cornelius
4 Jane Blalock
4 Sandra Palmer
4 Carol Mann
4 Hollis Stacy
4 Tracy Kerdyk.

Holes-in-one, tournament

2 Jo Ann Washam, at Mesa Verde CC in the 1979 Women's Kemper Open. In the second round Washam aced the 165-yard 16th hole with a 5-iron. In the fourth round she holed a 3-iron shot at the 168-yard seventh hole.

Fastest round

1:35:33 Lynn Adams and Catherine Duggan, 1984 Sarasota Classic, final round. Adams shot 78, Duggan 72.

All-time scoring leaders

Beth Daniel	1989	93	70.38
Beth Daniel	1990	78	70.54
Patty Sheehan	1990	86	70.62
Pat Bradley	1991	94	70.66
Nancy Lopez	1985	93	70.73
Dottie Mochrie	1992	91	70.80
Nancy Lopez	1993	65	70.83
Betsy King	1993	93	70.85
Beth Daniel	1991	62	70.94
Meg Mallon	1992	84	70.99
Meg Mallon	1993	78	71.02
Patty Sheehan	1993	75	71.04
Nancy Lopez	1992	73	71.05
Dottie Mochrie	1993	91	71.09
Helen Alfredsson	1993	77	71.40
Pat Bradley	1986	100	71.10
Pat Bradley	1990	94	71.13
Betsy King	1987	93	71.14
Nancy Lopez	1979	71	71.20
Colleen Walker	1988	100	71.26
Jan Stephenson	1988	87	71.29
Pat Bradley	1985	103	71.30
Patty Sheehan	1992	77	71.30

Brandie Burton	1992	83	71.30
Betsy King	1990	93	71.32
Nancy Lopez	1990	61	71.33
Ayako Okamoto	1987	86	71.36
Meg Mallon	1991	93	71.37
Patty Sheehan	1984	85	71.40
Helen Alfredsson	1993	77	71.40
Nancy Lopez	1988	75	71.40
JoAnne Carner	1983	82	71.41
Juli Inkster	1992	84	71.43
Dottie Mochrie	1991	98	71.44
Tammie Green	1993	79	71.46
Rosie Jones	1990	83	71.48
Ayako Okamoto	1992	52	71.48
JoAnne Carner	1982	95	71.49
Patty Sheehan	1991	76	71.49
Betsy King	1991	94	71.50

VICTORY RECORDS

Most tour victories, career

RANK	PLAYER	WINS
1	Kathy Whitworth	88
2	Mickey Wright	82
3	Patty Berg	*57
3	Betsy Rawls	55
5	Louise Suggs	50
6	Nancy Lopez	47
7	JoAnne Carner	42
7	Sandra Haynie	42
9	Carol Mann	38
10	Babe Zaharias	31
10	Patty Sheehan	31
12	Pat Bradley	30
13	Jane Blalock	29
13	Amy Alcott	29
13	Betsy King	29
16	Beth Daniel	27
17	Judy Rankin	26
18	Marlene Hagge	25
19	Donna Caponi	24
20	Marilynn Smith	22

*Includes 13 official professional wins prior to the organization of the LPGA.

Most tour victories, year-by-year

1948	Patty Berg	3
	Babe Zaharias	
1949	Patty Berg	3
	Louise Suggs	
1950	Babe Zaharias	6
1951	Babe Zaharias	7
1952	Betsy Rawls	6
	Louise Suggs	
1953	Louise Suggs	8
1954	Louise Suggs	5
	Babe Zaharias	
1955	Patty Berg	6
1956	Marlene Hagge	8
1957	Patty Berg	5
	Betsy Rawls	10
1958	Mickey Wright	5
1959	Betsy Rawls	0
1960	Mickey Wright	6
1961	Mickey Wright	10
1962	Mickey Wright	10
1963	Mickey Wright	13
1964	Mickey Wright	11
1965	Kathy Whitworth	8
1966	Kathy Whitworth	9
1967	Kathy Whitworih	8
1968	Kathy Whitworth	10
	Carol Mann	
1969	Carol Mann	8
1970	Shirley Englehorn	4
1971	Kathy Whitworth	5
1972	Kathy Whitworth	5
	Jane Blalock	
1973	Kathy Whitworth	7
1974	JoAnne Carner	6
	Sandra Haynie	
1975	Carol Mann	4
	Sandra Haynie	
1976	Judy Rankin	6
1977	Judy Rankin	5
	Debbie Austin	
1978	Nancy Lopez	9
1979	Nancy Lopez	8
1980	JoAnne Carner	5
	Donna Caponi	
1981	Donna Caponi	5
1982	JoAnne Carner	5
	Beth Daniel	
1983	Pat Bradley	4
	Patty Sheehan	
1984	Patty Sheehan	4
	Amy Alcott	
1985	Nancy Lopez	5
1986	Pat Bradley	5
1987	Jane Geddes	5
1988	Juli Inkster	3
	Rosie Jones	
	Betsy King	
	Nancy Lopez	
	Ayako Okamoto	
1989	Betsy King	6
	Beth Daniel	4
	Nancy Lopez	3
1990	Beth Daniel	7
	Patty Sheehan	5
	Pat Bradley	3
	Betsy King	
	Cathy Gerring	
1991	Pat Bradley	4
	Meg Mallon	
1992	Dottie Mochrie	4
	Danielle Ammaccapane	3
	Patty Sheehan	
	Colleen Walker	
	Betsy King	
1993	Brandie Burton	3

Official tournament victories as a professional

88 Kathy Whitworth.

Quickest first victory

1st tournament, Beverly Hanson, 1951 Eastern Open.

Longest period between victories

14 years, Shelley Hamlin, 1978 Patty Berg Classic to 1992 Phar-Mor at Inverrary.

Most consecutive victories in scheduled events

4   Mickey Wright in 1962 (Heart of America Invitational, August 10-12; Albuquerque Swing Parade, August 17-19; Salt Lake City Open, August 23-26; Spokane Open, August 31 -September 3).

4   Mickey Wright in 1963 (Alpine Open, May 10-12; Muskogee Open, May 16-19; Dallas Civitan Open, May 23-26; Babe Zaharias Open, May 31 -June 2).

4   Kathy Whitworth in 1969 (Orange Blossom Classic, March 14-16; Port Charlotte Invitational, March 21-23; Port Malabar Invitational, March 28-30; Lady Carling Open, April 25-27).

Consecutive victories in tournaments participated

5   Nancy Lopez in 1987 (Greater Baltimore Classic, May 12-14; Coca-Cola Classic, May 19-21; Golden Lights Championship, May 26-29; LPGA Championship, June 8-11; Bankers Trust Classic, June 16-18; Did not play Peter Jackson Classic, June 1-4).

Tournaments won in one calendar year

13 Mickey Wright in 1963.

First-time winners

9 1983, 1988 and 1993.

Different winners in a season

26 1991

Youngest winner

Marlene Hagge, 1952 Sarasota Open at 18 years, 14 days.

Oldest winner

JoAnne Carner, 1985 Safeco Classic at 46 years, 5 months, 9 days.

PLAYOFF RECORDS

Most players in a sudden-death playoff

5 three times, 1979 Women's Kemper Open, JoAnne Carner defeated Donna Caponi, Jan Stephenson, Nancy Lopez and Chako Higuchi; 1981 Florida Lady Citrus, Beth Daniel defeated Donna Caponi, Patty Sheehan, Cindy Hill and Patti Rizzo; 1981 West Virginia Classic, Hollis Stacy defeated Alice Ritzman, Penny Pulz, Kathy Postlewait and Susie McAllister.

Longest sudden-death playoff

10 holes. 1972 Corpus Christi Civitan Open. Jo Ann Prentice defeated Sandra Palmer and Kathy Whitworth. Record is unofficial.

MONEY WINNING RECORDS

Past leading money-winners, year-by-year

Year	Player	Amount
1950	Babe Zaharias	$14,800
1951	Babe Zaharias	15,087
1952	Betsy Rawls	14,505
1953	Louise Suggs	19,816
1954	Patty Berg	16,011
1955	Patty Berg	16,492
1956	Marlene Hagge	20,235
1957	Patty Berg	16,272
1958	Beverly Hanson	12,639
1959	Betsy Rawls	26,774
1960	Louise Suggs	16,892
1961	Mickey Wright	22,236
1962	Mickey Wright	21,641
1963	Mickey Wright	31,269
1964	Mickey Wright	29,800
1965	Kathy Whitworth	28,658
1966	Kathy Whitworth	33,517
1967	Kathy Whitworth	32,937
1968	Kathy Whitworth	48,379
1969	Carol Mann	49,152
1970	Kathy Whitworth	30,235
1971	Kathy Whitworth	41,181
1972	Kathy Whitworth	65,063
1973	Kathy Whitworth	82,864
1974	JoAnne Carner	87,094
1975	Sandra Palmer	76,374
1976	Judy Rankin	150,734
1977	Judy Rankin	122,890
1978	Nancy Lopez	189,814
1979	Nancy Lopez	197,489
1980	Beth Daniel	231,000
1981	Beth Daniel	206,998
1982	JoAnne Carner	310,400
1983	JoAnne Carner	291,404
1984	Betsy King	266,771
1985	Nancy Lopez	416,472
1986	Pat Bradley	492,021
1987	Ayako Okamoto	466,034
1988	Sherri Turner	350,851
1989	Betsy King	654,132
1990	Beth Daniel	863,578
1991	Pat Bradley	763,118
1992	Dottie Mochrie	693,335
1993	Betsy King	595,992

Youngest age to reach millionaire status

26 years, 2 months, 28 days, Nancy Lopez.

Most official money won in one calendar year

$863,578 by Beth Daniel in 1990.

Fastest to reach $1 million in career earnings

2 years, 180 days, Brandie Burton (1991-1993).

Fastest to reach $2 million in career earnings

8 years, 10 months, 22 days, Patty Sheehan.

Fastest to reach $3 million in career earnings

10 years, 8 months, 13 days, Patty Sheehan.

Fastest to reach $4 million in career earnings

17 years, 9 months, 29 days, Pat Bradley.

Fastest to $100,000 in single-season earnings

2nd event, 1991, Orix Hawaiian Ladies Open, Beth Daniel.

Fastest to $200,000 in single-season earnings

8th event, 1989, USX Golf Classic, Betsy King. 8th event, 1990, Nabisco Dinah Shore, Beth Daniel and Pat Bradley.

Fastest to $300,000 in single-season earnings

11th event, 1992 Centel Classic, Dottie Mochrie.

Fastest to $400,000 in single-season earnings

14th event, 1990 du Maurier Ltd. Classic, Pat Bradley. 1992 Oldsmobile Classic, Dottie Mochrie.

Fastest to $500,000 in single-season earnings

17th event, 1990, Mazda LPGA Championship, Patty Sheehan; 1990, Boston Five Classic, Beth Daniel; 17th event, 1991, LPGA Bay State Classic, Pat Bradley.

Fastest to $600,000 in single-season earnings

19th event, 1990, Northgate Classic, Beth Daniel.

Fastest to $700,000 in single-season earnings

22nd event, 1990, Centel Classic, Patty Sheehan.

Fastest to $800,000 in single-season earnings

22nd event, 1990, Centel Classic, Beth Daniel.

Most consecutive $100,000 seasons

13	Patty Sheehan,	1981-present
11	Amy Alcott	1979-1989

Most consecutive $200,000 seasons

12	Patty Sheehan,	1982-present
9	Betsy King	1984-1992

Most $100,000 earners in a single-season

55   1992

Most $200,000 earners in a single-season

26   1992

Most $300,000 earners in a single-season

14   1993

Most $400,000 earners in a single-season

6   1992

Most $500,000 earners in a single-season

3   1990 and 1993

Most official money won by a rookie

$262,115 by Helen Alfredsson in 1992.

Senior PGA Tour all-time records

SENIOR PGA TOUR PLAYER OF THE YEAR

1990 Lee Trevino
1991 Mike Hill/George Archer
1992 Lee Trevino
1993 Dave Stockton

SENIOR PGA TOUR ROOKIE OF THE YEAR

1990 Lee Trevino
1991 Jim Colbert
1992 Dave Stockton
1993 Bob Murphy

SCORING RECORDS

72 holes: (by winners only)
261 - (65-68-64-64) by Jack Nicklaus, 1990 Mazda Senior TPC (27-under).
263 - (64-66-70-63) by Orville Moody, 1988 Vintage Chrysler Invitational (25-under).
264 - (66-66-66-66) by Miller Barber, 1982 Suntree Classic (24-under).

54 holes:
193 - (63-65-65) by Bob Charles, 1989 NYNEX /Golf Digest Commemorative (17-under).
193 - (66-62-65) by Charles Coody, 1991 NYNEX Commemorative (17-under).
193 - (62-65-66) by Gibby Gilbert, 1992 Southwestern Bell Classic (17-under).
194 - (65-63-66) by Don January, 1984 du Maurier Champions (19-under).
194 - (65-65-64) by Raymond Floyd, 1993 Gulfstream Aerospace Invitational (22-under).
196 - (63-67-66) by Bob Charles, 1988 NYNEX/Golf Digest Commemorative (14-under).
197 - (65-67-65) by Bruce Crampton, 1987 MONY Syracuse Senior Classic (19-under).
197 - (64-65-68) by Miller Barber, 1988 Fairfield Barnett Classic (19-under).
197 - (65-68-64) by Jack Nicklaus, 1990 Mazda Senior TPC (19-under).
197 - (67-65-65) by Jimmy Powell, 1992 Aetna Challenge (19-under).
197 - (65-67-65) by Raymond Floyd, 1992 Senior TOUR Championship (19-under).

36 holes:
Opening Rounds
127 - (63-64) by Bruce Crampton, 1987 Vantage Bank One Classic (13-under).
127 - (66-61) by Jim Colbert, 1991 First Development Kaanapali Classic (13-under).
127 - (62-65) by Gibby Gilbert, 1992 Southwestern Bell Classic (13-under).
128 - (63-65) by Don January, 1984 du Maurier Champions (14-under).
128 - (63-65) by Bob Charles, 1989 NYNEX/Golf Digest Commemorative (12-under).
128 - (66-62) by Charles Coody, 1991 NYNEX Commemorative (12-under).
129 - (64-65) by Miller Barber, 1988 Fairfield Barnett Classic (15-under).
129 - (63-66) by Bob Charles, 1988 Vantage Bank One Classic (15-under).
Consecutive Rounds
127 - (63-64) by Bruce Crampton, 1987 Vantage Bank One Classic (13-under).
127 - (62-65) by Charles Coody, 1991 NYNEX Commemorative (13-under).
127 - (66-61) by Jim Colbert, 1991 First Development Kaanapali Classic (13-under).
127 - (62-65) by Gibby Gilbert, 1992 Southwestern Bell Classic (13-under).
127 - (65-62) by Raymond Floyd, 1992 Ralphs Senior Classic (15-under).

18 holes:
61 - by Lee Elder, 1985 Merrill Lynch/Golf Digest Commemorative (1-under).
61 - by Jim Colbert, 1991 First Development Kaanapali Classic (9-under).

9 holes:
28 - by Gene Littler, 1983 Suntree Classic (8-under).

Largest 36-hole lead

8 strokes - by Arnold Palmer, 1984 PGA Seniors Championship.
8 strokes - by Don Bies, 1989 Murata Seniors Reunion.

Largest 54-hole lead

8 strokes - by Jack Nicklaus, 1991 PGA Seniors Championship.

Largest winning margin

72 holes:
11 strokes - by Arnold Palmer, 1985 Senior TPC.
11 strokes - by Orville Moody, 1988 Vintage Chrysler Invitational.

54 holes:
9 strokes - by Rod Funseth, 1983 Hall of Fame Tournament.
9 strokes - by Gibby Gilbert, 1992 Southwestern Bell Classic.
9 strokes - by Dave Stockton, 1993 Franklin Quest Cup Championship.

Most birdies in a row

8 - by Chi Chi Rodriguez, 1987 Silver Pages Classic.
7 - by Gene Littler, 1983 Suntree Classic.
7 - by Gary Player, 1990 U.S. Senior Open.
7 - by Don January, 1991 Vantage at The Dominion.

Best (eagle-birdie) streak

- 1-4 by Chales Owens, 1986 Greenbrier/American Express.
- 1-4 by George Archer, 1991 Vantage Championship.
- 1-4 by Ben Smith, 1992 NYNEX Commemorative.
- 1-4 by Don January, 1992 Vantage Championship.
- 1-4 by Kermit Zarley, 1993 Las Vegas Sr. Classic.

Double eagle

Al Balding, 1982 Peter Jackson Champions.
Orville Moody, 1985 Denver Post Champions.
Jim Cochran, 1987 Silver Pages Classic.
Bobby Nichols, 1988 Northville Invitational.
Ben Smith, 1988 Northville Invitational.
Dick Rhyan, 1988 Showdown Classic.
Al Geiberger, 1989 Chrysler Cup.
Ted Neff, 1990 GTE Northwest Classic.
Jim Ferree, 1991 Murata Reunion Pro-Am.
Bob Brue, 1991 First Development Kaanapali Classic.

Eagle & double eagle in one round

Dick Rhyan, 1988 Showdown Classic.
Ted Neff, 1990 GTE Northwest Classic.

Three eagles in one round

Don January, 1985 Senior Roundup.
Jimmy Powell, 1985 Greenbrier/American Express Championship.
Rocky Thompson, 1992 Kaanapali Classic.

Consecutive eagles

Jim Ferree, 1983 Merrill Lynch/Golf Digest Commemorative.
Roland Stafford, 1987 Greater Grand Rapids Open.

Best scoring averages, all-time

68.89	Lee Trevino	1990
69.46	Don January	1983
69.46	Lee Trevino	1992
69.50	Lee Trevino	1991
69.57	Miller Barber	1981
69.59	Bob Charles	1993
69.65	Chi Chi Rodriguez	1986
69.71	Dave Stockton	1993
69.72	George Archer	1991
69.78	Bob Charles	1989

Most consecutive rounds par or less

27	Lee Trevino	1992

Most consecutive sub-par rounds

19	George Archer	1991

Most consecutive sub-70 rounds

11	Lee Trevino	1992

VICTORY RECORDS

Most Senior PGA Tour victories

24	Miller Barber
22	Don January
22	Chi Chi Rodriguez
21	Bob Charles
19	Bruce Crampton

All-time Senior Tour winners

RANK	PLAYER	WINS
1.	Miller Barber	24
2.	Don January	22
3.	Chi Chi Rodriguez	22
4.	Bob Charles	21
5.	Bruce Crampton	19
6.	Lee Trevino	18
7.	Gary Player	17
T8.	Mike Hill	15
	George Archer	15
T10.	Peter Thomson	11
	Orville Moody	11
T12.	Arnold Palmer	10
	Dale Douglass	10
14.	Billy Casper	9
T15.	Gene Littler	8
	Lee Elder	8
	Al Geiberger	8

Most Senior Tour victories year by year

1980	Don January	1
	Charles Sifford	1
	Arnold Palmer	1
	Roberto De Vicenzo	1
1981	Miller Barber	3
1982	Miller Barber	3
1983	Don January	6
1984	Miller Barber	4
1985	Peter Thomson	9
1986	Bruce Crampton	7
1987	Chi Chi Rodriguez	7
1988	Bob Charles	5
	Gary Player	5
1989	Bob Charles	5
1990	Lee Trevino	7
1991	Mike Hill	5
1992	Lee Trevino	5
1993	Dave Stockton	5

Most consecutive years winning at least one tournament

9	Miller Barber (1981-1989)
8	Don January (1980-1987)
8	Chi Chi Rodriguez (1986-present)
7	Gary Player (1985-1991)
7	Bruce Crampton (1986-1992)

Most consecutive victories

4	Chi Chi Rodriguez, 1987 Vantage at the Dominion, United Hospitals Classic, Silver Pages Classic (Senior Players Reunion).
3	Lee Trevino, The 1992 Tradition, PGA Seniors' Championship, Las Vegas Senior Classic.
3	Bob Charles, 1987 Vintage Chrysler Invitational, GTE Classic, Sunwest Bank/Charley Pride Senior Classic.

Most victories in a single event

3	Miller Barber, 1982, 1984, 1985 U.S. Senior Open.
3	Chi Chi Rodriguez, 1986, 1987, 1988 Digital Seniors Classic.
3	Miller Barber, 1981, 1982, 1988 Fairfield Barnett Classic.
3	Bob Charles, 1987, 1988,

1989 Sunwest Bank/Charley Pride Classic.
3 George Archer, 1990, 1991, 1992 Northville Long Island Classic.
3 George Archer, 1990, 1991, 1993 Raley Sr. Classic.

Most consecutive victories in a single event

3 Chi Chi Rodriguez, 1986, 1987, 1988 Digital Seniors Classic.
3 Bob Charles, 1987, 1988, 1989 Sunwest Bank/Charley Pride Classic.
3 George Archer, 1990, 1991, 1992 Northville Long Island Classic.

Most victories in a calendar year

9	Peter Thomson	1985
7	Bruce Crampton	1986
7	Chi Chi Rodriguez	1987
7	Lee Trevino	1990

Come-from-behind victories

6 strokes - by Chi Chi Rodriguez (over Dale Douglass), 1987 PGA Seniors Championship.
6 strokes - by Don January (over Arnold Palmer), 1981 Michelob-Egypt Temple Classic.
6 strokes - by Chi Chi Rodriguez (over Lee Elder), 1987 United Hospitals Classic.
6 strokes - by Jim Dent (over Gary Player), 1990 Crestar Classic.
6 strokes - by Don Massengale (over Gary Player), 1992 Royal Carribean Classic.

Youngest winners

George Archer, 50 years and 14 days, 1989 Gatlin Brothers Southwest Classic.
Ray Floyd, 50 years and 16 days, 1992 GTE North Classic.
Dale Douglass, 50 years and 18 days, 1986 Vintage Invitational.
Isao Aoki, 50 years and 27 days, 1992 Nationwide Championship.

Oldest winners

Mike Fetchick, 63 years to the day, 1985 Hilton Head Seniors International.
Roberto De Vicenzo, 61 years and 92 days, 1984 Merrill Lynch/Golf Digest Commemorative.
Jim Ferree, 59 years and 350 days, 1991 Bell Atlantic Classic.

PLAYOFF RECORDS

Most sudden-death playoff holes

8 - Orville Moody defeated Bob Betley, 1992 Franklin Showdown Classic.

Most players involved in a sudden-death playoff

4 - 1985 Citizens Union Classic-Lee Elder defeated Walt Zembriski, Dan Sikes and Orville Moody.
4 - 1988 Senior Players Reunion-Orville Moody defeated Bobby Nichols, Bob Charles and Don Massengale.
4 - 1989 GTE Suncoast Classic-Bob Charles defeated Jim Ferree, Dave Hill and Harold Henning.
4 - 1989 Northville Long Island Classic-Butch Baird defeated Frank Beard, Don Bies and Orville Moody.
4 - 1990 NYNEX Commemorative-Lee Trevino defeated Mike Fetchick, Chi Chi Rodriguez and Jimmy Powell.

MONEY WINNING RECORDS

Most money won in a single season

$1,190,518	Lee Trevino	1990
$1,115,944	Dave Stockton	1993
$1,065,657	Mike Hill	1991
$1,027,002	Lee Trevino	1992
$1,024,323	Bob Charles	1993
$ 963,455	George Archer	1991
$ 934,374	George Archer	1993

Most money won by a first-year player

$1,190,518	Lee Trevino	1990
$ 880,749	Jim Colbert	1991
$ 720,743	Bob Murphy	1993

Most money won in a single season without a victory

$529,315	Jim Dent	1991
$557,667	Isao Aoki	1993
$553,844	R. Thompson	1993

Most years leading money list

3	Don January
2	Miller Barber
2	Bob Charles
2	Lee Trevino

Most years Top 10 money list

8	Miller Barber
8	Bob Charles
7	Gene Littler
7	Don January
6	Chi Chi Rodriguez
5	Gary Player
5	Mike Hill

Past leading senior tour money-winners

1980	Don January	$44,100
1981	Miller Barber	$83,136
1982	Miller Barber	$106,890
1983	Don January	$237,571
1984	Don January	$328,597
1985	Peter Thomson	$386,724
1986	Bruce Crampton	$454,299
1987	Chi Chi Rodriguez	$509,145
1988	Bob Charles	$533,929
1989	Bob Charles	$725,887
1990	Lee Trevino	$1,190,518
1991	Mike Hill	$1,065,657
1992	Lee Trevino	$1,027,002
1993	Dave Stockton	$1,115,944

PGA TOUR TOURNAMENT HISTORIES

THE MASTERS

Augusta National Golf Club, Augusta, Ga.

YEAR	WINNER	SCORE	RUNNER UP
1934	Horton Smith	284	Craig Wood
1935	*Gene Sarazen (144)	282	Craig Wood (149)
1936	Horton Smith	285	Harry Cooper
1937	Byron Nelson	283	Ralph Guldahl
1938	Henry Picard	285	Ralph Guldahl, Harry Cooper
1939	Ralph Guldahl	279	Sam Snead
1940	Jimmy Demaret	280	Lloyd Mangrum
1941	Craig Wood	280	Byron Nelson
1942	*Byron Nelson (69)	280	Ben Hogan (70)
1943	*No Tournament-World War II*		
1944	*No Tournament-World War II*		
1945	*No Tournament-World War II*		
1946	Herman Keiser	282	Ben Hogan
1947	Jimmy Demaret	281	Byron Nelson, Frank Stranahan
1948	Claude Harmon	279	Cary Middlecoff
1949	Sam Snead	282	Johnny Bulla, Lloyd Mangrum
1950	Jimmy Demaret	283	Jim Ferrier
1951	Ben Hogan	280	Skee Riegel
1952	Sam Snead	286	Jack Burke, Jr.
1953	Ben Hogan	274	Ed Oliver, Jr.
1954	*Sam Snead (70)	289	Ben Hogan (71)
1955	Cary Middlecoff	279	Ben Hogan
1956	Jack Burke, Jr.	289	Ken Venturi
1957	Doug Ford	282	Sam Snead
1958	Arnold Palmer	284	Doug Ford, Fred Hawkins
1959	Art Wall, Jr.	284	Cary Middlecoff
1960	Arnold Palmer	282	Ken Venturi
1961	Gary Player	280	Charles R. Coe, Arnold Palmer
1962	*Arnold Palmer (68)	280	Gary Player (71), Dow Finsterwald (77)
1963	Jack Nicklaus	286	Tony Lema
1964	Arnold Palmer	276	Dave Marr, Jack Nicklaus
1965	Jack Nicklaus	271	Arnold Palmer, Gary Player
1966	*Jack Nicklaus (70)	288	Tommy Jacobs (72), Gay Brewer, Jr. (78)
1967	Gay Brewer, Jr.	280	Bobby Nichols
1968	Bob Goalby	277	Roberto DeVicenzo
1969	George Archer	281	Billy Casper, George Knudson, Tom Weiskopf
1970	*Billy Casper (69)	279	Gene Littler (74)
1971	Charles Coody	279	Johnny Miller, Jack Nicklaus
1972	Jack Nicklaus	286	Bruce Crampton, Bobby Mitchell, Tom Weiskopf
1973	Tommy Aaron	283	J. C. Snead
1974	Gary Player	278	Tom Weiskopf, Dave Stockton
1975	Jack Nicklaus	276	Johnny Miller, Tom Weiskopf
1976	Ray Floyd	271	Ben Crenshaw
1977	Tom Watson	276	Jack Nicklaus
1978	Gary Player	277	Hubert Green, Rod Funseth, Tom Watson
1979	*Fuzzy Zoeller	280	Ed Sneed, Tom Watson
1980	Seve Ballesteros	275	Gibby Gilbert, Jack Newton
1981	Tom Watson	280	Johnny Miller, Jack Nicklaus
1982	*Craig Stadler	284	Dan Pohl
1983	Seve Ballesteros	280	Ben Crenshaw, Tom Kite
1984	Ben Crenshaw	277	Tom Watson
1985	Bernhard Langer	282	Curtis Strange, Seve Ballesteros, Ray Floyd

*Winner in playoff. Figures in parentheses indicate scores.

1986	Jack Nicklaus	279	Greg Norman, Tom Kite
1987	*Larry Mize	285	Seve Ballesteros, Greg Norman
1988	Sandy Lyle	281	Mark Calcavecchia
1989	*Nick Faldo	283	Scott Hoch
1990	*Nick Faldo	278	Ray Floyd
1991	Ian Woosnam	277	Jose Maria Olazabal
1992	Fred Couples	275	Ray Floyd
1993	Bernhard Langer	277	Chip Beck

THE UNITED STATES OPEN

YEAR	WINNER	SCORE	RUNNER UP	COURSE
1895	Horace Rawlins	173-36 holes	Willie Dunn	Newport GC, Newport, R.I.
1896	James Foulis	152-36	Horace Rawlins	Shinnecock Hills GC, South Hampton, N.Y.
1897	Joe Lloyd	162-36	Willie Anderson	Chicago GC, Wheaton, Ill.
1898	Fred Herd	328-72	Alex Smith	Myopia Hunt Club, Hamilton, Mass.
1899	Willie Smith	315	George Low, Val Fitzjohn, W. H. Way	Baltimore CC, Baltimore
1900	Harry Vardon	313	J. H. Taylor	Chicago GC, Wheaton, Ill.
1901	*Willie Anderson (85)	331	Alex Smith (86)	Myopia Hunt Club, Hamilton, Mass.
1902	Laurie Auchterlonie	307	Stewart Gardner	Garden City GC, Garden City, L.I., N.Y.
1903	*Willie Anderson (82)	307	David Brown (84)	Baltusrol GC, Short Hills, N.Y.
1904	Willie Anderson	303	Gil Nicholls	Glen View Club, Golf, Ill.
1905	Willie Anderson	314	Alex Smith	Myopia Hunt Club, Hamilton, Mass.
1906	Alex Smith	295	Willie Smith	Onwentsia Club Lake Forest, Ill.
1907	Alex Ross	302	Gil Nicholls	Philadelphia Cricket Club, Chestnut Hill, Pa.
1908	*Fred McLeod (77)	322	Willie Smith (83)	Myopia Hunt Club, Hamilton, Mass.
1909	George Sargent	290	Tom McNamara	Englewood GC, Englewood, N.J.
1910	*Alex Smith (71)	298	John McDermott (75), Macdonald Smith (77)	Philadelphia Cricket Club, Chestnut Hill, Pa.
1911	*John McDermott (80)	307	Mike Brady (82), George Simpson (85)	Chicago GC, Wheaton, Ill.
1912	John McDermott	294	Tom McNamara	CC of Buffalo, Buffalo
1913	*Francis Ouimet (72)	304	Harry Vardon (77), Edward Ray (78)	The Country Club, Brookline, Mass.
1914	Walter Hagen	290	Charles Evans, Jr.	Midlothian CC, Blue Island, Ill.
1915	Jerome Travers	297	Tom McNamara	Baltusrol GC, Short Hills, N.J.
1916	Charles Evans, Jr.	286	Jock Hutchison	Minikahda Club, Minneapolis
1917-18	*No Championships Played-World War I*			
1919	*Walter Hagen (77)	301	Mike Brady (78)	Brae Burn CC, West Newton, Mass.
1920	Edward Ray	295	Harry Vardon, Jack Burke, Leo Diegel, Jock Hutchison	Inverness CC, Toledo, Ohio
1921	James M. Barnes	289	Walter Hagen, Fred McLeod	Columbia CC, Chevy Chase, Md.
1922	Gene Sarazen	288	John L. Black, Robert T. Jones, Jr.	Skokie CC, Glencoe, Ill.
1923	*R. T. Jones, Jr. (76)	296	Bobby Cruickshank (78)	Inwood CC, Inwood, L.I., N.Y.
1924	Cyril Walker	297	Robert T. Jones, Jr.	Oakland Hills CC, Birmingham, Mich.
1925	*W. MacFarlane (147)	291	R. T. Jones, Jr. (148)	Worcester CC, Worcester, Mass.
1926	Robert T. Jones, Jr.	293	Joe Turnesa	Scioto CC, Columbus, Ohio
1927	*Tommy Armour (76)	301	Harry Cooper (79)	Oakmont CC, Oakmont, Pa.
1928	*Johnny Farrell (143)	294	R. T. Jones, Jr. (144)	Olympia Fields CC, Matteson, Ill.
1929	*R.T. Jones, Jr. (141)	294	Al Espinosa (164)	Winged Foot GC, Mamaroneck, N.Y.
1930	Robert T. Jones, Jr.	287	Macdonald Smith	Interlachen CC, Hopkins, Minn.
1931	*Billy Burke (149-148)	292	George Von Elm (149-149)	Inverness Club, Toledo, Ohio
1932	Gene Sarazen	286	Phil Perkins, Bobby Cruickshank	Fresh Meadows CC, Flushing, N.Y.

Year	Winner	Score	Runner-up	Site
1933	Johnny Goodman	287	Ralph Guldahl	North Shore CC, Glenview, Ill.
1934	Olin Dutra	293	Gene Sarazen	Merion Cricket Club, Ardmore, Pa.
1935	Sam Parks, Jr.	299	Jimmy Thompson	Oakmont CC, Oakmont, Pa.
1936	Tony Manero	282	Harry Cooper	Baltusrol GC, Springfield, N.J.
1937	Ralph Guldahl	281	Sam Snead	Oakland Hills CC, Birmingham, Mich.
1938	Ralph Guldahl	284	Dick Metz	Cherry Hills CC, Denver
1939	*Byron Nelson (68-70)	284	Craig Wood (68-73) Denny Shute (76)	Philadelphia CC, Philadelphia
1940	*Lawson Little (70)	287	Gene Sarazen (73)	Canterbury GC, Cleveland
1941	Craig Wood	284	Denny Shute	Colonial Club, Fort Worth
1942-45	No Championships Played-World War II			
1946	*Lloyd Mangrum (72-72)	284	Vic Ghezzi (72-73) Byron Nelson (72-73)	Canterbury GC, Cleveland
1947	*Lew Worsham (69)	282	Sam Snead (70)	St. Louis CC, Clayton, Mo.
1948	Ben Hogan	276	Jimmy Demaret	Riviera CC, Los Angeles
1949	Cary Middlecoff	286	Sam Snead Clayton Heafner	Medinah CC, Medinah, Ill.
1950	*Ben Hogan (69)	287	Lloyd Mangrum (73) George Fazio (75)	Merion Golf Club, Ardmore, Pa.
1951	Ben Hogan	287	Clayton Heafner	Oakland Hills CC, Birmingham, Mich.
1952	Julius Boros	281	Ed Oliver	Northwood CC, Dallas
1953	Ben Hogan	283	Sam Snead	Oakmont CC, Oakmont, Pa.
1954	Ed Furgol	284	Gene Littler	Baltusrol GC, Springfield, N.J.
1955	*Jack Fleck (69)	287	Ben Hogan (72)	Olympic Club, San Francisco
1956	Cary Middlecoff	281	Ben Hogan Julius Boros	Oak Hill CC, Rochester, N.Y.
1957	*Dick Mayer (72)	282	Cary Middlecoff (79)	Inverness Club, Toledo, Ohio
1958	Tommy Bolt	283	Gary Player	Southern Hills CC, Tulsa
1959	Billy Casper	282	Bob Rosburg	Winged Foot GC, Mamaroneck, N.Y.
1960	Arnold Palmer	280	Jack Nicklaus	Cherry Hills CC, Denver
1961	Gene Littler	281	Bob Goalby Doug Sanders	Oakland Hills CC, Birmingham, Mich.
1962	*Jack Nicklaus (71)	283	Arnold Palmer (74)	Oakmont CC, Oakmont , Pa.
1963	*Julius Boros (70)	293	Jacky Cupit (73) Arnold Palmer (76)	The Country Club, Brookline, Mass.
1964	Ken Venturi	278	Tommy Jacobs	Congressional CC, Washington
1965	*Gary Player (71)	282	Kel Nagle (74)	Bellerive CC, St. Louis
1966	*Billy Casper (69)	278	Arnold Palmer (73)	Olympic Club, San Francisco
1967	Jack Nicklaus	275	Arnold Palmer	Baltusrol GC, Springfield, N.J.
1968	Lee Trevino	275	Jack Nicklaus	Oak Hill CC, Rochester N.Y.
1969	Orville Moody	281	Deane Beman Al Geiberger Bob Rosburg	Champions GC, Houston, Texas
1970	Tony Jacklin	281	Dave Hill	Hazeltine GC, Chaska, Minn.
1971	*Lee Trevino (68)	280	Jack Nicklaus (71)	Merion Golf Club, Ardmore, Pa.
1972	Jack Nicklaus	290	Bruce Crampton	Pebble Beach GL, Pebble Beach, Calif.
1973	Johnny Miller	279	John Schlee	Oakmont CC, Oakmont, Pa.
1974	Hale Irwin	287	Forrest Fezler	Winged Foot GC, Mamaroneck, N.Y.
1975	*Lou Graham (71)	287	John Mahaffey (73)	Medinah CC, Medinah, Ill.
1976	Jerry Pate	277	Tom Weiskopf Al Geiberger	Atlanta Athletic Club, Duluth, Ga.
1977	Hubert Green	278	Lou Graham	Southern Hills CC, Tulsa
1978	Andy North	285	Dave Stockton J. C. Snead	Cherry Hills CC, Denver
1979	Hale Irwin	284	Gary Player Jerry Pate	Inverness Club, Toledo, Ohio
1980	Jack Nicklaus	272	Isao Aoki	Baltusrol GC, Springfield, N.J.
1981	David Graham	273	George Burns Bill Rogers	Merion GC, Ardmore, Pa.
1982	Tom Watson	282	Jack Nicklaus	Pebble Beach GL, Pebble Beach, Calif.
1983	Larry Nelson	280	Tom Watson	Oakmont CC, Oakmont, Pa.

* Winner in playoff. Figures in parentheses indicate scores.

1984	*Fuzzy Zoeller (67)	276	Greg Norman (75)	Winged Foot GC, Mamaroneck, N.Y.
1985	Andy North	279	Dave Barr	Oakland Hills CC, Birmingham, Mich.
			T.C. Chen	
			Denis Watson	
1986	Ray Floyd	279	Lanny Wadkins	Shinnecock Hills GC,
			Chip Beck	Southampton, N.Y.
1987	Scott Simpson	277	Tom Watson	Olympic Club Lake Course,
				San Francisco
1988	*Curtis Strange (71)	278	Nick Faldo (75)	The Country Club, Brookline, Mass.
1989	Curtis Strange	278	Chip Beck	Oak Hill CC, Rochester, N.Y.
			Mark McCumber	
			Ian Woosnam	
1990	Hale Irwin (74)+3	280	Mike Donald (74)+4	Medinah CC, Medinah, Ill.
1991	Payne Stewart (75)	282	Scott Simpson (77)	Hazeltine National GC, Chaska, Minn.
1992	Tom Kite	285	Jeff Sluman	Pebble Beach GL, Pebble Beach, Calif.
1993	Lee Janzen	272	Payne Stewart	Baltusrol GC, Springfield, N.J.

THE BRITISH OPEN

YEAR	WINNER	SCORE	RUNNER UP	COURSE
1860	Willie Park	174	Tom Morris, Sr.	Prestwick, Scotland

(The First Event Was Open Only To Professional Golfers)

1861	Tom Morris, Sr.	163	Willie Park	Prestwick, Scotland

(The Second Annual Open Was Open To Amateurs Also)

1862	Tom Morris, Sr.	163	Willie Park	Prestwick, Scotland
1863	Willie Park	168	Tom Morris Sr.	Prestwick, Scotland
1864	Tom Morris, Sr.	160	Andrew Strath	Prestwick, Scotland
1865	Andrew Strath	162	Willie Park	Prestwick, Scotland
1866	Willie Park	169	David Park	Prestwick, Scotland
1867	Tom Morris, Sr.	170	Willie Park	Prestwick, Scotland
1868	Tom Morris, Jr.	154	Tom Morris, Sr.	Prestwick, Scotland
1869	Tom Morris, Jr.	157	Tom Morris, Sr.	Prestwick, Scotland
1870	Tom Morris, Jr.	149	David Strath	Prestwick, Scotland
			Bob Kirk	
1871	No Championship Played			
1872	Tom Morris, Jr.	166	David Strath	Prestwick, Scotland
1873	Tom Kidd	179	Jamie Anderson	St. Andrews, Scotland
1874	Mungo Park	159	No Record	Musselburgh, Scotland
1875	Willie Park	166	Bob Martin	Prestwick, Scotland
1876	Bob Martin	176	David Strath	St. Andrews, Scotland
1877	Jamie Anderson	160	R. Pringle	Musselburgh, Scotland
1878	Jamie Anderson	157	Robert Kirk	Prestwick, Scotland
1879	Jamie Anderson	169	A. Kirkaldy	St. Andrews, Scotland
			J. Allan	
1880	Robert Ferguson	162	No Record	Musselburgh, Scotland
1881	Robert Ferguson	170	Jamie Anderson	Prestwick, Scotland
1882	Robert Ferguson	171	Willie Fernie	St. Andrews, Scotland
1883	*Willie Fernie	159	Robert Ferguson	Musselburgh, Scotland
1884	Jack Simpson	160	D. Rolland	Prestwick, Scotland
			Willie Fernie	
1885	Bob Martin	171	Archie Simpson	St. Andrews, Scotland
1886	David Brown	157	Willie Campbell	Musselburgh, Scotland
1887	Willie Park, Jr.	161	Bob Martin	Prestwick, Scotland
1888	Jack Burns	171	B. Sayers	St. Andrews, Scotland
			D. Anderson	
1889	*Willie Park, Jr.	155 (158)	Andrew Kirkaldy (163)	Musselburgh, Scotland
1890	John Ball	164	Willie Fernie	Prestwick, Scotland
1891	Hugh Kirkaldy	166	Andrew Kirkaldy	St. Andrews, Scotland
			Willie Fernie	

(Championship Extended From 36 to 72 Holes)

1892	Harold H. Hilton	305	John Ball	Muirfield, Scotland
			Hugh Kirkaidy	

Year	Winner	Score	Runner-up	Location
1893	William Auchterlonie	322	John E. Laidlay	Prestwick, Scotland
1894	John H. Taylor	326	Douglas Rolland	Royal St. George's, England
1895	John H. Taylor	322	Alexander Herd	St. Andrews, Scotland
1896	*Harry Vardon	316 (157)	John H. Taylor (161)	Muirfield, Scotland
1897	Harold H. Hilton	314	James Braid	Hoylake, England
1898	Harry Vardon	307	Willie Park, Jr.	Prestwick, Scotland
1899	Harry Vardon	310	Jack White	Royal St. George's, England
1900	John H. Taylor	309	Harry Vardon	St. Andrews, Scotland
1901	James Braid	309	Harry Vardon	Muirfield, Scotland
1902	Alexander Herd	307	Harry Vardon	Hoylake, England
1903	Harry Vardon	300	Tom Vardon	Prestwick, Scotland
1904	Jack White	296	John H. Taylor	Royal St. George's, England
1905	James Braid	318	John H. Taylor Rolland Jones	St. Andrews, Scotland
1906	James Braid	300	John H. Taylor	Muirfield, Scotland
1907	Arnaud Massy	312	John H. Taylor	Hoylake, England
1908	James Braid	291	Tom Ball	Prestwick, Scotland
1909	John H. Taylor	295	James Braid Tom Ball	Deal, England
1910	James Braid	299	Alexander Herd	St. Andrews, Scotland
1911	Harry Vardon	303	Arnaud Massy	Royal St. George's, England
1912	Edward (Ted) Ray	295	Harry Vardon	Muirfield, Scotland
1913	John H. Taylor	304	Edward Ray	Hoylake, England
1914	Harry Vardon	306	John H. Taylor	Prestwick, Scotland
1915-1919 *No Championships Played*				
1920	George Duncan	303	Alexander Herd	Deal, England
1921	*Jock Hutchison	296 (150)	Roger Wethered (159)	St. Andrews, Scotland
1922	Walter Hagen	300	George Duncan James M. Barnes	Royal St. George's, England
1923	Arthur G. Havers	295	Walter Hagen	Troon, Scotland
1924	Walter Hagen	301	Ernest Whitcombe	Hoylake, England
1925	James M. Barnes	300	Archie Compston Ted Ray	Prestwick, Scotland
1926	Robert T. Jones, Jr.	291	Al Watrous	Royal Lytham, England
1927	Robert T. Jones, Jr.	285	Aubrey Boomer	St. Andrews, Scotland
1928	Walter Hagen	292	Gene Sarazen	Royal St. George's, England
1929	Walter Hagen	292	Johnny Farrell	Muirfield, Scotland
1930	Robert T. Jones, Jr.	291	Macdonald Smith Leo Diegel	Hoylake, England
1931	Tommy D. Armour	296	J. Jurado	Carnoustie, Scotland
1932	Gene Sarazen	283	Macdonald Smith	Prince's, England
1933	*Denny Shute(149)	292	Craig Wood (154)	St. Andrews, Scotland
1934	Henry Cotton	283	S. F. Brews	Royal St. George's, England
1935	Alfred Perry	283	Alfred Padgham	Muirfield, Scotland
1936	Alfred Padgham	287	J. Adams	Hoylake, England
1937	Henry Cotton	290	R. A. Whitcombe	Carnoustie, Scotland
1938	R. A. Whitcombe	295	James Adams	Royal St. George's, England
1939	Richard Burton	290	Johnny Bulla	St. Andrews, Scotland
1940-1945 *No Championships Played*				
1946	Sam Snead	290	Bobby Locke Johnny Bulla	St. Andrews, Scotland
1947	Fred Daly	293	R. W. Horne Frank Stranahan	Hoylake, England
1948	Henry Cotton	294	Fred Daly	Muirfield, Scotland
1949	*Bobby Locke	283 (135)	Harry Bradshaw(147)	Royal St. George's, England
1950	Bobby Locke	279	Roberto DeVicenzo	Troon, Scotland
1951	Max Faulkner	285	A. Cerda	Portrush, Ireland
1952	Bobby Locke	287	Peter Thomson	Royal Lytham, England

* Winner in playoff. Figures in parentheses indicate scores.

Year	Winner	Score	Runner(s)-up	Venue
1953	Ben Hogan	282	Frank Stranahan D. J. Rees Peter Thomson A. Cerda	Carnoustie, Scotland
1954	Peter Thomson	283	S. S. Scott Dai Rees Bobby Locke	Royal Birkdale, England
1955	Peter Thomson	281	John Fallon	St. Andrews, Scotland
1956	Peter Thomson	286	Flory Van Donck	Hoylake, England
1957	Bobby Locke	279	Peter Thomson	St Andrews, Scotland
1958	*Peter Thomson	278 (139)	Dave Thomas (143)	Royal Lytham, England
1959	Gary Player	284	Fred Bullock Flory Van Donck	Muirfield, Scotland
1960	Kel Nagle	278	Arnold Palmer	St. Andrews, Scotland
1961	Arnold Palmer	284	Dai Rees	Royal Birkdale, England
1962	Arnold Palmer	276	Kel Nagle	Troon, Scotland
1963	*Bob Charles	277 (140)	Phil Rodgers (148)	Royal Lytham, England
1964	Tony Lema	279	Jack Nicklaus	St. Andrews, Scotland
1965	Peter Thomson	285	Brian Huggett Christy O'Connor	Southport, England
1966	Jack Nicklaus	282	Doug Sanders Dave Thomas	Muirfield, Scotland
1967	Roberto DeVicenzo	278	Jack Nicklaus	Hoylake, England
1968	Gary Player	289	Jack Nicklaus Bob Charles	Carnoustie, Scotland
1969	Tony Jacklin	280	Bob Charles	Royal Lytham, England
1970	*Jack Nicklaus	283 (72)	Doug Sanders (73)	St. Andrews, Scotland
1971	Lee Trevino	278	Lu Liang Huan	Royal Birkdale, England
1972	Lee Trevino	278	Jack Nicklaus	Muirfield, Scotland
1973	Tom Weiskopf	276	Johnny Miller	Troon, Scotland
1974	Gary Player	282	Peter Oosterhuis	Royal Lytham, England
1975	*Tom Watson	279 (71)	Jack Newton (72)	Carnoustie, Scotland
1976	Johnny Miller	279	Jack Nicklaus S. Ballesteros	Royal Birkdale, England
1977	Tom Watson	268	Jack Nicklaus	Turnberry, Scotland
1978	Jack Nicklaus	281	Ben Crenshaw Tom Kite Ray Floyd Simon Owen	St. Andrews, Scotland
1979	Seve Ballesteros	283	Ben Crenshaw Jack Nicklaus	Royal Lytham, England
1980	Tom Watson	271	Lee Trevino	Muirfield, Scotland
1981	Bill Rogers	276	Bernhard Langer	Royal St. George's, England
1982	Tom Watson	284	Nick Price Peter Oosterhuis	Royal Troon, Scotland
1983	Tom Watson	275	Andy Bean	Royal Birkdale, England
1984	Seve Ballesteros	276	Tom Watson Bernhard Langer	St. Andrews, Scotland
1985	Sandy Lyle	282	Payne Stewart	Royal St. George's, England
1986	Greg Norman	280	Gordon Brand	Turnberry GL, Scotland
1987	Nick Faldo	279	Paul Azinger Rodger Davis	Muirfield, Gullane, Scotland
1988	Seve Ballesteros	273	Nick Price	Royal Lytham and St. Anne's, St. Anne's-On-The-Sea, England
1989	*Mark Calcavecchia	275	Wayne Grady Greg Norman	Royal Troon GC, Troon, Scotland
1990	Nick Faldo	270	Payne Stewart Mark McNulty	St. Andrews, Scotland
1991	Ian Baker-Finch	272	Mike Harwood	Royal Birkdale, England
1992	Nick Faldo	272	John Cook	Muirfield, Gullane, Scotland
1993	Greg Norman	267	Nick Faldo	Royal St. Georges's GC Sandwich England

PGA CHAMPIONSHIP

YEAR	WINNER	SCORE	RUNNER UP	COURSE
1916	James M. Barnes	1 up	Jock Hutchison	Siwanoy CC, Bronxville, N.Y.
1917-18	No Championships Played-World War I			
1919	James M. Barnes	6 & 5	Fred McLeod	Engineers CC, Roslyn, L.I., N.Y.
1920	Jock Hutchison	1 up	J. Douglas Edgar	Flossmoor CC, Flossmoor, Ill.
1921	Walter Hagen	3 & 2	James M. Barnes	Inwood CC, Far Rockaway, N.Y.
1922	Gene Sarazen	4 & 3	Emmet French	Oakmont CC, Oakmont, Pa.
1923	Gene Sarazen	1 up (38)	Walter Hagen	Pelham CC, Pelham, N.Y.
1924	Walter Hagen	2 up	James M. Barnes	French Lick CC, French Lick, Ind.
1925	Walter Hagen	6 & 5	William Mehlhorn	Olympia Fields, Olympia Fields, Ill.
1926	Walter Hagen	5 & 3	Leo Diegel	Salisbury GC, Westbury, L.I., N.Y.
1927	Walter Hagen	1 up	Joe Turnesa	Cedar Crest CC, Dallas
1928	Leo Diegel	6 & 5	Al Espinosa	Five Farms CC, Baltimore
1929	Leo Diegel	6 & 4	Johnny Farrell	Hillcrest CC, Los Angeles
1930	Tommy Armour	1 up	Gene Sarazen	Fresh Meadow CC, Flushing, N.Y.
1931	Tom Creavy	2 & 1	Denny Shute	Wannamoisett CC, Rumford, R.I.
1932	Olin Dutra	4 & 3	Frank Walsh	Keller GC, St. Paul, Minn.
1933	Gene Sarazen	5 & 4	Willie Goggin	Blue Mound CC, Milwaukee
1934	Paul Runyan	1 up (38)	Craig Wood	Park CC, Williamsville, N.Y.
1935	Johnny Revolta	5 & 4	Tommy Armour	Twin Hills CC, Oklahoma City
1936	Denny Shute	3 & 2	Jimmy Thomson	Pinehurst CC, Pinehurst, N.C.
1937	Denny Shute	1 up (37)	Harold McSpaden	Pittsburgh F.C, Aspinwali, Pa.
1938	PaulRunyan	8 & 7	Sam Snead	Shawnee CC, Shawnee-on-Delaware
1939	Henry Picard	1 up (37)	Byron Nelson	Pomonok CC, Flushing L.I., N.Y.
1940	Byron Nelson	1 up	Sam Snead	Hershey CC, Hershey, Pa.
1941	Vic Ghezzi	1 up (38)	Byron Nelson	Cherry Hills CC, Denver
1942	Sam Snead	2 & 1	Jim Turnesa	Seaview CC, Atlantic City
1943	No Championship Played-World War II			
1944	Bob Hamilton	1 up	Byron Nelson	Manito G & CC, Spokane, Wash.
1945	Byron Nelson	4 & 3	Sam Byrd	Morraine CC, Dayton, Ohio
1946	Ben Hogan	6 & 4	Ed Oliver	Portland GC, Portland, Ore.
1947	Jim Ferrier	2 & 1	Chick Harbert	Plum Hollow CC, Detroit
1948	Ben Hogan	7 & 6	Mike Turnesa	Norwood Hills CC, St. Louis
1949	Sam Snead	3 & 2	Johnny Palmer	Hermitage CC, Richmond, Va.
1950	Chandler Harper	4 & 3	Henry Williams, Jr.	Scioto CC, Columbus, Ohio
1951	Sam Snead	7 & 6	Walter Burkemo	Oakmont CC, Oakmont, Pa.
1952	Jim Turnesa	1 up	Chick Harbert	Big Spring CC, Louisville
1953	Walter Burkemo	2 & 1	Felice Torza	Birmingham CC, Birmingham, Mich.
1954	Chick Harbert	4 & 3	Walter Burkemo	Keller GC, St. Paul, Minn.
1955	Doug Ford	4 & 3	Cary Middlecoff	Meadowbrook CC, Detroit
1956	Jack Burke	3 & 2	Ted Kroll	Blue Hill CC, Boston
1957	Lionel Hebert	2 & 1	Dow Finsterwald	Miami Valley CC, Dayton, Ohio
1958	Dow Finsterwald	276	Billy Casper	Llanerch CC, Havertown, Pa.
1959	Bob Rosburg	277	Jerry Barber Doug Sanders	Minneapolis GC, St. Louis Park, Minn.
1960	Jay Hebert	281	Jim Ferrier	Firestone CC, Akron, Ohio
1961	*Jerry Barber (67)	277	Don January (68)	Olympia Fields CC, Olympia Fields, Ill.
1962	Gary Player	278	Bob Goalby	Aronomink GC, Newtown Square, Pa.
1963	Jack Nicklaus	279	Dave Ragan, Jr.	Dallas Athletic Club, Dallas
1964	Bobby Nichols	271	Jack Nicklaus Arnold Palmer	Columbus CC, Columbus, Ohio
1965	Dave Marr	280	Billy Casper Jack Nicklaus	Laurel Valley CC, Ligonier, Pa.
1966	Al Geiberger	280	Dudley Wysong	Firestone CC, Akron, Ohio
1967	*Don January (69)	281	Don Massengale (71)	Columbine CC, Littleton, Colo.
1968	Julius Boros	281	Bob Charles Arnold Palmer	Pecan Valley CC, San Antonio
1969	Ray Floyd	276	Gary Player	NCR CC, Dayton, Ohio

* Winner in playoff. Figures in parentheses indicate scores.

Year	Winner	Score	Runner-up	Site
1970	Dave Stockton	279	Arnold Palmer Bob Murphy	Southern Hills CC, Tulsa
1971	Jack Nicklaus	281	Billy Casper	PGA National GC, Palm Beach Gardens, Fla.
1972	Gary Player	281	Tommy Aaron Jim Jamieson	Oakland Hills CC, Birmingham, Mich.
1973	Jack Nicklaus	277	Bruce Crampton	Canterbury GC, Cleveland
1974	Lee Trevino	276	Jack Nicklaus	Tanglewood GC, Winston-Salem, N.C.
1975	Jack Nicklaus	276	Bruce Crampton	Firestone CC, Akron, Ohio
1976	Dave Stockton	281	Ray Floyd Don January	Congressional CC, Bethesda, Md.
1977	*Lanny Wadkins	282	Gene Littler	Pebble Beach GL, Pebble Beach, Calif.
1978	*John Mahaffey	276	Jerry Pate Tom Watson	Oakmont CC, Oakmont, Pa.
1979	*David Graham	272	Ben Crenshaw	Oakland Hills CC, Birmingham, Mich.
1980	Jack Nicklaus	274	Andy Bean	Oak Hill CC, Rochester, N.Y.
1981	Larry Nelson	273	Fuzzy Zoeller	Atlanta Athletic Club, Duluth, Ga.
1982	Raymond Floyd	272	Lanny Wadkins	Southern Hills CC, Tulsa
1983	Hal Sutton	274	Jack Nicklaus	Riviera CC, Pacific Palisades, Calif.
1984	Lee Trevino	273	Gary Player Lanny Wadkins	Shoal Creek, Birmingham, Ala.
1985	Hubert Green	278	Lee Trevino	Cherry Hills CC, Denver
1986	Bob Tway	276	Greg Norman	Inverness CC, Toledo, Ohio
1987	*Larry Nelson	287	Lanny Wadkins	PGA National, Palm Beach Gardens, Fla.
1988	Jeff Sluman	272	Paul Azinger	Oak Tree GC, Edmond, Okla.
1989	Payne Stewart	276	Mike Reid	Kemper Lakes GC, Hawthorn Woods, Ill.
1990	Wayne Grady	282	Fred Couples	Shoal Creek, Birmingham, Ala.
1991	John Daly	276	Bruce Lietzke	Crooked Stick GC, Carmel, Ind.
1992	Nick Price	278	John Cook Jim Gallagher Gene Sauers Nick Faldo	Bellerive CC, St. Louis
1993	*Paul Azinger	272	Greg Noman	Inverness Club, Toledo, Ohio

*Winners in playoffs. Figures in parentheses indicate scores.

INFINITI TOURNAMENT OF CHAMPIONS

TOURNAMENT OF CHAMPIONS

Desert Inn CC, Las Vegas (1953-66). Stardust CC, Las Vegas (1967-68). LaCosta CC, Carlsbad, Calif. (1969-93).

Year	Winner	Score
1953	Al Besselink	280
1954	Art Wall	278
1955	Gene Littler	280
1956	Gene Littler	281
1957	Gene Littler	285
1958	Stan Leonard	275
1959	Mike Souchak	281
1960	Jerry Barber	268
1961	Sam Snead	273
1962	Arnold Palmer	276
1963	Jack Nicklaus	273
1964	Jack Nicklaus	279
1965	Arnold Palmer	277
1966	*Arnold Palmer	283
1967	Frank Beard	278
1968	Don January	276
1969	Gary Player	284
1970	Frank Beard	273
1971	Jack Nicklaus	279
1972	*Bobby Mitchell	280
1973	Jack Nicklaus	276
1974	Johnny Miller	280

MONY TOURNAMENT OF CHAMPIONS

Year	Winner	Score
1975	*Al Geiberger	277
1976	Don January	277
1977	*Jack Nicklaus	281
1978	Gary Player	281
1979	Tom Watson	275
1980	Tom Watson	276
1981	Lee Trevino	273
1982	Lanny Wadkins	280
1983	Lanny Wadkins	280
1984	Tom Watson	274
1985	Tom Kite	275
1986	Calvin Peete	267
1987	Mac O'Grady	278
1988	@Steve Pate	202
1989	Steve Jones	279

IINFINITI TOURNAMENT OF CHAMPIONS

Year	Winner	Score
1990	Paul Azinger	272
1991	Tom Kite	272
1992	*Steve Elkington	279
1993	Davis Love III	272

UNITED AIRLINES HAWAIIAN OPEN

HAWAIIAN OPEN

Waialae CC, Honolulu.

Year	Winner	Score
1965	*Gay Brewer	281
1966	Ted Makalena	271
1967	*Dudley Wysong	284
1968	Lee Trevino	272
1969	Bruce Crampton	274
1970	No Tournament	
1971	Tom Shaw	273
1972	*Grier Jones	274
1973	John Schlee	273
1974	Jack Nicklaus	271
1975	Gary Groh	274
1976	Ben Crenshaw	270
1977	Bruce Lietzke	273
1978	*Hubert Green	274
1979	Hubert Green	267
1980	Andy Bean	266
1981	Hale Irwin	265
1982	Wayne Levi	277
1983	Isao Aoki	268
1984	*Jack Renner	271
1985	Mark O'Meara	267
1986	Corey Pavin	272
1987	*Corey Pavin	270
1988	Lanny Wadkins	271
1989	@Gene Sauers	197
1990	David Ishii	279

UNITED HAWAIIAN OPEN

Year	Winner	Score
1991	Lanny Wadkins	270

UNITED AIRLINES HAWAIIAN OPEN

Year	Winner	Score
1992	John Cook	265
1993	Howard Twitty	269

NORTHERN TELECOM OPEN

El Rio G&CC, Tucson, Ariz. (1945-62). 49er CC, Tucson, Ariz. (1963-64). Tucson National GC, Tucson, Ariz. (1965-78, 1980). Randolph Park Municipal GC, Tucson, Ariz. (1979, 1981-86). TPC at StarPass, Tucson, Ariz. (1987-1993).

TUCSON OPEN

Year	Winner	Score
1945	Ray Mangrum	268
1946	Jimmy Demaret	268
1947	Jimmy Demaret	264
1948	Skip Alexander	264
1949	Lloyd Mangrum	263
1950	Chandler Harper	267
1951	Lloyd Mangrum	269
1952	Henry Williams	274
1953	Tommy Bolt	265
1954	No Tournament	
1955	Tommy Bolt	265
1956	Ted Kroll	264
1957	Dow Finsterwald	269
1958	Lionel Hebert	265
1959	Gene Littler	266
1960	Don January	271

HOME OF THE SUN INVITATIONAL

Year	Winner	Score
1961	*Dave Hill	269

TUCSON OPEN

Year	Winner	Score
1962	Phil Rodgers	263
1963	Don January	266
1964	Jack Cupit	274
1965	Bob Charles	271
1966	*Joe Campbell	278
1967	Arnold Palmer	273
1968	George Knudson	273
1969	Lee Trevino	271
1970	*Lee Trevino	275
1971	J.C. Snead	273
1972	Miller Barber	273

DEAN MARTIN TUCSON OPEN

Year	Winner	Score
1973	Bruce Crampton	277
1974	Johnny Miller	272
1975	Johnny Miller	263

NBC TUCSON OPEN

Year	Winner	Score
1976	Johnny Miller	274

JOE GARAGIOLA TUCSON OPEN

Year	Winner	Score
1977	*Bruce Lietzke	275
1978	Tom Watson	276
1979	Bruce Lietzke	265
1980	Jim Colbert	270
1981	Johnny Miller	265
1982	Craig Stadler	266
1983	*Gil Morgan	271

SEIKO-TUCSON MATCH PLAY CHAMPIONSHIPS

Year	Winner	Score
1984	Tom Watson	2&1
1985	Jim Thorpe	4&3
1986	Jim Thorpe	67

SEIKO-TUCSON OPEN

Year	Winner	Score
1987	Mike Reid	268

NORTHERN TELECOM TUCSON OPEN

Year	Winner	Score
1988	David Frost	266
1989	No tournament	
1990	Robert Gamez	270

NORTHERN TELECOM OPEN

Year	Winner	Score
1991	#Phil Mickelson	272
1992	Lee Janzen	270
1993	Larry Mize	271

PHOENIX OPEN INVITATIONAL

Phoenix CC, Phoenix (1935-86), alternating with Arizona CC, Phoenix (1955-73. TPC of Scottsdale, Scottsdale, Ariz. (1987-93).

Year	Winner	Score
1935	Ky Laffoon	281
1936-1938 No Tournaments		
1939	Byron Nelson	198
1940	Ed Oliver	205
1941-1943 No Tournaments		
1944	*Harold McSpaden	273

KEY: * = Playoff # = Amateur @ = Rain-curtailed

Year	Winner	Score
1945	Byron Nelson	274
1946	*Ben Hogan	273
1947	Ben Hogan	270
1948	Bobby Locke	268
1949	*Jimmy Demaret	278
1950	Jimmy Demaret	269
1951	Lew Worsham	272
1952	Lloyd Mangrum	274
1953	Lloyd Mangrum	272
1954	*Ed Furgol	272
1955	Gene Littler	275
1956	Cary Middlecoff	276
1957	Billy Casper	271
1958	Ken Venturi	274
1959	Gene Littler	268
1960	*Jack Fleck	273
1961	*Arnold Palmer	270
1962	Arnold Palmer	269
1963	Arnold Palmer	273
1964	Jack Nicklaus	271
1965	Rod Funseth	274
1966	Dudley Wysong	278
1967	Julius Boros	272
1968	George Knudson	272
1969	Gene Littler	263
1970	Dale Douglass	271
1971	Miller Barber	261
1972	Homero Blancas	273
1973	Bruce Crampton	268
1974	Johnny Miller	271
1975	Johnny Miller	260
1976	Bob Gilder	268
1977	*Jerry Pate	277
1978	Miller Barber	272
1979	@Ben Crenshaw	199
1980	Jeff Mitchell	272
1981	David Graham	268
1982	Lanny Wadkins	263
1983	*Bob Gilder	271
1984	Tom Purtzer	268
1985	Calvin Peete	270
1986	Hal Sutton	267
1987	Paul Azinger	268
1988	*Sandy Lyle	269
1989	Mark Calcavecchia	263
1990	Tommy Armour III	267
1991	Nolan Henke	268
1992	Mark Calcavecchia	264
1993	Lee Janzen	273

AT&T PEBBLE BEACH NATIONAL PRO-AM

Rotates between Rancho Santa Fe CC, San Diego (1937-42); Cypress Point CC, Monterey Peninsula, Calif. (1947-90); Monterey Peninsula CC, Monterey Peninsula, Calif. (1947-67); Pebble Beach GC, Monterey Peninsula, Calif. (1947-93); Spyglass Hill GC, Monterey Peninsula, Calif. (1968-93);
Poppy Hills GC, Monterey Peninsula, Calif. (1991-93).

BING CROSBY PROFESSIONAL-AMATEUR

Year	Winner	Score
1937	Sam Snead	68
1938	Sam Snead	139
1939	Dutch Harrison	138
1940	Ed Oliver	135
1941	Sam Snead	136
1942	Tie-Lloyd Mangrum Leland Gibson	133
1943-1946	*No Tournaments*	
1947	Tie-Ed Furgol George Fazio	213
1948	Lloyd Mangrum	205
1949	Ben Hogan	208
1950	Tie-Sam Snead Jack Burke, Jr Smiley Quick Dave Douglas	214
1951	Byron Nelson	209
1952	Jimmy Demaret	145

THE BING CROSBY PROFESSIONAL-AMATEUR INVITATIONAL

Year	Winner	Score
1953	Lloyd Mangrum	204
1954	Dutch Harrison	210
1955	Cary Middlecoff	209

BING CROSBY NATIONAL PROFESSIONAL-AMATEUR GOLF CHAMPIONSHIP

Year	Winner	Score
1956	Cary Middlecoff	202
1957	Jay Heber	213
1958	Billy Casper	277

BING CROSBY NATIONAL

Year	Winner	Score
1959	Art Wall	279
1960	Ken Venturi	286
1961	Bob Rosburg	282
1962	*Doug Ford	286
1963	Billy Casper	285

BING CROSBY NATIONAL PROFESSIONAL-AMATEUR

Year	Winner	Score
1964	Tony Lema	284
1965	Bruce Crampton	284
1966	Don Massengale	283
1967	Jack Nicklaus	284
1968	*Johnny Pott	285
1969	George Archer	283
1970	Bert Yancey	278
1971	Tom Shaw	278
1972	*Jack Nicklaus	284
1973	*Jack Nicklaus	282
1974	@Johnny Miller	208
1975	Gene Littler	280
1976	Ben Crenshaw	281
1977	Tom Watson	273
1978	*Tom Watson	280
1979	Lon Hinkle	284
1980	George Burns	280
1981	@*John Cook	209
1982	Jim Simons	274
1983	Tom Kite	276
1984	*Hale Irwin	278
1985	Mark O'Meara	283

AT&T PEBBLE BEACH NATIONAL PRO-AM

Year	Winner	Score
1986	@Fuzzy Zoeller	205
1987	Johnny Miller	278
1988	*Steve Jones	280
1989	Mark O'Meara	277
1990	Mark O'Meara	281
1991	Paul Azinger	274
1992	*Mark O'Meara	275
1993	Brett Ogle	276

BOB HOPE CHRYSLER CLASSIC

Rotates among Bermuda Dunes CC, Palm Springs, Calif.; Tamarisk CC, Palm Springs, Calif.; Thunderbird CC, Palm Springs Calif.; La Quinta CC, La Quinta, Calif.; Indian Wells CC, Indian Wells, Calif.; Eldorado CC, Palm Springs, Calif.; and PGA West/Palmer Course, La Quinta, Calif. (1960-93).

PALM SPRINGS GOLF CLASSIC

Year	Winner	Score
1960	Arnold Palmer	338
1961	Billy Maxwell	345
1962	Arnold Palmer	342
1963	*Jack Nicklaus	345
1964	*Tommy Jacobs	348

BOB HOPE DESERT CLASSIC

Year	Winner	Score
1965	Billy Casper	348
1966	*Doug Sanders	349
1967	Tom Nieporte	349
1968	*Arnold Palmer	348
1969	Billy Casper	345
1970	Bruce Devlin	339
1971	*Arnold Palmer	342
1972	Bob Rosburg	344
1973	Arnold Palmer	343
1974	Hubert Green	341
1975	Johnny Miller	339
1976	Johnny Miller	344
1977	Rik Massengale	337
1978	Bill Rogers	339
1979	John Mahaffey	343
1980	Craig Stadler	343
1981	Bruce Lietzke	335
1982	*Ed Fiori	335
1983	*Keith Fergus	335

BOB HOPE CLASSIC

Year	Winner	Score
1984	*John Mahaffey	340
1985	*Lanny Wadkins	333

BOB HOPE CHRYSLER CLASSIC

Year	Winner	Score
1986	*Donnie Hammond	335
1987	Corey Pavin	341
1988	Jay Haas	338

1989	*Steve Jones	343
1990	Peter Jacobsen	339
1991	*Corey Pavin	331
1992	*John Cook	336
1993	Tom Kite	325

BUICK INVITATIONAL OF CALIFORNIA

Moved annually (1952-61). Stardust CC, San Diego (1962-67). Torrey Pines GC, San Diego (1968-93).

SAN DIEGO OPEN
1952	Ted Kroll	276
1953	Tommy Bolt	274
1954	#Gene Littler	274

CONVAIR-SAN DIEGO OPEN
| 1955 | Tommy Bolt | 274 |
| 1956 | Bob Rosburg | 270 |

SAN DIEGO OPEN INVITATIONAL
1957	Arnold Palmer	271
1958	*No Tournament*	
1959	Marty Furgol	274
1960	Mike Souchak	269
1961	*Arnold Palmer	271
1962	*Tommy Jacobs	277
1963	Gary Player	270
1964	Art Wall	274
1965	*Wes Ellis	267
1966	Billy Casper	268
1967	Bob Goalby	269

ANDY WILLIAMS-SAN DIEGO OPEN INVITATIONAL
1968	Tom Weiskopf	273
1969	Jack Nicklaus	284
1970	*Pete Brown	275
1971	George Archer	272
1972	Paul Harney	275
1973	Bob Dickson	278
1974	Bobby Nichols	275
1975	*J. C. Snead	279
1976	J. C. Snead	272
1977	Tom Watson	269
1978	Jay Haas	278
1979	Fuzzy Zoeller	282
1980	*Tom Watson	275

WICKES/ANDY WILLIAMS SAN DIEGO OPEN
| 1981 | *Bruce Lietzke | 278 |
| 1982 | Johnny Miller | 270 |

ISUZU/ANDY WILLIAMS SAN DIEGO OPEN
1983	Gary Hallberg	271
1984	*Gary Koch	272
1985	*Woody Blackburn	269

SHEARSON LEHMAN BROTHERS ANDY WILLIAMS OPEN
| 1986 | @*Bob Tway | 204 |
| 1987 | George Burns | 266 |

SHEARSON LEHMAN HUTTON ANDY WILLIAMS OPEN
| 1988 | Steve Pate | 269 |

SHEARSON LEHMAN HUTTON OPEN
| 1989 | Greg Twiggs | 271 |
| 1990 | Dan Forsman | 275 |

SHEARSON LEHMAN BROTHERS OPEN
| 1991 | Jay Don Blake | 268 |

BUICK INVITATIONAL OF CALIFORNIA
| 1992 | @Steve Pate | 200 |
| 1993 | Phil Mickelson | 278 |

NISSAN LOS ANGELES OPEN

Moved annually (1926-44, 1954-55, 1968). Riviera CC, Pacific Palisades, Calif. (1945-53, 1973-93). Rancho Municipal GC, Los Angeles (1956-67, 1969-72).

LOS ANGELES OPEN
1926	Harry Cooper	279
1927	Bobby Cruikshank	282
1928	Mac Smith	284
1929	Mac Smith	285
1930	Densmore Shute	296
1931	Ed Dudley	285
1932	Mac Smith	281
1933	Craig Wood	281
1934	Mac Smith	280
1935	*Vic Ghezzi	285
1936	Jimmy Hines	280
1937	Harry Cooper	274
1938	Jimmy Thomson	273
1939	Jimmy Demaret	274
1940	Lawson Little	282
1941	Johnny Bulla	281
1942	*Ben Hogan	282
1943	*No Tournament*	
1944	Harold McSpaden	278
1945	Sam Snead	283
1946	Byron Nelson	284
1947	Ben Hogan	280
1948	Ben Hogan	275
1949	Lloyd Mangrum	284
1950	*Sam Snead	280
1951	Lloyd Mangrum	280
1952	Tommy Bolt	289
1953	Lloyd Mangrum	280
1954	Fred Wampler	281
1955	Gene Littler	276
1956	Lloyd Mangrum	272
1957	Doug Ford	280
1958	Frank Stranahan	275
1959	Ken Venturi	278
1960	Dow Finsterwald	280
1961	Bob Goalby	275
1962	Phil Rodgers	268
1963	Arnold Palmer	274
1964	Paul Harney	280
1965	Paul Harney	276
1966	Arnold Palmer	273
1967	Arnold Palmer	269
1968	Billy Casper	274
1969	*Charles Sifford	276
1970	*Billy Casper	276

GLEN CAMPBELL LOS ANGELES OPEN
1971	*Bob Lunn	274
1972	*George Archer	270
1973	Rod Funseth	276
1974	Dave Stockton	276
1975	Pat Fitzsimons	275
1976	Hale Irwin	272
1977	Tom Purtzer	273
1978	Gil Morgan	278
1979	Lanny Wadkins	276
1980	Tom Watson	276
1981	Johnny Miller	270
1982	*Tom Watson	271
1983	Gil Morgan	270

LOS ANGELES OPEN
1984	David Edwards	279
1985	Lanny Wadkins	264
1986	Doug Tewell	270

LOS ANGELES OPEN PRESENTED BY NISSAN
| 1987 | *Tze-Chung Chen | 275 |
| 1988 | Chip Beck | 267 |

NISSAN LOS ANGELES OPEN
1989	Mark Calcavecchia	272
1990	Fred Couples	266
1991	Ted Schulz	272
1992	*Fred Couples	269
1993	Tom Kite	206

DORAL RYDER OPEN

Doral CC (Blue), Miami.

DORAL CC OPEN INVITATIONAL
1962	Billy Casper	283
1963	Dan Sikes	283
1964	Billy Casper	277
1965	Doug Sanders	274
1966	Phil Rodgers	278
1967	Doug Sanders	275
1968	Gardner Dickinson	275
1969	Tom Shaw	276

DORAL-EASTERN OPEN INVITATIONAL
1970	Mike Hill	279
1971	J.C. Snead	275
1972	Jack Nicklaus	276
1973	Lee Trevino	276
1974	Brian Allin	272

KEY * = Playoff # = Amateur
@ = Rain-curtailed

1975	Jack Nicklaus	276
1976	Hubert Green	270
1977	Andy Bean	277
1978	Tom Weiskopf	272
1979	Mark McCumber	279
1980	*Raymond Floyd	279
1981	Raymond Floyd	273
1982	Andy Bean	278
1983	Gary Koch	271
1984	Tom Kite	272
1985	Mark McCumber	284
1986	*Andy Bean	276

DORAL RYDER OPEN

1987	Lanny Wadkins	277
1988	Ben Crenshaw	274
1989	Bill Glasson	275
1990	*Greg Norman	273
1991	*Rocco Mediate	276
1992	Raymond Floyd	271
1993	Greg Norman	265

HONDA CLASSIC

Inverrary G&CC (East), Lauderhill, Fla. (1972-83). TPC at Eagle Trace, Coral Springs, Fla. (1984-91). Weston Hills G&CC, Fort Lauderdale, Fla. (1992-1993).

JACKIE GLEASON'S INVERRARY CLASSIC

1972	Tom Weiskopf	278

JACKIE GLEASON'S INVERRARY NATIONAL AIRLINES CLASSIC

1973	Lee Trevino	279

JACKIE GLEASON'S INVERRARY CLASSIC

1974	Leonard Thompson	278
1975	Bob Murphy	273
1976	Hosted Tournament Players Championship	
1977	Jack Nicklaus	275
1978	Jack Nicklaus	276
1979	Larry Nelson	274
1980	Johnny Miller	274

AMERICAN MOTORS INVERRARY CLASSIC

1981	Tom Kite	274

HONDA INVERRARY CLASSIC

1982	Hale Irwin	269
1983	Johnny Miller	278

HONDA CLASSIC

1984	*Bruce Lietzke	280
1985	*Curtis Strange	275
1986	Kenny Knox	287
1987	Mark Calcavecchia	279
1988	Joey Sindelar	276
1989	Blaine McCallister	266
1990	John Huston	282
1991	Steve Pate	279
1992	*Corey Pavin	273
1993	*Fred Couples	207

THE NESTLE INVITATIONAL

Rio Pinar CC, Orlando. (1966-78). Bay Hill Club, Orlando. (1979-93).

FLORIDA CITRUS OPEN INVITATIONAL

1966	Lionel Hebert	279
1967	Julius Boros	274
1968	Dan Sikes	274
1969	Ken Still	278
1970	Bob Lunn	271
1971	Arnold Palmer	270
1972	Jerry Heard	276
1973	Brian Allin	265
1974	Jerry Heard	273
1975	Lee Trevino	276
1976	*Hale Irwin	270
1977	Gary Koch	274
1978	Mac McLendon	271

BAY HILL CITRUS CLASSIC

1979	*Bob Byman	278

BAY HILL CLASSIC

1980	Dave Eichelberger	279
1981	Andy Bean	266
1982	*Tom Kite	278
1983	*Mike Nicolette	283
1984	*Gary Koch	272

HERTZ BAY HILL CLASSIC

1985	Fuzzy Zoeller	275
1986	@Dan Forsman	202
1987	Payne Stewart	264
1988	Paul Azinger	271

THE NESTLE INVITATIONAL

1989	*Tom Kite	278
1990	Robert Gamez	274
1991	@Andrew Magee	203
1992	Fred Couples	269
1993	Ben Crenshaw	280

THE PLAYERS CHAMPIONSHIP

Moved annually (1974-1976). Sawgrass, Ponte Vedra, Fla. (1977-81). TPC at Sawgrass, Ponte Vedra, Fla. (1982-93).

TOURNAMENT PLAYERS CHAMPIONSHIP

1974	Jack Nicklaus	272
1975	Al Geiberger	270
1976	Jack Nicklaus	269
1977	Mark Hayes	289
1978	Jack Nicklaus	289
1979	Lanny Wadkins	283
1980	Lee Trevino	278
1981	*Raymond Floyd	285
1982	Jerry Pate	280
1983	Hal Sutton	283
1984	Fred Couples	277
1985	Calvin Peete	274
1986	John Mahaffey	275
1987	*Sandy Lyle	274

THE PLAYERS CHAMPIONSHIP

1988	Mark McCumber	273
1989	Tom Kite	279
1990	Jodie Mudd	278
1991	Steve Elkington	276
1992	Davis Love III	273
1993	Nick Price	270

FREEPORT-MCMORAN CLASSIC

City Park GC, New Orleans, (1938-62). Lakewood CC, New Orleans, (1963-88). English Turn G&CC, New Orleans, (1989-93).

GREATER NEW ORLEANS OPEN INVITATIONAL

1938	Harry Cooper	285
1939	Henry Picard	284
1940	Jimmy Demaret	286
1941	Henry Picard	276
1942	Lloyd Mangrum	281
1943	*No Tournament*	
1944	Sammy Byrd	285
1945	*Byron Nelson	284
1946	Byron Nelson	277
1947	*No Tournament*	
1948	Bob Hamilton	280
1949-1957	*No Tournaments*	
1958	*Billy Casper	278
1959	Bill Collins	280
1960	Dow Finsterwald	270
1961	Doug Sanders	272
1962	Bo Wininger	281
1963	Bo Wininger	279
1964	Mason Rudolph	283
1965	Dick Mayer	273
1966	Frank Beard	276
1967	George Knudson	277
1968	George Archer	271
1969	*Larry Hinson	275
1970	*Miller Barber	278
1971	Frank Beard	276
1972	Gary Player	279
1973	*Jack Nicklaus	280
1974	Lee Trevino	267

FIRST NBC NEW ORLEANS OPEN

1975	Billy Casper	271
1976	Larry Ziegler	274
1977	Jim Simons	273
1978	Lon Hinkle	271
1979	Hubert Green	273

GREATER NEW ORLEANS OPEN
| 1980 | Tom Watson | 273 |

USF&G NEW ORLEANS OPEN
| 1981 | Tom Watson | 270 |

USF&G CLASSIC
1982	@Scott Hoch	206
1983	Bill Rogers	274
1984	Bob Eastwood	272
1985	@Seve Ballesteros	205
1986	Calvin Peete	269
1987	Ben Crenshaw	268
1988	Chip Beck	262
1989	Tim Simpson	274
1990	David Frost	276
1991	*Ian Woosnam	275

FREEPORT-MCMORAN CLASSIC
| 1992 | Chip Beck | 276 |
| 1993 | Mike Standly | 281 |

DEPOSIT GUARANTY GOLF CLASSIC

Hattiesburg CC, Hattiesburg, Miss.

MAGNOLIA STATE CLASSIC
1968	*B.R. McLendon	269
1969	Larry Mowry	272
1970	Chris Blocker	271
1971	Roy Pace	270
1972	Mike Morey	269
1973	Dwight Nevil	268
1974	@Dwight Nevil	133
1975	Bob Wynn	270
1976	Dennis Meyer	271
1977	Mike McCullough	269
1978	Craig Stadler	268
1979	Bobby Walzel	272
1980	@*Roger Maltbie	65
1981	*Tom Jones	268
1982	Payne Stewart	270
1983	@Russ Cochran	203
1984	@*Lance Ten Broeck	201
1985	@*Jim Gallagher, Jr.	131

DEPOSIT GUARANTY CLASSIC
1986	Dan Halldorson	263
1987	David Ogrin	267
1988	Frank Conner	267
1989	@*Jim Booros	199
1990	Gene Sauers	268
1991	*Larry Silveira	266
1992	Richard Zokol	267
1993	Greg Kraft	267

Note: 1983-85 TPS Event

MCI HERITAGE CLASSIC

Harbour Town GL, Hilton Head, S.C.

HERITAGE CLASSIC
| 1969 | Arnold Palmer | 283 |
| 1970 | Bob Goalby | 280 |

SEA PINES HERITAGE CLASSIC
1971	Hale Irwin	279
1972	Johnny Miller	281
1973	Hale Irwin	272
1974	Johnny Miller	276
1975	Jack Nicklaus	271
1976	Hubert Green	274
1977	Graham Marsh	273
1978	Hubert Green	277
1979	Tom Watson	270
1980	*Doug Tewell	280
1981	Bill Rogers	278
1982	*Tom Watson	280
1983	Fuzzy Zoeller	275
1984	Nick Faldo	270
1985	*Bernhard Langer	273
1986	Fuzzy Zoeller	276

MCI HERITAGE CLASSIC
1987	Davis Love III	271
1988	Greg Norman	271
1989	Payne Stewart	268
1990	*Payne Stewart	276
1991	Davis Love III	271
1992	Davis Love III	269
1993	David Edwards	273

K MART GREATER GREENSBORO OPEN

Rotated between Sedgefield CC, Greensboro, N.C. and Starmount Forest CC, Greensboro, N.C. (1938-60). Sedgefield CC (1961-76). Forest Oaks CC, Greensboro, N.C. (1977-93).

GREATER GREENSBORO OPEN
1938	Sam Snead	272
1939	Ralph Guldahl	280
1940	Ben Hogan	270
1941	Byron Nelson	276
1942	Sam Byrd	279
1943-1944	No Tournaments	
1945	Byron Nelson	271
1946	Sam Snead	270
1947	Vic Ghezzi	286
1948	Lloyd Mangrum	278
1949	*Sam Snead	276
1950	Sam Snead	269
1951	Art Doering	279
1952	Dave Douglas	277
1953	*Earl Stewart	275
1954	*Doug Ford	283
1955	Sam Snead	273
1956	*Sam Snead	279
1957	Stan Leonard	276
1958	Bob Goalby	275
1959	Dow Finsterwald	278
1960	Sam Snead	270
1961	Mike Souchak	276
1962	Billy Casper	275
1963	Doug Sanders	270
1964	*Julius Boros	277
1965	Sam Snead	273
1966	*Doug Sanders	276
1967	George Archer	267
1968	Billy Casper	267
1969	*Gene Littler	274
1970	Gary Player	271
1971	*Bud Allin	275
1972	*George Archer	272
1973	Chi Chi Rodriguez	267
1974	Bob Charles	270
1975	Tom Weiskopf	275
1976	Al Geiberger	268
1977	Danny Edwards	276
1978	Seve Ballesteros	282
1979	Raymond Floyd	282
1980	Craig Stadler	275
1981	*Larry Nelson	281
1982	Danny Edwards	285
1983	Lanny Wadkins	275
1984	Andy Bean	280
1985	Joey Sindelar	285
1986	Sandy Lyle	275
1987	Scott Simpson	282

K MART GREATER GREENSBORO OPEN
1988	*Sandy Lyle	271
1989	Ken Green	277
1990	Steve Elkington	282
1991	*Mark Brooks	275
1992	Davis Love III	272
1993	*Rocco Mediate	281

SHELL HOUSTON OPEN

Moved annually (1946-50, 1972-74). Memorial Park GC, Houston (1951-63). Sharpstown CC, Houston (1964-65). Champions GC, Houston (1966-71). Woodlands CC, The Woodlands, Texas (1975-84). TPC at The Woodlands, The Woodlands, Texas (1985-93).

TOURNAMENT OF CHAMPIONS
1946	Byron Nelson	274
1947	Bobby Locke	277
1948	No Tournament	
1949	John Palmer	272

KEY * = Playoff # = Amateur @ = Rain-curtailed

HOUSTON OPEN
Year	Winner	Score
1950	Cary Middlecoff	277
1951	Marty Furgol	277
1952	Jack Burke, Jr.	277
1953	*Cary Middlecoff	283
1954	Dave Douglas	277
1955	Mike Souchak	273
1956	Ted Kroll	277
1957	Arnold Palmer	279
1958	Ed Oliver	281

HOUSTON CLASSIC
Year	Winner	Score
1959	*Jack Burke, Jr.	277
1960	*Bill Collins	280
1961	*Jay Hebert	276
1962	*Bobby Nichols	278
1963	Bob Charles	268
1964	Mike Souchak	278
1965	Bobby Nichols	273

HOUSTON CHAMPION INTERNATIONAL
Year	Winner	Score
1966	Arnold Palmer	275
1967	Frank Beard	274
1968	Roberto De Vicenzo	274
1969	Hosted U.S. Open	
1970	*Gibby Gilbert	282
1971	*Hubert Green	280

HOUSTON OPEN
Year	Winner	Score
1972	Bruce Devlin	278
1973	Bruce Crampton	277
1974	Dave Hill	276
1975	Bruce Crampton	273
1976	Lee Elder	278
1977	Gene Littler	276
1978	Gary Player	270
1979	Wayne Levi	268

MICHELOB HOUSTON OPEN
Year	Winner	Score
1980	*Curtis Strange	266
1981	@Ron Streck	198
1982	*Ed Sneed	275

HOUSTON COCA-COLA OPEN
Year	Winner	Score
1983	David Graham	275
1984	Corey Pavin	274

HOUSTON OPEN
Year	Winner	Score
1985	Raymond Floyd	277
1986	*Curtis Strange	274

BIG I HOUSTON OPEN
Year	Winner	Score
1987	*Jay Haas	276

INDEPENDENT INSURANCE AGENT OPEN
Year	Winner	Score
1988	*Curtis Strange	270
1989	Mike Sullivan	280
1990	@*Tony Sills	204
1991	Fulton Allem	273

SHELL HOUSTON OPEN
Year	Winner	Score
1992	Fred Funk	272
1993	*Jim McGovern	199

BELLSOUTH CLASSIC

Atlanta CC, Marietta, Ga.

ATLANTA CLASSIC
Year	Winner	Score
1967	Bob Charles	282
1968	Bob Lunn	280
1969	*Bert Yancey	277
1970	Tommy Aaron	275
1971	*Gardner Dickinson	275
1972	Bob Lunn	275
1973	Jack Nicklaus	272
1974	Hosted TPC	
1975	Hale Irwin	271
1976	Hosted U.S. Open	
1977	Hale Irwin	273
1978	Jerry Heard	269
1979	Andy Bean	265
1980	Larry Nelson	270
1981	*Tom Watson	277

GEORGIA-PACIFIC ATLANTA GOLF CLASSIC
Year	Winner	Score
1982	*Keith Fergus	273
1983	@*Calvin Peete	206
1984	Tom Kite	269
1985	*Wayne Levi	273
1986	Bob Tway	269
1987	Dave Barr	265
1988	Larry Nelson	268

BELLSOUTH ATLANTA GOLF CLASSIC
Year	Winner	Score
1989	*Scott Simpson	278
1990	Wayne Levi	275
1991	*Corey Pavin	272

BELLSOUTH CLASSIC
Year	Winner	Score
1992	Tom Kite	272
1993	Nolan Henke	271

GTE BYRON NELSON CLASSIC

Oak Cliffs CC, Dallas (1958-67). Preston Trail Golf Club, Dallas (1968-82). Las Colinas Sports Club, Irving, Texas (1983-85). TPC at Las Colinas, Irving, Texas (1986-93).

DALLAS OPEN
Year	Winner	Score
1944	Byron Nelson	276
1945	Sam Snead	276
1946	Ben Hogan	284
1947-1955	No Tournaments	
1956	Don January	268
1956A	*Peter Thomson	267
1957	Sam Snead	264
1958	*Sam Snead	272
1959	Julius Boros	274
1960	*Johnny Pott	275
1961	Earl Stewart, Jr.	278
1962	Billy Maxwell	277
1963	No Tournament	
1964	Charles Coody	271
1965	No Tournament	
1966	Roberto De Vicenzo	276
1967	Bert Yancey	274

BYRON NELSON GOLF CLASSIC
Year	Winner	Score
1968	Miller Barber	270
1969	Bruce Devlin	277
1970	*Jack Nicklaus	274
1971	Jack Nicklaus	274
1972	*Chi Chi Rodriquez	273
1973	*Lanny Wadkins	277
1974	Brian Allin	269
1975	Tom Watson	269
1976	Mark Hayes	273
1977	Raymond Floyd	276
1978	Tom Watson	272
1979	*Tom Watson	275
1980	Tom Watson	274
1981	*Bruce Lietzke	281
1982	Bob Gilder	266
1983	Ben Crenshaw	273
1984	Craig Stadler	276
1985	*Bob Eastwood	272
1986	Andy Bean	269
1987	*Fred Couples	266

GTE BYRON NELSON GOLF CLASSIC
Year	Winner	Score
1988	*Bruce Lietzke	271
1989	*Jodie Mudd	265
1990	@Payne Stewart	202
1991	Nick Price	270
1992	@*Billy Ray Brown	199
1993	Scott Simpson	270

KEMPER OPEN

Pleasant Valley CC, Sutton, Mass. (1968). Quail Hollow CC, Charlotte, N.C. (1969-79). Congressional CC, Bethesda, Md. (1980-86). TPC at Avenel, Potomac, Md. (1987-93).

KEMPER OPEN
Year	Winner	Score
1968	Arnold Palmer	276
1969	Dale Douglass	274
1970	Dick Lotz	278
1971	*Tom Weiskopf	277
1972	Doug Sanders	275
1973	Tom Weiskopf	271
1974	*Bob Menne	270
1975	Raymond Floyd	278
1976	Joe Inman	277
1977	Tom Weiskopf	277
1978	Andy Bean	273
1979	Jerry McGee	272
1980	John Mahaffey	275
1981	Craig Stadler	270
1982	Craig Stadler	275
1983	*Fred Couples	287
1984	Greg Norman	280
1985	Bill Glasson	278
1986	*Greg Norman	277
1987	Tom Kite	270
1988	*Morris Hatalsky	274
1989	Tom Byrum	268

1990	Gil Morgan	274
1991	*Billy Andrade	263
1992	Bill Glasson	276
1993	Grant Waite	275

SOUTHWESTERN BELL COLONIAL

Colonial CC, Fort Worth.

COLONIAL NATIONAL INVITATION TOURNAMENT

1946	Ben Hogan	279
1947	Ben Hogan	279
1948	Clayton Heafner	272
1949	No Tournament	
1950	Sam Snead	277
1951	Cary Middlecoff	282
1952	Ben Hogan	279
1953	Ben Hogan	282
1954	Johnny Palmer	280
1955	Chandler Harper	276
1956	Mike Souchak	280
1957	Roberto De Vicenzo	284
1958	Tommy Bolt	282
1959	*Ben Hogan	285
1960	Julius Boros	280
1961	Doug Sanders	281
1962	*Arnold Palmer	281
1963	Julius Boros	279
1964	Billy Casper	279
1965	Bruce Crampton	276
1966	Bruce Devlin	280
1967	Dave Stockton	278
1968	Billy Casper	275
1969	Gardner Dickinson	278
1970	Homero Blancas	273
1971	Gene Littler	283
1972	Jerry Heard	275
1973	Tom Weiskopf	276
1974	Rod Curl	276
1975	Hosted TPC	
1976	Lee Trevino	273
1977	Ben Crenshaw	272
1978	Lee Trevino	268
1979	Al Geiberger	274
1980	Bruce Lietzke	271
1981	Fuzzy Zoeller	274
1982	Jack Nicklaus	273
1983	*Jim Colbert	278
1984	*Peter Jacobsen	270
1985	Corey Pavin	266
1986	@*Dan Pohl	205
1987	Keith Clearwater	266
1988	Lanny Wadkins	270

SOUTHWESTERN BELL COLONIAL

1989	Ian Baker-Finch	270
1990	Ben Crenshaw	272
1991	Tom Purtzer	267
1992	*Bruce Lietzke	267
1993	Fulton Allem	264

THE MEMORIAL TOURNAMENT

Muirfield Village GC, Dublin, Ohio.

THE MEMORIAL TOURNAMENT

1976	*Roger Maltbie	288
1977	Jack Nicklaus	281
1978	Jim Simons	284
1979	Tom Watson	285
1980	David Graham	280
1981	Keith Fergus	284
1982	Raymond Floyd	281
1983	Hale Irwin	281
1984	*Jack Nicklaus	280
1985	Hale Irwin	281
1986	Hal Sutton	271
1987	Don Pooley	272
1988	Curtis Strange	274
1989	Bob Tway	277
1990	@Greg Norman	216
1991	*Kenny Perry	273
1992	*David Edwards	273
1993	Paul Azinger	274

BUICK CLASSIC

Westchester CC, Harrison, N.Y.

WESTCHESTER CLASSIC

1967	Jack Nicklaus	272
1968	Julius Boros	272
1969	Frank Beard	275
1970	Bruce Crampton	273
1971	Arnold Palmer	270
1972	Jack Nicklaus	270
1973	*Bobby Nichols	272
1974	Johnny Miller	269
1975	*Gene Littler	271

AMERICAN EXPRESS WESTCHESTER CLASSIC

1976	David Graham	272
1977	Andy North	272
1978	Lee Elder	274

MANUFACTURERS HANOVER WESTCHESTER CLASSIC

1979	Jack Renner	277
1980	Curtis Strange	273
1981	Raymond Floyd	275
1982	Bob Gilder	261
1983	Seve Ballesteros	276
1984	Scott Simpson	269
1985	*Roger Maltbie	275
1986	Bob Tway	272
1987	*J.C. Snead	276
1988	*Seve Ballesteros	276
1989	*Wayne Grady	277

BUICK CLASSIC

1990	Hale Irwin	269
1991	Billy Andrade	273
1992	David Frost	268
1993	Vijay Singh	280

CANON GREATER HARTFORD OPEN

Wethersfield CC, Hartford, Conn. (1952-83). TPC of Connecticut, Cromwell, Conn. (1984-90). TPC at River Highlands, Cromwell, Conn. (1991-93).

INSURANCE CITY OPEN

1952	Ted Kroll	273
1953	Bob Toski	269
1954	*Tommy Bolt	271
1955	Sam Snead	269
1956	*Arnold Palmer	274
1957	Gardner Dickinson	272
1958	Jack Burke, Jr.	268
1959	Gene Littler	272
1960	*Arnold Palmer	270
1961	*Billy Maxwell	271
1962	*Bob Goalby	271
1963	Billy Casper	271
1964	Ken Venturi	273
1965	*Billy Casper	274
1966	Art Wall	266

GREATER HARTFORD OPEN INVITATIONAL

1967	Charlie Sifford	272
1968	Billy Casper	266
1969	*Bob Lunn	268
1970	Bob Murphy	267
1971	*George Archer	268
1972	*Lee Trevino	269

SAMMY DAVIS JR. GREATER HARTFORD OPEN

1973	Billy Casper	264
1974	Dave Stockton	268
1975	*Don Bies	267
1976	Rik Massengale	266
1977	Bill Kratzert	265
1978	Rod Funseth	264
1979	Jerry McGee	267
1980	*Howard Twitty	266
1981	Hubert Green	264
1982	Tim Norris	259
1983	Curtis Strange	268
1984	Peter Jacobsen	269
1985	*Phil Blackmar	271

CANON SAMMY DAVIS JR. GREATER HARTFORD OPEN

1986	*Mac O'Grady	269
1987	Paul Azinger	269
1988	*Mark Brooks	269

CANON GREATER HARTFORD OPEN

1989	Paul Azinger	267
1990	Wayne Levi	267
1991	*Billy Ray Brown	271

*KEY * = Playoff # = Amateur @ = Rain-curtailed. A = Second tournament that year.*

1992	Lanny Wadkins	274
1993	Nick Price	271

SPRINT WESTERN OPEN

Moved annually (1899-1973). Butler National GC, Oak Brook, Ill. (1974-90). Cog Hill CC (Dubsdread), Lemont, Ill. (1991-93).

WESTERN OPEN

Year	Winner	Score
1899	*Willie Smith	156
1900	No Tournament	
1901	Laurie Auchterlonie	160
1902	Willie Anderson	299
1903	Alex Smith	318
1904	Willie Anderson	304
1905	Arthur Smith	278
1906	Alex Smith	306
1907	Robert Simpson	307
1908	Willie Anderson	299
1909	Willie Anderson	288
1910	#Chick Evans, Jr.	6&5
1911	Robert Simpson	2&1
1912	Mac Smith	299
1913	John McDermott	295
1914	Jim Barnes	293
1915	Tom McNamara	304
1916	Walter Hagen	286
1917	Jim Barnes	283
1918	No Tournament	
1919	Jim Barnes	283
1920	Jock Hutchinson	296
1921	Walter Hagen	287
1922	Mike Brady	291
1923	Jock Hutchinson	281
1924	Bill Mehlhorn	293
1925	Mac Smith	281
1926	Walter Hagen	279
1927	Walter Hagen	281
1928	Abe Espinosa	291
1929	Tommy Armour	273
1930	Gene Sarazen	278
1931	Ed Dudley	280
1932	Walter Hagen	287
1933	Mac Smith	282
1934	*Harry Cooper	274
1935	John Revolta	290
1936	Ralph Guldahl	274
1937	*Ralph Guldahl	288
1938	Ralph Guldahl	279
1939	Byron Nelson	281
1940	*Jimmy Demaret	293
1941	Ed Oliver	275
1942	Herman Barron	276
1943-1945	No Tournaments	
1946	Ben Hogan	271
1947	Johnny Palmer	270
1948	*Ben Hogan	281
1949	Sam Snead	268
1950	Sam Snead	282
1951	Marty Furgol	270
1952	Lloyd Mangrum	274
1953	Dutch Harrison	278
1954	*Lloyd Mangrum	277
1955	Cary Middlecoff	272
1956	*Mike Fetchick	284
1957	*Doug Ford	279
1958	Doug Sanders	275
1959	Mike Souchak	272
1960	*Stan Leonard	278
1961	Arnold Palmer	271
1962	Jacky Cupit	281
1963	*Arnold Palmer	280
1964	Chi Chi Rodriguez	268
1965	Billy Casper	270
1966	Billy Casper	283
1967	Jack Nicklaus	274
1968	Jack Nicklaus	273
1969	Billy Casper	276
1970	Hugh Royer	273
1971	Bruce Crampton	279
1972	Jim Jamieson	271
1973	Billy Casper	272
1974	Tom Watson	287
1975	Hale Irwin	283
1976	Al Geiberger	288
1977	Tom Watson	283
1978	*Andy Bean	282
1979	*Larry Nelson	286
1980	Scott Simpson	281
1981	Ed Fiori	277
1982	Tom Weiskopf	276
1983	Mark McCumber	284
1984	*Tom Watson	280
1985	#Scott Verplank	279
1986	*Tom Kite	286

BEATRICE WESTERN OPEN

1987	@D. A. Weibring	207
1989	*Mark McCumber	275

CENTEL WESTERN OPEN

1990	Wayne Levi	275
1991	Russ Cochran	275
1992	Ben Crenshaw	276

SPRINT WESTERN OPEN

1993	Nick Price	269

ANHEUSER-BUSCH GOLF CLASSIC

Silverado CC, Napa, Calif. (1968-80). Kingsmill GC, Kingsmill, Va. (1981-93).

KAISER INTERNATIONAL OPEN INVITATIONAL

1968	Kermit Zarley	273
1969	@Miller Barber	135
1969+	*Jack Nicklaus	273
1970	*Ken Still	278
1971	Billy Casper	269
1972	George Knudson	271
1973	*Ed Sneed	275
1974	Johnny Miller	271
1975	Johnny Miller	272
1976	J. C. Snead	274

ANHEUSER-BUSCH GOLF CLASSIC

1977	Miller Barber	272
1978	Tom Watson	270
1979	John Fought	277
1980	Ben Crenshaw	272
1981	John Mahaffey	276
1982	@Calvin Peete	203
1983	Calvin Peete	276
1984	Ronnie Black	267
1985	*Mark Wiebe	273
1986	Fuzzy Zoeller	274
1987	Mark McCumber	267
1988	*Tom Sieckmann	270
1989	*Mike Donald	268
1990	Lanny Wadkins	266
1991	*Mike Hulbert	266
1992	David Peoples	271
1993	Jim Gallagher	269

NEW ENGLAND CLASSIC

Pleasant Valley CC, Sutton, Mass.

CARLING WORLD OPEN

1965	Tony Lema	279

KEMPER OPEN

1968	Arnold Palmer	276

AVCO GOLF CLASSIC

1969	Tom Shaw	280
1970	Billy Casper	277

MASSACHUSETTS CLASSIC

1971	Dave Stockton	275

USI CLASSIC

1972	Bruce Devlin	275
1973	Lanny Wadkins	279

PLEASANT VALLEY CLASSIC

1974	Victor Regalado	278
1975	Roger Maltbie	276
1976	Bud Allin	277
1977	Raymond Floyd	271

AMERICAN OPTICAL CLASSIC

1978	John Mahaffey	270
1979	Lou Graham	275

PLEASANT VALLEY JIMMY FUND CLASSIC

1980	*Wayne Levi	273
1981	Jack Renner	273

BANK OF BOSTON CLASSIC

1982	Bob Gilder	271
1983	Mark Lye	273
1984	George Archer	270
1985	George Burns	267
1986	*Gene Sauers	274
1987	@Sam Randolph	199
1988	Mark Calcavecchia	274
1989	Blaine McCallister	271
1990	Morris Hatalsky	275

NEW ENGLAND CLASSIC

1991	*Bruce Fleisher	268

| 1992 | Brad Faxon | 268 |
| 1993 | Paul Azinger | 268 |

FEDERAL EXPRESS ST. JUDE CLASSIC

Colonial CC, Memphis. (1958-71). Colonial CC, Cordova, Tenn. (1972-88). TPC at Southwind, Germantown, Tenn. (1989-93).

MEMPHIS INVITATIONAL OPEN
1958	Billy Maxwell	267
1959	*Don Whitt	272
1960	*Tommy Bolt	273
1961	Cary Middlecoff	266
1962	*Lionel Hebert	267
1963	*Tony Lema	270
1964	Mike Souchak	270
1965	*Jack Nicklaus	271
1966	Bert Yancey	265
1967	Dave Hill	272
1968	Bob Lunn	268
1969	Dave Hill	265

DANNY THOMAS MEMPHIS CLASSIC
1970	Dave Hill	267
1971	Lee Trevino	268
1972	Lee Trevino	281
1973	Dave Hill	283
1974	Gary Player	273
1975	Gene Littler	270
1976	Gibby Gilbert	273
1977	Al Geiberger	273
1978	*Andy Bean	277
1979	*Gil Morgan	278
1980	Lee Trevino	272
1981	Jerry Pate	274
1982	Raymond Floyd	271
1983	Larry Mize	274
1984	Bob Eastwood	280

ST. JUDE MEMPHIS CLASSIC
| 1985 | *Hal Sutton | 279 |

FEDERAL EXPRESS ST. JUDE CLASSIC
1986	Mike Hulbert	280
1987	Curtis Strange	275
1988	Jodie Mudd	273
1989	John Mahaffey	272
1990	*Tom Kite	269
1991	Fred Couples	269
1992	Jay Haas	263
1993	Nick Price	266

BUICK OPEN

Warwick Hills CC, Grand Blanc, Mich. (1958-69, 1978-93). Flint Elks CC, Flint, Mich. (1972, 1974-77). Benton Harbor Elks CC, Benton Harbor, Mich. (1973).

BUICK OPEN INVITATIONAL
1958	Billy Casper	285
1959	Art Wall	282
1960	Mike Souchak	282
1961	Jack Burke, Jr.	284
1962	Bill Collins	284
1963	Julius Boros	274
1964	Tony Lema	277
1965	Tony Lema	280
1966	Phil Rodgers	284
1967	Julius Boros	283
1968	Tom Weiskopf	280
1969	Dave Hill	277

VERN PARSELL BUICK OPEN
| 1972 | Gary Groh | 273 |

LAKE MICHIGAN CLASSIC
| 1973 | (2T) Wilf Homenuik | 215 |

FLINT ELKS OPEN
1974	(2T) Bryan Abbott	135
1975	(2T) Spike Kelley	208
1976	(2T) Ed Sabo	279
1977	Bobby Cole	271

BUICK GOODWRENCH OPEN
1978	*Jack Newton	280
1979	*John Fought	280
1980	Peter Jacobsen	276

BUICK OPEN
1981	*Hale Irwin	277
1982	Lanny Wadkins	273
1983	Wayne Levi	272
1984	Denis Watson	271
1985	Ken Green	268
1986	Ben Crenshaw	270
1987	Robert Wrenn	262
1988	Scott Verplank	268
1989	Leonard Thompson	273
1990	Chip Beck	272
1991	*Brad Faxon	271
1992	*Dan Forsman	276
1993	Larry Mize	272

THE INTERNATIONAL

Castle Pines GC, Castle Rock, Colo.

1986	Ken Green	Plus 12
1987	John Cook	Plus 11
1988	Joey Sindelar	Plus 17
1989	Greg Norman	Plus 13
1990	Davis Love III	Plus 14
1991	Jose M. Olazabal	Plus 10
1992	Brad Faxon	Plus 14
1993	Phil Mickelson	45

GREATER MILWAUKEE OPEN

Northshore CC, Mequon, Wis. (1968-70). Tripoli GC, Milwaukee (1971-72). Tuckaway CC, Franklin, Wis. (1973-93).

GREATER MILWAUKEE OPEN
1968	Dave Stockton	275
1969	Ken Still	277
1970	Deane Beman	276
1971	Dave Eichelberger	270
1972	Jim Colbert	271
1973	Dave Stockton	276
1974	Ed Sneed	276
1975	Art Wall	271
1976	Dave Hill	270
1977	Dave Eichelberger	278
1978	*Lee Elder	275
1979	Calvin Peete	269
1980	Bill Kratzert	266
1981	Jay Haas	274
1982	Calvin Peete	274
1983	*Morris Hatalsky	275
1984	Mark O'Meara	272
1985	Jim Thorpe	274
1986	*Corey Pavin	272
1987	Gary Hallberg	269
1988	Ken Green	268
1989	Greg Norman	269
1990	*Jim Gallagher, Jr.	271
1991	Mark Brooks	270
1992	Richard Zokol	269
1993	Billy Mayfair	270

CANADIAN OPEN

Moved annually (1904-76). Glen Abbey GC, Oakville, Ontario (1977-79, 1981-93).

1904	J. H. Oke	156
1905	George Cumming	148
1906	Charles Murray	170
1907	Percy Barrett	306
1908	Albert Murray	300
1909	Karl Keller	309
1910	Daniel Kenny	303
1911	Charles Murray	314
1912	George Sargent	299
1913	Albert Murray	295
1914	Karl Keller	300
1915-1918	No Tournaments	
1919	J. Douglas Edgar	278
1920	*J. Douglas Edgar	298
1921	W. H. Trovinger	293
1922	Al Watrous	303
1923	C. W. Hackney	295
1924	Leo Diegel	285
1925	Leo Diegel	295
1926	Mac Smith	283
1927	Tommy Armour	288
1928	Leo Diegel	282
1929	Leo Diegel	274
1930	*Tommy Armour	273
1931	*Walter Hagen	292
1932	Harry Cooper	290

*KEY * = Playoff # = Amateur @ = Rain-curtailed + = Second tournament that year 2T = Second Tour*

Year	Winner	Score
1933	Joe Kirkwood	282
1934	Tommy Armour	287
1935	Gene Kunes	280
1936	Lawson Little	271
1937	Harry Cooper	285
1938	*Sam Snead	277
1939	Harold McSpaden	282
1940	*Sam Snead	281
1941	Sam Snead	274
1942	Craig Wood	275
1943-1944	No Tournaments	
1945	Byron Nelson	280
1946	*George Fazio	278
1947	Bobby Locke	268
1948	C. W. Congdon	280
1949	Dutch Harrison	271
1950	Jim Ferrier	271
1951	Jim Ferrier	273
1952	John Palmer	263
1953	Dave Douglas	273
1954	Pat Fletcher	280
1955	Arnold Palmer	265
1956	#Doug Sanders	273
1957	George Bayer	271
1958	Wesley Ellis, Jr.	267
1959	Doug Ford	276
1960	Art Wall, Jr.	269
1961	Jacky Cupit	270
1962	Ted Kroll	278
1963	Doug Ford	280
1964	Kel Nagle	277
1965	Gene Littler	273
1966	Don Massengale	280
1967	*Billy Casper	279
1968	Bob Charles	274
1969	*Tommy Aaron	275
1970	Kermit Zarley	279
1971	*Lee Trevino	275
1972	Gay Brewer	275
1973	Tom Weiskopf	278
1974	Bobby Nichols	270
1975	*Tom Weiskopf	274
1976	Jerry Pate	267
1977	Lee Trevino	280
1978	Bruce Lietzke	283
1979	Lee Trevino	281
1980	Bob Gilder	274
1981	Peter Oosterhuis	280
1982	Bruce Lietzke	277
1983	*John Cook	277
1984	Greg Norman	278
1985	Curtis Strange	279
1986	Bob Murphy	280
1987	Curtis Strange	276
1988	Ken Green	275
1989	Steve Jones	271
1990	Wayne Levi	278
1991	Nick Price	273
1992	*Greg Norman	280
1993	David Frost	279

HARDEE'S GOLF CLASSIC

Crow Valley CC, Bettendorf, Iowa (1972-74). Oakwood CC, Coal Valley, Ill. (1975-93).

QUAD CITIES OPEN
Year	Winner	Score
1972	Deane Beman	279
1973	Sam Adams	268
1974	Dave Stockton	271

ED MCMAHON-JAYCEES QUAD CITY OPEN
Year	Winner	Score
1975	Roger Maltbie	275
1976	John Lister	268
1977	Mike Morley	267
1978	Victor Regalado	269
1979	D. A. Weibring	266

QUAD CITIES OPEN
Year	Winner	Score
1980	Scott Hoch	266
1981	*Dave Barr	270

MILLER HIGH-LIFE QUAD CITIES OPEN
Year	Winner	Score
1982	Payne Stewart	268
1983	*Danny Edwards	266
1984	Scoff Hoch	266

LITE QUAD CITIES OPEN
Year	Winner	Score
1985	Dan Forsman	267

HARDEE'S GOLF CLASSIC
Year	Winner	Score
1986	Mark Wiebe	268
1987	Kenny Knox	265
1988	Blaine McCallister	261
1989	Curt Byrum	268
1990	*Joey Sindelar	268
1991	D. A. Weibring	267
1992	David Frost	266
1993	David Frost	259

B. C. OPEN

En Joie GC, Endicott, N.Y.

BROOME COUNTY OPEN
Year	Winner	Score
1971	*Claude Harmon, Jr.	69

B. C. OPEN
Year	Winner	Score
1972	Bob Payne	136
1973	Hubert Green	266
1974	*Richie Karl	273
1975	Don Iverson	274
1976	Bob Wynn	271
1977	Gil Morgan	270
1978	Tom Kite	267
1979	Howard Twitty	270
1980	Don Pooley	271
1981	Jay Haas	270
1982	Calvin Peete	265
1983	Pat Lindsey	268
1984	Wayne Levi	275
1985	Joey Sindelar	274
1986	Rick Fehr	267
1987	Joey Sindelar	266
1988	Bill Glasson	268
1989	*Mike Hulbert	268
1990	Nolan Henke	268
1991	Fred Couples	269
1992	John Daly	266
1993	Blaine McCallister	271

BUICK SOUTHERN OPEN

Green Island CC, Columbus, Ga. (1970-90). Callaway Gardens Resort, Pine Mountain, Ga. (1991-93).

GREEN ISLAND OPEN INVITATIONAL
Year	Winner	Score
1970	Mason Rudolph	274

SOUTHERN OPEN INVITATIONAL
Year	Winner	Score
1971	Johnny Miller	267
1972	*DeWitt Weaver	276
1973	Gary Player	270
1974	Forrest Fezler	271
1975	Hubert Green	264
1976	Mac McClendon	274
1977	Jerry Pate	266
1978	Jerry Pate	269
1979	*Ed Fiori	274
1980	Mike Sullivan	269
1981	*J. C. Snead	271
1982	Bobby Clampett	266
1983	*Ronnie Black	271
1984	Hubert Green	265
1985	Tim Simpson	264
1986	Fred Wadsworth	269
1987	Ken Brown	266
1988	*David Frost	270
1989	Ted Schulz	266

BUICK SOUTHERN OPEN
Year	Winner	Score
1990	*Kenny Knox	265
1991	David Peoples	276
1992	@Gary Hallberg	206
1993	*John Inman	278

LAS VEGAS INVITATIONAL

Rotates among Las Vegas CC, Las Vegas; Desert Inn CC, Las Vegas; Dunes CC, Las Vegas; Showboat CC, Las Vegas; and (from 1992-1993) TPC at Summerlin, Las Vegas.

PANASONIC LAS VEGAS PRO-CELEBRITY CLASSIC
Year	Winner	Score
1983	Fuzzy Zoeller	340

PANASONIC LAS VEGAS INVITATIONAL
Year	Winner	Score
1984	Denis Watson	341
1985	Curtis Strange	338
1986	Greg Norman	333
1987	@Paul Azinger	271
1988	@Gary Koch	274

LAS VEGAS INVITATIONAL

1989	*Scott Hoch	336
1990	*Bob Tway	334
1991	*Andrew Magee	329
1992	John Cook	334
1993	John Inman	331

WALT DISNEY WORLD/OLDSMOBILE CLASSIC

Rotates among Palm, Walt Disney World, Lake Buena Vista, Fla. Magnolia, Walt Disney World, Lake Buena Vista, Fla. Lake Buena Vista CC, Lake Buena Vista, Fla.

WALT DISNEY WORLD OPEN INVITATIONAL

1971	Jack Nicklaus	273
1972	Jack Nicklaus	267
1973	Jack Nicklaus	275

WALT DISNEY WORLD NATIONAL TEAM CHAMPIONSHIP

1974	Hubert Green/ Mac McClendon	255
1975	Jim Colbert/ Dean Refram	252
1976	*Woody Blackburn/ Bill Kratzert	260
1977	Gibby Gilbert/ Grier Jones	253
1978	Wayne Levi/ Bob Mann	254
1979	George Burns/ Ben Crenshaw	255
1980	Danny Edwards/ Dave Edwards	253
1981	Vance Heafner/ Mike Holland	275

WALT DISNEY WORLD GOLF CLASSIC

1982	*Hal Sutton	269
1983	Payne Stewart	269
1984	Larry Nelson	266

WALT DISNEY WORLD OLDSMOBILE CLASSIC

1985	Lanny Wadkins	267
1986	*Ray Floyd	275
1987	Larry Nelson	268
1988	*Bob Lohr	263
1989	Tim Simpson	272
1990	Tim Simpson	264
1991	Mark O'Meara	267
1992	John Huston	262
1993	Jeff Maggert	265

H-E-B TEXAS OPEN

Rotated among several courses (1922-60, 1967-76). Oak Hills CC, San Antonio (1961-66, 1977-93).

TEXAS OPEN

1922	Bob MacDonald	281
1923	Walter Hagen	279
1924	Joe Kirkwood	279
1925	Joe Turnesa	284
1926	Mac Smith	288
1927	Bobby Cruikshank	272
1928	Bill Mehlhorn	297
1929	Bill Mehlhorn	277
1930	Denny Shute	277
1931	Abe Espinosa	281
1932	Clarence Clark	287
1933	*No Tournament*	
1934	Wiffy Cox	283
1935-1938	*No Tournaments*	
1939	Dutch Harrison	271
1940	Byron Nelson	271
1941	Lawson Little	273
1942	*Chick Harbert	272
1943	*No Tournament*	
1944	Johnny Revolta	273
1945	Sam Byrd	268
1946	Ben Hogan	264
1947	Ed Oliver	265
1948	Sam Snead	264
1949	Dave Douglas	268
1950	Sam Snead	265
1951	*Dutch Harrison	265
1952	Jack Burke, Jr.	260
1953	Tony Holguin	264
1954	Chandler Harper	259
1955	Mike Souchak	257
1956	Gene Littler	276
1957	Jay Hebert	271
1958	Bill Johnston	274
1959	Wes Ellis	276
1960	Arnold Palmer	276
1961	Arnold Palmer	270
1962	Arnold Palmer	273
1963	Phil Rodgers	268
1964	Bruce Crampton	273
1965	Frank Beard	270
1966	Harold Henning	272
1967	Chi Chi Rodriquez	277
1968	*No Tournament*	
1969	*Deane Beman	274

SAN ANTONIO TEXAS OPEN

1970	Ron Cerrudo	273
1971	*No Tournament*	
1972	Mike Hill	273
1973	Ben Crenshaw	270
1974	Terry Diehl	269
1975	*Don January	275
1976	*Butch Baird	273
1977	Hale Irwin	266
1978	Ron Streck	265
1979	Lou Graham	268
1980	Lee Trevino	265

TEXAS OPEN

1981	*Bill Rogers	266
1982	Jay Haas	262
1983	Jim Colbert	261
1984	Calvin Peete	266
1985	*John Mahaffey	268

VANTAGE CHAMPIONSHIP

1986	@Ben Crenshaw	196

NABISCO CHAMPIONSHIPS OF GOLF

1987	Tom Watson	268

TEXAS OPEN PRESENTED BY NABISCO

1988	Corey Pavin	259
1989	Donnie Hammond	258

H-E-B TEXAS OPEN

1990	Mark O'Meara	261
1991	*Blaine McCallister	269
1992	*Nick Price	263
1993	Jay Haas	269

THE TOUR CHAMPIONSHIP

Oak Hill CC, San Antonio (1986-87). Pebble Beach (Calif.) GL (1988). Harbour Town GL, Hilton Head, S.C. (1989). Champions GC, Houston, Texas (1990). Pinehurst No. 2, Pinehurst, N.C. (1991-92). The Olympic Club, San Francisco (1993).

VANTAGE CHAMPIONSHIP

1986	@Ben Crenshaw	196

NABISCO CHAMPIONSHIPS OF GOLF

1987	Tom Watson	268

NABISCO GOLF CHAMPIONSHIPS

1988	*Curtis Strange	279

NABISCO CHAMPIONSHIPS

1989	*Tom Kite	276
1990	*Jodie Mudd	273

THE TOUR CHAMPIONSHIP

1991	*Craig Stadler	279
1992	Paul Azinger	276
1993	Jim Gallagher	277

LINCOLN-MERCURY KAPALUA INTERNATIONAL

Bay Course, Kapalua GC, Kapalua, Maui, Hawaii (1983-90). Plantation Course, Kapalua GC, Kapalua, Maui, Hawaii (1991-93).

KEY * =Playoff # Amateur
@ = Rain-curtailed

KAPALUA INTERNATIONAL
1983	Greg Norman	268
1984	Sandy Lyle	266

ISUZU KAPALUA INTERNATIONAL
1985	Mark O'Meara	275
1986	Andy Bean	278
1987	Andy Bean	267
1988	Bob Gilder	266
1989	*Peter Jacobsen	270
1990	David Peoples	264

PING KAPALUA INTERNATIONAL
1991	*Mike Hulbert	276

LINCOLN-MERCURY KAPALUA INTERNATIONAL
1992	Davis Love III	275
1993	Fred Couples	

FRANKLIN FUNDS SHARK SHOOTOUT

Sherwood CC, Thousand Oaks, Calif.

RMCC INVITATIONAL
1989	Curtis Strange/ Mark O'Meara	190
1990	Ray Floyd/ Fred Couples	182

SHARK SHOOTOUT BENEFITING RMCC
1991	Tom Purtzer/ Lanny Wadkins	189

FRANKLIN FUNDS SHARK SHOOT OUT
1992	Davis Love III/ Tom Kite	191
1993	Steve Elkington/ Ray Floyd	188

SKINS GAME

Desert Highlands CC, Scottsdale, Ariz. (1983-84). Bear Creek CC, Murietta, Calif. (1985). TPC at PGA West, La Quinta, Calif. (1986-91). Bighorn GC, Palm Desert, Calif. (1992-93).

1983	Gary Player	$170,000
1984	Jack Nicklaus	$240,000
1985	Fuzzy Zoeller	$255,000
1986	Fuzzy Zoeller	$370,000
1987	Lee Trevino	$310,000
1988	Ray Floyd	$290,000
1989	Curtis Strange	$265,000
1990	Curtis Strange	$225,000
1991	Payne Stewart	$260,000
1992	Payne Stewart	$220,000
1993	Payne Stewart	$280,000

JCPENNEY CLASSIC

Rotated annually (1960-76). Bardmoor CC, Largo, Fla. (1977-89). Innisbrook Resort, Tarpon Springs, Fla. (1990-93).

HAIG & HAIG SCOTCH FOURSOME
1960	*Jim Turnesa Gloria Armstrong	+139
1961	Dave Ragan Mickey Wright	272
1962	Mason Rudolph Kathy Whitworth	272
1963	Dave Ragan Mickey Wright	273
1964	Sam Snead Shirley Englehorn	272
1965	Gardner Dickinson Ruth Jessen	281
1966	Jack Rule Sandra Spuzich	276

PEPSI-COLA MIXED TEAM
1976	Chi Chi Rodriguez JoAnn Washam	275
1977	Jerry Pate Hollis Stacy	270

JCPENNEY CLASSIC
1978	*Lon Hinkle Pat Bradley	267
1979	Dave Eichelberger Murle Breer	268
1980	Curtis Strange Nancy Lopez	268
1981	Tom Kite Beth Daniel	270
1982	John Mahaffey JoAnne Carner	268
1983	Fred Couples Jan Stephenson	264
1984	Mike Donald Vicki Alvarez	270
1985	Larry Rinker Laurie Rinker	267
1986	Tom Purtzer Juli Inkster	267
1987	Steve Jones Jane Crafter	268
1988	John Huston Amy Benz	269
1989	*Bill Glasson Pat Bradley	267
1990	Davis Love III Beth Daniel	266
1991	*Billy Andrade Kris Tschetter	266
1992	Dan Forsman Dottie Mochrie	264
1993	Mike Spring Melissa McNamara	265

MERRILL LYNCH SHOOT-OUT FINALS

Rotated annually (1987-93).
1987	Fuzzy Zoeller
1988	David Frost
1989	Chip Beck
1990	John Mahaffey
1991	Davis Love III
1992	Chip Beck
1993	Vijay Singh

NEC WORLD SERIES OF GOLF

Firestone Country Club, South Course, Akron, Ohio. (From 1962-1975, played as a four-man, 36 hole exhibition.)

1962	Jack Nicklaus (135)	
1963	Jack Nicklaus (140)	
1964	Tony Lema (138)	
1965	Gary Player (139)	
1966	Gene Littler (143)	
1967	Jack Nicklaus (144)	
1968	Gary Player (143)	
1969	Orville Moody (141)	
1970	Jack Nicklaus (136)	
1971	Charles Coody (141)	
1972	Gary Player (142)	
1973	Tom Weiskopf (137)	
1974	Lee Trevino (139)	
1975	Tom Watson (140)	
1976	Jack Nicklaus	275
1977	Lanny Wadkins	267
1978	*Gil Morgan	278
1979	Lon Hinkle	272
1980	Tom Watson	270
1981	Bill Rogers	275
1982	*Craig Stadler	278
1983	Nick Price	270
1984	Denis Watson	271
1985	Roger Maltbie	268
1986	Dan Pohl	277
1987	Curtis Strange	275
1988	*Mike Reid	275
1989	*David Frost	276
1990	Jose Maria Olazabal	262
1991	*Tom Purtzer	279
1992	Craig Stadler	273
1993	Fulton Allem	270

The Ryder Cup

Year	Venue	Dates	Winner	Score	Loser	Score
1927	Worcester Country Club, Worcester, Mass.	June 3-4	U.S.	9½	Britain	2½
1929	Moortown, England	May 26-27	Britain	7	U.S.	5
1931	Scioto Country Club, Columbus, Ohio	June 26-27	U.S.	9	Britain	3
1933	Southport & Ainsdale Courses, England	June 26-27	Britain	6½	U.S.	5½
1935	Ridgewood Country Club, Ridgewood, N.J.	Sept. 28-29	U S.	9	Britain	3
1937	Southport & Ainsdale Courses, England	June 29-30	U.S.	8	Britain	4
1938-1946	*Ryder Cup Matches not held during World War II.*					
1947	Portland Golf Club, Portland, Ore.	Nov. 1-2	U.S.	11	Britain	1
1949	Ganton Golf Course, Scarborough, England	Sept 16-17	U.S.	7	Britain	5
1951	Pinehurst Country Club, Pinehurst, N.C.	Nov. 2-4	U.S.	9½	Britain	2½
1953	Wentworth, England	Oct. 2-3	U.S.	6½	Britain	5½
1955	Thunderbird Ranch and CC, Palm Springs, Calif.	Nov. 5-6	U. S.	8	Britain	4
1957	Lindrick Golf Club, Yorkshire, England	Oct. 4-5	Britain	7½	U.S	4½
1959	Eldorado Country Club, Palm Desert, Calif.	Nov. 6-7	U.S.	8½	Britain	3½
1961	Royal Lytham and St. Anne's Golf Club, St. Anne's-On-The-Sea, England	Oct. 13-14	U.S.	14½	Britain	9½
1963	East Lake Country Club, Atlanta	Oct. 11-13	U.S.	23	Britain	9
1965	Royal Birkdale Golf Club, Southport, England	Oct. 7-9	U.S.	19½	Britain	12½
1967	Champions Golf Club, Houston	Oct. 20-22	U.S.	23½	Britain	8½
1969	Royal Birkdale Golf Club, Southport, England	Sept. 18-20	U.S.	16 Tie	Britain	16
1971	Old Warson Country Club, St. Louis	Sept. 16-18	U.S.	18½	Britain	13½
1973	Muirfield, Scotland	Sept. 20-22	U.S.	19	Britain	13
1975	Laurel Valley Golf Club, Ligonier, Pa.	Sept. 19-21	U.S.	21	Britain	11
1977	Royal Lytham and St. Anne's Golf Club, St. Anne's-On-The-Sea, England	Sept. 15-17	U.S	12½	Britain	7½
1979	Greenbrier, White Sulphur Springs, W.Va.	Sept. 13-15	U.S.	17	Europe	11
1981	Walton Heath Golf Club, Surrey, England	Sept. 18-20	U.S.	18½	Europe	9½
1983	PGA National GC, Palm Beach Gardens, Fla.	Oct. 14-16	U.S.	14½	Europe	13½
1985	The Belfry GC Sutton, Coldfield, England	Sept. 13-15	Europe	16½	U.S.	11½
1987	Muirfield Village Golf Club, Dublin, Ohio	Sept. 24-27	Europe	15	U.S.	13
1989	The Belfry GC, Sutton Coldfield, England	Sept. 22-24	U.S.	14 Tie	Europe	14
1991	The Ocean Course, Kiawah Island, S.C.	Sept. 26-29	U.S.	14½	Europe	13½
1993	The Belfry GC, Sutton Coldfield, England	Sept. 24-26	U.S.	15	Europe	13

RECAPITULATION: 29 Events, U.S. 22 wins-Europe 5 wins-Ties 2.

MAJOR U.S. AMATEUR EVENTS

NCAA CHAMPIONS

- 1949 Harvie Ward, North Carolina
- 1950 Fred Wampler, Purdue
- 1951 Tom Nieporte, Ohio State
- 1952 Jim Vickers, Oklahoma
- 1953 Earl Moeller, Okla. State
- 1954 Hillman Robbins, Memphis State
- 1955 Joe Campbell, Purdue
- 1956 Rick Jones, Ohio State
- 1957 Rex Baxter Jr. Houston
- 1958 Phil Rodgers, Houston
- 1959 Dick Crawford, Houston
- 1960 Dick Crawford, Houston
- 1961 Jack Nicklaus, Ohio State
- 1962 Kermit Zarley, Houston
- 1963 R.H. Sikes, Arkansas
- 1964 Terry Small, San Jose State
- 1965 Marty Fleckman, Houston
- 1966 Bob Murphy, Florida
- 1967 Hale Irwin, Colorado
- 1968 Grier Jones, Okla. State
- 1969 Bob Clark, Los Angeles State
- 1970 John Mahaffey, Houston
- 1971 Ben Crenshaw, Texas
- 1972 Ben Crenshaw, Texas
  Tom Kite, Texas
- 1973 Ben Crenshaw, Texas
- 1974 Curtis Strange, Wake Forest
- 1975 Jay Haas, Wake Forest
- 1976 Scott Simpson, Southern California
- 1977 Scott Simpson, Southern California
- 1978 David Edwards, Okla. State
- 1979 Gary Hallberg, Wake Forest
- 1980 Jay Don Blake, Utah State
- 1981 Ron Commans, Southern California
- 1982 Billy Ray Brown, Houston
- 1983 Jim Carter, Arizona State
- 1984 John Inman, North Carolina
- 1985 Clark Burroughs, Ohio State
- 1986 Scott Verplank, Okla. State
- 1987 Brian Watts, Okla. State
- 1988 E.J. Pfister, Oklahoma State
- 1989 Phil Mickelson, Arizona State
- 1990 Phil Mickelson, Arizona State
- 1991 Warren Schutte, Nevada-Las Vegas
- 1992 Phil Mickelson, Arizona State
- 1993 Todd Demsey, Arizona State

U.S. AMATEUR CHAMPIONS

- 1949 Charles R. Coe
- 1950 Sam Urzetta
- 1951 Billy Maxwell
- 1952 Jack Westland
- 1953 Gene A. Littler
- 1954 Arnold Palmer
- 1955 E. Harvie Ward, Jr.
- 1956 E. Harvie Ward, Jr.
- 1957 Hillman Robbins, Jr
- 1958 Charles R. Goe
- 1959 Jack W. Nicklaus
- 1960 Deane R. Beman
- 1961 Jack W. Nicklaus
- 1962 Labron E. Harris Jr.
- 1963 Deane R. Beman
- 1964 William C. Campbell

STROKE PLAY

- 1965 Robert J. Murphy 291
- 1966 Gary Cowan 285
- 1967 Robert B. Dickson 285
- 1968 Bruce Fleisher 284
- 1969 Steven N. Melnyk 286
- 1970 Lanny Wadkins 279
- 1971 Gary Cowan 280
- 1972 Vinny Giles 285

MATCH PLAY

- 1973 Craig Stadler
- 1974 Jerry Pate
- 1975 Fred Ridley
- 1976 Bill Sander
- 1977 John Fought
- 1978 John Cook
- 1979 Mark O'Meara
- 1980 Hal Sutton
- 1981 Nathaniel Crosby
- 1982 Jay Sigel
- 1983 Jay Sigel
- 1984 Scott Verplank
- 1985 Sam Randolph
- 1986 Buddy Alexander
- 1987 Bill Mayfair
- 1988 Eric Meeks
- 1989 Chris Patton
- 1990 Phil Mickelson
- 1991 Mitch Voges
- 1992 Justin Leonard
- 1993 John Harris

U.S. PUBLIC LINKS CHAMPIONS

- 1949 Kenneth J. Towns
- 1950 Stanley Bielat
- 1951 Dave Stanley
- 1952 Omer L. Bogan
- 1953 Ted Richards, Jr.
- 1954 Gene Andrews
- 1955 Sam D. Kocsis
- 1956 James H. Buxbaum
- 1957 Don Essig, III
- 1958 Daniel D. Sikes, Jr.
- 1959 William A. Wright
- 1960 Verne Callison
- 1961 Richard H. Sikes
- 1962 Richard H. Sikes
- 1963 Robert Lunn
- 1964 William McDonald
- 1965 Arne Dokka
- 1966 Lamont Kaser

STROKE PLAY

- 1967 Verne Callison 287
- 1968 Gene Towry 292
- 1969 J. M. Jackson 292
- 1970 Robert Risch 293
- 1971 Fred Haney 290
- 1972 Bob Allard 285
- 1973 Stan Stopa 294
- 1974 Chas. Barenaba 290

MATCH PLAY

- 1975 Randy Barenaba
- 1976 Eddie Mudd
- 1977 Jerry Vidovic
- 1978 Dean Prince
- 1979 Dennis Walsh
- 1980 Jodie Mudd
- 1981 Jodie Mudd
- 1982 Billy Tuten
- 1983 Billy Tuten
- 1984 Bill Malley
- 1985 Jim Sorenson
- 1986 Bill Mayfair
- 1987 Kevin Johnson
- 1988 Ralph Howe
- 1989 Tim Hobby
- 1990 Mike Combs
- 1991 David Berganio, Jr.
- 1992 Warren Schutte
- 1993 David Berganio Jr.

LPGA TOURNAMENT HISTORIES

U.S. WOMEN'S OPEN CHAMPIONSHIP

YEAR	WINNER	SCORE	RUNNER UP	COURSE
1946	Patty Berg	5 & 4	Betty Jameson	Spokane CC, Spokane, Wash.
1947	Betty Jameson	295	(a) Sally Sessions (a) Rolly Riley	Starmount Forest CC Greensboro, N.C.
1948	Babe Zaharias	300	Betty Hicks	Atlantic City CC, Northfield, N.J.
1949	Louise Suggs	291	Babe Zaharias	Prince Georges CC, Landover, Md.
1950	Babe Zaharias	291	(a) Betsy Rawls	Rolling Hills CC, Wichita, Kan.
1951	Betsy Rawls	293	Louise Suggs	Druid Hills GC, Atlanta
1952	Louise Suggs	284	Marlene Hagge Betty Jameson	Bala GC, Philadelphia
1953	† Betsy Rawls (70)	302	Jackie Pung (77)	CC of Rochester, Rochester, N.Y.
1954	Babe Zaharias	291	Betty Hicks	Salem CC, Peabody, Mass.
1955	Fay Crocker	299	Mary Lena Faulk Louise Suggs	Wichita CC, Wichita, Kan.
1956	† Kathy Cornelius (75)	302	B. McIntire (82)	Northland CC, Duluth, Minn.
1957	Betsy Rawls	299	Patty Berg	Winged Foot GC, Mamaroneck, N.Y.
1958	Mickey Wright	290	Louise Suggs	Forest Lake CC, Detroit
1959	Mickey Wright	287	Louise Suggs	Churchill Valley CC, Pittsburgh
1960	Betsy Rawls	292	Joyce Ziske	Worcester CC, Worcester, Mass.
1961	Mickey Wright	293	Betsy Rawls	Baltusrol GC, Springfield, N.J.
1962	Murle Breer	301	Jo Anne Prentice Ruth Jessen	Dunes GC, Myrtle Beach, S.C.
1963	Mary Mills	289 (-3)	Sandra Haynie Louise Suggs	Kenwood CC, Cincinnati
1964	† Mickey Wright (70)	290 (-2)	Ruth Jessen (72)	San Diego CC, Chula Vista, Calif.
1965	Carol Mann	290 (+2)	Kathy Cornelius	Atlantic City CC, Northfield, N.J.
1966	Sandra Spuzich	297 (+9)	Carol Mann	Hazeltine Nat. GC, Minneapolis
1967	(a)Catherine LaCoste	294 (+10)	Susie Berning Beth Stone	Hot Springs GC, Hot Springs, Va.
1968	Susie Berning	289 (+5)	Mickey Wright	Moselem Springs GC, Fleetwood, Pa.
1969	Donna Caponi	294 (-2)	Peggy Wilson	Scenic Hills CC, Pensacola, Fla.
1970	Donna Caponi	287 (-1)	Sandra Haynie Sandra Spuzich	Muskogee CC, Muskogee, Okla.
1971	JoAnne Carner	288 (E)	Kathy Whitworth	Kahkwa CC, Erie, Pa.
1972	Susie Berning	299 (+11)	Kathy Ahern Pam Barnett Judy Rankin	Winged Foot GC, Mamaroneck, N.Y.
1973	Susie Berning	290 (+2)	Gloria Ehret	CC of Rochester, Rochester, N.Y.
1974	Sandra Haynie	295 (+7)	Carol Mann Beth Stone	La Grange CC, La Grange, Ill.
1975	Sandra Palmer	295 (+7)	JoAnne Carner Sandra Post (a) Nancy Lopez	Atlantic City CC, Northfield, N.J.
1976	† JoAnne Carner (76)	292 (+8)	Sandra Palmer (78)	Rolling Green CC, Springfield, Pa.
1977	Hollis Stacy	292 (+4)	Nancy Lopez	Hazeltine Nat. GC, Chaska, Minn.
1978	Hollis Stacy	289 (+5)	JoAnne Carner Sally Little	CC of Indianapolis, Indianapolis
1979	Jerilyn Britz	284 (E)	Debbie Massey Sandra Palmer	Brooklawn CC, Fairfield, Conn.
1980	Amy Alcott	280 (-4)	Hollis Stacy	Richland CC, Nashville, Tenn.
1981	Pat Bradley	279 (-9)	Beth Daniel	La Grange CC, La Grange, Ill.
1982	Janet Anderson	283 (-5)	Beth Daniel Sandra Haynie Donna White	Del Paso CC, Sacramento

* Winner in playoff. Figures in parentheses indicate scores.

Year	Winner	Score	Runner Up	Course
1983	Jan Stephenson	290 (+6)	JoAnne Carner JoAnne Carner Patty Sheehan	Cedar Ridge CC, Tulsa
1984	Hollis Stacy	290 (+2)	Rosie Jones	Salem CC, Peabody, Mass.
1985	Kathy Baker	280 (-8)	Judy Dickinson	Baltusrol GC, Springfield, N.J.
1986	† Jane Geddes (71)	287 (-1)	Sally Little (73)	NCR GC, Dayton, Ohio
1987	† Laura Davies (71)	285 (-3)	Ayako Okamoto (73) JoAnne Carner (74)	Plainfield CC, Plainfield, N.J.
1988	Liselotte Neumann	277 (-7)	Patty Sheehan	Baltimore CC, Baltimore
1989	Betsy King	278 (-4)	Nancy Lopez	Indian Wood G&CC, Lake Orion, Mich.
1990	Betsy King	284 (-4)	Patty Sheehan	Atlanta Athletic Club, Duluth, Ga.
1991	Meg Mallon	283 (-1)	Pat Bradley	Colonial CC, Ft. Worth
1992	† Patty Sheehan	280 (-4)	Juli Inkster	Oakmont CC, Oakmont, Pa.
1993	Lauri Merten	280	Donna Andrews Helen Alfredsson	Crooked Stick GC, Carmel, Ind.

MAZDA LPGA CHAMPIONSHIP

YEAR	WINNER	SCORE	RUNNER UP	COURSE
1955	†† Beverly Hanson	220 (4 & 3)	Louise Suggs	Orchard Ridge CC, Ft. Wayne, Ind.
1956	*Marlene Hagge	291	Patty Berg	Forest Lake CC, Detroit
1957	Louise Suggs	285	Wiffi Smith	Churchill Valley CC, Pittsburgh
1958	Mickey Wright	288	Fay Crocker	Churchill CC, Pittsburgh
1959	Betsy Rawls	288	Patty Berg	Sheraton Hotel CC, French Lick, Ind.
1960	Mickey Wright	292	Louise Suggs	Sheraton Hotel CC, French Lick, Ind.
1961	Mickey Wright	287	Louise Suggs	Stardust CC, Las Vegas
1962	Judy Kimball	282	Shirley Spork	Stardust CC, Las Vegas
1963	Mickey Wright	294 (+10)	Mary Lena Faulk Mary Mills Louise Suggs	Stardust CC, Las Vegas
1964	Mary Mills	278 (-6)	Mickey Wright	Stardust CC, Las Vegas
1965	Sandra Haynie	279 (-5)	Clifford A. Creed	Stardust CC, Las Vegas
1966	Gloria Ehret	282 (-2)	Mickey Wright	Stardust CC, Las Vegas
1967	Kathy Whitworth	284 (-8)	Shirley Englehorn	Pleasant Valley CC, Sutton, Mass.
1968	Sandra Post (68)	294 (+2)	Kathy Whitworth (75)	Pleasant Valley CC, Sutton, Mass.
1969	Betsy Rawls	293 (+1)	Susie Berning Carol Mann	Concord GC, Kiameshia Lake, N.Y.
1970	Shirley Englehorn	285 (-7)	Kathy Whitworth	Pleasant Valley CC, Sutton, Mass.
1971	Kathy Whitworth	288 (-4)	Kathy Ahern	Pleasant Valley CC, Sutton, Mass.
1972	Kathy Ahern	293 (+1)	Jane Blalock	Pleasant Valley CC, Sutton, Mass.
1973	Mary Mills	288 (-4)	Betty Burfeindt	Pleasant Valley CC, Sutton, Mass.
1974	Sandra Haynie	288 (-4)	JoAnne Carner	Pleasant Valley CC, Sutton, Mass.
1975	Kathy Whitworth	288 (-4)	Sandra Haynie	Pine Ridge GC, Baltimore
1976	Betty Burfeindt	287 (-5)	Judy Rankin	Pine Ridge GC, Baltimore
1977	Chako Higuchi	279 (-9)	Pat Bradley Sandra Post Judy Rankin	Bay Tree Golf Plantation N. Myrtle Beach, S.C.
1978	Nancy Lopez	275 (-13)	Amy Alcott	Jack Nicklaus GC, Kings Island, Ohio
1979	Donna Caponi	279 (-9)	Jerilyn Britz	Jack Nicklaus GC, Kings Island, Ohio
1980	Sally Little	285 (-3)	Jane Blalock	Jack Nicklaus GC, Kings Island, Ohio
1981	Donna Caponi	280 (-8)	Jerilyn Britz Pat Meyers	Jack Nicklaus GC, King's Island, Ohio
1982	Jan Stephenson	279 (-9)	JoAnne Carner	Jack Nicklaus GC, Kings Island, Ohio
1983	Patty Sheehan	279 (-9)	Sandra Haynie	Jack Nicklaus GC, Kings Island, Ohio
1984	Patty Sheehan	272 (-16)	Beth Daniel Pat Bradley	Jack Nicklaus GC, Kings Island, Ohio
1985	Nancy Lopez	273 (-15)	Alice Miller	Jack Nicklaus GC, Kings Island, Ohio
1986	Pat Bradley	277 (-11)	Patty Sheehan	Jack Nicklaus GC, Kings Island, Ohio
1987	Jane Geddes	275 (-13)	Betsy King	Jack Nicklaus GC, Kings Island, Ohio
1988	Sherri Turner	281 (-7)	Amy Alcott	Jack Nicklaus GC, Kings Island, Ohio
1989	Nancy Lopez	274 (-14)	Ayako Okamoto	Jack Nicklaus GC, Kings Island, Ohio
1990	Beth Daniel	280 (-4)	Rosie Jones	Bethesda CC, Bethesda, Md.

1991	Meg Mallon	274 (-10)	Pat Bradley	Bethesda CC, Bethesda, Md.
			Ayako Okamoto	
1992	Betsy King	267 (-17)	JoAnne Carner	Bethesda CC, Bethesda, Md.
			Karen Noble	
			Liselotte Neumann	
1993	Patty Sheehan	275	Lauri Merten	Bethesda CC, Bethesda, Md.

NABISCO DINAH SHORE

Mission Hills Country Club, Rancho Mirage, Calif.
(Designated Major Commencing 1983.)

YEAR	WINNER	SCORE	RUNNER UP
COLGATE DINAH SHORE			
1972	Jane Blalock	213 (-3)	Carol Mann, Judy Rankin
1973	Mickey Wright	284 (-4)	Joyce Kazmierski
1974	*Jo Ann Prentice	289 (+1)	Jane Blalock, Sandra Haynie
1975	Sandra Palmer	283 (-5)	Kathy McMullen
1976	Judy Rankin	285 (-3)	Betty Burfeindt
1977	Kathy Whitworth	289 (+1)	JoAnne Carner, Sally Little
1978	*Sandra Post	283 (-5)	Penny Pulz
1979	Sandra Post	276 (-12)	Nancy Lopez
1980	Donna Caponi	275 (-13)	Amy Alcott
1981	Nancy Lopez	277 (-11)	Carolyn Hill
NABISCO DINAH SHORE			
1982	Sally Little	278 (-10)	Hollis Stacy, Sandra Haynie
1983	Amy Alcott	282 (-6)	Beth Daniel, Kathy Whitworth
1984	*Juli Inkster	280 (-8)	Pat Bradley
1985	Alice Miller	275 (-13)	Jan Stephenson
1986	Pat Bradley	280 (-8)	Val Skinner
1987	*Betsy King	283 (-5)	Patty Sheehan
1988	Amy Alcott	274 (-14)	Colleen Walker
1989	Juli Inkster	279 (-9)	Tammie Green
			JoAnne Carner
1990	Betsy King	283 (-5)	Kathy Postlewait, Shirley Furlong
1991	Amy Alcott	273 (-15)	Dottie Mochrie
1992	*Dottie Mochrie	279 (-9)	Juli Inkster
1993	Helen Alfredsson	284 (-4)	Amy Benz, Tina Barrett

DU MAURIER LTD. CLASSIC

(Designated Major commencing 1979.)

YEAR	WINNER	SCORE	RUNNER UP	COURSE
LA CANADIENNE				
1973	*Jocelyne Bourassa	214 (-5)	Sandra Haynie	Montreal GC, Montreal
			Judy Rankin	
PETER JACKSON CLASSIC				
1974	Carole Jo Callison	208 (-11)	JoAnne Carner	Candiac GC, Montreal
1975	*JoAnne Carner	214 (-5)	Carol Mann	St. George's CC, Toronto
1976	*Donna Caponi	212 (-4)	Judy Rankin	Cedar Brae G & CC Toronto
1977	Judy Rankin	214 (-4)	Pat Meyers	Lachute G & CC, Montreal
			Sandra Palmer	
1978	JoAnne Carner	278 (-14)	Hollis Stacy	St. George's CC, Toronto
1979	Amy Alcott	285 (-7)	Nancy Lopez	Richelieu Valley CC Montreal
1980	Pat Bradley	277 (-11)	JoAnne Carner	St. George's CC, Toronto
1981	Jan Stephenson	278 (-10)	Nancy Lopez	Summerlea CC, Dorion, Quebec
			Pat Bradley	
1982	Sandra Haynie	280 (-8)	Beth Daniel	St. George's CC, Toronto

DU MAURIER LTD. CLASSIC

Year	Winner	Score	Runner-up	Venue
1983	Hollis Stacy	277(-11)	JoAnne Carner Alice Miller	Beaconsfield GC, Montreal
1984	Juli Inkster	279(-9)	Ayako Okamoto	St. George's G & CC, Toronto
1985	Pat Bradley	278(-10)	Jane Geddes	Beaconsfield CC, Montreal
1986	*Pat Bradley	276 (-12)	Ayako Okamoto	Board of Trade CC, Toronto
1987	Jody Rosenthal	272 (-16)	Ayako Okamoto	Islesmere GC, Laval, Quebec
1988	Sally Little	279 (-9)	Laura Davies	Vancouver GC, Coquitlam, Canada
1989	Tammie Green	279 (-9)	Pat Bradley Betsy King	Beaconstield GC, Montreal
1990	Cathy Johnston	276 (-16)	Patty Sheehan	Westmount G & CC, Kitchener, Ontario, Canada
1991	Nancy Scranton	279 (-9)	Debbie Massey	Vancouver GC, Coquitiam, B.C., Canada
1992	Sherri Steinhauer	277 (-11)	Judy Dickinson	St. Charles CC, Winnipeg, Canada
1993	*Brandie Burton	277 (-11)	Betsy King	London Hunt and CC, London, Ontario

 # Amateur
@ Rain shortened
@@ Rain delayed
*Won sudden-death playoff
† Won 18-hole playoff
†† Won match play final

ATLANTA WOMEN'S CHAMPIONSHIP

Eagle's Landing CC, Stockbridge, Ga.

SEGA WOMEN'S CHAMPIONSHIP
1992 Dottie Mochrie 277 (-11)

ATLANTA WOMEN'S CHAMPIONSHIP
1993 Trish Johnson 282(-6)

SPRINT CLASSIC

Killearn CC & Inn, Tallahassee, Fla.

CENTEL CLASSIC
1990 Beth Daniel 271 (-17)
1991 Pat Bradley 278 (-10)
1992 Da. Ammaccapane 208 (-8)

SPRINT CLASSIC
1993 Kristi Albers 279(-9)

CENTEL SENIOR CHALLENGE

Killearn CC & Inn, Tallahassee, Fla.
1991 Sandra Palmer 143 (-3)
1992 Sandra Palmer 139 (-7)
1993 Sandra Palmer 138 (-8)

GOLF FOR WOMEN MAGAZINE LPGA T&CP DIVISION NATIONAL CHAMPIONSHIP

Moved annually (1983-91).
1983 H.B. Duntz
      Peggy Kirk Bell
      (senior champion)
1985 Sharon Miller
      Barbara Romack
      (senior champion)
1987 Kelley Spooner
      Patricia Kimball
      (senior champion)
1989 Kathy Kostas
      Linda Maurer
      (senior champion)
1991 Marlene Davis
      Barbara Romack
      (senior champion)

INAMORI CLASSIC

Moved annually (1980-87). StoneRidge CC, Poway, Calif. (1988-93).

INAMORI CLASSIC
1980 Amy Alcott 280 (-12)
1981 *Hollis Stacy 286 (-6)
1982 Patty Sheehan 277 (-15)
1983 @Patty Sheehan 209 (-10)
1984 *No Tournament*

KYOCERA INAMORI GOLF CLASSIC
1985 Beth Daniel 286 (-2)
1986 Patty Sheehan 278 (-10)
1987 Ayako Okamoto 275 (-13)

SAN DIEGO INAMORI GOLF CLASSIC
1988 Ayako Okamoto 272 (-12)

RED ROBIN KYOCERA INAMORI CLASSIC
1989 Patti Rizzo 277 (-7)
1990 Kris Monaghan 276 (-8)

INAMORI CLASSIC
1991 Laura Davies 277 (-11)
1992 Judy Dickinson 277 (-11)
1993 Kris Monaghan 275(-13)

ITOKI HAWAIIAN LADIES OPEN

Turtle Bay Resort (1987-89). Ko Olina GC, Ewa Beach, Oahu, Hawaii (1990-93).

TSUMURA LADIES OPEN
1987 Cindy Rarick 207 (-9)

ORIENT LEASING HAWAIIAN LADIES OPEN
1988 Ayako Okamoto 213 (-3)

ORIX HAWAIIAN LADIES OPEN
1989 Sherri Turner 205 (-11)
1990 Beth Daniel 210 (-6)
1991 Patty Sheehan 207 (-9)

ITOKI HAWAIIAN LADIES OPEN
1992 Lisa Walters 208 (-8)
1993 Lisa Walters 210(-6)

JAL BIG APPLE CLASSIC

Wykagyl CC, New Rochelle, N.Y.
1990 Betsy King 273 (-15)
1991 Betsy King 279 (-5)
1992 Juli Inkster 273 (-11)
1993 Hiromi Kobayashi 278(-6)

JAMIE FARR TOLEDO CLASSIC

Glengarry CC (1984-88). Highland Meadows GC, Sylvania, Ohio (1989-93).
1984 Lauri Peterson 278 (-10)
1985 Penny Hammel 278 (-10)
1986 *No Tournament*
1987 Jane Geddes 280 (-8)
1988 Laura Davies 277 (-11)
1989 Penny Hammel 206 (-7)
1990 Tina Purizer 205 (-8)
1991 *Alice Miller 205 (-8)
1992 Patty Sheehan 209 (-4)
1993 Brandie Burton 201(-12)

TORAY QUEENS CUP

Moved annually (1973-92).

LPGA JAPAN CLASSIC
(Unofficial event.)
1973 Jan Ferraris 216 (even)
1974 Chako Higuchi 218 (-4)
1975 Shelley Hamlin 218 (-1)

MIZUNO JAPAN CLASSIC
1976 Donna Caponi 217 (-5)
1977 Debbie Massey 220 (-2)
1978 *Michiko Okada 216 (-6)
1979 Amy Alcott 211 (-11)

MAZDA JAPAN CLASSIC
1980 Tatsuko Ohsako 213 (-9)
1981 Patty Sheehan 213 (-9)
1982 Nancy Lopez 207 (-9)
1983 Pat Bradley 206 (-10)
1984 Nayoko Yoshikawa 210 (-6)
1985 Jane Blalock 206 (-10)
1986 *Ai-Yu Tu 213 (-3)
1987 Yuko Moriguchi 206 (-10)
1988 *Patty Sheehan 206 (-10)
1989 Elaine Crosby 205 (-11)
1990 @Debbie Massey 133 (-11)
1991 Liselotte Neumann 211 (-5)
1992 *Betsy King 205 (-11)

TORAY QUEENS CUP
1993 Betsy King 205 (-11)

JCPENNEY LPGA SKINS GAME

Stonebriar CC., Frisco, Texas (Unofficial event).
1990 Jan Stephenson 6 skins
1991 *No Tournament*
1992 Pat Bradley 8 skins
1993 Betsy King 7 skins

JCPENNEY CLASSIC

Doral CC, Miami (1976). Bardmoor CC, Largo, Fla. (1977-89). Innisbrook Resort, Tarpon Springs, Fla. (1990-93). (Unofficial event.)

PEPSI-COLA MIXED TEAM CHAMPIONSHIP
1976 JoAnn Washam/
      Chi Chi Rodriguez 275 (-13)
1977 Hollis Stacy/
      Jerry Pate 270 (-18)

JC PENNEY CLASSIC
1978 Pat Bradley/
      Lon Hinkle 267 (-21)

KEY * =Playoff # Amateur
@ = Rain-curtailed

1979 Murle Breer/
Dave Eichelberger 268 (-20)
1980 Nancy Lopez/
Curtis Strange 268 (-24)
1981 Beth Daniel/
Tom Kite 270 (-18)
1982 JoAnne Carner/
John Mahaffey 268 (-20)
1983 Jan Stephenson/
Fred Couples 264 (-24)
1984 Vicki Alvarez/
Mike Donald 270 (-18)
1985 Laurie Rinker/
Larry Rinker 267 (-21)
1986 Juli Inkster/
Tom Purtzer 265 (-23)
1987 Jane Crafter/
Steve Jones 268 (-20)
1988 Amy Benz/
John Huston 269 (-19)
1989 Pat Bradley/
Bill Glasson 267 (-21)
1990 Beth Daniel/
Davis Love III 266 (-18)
1991 *Kris Tschetter/
Billy Andrade 266 (-18)
1992 Dottie Mochrie/
Dan Forsman 264 (-20)
1993 Melissa McNamara/
Mike Spring 265 (-19)

LADY KEYSTONE OPEN

Sportman's GC (1975-76). Armitage GC (1977). Hershey (Pa.) CC (1978-93).
1975 Susie Berning 142 (-2)
1976 Susie Berning 215 (-1)
1977 Sandra Spuzich 201 (-9)
1978 Pat Bradley 206 (-10)
1979 Nancy Lopez 212 (-4)
1980 JoAnne Carner 207 (-9)
1981 JoAnne Carner 203 (-13)
1982 Jan Stephenson 211 (-5)
1983 Jan Stephenson 205 (-11)
1984 Amy Alcott 208 (-8)
1985 Juli Inkster 209 (-7)
1986 *Juli Inkster 210 (-6)
1987 Ayako Okamoto 208 (-8)
1988 *Shirley Furlong 205 (-11
1989 Laura Davies 207 (-9)
1990 Cathy Gerring 208 (-8)
1991 Colleen Walker 207 (-9)
1992 Da. Ammaccapane 208 (-8)
1993 Val Skinner 210 (-6)

LAS VEGAS LPGA AT CANYON GATE

Desert Inn CC, Las Vegas.
DESERT INN LPGA INTERNATIONAL
1990 Maggie Will 214 (-2)
1991 Penny Hammel 211 (-5)
LAS VEGAS LPGA INTERNATIONAL
1992 Dana Lofland 212 (-4)
LAS VEGAS LPGA AT CANYON GATE
1993 Trish Johnson 209 (-7)

LPGA CORNING CLASSIC

Corning CC.
1979 Penny Pulz 284 (+4)
1980 Donna Caponi 281 (-7)
1981 Kathy Hite 282 (-6)
1982 Sandra Spuzich 280 (-8)
1983 Patty Sheehan 272 (-16)
1984 JoAnne Carner 281 (-7)
1985 Patti Rizzo 272 (-16)
1986 Laurie Rinker 278 (-10)
1987 Cindy Rarick 275 (-13)
1988 Sherri Turner 273 (-15)
1989 Ayako Okamoto 272 (-12)
1990 Pat Bradley 274 (-10)
1991 Betsy King 273 (-15)
1992 Colleen Walker 276 (-12)
1993 *Kelly Robbins 277 (-11)

LPGA MATCH PLAY CHAMPIONSHIP

Princeville Makai GC (1990-91). Waikolo Beach GC, Waikoloa, Hawaii (1992-93).
ITOMAN LPGA WORLD MATCH PLAY CHAMPIONSHIP
1990 Betsy King
JBP CUP LPGA MATCH PLAY CHAMPIONSHIP
1991 Deb Richard
PIZZA-LA LPGA MATCH PLAY CHAMPIONSHIP
1992 Dawn Coe-Jones

McCALL'S LPGA CLASSIC AT STRATTON MOUNTAIN

Stratton Mountain (Vt.) CC.
STRATTON MOUNTAIN LPGA CLASSIC
1990 *Cathy Gerring 281 (-7)
1991 M. McNamara 278 (-10)
McCALL'S LPGA CLASSIC AT STRATTON MOUNTAIN
1992 F. Descampe 278 (-6)
1993 D. Lofland-Dormann 275 (-13)

McDONALD'S CHAMPIONSHIP

White Manor CC (1981-86). Du Pont CC, Wilmington, Del. (1987-93).
McDONALD'S KIDS CLASSIC
1981 Sandra Post 282 (-6)
1982 JoAnne Carner 276 (-12)
1983 *Beth Daniel 286 (-2)
1984 Patty Sheehan 281 (-7)
McDONALD'S CHAMPIONSHIP
1985 Alice Miller 272 (-16)
1986 Juli Inkster 281 (-7)
1987 Betsy King 278 (-6)
1988 Kathy Postlewait 276 (-8)
1989 Betsy King 272 (-12)
1990 Patty Sheehan 275 (-9)
1991 Beth Daniel 273 (-11)
1992 Ayako Okamoto 205 (-8)
1993 Laura Davies 277 (-7)

MINNESOTA LPGA CLASSIC

Edinburgh USA GC, Brooklyn Park, Minn.
NORTHGATE CLASSIC
1990 Beth Daniel 203 (-13)
NORTHGATE COMPUTER CLASSIC
1991 *Cindy Rarick 211 (-5)
1992 Kris Tschetter 211 (-5)
1993 Hiromi Kobayashi 205 (-11)

NICHIREI INTERNATIONAL US-JAPAN TEAM CHAMPIONSHIP

Moved annually (1979-93). (Unofficial event.)

	INDIVIDUAL	TEAM
PIONEER CUP		
1979	Yuko Moriguchl	USA
1980	Amy Alcott	USA
1981	Chako Higuchi	Japan
1982	Nayako Yoshikawa	USA
SPORTS NIPPON TEAM		
		Mass.TCH
1983	Chako Higuchi	USA
NICHIREI INTERNATIONAL US-JAPAN TEAM CHAMPIONSHIP		
1984	Hollis Stacy	Japan
1985	Jan Stephenson	USA
1986	Ayako Okamoto	USA
1987	Fukumi Tani	USA
1988	Beth Daniel	USA
1989	Colleen Walker	USA
1990	*No individual competition*	

1991 No individual competition
1992 No individual competition
1993 Laura Davies   USA

OLDSMOBILE CLASSIC

Walnut Hills CC, East Lansing, Mich.
1992 Barb Mucha   276 (-12)
1993 Jane Geddes   277 (-11)

HEALTHSOUTH PALM BEACH CLASSIC

Deer Creek CC (1980-85). Stonebridge G&CC (1986-89). Wycliffe G&CC, Lake Worth, Fla. (1990-93).

WHIRLPOOL CHAMPIONSHIP OF DEER CREEK
1980 JoAnne Carner   282 (-10)
1981 Sandra Palmer   284 (-8)
1982 *Hollis Stacy   282 (-6)

MAZDA CLASSIC OF DEER CREEK
1983 Pat Bradley   272 (-16)
1984 Silvia Bertolaccini 280 (-8)
1985 Hollis Stacy   280 (-8)

MAZDA CLASSIC
1986 Val Skinner   280 (-8)
1987 *Kathy Postlewait   286 (-2)
1988 Nancy Lopez   283 (-5)

OLDSMOBILE LPGA CLASSIC
1989 *Dottie Mochrie   279 (-9)
1990 *Pat Bradley   281 (-7)
1991 Meg Mallon   276 (-12)
1992 *Colleen Walker   279 (-9)

HEALTHSOUTH PALM BEACH CLASSIC
1993 *Tammie Green   208 (-8)

PING-CELLULAR ONE GOLF CHAMPIONSHIP

Rotated among Portland GC, Columbia Edgewater CC, and Riverside G & CC, Portland, Ore. (1972-93).

PORTLAND CLASSIC
1972 Kathy Whitworth   212 (-7)
1973 @Kathy Whitworth   144 (-2)
1974 JoAnne Carner   211 (-5)
1975 Jo Ann Washam   215 (-l)
1976 *Donna Caponi   217 (-2)

PORTLAND PING TEAM CHAMPIONSHIP
(Unofficial event.)
1977 *JoAnne Carner/
       Judy Rankin   202 (-17)
1978 *Donna Caponi/
       Kathy Whitworih   203 (-16)
1979 Nancy Lopez/
       Jo Ann Washam   198 (-21)
1980 Donna Caponi/
       Kathy Whitworth   195 (-24)
1981 *Donna Caponi/
       Kathy Whitworth   203 (-16)
1982 *Sandra Haynie/
       Kathy McMullen   196 (-20)

PORTLAND PING CHAMPIONSHIP
1983 *JoAnne Carner   212 (-4)
1984 Amy Alcott   212 (-4)
1985 Nancy Lopez   215 (-1)

PING-CELLULAR ONE GOLF CHAMPIONSHIP
1986 Ayako Okamoto   207 (-9)
1987 Nancy Lopez   210 (-6)
1988 Betsy King   213 (-3)
1989 M. Spencer-Devlin   214 (-2)
1990 Patty Sheehan   208 (-8)
1991 Michelle Estill   208 (-8)
1992 *Nancy Lopez   209 (-9)
1993 Donna Andrews   208 (-8)

PING/WELCH'S CHAMPIONSHIP (Boston)

Radisson-Ferncroft CC (1980-84). Sheraton Tara Hotel/Resort at Ferncroft (1985-90). Blue Hill CC, Canton, Mass. (1992-1993).

BOSTON FIVE CLASSIC
1980 Dale Eggering   276 (-12)
1981 Donna Caponi   276 (-12)
1982 Sandra Palmer   281 (-7)
1983 Patti Rizzo   277 (-11)
1984 Laurie Rinker   286 (-2)
1985 Judy Dickinson   280 (-8)
1986 Jane Geddes   281 (-7)
1987 Jane Geddes   277 (-11)
1988 Colleen Walker   274 (-14)
1989 Amy Alcott   272 (-16)
1990 *Barb Mucha   277 (-11)

LPGA BAY STATE CLASSIC
1991 Juli Inkster   275 (-13)

WELCH'S CLASSIC
1992 Dottie Mochrie   278 (-10)

PING/WELCH'S CHAMPIONSHIP (Boston)
1993 *Missie Berteotti   276 (-12)

PING/WELCH'S CHAMPIONSHIP (Tucson)

Randolph Park North, Tucson, Ariz.

ARIZONA COPPER CLASSIC
1981 Nancy Lopez   278 (-14)
1982 *Ayako Okamoto   281 (-7)

TUCSON CONQUISTADORES OPEN
1983 Jan Stephenson   207 (-9)
1984 Chris Johnson   272 (-16)

CIRCLE K LPGA TUCSON OPEN
1985 Amy Alcott   279 (-9)
1986 Penny Pulz   276 (-12)
1987 Betsy King   281 (-7)
1988 Laura Davies   278 (-10)
1989 Lori Garbacz   274 (-14)
1990 Colleen Walker   276 (-12)

PING/WELCH'S CHAMPIONSHIP (Tucson)
1991 Chris Johnson   273 (-15)
1992 Brandie Burton   277 (-11)
1993 Meg Mallon   272 (-16)

ROCHESTER INTERNATIONAL

Locust Hill CC, Pittsford, N.Y.

BANKERS TRUST CLASSIC
1977 Pat Bradley   213 (-6)
1978 Nancy Lopez   214 (-5)

SARAH COVENTRY
1979 Jane Blalock   280 (-12)
1980 Nancy Lopez   283 (-9)
1981 Nancy Lopez   285 (-7)

ROCHESTER INTERNATIONAL
1982 *Sandra Haynie   276 (-12)
1983 Ayako Okamoto   282 (-6)
1984 *Kathy Whitworth   281 (-7)
1985 Pat Bradley   280 (-8)
1986 Judy Dickinson   281 (-7)
1987 Deb Richard   280 (-8)
1988 *Mei-Chi Cheng   287 (-l)
1989 *Patty Sheehan   278 (-10)
1990 Patty Sheehan   271 (-17)
1991 Rosie Jones   276 (-12)
1992 Patty Sheehan   269 (-19)
1993 Tammie Green   276 (-12)

SAFECO CLASSIC

Meridian Valley CC, Kent, Wash.
1982 Patty Sheehan   276 (-12)
1983 Juli Inkster   283 (-5)
1984 Kathy Whitworth   279 (-9)
1985 JoAnne Carner   279 (-9)
1986 Judy Dickinson   274 (-14)
1987 Jan Stephenson   277 (-11)
1988 Juli Inkster   278 (-10)
1989 Beth Daniel   273 (-15)
1990 Patty Sheehan   270 (-18)
1991 *Pat Bradley   280 (-8)
1992 Colleen Walker   277 (-11)
1993 Brandie Burton   274 (-14)

KEY * =Playoff # Amateur
@ = Rain-curtailed

SARA LEE CLASSIC

Hermitage GC, Old Hickory, Tenn.

1988	*Patti Rizzo	207 (-9)
1989	Kathy Postlewait	203 (-13)
1990	Ayako Okamoto	210 (-6)
1991	Nancy Lopez	206 (-10)
1992	*Maggie Will	207 (-9)
1993	*Meg Mallon	205 (-11)

SHOPRITE LPGA CLASSIC

Marriott Seaview CC& Resort (1986-87). Sands CC (1988-90). Greate Bay Resort & CC, Somers Point, N.J. (1991-93).

ATLANTIC CITY CLASSIC

1986	Juli Inkster	209 (-4)
1987	Betsy King	207 (-6)
1988	*Juli Inkster	206 (-7)
1989	Nancy Lopez	206 (-4)
1990	Chris Johnson	275 (-5)
1991	Jane Geddes	208 (-5)

SHOPRITE LPGA CLASSIC

1992	Anne-Marie Palli	207 (-6)
1993	Shelley Hamlin	204 (-9)

STANDARD REGISTER PING

Hillcrest GC (1980-82). Arizona Biltmore CC (1983-86). Moon Valley CC, Phoenix (1987-93).

SUN CITY CLASSIC

1980	Jan Stephenson	275 (-13)
1981	Patty Hayes	277 (-15)
1982	*Beth Daniel	278 (-10)

SAMARITAN TURQUOISE CLASSIC

1983	Anne-Marie Palli	205 (-14)
1984	Chris Johnson	276 (-12)
1985	*Betsy King	280 (-8)

STANDARD REGISTER TURQUOISE CLASSIC

1986	M. B. Zimmerman	278 (-10)
1987	Pat Bradley	286 (-6)
1988	Ok-Hee Ku	281 (-7)
1989	Allison Finney	282 (-6)
1990	Pat Bradley	280 (-12)

STANDARD REGISTER PING

1991	Da. Ammaccapane	283 (-9)
1992	Da. Ammaccapane	279 (-13)
1993	Patty Sheehan	275 (-17)

STATE FARM RAIL CHARITY GOLF CLASSIC

Rail GC, Springfield, Ill.

JERRY LEWIS MUSCULAR DYSTROPHY CLASSIC

1976	*Sandra Palmer	213 (-3)

STATE FARM RAIL CHARITY GOLF CLASSIC

1977	Hollis Stacy	271 (-17)
1978	Pat Bradley	276 (-12)
1979	Jo Ann Washam	275 (-13)
1980	Nancy Lopez	275 (-13)
1981	JoAnne Carner	205 (-11)
1982	JoAnne Carner	202 (-14)
1983	*Lauri Peterson	210 (-6)
1984	Cindy Hill	207 (-9)
1985	Betsy King	205 (-11)
1986	*Betsy King	205 (-11)
1987	Rosie Jones	208 (-8)
1988	Betsy King	207 (-9)
1989	Beth Daniel	203 (-13)
1990	Beth Daniel	203 (-13)
1991	Pat Bradley	197 (-19)
1992	*Nancy Lopez	199 (-17)
1993	*Helen Dobson	203 (-13)

SUN-TIMES CHALLENGE

Oak Brook GC (1991). White Eagle CC Naperville, Ill. (1992-1993).

CHICAGO SUN-TIMES SHOOT-OUT

1991	Martha Nause	275 (-13)

SUN-TIMES CHALLENGE

1992	*Dottie Mochrie	216 (E)
1993	Cindy Schreyer	272 (-16)

WORLD CHAMPIONSHIP OF WOMEN'S GOLF

Moved annually (1980-93).

CHEVROLET WORLD CHAMPIONSHIP OF WOMEN'S GOLF

1980	Beth Daniel	282 (-6)
1981	Beth Daniel	284 (-4)
1982	JoAnne Carner	284 (-4)
1983	JoAnne Carner	282 (-6)
1984	Nancy Lopez	281 (-7)

NESTLE WORLD CHAMPIONSHIP

1985	Amy Alcott	274 (-14)
1986	Pat Bradley	279 (-9)
1987	Ayako Okamoto	282 (-6)
1988	Rosie Jones	279 (-9)
1989	Betsy King	275 (-13)

TROPHEE URBAN-WORLD CHAMPIONSHIP OF WOMEN'S GOLF

1990	Cathy Gerring	278 (-10)

DAIKYO WORLD CHAMPIONSHIP OF WOMEN'S GOLF

1991	Meg Mallon	216 (-3)

WORLD CHAMPIONSHIP OF WOMEN'S GOLF

1992	DNP	
1993	Dottie Mochrie	283 (-5)

YOUNGSTOWN-WARREN LPGA CLASSIC

Squaw Creek CC, Warren, Ohio.

PHAR-MOR IN YOUNGSTOWN

1990	*Beth Daniel	207 (-9)
1991	*Deb Richard	207 (-9)
1992	*Betsy King	209 (-7)

YOUNGSTOWN-WARREN LPGA CLASSIC

1993	Nancy Lopez	203 (-13)

KEY * =Playoff # Amateur
@ = Rain-curtailed

Senior PGA Tour Tournament Histories

PGA SENIORS' CHAMPIONSHIP

YEAR	WINNER	SCORE	COURSE
PGA SENIORS CHAMPIONSHIP			
1937	Jock Hutchinson	223	Augusta National GC, Augusta, Ga.
1938	*Fred McLeod	154	Augusta National GC, Augusta, Ga.
1939	*No Tournament*		
1940	*Otto Hackbarth	146	North Shore CC & Bobby Jones GC, Sarasota, Fla.
1941	Jack Burke, Sr.	142	Sarasota Bay CC & Bobby Jones GC, Sarasota, Fla.
1942	Eddie Williams	1 3	Ft. Myers G & CC, Ft. Myers, Fla.
1943-1944	*No Tournament*		
1945	EddieWilliams	148	PGA National GC, Dunedin, Fla.
1946	*Eddie Williams	146	PGA National GC, Dunedin, Fla.
1947	Jock Hutchinson	145	PGA National GC, Dunedin, Fla.
1948	Charles McKenna	141	PGA National GC, Dunedin, Fla.
1949	Marshall Crichton	145	PGA National GC, Dunedin, Fla.
1950	Al Watrous	142	PGA National GC, Dunedin, Fla.
1951	*Al Watrous	142	PGA National GC, Dunedin, Fla.
1952	Ernie Newnham	146	PGA National GC, Dunedin, Fla.
1953	Harry Schwab	142	PGA National GC, Dunedin, Fla.
1954	Gene Sarazen	214	PGA National GC, Dunedin, Fla.
1955	Mortie Dutra	213	PGA National GC, Dunedin, Fla.
1956	Pete Burke	215	PGA National GC, Dunedin, Fla.
1957	*Al Watrous	210	PGA National GC, Dunedin, Fla.
1958	Gene Sarazen	288	PGA National GC, Dunedin, Fla.
1959	Willie Goggin	284	PGA National GC, Dunedin, Fla.
1960	Dick Metz	284	PGA National GC, Dunedin, Fla.
1961	Paul Runyan	278	PGA National GC, Dunedin, Fla.
1962	Paul Runyan	278	PGA National GC, Dunedin, Fla.
1963	Herman Barron	272	Port St. Lucie CC, Port St. Lucie, Fla.
1964	Sam Snead	279	PGA National GC, Palm Beach Gardens, Fla.
1965	Sam Snead	278	Ft. Lauderdale CC, Ft. Lauderdale, Fla.
1966	Freddie Haas	286	PGA National GC, Palm Beach Gardens, Fla.
1967	Sam Snead	279	PGA National GC, Palm Beach Gardens, Fla.
1968	Chandler Harper	279	PGA National GC, Palm Beach Gardens, Fla.
1969	Tommy Bolt	278	PGA National GC, Palm Beach Gardens, Fla.
1970	Sam Snead	290	PGA National GC, Palm Beach Gardens, Fla.
1971	Julius Boros	285	PGA National GC, Palm Beach Gardens, Fla.
1972	Sam Snead	286	PGA National GC, Palm Beach Gardens, Fla.
1973	Sam Snead	268	PGA National GC, Palm Beach Gardens, Fla.
1974	Roberto De Vicenzo	273	Port St. Lucie CC, Port St. Lucie, Fla.
1975	*Charlie Sifford	280	Walt Disney World (Magnolia), Orlando
1976	Pete Cooper	283	Walt Disney World (Magnolia), Orlando
1977	Julius Boros	283	Walt Disney World (Magnolia), Orlando
1978	*Joe Jimenez	286	Walt Disney World (Magnolia), Orlando
1979	*Jack Fleck	289	Walt Disney World (Magnolia), Orlando
1979	+Don January	270	Turnberry Isle CC, North Miami, Fla.
1980	*Arnold Palmer	289	Turnberry Isle CC, North Miami, Fla.
1981	Miller Barber	281	Turnberry Isle CC, North Miami, Fla.
1982	Don January	288	PGA National GC (Champion), Palm Beach Gardens, Fla.
1983	*No Tournament*		
1984	Arnold Palmer	282	PGA National GC (Champion), Palm Beach Gardens, Fla.

KEY: * = Playoff   + = Second tournament that year.

GENERAL FOODS PGA SENIORS CHAMPIONSHIP

Year	Winner	Score	Course
1984	+Peter Thomson	286	PGA National GC (Champion), Palm Beach Gardens, Fla.
1985	*No Tournament*		
1986	Gary Player	281	PGA National GC (Champion), Palm Beach Gardens, Fla.
1987	Chi Chi Rodriguez	282	PGA National GC (Champion), Palm Beach Gardens, Fla.
1988	Gary Player	284	PGA National GC (Champion), Palm Beach Gardens, Fla.
1989	Larry Mowry	281	PGA National GC (Champion), Palm Beach Gardens, Fla.

PGA SENIORS CHAMPIONSHIP

Year	Winner	Score	Course
1990	Gary Player	281	PGA National GC (Champion), Palm Beach Gardens, Fla.
1991	Jack Nicklaus	271	PGA National GC (Champion), Palm Beach Gardens, Fla.
1992	Lee Trevino	278	PGA National GC (Champion), Palm Beach Gardens, Fla.
1993	*Tom Wargo	275	PGA National GC (Champion), Palm Beach Gardens, Fla.

THE TRADITION

YEAR	WINNER	SCORE	COURSE
THE TRADITION AT DESERT MOUNTAIN			
1989	Don Bies	275	GC at Desert Mountain (Cochise), Scottsdale, Ariz.
1990	@Jack Nicklaus	206	GC at Desert Mountain (Cochise), Scottsdale, Ariz.
1991	Jack Nicklaus	277	GC at Desert Mountain (Cochise), Scottsdale, Ariz.
THE TRADITION			
1992	Lee Trevino	274	GC at Desert Mountain (Cochise), Scottsdale, Ariz.
1993	Tom Shaw	269	GC at Desert Mountain (Cochise), Scottsdale, Ariz.

FORD SENIOR PLAYERS CHAMPIONSHIP

YEAR	WINNER	SCORE	COURSE
SENIOR TOURNAMENT PLAYERS CHAMPIONSHIP			
1983	Miller Barber	278	Canterbury GC, Cleveland
1984	Arnold Palmer	276	Canterbury GC, Cleveland
1985	Arnold Palmer	274	Canterbury GC, Cleveland
1986	@Chi Chi Rodriguez	206	Canterbury GC, Cleveland
MAZDA SENIOR TOURNAMENT PLAYERS CHAMPIONSHIP			
1987	Gary Player	280	Sawgrass CC, Ponte Vedra, Fla.
1988	Billy Casper	278	PC at Sawgrass (Valley), Ponte Vedra, Fla.
1989	Orville Moody	271	PC at Sawgrass (Valley), Ponte Vedra, Fla.
1990	Jack Nicklaus	261	Dearborn CC, Dearborn, Mich.
MAZDA PRESENTS THE SENIOR PLAYERS CHAMPIONSHIP			
1991	Jim Albus	279	Dearborn CC, Dearborn, Mich.
1992	Dave Stockton	277	Dearborn CC, Dearborn, Mich.
MAZDA PRESENTS THE SENIOR FORD SENIOR PLAYERS CHAMPIONSHIP			
1993	Jim Colbert	278	Dearborn CC, Dearborn, Mich.

U.S. SENIOR OPEN

YEAR	WINNER	SCORE	COURSE
1980	Roberto DeVicenzo	285	Winged Foot GC (East), Mamaroneck, N.Y.
1981	*Arnold Palmer	289	Oakland Hills CC (South), Birmingham, Mich.
1982	Miller Barber	282	Portland GC, Portland, Ore.
1983	*Billy Casper	288	Hazeltine National GC, Chaska, Minn.
1984	Miller Barber	286	Oak Hill CC, Rochester, N.Y.
1985	Miller Barber	285	Edgewood Tahoe GC, Stateline, Nev.
1986	Dale Douglass	279	Scioto CC, Columbus, Ohio
1987	Gary Player	270	Brooklawn CC, Fairfield, Conn.
1988	*Gary Player	288	Medinah CC, Medinah, Ill.
1989	Orville Moody	279	Laurel Valley CC, Ligonier, Pa.
1990	Lee Trevino	275	Ridgewood CC, Paramus, N.J.
1991	*Jack Nicklaus	282	Oakland Hills CC (South), Birmingham, Mich.
1992	Larry Laoretti	275	Saucon Valley CC, Bethlehem, Pa.
1993	Jack Nicklaus	278	Cherry Hills CC, Englewood, Colo.

SENIOR INFINITI TOURNAMENT OF CHAMPIONS

LaCosta CC, Carlsbad, Calif.

MONY SENIOR TOURNAMENT OF CHAMPIONS

1984	Orville Moody	288
1985	Peter Thomson	284
1986	Miller Barber	282
1987	*Don January	287
1988	@Dave Hill	211
1989	Miller Barber	280
1990	George Archer	283

INFINITI SENIOR TOURNAMENT OF CHAMPIONS

1991	Bruce Crampton	279
1992	Al Geiberger	282
1993	Al Geiberger	280

SENIOR SKINS GAME

Turtle Bay GC, Oahu, Hawaii (1988). La Quinta GC, La Quinta, Calif. (1989). Mauna Lani Resort, Kohala Coast, Hawaii (1990-93). (Unofficial event.)

1988	Chi Chi Rodriguez	$300,000
1989	Chi Chi Rodriguez	$120,000
1990	Arnold Palmer	$240,000
1991	Jack Nicklaus	$310,000
1992	Arnold Palmer	$205,000
1993	Arnold Palmer	$190,000

ROYAL CARIBBEAN CLASSIC

Links at Key Biscayne, Key Biscayne, Fla.

GUS MACHADO SENIOR CLASSIC

1987	Gene Littler	207
1988	Lee Elder	202
1989	No Tournament	

ROYAL CARIBBEAN CLASSIC

1990	Lee Trevino	206
1991	Gary Player	200
1992	Don Massengale	205
1993	Jim Colbert	199

THE CHALLENGE

The Club at Pelican Bay, Naples, Fla. (1988-90). The Vineyards G & CC (South), Naples, Fla. (1991-93).

AETNA CHALLENGE

1988	Gary Player	207
1989	Gene Littler	209
1990	Lee Trevino	200
1991	Lee Trevino	205
1992	Jimmy Powell	197
1993	Mike Hill	202

GTE SUNCOAST CLASSIC

Tampa Palms CC, Tampa (1988-91). TPC of Tampa Bay at Cheval, Tampa (1992-93).

GTE SUNCOAST SENIORS CLASSIC

1988	Dale Douglass	210
1989	*Bob Charles	207

GTE SUNCOAST CLASSIC

1990	Mike Hill	207
1991	Bob Charles	210
1992	*Jim Colbert	200
1993	Jim Albus	206

CHRYSLER CUP

TPC at Avenel, Potomac, Md. (1986). TPC at Prestancia, Sarasota, Fla. (1987-93). (Unofficial Event.)

1986	United States	68.5
1987	International	59.9
1988	United States	55.0
1989	United States	71.0
1990	United States	53.5
1991	United States	58.5
1992	United States	54.0
1993	United States	

GTE WEST CLASSIC

Mountaingate CC, Los Angeles (1985-86). Wood Ranch GC, Simi Valley, Calif. (1987-88). Ojai Valley Inn & CC, Ojai, Calif. (1989-93).

AMERICAN GOLF CARTA BLANCA JOHNNY MATHIS CLASSIC

1985	Peter Thomson	205

JOHNNY MATHIS SENIOR CLASSIC

1986	Dale Douglass	202

GTE CLASSIC

1987	Bob Charles	208
1988	Harold Henning	214

GTE WEST CLASSIC

1989	WalterZembriski	197
1990	No Tournament	
1991	@Chi Chi Rodriguez	132
1992	Bruce Crampton	195
1993	Al Geiberger	198

VANTAGE AT THE DOMINION

Dominion CC, San Antonio.

THE DOMINION SENIORS

1985	Don January	206

BENSON & HEDGES INVITATIONAL AT THE DOMINION

1986	Bruce Crampton	202

VANTAGE AT THE DOMINION

1987	Chi Chi Rodriguez	203
1988	Billy Casper	205

RJR AT THE DOMINION

1989	Larry Mowry	201

VANTAGE AT THE DOMINION

1990	Jim Dent	205
1991	@Lee Trevino	137
1992	Lee Trevino	201
1993	J.C. Snead	214

GULFSTREAM AEROSPACE INVITATIONAL

Vintage Club (Mountain), Indian Wells, Calif. (Desert, Indian Wells, Calif. (Unofficial Event 1981-83.)

VINTAGE CLASSIC

1981	Gene Littler	271

VINTAGE INVITATIONAL

1982	Miller Barber	282
1983	Gene Littler	280
1984	Don January	280
1985	Peter Thomson	280
1986	Dale Douglass	272

VINTAGE CHRYSLER INVITATIONAL

1987	Bob Charles	285
1988	Orville Moody	263
1989	Miller Barber	281
1990	LeeTrevino	205

VINTAGE ARCO INVITATIONAL

1991	Chi Chi Rodriguez	206
1992	*Mike Hill	203

GULFSTREAM AEROSPACE INVITATIONAL

1993	Ray Floyd	194

DOUG SANDERS KING-WOOD CELEBRITY CLASSIC

Deerwood Club, Houston.

1988	Chi Chi Rodriguez	208
1989	Homero Blancas	208
1990	Lee Trevino	203
1991	Mike Hill	203
1992	@Mike Hill	134
1993	Bob Charles	208

KEY: * = Playoff @ Rain-curtailed + = Second tournament that year

FUJI ELECTRIC GRANDSLAM

Oak Hills CC, Kurimotomachi, Japan. (Unofficial event.)
1989	Bob Charles	207
1990	Bob Charles	214
1991	Miller Barber	202
1992	Ray Floyd	197

MURATEC REUNION PRO-AM

Bent Tree CC, Dallas (1985-88). Stonebriar CC, Frisco, Texas (1989-93).

SENIOR PLAYERS REUNION PRO-AM
1985	Peter Thomson	202
1986	Don January	203
1987	Chi Chi Rodriguez	201
1988	*Orville Moody	206

MURATA SENIORS REUNION
1989	Don Bies	208

MURATA REUNION PRO-AM
1990	Frank Beard	207
1991	*Chi Chi Rodriguez	208
1992	*George Archer	211
1993	Dave Stockton	211

LAS VEGAS SENIOR CLASSIC

Desert Inn CC, Las Vegas.

LAS VEGAS SENIOR CLASSIC
1986	Bruce Crampton	206
1987	Al Geiberger	203

GENERAL TIRE LAS VEGAS CLASSIC
1988	Larry Mowry	204
1989	*Charles Coody	205

LAS VEGAS SENIOR CLASSIC
1990	Chi Chi Rodriguez	204
1991	Chi Chi Rodriguez	204
1992	Lee Trevino	206
1993	Gibby Gilbert	204

LIBERTY MUTUAL LEGENDS OF GOLF

Onion Creek CC, Austin, Texas (1978-89). Barton Creek CC, Austin, Texas (1990-93). (Unofficial event.)

LEGENDS OF GOLF
1978	Sam Snead/ Gardner Dickinson	193
1979	Julius Boros/ Roberto De Vicenzo	195

LIBERTY MUTUAL LEGENDS OF GOLF
1980	Tommy Bolt/ Art Wall	187
1981	Gene Littler/ Bob Rosburg	257
1982	@SamSnead/ Don January	183
1983	Rod Funseth/ Roberto De Vicenzo	258
1984	Billy Casper/ Gay Brewer	258
1985	Don January/ Gene Littler	257
1986	Don January/ Gene Littler	255
1987	Bruce Crampton/ Orville Moody	251
1988	*Bruce Crampton/ Orville Moody	254
1989	Harold Henning/ Al Geiberger	251
1990	Dale Douglass/ Charles Coody	249
1991	Lee Trevino/ Mike Hill	252
1992	Lee Trevino/ Mike Hill	251
1993	*Harold Henning	204

PAINEWEBBER INVITATIONAL

Quail Hollow CC, Charlotte, N.C. (1980-88). PC at Piper Glen, Charlotte, N.C. (1989-93). (Unofficial event 1980-82.)

WORLD SENIORS INVITATIONAL
1980	*Gene Littler	211
1981	Miller Barber	282
1982	Gene Littler	280
1983	Doug Sanders	283

WBTV WORLD SENIORS INVITATIONAL
1984	Peter Thomson	281

PAINEWEBBER WORLD SENIORS INVITATIONAL
1985	Miller Barber	277
1986	Bruce Crampton	279
1987	@*Gary Player	207

PAINEWEBBER INVITATIONAL
1988	Dave Hill	206
1989	no event (Hurricane Hugo)	
1990	Bruce Crampton	205
1991	Orville Moody	207
1992	Don Bies	203
1993	Mike Hill	204

BELL ATLANTIC CLASSIC

Chester Valley GC, Malvern, Pa.

UNITED HOSPITALS SENIOR GOLF CHAMPIONSHIP
1985	@Don January	135
1986	Gary Player	206
1987	Chi Chi Rodriguez	202

UNITED HOSPITALS CLASSIC
1988	*Bruce Crampton	205

BELL ATLANTIC/ ST. CHRISTOPHER'S CLASSIC
1989	*Dave Hill	206

BELL ATLANTIC CLASSIC
1990	*Dale Douglass	204
1991	Jim Ferree	208
1992	Lee Trevino	205
1993	Bob Charles	204

CADILLAC/NFL GOLF CLASSIC

Upper Montclair CC, Clinton N.J.
1993	Lee Travino	209

NYNEX COMMEMORATIVE

Newport CC, Newport, R.I. (1980-85). Sleepy Hollow CC, Scarborough, N.Y. (1986-93).

GOLF DIGEST COMMEMORATIVE PRO-AM
(Unofficial event.)
1980	*Sam Snead	136
1981	*Doug Ford	208

MERRILL LYNCH/GOLF DIGEST COMMEMORATIVE PRO-AM
1982	*Billy Casper	206
1983	Miller Barber	200
1984	Roberto De Vicenzo	206
1985	@*Lee Elder	133

MERRILL LYNCH/GOLF DIGEST COMMEMORATIVE
1986	Lee Elder	199

NYNEX/GOLF DIGEST COMMEMORATIVE
1987	Gene Littler	200
1988	Bob Charles	196
1989	Bob Charles	193

NYNEX COMMEMORATIVE
1990	*Lee Trevino	199
1991	Charles Coody	193
1992	*Dale Douglass	133
1993	Bob Wynn	203

SOUTHWESTERN BELL CLASSIC

Quail Creek G & CC, Oklahoma City (1987-90). Loch Lloyd CC, Belton, Mo. (1991-93).

SILVER PAGES CLASSIC
1987	Chi Chi Rodriguez	200

SOUTHWESTERN BELL CLASSIC
1988	*Gary Player	203
1989	*Bobby Nichols	209
1990	Jimmy Powell	208
1991	Jim Colbert	201
1992	Gibby Gilbert	193
1993	Dave Stockton	204

BURNET SENIOR CLASSIC

Bunker Hills GC, Coon Rapids, Minn.

1993	Chi Chi Rodriguez	201

KROGER SENIOR CLASSIC

Jack Nicklaus Sports Center (Grizzly), Kings Island, Ohio.

1990	@Jim Dent	133
1991	Al Geiberger	203
1992	*Gibby Gilbert	203
1993	Simon Hobday	202

AMERITECH SENIOR OPEN

Canterbury, GC, Cleveland (1989). Grand Traverse Village, Mich. (1990). Stonebridge CC, Aurora, Ill. (1991-93).

1989	Bruce Crampton	205
1990	Chi Chi Rodriguez	203
1991	Mike Hill	200
1992	Dale Douglass	201
1993	George Archer	133

FIRST OF AMERICA CLASSIC

Elks CC, Grand Rapids, Mich. (1986-89). The Highlands, Grand Rapids, Mich. (1990-93).

GREATER GRAND RAPIDS OPEN
1986	*Jim Ferree	204
1987	Billy Casper	200
1988	Orville Moody	203
1989	John Paul Cain	203
1990	@Don Massengale	134

FIRST OF AMERICA CLASSIC
1991	*Harold Henning	202
1992	Gibby Gilbert	202
1993	*George Archer	199

NORTHVILLE LONG ISLAND CLASSIC

Meadow Brook Club, Jericho, N.Y.

THE NORTHVILLE INVITATIONAL
1988	Don Bies	202

NORTHVILLE LONG ISLAND CLASSIC
1989	@*Butch Baird	183
1990	George Archer	208
1991	George Archer	204
1992	George Archer	205
1993	Ray Floyd	208

BANK OF BOSTON CLASSIC

Marlboro CC, Marlborough, Mass. (1981-83). Nashawtuc CC, Concord, Mass. (1984-93).

MARLBORO CLASSIC
1981	Bob Goalby	208
1982	Arnold Palmer	276
1983	Don January	273

DIGITAL MIDDLESEX CLASSIC
1984	Don January	209

DIGITAL SENIORS CLASSIC
1985	*Lee Elder	208
1986	Chi Chi Rodriguez	203
1987	Chi Chi Rodriguez	198
1988	Chi Chi Rodriguez	202
1989	Bob Charles	200
1990	Bob Charles	203
1991	Rocky Thompson	205
1992	@*Mike Hill	136

BANK OF BOSTON CLASSIC
1993	Bob Betley	204

FRANKLIN QUEST CHAMPIONSHIP

Jeremy Ranch GC, Park City, Utah. (Unofficial event 1983-86.)

THE SHOOTOUT AT JEREMY RANCH
1982	Billy Casper	279
1983	Bob Goalby/ Mike Reid	256
1984	Don January/ Mike Sullivan	250
1985	Miller Barber/ Ben Crenshaw	257

SHOWDOWN CLASSIC
1986	Bobby Nichols/ Curt Byrum	249
1987	Miller Barber	210
1988	Miller Barber	207
1989	Tom Shaw	207
1990	Rives McBee	202
1991	Dale Douglass	209

FRANKLIN SHOWDOWN CLASSIC
1992	@*Orville Moody	137
1993	Dave Stockton	197

BRUNO'S MEMORIAL CLASSIC

Greystone GC, Birmingham, Ala.

1992	George Archer	208
1993	Bob Murphy	203

QUICKSILVER CLASSIC

Quicksilver CC, Midway, Pa.

1993	Bob Charles	207

GTE NORTHWEST CLASSIC

Sahalle CC, Redmond, Wash. (1986). Inglewood CC, Kenmore, Wash. (1987-93).

1986	Bruce Crampton	210
1987	Chi Chi Rodriguez	206
1988	Bruce Crampton	207
1989	Al Geiberger	204
1990	George Archer	205
1991	Mike Hill	198
1992	Mike Joyce	204
1993	Dave Stockton	200

GTE NORTH CLASSIC

Broadmoor CC, Indianapolis.

1988	Gary Player	201
1989	@Gary Player	135
1990	*Mike Hill	201
1991	George Archer	199
1992	Ray Floyd	199
1993	Bob Murphy	134

BANK ONE SENIOR CLASSIC

Griffin Gate GC, Lexington, Ky. (1983-1989). Kearney Hill Links, Lexington, Ky. (1990-93).

CITIZENS UNION SENIOR GOLF CLASSIC
1983	Don January	269
1984	Gay Brewer	204
1985	@Lee Elder	135

BANK ONE SENIOR GOLF CLASSIC
1986	*Gene Littler	201

VANTAGE PRESENTS BANK ONE SENIOR GOLF CLASSIC
1987	Bruce Crampton	197
1988	Bob Charles	200

KEY: * = Playoff @ = Rain-curtailed + = Second tournament that year

RJR BANK ONE CLASSIC
1989 Rives McBee 202

VANTAGE BANK ONE CLASSIC
1990 Rives McBee 201

BANK ONE SENIOR CLASSIC
1991 *DeWitt Weaver 207
1992 Terry Dill 203
1993 Gary Player 202

NATIONWIDE CHAMPIONSHIP

CC of the South, Alpharetta, Ga.
1991 Mike Hill 212
1992 @Isao Aoki 208
1993 Lee Trevino 205

VANTAGE CHAMPIONSHIP

Tanglewood Park, Clemmons, N.C.

VANTAGE CHAMPIONSHIP
1987 Al Geiberger 206
1988 Walt Zembriski 278

RJR CHAMPIONSHIP
1989 Gary Player 207

VANTAGE CHAMPIONSHIP
1990 Charles Coody 202
1991 Jim Colbert 205
1992 @Jim Colbert 132
1993 Lee Trevino 198

THE TRANSAMERICA

Silverado CC (South), Napa, Calif.

TRANSAMERICA SENIOR GOLF CHAMPIONSHIP
1989 Billy Casper 207
1990 Lee Trevino 205
1991 Charles Coody 204
1992 Bob Charles 200
1993 Dave Stockton 203

RALEY'S SENIOR GOLD RUSH

Rancho Murieta CC (North), Rancho Murieta, Calif.

RANCHO MURIETA SENIOR GOLD RUSH
1987 Orville Moody 205
1988 Bob Charles 207
1989 Dave Hill 207

GOLD RUSH AT RANCHO MURIETA
1990 George Archer 204

RALEY'S SENIOR GOLD RUSH
1991 George Archer 206
1992 Bob Charles 201
1993 George Archer 202

RALPHS SENIOR CLASSIC

Rancho Park GC, Los Angeles.

SECURITY PACIFIC SENIOR CLASSIC
1990 Mike Hill 201
1991 *John Brodie 200

RALPHS SENIOR CLASSIC
1992 Ray Floyd 195
1993 *Dale Douglas 196

KAANAPALI CLASSIC

Royal Kaanapali GC (North), Maui, Hawaii.

GTE KAANAPALI CLASSIC
1987 @Orville Moody 132
1988 Don Bies 204
1989 @Don Bies 132
1990 Bob Charles 206

FIRST DEVELOPMENT KAANAPALI CLASSIC
1991 Jim Colbert 195

KAANAPALI CLASSIC
1992 Tommy Aaron 198
1993 George Archer 199

DUPONT CUP JAPAN VS. USA SENIOR GOLF MATCH

TPC at Batoh, Bato-machi, Japan (1989-90). Sawara Springs CC, Sawara City, Japan (1991-92). Kitaura GC, Ibaragi, Japan (1993).
1989 United States 1,493
1990 United States 20-12
1991 United States 24-8
1992 United States 22-10
1993 United States 26-6

SENIOR TOUR CHAMPIONSHIP

Tryall Golf & Beach Club, Sandy Bay, Jamaica (1985-87). Hyatt Dorado Beach (East) Dorado, Puerto Rico (1988-93).

MAZDA CHAMPIONS
(Unofficial event 1985-89.)
1985 Don January/ 127
    Alice Miller
1986 Bob Charles/ 193
    Amy Alcott
1987 Miller Barber/ 191
    Nancy Lopez
1988 Dave Hill/ 186
    Colleen Walker
1989 Mike Hill/ 191
    Patti Rizzo

NEW YORK LIFE CHAMPIONS
1990 *Mike Hill 201

SENIOR TOUR CHAMPIONSHIP
1991 Mike Hill 202
1992 Ray Floyd 197
1993 Simon Hobday 199

KEY * = Playoff
@ = Rain-curtailed

1993 PGA Tour: Top 100 Money Leaders

Player	Tournaments	Money
1. Nick Price	18	$1,478,557
2. Paul Azinger	24	$1,458,456
3. Greg Norman	15	$1,359,653
4. Jim Gallagher, Jr.	27	$1,078,870
5. David Frost	22	$1,030,717
6. Payne Stewart	26	$982,875
7. Lee Janzen	26	$932,335
8. Tom Kite	20	$887,811
9. Fulton Allem	28	$851,345
10. Fred Couples	19	$796,579
11. Jeff Maggert	28	$793,023
12. Davis Love III	26	$777,059
13. Larry Mize	22	$724,660
14. Scott Simpson	22	$707,166
15. John Huston	30	$681,441
16. Rocco Mediate	24	$680,623
17. Steve Elkington	23	$675,383
18. Corey Pavin	24	$675,087
19. Vijay Singh	14	$657,831
20. David Edwards	21	$653,086
21. Mark Calcavecchia	30	$630,366
22. Phil Mickelson	24	$628,735
23. Bernhard Langer	6	$626,938
24. Gil Morgan	24	$610,312
25. Chip Beck	27	$603,376
26. Jay Haas	29	$601,603
27. Jim McGovern	34	$587,495
28. Rick Fehr	26	$556,322
29. Craig Stadler	24	$553,623
30. Billy Mayfair	32	$513,072
31. Nolan Henke	26	$502,375
32. Bob Estes	28	$447,187
33. Tom Lehman	28	$422,761
34. Howard Twitty	29	$416,833
35. Grant Waite	30	$411,405
36. Dan Forsman	25	$410,150
37. Scott Hoch	28	$403,742
38. Joey Sindelar	22	$391,649
39. Fuzzy Zoeller	18	$378,175
40. Billy Andrade	29	$365,759
41. Mark McCumber	21	$363,269
42. Mark Wiebe	27	$360,213
43. Mark O'Meara	26	$349,516
44. Keith Clearwater	31	$348,763
45. John Cook	23	$342,321
46. Tom Watson	16	$342,023
47. Donnie Hammond	23	$340,432
48. Brett Ogle	18	$337,374
49. Mike Standly	30	$323,886
50. Craig Parry	23	$323,068
51. Ben Crenshaw	22	$318,605
52. Dudley Hart	30	$316,750
53. Loren Roberts	28	$316,506
54. Bob Lohr	26	$314,982
55. Brad Faxon	25	$312,023
56. Fred Funk	34	$309,435
57. Bill Glasson	22	$299,799
58. D.A. Weibring	22	$299,293
59. Russ Cochran	27	$293,868
60. Greg Kraft	24	$290,581
61. Blaine McCallister	27	$290,434
62. Andrew Magee	25	$269,986
63. Curtis Strange	24	$262,697
64. Steve Pate	28	$254,841
65. Hale Irwin	21	$252,686
66. Mark Brooks	31	$249,696
67. Dave Rummells	28	$247,963
68. Lanny Wadkins	22	$244,544
69. John Inman	32	$242,140
70. Robert Gamez	25	$236,458
71. Jay Delsing	29	$233,484
72. Greg Twiggs	29	$231,823
73. Michael Allen	27	$231,072
74. Brad Bryant	31	$230,139
75. Ken Green	22	$229,750
76. John Daly	24	$225,591
77. Peter Jacobsen	23	$222,291
78. John Adams	29	$221,753
79. Mike Springer	30	$214,729
80. Richard Zokol	25	$214,419
81. Bruce Fleisher	28	$214,279
82. Dick Mast	28	$210,125
83. Phil Blackmar	30	$207,310
84. Duffy Waldorf	25	$202,638
85. Brian Claar	32	$202,624
86. Jay Don Blake	26	$202,482
87. Tom Sieckmann	31	$201,429
88. Kenny Perry	29	$196,863
89. Mike Hulbert	31	$193,833
90. Kirk Triplett	27	$189,418
91. Nick Faldo	6	$188,886
92. Steve Lowery	32	$188,287
93. Jeff Sluman	27	$187,841
94. Brian Kamm	27	$183,185
95. Wayne Levi	25	$179,521
96. Dave Barr	28	$179,264
97. Billy Ray Brown	15	$173,662
98. Dillard Pruitt	26	$168,053
99. Ed Dougherty	35	$167,651
100. Ted Schulz	31	$164,260

1993 LPGA Tour: Top 50 Money Leaders

Player	Tournaments	Money
1. Betsy King	27	$595,992
2. Patty Sheehan	21	$540,547
3. Brandie Burton	26	$517,741
4. Dottie Mochrie	25	$429,118
5. Helen Alfredsson	22	$402,685
6. Lauri Merten	23	$394,744
7. Tammie Green	23	$356,579
8. Hiromi Kobayashi	24	$347,060
9. Donna Andrews	23	$334,285
10. Trish Johnson	16	$331,745
11. Rosie Jones	24	$320,964
12. Michelle McGann	27	$315,921
13. Sherri Steinhauer	28	$311,967
14. Nancy Lopez	18	$304,480
15. Meg Mallon	23	$276,291
16. Dawn Coe-Jones	25	$271,978
17. Kristi Albers	25	$263,483
18. Jane Geddes	23	$263,149
19. Tina Barrett	25	$261,491
20. Laura Davies	16	$240,643
21. D. Lofland-Dormann	26	$234,415
22. Deb Richard	23	$223,282
23. Kris Monaghan	24	$208,987
24. Kelly Robbins	22	$200,744
25. Kris Tschetter	26	$196,913
26. Hollis Stacy	21	$191,257
27. Pat Bradley	24	$188,135
28. Dan. Ammaccapane	23	$187,862
29. Jane Crafter	22	$187,190
30. Judy Dickinson	24	$186,317
31. Missie Berteotti	27	$184,553
32. Missie McGeorge	25	$180,311
33. Elaine Crosby	27	$177,726
34. Cindy Rarick	26	$174,407
35. Amy Benz	23	$166,968
36. Jan Stephenson	24	$161,123
37. Lisa Walters	24	$149,260
38. Dale Eggeling	26	$145,789
39. Barb Bunkowsky	22	$142,907
40. Beth Daniel	23	$140,001
41. JoAnne Carner	18	$134,956
42. Nancy Scranton	27	$129,766
43. Val Skinner	25	$129,665
44. Shelley Hamlin	25	$129,447
45. Gail Graham	24	$126,048
46. M. Beth Zimmerman	25	$118,626
47. Juli Inkster	21	$116,583
48. Alice Ritzman	21	$113,992
49. Patti Rizzo	20	$111,371
50. Chris Johnson	23	$111,027

1993 Sr. PGA Tour: Top 50 Money Leaders

Player	Tournaments	Money
1. Dave Stockton	34	$1,115,944
2. Bob Charles	29	$1,046,823
3. George Archer	32	$963,124
4. Lee Trevino	25	$956,591
5. Chi Chi Rodriguez	32	$798,857
6. Mike Hill	29	$798,116
7. Jim Colbert	31	$779,889
8. Bob Murphy	27	$768,743
9. Ray Floyd	14	$713,168
10. Simon Hobday	34	$670,417
11. Gibby Gilbert	32	$661,378
12. Jim Albus	35	$627,883
13. Al Geiberger	26	$608,877
14. Rocky Thompson	37	$571,844
15. Isao Aoki	23	$557,667
16. Tom Wargo	32	$557,270
17. Larry Gilbert	32	$515,790
18. Jim Dent	30	$513,515
19. Dale Douglass	32	$499,858
20. J.C. Snead	28	$487,500
21. Dewitt Weaver	33	$472,220
22. Jim Ferree	29	$424,333
23. Kermit Zarley	33	$414,715
24. Bob Betley	26	$407,300
25. Bruce Crampton	32	$366,762
26. Gary Player	22	$360,272
27. Jack Kiefer	32	$333,511
28. Walter Zembriski	33	$331,960
29. Tom Shaw	30	$324,385
30. Miller Barber	35	$318,986
31. Harold Henning	30	$314,104
32. Tom Weiskopf	12	$296,528
33. Don January	25	$274,338
34. Tommy Aaron	31	$266,611
35. Dick Hendrickson	34	$243,262
36. Don Bies	26	$239,781
37. Charles Coody	29	$221,982
38. Larry Ziegler	31	$216,073
39. Tommy Aycock	26	$211,826
40. Ben Smith	33	$209,427
41. Richard Rhyan	32	$208,374
42. Jack Nicklaus	6	$206,028
43. Harry Toscano	32	$201,150
44. Dick Lotz	30	$199,244
45. Orville Moody	32	$196,565
46. Larry Laoretti	35	$183,694
47. Rives Mcbee	33	$181,803
48. Bobby Nichols	26	$181,433
49. Larry Mowry	22	$180,703
50. Terry Dill	33	$179,976

1993 PGA Tour: Statistical Leaders

DRIVING DISTANCE

1	DALY, JOHN	288.9
2	LOVE III, DAVIS	280.2
3	JACKSON, DAVID	278.7
4	CHEESMAN, BARRY	278.6
5	ADAMS, JOHN	277.6
6	OGLE, BRETT	276.9
7	COUPLES, FRED	275.0
8	DELSING, JAY	274.8
9	NORMAN, GREG	274.4
10	ELLIOTT, JOHN	274.2
11	PRICE, NICK	273.9
12T	AZINGER, PAUL	273.3
12T	MUDD, JODIE	273.3
12T	ZOELLER, FUZZY	273.3
15	HUMENIK, ED	272.7
16	BLACKMAR, PHIL	271.4
17	GIBSON, KELLY	270.9
18T	ANDERSON, JC	270.6
18T	HUSTON, JOHN	270.6
20	POHL, DAN	270.5

DRIVING ACCURACY (%)

1	TEWELL, DOUG	82.5
2	PRUITT, DILLARD	81.7
3	FUNK, FRED	80.6
4	IRWIN, HALE	79.8
5	EDWARDS, DAVID	78.3
6	WEIBRING, D.A.	77.9
7	ALLEM, FULTON	77.6
8	FIORI, ED	77.3
9	ROBERTS, LOREN	77.2
10	BYRUM, TOM	76.9
11	LOHR, BOB	76.8
12	LIETZKE, BRUCE	76.6
12	PAVIN, COREY	76.6
14	MAGGERT, JEFF	76.3
15	MAYFAIR, BILLY	76.2
16	MORGAN, GIL	76.1
17	HATALSKY, MORRIS	76.0
18	FLEISHER, BRUCE	75.6
19	MCCALLISTER, BLAINE	75.5
19	STRANGE, CURTIS	75.5

GREENS IN REGULATION (%)

1	ZOELLER, FUZZY	73.6
2	GLASSON, BILL	72.3
3	EDWARDS, DAVID	72.1
4	COOK, JOHN	71.7
5	POHL, DAN	71.5
6	PRICE, NICK	71.3
7	HOCH, SCOTT	71.2
8	MORGAN, GIL	71.1
8	PRUITT, DILLARD	71.1
10	PAVIN, COREY	70.9
11	BARR, DAVE	70.7
12	AZINGER, PAUL	70.6
13	MCCALLISTER, BLAINE	70.3
14	PEOPLES, DAVID	70.2
15	MAYFAIR, BILLY	70.1
16	NORMAN, GREG	70.0
17	LIETZKE, BRUCE	69.9
18	SIMPSON, TIM	69.8
19	HAAS, JAY	69.7

TOTAL EAGLES

1	LOVE III, DAVIS	15
2	DELSING, JAY	13
3	DALY, JOHN	12
3	HUMENIK, ED	12
3	LANCASTER, NEAL	12
6	CLEARWATER, KEITH	11
6	LEHMAN, TOM	11
6	RUMMELLS, DAVE	11
9	CALCAVECCHIA, MARK	10
9	GIBSON, KELLY	10
9	LAMONTAGNE, STEVE	10
9	LOWERY, STEVE	10
9	MAGEE, ANDREW	10
9	MCGOVERN, JIM	10
9	ZOELLER, FUZZY	10
16	DAWSON, MARCO	9
16	HENNINGER, BRIAN	9
16	HULBERT, MIKE	9
16	JACOBSEN, PETER	9
16	MORGAN, GIL	9
16	RHYAN, TAD	9
16	SAUERS, GENE	9
16	SIECKMANN, TOM	9
16	TRIPLETT, KIRK	9

TOTAL BIRDIES

1	HUSTON, JOHN	426
2	MCGOVERN, JIM	412
3	FUNK, FRED	394
4	CLEARWATER, KEITH	384
5	HAAS, JAY	374
6	LOWERY, STEVE	372
7	FLANNERY, JOHN	370
8	STEWART, PAYNE	365
9	CLAAR, BRIAN	364
10	LOVE III, DAVIS	361
11	MAYFAIR, BILLY	356
12	BRYANT, BRAD	353
13	BEIERSDORF, RUSS	350
14	HOCH, SCOTT	347
15	COCHRAN, RUSS	344
16	ESTES, BOB	343
16	FEHR, RICK	343
18	DOUGHERTY, ED	341
19	JANZEN, LEE	340
20	HENKE, NOLAN	339

PUTTING AVERAGE

1	FROST, DAVID	1.739
2	FAXON, BRAD	1.741
3	GREEN, KEN	1.750
4	NORMAN, GREG	1.751
5	SIMPSON, SCOTT	1.752
6	FLANNERY, JOHN	1.753
7	MAST, DICK	1.754
8	CRENSHAW, BEN	1.755
9	HAMMOND, DONNIE	1.758
9	LEVI, WAYNE	1.758
11	COCHRAN, RUSS	1.760
11	KRAFT, GREG	1.760
11	PAVIN, COREY	1.760
14	WADKINS, LANNY	1.764
14	WATSON, DENIS	1.764
16	LOHR, BOB	1.765
16	STEWART, PAYNE	1.765
18	JANZEN, LEE	1.766
18	PRICE, NICK	1.766
18	WATSON, TOM	1.766

SAND SAVES (%)

1	GREEN, KEN	64.4
2	HATALSKY, MORRIS	63.7
3	JOHNSTON, JIMMY	63.6
3	PRICE, NICK	63.6
5	HALLBERG, GARY	63.3
6	MIZE, LARRY	62.7
7	BECK, CHIP	62.6
8	NORMAN, GREG	62.4
9	PATE, STEVE	61.9
10	BRADLEY, MICHAEL	61.7
10	MAST, DICK	61.7
12	MUDD, JODIE	61.4
13	GILDER, BOB	60.6
13	LIETZKE, BRUCE	60.6
15	HART, DUDLEY	60.4
16	CLEARWATER, KEITH	59.9
17	WATSON, TOM	59.3
18	FIORI, ED	59.2
19	SIMPSON, SCOTT	58.9
19	WEIBRING, D.A.	58.9

ALL-AROUND

1	MORGAN, GIL	252
2	STEWART, PAYNE	266
3	AZINGER, PAUL	286
4	PRICE, NICK	296
5	MAGGERT, JEFF	328
6	ZOELLER, FUZZY	329
7	NORMAN, GREG	374
8	LOVE III, DAVIS	381
9	ELKINGTON, STEVE	384
10	MCGOVERN, JIM	389
11	MIZE, LARRY	397
12	COCHRAN, RUSS	405
13	GLASSON, BILL	434
14	ALLEM, FULTON	439
15	CLEARWATER, KEITH	440
16	LEHMAN, TOM	448
17	WATSON, TOM	451
18	ESTES, BOB	463
19	HAAS, JAY	478
20	JACOBSEN, PETER	480

SCORING AVERAGE (VARDON TROPHY)

1	NORMAN, GREG	68.90
2	PRICE, NICK	69.11
3	FROST, DAVID	69.48
4	KITE, TOM	69.74
5	AZINGER, PAUL	69.75
6	STEWART, PAYNE	69.82
7	COUPLES, FRED	69.85
8	ELKINGTON, STEVE	69.97
9	PAVIN, COREY	70.00
10	FEHR, RICK	70.09
11	MORGAN, GIL	70.12
12	ZOELLER, FUZZY	70.14
13	LEHMAN, TOM	70.18
13	MIZE, LARRY	70.18
15	WATSON, TOM	70.19
16	JANZEN, LEE	70.21
17	MAGGERT, JEFF	70.24
18	ESTES, BOB	70.25
19	MCCUMBER, MARK	70.27
20	LOVE III, DAVIS	70.28
21	IRWIN, HALE	70.30
22	EDWARDS, DAVID	70.32
22	HAAS, JAY	70.32
22	KRATZERT, BILL	70.32
25	SIMPSON, SCOTT	70.33
26	HOCH, SCOTT	70.36
27	FORSMAN, DAN	70.38
27	JACOBSEN, PETER	70.38
29	COOK, JOHN	70.45
30	GLASSON, BILL	70.49
31	HAMMOND, DONNIE	70.51
31	STRANGE, CURTIS	70.51
33	CLEARWATER, KEITH	70.53
34	HATALSKY, MORRIS	70.55
35	BROOKS, MARK	70.58
36	MEDIATE, ROCCO	70.59
37	HUSTON, JOHN	70.60
37	STADLER, CRAIG	70.60
39	ROBERTS, LOREN	70.61
40	SINDELAR, JOEY	70.65
41	CALCAVECCHIA, MARK	70.66
42	FAXON, BRAD	70.68
43	TWITTY, HOWARD	70.70
44	MCGOVERN, JIM	70.71
45	CLEMENTS, LENNIE	70.73
46	BURKE, PATRICK	70.75
46	WEIBRING, D.A.	70.75
48	COCHRAN, RUSS	70.76
48	LOHR, BOB	70.76
50	BECK, CHIP	70.77

1993 LPGA TOUR: STATISTICAL LEADERS

DRIVING DISTANCE

1	DAVIES, LAURA	253.9
2	MCGANN, MICHELLE	251.3
3	DESCAMPE, FLORENCE	246.2
4	ROBBINS, KELLY	245.5
5	BURTON, BRANDIE	245.3
6	ALFREDSSON, HELEN	243.1
7	LOPEZ, NANCY	243.0
8	BRILES-HINTON, JILL	242.0
9	JOHNSON, CHRIS	242.0
10	HOOD, ROBIN	240.5
11	ESTILL, MICHELLE	239.5
12	MORRIS, MARIANNE	239.3
13	TSCHETTER, KRIS	238.6
14	SKINNER, VAL	238.5
15	LUNN, KAREN	238.2
16	INKSTER, JULI	238.1
17	TURNER, SHERRI	238.0
18	COE-JONES, DAWN	237.6
19	ABITBOL, TANIA	237.2
20	ZEDLITZ, JEAN	237.1

DRIVING ACCURACY (%)

1	RAMSBOTTOM, NANCY	83.4
2	ANDREWS, DONNA	82.4
3	BARRETT, TINA	81.2
4	FIGUERAS-DOTTI, MARTA	81.1
5	KOBAYASHI, HIROMI	80.8
6	ANSCHUTZ, JODY	79.5
7	DIBOS, ALICIA	79.3
8	CONNELLY, LYNN	77.7
9	AMMACCAPANE, DANIELLE	77.5
10	FRUHWIRTH, AMY	77.4
11	MOCHRIE, DOTTIE	77.0
12	BERNING, SUSIE	76.6
13	CROSBY, ELAINE	76.5
14	POSTLEWAIT, KATHY	75.4
15	LISCIO, PATTI	75.3
16	STRUDWICK, SUZANNE	75.1
17	SCHREYER, CINDY	74.9
18	BUNKOWSKY, BARB	74.8
19	WYATT, JENNIFER	74.5
20	STEINHAUER, SHERRI	74.3

GREENS IN REGULATION (%)

1	MOCHRIE, DOTTIE	74.1
2	STEINHAUER, SHERRI	71.8
3	SCRANTON, NANCY	71.4
4	KING, BETSY	71.1
5	MCGANN, MICHELLE	70.3
6	LOPEZ, NANCY	69.8
7	ALFREDSSON, HELEN	69.5
8	BURTON, BRANDIE	69.3
9	SHEEHAN, PATTY	69.2
10	EGGELING, DALE	69.1
11	COE-JONES, DAWN	69.0
12	MONAGHAN, KRIS	69.0
13	BETH ZIMMERMAN, MARY	68.9
14	RIZZO, PATTI	68.6
15	BRADLEY, PAT	68.6
16	ROBBINS, KELLY	68.2
17	CROSBY, ELAINE	68.1
18	GUADAGNINO, KATHY	68.0
19	DICKINSON, JUDY	68.0
20	MALLON, MEG	68.0

TOTAL EAGLES

1	ROBBINS, KELLY	11
2T	ALBERS, KRISTI	8
2T	BERTEOTTI, MISSIE	8
2T	KING, BETSY	8
2T	MCGANN, MICHELLE	8
2T	MORRIS, MARIANNE	8
2T	RIZZO, PATTI	8
8T	BARRETT, TINA	7
8T	KIGGENS, LISA	7
8T	LOPEZ, NANCY	7
8T	NOBLE, KAREN	7
8T	SCRANTON, NANCY	7
8T	TOMBS, TINA	7
8T	TSCHETTER, KRIS	7
8T	WALTERS, LISA	7
16T	ALFREDSSON, HELEN	6
16T	CARNER, JOANNE	6
16T	DANIEL, BETH	6
16T	DAVIES, LAURA	6
16T	FERGON, VICKI	6
16T	LUNN, KAREN	6
16T	MALLON, MEG	6
16T	RITZMAN, ALICE	6
16T	STEINHAUER, SHERRI	6

TOTAL BIRDIES

1	BURTON, BRANDIE	334
2	KING, BETSY	320
3	MCGANN, MICHELLE	298
4	STEINHAUER, SHERRI	296
5	MOCHRIE, DOTTIE	293
6	CROSBY, ELAINE	292
7	ANDREWS, DONNA	284
8	TSCHETTER, KRIS	282
9	COE-JONES, DAWN	272
10T	ALFREDSSON, HELEN	265
10T	GREEN, TAMMIE	265
12	RARICK, CINDY	261
13T	KOBAYASHI, HIROMI	257
13T	SCRANTON, NANCY	257
15T	DICKINSON, JUDY	255
15T	WALTERS, LISA	255
17	JONES, ROSIE	254
18	SHEEHAN, PATTY	253
19	MONAGHAN, KRIS	252
20	DANIEL, BETH	250

PUTTS PER ROUND

1	NEUMANN, LISELOTTE	29.17
2	MERTEN, LAURI	29.33
3	JOHNSON, TRISH	29.35
4	JOHNSTON-FORBES, CATHY	29.36
5	JONES, ROSIE	29.41
6	GEDDES, JANE	29.41
7	KOBAYASHI, HIROMI	29.43
8	CRAFTER, JANE	29.45
9	HARVEY, NANCY	29.51
10	DAVIES, LAURA	29.52
11	WALKER, COLLEEN	29.56
12	SHEEHAN, PATTY	29.57
13	STACY, HOLLIS	29.62
14	OKAMOTO, AYAKO	29.63
15	BUNKOWSKY, BARB	29.66
16	TOMBS, TINA	29.73
17	GREEN, TAMMIE	29.74
18	THOMAS, BARB	29.74
19	WILKINS, DONNA	29.75
20	BERNING, SUSIE	29.76

SAND SAVES (%)

1	AMBROSE, JAYNE	58.5
2	PIERCE, CAROLINE	56.1
3	MILLER, ALICE	55.7
4	FARWIG, STEPHANIE	54.8
5	ZEDLITZ, JEAN	54.7
6	WALKER, COLLEEN	54.7
7	PRECHTL, KIERNAN	54.5
8	MERTEN, LAURI	53.4
9	ADAMS, LYNN	52.7
10	BARRETT, TINA	52.4
11	CARNER, JOANNE	51.9
12	PITCOCK, JOAN	51.8
13	SHEEHAN, PATTY	51.4
14	MUCHA, BARB	49.5
15	DESCAMPE, FLORENCE	49.3
16	GARBACZ, LORI	48.9
17	MASSEY, DEBBIE	48.6
18	KERDYK, TRACY	48.3
19	GIBSON, ELLIE	48.1
20	MCGANN, MICHELLE	48.1

SCORING AVERAGE (VARE TROPHY)

1	LOPEZ, NANCY	70.83
2	KING, BETSY	70.85
3	BURTON, BRANDIE	71.02
4	SHEEHAN, PATTY	71.04
5	MOCHRIE, DOTTIE	71.09
6	ALFREDSSON, HELEN	71.40
7	GREEN, TAMMIE	71.46
8	ANDREWS, DONNA	71.54
9	ROBBINS, KELLY	71.59
10	DICKINSON, JUDY	71.59
11	MCGANN, MICHELLE	71.63
12	STEINHAUER, SHERRI	71.64
13	JOHNSON, TRISH	71.64
14	CRAFTER, JANE	71.71
15	COE-JONES, DAWN	71.71
16	KOBAYASHI, HIROMI	71.78
17	MALLON, MEG	71.82
18	JONES, ROSIE	71.85
19	BARRETT, TINA	71.87
20	STACY, HOLLIS	71.87
21	AMMACCAPANE, DANIELLE	71.88
22	WEST, LORI	71.93
23	EGGELING, DALE	71.93
24	GEDDES, JANE	71.93
25	BRADLEY, PAT	71.96
26T	DAVIES, LAURA	72.00
26T	MONAGHAN, KRIS	72.00
28	LIDBACK, JENNY	72.02
29	MERTEN, LAURI	72.03
30	RARICK, CINDY	72.08
31	WALKER, COLLEEN	72.16
32	ALBERS, KRISTI	72.17
33	MCGEORGE, MISSIE	72.17
34	STEPHENSON, JAN	72.19
35	CROSBY, ELAINE	72.20
36	DANIEL, BETH	72.25
37	BENZ, AMY	72.25
38	RICHARD, DEB	72.25
39	NICHOLAS, ALISON	72.25
40T	BERTEOTTI, MISSIE	72.29
40T	TSCHETTER, KRIS	72.29
42	LOFLAND-DORMANN, DANA	72.31
43	RIZZO, PATTI	72.32
44	BUNKOWSKY, BARB	72.32
45	FIGUERAS-DOTTI, MARTA	72.32
46	RITZMAN, ALICE	72.34
47	SCRANTON, NANCY	72.35
48	WALTERS, LISA	72.43
49	ZIMMERMAN, MARY BETH	72.45
50	CARNER, JOANNE	72.46

1993 Sr. PGA Tour: Statistical leaders

DRIVING DISTANCE

1	DENT, JIM	277.8
2	DILL, TERRY	275.1
3	WEAVER, DEWITT	274.3
4	AYCOCK, TOMMY	272.9
5	SNEAD, J.C.	269.0
6	THOMPSON, ROCKY	268.9
7	FERREE, JIM	268.7
8	GILBERT, LARRY	267.5
9	HENDRICKSON, DICK	266.2
10	ZIEGLER, LARRY	266.1
11	MORGAN, WALTER	265.5
11	TREVINO, LEE	265.5
13	WARGO, TOM	263.5
14	AOKI, ISAO	262.9
14	TOSCANO, HARRY	262.9
16	JIMENEZ, JOE	262.6
17	ZARLEY, KERMIT	262.5
18	ALBUS, JIM	262.1
19	YANCEY, BERT	261.8
20	BETLEY, BOB	261.1

DRIVING ACCURACY (%)

1	SIFFORD, CHARLES	78.2
2	ZEMBRISKI, WALTER	77.0
3	CHARLES, BOB	76.1
4	COLBERT, JIM	75.0
5	GILBERT, LARRY	74.9
6	RHYAN, RICHARD	74.4
7	ELDER, LEE	73.9
8	KIEFER, JACK	73.7
9	ALBUS, JIM	73.5
9	FORD, DOUG	73.5
11	MURPHY, BOB	73.3
12	HILL, MIKE	73.0
13	FERREE, JIM	72.9
14	BARBER, MILLER	72.5
14	CAIN, JOHN PAUL	72.5
16	AOKI, ISAO	71.7
16	DOUGLASS, DALE	71.7
18	GEIBERGER, AL	71.5
19	MORGAN, WALTER	71.2
19	TREVINO, LEE	71.2

GREENS IN REGULATION (%)

1	CHARLES, BOB	75.9
2	TREVINO, LEE	74.4
3	GEIBERGER, AL	74.1
4	MURPHY, BOB	73.8
5	HILL, MIKE	73.4
6	RODRIGUEZ, CHI CHI	73.3
7	FERREE, JIM	72.9
8	WARGO, TOM	72.1
9	AOKI, ISAO	71.7
10	STOCKTON, DAVE	71.6
11	ARCHER, GEORGE	71.5
12	ALBUS, JIM	71.3
13	ZARLEY, KERMIT	71.2
14	COLBERT, JIM	70.9
15	SNEAD, J.C.	70.5
16	DENT, JIM	70.2
16	GILBERT, GIBBY	70.2
18	KIEFER, JACK	70.1
19	WEAVER, DEWITT	69.9
20	DOUGLASS, DALE	69.8

TOTAL EAGLES

1	WEAVER, DEWITT	17
2	ZARLEY, KERMIT	13
3	HENDRICKSON, DICK	12
4	THOMPSON, ROCKY	11
5	AOKI, ISAO	10
5	BARBER, MILLER	10
7	BAIRD, BUTCH	9
7	BIES, DON	9
7	DENT, JIM	9
7	SNEAD, J.C.	9
11	GEIBERGER, AL	8
11	GILBERT, GIBBY	8
11	GILBERT, LARRY	8
11	HILL, MIKE	8
11	LEHNHARD, BRUCE	8
11	MURPHY, BOB	8
11	STOCKTON, DAVE	8
18	CHARLES, BOB	7
18	JANUARY, DON	7
18	MCBEE, RIVES	7
18	WARGO, TOM	7

TOTAL BIRDIES

1	THOMPSON, ROCKY	420
2	STOCKTON, DAVE	419
3	ARCHER, GEORGE	397
4	ALBUS, JIM	387
5	RODRIGUEZ, CHI CHI	378
6	WARGO, TOM	371
7	GILBERT, GIBBY	365
8	HOBDAY, SIMON	353
9	CHARLES, BOB	349
10	COLBERT, JIM	343
11	ZARLEY, KERMIT	338
12	BARBER, MILLER	337
13	WEAVER, DEWITT	332
14	DENT, JIM	330
15	HILL, MIKE	328
16	GILBERT, LARRY	327
17	DOUGLASS, DALE	326
17	HENDRICKSON, DICK	326
19	SHAW, TOM	320
20	TREVINO, LEE	319

PUTTING AVERAGE

1	STOCKTON, DAVE	1.742
2	ARCHER, GEORGE	1.748
3	TREVINO, LEE	1.750
4	THOMPSON, ROCKY	1.755
5	AOKI, ISAO	1.762
5	GEIBERGER, AL	1.762
7	CHARLES, BOB	1.768
8	GILBERT, GIBBY	1.775
9	WARGO, TOM	1.776
10	COLBERT, JIM	1.778
11	PLAYER, GARY	1.779
12	HILL, MIKE	1.780
12	MURPHY, BOB	1.780
14	RODRIGUEZ, CHI CHI	1.785
15	BETLEY, BOB	1.789
16	JANUARY, DON	1.792
17	DENT, JIM	1.797
18	ALBUS, JIM	1.798
19	SMITH, BEN	1.800
20	DILL, TERRY	1.802
20	SHAW, TOM	1.802

SAND SAVES (%)

1	ARCHER, GEORGE	64.2
2	HENNING, HAROLD	61.3
3	BREWER, GAY	57.9
4	COLBERT, JIM	57.8
5	STOCKTON, DAVE	57.4
6	RODRIGUEZ, CHI CHI	55.2
6	SNEAD, J.C.	55.2
8	CASPER, BILLY	54.9
9	CHARLES, BOB	54.8
10	MOODY, ORVILLE	53.8
11	ELDER, LEE	53.4
12	MASSENGALE, DON	53.0
13	MURPHY, BOB	52.8
14	TREVINO, LEE	52.6
15	BRUE, BOB	52.2
16	PLAYER, GARY	51.6
17	CRAMPTON, BRUCE	51.1
18	DOUGLASS, DALE	50.3
19	GILBERT, GIBBY	50.0
19	MCBEE, RIVES	50.0

ALL-AROUND

1	TREVINO, LEE	101
2	CHARLES, BOB	111
3	RODRIGUEZ, CHI CHI	112
4	MURPHY, BOB	120
5	AOKI, ISAO	124
6	ALBUS, JIM	125
7	STOCKTON, DAVE	137
8	GILBERT, LARRY	147
9	WARGO, TOM	148
10	COLBERT, JIM	153
11	GILBERT, GIBBY	156
12	DENT, JIM	160
13	GEIBERGER, AL	161
14	HILL, MIKE	162
15	SNEAD, J.C.	186
15	THOMPSON, ROCKY	186
17	DOUGLASS, DALE	190
18	WEAVER, DEWITT	203
19	FERREE, JIM	207
20	ARCHER, GEORGE	217

SCORING AVERAGE

1	CHARLES, BOB	69.59
2	STOCKTON, DAVE	69.71
3	ARCHER, GEORGE	69.86
4	GEIBERGER, AL	69.89
5	HILL, MIKE	69.97
6	TREVINO, LEE	70.00
7	AOKI, ISAO	70.21
8	MURPHY, BOB	70.24
9	RODRIGUEZ, CHI CHI	70.41
10	COLBERT, JIM	70.57
11	WARGO, TOM	70.60
12	GILBERT, GIBBY	70.72
13	PLAYER, GARY	70.81
14	ALBUS, JIM	70.82
15	DENT, JIM	70.84
16	SNEAD, J.C.	70.91
17	GILBERT, LARRY	70.98
18	THOMPSON, ROCKY	71.00
19	ZARLEY, KERMIT	71.05
20	DOUGLASS, DALE	71.06
21	FERREE, JIM	71.18
22	WEAVER, DEWITT	71.34
23	HOBDAY, SIMON	71.40
24	JANUARY, DON	71.44
25	BIES, DON	71.49
26	AYCOCK, TOMMY	71.54
27	BETLEY, BOB	71.55
28	CRAMPTON, BRUCE	71.60
28	KIEFER, JACK	71.60
30	ZEMBRISKI, WALTER	71.70
31	AARON, TOMMY	71.73
32	HENDRICKSON, DICK	71.77
32	LOTZ, DICK	71.77
34	SHAW, TOM	71.89
35	BARBER, MILLER	71.92
36	HENNING, HAROLD	72.02
37	MORGAN, WALTER	72.05
38	COODY, CHARLES	72.13
39	ZIEGLER, LARRY	72.18
40	MCBEE, RIVES	72.20
41	MOODY, ORVILLE	72.23
41	MOWRY, LARRY	72.23
43	BAIRD, BUTCH	72.38
44	DILL, TERRY	72.50
45	BREWER, GAY	72.64
46	RHYAN, RICHARD	72.67
47	TOSCANO, HARRY	72.69
48	KELLEY, AL	72.70
48	LAORETTI, LARRY	72.70
50	JOYCE, MIKE	72.76

GOLF ALMANAC 1994

Minors

Nike Tour ...344

T.C. Jordan Tour...351

USA SNAPSHOTS®
A look at statistics that shape the sports world

Company on the course
States with the lowest, highest ratio of resident golfers to golf courses:

Number of golfers for every 18 holes

- 3,286 Ore.
- 3,021 Utah
- 889 Vt.
- 3,182 Md.
- 1,009 Ark.
- 1,030 Miss.

Lowest ratio | Highest ratio

Source: National Golf Foundation

By Marty Baumann, Web Bryant, USA TODAY

1993 Nike Tour: Staging ground for PGA

All those long-hitting, straight-putting stars of the pro golf tours couldn't possibly just pick up a club and become top-flight players.

Somewhere, after learning to play the game, they had to develop the mental toughness to compete on a high level.

Aha! The "minor league" tours.

Under the umbrella of the PGA Tour falls the Nike Tour. Begun in 1988 as the Ben Hogan Tour, this proving ground for young players is a ticket to the "major league."

Players have moved up and been successful, and will again in 1994. The top 10 Nike players each year are awarded PGA Tour cards for the next year.

Others in the top 55 on the '93 Nike Tour money list received exemptions through all or part of the qualifying for the 1994 PGA Tour.

—by Don Cronin

Sean Murphy won four times, ready to move on

Sean Murphy did a lot more than win four times and finish first in money on the Nike Tour in 1993. He may have figured out what it takes to compete with the Fred Couples and Greg Normans of golf.

Murphy, 28, goes into 1994 with more experience and confidence than ever in a frustrating struggle to make a living on the PGA Tour.

Things haven't been easy for the 1988 Western Athletic Conference player of the year at the University of New Mexico. He went to the PGA Tour Qualifying Tournament five years in a row, gaining his playing card twice, then losing it each time by playing poorly. He was 22nd in '92 Hogan (now Nike) Tour earnings ($54,283).

Suddenly last year, drives started to find the fairway with more frequency, approach shots nestled closer to the hole and putts fell. In the second round of the Nike Central Georgia Open in April, he shot 61.

Murphy won that week, and his season took off. Two weeks later, he eagled the 525-yard final hole, sinking a 51-foot putt to win the South Carolina Classic in Florence by a stroke.

"Once I had a little success, it just seemed to snowball," Murphy said. "I didn't make any swing changes, didn't have any specific lessons or tips. It was a mental thing."

Some outside conflicts, including changing girlfriends, distracted Murphy in 1992, causing his mind to wander as much as his rambling station wagon, which rolled up about 30,000 miles.

"I had some problems, but they were all resolved in December," he said. "I approached this season as a brand-new year. I set some definite goals and concentrated on staying focused every week."

A maturing process more than anything mechanical has Murphy hoping to emulate past Nike Players of the Year Jeff Maggert in 1990, Tom Lehman '91 and John Flannery '92.

Maggert won the PGA Tour Walt Disney World/Oldsmobile Classic in 1993 and finished No. 11 on the money list with $793,023. In three years, he's earned $1,411,371.

Lehman had nine top-10 finishes in 1992 and was 24th on the money list. This year, he was 33rd ($422,761) and cleared $1 million in career earnings in just two years.

Flannery, a three-time winner and money leader on the Hogan Tour in 1992, was 102nd on the PGA Tour money list with $161,234.

"Those guys have just learned to play the golf course and not worry about who they're playing against," Murphy said. "When I was on the (PGA) Tour those two years, I was a little bit in awe. Now, I've learned. I'm playing the course, and that's what I focus on. This time, I'll be ready."

—by Steve Hershey

FINAL NIKE TOUR MONEY LEADERS

Top 10 qualified for 1994 PGA Tour.

1. Sean Murphy		$166,273
2. Doug Martin		$147,003
3. Stan Utley		$143,127
4. Bob May		$132,656
5. John Morse		$122,627
6. Olin Browne		$107,754
7. Tommy Moore		$102,004
8. Larry Silveira		$93,098
9. Chris Dimarco		$90,687
10. Curt Byrum		$88,757
11. David Duval		$85,882
12. Hugh Royer III		$76,401
13. Guy Boros		$75,104
14. Emlyn Aubrey		$72,944
15. Danny Briggs		$72,437
16. Mike Heinen		$71,706
17. Steve Rintoul		$71,579
18. Franklin Langham		$71,235
19. R.W. Eaks		$68,737
20. Gary Rusnak		$67,207
21. Ron Streck		$65,718
22. Clark Dennis		$64,779
23. Dave Stockton Jr.		$64,214
24. Tommy Tolles		$61,391
25. Jerry Kelly		$61,074
26. Jim Furyk		$58,240
27. Jim Carter		$55,502
28. Sonny Skinner		$54,998
29. Frank Conner		$53,258
30. Jerry Haas		$51,147

NIKE YUMA OPEN

- **Course:** Desert Hills Golf Course
- **Location:** Lake Worth, Fla.
- **When:** Feb. 19-21, 1993
- **Purse:** $150,000
- **Par:** 71
- **Yards:** 6,822

Scores and earnings
#Ron Streck, $27,000	71-64-66–201
Chris Dimarco, $17,025	66-70-65–201
Greg Bruckner, $11,250	70-67-66–203
Olin Browne, $11,250	68-66-69–203
Franklin Langham, $7,500	70-66-68–204
Bob May, $7,500	68-67-69–204
Taylor Smith, $5,250	70-69-66–205
Steve Haskins, $5,250	67-68-70–205
Jim Carter, $5,250	67-66-72–205
Jeff Brehaut, $2,763	70-70-66–206
Rick Pearson, $2,763	67-72-67–206
Bart Bryant, $2,763	70-65-71–206
Guy Boros, $2,763	67-68-71–206
Danny Briggs, $2,763	68-67-71–206
Tim Loustalot, $2,763	71-63-72–206

#-won on second playoff hole

NIKE MONTERREY OPEN

- **Course:** Club Campestre
- **Location:** Monterrey, Mexico
- **When:** March 4-7, 1993
- **Purse:** $200,000
- **Par:** 72
- **Yards:** 6,969

Scores and earnings
Olin Browne, $36,000	71-71-67-67–276
Stan Utley, $19,850	69-74-66-68–277
Lon Hinkle, $19,850	73-68-68-68–277
J.P. Hayes, $12,000	72-68-67-71–278
Frank Conner, $12,000	69-69-66-74–278
Steve Haskins, $7,500	68-72-71-68–279
Morris Hatalsky, $7,500	66-69-74-70–279
Christian Pena, $7,500	71-69-69-70–279
Peter Jordan, $7,500	68-68-71-72–279
Greg Cesario, $3,435	73-63-74-70–280
Skeeter Heath, $3,435	67-71-72-70–280
Rick Todd, $3,435	73-70-67-70–280
R.W. Eaks, $3,435	69-67-73-71–280
Victor Regalado, $3,435	69-68-72-71–280
Ben Bates, $3,435	68-71-70-71–280
Chris Tucker, $3,435	75-67-66-72–280
Bob Burns, $3,435	71-68-66-75–280

NIKE LOUISIANA OPEN

- **Course:** Le Triomphe Country Club
- **Location:** Broussard, La.
- **When:** March 18-21, 1993
- **Purse:** $150,000
- **Par:** 72
- **Yards:** 6,978

Scores and earnings
R.W. Eaks, $27,000	67-63-72-71–273
Karl Kimball, $17,025	65-68-71-71–275
Eric Johnson, $11,250	67-66-73-71–277
JC Anderson, $11,250	65-72-68-72–277
Jaime Gomez, $7,000	69-66-73-70–278
Chris Dimarco, $7,000	67-74-67-70–278
Mike Heinen, $7,000	69-70-67-72–278
Matt Ewing, $4,500	71-71-67-70–279
Brad Lardon, $4,500	71-68-69-71–279
Peter Jordan, $4,500	71-67-70-71–279

NIKE PANAMA CITY BEACH CLASSIC

- **Course:** Hombre Golf Club
- **Location:** Panama City Beach, Fla.
- **When:** March 26-28, 1993
- **Purse:** $150,000
- **Par:** 72
- **Yards:** 6,920

Scores and earnings
Mike Schuchart, $27,000	69-71-68–208
Ron Streck, $17,025	69-70-71–210
Ben Bates, $11,250	71-73-67–211
Skip Kendall, $11,250	67-72-72–211
Rick Pearson, $7,500	65-71-76–212

Mike San Filippo, $7,500	72-66-74—212
Jon Christian, $5,250	75-70-68—213
Greg Kraft, $5,250	71-71-71—213
Ty Armstrong, $5,250	67-74-72—213
David Canipe, $3,375	72-72-70—214
Harry Taylor, $3,375	68-75-71—214

NIKE SOUTH TEXAS OPEN

▸**Course:** North Shore Country Club
▸**Location:** Portland, Texas
▸**When:** April 1-4, 1993
▸**Purse:** $150,000
▸**Par:** 72
▸**Yards:** 6,905

Scores and earnings
#Doug Martin, $27,000	70-76-70-71—287
Guy Boros, $17,025	67-70-74-76—287
Roger Salazar, $11,250	71-71-72-74—288
Rick Pearson, $11,250	72-69-70-77—288
Rick Todd, $5,750	68-74-75-72—289
Jeff Hart, $5,750	71-74-70-74—289
John Morse, $5,750	67-75-72-75—289
Remi Bouchard, $5,750	69-72-72-76—289
Keith Fergus, $5,750	66-74-72-77—289
Stan Utley, $5,750	70-74-69-76—289

#-won on first playoff hole

NIKE SHREVEPORT OPEN

▸**Course:** Southern Trace Country Club
▸**Location:** Shreveport, La.
▸**When:** April 15-18, 1993
▸**Purse:** $150,000
▸**Par:** 72
▸**Yards:** 6,916

Scores and earnings
Sonny Skinner, $27,000	74-70-69-65—278
Bob May, $17,025	70-71-67-71—279
Stan Utley, $12,750	69-74-70-68—281
Ben Bates, $9,000	72-75-69-67—283
Sean Murphy, $9,000	74-70-70-69—283
Steve Rintoul, $6,375	75-70-69-70—284
Perry Arthur, $6,375	73-72-67-72—284
Mike Heinen, $4,125	74-73-71-67—285
Jim Carter, $4,125	73-74-70-68—285
Webb Heintzelman, $4,125	71-74-70-70—285
Doug Martin, $4,125	73-73-69-70—285
Don Reese, $2,550	76-71-71-68—286
Greg Bruckner, $2,550	70-74-71-71—286
Tommy Moore, $2,550	72-74-69-71—286

NIKE CENTRAL GEORGIA OPEN

▸**Course:** River North Country Club
▸**Location:** Macon, Ga.
▸**When:** April 23-25, 1993
▸**Purse:** $150,000
▸**Par:** 72
▸**Yards:** 6,714

Scores and earnings
Sean Murphy, $27,000	73-61-71—205
Don Walsworth, $17,025	71-68-68—207
Morris Hatalsky, $11,250	72-68-69—209
Doug Martin, $11,250	69-67-73—209
Tom Harding, $5,750	74-68-68—210
Tim Conley, $5,750	71-69-70—210
John Morse, $5,750	71-69-70—210
Gene Jones, $5,750	68-72-70—210
Michael Weeks, $5,750	64-75-71—210
Bob May, $5,750	71-68-71—210

NIKE SOUTH CAROLINA CLASSIC

▸**Course:** Country Club of South Carolina
▸**Location:** Florence, S.C.
▸**When:** April 29-May 2, 1993
▸**Purse:** $150,000
▸**Par:** 72
▸**Yards:** 7,150

Scores and earnings
Hugh Royer III, $27,000	68-65-69-71—273
Chris Dimarco, $14,888	67-71-68-68—274
Steve Haskins, $14,888	68-67-70-69—274
Bob May, $9,750	66-68-66-75—275
Oswald Drawdy, $8,250	74-68-67-67—276
Greg Whisman, $6,000	68-69-68-72—277
R.W. Eaks, $6,000	68-67-68-74—277
Jerry Haas, $6,000	71-66-68-72—277
Mike Blewett, $3,506	68-74-71-65—278
Rick Pearson, $3,506	73-66-70-69—278

NIKE GREATER GREENVILLE CLASSIC

▸**Course:** Verdae Greens Golf Club
▸**Location:** Greenville, S.C.
▸**When:** May 6-9, 1993
▸**Purse:** $150,000
▸**Par:** 72
▸**Yards:** 6,799

Scores and earnings
Sean Murphy, $27,000	72-65-67-67—271
Doug Martin, $17,025	66-70-69-67—272
Chris Peddicord, $12,750	67-72-68-68—275
Jeff Brehaut, $9,750	70-70-69-67—276
Larry Silveira, $8,250	72-66-70-69—277
Bob May, $6,375	70-72-70-66—278
Don Reese, $6,375	72-67-70-69—278
Esteban Toledo, $3,450	71-70-74-64—279
Eric Johnson, $3,450	71-70-70-68—279
Jerry Haas, $3,450	69-70-71-69—279
Hugh Royer III, $3,450	68-72-70-69—279
Tommy Moore, $3,450	71-67-71-70—279
Joe Mccormick, $3,450	67-71-70-71—279
Tommy Tolles, $3,450	69-70-65-75—279

NIKE KNOXVILLE OPEN

▶**Course:** Willow Creek Golf Course
▶**Location:** Knoxville, Tenn.
▶**When:** May 13-16, 1993
▶**Purse:** $175,000
▶**Par:** 6,869
▶**Yards:** 71

Scores and earnings
Tim Conley, $31,500	65-63-66-67–261
Greg Whisman, $13,934	69-68-65-66–268
Larry Silveira, $13,934	66-66-67-69–268
Jerry Haas, $13,934	68-65-67-68–268
Tommy Tolles, $13,934	67-67-65-69–268
Franklin Langham, $7,875	66-67-68-68–269
Rick Todd, $6,125	68-70-69-64–271
Bob May, $6,125	66-66-70-69–271
Jeff Brehaut, $6,125	66-69-66-70–271
Jeff Hart, $3,938	68-66-70-68–272
Sean Murphy, $3,938	68-70-66-68–272

NIKE MIAMI VALLEY OPEN

▶**Course:** Heatherwoode Golf Club
▶**Location:** Springboro, Ohio
▶**When:** April 21-23, 1993
▶**Purse:** $175,000
▶**Par:** 71
▶**Yards:** 6,730

Scores and earnings
Emlyn Aubrey, $31,500	65-72-65–202
Larry Silveira, $19,863	70-69-67–206
Guy Boros, $13,125	66-72-69–207
Omar Uresti, $13,125	64-71-72–207
Tommy Moore, $8,167	69-70-69–208
Ricky Smallridge, $8,167	65-73-70–208
Doug Martin, $8,167	66-71-71–208
Danny Briggs, $5,250	71-70-68–209
Chris Dimarco, $5,250	70-68-71–209
Chris Kaufman, $5,250	69-68-72–209

NIKE DOMINION OPEN

▶**Course:** The Dominion Club
▶**Location:** Glen Allen, Va.
▶**When:** June 3-6, 1993
▶**Purse:** $175,000
▶**Par:** 72
▶**Yards:** 7,040

Scores and earnings
Angel Franco, $31,500	68-66-67-71–272
Rocky Walcher, $19,863	69-64-71-70–274
Taylor Smith, $14,875	67-71-65-72–275
Jerry Haas, $8,400	68-70-68-70–276
Steve Isley, $8,400	70-68-68-70–276
Hicks Malonson, $8,400	68-70-67-71–276
Mike Heinen, $8,400	69-69-67-71–276
Eric Hoos, $8,400	68-65-69-74–276
Gary Rusnak, $3,675	68-69-72-68–277
Peter Jordan, $3,675	68-67-73-69–277
Greg Whisman, $3,675	66-73-68-70–277
Doug Martin, $3,675	73-65-70-69–277
Hugh Royer III, $3,675	69-70-68-70–277
Tony Sills, $3,675	70-68-68-71–277

NIKE CLEVELAND OPEN

▶**Course:** Quail Hollow Resort
▶**Location:** Concord, Ohio
▶**When:** June 10-13, 1993
▶**Purse:** $275,000
▶**Par:** 72
▶**Yards:** 6,712

Scores and earnings
Stan Utley, $49,500	69-69-68-65–271
Jerry Kelly, $31,213	70-70-68-66–274
Frank Conner, $23,375	68-70-69-68–275
Sean Murphy, $16,500	71-66-70-69–276
Danny Briggs, $16,500	65-71-67-73–276
Jeff Gallagher, $11,688	74-65-69-69–277
John Morse, $11,688	70-68-69-70–277
Deane Pappas, $9,625	67-71-69-71–278
Doug Martin, $8,250	69-70-70-70–279
Lon Hinkle, $5,534	72-70-75-63–280
Tim Conley, $5,534	70-71-70-69–280
Tim Loustalot, $5,534	70-72-69-69–280
Barry Jaeckel, $5,534	71-69-70-70–280

NIKE CONNECTICUT OPEN

▶**Course:** Yale Golf Club
▶**Location:** New Haven, Conn.
▶**When:** June 18-20, 1993
▶**Purse:** $150,000
▶**Par:** 70
▶**Yards:** 6,622

Scores and earnings
Dave Stockton Jr, $27,000	66-67-71–204
Jeff Coston, $17,025	70-66-69–205
Bob May, $9,375	67-70-69–206
Tim Simpson, $9,375	68-68-70–206
Stan Utley, $9,375	68-68-70–206
David Ogrin, $9,375	69-66-71–206
Greg Parker, $5,250	71-70-66–207
Jeff Woodland, $5,250	70-67-70–207
Skip Kendall, $5,250	71-66-70–207
Robert Thompson, $3,750	69-73-66–208

NIKE NEW ENGLAND CLASSIC

▶**Course:** The Woodlands Club
▶**Location:** Falmouth, Mass.
▶**When:** June 24-27, 1993
▶**Purse:** $200,000
▶**Par:** 72
▶**Yards:** 6,848

Scores and earnings
John Morse, $27,000	72-70-68-68–278
Sam Randolph, $11,944	74-73-70-65–282
Larry Silveira, $11,944	69-72-73-68–282
Emlyn Aubrey, $11,944	70-75-70-67–282
Peter Jordan, $11,944	70-67-72-73–282

Tommy Moore, $6,750	73-70-72-69–284
Gary Rusnak, $5,625	70-73-73-69–285
Jeff Gallagher, $5,625	73-71-68-73–285
Mark Mielke, $3,506	73-71-74-68–286
Karl Kimball, $3,506	74-71-71-70–286
Tom Jenkins, $3,506	70-78-68-70–286
Taylor Smith, $3,506	70-73-71-72–286

NIKE WHITE ROSE CLASSIC

▸**Course:** Honey Run Golf & C C
▸**Location:** York, Penn.
▸**When:** July 1-4, 1993
▸**Purse:** $200,000
▸**Par:** 72
▸**Yards:** 6,797

Scores and earnings
Curt Byrum, $36,000	69-70-64-67–270
E. Toledo, $17,567	68-69-69-65–271
M. Hatalsky, $17,567	69-66-69-67–271
Gary Rusnak, $17,567	71-65-64-71–271
R. Smallridge, $9,333	69-72-65-66–272
Sean Murphy, $9,333	70-65-70-67–272
Jeff Coston, $9,333	65-69-68-70–272
M. Cunning, $6,000	70-67-68-68–273
Bob Friend, $6,000	66-69-69-69–273
Karl Kimball, $6,000	69-68-65-71–273

NIKE HAWKEYE OPEN

▸**Course:** Finkbine Golf Club
▸**Location:** Iowa City, Iowa
▸**When:** July 8-11, 1993
▸**Purse:** $150,000
▸**Par:** 71
▸**Yards:** 6,732

Scores and earnings
Dave Stockton Jr., $27,000	70-64-66-200
Mike Heinen, $17,025	65-71-68-204
Clark Dennis, $9,375	71-68-66-205
John Morse, $9,375	71-66-68-205
Lonnie Nielsen, $9,375	68-69-68-205
Bill Porter, $9,375	66-68-71-205
Jim Schuman, $5,250	67-74-65-206
R.W. Eaks, $5,250	72-69-65-206
Angel Franco, $5,250	64-72-70-206
Jack Kay Jr., $2,664	72-68-67-207
Franklin Langham, $2,664	69-71-67-207
Gary Rusnak, $2,664	69-69-69-207
Curt Byrum, $2,664	68-70-69-207
Rob Boldt, $2,664	71-70-66-207
Jim Carter, $2,664	71-67-69-207
Guy Boros, $2,664	77-64-66-207

NIKE DAKOTA DUNES OPEN

▸**Course:** Dakota Dunes Country Club
▸**Location:** Dakota Dunes, S.D.
▸**When:** July 15-18, 1993
▸**Purse:** $175,000
▸**Par:** 72
▸**Yards:** 7,165

Scores and earnings
Alan Pate, $31,500	69-65-61-65–260
Stan Utley, $19,863	65-68-66-62–261
Curt Byrum, $11,958	67-64-68-63–262
R. Thompson, $11,958	67-64-67-64–262
Gary Rusnak, $11,958	68-62-64-68–262
Olin Browne, $7,438	67-66-66-64–263
Jeff Brehaut, $7,438	62-67-67-67–263
Guy Boros, $4,813	71-63-68-63–265
Hugh Royer III, $4,813	70-65-67-63–265
Dennis Trixler, $4,813	64-69-67-65–265

NIKE GREATER OZARKS OPEN

▸**Course:** Highland Springs C C
▸**Location:** Springfield, Mo.
▸**When:** July 22-25, 1993
▸**Purse:** $175,000
▸**Par:** 72
▸**Yards:** 7,058

Scores and earnings
Tommy Tolles, $31,500	68-68-69-66–271
Bob May, $17,369	68-65-72-68–273
Bob Burns, $17,369	71-67-67-68–273
Greg Bruckner, $11,375	71-69-63-71–274
Larry Silveira, $9,625	68-70-66-71–275
Tom Garner, $7,438	69-72-67-68–276
Emlyn Aubrey, $7,438	69-67-71-69–276
Clark Dennis, $5,250	68-73-69-67–277
Bob Wolcott, $5,250	69-67-72-69–277
Chris Dimarco, $5,250	66-67-73-71–277

NIKE MISSISSIPPI GULF COAST CLASSIC

▸**Course:** Windance Golf & Country Club
▸**Location:** Gulfport, Miss.
▸**When:** July 29-Aug. 1, 1993
▸**Purse:** $150,000
▸**Par:** 72
▸**Yards:** 6,705

Scores and earnings
#Jim Furyk, $27,000	72-68-66-206
Bob Friend, $17,025	70-66-70-206
J.P. Hayes, $12,750	72-72-65-209
Kim Young, $9,000	71-70-69-210
Tommy Moore, $9,000	69-70-71-210
Bill Porter, $5,625	70-74-67-211
Chris DiMarco, $5,625	68-74-69-211
Frank Conner, $5,625	70-71-70-211
Bob Wolcott, $5,625	69-70-72-211
Karl Zoller, $3,375	75-68-69-212
Jim Carter, $3,375	70-71-71-212

#-won on first playoff hole

NIKE PERMIAN BASIN OPEN

▶ **Course:** The Club at Mission Dorado
▶ **Location:** Odessa, Texas
▶ **When:** Aug. 6-8, 1993
▶ **Purse:** $150,000
▶ **Par:** 72
▶ **Yards:** 7,135

Scores and earnings
#Franklin Langham, $27,000	67-66-69–202
Doug Martin, $17,025	67-68-67–202
Steve Rintoul, $12,750	66-68-70–204
Jerry Kelly, $9,750	67-68-70–205
Andrew Morse, $7,000	74-66-66–206
Rob Boldt, $7,000	71-65-70–206
Ty Armstrong, $7,000	66-70-70–206
Jon Christian, $4,500	70-69-68–207
Joe Durant, $4,500	69-69-69–207
Michael Cunning, $4,500	68-68-71–207

won on first playoff hole

NIKE NEW MEXICO CHARITY CLASSIC

▶ **Course:** Valle Grande Golf Club
▶ **Location:** Bernalillo, N.M.
▶ **When:** Aug. 12-15, 1993
▶ **Purse:** $175,000
▶ **Par:** 71
▶ **Yards:** 7,082

Scores and earnings
Chris Patton, $31,500	64-66-65-67–262
John Morse, $17,369	66-66-66-69–267
Doug Martin, $17,369	65-66-65-71–267
Steve Rintoul, $8,400	68-66-71-64–269
Clark Dennis, $8,400	69-66-67-67–269
Larry Silveira, $8,400	70-63-68-68–269
T. Gene Jones, $8,400	68-66-66-69–269
R.W. Eaks, $8,400	68-65-67-69–269
David Duval, $4,813	64-69-70-67–270
Bill Porter, $4,813	69-68-64-69–270

NIKE WICHITA OPEN

▶ **Course:** Reflection Ridge Golf Club
▶ **Location:** Wichita, Kan.
▶ **When:** Aug. 19-22, 1993
▶ **Purse:** $150,000
▶ **Par:** 72
▶ **Yards:** 6,730

Scores and earnings
David Duval, $27,000	62-70-69-70–271
Jeff Lee, $14,888	66-70-68-68–272
John Morse, $14,888	65-69-66-72–272
Doug Martin, $9,750	67-65-71-70–273
Hicks Malonson, $8,250	66-70-64-74–274
Guy Boros, $6,000	70-70-67-68–275
Jim Kane, $6,000	70-67-67-71–275
Alan Pate, $6,000	67-71-66-71–275
Bob Burns, $3,011	70-68-69-69–276
Omar Uresti, $3,011	70-70-66-70–276
Curt Byrum, $3,011	66-71-67-72–276
Clark Dennis, $3,011	69-68-66-73–276
Gary Rusnak, $3,011	68-66-67-75–276
Mike Heinen, $3,011	69-65-67-75–276
Tom Garner, $3,011	68-66-65-77–276

NIKE TEXARKANA OPEN

▶ **Course:** Texarkana Country Club
▶ **Location:** Texarkana, Texas
▶ **When:** Aug. 26-29, 1993
▶ **Purse:** $150,000
▶ **Par:** 72
▶ **Yards:** 6,588

Scores and earnings
Hugh Royer III, $27,000	67-67-66-67–267
Steve Rintoul, $17,025	70-65-68-66–269
Bob Burns, $10,250	68-66-72-66–272
John Morse, $10,250	70-69-64-69–272
David Duval, $10,250	68-68-67-69–272
Jeff Coston, $6,000	69-67-71-66–273
Mike Foster, $6,000	71-67-67-68–273
Larry Silveira, $6,000	69-68-67-69–273
Rob Boldt, $4,125	69-70-66-69–274
Doug Martin, $4,125	66-69-68-71–274

NIKE TRI-CITIES OPEN

▶ **Course:** Meadow Springs Country Club
▶ **Location:** Richland, Wash.
▶ **When:** Sept. 10-12, 1993
▶ **Purse:** $150,000
▶ **Par:** 72
▶ **Yards:** 6,926

Scores and earnings
Steve Jurgensen, $27,000	67-73-67–207
Stan Utley, $17,025	69-69-70–208
Jeff Lee, $9,375	71-72-66–209
Bob Friend, $9,375	69-73-67–209
Steve Haskins, $9,375	68-71-70–209
Perry Parker, $9,375	68-69-72–209
Bob May, $5,625	69-71-71–211
Tim Loustalot, $5,625	69-70-72–211
Dave Sutherland, $4,125	68-74-70–212
Don Reese, $4,125	66-76-70–212

NIKE UTAH CLASSIC

▶ **Course:** Riverside Country Club
▶ **Location:** Provo, Utah
▶ **When:** Sept. 17-19, 1993
▶ **Purse:** $150,000
▶ **Par:** 72
▶ **Yards:** 6,950

Scores and earnings
Sean Murphy, $27,000	68-70-66–204
Tommy Moore, $13,175	68-69-67–204
Curt Byrum, $13,175	68-69-67–204

Jim Carter, $13,175	68-68-68–204
John Morse, $8,250	68-69-68–205
Emlyn Aubrey, $4,875	67-72-67–206
Roger Salazar, $4,875	67-72-67–206
Dave Sutherland, $4,875	70-69-67–206
Jerry Kelly, $4,875	70-69-67–206
Steve Brodie, $4,875	68-69-69–206

NIKE BOISE OPEN

▸**Course**: Hillcrest Country Club
▸**Location**: Boise, Idaho
▸**When**: Sept. 24-26, 1993
▸**Purse**: $200,000
▸**Par**: 71
▸**Yards**: 6,773

Scores and earnings
Tommy Moore, $36,000	68-67-64–199
Olin Browne, $22,700	67-67-68–202
Chris Patton, $12,500	67-71-65–203
Chris Peddicord, $12,500	69-68-66–203
Bob May, $12,500	72-64-67–203
Tom Garner, $12,500	69-65-69–203
Perry Parker, $7,500	70-67-67–204
Chris Dimarco, $7,500	68-68-68–204
Jim Carter, $5,000	70-69-66–205
Gary Rusnak, $5,000	71-68-66–205
Guy Boros, $5,000	71-67-67–205

NIKE SONOMA COUNTY OPEN

▸**Course**: Windsor Golf Club
▸**Location**: Windsor, Calif.
▸**When**: Sept. 30-Oct. 3, 1993
▸**Purse**: $150,000
▸**Par**: 72
▸**Yards**: 6,650

Scores and earnings
Sean Murphy, $27,000	67-71-68-68–274
Joey Rassett, $17,025	70-68-69-68–275
Danny Briggs, $12,750	67-68-69-72–276
Curt Byrum, $9,750	72-70-67-68–277
Kevin Sutherland, $6,563	73-69-68-68–278
Olin Browne, $6,563	70-69-70-69–278
Louis Brown, $6,563	70-72-67-69–278
Taylor Smith, $6,563	70-71-66-71–278
David Duval, $4,500	67-71-71-70–279
Tommy Moore, $3,375	68-71-70-71–280
Tim Loustalot, $3,375	70-69-67-74–280

NIKE BAKERSFIELD OPEN

▸**Course**: Seven Oaks Country Club
▸**Location**: Bakersfield, Calif.
▸**When**: Oct. 8-10, 1993
▸**Purse**: $150,000
▸**Par**: 72
▸**Yards**: 7,119

Scores and earnings
#Clark Dennis, $27,000	64-69-69–202
Jim Furyk, $14,888	69-68-65–202
Sonny Skinner, $14,888	68-65-69–202
Karl Kimball, $9,000	70-67-66–203
Mike Heinen, $9,000	62-68-73–203
Steve Brodie, $6,375	69-70-65–204
Guy Boros, $6,375	72-67-65–204
Tom Garner, $4,875	70-69-66–205
Doug Martin, $4,875	70-65-70–205
Bryan Gorman, $3,019	71-68-67–206
Gary Rusnak, $3,019	67-72-67–206
Greg Bruckner, $3,019	67-70-69–206
Chris DiMarco, $3,019	69-68-69–206

 # won on first playoff hole

NIKE TOUR CHAMPIONSHIP

▸**Course**: Pumpkin Ridge Golf Club (Ghost Creek Course)
▸**Location**: Cornelius, Ore.
▸**When**: Oct. 14-17, 1993
▸**Purse**: $200,000
▸**Par**: 71
▸**Yards**: 6,839

Scores and earnings
David Duval, $36,000	69-68-72-68–277
Danny Briggs, $22,700	69-66-71-72–278
Bob May, $17,000	72-70-69-69–280
Franklin Langham, $13,000	70-72-69-70–281
Mike Heinen, $11,000	73-69-68-72–282
Tim Loustalot, $9,000	71-70-70-73–284
Chris Dimarco, $7,000	72-71-72-70–285
Jeff Coston, $7,000	74-68-71-72–285
Steve Rintoul, $7,000	71-71-70-73–285
Jim Furyk, $4,500	77-70-70-69–286
Doug Martin, $4,500	70-72-72-72–286
Sean Murphy, $3,550	76-67-73-71–287
Ron Streck, $3,550	74-67-71-75–287

1993 T.C. Jordan Tour: Up and coming

The T.C. Jordan Tour has become an important, alternative proving ground for young golfers. It just completed its fifth season, with 18 events and purses totaling nearly $1.2 million.

Charlie Rymer of Atlanta led the Jordan Tour in earnings, banking $46,600. Rymer, a three-time All-American at Georgia Tech, won at Savannah, Ga., and Natchez, Miss.

Chris Perks of Lafayette, La., also won twice—in New Bern, N.C., and Louisville.

Perks and Marion Dantzler of Orangeburg, S.C., were co-players of the year and Dantzler led the tour with a 70.1 average. They were honored at the annual awards banquet Sept. 25, 1993, in Venice, Fla., where Jeff Cook of Chattanooga, Tenn., was named rookie of the year and Steven Schaff of Sylvania, Ohio, was honored for special achievements in golf.

The Jordan Tour has sent about 30% of its players on to the Nike Tour or PGA Tour. In 1992, 80 of the 180 players in the final PGA Tour qualifying tournament had Jordan Tour experience.

Lee Janzen, who won the U.S. Open last June, led the Jordan Tour in earnings in 1989. John Daly, who won the 1991 PGA Championship and 1992 B.C. Open, played the Jordan Tour in '88-'89.

No group of golfers could have imagined better weather than the Jordan Tour enjoyed in 1993: in the 18 tournaments (72 rounds) just one round was rained out, in El Paso, Ill., during the heavy summer flooding in the Midwest.

Tour originator and sponsor Rick Jordan gives special consideration to players who get into Nike and PGA Tour events through local qualifying. If they have previously entered that week's Jordan event, they are excused with no financial penalties.

"Our whole purpose is to provide a place for young men to hone their (golf) games for the move toward the major leagues of golf," Jordan says. "Our record speaks for itself. Our players and host cities have been our biggest boosters. I continue to think we are the best kept secret in pro golf, and the secret is almost out to the sports world."

In 1994, the Jordan Tour will stage its first $100,000 event, the Decatur (Ala.) Daily Classic, sponsored by the *Decatur Daily* newspaper.

1993 Futures Golf Tour: Wrapup

Nanci Bowen of Tifton, Ga., led the women's Futures Golf Tour in earnings, amassing $20,443 while playing 11 of the 13 tournaments. She also won twice, at Florien, La., and Victoria, Texas, the second and third tournaments of the year.

Margaret Platt of Hastings-on-Hudson, N.Y., was the other two-time winner on the '93 Futures Tour, winning June 13 at Decatur, Ill., and July 18 at York, Pa. She finished ninth on the Futures Tour money list with $10,478.

In qualifying for the 1994 LPGA tour in November in Daytona Beach, Fla., 35 players with Futures Tour experience earned their cards, including nine who are moving onto the tour for the first time.

Of those qualifiers, several were winners or runners-up at Futures Tour events: Bowen; Jodi Figley of Aliquippa, Pa., who finished seond in earnings with $14,648; Susan Thielbar of Palm Harbor, Fla.; and Jackie Gallagher-Smith of Ponte Vedra Beach, Fla., who was seventh on the money list with $11,339. Gallagher-Smith is the sister of PGA Tour pro Jim Gallagher Jr., who won the 1993 Tour Championship and was on the winning U.S Ryder Cup team.

Bowen, who played the LPGA Tour in 1992, is among those who regained their cards.

—by Don Cronin

Final T.C. Jordan Tour Money List

1. Charlie Rymer		$46,600.36
2. Craig Perks		$37,863.74
3. Marion Dantzler		$36,350.25
4. Ray Franz		$35,112.21
5. Rob McKelvey		$34,189.74
6. Paul Claxton		$28,708.75
7. Eric Johnson		$27,920.33
8. Tee Burton		$25,508.51
9. Jeff Lee		$24,338.54
10. Ralph Howe III		$23,701.76
11. Mike Brisky		$22,760.42
12. Jeff Cook		$20,914.71
13. Doug Weaver		$20,650.79
14. Mark Jordan		$18,635.00
15. Javier Sanchez		$18,209.50
16. Craig Bowden		$18,122.32
17. Steve Pope		$17,611.86
18. Spike McRoy		$15,994.04
19. Tim Holt		$15,932.61
20. Jeff Barlow		$15,249.83

Douglas Golf Classic

▸**Course:** Douglas Golf & Country Club
▸**Location:** Douglas, Ga.
▸**When:** April 12-18, 1993
▸**Purse:** $65,000
▸**Par:** 72
▸**Yards:** 6,800

Scores and earnings
Ray Franz $11,000	67-72-73-67–279
Rob McElvey $6,000	63-74-73-71–281
Bo Fennell $3,400	73-71-69-70–283
Steve Pope $2,342	69-74-72-69–284
Joe McCormick $2,342	70-74-72-69–284
Eric Johnson $1,775	73-70-73-69–285
Mike Brisky $1,775	66-71-74-74–285
Spike McRoy $1,498	71-76-72-67–286
Marion Dantlzer $1,498	70-71-74-71–286
Paul Claxton $1,498	69-74-69-74–286

John Crosland/Charleston National Golf Classic

▸**Course:** Charleston National Golf Course
▸**Location:** Mount Pleasant, S.C.
▸**When:** April 19-25, 1993
▸**Purse:** $65,000
▸**Par:** 72
▸**Yards:** 6,928

Scores and earnings
Paul Claxton $11,000	73-69-73-72–287
Marion Dantzler $6,000	73-72-73-71–289
Jeff Thorsen $3,400	76-72-72-70–290
Rob McKelvey $2,600	79-69-73-70–291
Alan Schulte $2,000	72-76-74-70–292
Ray Franz $1,673.34	77-73-73-70–293
Jeff Barlow $1,673.33	75-73-74-71–293
Eric Johnson $1,673.33	79-74-67-73–293
Mark Strickland $1,322.50	74-76-73-72–295
Mike Bolding $1,322.50	75-71-75-74–295
Chris Hunsucker $1,322.50	74-66-80-75–295
Tom Hearn $1,322.50	77-71-73-74–295

Sumter Classic

▸**Course:** Links at Lakewood
▸**Location:** Sumter, S.C.
▸**When:** May 6-9, 1993
▸**Purse:** $70,000
▸**Par:** 72
▸**Yards:** 6,625

Scores and earnings
Mark Jordan, $14,000	66-66-71-68–271
Doug Weaver, $4,700	68-68-66-70–272
Joe Shahady, $4,700	70-63-68-71–272
Mike Brisky, $2,127	71-66-70-66–273
Rob McKelvey, $2,127	75-64-66-68–273
Jason Larson, $2,127	66-68-69-70–273
David Patterson, $1,567	66-70-68-70–274
Paul Claxton, $1,567	70-69-65-70–274
Bo Fennell, $1,567	69-64-68-73–274
Skhaun Michoel, $1,315	74-65-70-66–275
T.J. Jackson, $1,315	65-70-71-69–275

Western Sizzlin Classic

▸**Course:** Willowpeg Golf Club
▸**Location:** Rincon, Ga.
▸**When:** April 26-May 2, 1993
▸**Par:** 72
▸**Yards:** 6,795

Charlie Rymer, of Atlanta, defeated Eric Johnson, of Eugene, Ore., on the first playoff hole.

Coca-Cola Classic

▸**Course:** Belwood Country Club
▸**Location:** Natchez, Miss.
▸**When:** May 24-30, 1993
▸**Par:** 71
▸**Yards:** 6,645

Scores and earnings
Charlie Rymer, $11,000	66-67-66-62–261
Winston Walker, $6,000	62-70-70-65–267
Jeff Lee, $2,980	66-67-69-66–268
Craig Perks , $2,980	68-65-65-70–268
Mark Strickland, $1,848	68-65-70-66–269
Rob McKelvey, $1,848	67-68-64-70–269
Javier Sanchz, $1,508	68-68-70-64–270
Shaun Micheel, $1,508	67-70-67-66–270
Tee Burton, $1,508	67-63-72-68–270
Ralph Howe III, $1,147	69-68-67-67–271
Michael Clark II, $1,147	64-70-69-68–271
Gibby Gilbert, III, $1,147	69-67-67-68–271
Jay Williamson, $1,147	70-66-65-70–271
Jeff Cook, $1,147	67-70-65-69–271

Gray Daniels Ford/APT 16 Classic

- **Course:** Bay Pointe Resort & Golf Club
- **Location:** Brandon, Miss.
- **When:** May 31-June 6, 1993
- **Par:** 72
- **Yards:** 6,630

Scores and earnings
Jeff Lee, $11,000	66-69-69-72–276
Steve Ford, $4,700	70-70-69-68–277
Spike McRoy, $4,700	69-68-69-71–277
Rob McKelvey, $2,650	74-69-68-68–279
Ray Franz, $2,035	74-72-66-68–280
Todd Gleaton, $1,830	71-72-67-71–281
Doug Weaver, $1,720	73-69-72-69–283
Gibby Gilbert III, $1,498	72-75-72-65–284
Ralph Howe III, $1,498	71-72-70-71–284
Jimmy Green, $1,498	69-75-68-72–284

Decatur Daily Classic

- **Course:** Point Mallard Golf Club
- **Location:** Decatur, Ala.
- **When:** June 7-13, 1993
- **Purse:** $65,000
- **Par:** 72
- **Yards:** 7,098

Scores and earnings
Tee Burton, $11,000	66-69-71-68–274
Ray Franz, $4,700	66-72-69-70–277
Doug Weaver, $4,700	68-71-68-70–277
Paul Claxton, $2,265	72-71-69-66–278
Michael Clark II, $2,265	69-71-69-69–278

Foxfire Golf Classic

- **Course:** Foxfire Inn & Country Club
- **Location:** Pinehurst, N.C.
- **When:** June 21-27, 1993
- **Par:** 72
- **Yards:** 6,650

Scores and earnings
Scott Medlin, $11,500	67-66-69-63–265
Ray Franz, $6,200	67-69-65-67–268
Jeff Lee $3,137	68-66-69-67–270
Brian Lamb, $3,137	66-68-68-68–270
Craig Bowden, $2,100	69-65-69-69–272
Chris Haarlow, $1,812	70-72-67-64–273
Ray Williamson, $1,812	69-64-72-68–273
Charlie Whittington, $1,595	70-71-66-67–274
Charlie Rymer, $1,595	67-67-70-70–274
David Patterson, $1,400	68-69-69-69–275
Marion Dantzler, $1,400	67-71-66-71–275

Croatan Classic

- **Course:** Fairfield Harbour Country Club
- **Location:** New Bern, N.C.
- **When:** June 28-July 4, 1993
- **Par:** 72
- **Yards:** 6,825

Scores and earnings
Craig Perks, $11,500	66-67-71-71–275
Mike Brisky, $6,200	70-70-68-69–277
Mark Strickland, $3,147	68-64-76-70–278
Jeff Lee, $3,147	68-65-73-72–278
Jeff Thorsen, $1,778	70-74-70-66–280
Lan Gooch, $1,778	73-71-67-69–280
Harold Wallace, $1,778	69-71-70-70–280
Dave Schreyer, $1,778	68-69-72-71–280
Vance Heafner, $1,778	70-71-68-71–280
Tom Hearn, $1,291	70-71-70-70–281
John Riegger, $1,291	71-70-69-71–281
Clark Burroughs, $1,291	69-68-71-73–281
Shaun Micheel, $1,291	71-70-65-75–281

B&A Travel Classic

- **Course:** Oak Hills Golf Club
- **Location:** Columbia, S.C.
- **When:** July 5-11, 1993
- **Par:** 72
- **Yards:** 6,785

Scores and earnings
Rob McKelvey, $11,000	72-66-68-71–277
Steve Pope, $6,000	68-70-71-69–278
Jeff Lee, $3,025	67-71-70-71–279
Tee Burton, $3,025	69-71-65-74–279
Spike McRoy, $1,932	72-71-70-68–281
Chris Hunsucker, $1,932	68-71-71-71–281
Mike Brisky, $1,640	69-70-73-70–282
Shaun Micheel, $1,640	71-70-70-71–282
Vance Veazey, $1,448	68-70-72-73–283
Jeff Thorsen, $1,448	73-70-67-73–283
Matt Peterson, $1,448	67-72-69-75–283

Bud Light/WBKO 13 Classic

- **Course:** Hartland Municipal Golf Course
- **Location:** Bowling Green, Ky.
- **When:** July 26-Aug. 1, 1993
- **Par:** 72
- **Yards:** 6,425

Scores and earnings
Tim Holt, $11,000	66-70-64-66–266
Brian Lamb, $4,700	70-69-63-69–271
Jamie Miller, $4,700	71-65-65-70–271
Sean Noonan, $2,176	69-73-67-64–273
Marion Dantzler, $2,176	68-69-71-65–273
Shaw Prtichett, $2,176	67-69-72-65–273
Dave Schreyer, $1,665	71-67-69-67–274
Tom Hearn, $1,665	68-69-69-68–274
Jeff Guest, $1,413	68-69-69-69–275
Ray Franz, $1,413	69-67-69-70–275
Vance Veazey, $1,413	67-71-65-72–275

Collins Pro Classic

- **Course:** Seneca Golf Club
- **Location:** Louisville, Ky.
- **When:** Aug. 2-8, 1993
- **Purse:** $65,000

▸**Par:** 72
▸**Yards:** 6,975

Scores and earnings
Craig Perks, $11,000	73-68-67-71–279
Jeff Barlow, $6,000	71-68-69-72–280
Todd Gleaton, $3,400	67-71-72-71–281
Marion Dantzler, $2,352.50	72-72-70-69–283
Shaun Micheel, $2,352.50	67-73-73-70–283
Brad Lehmann, $1,767.50	69-71-72-72–284
John Wells, $1,767.50	77-69-66-72–284
Mike Brisky, $1,465	71-69-73-72–285
Joe McCormick, $1,465	67-71-73-74–285
Dave Schreyer, $1,465	72-70-69-74–285
David Wall, $1,465	72-67-71-75–285

BUD DRY GOLF CLASSIC

▸**Course:** El Paso Golf Club
▸**Location:** El Paso, Ill.
▸**When:** Aug. 9-15, 1993
▸**Purse:** $65,000
▸**Par:** 72
▸**Yards:** 6,530

Scores and earnings
Steve Novarro, $11,000	66-65-73–204
Eric Johnson, $6,000	68-69-68–205
Doug Weaver, $3,400	72-66-68–206
Robert Huxtable, $2,650	67-70-70–207
Jeff Cook, $1,875	70-70-68–208
Scott Gardner, $1,875	70-70-68–208
Steven Schaff, $1,553	68-71-70–209
Jon Hough, $1,553	68-71-70–209
Chan Reeves, $1,553	68-69-72–209
Craig Bowden, $1,231	71-73-66–210
Michael Clark I$1,231	71-72-67–210
Carl Paulson, $1,231	69-70-71–210
Rob McKelvey, $1,231	68-71-71–210

PEPSI OPEN

▸**Course:** Elks Country Club
▸**Location:** Portsmouth, Ohio
▸**When:** Aug. 16-22, 1993
▸**Purse:** $65,000
▸**Par:** 72
▸**Yards:** 6,675

Scores and earnings
#Eric Johnson, $11,000	67-65-71-67–270
Charlie Rymer, $6,000	65-67-71-67–270
Craig Perks, $3,400	66-69-66-70–271
Marion Dantzler, $2,343	65-68-69-70–272
Ralph Howe III, $2,343	66-67-69-70–272
Javier Sanchez, $1,775	71-68-70-66–275
Bill Brown III, $1,775	68-71-66-70–275
Steve Pope, $1,451	69-67-71-69–276
Chris Haarlow, $1,451	68-68-70-70–276
Jimmy Green, $1,451	68-70-68-70–276
Bo Beard, $1,451	69-67-68-72–276

won on second playoff hole

HERITAGE LINKS CLASSIC

▸**Course:** Heritage Links Country Club
▸**Location:** Alachua, Fla.
▸**When:** Sept. 6-12, 1993

▸**Par:** 72
▸**Yards:** 6,725

Scores and earnings
Jeff Cook, $11,000	64-70-67-70–271
Javier Sanchez, $6,000	66-66-70-69–271
Marion Dantzler, $3,025	69-63-72-69–273
Charlie Rymer, $3,025	70-68-66-69–273
Craig Bowden, $1,938	69-69-67-69–274
Paul Claxton, $1,938	68-65-71-70–274
Don Abbott, $1,710	68-65-71-71–275
Ray Franz, $1,620	70-69-71-66–276
Lan Gooch, $1,363	70-67-71-69–277
Jason Brown, $1,363	69-69-70-69–277
Ralph Howe III, $1,363	67-71-68-71–277
Mike Brisky, $1,363	69-68-70-70–277

FOX 30 GOLF CLASSIC

▸**Course:** Magnolia Point Country Club
▸**Location:** Orange Park, Fla.
▸**When:** Sept. 13-19, 1993
▸**Purse:** $65,000
▸**Par:** 72
▸**Yards:** 6,855

Scores and earnings
Craig Bowden, $11,000	66-70-74-69–279
Paul Claxton, $6,000	70-70-68-73–281
Eric Brito, $3,025	69-69-74-71–283
Tee Burton, $3,025	69-70-72-72–283
Craig Perks, $1,875	69-71-72-72–284
Britt Pavelonis, $1,875	71-71-69-73–284
Michael Clark II, $1,553	73-71-71-70–285
Jon Hough, $1,553	69-75-70-71–285
Clark Burroughs, $1,553	78-66-69-72–285
David Patterson, $1,270	71-70-73-72–286
Javier Sanchez, $1,270	73-72-70-71–286
Michael Christie, $1,270	71-74-67-74–286

ATHENS GOLF CLASSIC

▸**Course:** Lane Creek Golf Club
▸**Location:** Watkinsville, Ga.
▸**When:** Sept. 20-26, 1993
▸**Purse:** $65,000
▸**Par:** 72
▸**Yards:** 6,620

Scores and earnings
Ralph Howe III, $11,000	68-66-71-70–275
Charlie Rymer, $6,000	65-65-75-71–276
Chris Haarlow, $2,666	71-68-71-67–277
Michael Christie, $2,666	73-69-67-68–277
Matt Peterson, $2,666	69-66-70-72–277
John Slinger, $1,780	67-69-72-70–278
Chris Van Der Velde, $1,466	72-67-73-67–279
Don Abbott, $1,466	67-73-72-67–279
Bill Brown III, $1,466	71-69-69-70–279
Rob McKelvey, $1,466	71-66-71-71–279
Jeff Jordan, $1,466	75-65-67-72–279

GOLF ALMANAC 1994

COLLEGE

NCAA DIV. I MEN'S CHAMPIONSHIP...356

NCAA DIV. I WOMEN'S CHAMPIONSHIP...357

OTHER MAJOR COLLEGE TOURNAMENTS...358

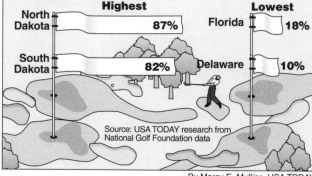

NCAA Div. I Men's Golf Championship

AT A GLANCE

- **Course:** The Champions Golf Club
- **Location:** Lexington, Ky.
- **When:** June 2–5, 1993
- **Par:** 72
- **Yards:** 7,064

Team scores

Team	Scores
Florida	291-277-294-283–1145
Ga. Tech	288-293-278-287–1146
North Carolina	284-286-293-284–1147
Clemson	293-284-288-288–1153
Texas	286-292-295-283–1156
Arizona St.	296-282-295-289–1162
Arkansas	293-290-300-286–1169
UNLV	296-290-304-286–1176
Oklahoma	300-295-294-288–1177
Duke	293-293-300-293–1179
Wake Forest	293-292-300-299–1184
Oklahoma St.	301-294-300-293–1188
Augusta	291-302-301-295–1189
SW Louisiana	294-300-308-288–1190
Kansas	294-299-309-298–1200

Individual scores (partial)

Player	Score
Todd Demsey, Arizona St.	73-65-71-69–278
David Duval, Ga. Tech	73-71-65-70–279
Chris Riley, UNLV	73-69-77-68–287
Guy Hill, Florida	73-69-77-68–287
Jean-Paul Hebert, Texas	68-72-78-69–287
Thump Delk, Clemson	71-71-73-72–287
Tim Herron, New Mexico	68-73-75-72–288
Chris Couch, Florida	71-65-76-76–288
Lee McEntee, North Carolina	73-70-72-73–288
Rob Bradley, North Carolina	67-76-74-71–288
Mark Swygert, Clemson	73-73-71-71–288
Stewart Cink, Ga. Tech	70-74-71-74–289
Carlos Beautell, Ga. Tech	72-76-68-73–289
Bud Still, Arkansas	71-71-76-71–289
Mike Etherington, SW La.	72-76-74-68–290
Bill Smith, North Carolina	76-71-72-71–290
Warren Schutte, UNLV	72-74-72-72–290
Brad Lehmann, Florida	74-72-78-67–291
Bobby Murray, North Carolina	72-71-79-69–291
Brian Gay, Florida	73-77-70-71–291
Jason Widener, Duke	73-75-74-70–292
Nicky Goetze, Clemson	76-70-68-78–292
Grant Masson, Oklahoma	74-72-72-75–293
Mikko Rantanen, Ga. Tech	73-72-78-70–293
Justin Leonard, Texas	71-74-76-72–293
Joe Guillion, Minnesota	73-71-77-72–292
Mike Muehr, Duke	72-70-76-76–294
Taylor Tipton, Texas	76-76-70-72–294
Cade Stone, Arizona St.	75-71-77-71–294
Chris Tidland, Oklahoma St.	75-73-76-70–294
Ron Whittaker, Wake Forest	69-72-75-78–294
Kevin Kemp, Wake Forest	72-72-76-74–294
Matt Gogel, Kansas	73-72-78-72–295
Larry Barber, Arizona St.	74-71-75-75–295
Chris Popp, SW Louisiana	73-71-73-78–295
Alan Bratton, Oklahoma St.	71-76-73-75–295
Brad Bruno, Kansas	75-77-74-69–295
David White, Arkansas	77-74-73-72–296
Dax Johnston, Oklahoma	74-77-78-67–296
Richard Johnson, Augusta	72-77-75-72–296
Gary Murphy, Augusta	74-76-75-71–296
Jack O'Keefe, Arkansas	72-73-73-79–297
Danny Ellis, Clemson	77-70-76-74–297
Ryan Parnell, North Carolina	72-74-75-76–297
Rob Mangini, Arizona St.	75-75-72-75–297
Bob Fisher, Wake Forest	76-74-72-75–297
Tom Hurley, Duke	76-74-74-73–297
Gary Clark, Arkansas	76-72-78-72–298
Marten Olander, Alabama	74-70-78-76–298
John Pettit, Florida	76-71-72-79–298
Justin Klein, Duke	75-74-76-74–299
Bobby Doolittle, Clemson	73-79-76-71–299
Rich Mayo, Oklahoma	76-73-74-77–300
Stuart Wallace, Texas	77-78-75-70–300
Craig Young, Arkansas	74-78-78-71–301
Eric Schroeder, UNLV	75-74-77-75–301
Craig Cozby, Oklahoma	79-73-74-75–301

Chris Couch rolled in a 4-foot putt for par on the final hole to give the University of Florida a one-stroke victory over Georgia Tech in the NCAA Div. I men's championship.

Tech's Dave Duval, who had played steadily the entire day, bogeyed the last hole on The Champions course. The bogey was doubly disastrous for Duval, as it also allowed Arizona State's Todd Demsey to win the individual championship by a single stroke.

"It was unexpected," Demsey said of his victory. "I figured David would probably sink that putt."

Demsey, who had a 3-under 69 in the final round, finished at 10-under 278. Duval settled for 70–279.

"I feel good about my performance," Duval said. "I gave myself the chance to make birdies, but none were falling in during the last few holes."

Duval had potential birdie putts stop inches short on 16 and 17. His tee shot on the par-4 18th landed in a sand bunker, and his subsequent chip shot for par from the fringe of the green skipped 12 feet past the hole. Duval calmly sank the next shot for bogey.

Couch, however, was a bundle of nerves on his putt.

"I was so nervous, I had to put my glove on," he said. "I couldn't feel my hand."

Gator freshman Brad Lehmann led Florida on the final day with a 67, while Guy Hill shot a 69, Brian Guy 71 and Couch 76. The Gators also won the title in 1968 and 1973.

North Carolina, the first-round leader, finished third, at 5-under 1,147, with Clemson fourth at 1,153 and Texas fifth at 1,156.

NCAA Div. I Women's Golf Championship

AT A GLANCE

- **Course:** University of Ga. Golf Course
- **Location:** Athens, Ga.
- **When:** May 26-29, 1993
- **Par:** 73
- **Yards:** 6,114

Team scores
1. Arizona State — 299-300-293-295–1,187
2. Texas — 305-289-295-300–1,189
3. San Jose State — 295-300-297-298–1,190
4. Georgia — 294-298-308-297–1,197
5. Southern Cal. — 310-307-300-295–1,212
6. Furman — 309-310-301-293–1,213
7. Wake Forest — 313-300-293-309–1,215
8. Indiana — 307-305-301-305–1,218
9. North Carolina — 306-304-301-307–1,218
10. UCLA — 311-306-304-303–1,224
11. Stanford — 310-310-311-301–1,232
12. South Carolina — 309-310-315-304–1,238
13. Oklahoma — 315-306-313-306–1,240
14. Arizona — 312-313-301-316–1,242
15. Ohio State — 318-311-319-304–1,252
16. New Mexico — 322-315-312-318–1,267
17. Oregon — 322-322-317-332–1,293

Individual scores (partial)
- 287 - Charlotta Sorenstam, Texas, 74-70-70-73
- 289 - Angela Buzminski, Indiana, 73-73-73-70
- 290 - Leta Lindley, Arizona, 74-76-68-72; Wendy Ward, Arizona State, 71-74-73-72
- 292 - Vicki Goetze, Georgia, 72-75-72-73
- 293 - Renee Heiken, Illinois, 74-73-73-73; Nadine Ash, Texas, 73-73-74-73
- 294 - Stephanie Neill, Wake Forest, 81-71-71-71
- 295 - Kristel Mourgue d'Algue, Furman, 78-74-73-70; Tracy Hanson, San Jose State, 70-79-72-74
- 297 - Lisa Walton, San Jose State, 80-73-71-73
- 298 - Moira Dunn, Fla. International, 72-76-77-73; Heidi Voorhees, Southern Cal, 74-75-70; Justine Richards, North Carolina, 76-73-77-72
- 299 - Kristin Milligan, Georgia, 73-74-78-74; Ninni Sterner, San Jose State, 74-72-77-76; Emilee Klein, Arizona State, 79-75-72-73; Holly Reynolds, Kansas, 77-72-76-74; Vibeke Stensrud, San Jose State, 71-76-77-75
- 300 - Dagmar de Vries, Furman, 76-77-74-73
- 301 - Abby Pearson, Tennessee, 78-74-82-67; Kim Augusta, Miami, Fla, 77-73-72-79; Martha Richards, Stanford, 72-80-74-75
- 302 - Elizabeth Bowman, UCLA, 78-74-76-74; Tracy Cone, Arizona State, 73-76-72-81
- 303 - Jessica Wood, North Carolina, 78-77-73-75
- 304 - Jill McGill, Southern Cal, 79-78-74-73; Jenny Turner, Texas, 80-71-75-78; Linda Ericsson, Arizona State, 81-75-77-71; Kelly Doohan, Georgia, 74-72-79-79; Jane Kragh, TCU, 79-77-76-72; Sara Miley, Georgia, 75-79-79-71; Mia Loejdahl, UCLA, 72-76-78-78; Camie Hoshino, Southern Cal, 78-74-76-76 305 - Jamille Jose, Stanford, 78-76-75-76; Caroline Peek, Furman, 75-81-74-75
- 306 - Jennifer Biehn, Southern Cal, 77-78-75-76
- 307 - Lisa Christie, BYU, 79-75-78-75; Nicole Cooper, Texas, 78-77-76-76; Kim Marshall, Wake Forest, 79-76-74-78
- 308 - Tara Joy, South Carolina, 79-79-77-73; Tami Dougan, Ohio State, 78-78-76-76; Courtney Cox, Indiana, 74-78-77-79
- 309 - Kim O'Connor, Oklahoma, 80-77-79-73; Kimberly Byham, North Carolina, 75-79-77-78
- 310 - Alycya Rambin, Oklahoma, 81-76-78-75; Ulrika von Heijne, Arizona State, 76-79-76-79; Jennifer Choi UCLA, 83-79-74-74
- 311 - Rachel Bates, South Carolina, 75-76-77-83; Stacy Quilling, Indiana, 80-78-77-76; Ulrika Johansson, Arizona, 76-77-77-81; Kim Tyrer, Wake Forest, 74-73-84-80
- 312 - Siew Ai Lim, South Carolina, 77-77-82-76; Robin Berning, Ohio State, 77-81-79-75; Julie Bowen, Stanford, 79-79-81-73; Shannon Clark, New Mexico, 78-76-77-81

Charlotta Sorenstam of the University of Texas breezed to the NCAA Division I women's golf individual title. But her four-putt double bogey at No. 9—where the last three shots were from inside 2 feet—may have cost Texas the team race.

Arizona State won the team title with a 5-under-par 1,187 total. Defending champion San Jose State was third at 1,190.

Though it had only one player in the top 10 and two in the top 20, Arizona State played evenly as a team. With four of the five best individual scores each day, the Sun Devils counted only one score higher than 76 on the par-73 course.

Texas had led Arizona State and San Jose State by three strokes starting the final round. Georgia, which led by nine strokes midway through the third round, was eight shots back with 18 holes to play.

At one point in the final round, ASU had an eight-stroke lead after playing 10 through 13 4-under par.

The Sun Devils return their top four players in 1994 and add Kristel Mourgue d'Algue, a Furman University sophomore who transferred to Arizona State last fall.

Sorenstam, whose sister Annika won the individual title two years previously as a University of Arizona freshman, shot 74-70-70-73–287 and finished two strokes ahead of Indiana University's Angela Buzminski (73-73-73-70–289).

Other Major College Tournaments

NCAA Div. II Men's Golf Championship

Abilene Christian won the NCAA Div. II men's golf championship by five strokes over Columbus (Ga.), but the Georgians could take consolation in Jeev Milkha Singh's individual-title victory at Turlock (Calif.) Golf and Country Club.

California State-Stanislaus, a 12-time winner in Div. III before moving up in 1989, nearly became the first school to win golf titles in two divisions.

Stanislaus senior Brad Long injured his right wrist while shooting a 7-under-par 65 in the second round and managed only a 76 in the third before being forced to sit out the final day.

Singh and Martin Lonardi of Columbus tied at 6-under-par 282 after 72 holes, but Singh rolled in a 2-foot birdie putt on the second playoff hole to edge his teammate.

Abilene Christian shot an 8-over-par 1,160 total, Columbus 1,165, Florida Southern 1,167 and California State-Stanislaus 1,170.

NCAA Div. III Men's Golf Championship

California-San Diego rolled to a 12-stroke victory over runner-up Ohio Wesleyan in the NCAA Div. III golf championships at Torrey Pines Golf Club's South Course in La Jolla, Calif.

Ryan Jenkins of Methodist (N.C.) shot 6-over-par 294 to win the individual title by a stroke over San Diego's Dale Abraham. Tim Ailes of Ohio Wesleyan and Brock Shafer of San Diego tied at 296.

Ohio Wesleyan finished third in the team race, 23 shots behind the winner.

Nat'l Minority College Golf Championship

Sophomore Brian Diggs' 18-foot birdie-putt on the final hole gave St. Augustine's (N.C.) the team title by one stroke over Jackson (Miss.) State in the seventh annual minority championships at Mana-kiki Golf Club in Willoughby Hills, Ohio.

The Mighty Falcons, in coach Lawrence Coleman's 25th season with the program, ended a three-year reign by defending champion Jackson State, edging them 599-600.

Coleman told Diggs on the 18th tee that a birdie would win the team title. Diggs hit a 3-wood off the tee, a wedge to the green, and sank the putt.

Robert Ames of Florida A&M won the individual title with a 1-over-par 75-70–145. Michael Harmon of Texas Southern was second at 74-72–146; Diggs and teammate Jason Parris, Mike Sorpauru of Jackson State, and Davey Broughton of Prairie View were tied another shot back.

Texas Southern won the women's team title by 869-1,074 over Grambling.

Palmetto Dunes Collegiate Tournament

Oklahome State and Arizona State fired sub-par rounds to take the men's and women's titles in the *Golf World*-Palmetto Dunes Collegiate tournament.

The Cowboys had a 10-under-par team score of 278 for a 23-under 841 total, six strokes ahead of Wake Forest.

Nota Begay of Stanford shot 67—202, 14-under, to win the individual title by five strokes over Rob Bradley of North Carolina. Sophomore Emilee Klein (69—214) edged teammate Wendy Ward (70—215) for the individual title, leading ASU to the women's championship.

GOLF ALMANAC 1994

Hall of Fame

PATTY SHEEHAN QUALIFIES FOR LPGA

HALL OF FAME ...360

GOLF THEME PARK PLANNED...362

USA SNAPSHOTS®
A look at statistics that shape the sports world

Open provides toughest test
Of the four major LPGA tournaments, the U.S. Women's Open has been the most difficult. Tournament records for 72 holes:

Strokes under par

U.S. Women's Open Pat Bradley, 1981	**–9**
Dinah Shore Amy Alcott, 1991	**–15**
du Maurier Ltd. Classic Cathy Johnston, 1990	**–16**
LPGA Championship Betsy King, 1992	**–17**

Source: *1993 LPGA Tour Book* By Marty Baumann, USA TODAY

GOLF ALMANAC 1994

Sheehan won way into LPGA Hall of Fame

Sheehan's road to fame

Some highlights from Patty Sheehan's career:

▶ Won all four of her matches as member of 1980 U.S. Curtis Cup team.
▶ Joined LPGA Tour in July, 1980.
▶ Won first event at 1981 Mazda Japan Classic.
▶ Won first major title at 1983 LPGA Championship.
▶ Earned 1983 Rolex Player of the Year award, with four wins and $255,185.
▶ Repeated as LPGA Championship winner in 1984.
▶ Won four tournaments for second year in a row in 1984.
▶ Awarded 1984 Vare Trophy for low scoring average at 71.40.
▶ At 1985 Moss Creek Invitational, became fastest player to pass $1 million in career earnings (a mark since bettered by Brandie Burton).
▶ Won three tournaments in 1986.
▶ One of eight athletes festured on *Sports Illustrated's* annual Sportsmen of the Year cover in 1987.
▶ Played on victorious U.S. team at inaugural 1990 Solheim Cup.
▶ Won five tournaments in 1990, while posting career-best scoring average of 70.62.
▶ Won U.S. Women's Open in 1992.
▶ Entered LPGA Hall of Fame with her 30th victory, at 1993 Standard Register Ping.
▶ Won 1993 Mazda LPGA Championship, her fourth major title.

Patty Sheehan was all of 13 when she retired for the first time to a life of leisure by the pool at the country club in Middlebury, Vt.

She had earned the rest by advancing from the Vermont Lollipop Ski Races at age 4 to a national ranking in nine years.

"I didn't know what I wanted to do," recalled Sheehan, 36. "So I sat by the pool for a whole summer before I went back to practicing golf really hard."

The practice paid off for Sheehan on March 21, 1993, as she qualified for the LPGA's Hall of Fame by winning the Standard Register Ping tournament, the 30th victory of her career.

Bobo and Leslie Sheehan, her parents, have been wintering in the Southern California desert since Bobo retired. He was the driving force behind Patty, giving her lessons in both skiing and golf when she was 4.

Bobo coached at Middlebury College and legend has it that when Patty was born Oct. 27, 1956, Bobo was helping tutor Middlebury in a football game.

"I don't know that she's the best athlete on our tour, but she's among the top five," said Pat Bradley, who qualified for the Hall in 1991. "It was only a matter of time until she made it."

A champagne celebration after Patty Sheehan's 30th victory.

By winning the Standard Register Ping, Patty became the 13th woman to qualify for the LPGA's Hall of Fame since it was established in 1967.

Six players from the original Women's Golf Hall of Fame (established in 1950) were inducted before the current rules were in effect. Their performances created the high standards in the current rules: 30 official victories, including two major championships; or 35 victories and one major; or 40 victories.

Three other players—Amy Alcott, Betsy King and Beth Daniel—are knocking on the Hall's door. Alcott needs one victory, but she hasn't won since the 1991 Dinah Shore.

"I think with Betsy it's only a matter of a couple of months until she gets in," said Bradley, who qualified with victories in the final two domestic events in 1991.

Bradley said the 30th victory is the most difficult. "I thank God every day that I didn't have to sit around and wait for one victory," she said.

But she hasn't escaped the vacuum that exists in what she calls "life after fame," a period when there are no more goals to reach. Bradley hasn't won since qualifying for the Hall.

"I don't think that's going to happen to me," said Sheehan, who went on to win the Mazda LPGA Championship in June 1993. "I enjoy the competition. I don't expect any letdown."

Despite her success, Sheehan is familiar with adversity. She won the 1979 collegiate championship and was unbeaten in four matches in the 1980 Curtis Cup competition, but she says of pro golf, "I didn't think I wanted that lifestyle of being on the road."

After finishing in the top 10 in three of the six LPGA events she played in 1980, Sheehan was confident she could play golf on the tour.

She was right, but until 1992 it looked like the biggest prize—the U.S. Women's Open—would elude her. She led the 1990 Open for two rounds, but faltered in the final 36 holes. In 1992, in the Open at Oakmont, Pa., she birdied the final two holes of regulation to force a playoff with Juli Inkster and then won the tournament in the playoff.

"The Open victory meant so much because I had so many psychological hurdles to get over," says Sheehan. "That had to be my greatest win ever.

"I knew I was going to have a lot more chances to qualify for the Hall of Fame, but I wasn't so sure about the Open."

—*by Jerry Potter*

"ON A VENDETTA": SHEEHAN ENTERED HALL, DID NOT FADE AWAY

Patty Sheehan is determined to make a life for herself after the Hall of Fame.

"I don't feel old," said Sheehan, who won her way into the LPGA Hall of Fame last March.

Her subsequent victory in the Mazda LPGA Championship proved she wasn't about to go off into retirement at age 36.

"That's the way the Hall of Fame is set up. You get in and you go away."

Sheehan was a vocal critic of the Hall of Fame before she qualified with her 30th victory at the Standard Register Ping in Phoenix.

She said then that "if they don't change the requirements, there isn't going to be anything but a bunch of old ladies in the Hall of Fame. They're gonna die, and it'll be a dead Hall of Fame."

After winning the LPGA Championship at Bethesda (Md.) Country Club, Sheehan gave a couple of good reasons for changing the criteria.

"Look at Pat Bradley and Amy Alcott," Sheehan said. "See what it's done to their lives."

Bradley has struggled with her career and hasn't won since her 30th victory in '91.

She went from No. 1 on the money list in '91 to No. 19 in '92. Last year she was 27th.

"She hasn't been able to focus on new goals and she has lost a lot of motivation," said Sheehan. "I don't want that to happen to me."

Alcott presents an even more painful sight for Sheehan. She has been stuck on

29 wins for over two years.

"Amy is having a hard time," said Sheehan. "She says it isn't bothering her, but I know it's devastating.

"She's one of the greatest players we've ever had, but she's being judged by what she's doing now. I don't think that's fair."

Sheehan says the Hall of Fame puts too much emphasis on the 30th victory, but she offered no advice on changing the entrance requirements.

An LPGA players committee is studying the Hall requirements. Most think they're too strict for modern times.

"Everyone agrees it's pretty much impossible for players joining the tour now to qualify," says LPGA President Alice Miller. "When I joined the tour 14 years ago, there were 20 players who could win. Now, there are 120."

The problem: easing the requirements without diminishing the accomplishments of Hall members or losing the LPGA's distinction of having the toughest Hall of Fame in sports.

Miller says nothing has been decided, but she expects the guidelines to remain unchanged in the hope that Alcott, King and Daniel can qualify.

Sheehan favors change, "so some of the greatest players in the world" can be inducted.

In contrast to the stuggles faced by some of her fellow Hall-of-Famers, Sheehan lost no time getting back to work. She finished second on the 1993 LPGA money list, with 12 top 10 finishes.

Her performance in the LPGA Championship was noted by Betsy King, who hoped to enter the hall but stayed stuck at 28 victories until the final event of the year.

"I have a feeling this is going to be Patty's year," said King.

"She seems to be on a vendetta."

—by Jerry Potter

Golf theme park planned for Florida

More than a dozen golf governing bodies, clubs and organizations have joined to develop the International Golf Museum and World Golf Village, a 400-acre project along Interstate 95 about 22 miles south of Jacksonville and 8 miles north of St. Augustine, Fla.

The Museum is to honor the spirit of golf, its great players, supporters and heritage and the values that make the game special to so many people.

Also involved will be educational and entertaining exhibits involving displays of memorabilia and historical artifacts. State-of-the-art technology will be used to let visitors interact and become part of the experience.

The PGA Tour, LPGA and PGA of America will combine their Halls of Fame into the facility, and expand their present collections. The PGA of America is moving its World Hall of Fame from Pinehurst, N.C., and closed that building last December.

The U.S. Golf Association also is involved in the project but no decision has been made how much, if any, of the organization's memorabilia from its Golf House in Far Hills, N.J., might be included in the museum.

The facility also is to include hotel and office space, campgrounds and entertainment facilities plus at least one golf course.

Also involved in the project: American Golf Sponsors, an organization of groups sponsoring pro tour events; the Amerian Junior Golf Association; American Society of Golf Course Architects; Augusta (Ga.) National Golf Club, site of The Masters each April; Club Managers Association; Golf Course Superintendents Association; Golf Writers Association of America; National Golf Course Owners Association; National Golf Foundation; Royal and Ancient Golf Club of St. Andrews, Scotland, which governs golf in Europe and, along with the USGA, sets the rules of golf.

—by Don Cronin

GOLF ALMANAC 1994

Courses

NICKLAUS BUILDS A COURSE...364

1994 MAJORS' COURSES PREVIEWS...366

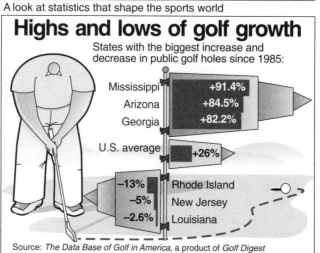

GOLF ALMANAC 1994

Dunes to greens: The course Jack built

Nicklaus as designer

In the past 25 years Jack Nicklaus has established himself among the top golf course architects in the world. In 1989 he became the only professional golfer to be accepted into the American Society of Golf Course Architects.

Nicklaus has over 100 courses he designed now open for play. Six of his courses are among *Golf Digest*'s top 100 courses in the USA and four are ranked among *Golf Magazine*'s greatest courses in the world. Nicklaus, who gets about five inquiries a week for new courses, has contracts for 73 to be completed.

Here are highlights of his accomplishments:

▶ **First Course:** 1968, Harbour Town Links, Hilton Head, S.C. (consultant for Pete Dye)

▶ **First Solo Design:** 1976, Glen Abbey Golf Club, Toronto.

▶ **First Solo Design in USA:** 1976, Shoal Creek, Brimingham, Ala.

▶ **100th Design:** 1993, Sunrise Course at Las Campanas, Santa Fe, N.M.

So, you want a new golf course and you want Jack Nicklaus to design it.

Well, bring your land and bring your money. Nicklaus can design a course for as little as $500,000, but to get the Nicklaus Signature it costs $1.25 million and takes at least 150 acres of land.

The process begins when Jim Lipe, a senior design associate, visits a client and looks at the property. "I ask if they want to build just a golf course or if they want a residential community," said Lipe. "If they want a community they need 400 acres."

If Lipe's report is favorable then the client meets with Nicklaus associates in Palm Beach, Fla., where they go over a budget for the project and enter into an agreement.

The first step is to review a topographical map of the property. That leads to a preliminary routing plan for the course. Nicklaus reviews the plans and decides if he wants to continue the project. He accepts about 90 percent of the jobs.

The third stage—strategy—is where Nicklaus puts his print on the course by deciding how he wants each hole to be played for every level of golfer. He determines where he wants the tees, greens, and bunkers.

Nicklaus then works with design associates to produce the preliminary contours of the course, which lead to the final set of contour plans. Those plans show the outline of the course, from drainage system to cart paths.

The final construction documents are made from these plans and construction begins. It takes from one to two years to build the course, depending on the climate and the quality of the course.

Nicklaus has various fees for design, ranging from $500,000 to $1.25 million. The more he's personally involved, the more it costs, with the Jack Nicklaus Signature Design the most expensive plan available.

One such course, Cabo del Sol, was built in Cabo San Lucas, Mexico, in 1993. Nicklaus worked on the design from the beginning and made numerous trips to the project, inspecting each stage of construction.

The 53-year-old legend visited the site in 100-degree summer heat, surveying construction from the bed of a four-wheel drive pickup truck.

The Sea of Cortez glistened in the background, but Nicklaus was focused only on the sandy ground that would become his 101st course.

In the industry such inspections are also known as "The day of the $50,000 wave." Meaning the designer visits, sees something about a hole that he doesn't like, waves his hand as if to move the offending hole, and the owner coughs up another $50,000.

Nicklaus does not like $50,000 waves. At Cabo del Sol, he only found one hole that wasn't as good as its design. He thought it was too difficult and instructed Lipe and the foreman to eliminate one bunker and move two others to give the golfers more room.

On most tees, he looked off into the distance, surveyed the hole and said, "As advertised," a sign that the hole was built as he designed it.

"We try to make sure that we don't have any big mistakes that aren't corrected until after the golf course is completed," said Nicklaus. "The reason we had to make very few changes (on Cabo del Sol) is that we'd made alterations as we went along."

Cabo del Sol is his second course in the area, but it's on a favorite piece of property, a stretch of land that includes desert, mountains and ocean.

"The most important thing to a developer are the 'Three L's,'" says Nicklaus. "That's location, location, location. We've gotten property that is good and property that is bad, but we can build a good golf course on bad property."

Nicklaus designed the TPC of Michigan in Dearborn, Mich., on an old dump for Ford Motor Company, and he built the Loxahatchee Club in Jupiter, Fla., on a swamp.

Loxahatchee is known for large mounds between the fairways, which some think is Nicklaus' attempt to give a South Florida a touch of Scotland. Not so, says Jack. "We had all this extra dirt," he said. "We had to have some place to put it, so we made mounds on the course."

Nicklaus' first effort in design came in 1968 when he was a consultant to Pete Dye on the construction of Harbour Town in Hilton Head, S.C. After doing nine courses as a consultant, Nicklaus went solo in 1976 with Glen Abbey Golf Club in Toronto.

Over the years Nicklaus has been criticized for making golf courses that are too expensive to build and too difficult to play. He takes issue with these criticisms, although he has altered his designs over the years.

"Most people only see my golf courses on TV when they're playing a major tournament on them," he says. "Sure, they're going to be playing 7,100 yards and they'll be tough.

"I try to design each hole so there are enough tees for every player. If I play a par-4 with a driver and a 5-iron I put tees in that allow the short hitter to play it in a driver and a 5-iron. The problem is most people try to play my courses from the back tees. I don't design them for everybody to play from there."

Nicklaus' standard course plays to a par 72 and measures 7,000 yards from the back tees. In between, he'll have tees that make the course play 6,400 to 5,000 yards.

The basic formula for his courses includes four par-5s and four par-3s, one of each playing north, south, east, and west, and 10 par-4s.

The sun and the direction of the prevailing wind plays into the design. Usually, the course starts to the west and finishes to the east, so golfers don't play into the sun. He likes the driving range to face north and south, again to avoid the sun.

Par-3s and par-5s are connecting holes, which explains, for example, why the 10th hole at Colleton River Plantation, Hilton Head, S.C., is 600 yards long. "I knew what I wanted to do with the 11th hole," says Nicklaus, "but I had to get there first. So, I made a 600-yard hole."

On top of Nicklaus' design fees are the actual construction costs. A public facility can be built for about $3 million, but a planned community project can cost as much as $25 million.

Nicklaus' costs are billed half during planning and half during construction. But, when it's over, you have a Jack Nicklaus Signature Course.

Said Nicklaus: "When they hire us, they hire us forever. If they've paid me once they've paid me forever."

Lyle Anderson, an Arizona developer who has hired Nicklaus for five projects, thinks its worth the money.

"Jack has only built 100 of these things all over the world," said Anderson. "And some day he won't build any more. When that happens these courses will be like a Rembrandt."

—by Jerry Potter

Previews of 1994 Majors' Courses

▸**The Masters, Augusta (Ga.) National Golf Club (April 7-10):** The "rite of spring" returns each April to Augusta, where Bobby Jones' dream course opened in 1933. Augusta National was built on a choice tract of land, formerly a landmark nursery owned by a Belgian horticulturist, which was purchased for $70,000—about $200 an acre. Jones, who had retired from competitive golf in 1930, established an annual invitational tourney to bring together "men of some means and devoted to the game of golf." Clifford Roberts, who helped form the club, suggested calling the competition the "Masters Tournament," but Jones thought the name too pretentious. Now, the Masters is one of the three most famous golf tournaments in the world (with the U.S. and British Opens) and stands as a tribute to the spirit of Jones, the only man to win golf's grand slam.

▸**U.S. Open, Oakmont (Pa.) Country Club (June 16-19):** This year's Open will be the seventh at this legendary course, which, counting three PGA Championships, has hosted the most grand slam events of any course. The original treacherous layout opened in 1904, with eight par-5s and a par-6 for a total par of 80. Its 220 sand bunkers have since been trimmed to a tad gentler 199.

Founded by Pittsburgh steel magnate Henry Fownes, a four-time U.S. Amateur champion, Oakmont is bisected by Hwy. 76.

In what is considered one of the top final rounds in championship golf, Johnny Miller, then 26, shot a final-round 63, including a putt for 62 that lipped out of the 18th hole at the 1973 Open.

Oakmont hosted the 1992 U.S. Women's Open, won by Patty Sheehan; U.S. Opens in 1927 (Tommy Armour won), 1935 (Sam Parks Jr.), 1953 (Ben Hogan), 1962 (Jack Nicklaus), 1973 (Johnny Miller) and 1983 (Larry Nelson); and PGA Championships in 1922 (Gene Sarazen), 1951 (Sam Snead), and 1978 (John Mahaffey).

▸**British Open, the Ailsa Course, Turnberry, Scotland (July 14-17):** A World War I training site for the Royal Flying Corps and a World War II landing strip for Spitfires, Turnberry sits along cliffs that border the Firth of Clyde.

Tom Watson won the 1977 British Open at Turnberry, besting Jack Nicklaus head-to-head over the final 36 holes. They had both opened 68-70-65 and Nicklaus led by two strokes with six holes to play the final day. But Watson rallied, birdying four of the final six holes. Down by a stroke on the final hole, Nicklaus made a 30-foot birdie putt, forcing Watson to sink a 2-footer for birdie to win. Third-place Hubert Green finished 10 strokes back.

Greg Norman won his first British Open at Turnberry in 1986, including a second-round 63 that just missed being a 60.

▸**PGA Championship, Southern Hills Country Club, Tulsa, Okla. (Aug. 11-14):** The 1994 PGA Championship was originally awarded to Oak Tree Country Club in Edmond, Okla. But, caught up in the Oak Tree Savings and Loan debacle, Oak Tree withdrew for business reasons.

Completed in 1936, Southern Hills was built on land that Waite Phillips (of the Phillips oil family) gave to organizers after they met his unusual challenge: Raise $150,000 in two weeks and agree to spend it over a two-year period on a true country club.

Temperatures often have reached 100 degrees during majors at Southern Hills, since they are played in the summer months. This year should be no exception.

Designed by Perry Maxwell, the course is formidably long and tight and is noted for its extra-thick Bermuda rough.

Southern Hills hosted the U.S. Open in 1958 (Tommy Bolt) and 1977 (Hubert Green) and the PGA Championship in 1970 (Dave Stockton) and 1982 (Ray Floyd).

GOLF ALMANAC 1994

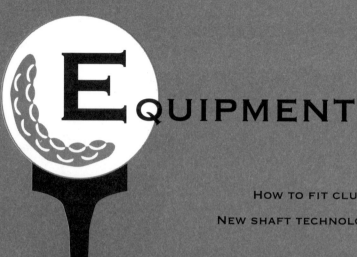

EQUIPMENT

HOW TO FIT CLUBS ...368

NEW SHAFT TECHNOLOGY...369

USA SNAPSHOTS®
A look at statistics that shape the sports world

Public golf courses growing

1988 1992

Private clubs: 4,897 / 4,568
Courses open to public: 7,685 / 8,642

Source: National Golf Foundation By Nick Galifianakis, USA TODAY

How to pick clubs that fit your swing

Lorraine Klippel wasn't trying to be funny, but she got a chuckle from her audience when she said, "Golf clubs do not have sex."

Klippel, a teaching pro from Mechanicsburg, Pa., was trying to say that there should be no gender attached to golf clubs. Rather, a pro should try to find the right combination of club head, shaft and grip to give the golfer the best chance to hit good shots.

Increasingly, club professionals are turning to club fitting as a means of matching equipment to a player's swing.

On a hot day last June, Klippel came to Charlotte, N.C., to teach a class of approximately 15 LPGA Teaching Pros the secrets of club fitting.

She spent last summer traveling the USA, giving these seminars for Square Two Golf, which has joined the LPGA's teaching pros in an ambitious program of customizing clubs.

Although there are secrets to the process, Square Two President George Nichols tells the students, "This is not rocket science."

A golf club has just three parts—head, shaft and grip—but each part has several variations, all of which can affect a golfer's chance to hit good shots.

"The only way to know for sure what's best for the individual is to take dynamic measurements," said Klippel. "A lot of companies are taking static measurements.

"They measure your height, the distance from your finger tips to the ground, etc. All you know when you do that is how tall they are and how far their fingers are from the ground."

The only true fit is one created from dynamic measurements, those taken while a golfer is in the process of striking a ball.

In recent years more and more equipment companies are teaching pros to take dynamic measurements.

Square Two has developed a simplified system that still gives the student and the teacher the information needed to fit clubs.

The process tests two important factors—clubhead speed and lie angle. The clubhead speed, measured from the driver with an electronic radar gun, determines the type of shaft that's best for the student.

The speed can range from 55 to 105 mph. The higher the golfer's swing speed, the stiffer the shaft needed in the clubs.

"With the advent of composite shafts," said Nichols, "the day will come when we can engineer a shaft that fits increments of speed down to 5 mph."

Typically, a student with average clubhead speed—80 mph—needs a more flexible shaft and a driver with more loft. Both shaft flex and loft help the player get the ball airborne.

Lie angle is a factor that's often overlooked, but it's critical to hitting accurate shots.

"The ideal place for the ball to strike the face of modern cavity-backed clubs is right in the center," said Nichols. "If the club face comes in contact with the ball and it's too upright or too flat then the ball goes off-line."

To check the lie angle, Klippel trains pros to test the students by taping the sole of the club and having them hit balls off a lie-board, made of Lexan. The board will mark the tape where it first hits.

If the mark is on the toe, then the club is too flat. If it's on the heel, then the club is too upright.

If the mark strikes in the middle, then the club is a fit, but that's seldom the case without some adjustments—bending of the hosel—to the club. Usually, the proper lie angle can only be determined by this test.

Kerry Graham, past President of the LPGA's Teaching Division, has preached the gospel of club fitting for years, or since the day that she compared her clubs to another golfer's clubs.

"I'm 5-foot-1 and she's 6-foot-2," said Graham. "Looking at us there's no way that we should have clubs with the same lie angle. But after the tests we both measured for clubs that were 2 degrees flat."

Nichols said Graham's experiences prove the point. "Lie angle is determined by swing plane," he said. "It doesn't necessarily match a person's body build."

Adds Graham: "For people between 5-feet and 6-feet tall, lie angle can vary all over the board. It's like a finger print. Each person is unique in that he or she has a different lie angle."

Although Graham believes in fitting clubs for all golfers, she cautions that the best fit comes from a working relationship between the teacher and the student.

As the student's swing develops then the teacher can better adjust the clubs to fit the normal pattern of the swing.

Graham also cautions that teachers and students should check the clubs to make sure they remain the measurements that fit. Golf clubs take a tremendous beating, which can alter their dimensions.

"The teacher has to be knowledgable and the company has to provide what's ordered," said Graham. "That link is the secret to the whole deal."

Does the deal work?

"There is no national champion, no player making a profit in the precarious occupation of tournament golf, who would ever come close to championship play if his clubs were as ill-fitted as those of the many thousands of golfers."

Pro Tommy Armour wrote that in 1953, when he recommended golfers play clubs with more flexible shafts, more upright lie angles and more lofted driving clubs.

—by Jerry Potter

New technology has made its mark

Gary Player won the 1965 U.S. Open using irons with Fiberglas shafts by Shakespeare, a maker of fishing equipment.

"I betcha I couldn't take that set of clubs and shoot 75 today," said Player. "They were so flexible you could almost hear them snapping back as you swung."

The old Shakespeares are long gone, but fishing poles are back in pro golf, thanks to Gary Loomis, who began making fishing rods of composite materials in 1973.

"I started to make golf shafts in 1974," said Loomis, from Woodland, Wash. "But the material wasn't good enough, so I got out."

Since coming back to golf in 1989, Loomis has persuaded about 40 members of the PGA Tour, as well as players on the Senior PGA Tour and LPGA, to use his G. Loomis shafts. Loomis got a double win Feb. 7, 1993, with Jim Colbert on the Senior Tour and Tammie Green in the LPGA.

Colbert used Ping irons and Green used Tommy Armour irons, but both had Loomis shafts of different flexes.

Colbert went to the Loomis shaft after Bob Murphy, another Senior Tour player, demonstrated them for him the previous fall.

Murphy, who has arthritis in his hands, thought the Loomis graphite shaft, which has less vibration, would enable him to play more tournaments.

Colbert tried several shafts before playing the Loomis. "Always before, you couldn't get any consistency out of the irons with composite shafts," he said. "One swing you'd hit the ball one distance, and another swing, the same club would hit it a different distance."

That was a common problem, which Loomis says he solved. Still, Loomis couldn't persuade Lee Trevino to change.

"They told me they were just like my metal shafts," said Trevino. "I said, 'If that's the case, why do I want to play them?'"

That's a good question, but some golfers are predicting graphite shafts will replace steel, just as steel replaced hickory.

"I don't think there has been a lot of technology in the golf shaft industry," said Loomis. "The window of design on the steel shaft is so small, there isn't a lot you can do with it."

Loomis says he solved the problem of inconsistency in the shafts with technology he used making fly rods, which also must remain consistent in their flex. He says composite shafts, made of epoxy with strands of graphite and boron, can be engineered to any golfer's swing.

Loomis' shafts, used by six club companies, retail for $60–$125 each.

—*by Jerry Potter*

DOES YOUR SHAFT HAVE THE RIGHT TORQUE?

If Hillerich & Bradsby, which makes baseball bats and golf clubs, had a candy store it would be in their manufacturing plant at Jeffersonville, Ind., across the Ohio River from the corporate headquarters in Louisville, Ky.

George Manning would run the store, dispensing golf club shafts like they're sticks of candy. As H & B's resident guru on shafts, he keeps up with products being offered in the industry, often lining them up in his office like candy on a shelf.

There's red. There's black. There's blue. Even a cream. And a few with swirling mixtures of colors that could blind your eyes.

"No," said Manning, chuckling at the question, "you don't select a shaft because you like the color. The color really has nothing to do with the performance of the shaft. It's just marketing."

With the popularity of the composite shaft—those made from epoxy and various types of space age material like graphite and boron—marketing experts are going batty with different colors and different designs on shafts. But that's only cosmetic.

"The club shaft, when it's swung, contorts in two ways," explained Manning. "The shaft actually bends or flexes, and it torques, or twists, at the bottom near the club head."

Those two characteristics affect the performace of clubs tremendously and determine which shaft should be used by each golfer. Basically, the stronger the player the less flex and less torque needed in the shaft.

"We use a different shaft for women's clubs, senior clubs, average player clubs and the low-handicap player's clubs," said Manning.

"You can do that with composite materials because you can take fibers and organize them in different directions to alter flex and torque."

The key marking on composite shafts is a number on the shaft that ranges from approximately 4.0 to 2.5. It means nothing to most people, but the number tells you about the torque. The higher the number the more it torques; the lower the number the less it torques.

A player with a slow swing speed—usually women and senior amateurs—need clubs with more torque and flex.

Both help them get the ball launched on a higher trajectory which will give them more distance and a more controlled shot.

"If a player has a tendency to slice we can build a shaft that can help him cut down on the slice," said Manning. "We can also make shafts lighter and stronger, so the player can swing the club faster and get more distance on his shots."

Another marking on some shafts is the phrase, "filament wound."

"That means the shaft was made by taking epoxy and a roll of fibers and spinning them on a mandrel," he explained. "You don't get a seam down the shaft with this method. Without a seam you can come much closer to matching a set of shafts in frequency of vibration."

As one might expect composite materials have made shafts more expensive. Manning estimates golfers can buy steel shafts for $2 to $10 apiece, while composite shafts cost from $6 to $100 apiece.

"We can build a top quality component shaft and keep the price below $15 a shaft," said Manning. "If you're an average player or below you don't need all the high-tech components that are used in the shaft of a touring pro's club."

—*by Jerry Potter*

GOLF ALMANAC 1994

INSTRUCTION

LPGA AND PGA OF AMERICA HOTLINES ...372

MORE TIPS...375

TEACHER SPOTLIGHT: LOUISE SUGGS...376

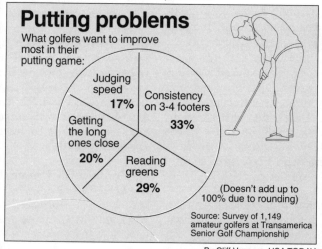

USA SNAPSHOTS®
A look at statistics that shape the sports world

Putting problems
What golfers want to improve most in their putting game:

- Judging speed: **17%**
- Consistency on 3-4 footers: **33%**
- Getting the long ones close: **20%**
- Reading greens: **29%**

(Doesn't add up to 100% due to rounding)

Source: Survey of 1,149 amateur golfers at Transamerica Senior Golf Championship

By Cliff Vancura, USA TODAY

Hotline: Talking Shop with the Pros

Every golfer—even Jack Nicklaus—needs advice from a good teacher once in a while. Whether to fine-tune a putting stance, work on sand shots or straighten out an unwanted slice. But the right golf doctor can sometimes be hard to find.

In recognition of the exquisite frustration caused by the ancient and royal sport, USA TODAY organized two free call-in advice days, where LPGA and PGA of America pros would try to help callers iron out the kinks in their game. Everyone from weekend high-handicappers to scratch golfers had questions, as USA TODAY logged thousands of calls. And everyone from LPGA Hall of Famer Patty Berg to CBS analyst Ken Venturi was waiting with their own tips and tricks—sometimes, not surprisingly, offering different takes on the same question.

After three hours of giving golf lessons on the telephone, pro Bill Strausbaugh concluded that people throughout the USA were eager to learn more about the game.

"There are so many people out there crying out for proper guidance that we as professionals have to be ready to meet their needs," said the 1992 PGA of America Instructor of the Year.

Strausbaugh was taken with the number of people who just wanted to know how to get started.

"It's terribly important that people be involved from Day 1 with a PGA member," said Strausbaugh, 69 and a teaching pro for 47 years. "And it's terribly important that the PGA have people ready and prepared to handle their problems."

A typical phone call for Strusbaugh: I'm just starting, do I need to buy equipment now?

"Heavens, no," he answered. "Go to your PGA teacher and let him be your guiding light."

Strausbaugh, the pro at Columbia Country Club in Chevy Chase, Md., believes the key to success is getting the proper start. "Our mothers always said, 'Well-begun is half done.' That's what golf is all about."

Meanwhile, when LPGA touring pros manned the phone lines for a day last June, Kathy Whitworth also had lots of answers, but one response was a bit unusual.

"One guy was so messed up that I finally told him just to watch the telecast of the (Mazda LPGA Championship) on Saturday and Sunday," Whitworth said, "and he'd see what I was talking about."

A sampling of the most oft-asked questions and some pro opinions follows.

—by Jerry Potter

LPGA Pros Answer Callers' Questions

Q: How do I stop shanking?
—Mary Jane Dennis, Whispering Pines, N.C.
A: Stay level in backswing and downswing; visualize a string attached to your head and someone is pulling it up. This will help to keep you from dropping.
—Lynn Connelly

Q: If you have had a hip injury, or you're a senior golfer with a hip injury, how can you adjust your swing and still enjoy the game?
—Fran Eward, 86, Richmond, Ind.
A: Use more of your upper body in the pivot and be sure to swing with a slow and steady rhythm.
—Shelley Hamlin

Q: I'm 6-4. Do I need longer (than normal) clubs?
—John Millen, Butler, Pa.
A: Definitely. Graphite shafts are a good idea as long as you get the right flex. See a pro in your area to get the right flex for the graphite shaft and for measurements to see how much longer your clubs should be.
—Nina Foust

Q: I'm 80 years old and want to know

how to swing the club and not just hit it.

—Jack Cohn, Pembroke Pines, Fla.

A: It doesn't really matter how old you are. If you take a good shoulder turn, the swing will be fine. You have to remember to initiate the swing with the left shoulder and don't let the hands and wrists take over. Heck, you've got another 30 years of golf to play.

—Lynn Adams

Q: **How important is it to raise the left foot on the backswing?**

—Sheri Martin, Wooster, Ohio

A: Lifting the left foot should only be a result of taking the club away from the body and making a wide swing—not a long swing.

—Shelley Hamlin

Q: **What is the value of new technology? I have an old set of clubs, but they work fine. Should I be thinking about new equipment?**

—Gary Myers, Bellingham, Wash.

A: You can't deny that golf technology has come a long way. New clubs—such as those with graphite shafts—are very forgiving, both on bad swings and on the body when you hit the ground. But the bottom line is: If you enjoy your game and the old clubs are holding up OK, then stick with them and have a good time.

—Nancy Ramsbottom

Q: **How should I set up to the ball to be consistent?**

—Bill O'Conner, New York

A: This is a good tip for anybody. Try to keep the set-up as relaxed as possible. Many people want to make their set-up very contorted, but the more contorted and still they get it, the harder it is to reproduce it every swing.

—Martha Nouse

PGA SAGES DIAGNOSE COMMON COMPLAINTS

Q: **Should I put 65% of my weight on the balls of my feet rather than 50-50 between the heels and toes?**

—Tim Clark, 37, Sterling, Va.

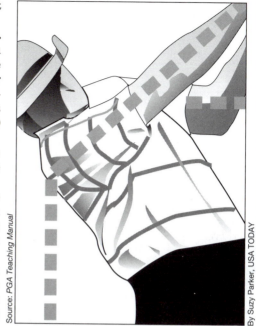

PERFECT FORM: Just as the left arm extends in the backswing, the right arm extends in the forward swing.

A: Balance your weight between the heels and the toes, because if you put too much weight in one area, you might have trouble shifting weight during the swing.

—Jock Olson, Cedar Rapids (Iowa) Country Club

Q: **I am a 5 handicapper who hits 200-plus balls per practice session, but can't seem to get my handicap lower. What should I do?**

—Scott Driver, 34, Memphis

A: You should track your game every time you go out. Keep track of fairways you hit, greens hit in regulation and putts. Use a scorecard to catalog every shot, which direction every iron and wood goes and how successful each type of shot is. After about 10 rounds you will be able to identify trends. Once you identify the problems, you can develop a program to improve those areas and that handicap could be down to 2 by next summer.

—Ed Ibarguen, Duke University Golf Club

Q: **Will a graphite driver help my game?**

—Joe Nolan, 47, Steubenville, Ohio

A: Yes. Within five years, all your clubs will be graphite. They have less torque and less shock when you hit them. The

SAND SHOT TIP: Don't use a closed-face grip to execute a "splash" sand shot. The toe will tend to lead and dig.

older a player gets, the more a shaft with a softer feel helps.

—John Haines, Teton Pines Country Club, Jackson, Wyo.

Q: I hit short irons well but have trouble with long irons.

—Mark Pillarelli, 38, Augusta, Ga.

A: When you address the ball, make sure your head is not too far forward. If you move your hands back to the center, you'll square up the club face and hit the ball straighter.

—Kip Puterbaugh, Golf Academy, Carlsbad, Calif.

Q: When I play with my local pro, I seem to play pretty well, but when I'm out on my own, I try to hit it too far.

—Jean McBride, 70, Newcastle, Pa.

A: When you're not playing with your pro, try to remember what he's told you. But most important, relax and don't overswing.

—CBS analyst Ken Venturi

Q: How will weight training affect my golf game?

—Jason Navarro, 14, Milwaukee

A: You should gear your workout to increase strength and flexibility. Do not try to bulk up with heavy weights. Start doing hand, forearm and leg exercises using a weight with which you can easily do 20 repetitions. Don't increase the weight until you are doing 40 repetitions.

—Ed Hester, Butte Creek Country Club, Chico, Calif.

Q: I'm a 3-handicap golfer and play well, except in tournaments. How can I improve?

—Dave Reynolds, 29, Greensboro, N.C.

A: You should play in more tournaments. The more you play, the less likely you'll get nervous. Another thing that might help is concentrating on holes 1-2-3 and 16-17-18. I find that if I can get off to a good start and finish strong, the tournament will go well.

—Paul Wilcox, Diablo (Calif.) Country Club

Q: How can I stop hitting my short irons to the right when I'm approaching the green?

—Patty Huffman, 65, Palm Desert, Calif.

A: Sometimes when people get close to the green, they try to steer the ball instead of swinging at it. Don't try to guide the ball and club, but swing the short irons like you do the driver.

—John Haines, Teton Pines Country Club, Jackson, Wyo.

Q: When should my son, who is 10, start taking lessons? He's been playing about three years.

—Len Thielk, 41, Ann Arbor, Mich.

A: Let him start taking serious lessons when he's about 14.

—Jerry Mowlds, Pumpkin Ridge C.C., Portland, Ore.

Q: I'm a club pro and professional player but have trouble with my mind wandering. How do I control that?

—J. Paul Leslie III, 27, Darien, Conn.

A: You need to think of ways to quiet the mind. I like to think of the "three Cs," calm, confidence, control. Sometimes it helps to hum a gentle tune. Just before you swing, take a deep cleansing breath.

—Joe Thiel, Capitol City Golf Club, Olympia, Wash.

MORE TIPS: SLICING, PUTTING, FITNESS, ETC.

The most-asked question by callers to the USA TODAY/LPGA Hotline: "How can I stop slicing the ball?"
LPGA players answered as follows.

▶**Heather Drew:** Almost everyone who has problems slicing has problems with foot alignment. What they think helps actually hurts. People try to compensate by opening their stance. They should be using a square alignment and swinging from the inside out.

▶**Missie Berteotti:** One good drill to eliminate the slice is to keep the feet together and swing naturally. This forces golfers to practice the full range of motion.

▶**Joan Pitcock:** If you are having consistent problems with slices, you need to spend more time on the practice range and less on the course. That can be hard to take when you are playing just once or twice a month, but it's true.

▶**Julie Larson:** To check your alignment, put a club on the ground pointing downrange where you want to hit the ball. Then set up and put another club in front of your toes. If the two clubs are not parallel, your alignment is off.

Some other responses to common questions:

▶Touring pro **Kathy Whitworth** advised a symmetrical swing for the short game: "Keep the backswing and the follow-through even on both sides."
Her advice for golfers who sway on their backswing: "A sway usually means you're starting the swing with the body and not the club head."
If you can't stop swaying, keep the club head in line with your sway. "You can sway all you want if you take the club head back with you."

▶Hall of famer **Patty Berg**, 75, got an array of questions from golfers whose

Slice and hook: How not to

Hook and slice: to hit a shot that curves sharply left (hook) or right (slice, for right-handed golfers), respectively. Players who do one or the other should consider changing the way they stand, hold the club or swing. Players who do both should consider changing the way they spend their weekends.
— Henry Beard and Roy McKie in *Golfing: A Duffer's Dictionary*

Ball flight

Hook   Straight   Slice

Club face in 10 o'clock position produces a hook with the ball rotation being counter-clockwise

Club face in 2 o'clock position produces a slice with the ball rotation being clockwise

By Julie Stacey, USA TODAY

skills ranged from the single-digit handicapper to the 20.
To the good player who duck-hooked tee shots, she advised checking the shoulder turn.
"If you forget to get a full shoulder turn, you come across the ball and get a duck hook," she said.
Her advice on putting fit any level of golfer: "You have to get a good stance and a good set-up. You have to keep your head and body still. If you move either one, you hit the putt off line. Watch the putter blade hit the ball. That'll help you stay still."

▶**Julie Barr** of the Palo Alto Hills Country Club in Palo Alto, Calif., got calls wanting to know about the right age to start youngsters in golf.
"I think five or six is too young, because at that age a child's attention span is too short," she said. "And if you start that young, you burn out and lose interest. I advise starting at age nine or 10."

▶**Tennye Ohr** from the Connemara Golf Club, Lexington, Ky., got calls from

TEACHER

Louise Suggs was one of the great names in women's golf who gave golfers advice on the USA TODAY/LPGA hotline.

"The major question I was asked was how to cure a slice," Suggs said. "I told one guy, 'If I knew the answer to that, I'd make a million bucks.'"

Suggs, who turned 70 last September, has seen about every golf problem and has decided that good golf instruction has to be individualized.

"You have to understand how each person learns," she said. "It's a slow process. I think people who go out and hit golf balls eight hours a day for five days come back with sore hands and sore arms and not much else."

Suggs believes in playing golf by feel: "I once had a student who couldn't hit a chip shot. One day I told her to close her eyes and hit it."

The woman hit the shot and Suggs says, "To this day, she's still hitting chip shots with her eyes closed."

Suggs still plays with persimmon woods but believes in modern equipment, especially the new composite shafts.

"Not long ago, a woman told me she couldn't hit her driver," Suggs said. "I looked at it and told her, 'This shaft is as stiff as a steel beam. King Kong couldn't hit with that golf club.'"

Suggs got the woman a new driver with a composite shaft. "Most women can't hit the ball hard enough to get the kick they need from a steel shaft."

She accepts exotic equipment as a part of the game but cautions that the only real improvement comes from a better swing: "The sweet spot might be bigger, but you can't get maximum performance until you hit the sweet spot. And you can only get there by developing a repeating swing."

—*by Jerry Potter*

SPOTLIGHT

people wanting to know how to stay in shape over the winter.

"Stretching exercises," she advised. "All stretching exercises are good, and your local library should have a couple of books that shows some basic stretches that help your lower back and your shoulders. Also, you can swing a weighted club."

▶**Ed Oldfield** of the Merit Club in Libertyville, Ill., was asked about indoor putting drills, which work indoors but don't produce under the pressure of competition.

His advice was a drill he used to develop Betsy King, who has won 28 events in the LPGA.

"You need to play games with yourself," said Oldfield. "One way is to practice putting one foot from the cup, then three feet and on back.

"Make yourself sink five putts without missing. If you do miss, then start over at the same distance. That puts you under pressure like you'd face on the golf course."

GOLF ALMANAC 1994

Tour Preview

QUALIFYING TOURNAMENTS ...378

PGA, LPGA, AND SENIOR PGA

TOUR SCHEDULES...380

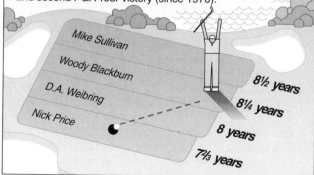

USA SNAPSHOTS®
A look at statistics that shape the sports world

Long wait for second win
When John Inman won the Southern Open Oct. 3, it had been six years since his first win. Most time between first and second PGA Tour victory (since 1970):

- Mike Sullivan — 8½ years
- Woody Blackburn — 8¼ years
- D.A. Weibring — 8 years
- Nick Price — 7⅔ years

Source: *Golf World* By John Riley and Sam Ward, USA TODAY

1994 QUALIFYING TOURNAMENTS

PGA TOUR QUALIFYING TOURNAMENT

▶ **Courses:** PGA West (Jack Nicklaus Resort Course) and La Quinta Golf Club (Dunes Course)
▶ **Location:** La Quinta, Calif.
▶ **When:** Dec. 1-6, 1993
▶ **Par:** 72, both courses
▶ **Yards:** Jack Nicklaus Resort Course, 7,126; Dunes Course, 6,861

Ty Armstrong, Dave Stockton Jr. and Robin Freeman tied for first at 17-under-par after the final round of the PGA Qualifying Tournament.

Armstrong, from Eden Prairie, Minn., shot a closing 68; Stockton, from La Quinta, and Freeman, from Rancho Mirage, Calif., each shot 71.

Jesper Parnevik of Sweden finished a shot back with a final-round 72 that put him among a group of three at 416.

Also in that group were Jeff Woodland of Orlando, and Pete Jordan, of Valrico, Fla., who each shot a final-round 71 over the Nicklaus Resort course at PGA West.

Bob Burns, the fifth-round leader, shot a closing 78 and dropped back into the pack, but still was among the 46 low scorers to qualify for the 1994 PGA Tour.

Qualified

Ty Armstrong, $11,000	71-70-68-71-67-68–415
Dave Stockton Jr., $11,000	68-72-66-68-70-71–415
Robin Freeman, $11,000	70-68-68-68-70-71–415
Jesper Parnevik, $5,000	65-66-79-67-67-72–416
Jeff Woodland, $5,000	68-69-71-69-68-71–416
Pete Jordan, $5,000	71-65-69-72-68-71–416
Joey Rassett, $3,000	74-71-66-66-72-68–417
Clark Dennis, $3,000	69-72-70-68-69-71–419
Morris Hatalsky, $3,000	69-71-70-71-68-70–419
Dennis Paulson, $3,000	70-70-71-69-69-71–420
Glen Day, $3,000	69-71-71-73-68-69–421
David Feherty, $3,000	76-70-69-66-68-72–421
Yoshi Mizumaki, $3,000	73-74-67-67-71-69–421
Todd Barranger, $3,000	67-73-71-68-73-69–421
Steve Rintoul, $3,000	68-71-68-72-73-69–421
Bob Burns, $3,000	70-69-67-70-67-78–421
Steve Gotsche, $3,000	74-68-74-68-67-70–421
Tim Simpson, $3,000	71-71-71-68-67-74–422
Guy Boros, $3,000	72-70-68-70-71-71–422
Paul Goydos, $3,000	71-71-72-65-72-71–422
John Wilson, $3,000	70-70-70-73-68-71–422
Thomas Levet, $3,000	67-71-66-76-72-70–422
Steve Stricker, $3,000	71-73-73-69-65-71–422
Mark Wurtz, $3,000	74-69-69-68-72-71–423
Dicky Pride, $3,000	70-71-65-72-68-77–423
Esteban Toledo, $3,000	70-68-73-70-70-73–424
Paul Stankowski, $3,000	66-71-74-70-71-72–424
Steve Brodie, $3,000	70-73-71-72-73-65–424
Rocky Walcher, $3,000	72-69-73-68-70-72–424
D.A. Russell, $3,000	73-71-67-72-67-74–424
Mike Heinen, $3,000	68-70-75-67-76-68–424
Don Reese, $3,000	71-67-76-72-69-70–425
Ed Kirby, $3,000	75-66-72-69-71-72–425
Steve Lamontagne, $3,000	73-71-72-70-70-69–425
Bill Britton, $3,000	73-75-66-68-74-69–425
Bill Kratzert, $3,000	70-71-73-70-72-69–425
Charles Raulerson, $3,000	70-72-71-70-69-74–426
Rob Boldt, $3,000	70-72-73-71-72-68–426
Shaun Micheel, $3,000	73-68-69-76-73-67–426
Mike Brisky, $3,000	69-69-72-72-69-75–426
Chris Kite, $3,000	68-75-71-71-69-72–426
Brad Lardon, $3,000	73-69-72-70-73-69–426
Phil Tataurangi, $3,000	68-72-69-75-71-71–426
Jim Furyk, $3,000	70-71-74-71-69-71–426
Brad King, $3,000	68-74-70-67-73-74–426
Tom Garner, $3,000	71-70-71-68-74-72–426

LPGA QUALIFYING TOURNAMENT

▶ **Course:** Indigo Lakes Golf & Tennis Resort
▶ **Location:** Daytona Beach, Fla.
▶ **When:** Oct. 19-22, 1993
▶ **Par:** 72
▶ **Yards:** 6,355

Leigh Ann Mills of Coral Springs, Fla., shot 2-under par 286 (72-71-70-73) to take first place in the LPGA Final Qualifying Tournament.

Mills finished 156th on the 1993 LPGA money list, earning $5,601 in 18 starts.

"I was pushing too hard," Mills said. "I had my conditional ('93) card and it always seemed like my back was against the wall, gritting my teeth all year."

Not in '94. In addition to winning $2,000, her qualifying spot means she can play every '94 LPGA event, if she chooses.

Connie Chillemi of Ocala, Fla., and Mardi Lunn of Australia finished a shot behind Mills. Vicki Goetze, who left the University of Georgia in the spring of 1993 after her sophomore season to play the LPGA tour, was another shot back at 288.

Lunn joins her older sister Karen to form the LPGA's second sister duo, along with Danielle and Dina Ammaccapane.

Lunn is among seven foreign players to earn exempt status for 1994: Alicia Dibos of Peru, Amaia Arruti and Tania Abitbol of Spain, Lu Bemvenuti of Brazil, Eva

Dahllof of Sweden and Kathryn Marshall of Scotland.

Earned 1994 playing cards

Leigh Ann Mills, $2,000		72-71-70-73–286
Connie Chillemi, $1,400		71-71-75-70–287
Mardi Lunn, $1,400		76-70-66-75–287
Vicki Goetze, $1,100		72-72-73-71–289
Nicole Jeray, $1,100		74-71-71-73–290
Alicia Dibos, $912		74-72-74-70–290
Stephanie Farwig, $912		76-73-69-72–290
Stephanie Manor, $862		72-74-71-74–291
Kate Rogerson, $862		75-69-73-74–291
Nancy Haravey, $787		74-76-70-72–292
Nina Foust, $787		75-72-72-73–292
Kim Saiki, $787		71-76-72-73–292
Amaia Arruti, $787		73-73-71-75–292
Patty Jordan, $233		74-73-76-70–293
Tania Abitbol, $233		78-72-71-72–293
Mary Murphy, $233		76-72-73-72–293
Pam Allen, $233		73-75-73-72–293
Heather Drew, $233		77-71-70-75–293
Nanci Bowen, $233		74-73-71-75–293
Lu Bemvenuti#		75-75-74-70–294
Eva Dahllof#		76-75-72-71–294
Jodi Figley#		76-73-73-72–294
Kathryn Marshall#		73-76-73-72–294
Kim Cathrein#		74-76-71-73–294
Noelle Daghe#		71-76-71-76–294

Earned conditional 1994 playing cards

Nancy Taylor		74-70-74-76–294
Susan Thielbar		73-74-74-73–294
Lauri Brower		77-71-75-72–295
Annika Sorenstam		75-72-75-73–295
Jan Kleiman		73-74-75-73–295
Terri Thompson		72-75-73-75–295
Kelly Leadbetter		74-77-74-71–296
Audrey Wooding		78-73-73-72–296
Kim Shipman		72-74-74-76–296
Karen Weiss		69-74-75-78–296
Debbie Parks		79-76-71-71–297
Karen Peterson-Parker		76-74-76-71–297
Amy Fruhwirth		77-76-71-73–297
Joal Rieder		74-78-72-73–297
Jackie Gallagher-Smith		78-73-73-73–297
Laura Witvoet		74-78-71-74–297
Michelle Bell		74-74-72-77–297
Sue Fogleman		77-74-76-71–298
Kay Cockerill		74-76-77-71–298
Stefanie Croce		77-75-74-72–298
Kate Golfen		75-73-77-73–298
Marty Dickerson		74-74-77-73–298
Patti Liscio		74-73-77-74–298
Becky Iverson		76-76-71-75–298
Margaret Platt		77-74-72-75–298
Carri Wod		72-76-73-77–298
Jenny Germs		70-77-74-77–298

#–won playoff for final spots

SENIOR PGA TOUR NATIONAL QUALIFYING TOURNAMENT

▸**Course:** Grenelefe Resort and Conference Center (West Course)
▸**Location:** Haines City, Fla.
▸**When:** Nov. 30-Dec. 3, 1993
▸**Par:** 72
▸**Yards:** 6,759

St. Louis club pro Bill Hall birdied two of his final three holes to pass Australian Graham Marsh and earn medalist honors in the Senior PGA Tour National Qualifying Tournament.

Hall, who led the tournament after the first and second rounds, shot a 2-under-par 69 the final day. He started the last round a shot behind Marsh, George Shortridge of Coon Rapids, Minn., and Dick Goetz of Richardson, Texas.

"It's a frightening experience," Hall said of the final two days. "I hit the ball good, but what really got me going was a bogey on the first hole (the final round). I really started grinding after that."

Hall, pro at Glen Echo Country Club, earned $10,500 for his two-stroke victory, but more important, he earned a full exemption for all Senior Tour events in 1994.

Two-time U.S. Amateur champion Jay Sigel shot 2-under 70 the final day for a 293 total to take the 11th spot. He defeated Marion Heck of Fort Myers Beach, Fla., on the fourth playoff hole, and is the third alternate.

"I knew I had to shoot a good (final-round) score and I played very well," Sigel said. "I had five putts lip out on me or my round could have been unbelievable. There was lots of pressure, but I'm glad to finish in the top 16, even though I think we all set our goal to finish in the top eight."

Qualifying results

Bill Hall#, St. Louis, $10,500	69-74-72-69–284
Graham Marsh#, Australia, $8,400	74-70-70-72–286
Randy Petri#, Austin, Texas, $7,000	73-73-72-70–288
G. Shortridge#, Mn.., $5,740	73-74-67-75–289
D. Goetz#, Richardson, Tex., $5,740	75-72-67-75–289
Fred Ruiz#, Mission, Texas, $4,620	77-74-69-70–290
Richard Bassett#, Fla., $3,453	72-73-76-70–291
Bob Panasik#, Canada, $3,453	72-74-74-71–291
Bob E. Smith#, Fla., $3,453	70-77-74-70–291
Bob Dickson##, Fla., $2,940	78-70-72-72–292
Jay Sigel##, Berwyn, Pa., $2,730	75-75-73-70–293
Marion Heck##, Fla., $2,730	75-74-72-75–293
Tommy Horton##, Britain, $2,450	74-74-73-73–294
Bob Carson##, Fla., $2,450	75-76-72-71–294
Robert Gaona##, Ariz., $1,446	72-77-69-72–295
Bob Zimmerman##, Ohio, $1,446	72-73-77-73–295
John Brodie###,Calif., $1,446	74-79-71-71–295

#–earned 1994 Senior PGA Tour cards
##–alternates
###–lost playoff for final alternate spot

1994 PGA TOUR SCHEDULE

Date	Tournament	Site
Jan. 6-9	Mercedes Championship	La Costa CC, Carlsbad, Calif.
Jan. 13-16	United Airlines Hawaiian Open	Waialae CC, Honolulu.
Jan. 20-23	Northern Telcom Open	TPC at Starpass and Tucson National, Tucson, Ariz.
Jan. 27-30	Phoenix Open	TPC of Scottsdale, Phoenix
Feb. 3-6	AT&T Pebble Beach National Pro-Am	Pebble Beach GL, Spyglass Hill GC, and Poppy Hills, Monterey, Calif.
Feb. 10-13	Nissan Los Angeles Open	Riviera CC, Pacific Palisades, Calif.
Feb. 17-20	Bob Hope Chrysler Classic	PGA West (Palmer Course), Bermuda Dunes CC, Indian Wells CC, Tamarisk CC, Palm Desert, Calif.
Feb. 24-27	Buick Invitational of California	Torrey Pines GC, San Diego
March 3-6	Doral Ryder Open	Doral CC (Blue Course) Miami
March 10-13	Honda Classic	Weston Hills CC, Fort Lauderdale, Fla.
March 17-20	Nestlé Invitational	Bay Hill Club, Orlando
March 24-27	The Players Championship	TPC at Sawgrass (Stadium Course) Jacksonville, Fla.
March 31-April 3	Freeport-McMoRan Classic	English Turn G&CC, New Orleans
April 7-10	The Masters	Augusta (Ga.) National GC
April 14-17	MCI Heritage Classic	Harbour Town GL, Hilton Head Island, S.C.
April 21-24	K mart Greater Greensboro Open	Forest Oaks CC, Greensboro, N.C.
April 28-May 1	Shell Houston Open	TPC at The Woodlands, The Woodlands, Texas
May 5-8	BellSouth Classic	Atlanta CC, Marietta, Ga.
May 12-15	GTE Byron Nelson Classic	TPC at Los Colinas, Irving, Texas
May 19-22	Memorial Tournament	Muirfield Village GC, Dublin, Ohio
May 26-29	Southwestern Bell Colonial	Colonial CC, Fort Worth, Texas
June 2-5	Kemper Open	TPC at Avenel, Potomac, Md.
June 9-12	Buick Classic	Westchester CC, Rye, N.Y.
June 16-19	U.S. Open	Oakmont (Pa.) CC
June 23-26	Canon Greater Hartford Open	TPC at River Highlands, Cromwell, Conn.
June 30-July 3	Centel Western Open	Cog Hill CC, Lemont, Ill.
July 7-10	Anheuser-Busch Classic	Kingsmill GC, Williamsburg, Va.
July 14-17	British Open	The Ailsa Course, Turnberry, Scotland
July 14-17	Deposit Guaranty Classic	Annadale GC, Madison, Miss.
July 21-24	New England Classic	Pleasant Valley CC, Sutton, Mass.
July 28-31	Federal Express St. Jude Classic	TPC at Southwind, Memphis
Aug. 4-7	Buick Open	Warwick Hills G&CC, Grand Blanc, Mich.
Aug. 11-14	PGA Championship	Southern Hills CC, Tulsa, Okla.
Aug. 18-21	The International	Castle Pines GC, Castle Rock, Colo.
Aug. 25-28	NEC World Series of Golf	Firestone CC (South Course), Akron, Ohio
Sept. 1-4	Greater Milwaukee Open	Brown Deer GC, Franklin, Wis.
Sept. 8-11	Canadian Open	Glen Abbey GC, Oakville, Ontario
Sept. 15-18	Quad Cities Golf Classic	Oakwood CC, Coal Valley, Ill.
Sept. 22-25	B.C. Open	En-Joie GC, Endicott, N.Y.
Sept. 29-Oct. 2	Buick Southern Open	Callaway Gardens Resort, Pine Mountain, Ga.
Oct. 6-9	Walt Disney World/ Oldsmobile Classic	Magnolia, Palm and Buena Vista Golf Courses, Lake Burna Vista, Fla.
Oct. 13-16	H-E-B Texas Open	Oak Hills C, San Antonio.

Oct. 19-23	Las Vegas Invitational	TPC at Summerlin, Desert Inn & CC, Las Vegas CC, Las Vegas
Oct. 27-30	TOUR Championship	Olympic Club, San Francisco
Nov. 3-6	Lincoln-Merury Kapalua International	Kapalua Resort, Kapalua, Maui, Hawaii
Nov. 17-20	Franklin Funds Shark Shootout	Sherwood CC, Thousand Oaks, Calif.
Nov. 26-27	The Skins Game	BIGHORN, Palm Desert, Calif.
Dec. 1-4	JCPenney Classic	Innisbrook Resort (Copperhead Course), Tarpon Springs, Fla.

1994 LPGA SCHEDULE

Date	Tournament	Site
Feb. 4-6	Healthsouth Palm Beach Classic	Wycliffe G&CC, Lake Worth, Fla.
Feb. 17-19	Hawaiian Ladies Open	Ko Olina GC, Ewa Beach, Hawaii
March 2-5	Chrysler-Plymouth T. of C.	Grand Cypress Resort, Orlando
March 10-13	Ping/Welch's Championship	Randolph Park, Tucson, Ariz.
March 17-20	Standard Register Ping	Moon Valley CC, Phoenix
March 24-27	Nabisco Dinah Shore	Mission Hills CC, Rancho Mirage, Calif.
April 15-17	Atlanta Women's Champ.	Eagle's Landing CC, Stockbridge, Ga.
April 28-May 1	Sprint Championship	Indigo Lakes DD, Daytona Beach, Fla.
May 6-8	Sara Lee Classic	Hermitage GC, Old Hickory, Tenn.
May 12-15	McDonald's LPGA Champ.	DuPont CC, Wilmington, Del.
May 20-22	Lady Keystone Open	Hershey (Pa.) CC
May 26-29	LPGA Corning Classic	Corning (N.Y.) CC
June 2-5	Oldsmobile Classic	Walnut Hills CC, East Lansing, Mich.
June 10-12	Minnesota Classic	Edinburgh USA, Brooklyn Park, Minn.
June 16-19	Rochester International	Locust Hill CC, Pittsford, N.Y.
June 24-26	ShopRite Classic	Great Bay Resort, Somers Point, N.J.
July 1-3	Youngstown-Warren Classic	Avalon Lakes GC, Warren, Ohio
July 8-10	Jamie Farr Toledo Classic	Highland Meadows GC, Sylvania, Ohio
July 14-17	JAL Big Apple Classic	Wykagyl CC, New Rochelle, N.Y.
July 21-24	U.S. Women's Open	Indianwood GC, Lake Orion, Mich.
July 28-31	Ping/Welch's Championship	Blue Hill CC, Canton, Mass.
Aug. 4-7	McCalls Classic	Stratton Mountain (Vt.) CC
Aug. 11-14	Weetabix Women's British Open	Woburn G&CC, Milton Keynes, Eng.
Aug. 12-14	Dayton Classic	CC of the North, Dayton, Ohio
Aug. 18-21	Chicago Challenge	White Eagle GC, Naperville, Ill.
Aug. 25-28	du Maurier Ltd. Classic	Ottawa (Ont.) Hunt Club
Sept. 3-5	State Farm Rail Classic	Rail GC, Springfield, Ill
Sept. 9-11	Ping-Cellular One Champ.	Columbia Edgewater CC, Portland, Ore.
Sept. 15-18	Safeco Classic	Meridian Valley CC, Kent, Wash.
Sept. 29-Oct. 2	Heartland Classic	Forest Hills CC, St. Louis
Oct. 13-16	World Champ. of Women's Golf	TBA
Oct. 21-23	Solheim Cup	The Greenbrier, White Sulphur Springs, W. Va.
Oct. 28-30	Nichirei International	Ami GC, Ibaragi-Ken, Japan
Nov. 4-6	Toray Queens Cup	TBA, Japan
Dec. 1-4	JCPenney Classic	Innisbrook Resort, Tarpon Springs, Fla.
Dec. 9-11	Diner's Club Matches	TBA

1994 Senior PGA Tour Schedule

Date	Tournament	Site
Jan. 6-9	Mercedes Championship	La Costa CC, Carlsbad, Calif.
Jan. 29-30	Senior Skins Game	Mauna Lani Resort, Hawaii
Feb. 4-6	Royal Caribbean Classic	Links at Key Biscayne, Fla.
Feb. 7-8	Senior Slam of Golf	Club Campostro de Queretaro, Mexico
Feb. 11-13	GTE Suncoast Classic	TPC at Tampa Bay, Lutz, Fla.
Feb. 18-20	Intellinet Challenge	The Vineyards, Naples, Fla.
Feb. 25-27	Chrysler Cup	TPC at Prestancia, Sarasota, Fla.
March 4-6	GTE West Classic	Ojai (Calif.) Valley Inn & CC
March 11-13	Vantage at The Dominion	The Dominion CC, San Antonio
March 25-27	Doug Sanders Classic	Deerwood CC, Kingswood, Texas
March 25-27	American Express Grandslam	Oak Hills CC, Narita Japan
March 31-April 3	The Tradition	Desert Mountain, Scottsdale, Ariz.
April 14-17	PGA Seniors	PGA National GC, Palm Beach, Fla.
April 22-24	Muratec Reunion Pro-Am	Oak Cliff CC, Dallas
April 30-May 1	Las Vegas Classic	TPC at Summerlin, Las Vegas
May 6-8	Liberty Mutual Legends	Barton Creek CC, Austin, Texas
May 13-15	PaineWebber Invitational	TPC at Piper Glen, Charlotte, N.C.
May 20-22	Cadillac NFL Classic	Upper Montclair CC, Clifton, N.J.
May 27-29	Bell Atlantic Classic	Chester Valley CC, Malvern, Pa.
June 3-5	Bruno's Memorial Classic	Greystone GC, Birmingham, Ala.
June 10-12	Nationwide Championship	CC of the South, Alpharetta, Ga.
June 17-19	Senior Classic at Opryland	Springhouse GC, Nashville
June 23-26	Ford Senior Players Champ.	TPC of Michigan, Dearborn, Mich.
June 30-July 3	U.S. Senior Open	Pinehurst (N.C.) Resort and CC
July 8-10	Kroger Classic	Nicklaus GC, Kings Island, Ohio
July 15-17	Ameritech Senior Open	Stonebridge CC, Aurora, Ill.
July 22-24	Southwestern Bell Classic	Loch Lloyd CC, Belton, Mo.
July 29-31	Northville Long Island Cl.	Meadowbrook CC, Jericho, N.Y.
Aug. 5-7	Bank of Boston Sr. Classic	Nashawtuc CC, Concord, Mass.
Aug. 12-14	First of America Classic	TBA, Grand Rapids, Mich.
Aug. 19-21	Burnet Sr. Classic	Bunker Hills GC, Coon Rapids, Minn.
Aug. 26-28	Franklin Quest Champ.	Park Meadows, Park City, Utah
Sept. 2-4	GTE Northwest Classic	Inglewood CC, Kenmore, Wash.
Sept. 9-11	Quicksilver Classic	Quicksilver CC, Midway, Pa.
Sept. 16-18	Bank One Classic	Kearney Hill Links, Lexington, Ky.
Sept. 23-25	Brickyard Crossing Champ.	Brickyard Crossing, Speedway, Ind.
Sept. 30-Oct. 3	Vantage Championship	Tanglewood Park, Clemmons, N.C.
Oct. 7-9	The Transamerica	Silverado CC, Napa, Calif.
Oct. 14-16	Raley's Senior Gold Rush	Rancho Murieta (Calif.) CC
Oct. 21-23	Ralph's Senior Classic	Rancho Park GC, Los Angeles
Oct. 28-30	Kaanapali Classic	Royal Kaanapali GC, Maui, Hawaii
Nov. 10-13	Senior Tour Championship	Dunes Golf & Beach Club, Myrtle Beach, S.C.

Golf is the only sport totally dedicated to charity, and the **Ladies Professional Golf Association** is proud to align itself with that theme. Charitable contributions from **LPGA tournaments** totaled nearly $7 million in 1993.

As a women's organization with strong family priorities, the **LPGA** unfortunately has been affected first-hand by breast cancer and knows only too well the devastating results of the disease on the patients, family and friends.

In April, 1992, the LPGA named the **Susan G. Komen Breast Cancer Foundation** as its Official National Charity. The **Susan G. Komen Breast Cancer Foundation** has made remarkable strides to raise funds for advanced research into the disease and to provide further education for early detection and prevention. The **LPGA** provides the **Komen Foundation** with another avenue through which to focus its goals and to spread its message.

The Susan G. Komen Breast Cancer Foundation was founded in 1983 in Dallas, Texas, by Nancy Brinker in memory of her sister, Susan G. Komen, who succumbed to breast cancer in 1980 at the age of 36. Brinker is an outstanding civic and community leader and Presidential appointee to the National Cancer Advisory Board.

The **LPGA** lost a very good friend on November 20, 1993. **Heather Farr**, who joined the **LPGA Tour** in 1985, fought a four and one-half year battle with breast cancer after having been diagnosed in 1989 at the age of 24. Although Heather may be gone, her spirit will live forever in the heart of the **LPGA**.

This card

These courses

These players

This number
1-800-545-9920

Get your **PGA TOUR Partners** card and step into a whole new world of golf excitement. Play with a top PGA TOUR professional in THE TOUR Championship pro-am by winning the Partners' Team Competition fantasy golf game. Play legendary golf courses like Pebble Beach and Pinehurst in Partners-only tournaments, played under actual TOUR conditions. Attend a PGA TOUR tournament with your complimentary Partner's pass. Receive a yearly subscription to ON TOUR, the only magazine that shows you the PGA TOUR from the inside. Get the PGA TOUR's Official Media Guide containing all the game's facts and figures, and receive other unique Partners benefits. Just $38 makes you a **PGA TOUR Partner**. Proceeds support over 900 charities nationwide. ***Call and join today!***

Major credit cards accepted.